Between Worlds

BETWEEN

WORLDS

Early Exchanges Between
Maori and Europeans
1773-1815

Anne Salmond

UNIVERSITY OF HAWAI'I PRESS
Honolulu

Published in North America by
UNIVERSITY OF HAWAI'I PRESS
2840 Kolowalu Street
Honolulu, Hawai'i 96822

First published in New Zealand by
PENGUIN BOOKS (NZ) LTD
Cnr Rosedale & Airborne Roads
Albany, Auckland
New Zealand

Printed in Hong Kong

LIBRARY OF CONGRESS CATALOGUING-IN-PUBLICATION DATA

Salmond, Anne
Between worlds: early meetings between Maori and Europeans,
1773–1815 / Anne Salmond
p.   cm.
Includes bibliographical references and index.

ISBN 0-8248-2020-7

1. Maori (New Zealand people) – History.
2. New Zealand – History – To 1840.
3. New Zealand – Race relations
I. Title
DU423.A1825   1997
993.01 – dc21
97-24190
CIP

For Joyce and Jack,
my parents;

Jeremy,
my love;

Amiria Manutahi, Stephen Jeremy and Timothy Potiki,
our children;

and all of the family.

Contents

PART THREE: TAPU AND RELIGION

Acknowledgements

In acknowledging the people who shaped this work, I begin with ancestors and elders. The curiosity about Te Ao Maori (the Maori 'world') that inspired it began when I was young, provoked by stories about my great-grandfather, James McDonald. He worked with Elsdon Best, Sir Apirana Ngata and Te Rangi-hiroa, among others, photographing and sketching Maori people and activities, and producing a series of ethnological films early this century. Curiosity became fascination as I met various elders in my home town of Gisborne, on the East Coast of New Zealand – Peggy Kaua, Sir Henry and Lady Lorna Ngata, George and Pare Marsden, and Pax and Maaka Jones. I began to learn Maori then, along with action songs and the first rudiments of Maori knowledge. Soon afterwards I went to the University of Auckland, where I enrolled in Maori Studies papers (with Bruce Biggs, Merimeri Penfold, Patu Hohepa, Hirini Mead and Hugh Kawharu as mentors) and joined the University Maori club. It was glorious fun, and by the time I encountered Eruera and Amiria Stirling at the end of that year, fascination had become a passion.

That relationship with Eruera and Amiria Stirling was one of the most important in my life. I spent a good deal of time at their home in Mercer Road (now Amiria Street) in Herne Bay, and travelled with them to ceremonial gatherings. They became godparents to two of our children, friends to our extended family, and counsellors to me and my husband. In the process, I produced three books in collaboration with them, while Eruera tried to instruct me in esoteric aspects of Maori philosophies of living. When I left New Zealand for a year at Cambridge University in 1980, soon after completing *Eruera: The Teachings of a Maori Elder*, I began to delve into theoretical writings of various kinds, seeking to understand the relationships between Maori and Western ways of knowing.

I have received much help from students and colleagues in Maori Studies at Auckland in debating the deeper questions involved – including Sir Hugh Kawharu, Ranginui Walker, Cleve Barlow, Waerete Norman, Jane McRae, Maureen Lander, Paul Tapsell and the late Taimihinga Potaka; and from anthropological colleagues, including (outside of New Zealand) Ward Goodenough, Marilyn Strathern, Stephen Hugh-Jones, Keith Hart, Anna Grimshaw, Peter Gathercole, David Parkin, Joanna Overing, Mark Hobart, Anthony Cohen, Marshall Sahlins, Barbara Kirshenblatt-Gimblett, James Fox, Nicholas Thomas, and Bronwen Douglas; and (at the Department of Anthropology in Auckland) Roger Green, Ralph Bulmer, Mark

Mosko, Max Rimoldi, Jeff Sissons, Judith Huntsman and Karen Nero. In this regard I would also like to acknowledge my friend the historian Judith Binney. In addition, international debates have also helped to shape my thinking. The Association of Social Anthropologists in the United Kingdom took me to a number of conferences in Britain; the Royal Anthropological Institute invited me to deliver the 1996–97 Henry Myers lecture in Edinburgh; and the Australian National University awarded me a visiting Fellowhip in 1996, honours for which I am deeply grateful. Julian Young invited me to an international meeting of philosophers at the Bay of Islands in 1996, which helped me to think about the fate of Ruatara. These invitations resulted in a series of papers. Readers who find interest in the more reflective sections of this book may wish to consult those writings.

The family, close and extended, have shared in many of my cross-cultural adventures. One of the greatest joys has been their support and encouragement. My husband Jeremy's contribution to this work has been inestimable. Our children have also left their mark on the project. Amiria Manutahi, now studying anthropology at Cambridge University, extended my thinking in new and unexpected directions. Stephen, a student of computer science at the University of Auckland, wrote a database for European shipping in the period. Tim, a student of science at Lincoln University, showed an interest in the book that lifted my spirits. Through my attachment to them, and to our ancestors, I have been drawn to reflect about the colonial processes that brought those forebears to New Zealand.

That history, as well as more ancient tribal stories, is active in the New Zealand landscape. It animates current controversies about how Maori and Pakeha can best inhabit the place together. In this context, close attention to the details of past relationships between Maori and Pakeha may prove helpful. Stark stereotypes can be replaced by more complex, subtle interplays. Many pivotal relationships, it is plain, were constructed across cultural boundaries and edges. These processes continue, and have shaped this work. In this connection I would like to thank Merimeri Penfold of Ngaati Kurii and Patu Hohepa of Te Maahurehure, my friends of many years, for their guidance on northern inter-hapuu exchanges, and the intricacies of cross-cultural interaction. Hori Parata of Ngaati Wai gave counsel on the background of his ancestor Te Mahanga. Maui John Mitchell of Te Ati Awa and his wife Hilary brought their expertise and zest to our shared work on Cook's sojourns in Totaranui. The research into Tuki and Huru's adventures on Norfolk Island involved many people, both on Norfolk Island and in Tai Tokerau – Pauline Thompson, Les Brown, Merval Hoare, Alice Buffet, Mera Martin, Bob Toft and Kathy Le Cren on Norfolk Island, and Selwyn Muru, Dame Mira Szazy, Atihana Johns and the descendants of Tuki-tahua from Tai Tokerau. Our trip to Norfolk in 1993 for the bicentennial commemoration of Tuki and Huru's sojourn on the island was an unforgettable experience.

Without good access to documents, too, this project would have been impossible. I would like to acknowledge staff in the following libraries for their help: the University of Auckland Library (particularly Janny Jonkers, John Laurie and the Chief Librarian, Peter Durey), the Auckland Institute and Museum Library, the Alexander Turnbull Library in Wellington (especially Marian Minson and David Retter) and the Hocken Library in Dunedin (Beverley Booth, Janine Delaney and Stuart Strachan), in New Zealand; the National Library of Australia (Graeme Powell) and the Australian National University library in Canberra, the Mitchell and Dixson Libraries (especially Martin Beckett, the Mitchell microfilms librarian) and the New South Wales Archive in Sydney, in Australia; the British Museum Manuscripts Room and Reading Room, the Public Record Office, the libraries of the Royal Commonwealth Society and the Royal Geographical Society, the St Bride Printing Library, the National Maritime Museum, the libraries of the School of Oriental and African Studies, University College and the India Office, in London; the University of Cambridge Library; Trinity House, Hull; the Hydrographic Office, Taunton (Richard Campbell); the University of Birmingham Library, the National Library of Scotland and the Scottish Record Office, in the United Kingdom; the libraries of the University of Hawaii and the Bernice P. Bishop Museum in Hawai‘i; the Harvard University Library, the Peabody Essex Museum in Salem (Jane Ward and Christina Scarangello), the Whaling Museum and the Atheneum on Nantucket, the Providence Public Library, the Kendall Whaling Museum in Sharon, Massachusetts, the Mystic Seaport Museum (Paul O'Pecko) in Mystic, Connecticut, and the New Bedford/Old Dartmouth Historical Society and Whaling Museum, in the United States of America. In addition I am grateful to Lady Aileen Fox, Harold Carter of the Banks Archive Project in London, and Patricia Fara at Darwin College, Cambridge in the United Kingdom; Robin Fisher, Hugh Johnson and Andrew David of the Vancouver Conference on Discovery and Exploration in Vancouver, Canada; Lilikala Kame‘eleihiwa and David Chappell at the University of Hawaii; Ian Nicholson, Jeffrey Hopkins, Joan Kerr, Dorothy Shineberg, and Michael Williams of the Aboriginal and Torres Strait Islander Studies Unit at the University of Queensland, in Australia; and Nicholas Tarling, Jenny Curnow, Andrew Sharp, Geoffrey Irwin, Taane Malcolm of Ngaati Tumutumu, Phillip Eadie, W. A. Laxon, Clifford Hawkins, Roger Neich of the Auckland Institute and Museum, Grant Phillipson of the Waitangi Tribunal, Wayne Marriott of the Southland Museum, June McDougall, Dr Alan Davidson of St John's Theological College, and Joanne Wilkes in New Zealand for their help with particular matters.

I am indebted to Caroline Phillips, Louise Furey and Paul Monin, who have checked the Hauraki section of this work. Roger Morris and Caroline Phillips each carried out a meticulous reconstruction of the *Fancy*'s movements up the Waihou River. Rhys Richards offered searching comments on Part II, and access to the Jorgen Jorgensen papers. Isabel Ollivier carried out research into French newspapers of the period and the writings of Jules de Blosseville in Paris. Sarah Joynes collected newspaper reports of the return of Cook's expeditions in London. Felicity Stewart examined every issue of the *Sydney Gazette* up to 1810 for reports relevant to New Zealand. Maxine Iverson completed the search up to

1815, examined the Colonial Office records on microfilm for this period, painstakingly checked the shipping records to ensure that the Shipping Appendices I had compiled were accurate, and checked the missionary records. Their labours, more than mine, have resulted in a Shipping Archive covering all European ship visits to New Zealand between 1642 and 1814, now lodged in the University of Auckland Library. M. G. S. Parsonson checked Part Three against his own extensive knowledge of Samuel Marsden's missionary endeavours.

My aroha to Patu Hohepa, Merimeri Penfold, Jock Phillips, Dame Joan Metge, Judith Binney, Michael King, David Mackay, Nicholas Thomas, Caroline Phillips, Fergus Clunie, Maxine Iversen, Grace Smit and Jane McRae, for acting as readers of the final manuscript (either whole or in part). I thank them for their honest and expert advice, and generosity beyond the call of duty. Any errors that remain are all my own. The project could not have happened without a grant from the Foundation for Research, Science and Technology, which supported the research. I am grateful to the University of Auckland and colleagues in my two departments – Maori Studies and Anthropology – for giving me time to tackle so challenging a project. And Geoff Walker of Penguin Books, and Richard King, my editor, for their faith and encouragement. A whakatauki from Eruera Stirling will help to express my feelings of gratitude:

| E paru i te tinana, e maa i te wai | If you're touched by mud, you can wash it off |
| E paru i te aroha, ka mau tonu e. | If you're touched by aroha, it lasts always. |

Anne Salmond
June 1997

This has been a difficult but exciting book to write. It tells of a time when Maori warriors went to sea on European ships and explored the world, visiting Norfolk Island, Australia, the Pacific Islands, India, South-East Asia, North and South America, and Europe. At the same time, white men and women began to live on shore in New Zealand, taking the moko (tattoo) as well as Maori wives or husbands. It was a swashbuckling period of cross-cultural trial and error.

Between Worlds is the sequel to an earlier work, *Two Worlds: First Meetings Between Maori and Europeans 1642–1772*. *Two Worlds* discussed the first encounters between Maori and Europeans – Abel Tasman's visit to Taitapu (Golden Bay) in 1642; Captain James Cook's circumnavigation of the two main islands in the *Endeavour* during 1769–70; Jean-François-Marie de Surville's sojourn at Tokerau (Doubt-less Bay) in 1769; and Marc-Joseph Marion du Fresne's disastrous stay in the Bay of Islands in 1772. *Two Worlds* took its title from the image of Te Ao Maori and Te Ao Pakeha, the Maori and European 'worlds', for in the very first meetings between Maori people and Europeans – those short, sharp and often violent encounters – the boundaries between the European ships and the people on the beaches were only briefly breached. For the period that followed, however, as visits by European vessels became more frequent and finally commonplace, the idea of a middle ground for action seems to fit. *Between Worlds* echoes the idea of the 'pae' in Maori – that edge or horizon between earth and sky, worlds of light or darkness – where people and ancestor gods enter into exchanges that separate and bind them. The pae is a place of action, where history is made.

The challenge of writing history across the pae, though, is formidable. Early meetings between Maori and Europeans were shaped by strategic choices. When Europeans arrived, some Maori leaders kept their distance, while others engaged with them. European sailors visited certain harbours often – Totaranui (Queen Charlotte Sound), Tamatea (Dusky Sound), Hauraki and the Bay of Islands (all sheltered anchorages charted by Cook) – while avoiding others. On both sides, fighting men frequently initiated encounters, while women, children and elders stayed in the background. Some Europeans recorded their experiences of Maori in logs, journals, letters, charts and sketches, while others (including all of the women who visited New Zealand in this period) remained silent. Tribal histories described the adventures of rangatira (aristocratic people), while saying little about the lives of lesser mortals.

Documentary and oral accounts illuminate the past in bits and pieces, and from particular angles. In writing this work, I have gathered these fragments like a magpie, storing them in archive boxes and filing cabinets. Documents from both Maori and European sources have been gathered from around the world, recorded on cards in a master index, and placed in a 'Ships Archive', with one file for every ship known to have visited New Zealand between 1773 and 1815. While trying to master the myriad details of these vessels, their crews and their movements, and of tribal histories, I have sought to grasp key patterns in European and Maori forms of life that influenced those early meetings.

Between Worlds is written in three main sections. The first, 'Science and Whaka-papa', looks at scientific voyages to New Zealand as encounters between European and Maori ways of knowing. The second, 'Utu, Law and Commerce', describes the founding of penal colonies in Australia and Norfolk Island, the beginning of European commercial activity in New Zealand, and Maori exploration of the world on European vessels. The third section, 'Tapu and Religion', tells of the first European evangelical voyages to Aotearoa as exchanges between Maori and European belief systems. The book traces a process of cross-cultural entanglement – in fighting, friendship, gift exchange, talk and sex – as across the pae, new ways of living emerged between Maori and Europeans.

He iwi kee, he iwi kee
Titiro atu, titiro mai!

One strange people and another,
Looking at each other!

FROM A HAKA BY MERIMERI PENFOLD

The image overleaf and on the part-title pages, of Joseph Banks
exchanging bark cloth (?) for a crayfish, was evidently drawn by Tupaia,
the high priest-navigator who visited New Zealand in 1769–70.
On 12 December 1812, Banks wrote to a friend: 'Tupaia the Indian
who came with me from Otaheite Learned to draw in a way not
Quite unintelligible. The genius for Caricature which all
wild people Possess Led him to Caricature me & he drew
me with a nail in my hand delivering it to an Indian
who sold me a Lobster.'

Prologue

The *Endeavour*'s arrival at Tuuranga-nui (Poverty Bay)
October 1769

Like all strange, powerful things, it came from the horizon between night and day, sea and sky. It was large, floating out there on the water, with white, curved shapes that shifted in the breeze. People were already up and moving about, and the news spread quickly. As they crowded onto the beach, staring out to sea, signal fires were lit and smoke plumed up, telling the inland settlements to be on the alert. No one could say for certain what it was, although when they saw the white-skinned beings that it carried, they remembered their tohunga (priest) Toiroa some years before, when the spirit of prophecy had entered him, arching his back and splaying out his fingers like a lizard, singing of white-skinned people coming out of the darkness to their land . . .[1]

A sketch of the Endeavour *at sea during Cook's first Pacific voyage.*

In the aftermath of their very first meetings, how did Maori and European understand each other? Who, or what, did they think that they had seen? In the case of
Maori, those meetings provoked debates that went on for years. Until Europeans
arrived, they had lived in a world peopled only by their ancestors and themselves.
At first they thought these new arrivals might be atua (supernatural beings) or
tiipuna (ancestors) come to visit their descendants. Some ancestors had come
from other islands, called Raiatea or Hawaiki in the origin stories, and for a time
at least, there had been voyages back and forth. Another good guess, then, was
that the Europeans were people from Hawaiki, come to visit them. They were
white, however, and strange in many other ways. If they were neither atua nor
ancestors, nor people from Hawaiki, then the world must be a different place
from what they had supposed. As Maori thinkers reflected upon these matters,
their understandings of the world, and of themselves, began to change.

Surviving Maori versions of the earliest meetings between Maori and Europeans suggest that at first, local people thought that Europeans were part of the
world of supernatural beings rather than the everyday world of light. In Tuuranga-
nui (Poverty Bay) in 1769, some people had guessed that James Cook's *Endeavour*
might be Waikawa, a sacred island off the Maahia Peninsula, floating into their
harbour. When they saw its sails, they cried out, 'Aha. Ha! The sails of this travelling island are like clouds in the sky!'[2] Others thought it was a great bird, and they
marvelled at the beauty and the size of its wings. When it came right into their bay
(according to Joel Polack's East Coast informants in 1838), they saw 'a smaller
bird, unfledged (without sails), descending into the water, and a number of parti-
coloured beings, but apparently in the human shape, also descending, [and] the
bird was regarded as a houseful of divinities. Nothing could exceed the astonishment of the people.'[3] In Te Matau-a-Maaui (Hawke's Bay), when the *Endeavour*'s
Raiatean pilot Tupaia warned the local people not to approach the ship in a hostile
manner, the chiefs contemptuously over-ruled him, saying, 'Kahore he raakau o
te hunga o Hawaiki; he puu kaakaho, he korari!' (The people of Hawaiki have
no weapons, only reeds and flax-stalks!)[4] They understood the *Endeavour* to be a
vessel from the homeland, Hawaiki, but were far from awe-struck by the new
arrivals.

In Whitianga, according to Horeta Te Taniwha, Cook's crew were thought to
be 'goblins' or 'tupua', a kind of supernatural being.[5] Te Taniwha was given a nail
that he treasured as an atua until he lost it one day when his canoe capsized. In the
north of New Zealand they called them 'maitai' (literally, 'from the sea'), a term
they also gave to iron.[6] In all of these meetings, though, local people challenged
the Europeans vigorously with haka (chants), the ritual throwing of spears and
with karakia (incantations). Interestingly, 'Maori' (as they came to define themselves in contradistinction to 'Pakeha' or Europeans) seem to have treated human-
like atua much the same as other unidentified visitors. Given the notion that visiting
parties might include ancestors, this is not surprising. Indeed, the first Maori
visitors on board European vessels acted with aplomb, examining the crews,

*Horeta Te Taniwha, painted by
Gottfried Lindauer.*

guns and physical lay-out of the ships, and often staying on board all night.

Te Taniwha's account of the *Endeavour*'s arrival at Whitianga in 1769 gives some idea of the rapidity with which local people relaxed once they decided that the Europeans were not intent on fighting them:

> We lived at Whitianga, and a vessel came there, and when our old men saw the ship they said it was an atua, and the people on board were tupua, strange beings or 'goblins'. The ship came to anchor, and the boats pulled on shore. As our old men looked at the manner in which they came on shore, the rowers pulling with their backs to the bows of the boat, the old people said, 'Yes, it is so: these people are goblins, their eyes are at the back of their heads; they pull on shore with their backs to the land to which they are going.' When these goblins came on shore we (the children and women) took notice of them, but we ran away from them into the forest, and the warriors alone stayed in the presence of those goblins; but, as the goblins stayed some time, and did not do any evil to our braves, we came back one by one, and gazed at them, and we stroked their garments with our hands, and we were pleased with the whiteness of their skins and the blue of the eyes of some of them.
>
> These goblins began to gather oysters, and we gave some kumara, fish and fern root to them. These they accepted, and we (the women and children) began to roast cockles for them; and as we saw that these goblins were eating kumara, fish and cockles, we were startled, and said, 'Perhaps they are not goblins like the Maori goblins.' These goblins went into the forest, and also climbed up the hill to our pa (fort) at Whitianga. They collected grasses from the cliffs, and kept knocking at the stones on the beach [no doubt Banks and Solander, 'botanising' and 'geologising' on behalf of the Royal Society]. We said, 'Why are these acts done by these goblins?'

We and the women gathered stones and grass of all sorts, and gave to these goblins. Some of the stones they liked, and put them into their bags, the rest they threw away; and when we gave them the grass and branches of trees they stood and talked to us, or they uttered the words of their language. Perhaps they were asking questions, and, as we did not know their language, we laughed, and these goblins also laughed, so we were pleased.[7]

Before long, however, some Maori decided that Europeans were not tupua or atua, but human beings. In the north of New Zealand, that moment probably came during the sojourn of Marion du Fresne and his expedition in the Bay of Islands in 1772. Marion and his men stayed in the Bay for about a month, in largely peaceful intimacy with local groups. As Crozet later commented:

The friendship which they showed us was carried to the extremest familiarity; the chiefs on boarding our vessels entered our rooms without ceremony, and slept on our beds, examining all our furniture piece by piece; they asked about the meaning of our pictures, and of our mirrors, of which they of course understood nothing. Indeed, they spent whole days with us with the greatest demonstrations of friendship and confidence.[8]

For thirty-three days Marion lived among Maori in blissful ignorance of their politics and beliefs, assuring his officers that 'since I do them nothing but good, surely they will not do me any harm?'[9] Towards the end of his time in the Bay, Marion was taken to a high hill and installed as a chief (or prepared for sacrifice?):

He received many caresses from them, then they put a sort of crown of feathers on his head, showing him the whole expanse of land and making him understand that they recognised him as their king. They carried out several ceremonies and treated him with much respect; they made him a present of fish and of a stone on which an image of their deity was carved [probably an ancestral tiki ornament]. For his part he also gave them presents and many caresses and they escorted him back on board ship.[10]

Two days later he was dead, killed by one of the principal chiefs of the Bay. According to several tribal manuscript accounts from the 1850s, the event that finally provoked Marion's killing (after a series of lesser offences) was a fishing expedition, when, ignoring the advice of his Maori companions, he insisted on hauling his net in a tapu bay where two drowned men had recently been washed up. The kin groups (Ngaati Pou and Ngaati Uru) whose members had accompanied him were held responsible for this breach of tapu, and attacked his expedition in retribution. The tribal accounts are matter-of-fact about his fate:

Marion was cooked and eaten by . . . the chiefs Te Kauri and Tohitapu, as they were priests, and it was for them to eat these foreigners, so that evil might not come on their tribes for the evil of those people for ignoring the tapu of the beach where corpses had lain . . . The bones of the foreigners who had been killed were made into forks for picking up food, and the thigh bones were made into flutes.[11]

None of the Maori accounts of this episode asserts that Marion and his men, despite their peculiarity, were anything other than human. They had arrived in the Bay during a period of intertribal hostilities, and after various attempts by particular groups to acquire the French as allies, it was decided that they were too unpredictable and disrespectful of the gods, and must be got rid of. Marion himself was sacrificed, not as a god, but like any enemy chief who had desecrated a tapu place. Despite its fine beginnings, this proved to be one of the most destructive of all early Maori–European encounters; it led to the slaughter of hundreds of local Maori as well as many of Marion's companions, and consequential intertribal battles and expulsions of whole descent groups from the Bay of Islands.

One result of local reflection on these experiences was the emergence of the word 'Maori' to distinguish themselves from Europeans, or 'Pakeha'. Accounts of the origins of these two terms show how intertwined they were with each other, and with debates about the first meetings with Europeans.

In 1910, for instance, Te Waaka Te Ranui of Ruaatoki wrote a letter to the editor of *Te Pipiwharauroa,* a Maori-language newspaper, asking, 'He aha tatou i kiia ai he Maori?' – Why are we called Maori? In his letter, Te Waaka offered some answers both to this question and to another on the origin of the word 'Pakeha' (European). First, Te Waaka claimed that when Captain Cook arrived at Tuuranga-nui in 1769, he was almost out of potatoes, so he asked the local people if they had any. They answered that they had a similar root, and when he asked for its name, they said that it was 'maori' (ordinary). Cook turned to his companions and said, 'These people are Maori!' Second, according to Te Waaka, when the local people first saw Europeans' faces, they thought they were as pale as some of their garments, and so they called them 'Pakeha' after a particular type of flax.

In the next issue of *Te Pipiwharauroa*, there was a scathing response to Te Waaka's letter from Nikora Tautau of Uawa. Nikora began by rehearsing both Te Waaka's questions and his answers, dismissing these as 'koorero puuraakau', 'paki waitara' (incredible stories, fiction). He lampooned Te Waaka's account of the conversation with Captain Cook, asking whether he thought Cook was mad, for it was as though a person, having asked a horse its name and having been told 'horse', turned to his companion and said, 'This is a cow!' He then proceeded to give his own answers to Te Waaka's questions.

According to Nikora, the term 'maori' was a description for ancient things, ordinary things, things from inland and for local people. 'Wai maori', for instance, was fresh water, in contrast to 'wai tai', the salty waters of the sea. As for 'Pakeha', this was an ancient term for pale-skinned folk who were also called 'tuurehu, patupaiarehe, urukehu, pakepakeha'. When local people first saw Europeans with their pale skins, they called them 'pakepakeha' after an ancient people who had arrived from the sea, from outside Maori territories.

In the next issue of *Te Pipiwharauroa*, a letter was published from the East Coast tribal expert Mohi Tuurei, from the Taapere-nui whare waananga ('school of learning') and a deacon of the Church of England, in response to this exchange. He supported Nikora's account and further corrected Te Waaka's claims, but with a display of erudite authority that outmatched them both. He explained that the term 'maori' was indeed ancient, for in the old days there had been two peoples in the land, the tribe of atua and the tribe of 'taangata maori' (ordinary people). Everything in the everyday world was 'maori' – descent groups, chiefs, paa (fortified villages), treasures and food. When people died they were farewelled: 'Hei konei raa i te ao maori, i te ao tuuroa' (Farewell from the maori world, the established world). 'Maori' people were ordinary and everyday, unlike the new arrivals with their white skins and strange ways of speaking. He also told of the arrival of a boatload of pale-skinned people to the East Coast, called 'pakepakeha' after part of a haka (chant) they performed, long before the arrival of Captain Cook in the *Endeavour* in 1769. This chant, according to Tuurei, was the origin of the term 'pakeha'.[12]

From the outset, then, Maori people were formulating guesses about the nature of their extraordinary visitors; and as the debate in the pages of *Te Pipiwharauroa* indicates, it is unlikely that unanimity was quickly achieved. All the various surviving Maori accounts of first meetings with Europeans share the supposition, however, that these new arrivals were not 'maori', or ordinary. The newly constituted groups were defined in relation to each other; what are now commonplace ethnic labels in New Zealand ('Maori' and 'Pakeha') at first meant simply 'familiar, everyday', and 'extraordinary' in some way.

MAORI AS EUROPEANS' OTHERS

European images of Maori emerged out of the same volatile mix of puzzlement, preconception and violence. Although Maori memories of their first meetings with Europeans focused upon Cook and his six-month circumnavigation of the country in 1769–70, Europeans' first ideas about Maori were crafted from written records of Tasman's short visit to Taitapu in 1642. One early printed version of this meeting, by Dirk van Nierop in 1674, described Maori as 'opposite footers'; 'Antipodeans' who lived on the other side of the globe, with their feet directly opposite the Netherlands:

> [These opposite footers] were rough voiced, sturdy and big boned. They came no further than a shot from the boat. They blew many times on an instrument which gave off a sound like Moorish trumpets. Our people also blew back. Their colour was between brown and yellow, with black hair, tied directly above the crown, as the Japanese do behind the head. Their hair was as long and thick as the Japanese, and in this a great thick white feather stood. Some of them wore clothes of matting and some of cotton, but they were naked above the waist.
>
> On 19 December these opposite footers began to be somewhat bolder and more courageous, because they began to trade with the smaller ship and even

came on board. The commander, seeing this, feared that there might be an attack, and sent a small boat with seven men to warn his comrades not to trust these people too much. They put off from the ship, unarmed, and were themselves attacked by these Antipodeans. Three or four were killed and the rest swam away. Our people tried to avenge this attack, but the sea was rather rough and they could not do it. The Bay was therefore called Murderers' Bay, and it is now called such on the maps.[13]

This account centred upon a violent clash which led to Maori being described as 'murderers' on the world maps at the time. Later versions of this meeting were more lurid; for instance, one published by Prévost in 1746:

> The Barbarians dared to go on board one of the two vessels to trade. Tasman suspected a surprise attack of some sort. He immediately despatched his longboat, manned by seven men, to urge the captain of the other ship to take every precaution. The longboat was unarmed. It was attacked by the savages, who killed three of the seven Dutchmen and forced the others to swim for their lives. Tasman, pierced by grief, called this spot *Murderers' Bay*. He wanted to revenge such dark treachery, but bad weather prevented his men from landing. This land seemed to him pleasant and fertile.[14]

Prévost termed Maori 'savages' and 'barbarians', and their attack on the Dutch 'dark treachery', although from a local point of view they were simply defending their harbour from strangers who (in the exchange of trumpet calls) had accepted

'*Thus Appears the Murderers Bay*' — a sketch of the meeting between Tasman's ships and Ngaati Tuuma-takokiri in Taitapu (Golden Bay) in 1642, by Isaack Gilsemans.

a challenge to fight. Prévost's text influenced later meetings, for instance the visit by *St Jean Baptiste*, Surville's ship, to Tokerau in 1769.[15] It was consulted by officers on board the ship, and contributed to the negative way in which they viewed Maori (whom they described in advance as 'savages of bad repute'), and the kidnapping and burning of villages and canoes that marred their encounters with Ngaati Kahu, the people of that place.

Cook was also influenced by Tasman's account, which came on board the *Endeavour* in a copy of Dalrymple's *Historical Collection* (which termed Taitapu Maori 'villains' and 'murderers' and depicted them in their canoes), and a translated version of van Nierop's more matter-of-fact report. Whatever their initial expectations may have been, however, the scientists on board the *Endeavour*, and Cook himself, carefully observed Maori during their circumnavigation of the two main islands during 1769–70, and tried systematically to describe them and their ways of life.

In a set of 'Hints' supplied to the *Endeavour* expedition by the Royal Society, the Earl of Morton had talked of 'natives' as 'human creatures, the work of the same omnipotent Author, equally under His care with the most polished European', and instructed Cook to avoid violence wherever possible:

> They are the natural, and in the strictest sense of the word, the legal possessors of the several Regions they inhabit. No European Nation has a right to occupy any part of their country, or settle among them without their voluntary consent. Conquest over such people can give no just title; because they could never be the Agressors. They may naturally and justly attempt to repell intruders, whom they may apprehend are come to disturb them in the quiet possession of their country. Therefore should they in a hostile manner oppose a landing, and kill some men in the attempt, even this would hardly justify firing among them, 'till every other gentle method had been tried.[16]

Morton's liberalism construed 'natives' as 'unpolished' and inferior to Europeans, but fully entitled to human rights. Despite his 'Hints', there were a number of shootings during the voyage, and the *Endeavour* descriptions of Maori were distinctly mixed; sometimes respectful, even admiring, and sometimes – especially on the topic of cannibalism – scandalised.

Accounts of Maori from Cook's or Surville's voyages had little popular impact in Europe by the time that Cook's second expedition left England in July 1772. None of the official publications had yet appeared, and a close examination of French and British periodicals at the time shows a mixed reaction to news from those expeditions. Like the versions of Tasman's voyage, the brief reports that were published generally represented Maori as cruel, brave or warlike 'savages'. The *Gazette de France*, for instance, published short comments on Surville's voyage and the *Endeavour*'s return to England, noting that they had collected specimens of a 'thousand different species of plants unknown in Europe', including a kind of flax 'which yields a thread twice as strong as that of known varieties of hemp' (the New Zealand flax, or harakeke); and added:

the English travellers . . . went to New Zealand which has always been considered
to be a continent; but they verified that the bay known to date as Murderer's Bay
is really a strait which divides the island into two parts. They found that these two
parts are together bigger than Great Britain. They landed in several places, despite
the resistance of the inhabitants who are cannibals and very cruel. During their
stay in the two islands, they noticed that the savages, although often divided and at
war, adhere faithfully to the treaties they make with one another.[17]

The *Endeavour's* return provoked greater public interest in Britain, and British
periodicals published lengthy descriptions of the voyage, quoting from letters and
anonymous publications by members of the *Endeavour* crew. Again, however,
reports of New Zealand – 'an island near three hundred leagues in length, and
inhabited by cannibals' – focused on Maori violence (ironically, since the only
people killed or wounded during the *Endeavour* circumnavigation were Maori)
and the practical difficulties of landing in Maori territories.[18]

The British élite also learned about Maori by word of mouth. On their arrival
back in London, the wealthy young naturalist Joseph Banks and his colleague Dr
Daniel Solander became the talk of the town. They were summoned to Windsor,
honoured with doctorates from Oxford and invited everywhere to tell tales of
their great adventure. King George III befriended the young Banks, who had his
portrait painted by Benjamin West, draped in a Maori cloak and surrounded by a
carved taiaha (fighting staff), a painted paddle, a greenstone adze and other Pacific
'curiosities'. At a dinner at Sir John Pringle's, Banks and Solander met Benjamin
Franklin, who heard from them that 'the Inhabitants of New Zealand were . . . a
brave & sensible People, and seem'd to have a fine Country'.[19] Perhaps at this
same dinner, an expedition sponsored by the Royal Society to take the benefits of
civilisation to New Zealand was proposed, and the hydrographer Alexander
Dalrymple, who had hoped to head the *Endeavour* voyage, volunteered to lead
it.[20] Among others, Samuel Johnson was approached to join the expedition, but
he declined. The great poet and essayist was no enthusiast for 'savage life', and later
confessed that he had grave doubts about the scientific merits of the voyage.[21]

Cook's own impressions of Maori, like those of Banks and Solander, were
on the whole admiring. In a 1771 letter to Captain John Walker in Whitby, he
described Maori as

> a strong, well-made, active people, rather above the common size. They are also a
> brave, war-like people, with sentiments void of treachery . . . They live in strong-
> holds of fortified towns, built in well chosen situations, and according to art. We
> had frequent skirmishes with them, always where we were not known, but fire-
> arms gave us the superiority. At first some of them were killed, but we at last
> learned how to manage them without taking away their lives; and when once
> peace was settled, they ever after were our very good friends . . . Their chief food
> is fish and fern roots; they have, too, in places, large plantations of potatoes and
> likewise yams, etc. Land animals they have none, either wild or tame, except
> dogs, which they breed for food. This country produceth a grass plant like flags, of

*Joseph Banks cross-dressing in a Maori cloak, with a taiaha, painted paddle and
ceremonial adze — a portrait by Benjamin West.*

the nature of hemp or flax, but superior in quality to either. Of this the natives make clothing, lines, nets, etc. The men very often go naked, with only a narrow belt around their waists; the women, on the contrary, never appear naked. Their government, religion, notions of the creation of the world, mankind, &c., are much the same as those of the natives of the South Sea Islands.[22]

Cook's claim that European encounters with Maori were often violent because Europeans did not know the local protocols for meeting strangers is interesting. Both he and Tasman had misunderstood the challenges that were directed at their ships. In the case of Tasman, his men responded to blasts on shell trumpets (often an invitation to battle) with trumpet calls of their own, and interpreted these exchanges as a musical soirée; while Cook's men at first understood the throwing of a single spear and chants of challenge (which required strangers to declare their intentions) as hostile behaviour, and shot the challengers down. As in the case of Maori, Cook's letter shows that some Europeans, who had at first thought of Maori as savages, began on closer acquaintance to realise that these were people, and fellow human beings. Yet they were not considered to be Europeans' equals – a significant qualification – for, in the last resort, the voyagers believed that their superiority was guaranteed by their guns.

I

SCIENCE
AND
WHAKAPAPA

THE SCIENTIFIC VOYAGES

REFLECTIONS ON SCIENCE AND WHAKAPAPA

Early European ventures into the Pacific were inspired in part by scientific reasoning. Terra Australis Incognita – that fabled continent of gold and spices, princes and pearls – had been dreamed of for centuries. European philosophers supposed that a great southern land must exist to counterbalance the northern landmasses, and monarchs sent explorers out to find it. In 1642, Abel Tasman had sailed from Batavia to look for the 'Unknown South-land'. He found an isolated coastline deep in the southern Pacific (part of the west coast of New Zealand), which fuelled further speculation. For a time Europeans were preoccupied with their own domestic contests. In 1744, however, John Campbell urged British merchants to send expeditions to explore and colonise the region, and in 1756 Charles de Brosses published a detailed plan for French settlement and exploration of the Southern Continent that extolled its likely marvels:

> How many people differing among themselves and certainly very dissimilar to us, in appearance, manners, custom, ideas, religion. How many animals, insects, fishes, plants, trees, forests, medicinal herbs, rocks, precious stones, fossils and metals. There are doubtless, in all fields, countless of species of which we have not even a notion, since that world has never had any connection with ours, and is, so to speak, almost as alien as if it were another planet.[1]

Voyages to the South Seas by John Byron (1764–66), Samuel Wallis (1766–68) and Cook (1768–71) for the British, and by Louis-Antoine de Bougainville (1766–69), Surville (1769–70), and Marion du Fresne (1771–72) for the French quickly followed. The French and British governments attempted to keep their findings quiet, but news of new islands and coastlines came quickly back to Europe. Gossip, letters and illicitly published journals, as well as exchanges between voyaging scientists, made attempts at secrecy (except about precise bearings) almost futile.

The reports from Wallis's and Bougainville's expeditions were greeted with rapture; it seemed that a Pacific paradise had been discovered at Tahiti, and always there were distant peaks (possibly part of the elusive continent) still to be explored. Tasman's New Zealand coastline remained a candidate for continental status until Cook's circumnavigation in 1769–70 proved it to be islands, 'to the total demolition of our aerial fabrick calld continent',[2] as Joseph Banks ruefully observed at the time. There were other coastlines, however, and other seas that had not yet been explored, and there remained a hope that the continent might still be located and claimed for European powers. The British, French and Spanish governments each sponsored expeditions to systematically search the southern oceans and to document the new islands that had been found.

After 1773, expeditions led by Cook (1773–74 and 1777), Antoine-Raymond-Joseph de Bruni d'Entrecasteaux (1793), and Alejandro Malaspina (1793) visited New Zealand. These were primarily scientific voyages, equipped for systematic observation and enquiry. In the eighteenth century, European science was often an imperial instrument, investigating the world for the glory of monarchs and the interests of the state. Imperialism, on the other hand, was sometimes a scientific instrument. Science was understood as 'enlarging of the bounds of Human Empire', by 'conquest of the works of nature',[3] based on a power relation (between mind and matter, reason and nature) that put reason in charge of reality, and made this rule seem 'natural' and right.

During the Age of Enlightenment, science laid the world out for European exploration. Emergent modern science supposed that 'all bodies are alike. No motion is special. Every place is like every other, each moment like any other . . . The natural process is nothing but the space-time determination of the motion of points of mass.'[4] The cosmos, so defined, was framed in standard grids and measured, processes made visible in the instruments, tables, charts and logs of the explorers. At the same time, those aspects of the world that resisted measurement – for instance, plants, animals and people – were brought under other kinds of standardised description (particularly the languages of taxonomy).

Pressed, painted, written about, bottled and transported, exotic plants, animals and people were taken to the explorers' homelands to be sorted, stored and exhibited in herbaria, encyclopaedia, zoos, botanical gardens and museums. The Renaissance 'theatres of memory' – imagined spaces where knowledge was stored in ampitheatres whose tiers corresponded to levels of being (from base to divine) – became real institutions where Pacific and other 'curiosities' were brought under intellectual control.

These philosophical and political assumptions made encounters between Maori people and European scientists complicated affairs. The scientific visits to New Zealand between 1773 and 1793 brought European explorers into contact with people whose understandings of the world were very different from their own. Whereas European science sought to plumb the mind of God by means of mathematics and taxonomy, Maori philosophies described the world by means of whakapapa (genealogy), networks of interactive links between beings of different kinds, and sought to influence it by means of ancestral power.

According to the cosmological accounts of Maori kin groups, the universe had emerged in genealogical stages, from a surge of energy to states of potential pattern, including thought, memory, the mind-heart and desire. Once earth and sky were formed, ancestor gods generated various forms of life, including plants, animals and people. Ancestors could collapse space-time to become co-present with their descendants, moving from an invisible dimension of experience variously described (as Hawaiki, Poo, Tawhiti, etc.) into the being of their descendants. A contemporary self as the 'living face' of their ancestor could share their experiences, or act with them in Te Ao Maarama (The World of Light).

These genealogical nets joined people to each other and to other kinds of being in relations of various kinds. Utu (the principle of balance) was the stuff of life, where relationships were constantly being negotiated in reciprocal exchanges. Tapu (the power of the gods) marked out those people, places and things where ancestors were present in the world. Mana, or efficacy, was a sign that relations with ancestors were working well, allowing transactions with others to succeed. Mate, or ill-being, showed that relationships were out of kilter, while ora was well-being, when all relations were in balance and good heart.

When Maori supposed, therefore, that in meeting with Europeans they were negotiating with ancestors or other tapu kinds of being, they were following their own accustomed logic. European scientific descriptions of Maori as 'savages' were equally logical, given their beliefs about a Great Chain of Being that categorised and ranked all forms of life, including human beings. If European explorers, by and large, were certain of their power, Maori were as certain of their mana, and each scrutinised the other intently – 'titiro atu, titiro mai!' In these early encounters the scene was set for struggles and exchanges, not just between different ways of thinking, but between Maori and European ways of being.

Overleaf: *Map of New Zealand place names.*
Detailed maps are provided in the following chapters for those areas indicated*.

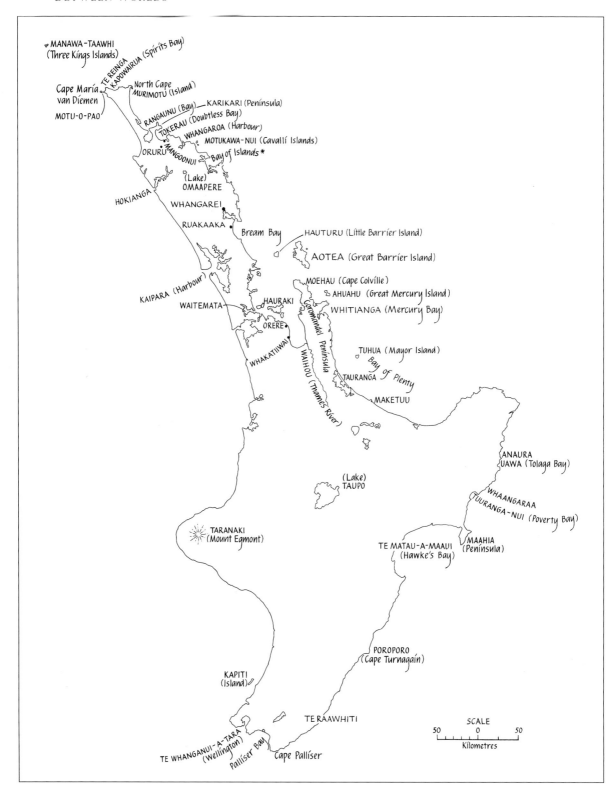

MANAWA-TAAWHI
(Three Kings Islands)

TE REINGA
KAPOWAIRUA (Spirits Bay)

North Cape
MURIMOTU (Island)

Cape Maria
van Diemen

KARIKARI (Peninsula)

MOTU-O-PAO

RANGAUNU (Bay)

TOKERAU (Doubtless Bay)

WHANGAROA (Harbour)

MOTUKAWA-NUI (Cavalli Islands)

ORURU MANGOONUI

Bay of Islands *

(Lake)
OMAAPERE

HOKIANGA

WHANGAREI

RUAKAAKA

Bream Bay

HAUTURU (Little Barrier Island)

AOTEA (Great Barrier Island)

MOEHAU (Cape Colville)

AHUAHU (Great Mercury Island)

KAIPARA (Harbour)

WAITEMATA

HAURAKI

WHITIANGA (Mercury Bay)

ORERE

Coromandel Peninsula

TUHUA (Mayor Island)

Bay of Plenty

WHAKATIIWAI

WAIHOU (Thames River)

TAURANGA

MAKETUU

ANAURA
UAWA (Tolaga Bay)

(Lake)
TAUPO

WHAANGARAA
TUURANGA-NUI (Poverty Bay)

TARANAKI
(Mount Egmont)

TE MATAU-A-MAAUI
(Hawke's Bay)

MAAHIA
(Peninsula)

POROPORO
(Cape Turnagain)

KAPITI
(Island)

TE RAAWHITI

SCALE

50   0   50

Kilometres

TE WHANGANUI-A-TARA
(Wellington)

Palliser Bay

Cape Palliser

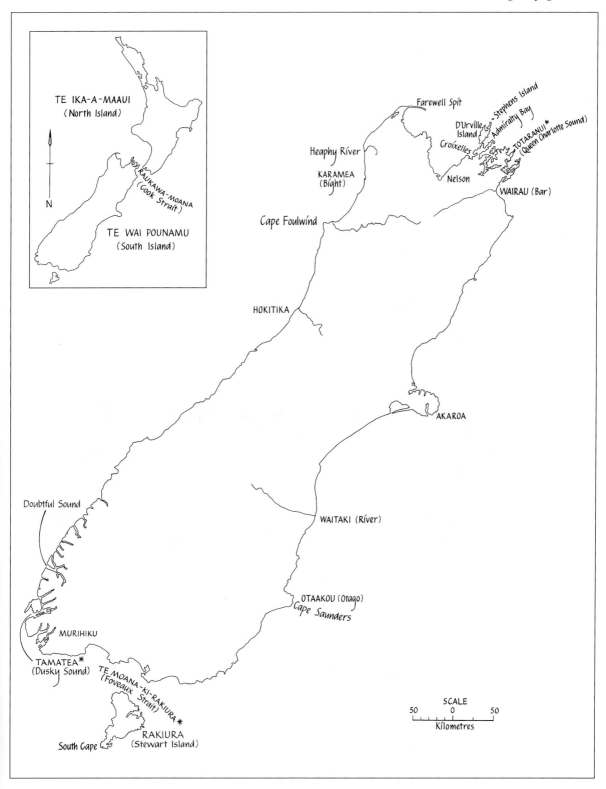

One

The Voyage of the *Resolution*
and *Adventure*
1772–1775

The first of the scientific voyages to visit New Zealand in this period was James Cook's second Pacific expedition. This was planned during Cook's first Pacific voyage, when his six-month circumnavigation of New Zealand brought him into frequent contact with Maori people. As we have noted, during those six months Cook formed a view of Maori as 'a brave, war-like people, with sentiments void of treachery'. His experiences of them, including skirmishes as well as friendly exchanges, did not discourage him from planning future visits. Once their circumnavigation of the main islands proved that New Zealand was not part of Terra Australis, Cook and Joseph Banks, the wealthy young naturalist who represented the Royal Society on that expedition, had spent long hours in the *Endeavour*'s great cabin debating how the 'continental question' might best be settled.[1] A strategy based on those discussions was outlined in Cook's journal when it was submitted to the Admiralty in 1771. While Banks basked in a blaze of public glory on their return to London, Cook drafted a chart showing the tracks of previous voyages in the Pacific, and the areas of unexplored ocean where a continent still might be. He concluded that if there was a Southern Continent, it must be in the high latitudes between 40° South and the South Pole, unless it was about the meridian of 140° West, where the northern seas had not yet been explored. Cook suggested to the Admiralty that a voyage leaving the Cape of Good Hope early in October could pick up the prevailing westerlies and sail east into high latitudes, circumnavigating the world during the summer months, while taking time out to collect wood and water at New Zealand or during the winter months to rest the crews and refit the ships at Tahiti.

The Admiralty accepted his reasoning and began to make arrangements for the voyage. Alexander Dalrymple and Benjamin Franklin's philanthropic scheme for a Royal Society expedition to New Zealand to carry 'the conveniencies of Life, as Fowls, Hogs, Goats, Cattle, Corn, Iron &c. to those remote regions' was rejected, despite Franklin's impassioned arguments published in a pamphlet at the time:

Britain is now the first maritime power in the world. Her ships are innumerable, capable by their form, size and strength of sailing all seas. Her seamen are equally bold, skilful, and hardy; dextrous in exploring the remotest regions, and ready to engage in voyages to unknown countries, although attended with the greatest dangers. The inhabitants of those countries, our fellow men, have canoes only. Not knowing iron, they cannot build ships. They have little astronomy, and no knowledge of the compass to guide them. They cannot therefore come to us, or obtain any of our advantages . . .

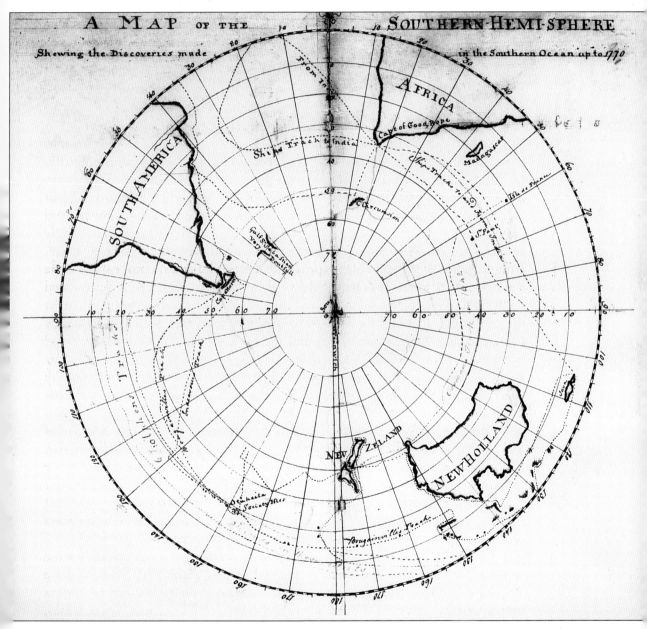

James Cook's chart of the Southern Hemisphere, showing the tracks of previous explorations.

Many voyages have been undertaken with views of profit or plunder, or to gratify resentment; to procure some advantage to ourselves, or to do some mischief to others; but a voyage is now proposed to visit a distant people on the other side the Globe; not to cheat them, not to rob them, not to seize their lands, or enslave their persons; but merely to do them good, and enable them as far as in our power lies, to live as comfortably as ourselves . . . From these circumstances, does not some duty seem to arise from us to them?[2]

The Admiralty voyage was to include a scientific party led by Joseph Banks, which would carry out experiments on new navigational instruments (including a kind of azimuth compass and four different types of chronometer), the distillation of fresh from salt water, and the prevention of scurvy by the use of carrot marmalade, sauerkraut and salted cabbage, beer brewed from juice of malt, portable soup (a meat extract) and the concentrated juice of oranges and lemons.

In the months leading up to the voyage, Banks was in his element, helping to organise the expedition. Cook had chosen the ships, two sturdy colliers built at Whitby by the shipwright who built the *Endeavour*, but Banks considered them to be too small. He spoke to his friend Lord Sandwich, First Lord of the Admiralty, and the ship in which Banks would sail, the *Resolution*, was altered to suit his requirements. Banks planned an entourage of fifteen people, including Daniel Solander, the Swedish naturalist who had accompanied him on the *Endeavour*; Dr James Lind, an Edinburgh physician and amateur astronomer; the artist John Zoffany and assorted draughtsmen, secretaries, servants and musicians; and ordered an array of scientific instruments, trade goods (including forty iron 'Patapatoes for New Zealand in imitation of their stone weapons'[3]), books and charts.

When the *Resolution* set out to sail from the shipyard to the Downs, though, the ship's new superstructure proved to be so top-heavy that she almost capsized. Charles Clerke, the ship's second lieutenant, exclaimed to Banks, 'By God, I'll go to sea in a grog-tub, if required, or in the *Resolution* as soon as you please, but must say I think her by far the most unsafe ship I ever saw or heard of.'[4] Cook told the Admiralty that the upper works would have to go. When Banks saw the results of these alterations, according to one of the midshipmen, 'He swore and stamp'd upon the Warfe, like a Mad Man; and instantly order'd his servants and all his things out of the Ship.'[5] He told the Navy Board that he would not sail in her, and from that time on lobbied for another expedition to be organised with another captain, in another vessel.

Despite all the public pressure that Banks could bring to bear, however, the Admiralty was unmoved. The *Resolution* and the *Adventure* had already been equipped with guns, stores, trade goods and crews, and the Comptroller of the Navy Board was not impressed by Banks's tantrums. Johann Forster and his son George were appointed to replace him and Solander as the expedition's naturalists, while William Wales and William Bayly were appointed as astronomers and William Hodges as the expedition's artist. In a fit of pique, Banks refused the Forsters access to the specimens from the *Endeavour* voyage, so that throughout the coming months they could never be sure whether the plants, animals and fishes they were collecting and describing were new to European science or not. All the same, Johann Forster ordered an assortment of scientific equipment and joined the ship, and on 25 June 1772, secret instructions were drafted ordering Cook to set sail in search of the Southern Continent, and instructing him to claim any uninhabited parts of it for the British Crown:

> If you find any Mines, Minerals or valuable Stones, you are to bring home Specimens of each, and also of the Seeds of Trees, Shrubs, Plants, Fruits & Grains peculiar to the Country, as you may be able to collect, & to transmit them to our Secretary that we may cause proper Examination & Experiments to be made of them; You are likewise to observe the Genius, Temper, Disposition and Number of the Natives or Inhabitants, if there be any, & endeavour by all proper means to cultivate a Friendship and Alliance with them, making them Presents of such Trinquets as they may value, inviting them to Trafick, & shewing them every kind of Civility & Regard; but taking care nevertheless not to suffer yourself to be surprized by them, but to be always on your guard against any Accident. You are with the consent of the Natives to take possession of convenient Situations in the Country in the Name of the King of Great Britain, and to distribute among the Inhabitants some of the Medals with which you have been furnished to remain as Traces of your having been there. But if you find the Country uninhabited you are to take possession of it for His Majesty by setting up proper Marks & Inscriptions as first Discoverers & Possessors.[6]

THE SHIPS

After those nerve-racked days during his first Pacific voyage when he had nearly lost the *Endeavour* on the Great Barrier Reef, Cook decided that he wanted two ships for this expedition; and he got them. His own ship, the *Resolution* was a sloop 110 feet long, weighing 462 tons, while the *Adventure* was slightly smaller, at 340 tons and 97 feet. In preparation for the voyage they were loaded with supplies (the *Resolution*, for instance, carried 59,531 pounds of biscuit, 17,437 pounds of flour, 21,851 pieces of salt meat, 19 tons of beer, 642 gallons of wine and 1,397 gallons of spirits, plus peas, wheat, oatmeal, butter, cheese, sugar, olive oil, vinegar, suet, raisins, salt, 45 tons of water and assorted anti-scorbutics[7]), as well as guns, nets and other fishing gear, carpenters' tools, scientific, surgical and cooking equipment, a forge, trade goods and other items. The trade goods 'to be exchanged for Refreshments with the Natives of such New discovered or unfrequented Countries as they may touch at, or to be distributed to them in presents towards obtaining their friendship, & winning them over to our Interest'[8]) included iron tools (adzes, axes, hatchets, chisels, saws, augers, hammers, knives, scissors and tweezers), wire, nails, combs, beads, looking glasses, kettles and pots, grindstones, cloth, old clothes and sheets. The *Resolution* had 118 men on board and the *Adventure* eighty-three, and there were also shipboard animals (including sheep, goats, poultry, cats and dogs) to be managed and provided with fresh food and water. When the *Resolution* and the *Adventure* sailed into a Pacific port, this would be a formidable arrival, involving two large ships, over two hundred men and a huge array of European material items.

A number of the men on this expedition, including Cook, had been in the Pacific before. Charles Clerke, for instance, second lieutenant of the *Resolution* and a 'general favorite', had sailed as a midshipman with Byron, and on the *Endeavour* as third lieutenant. Tobias Furneaux, commander of the *Adventure*, and Richard Pickersgill, the *Resolution*'s third lieutenant and formerly master's mate on the *Endeavour*, 'a good officer and astronomer but liking ye Grog',[9] had sailed with Wallis to Tahiti. Along with Cook himself, and Clerke and Pickersgill, there were a number of the *Endeavour*'s crew on board the *Resolution*, including the 'clever and steady' master's mate Isaac Smith, the midshipmen William Harvey and Isaac Manley, two marines, Lieutenant John Edgcumbe and Corporal Samuel Gibson, who had tried to desert in Tahiti, and eight seamen, including the Irish gunner's mate John Marra, who wrote a vivid account of the voyage.

Thus many of the *Resolution*'s men already had experience of Polynesian people, and none of them, according to the ships' muster rolls (unlike four of the *Adventure*'s crew), had 'the venereals' at the outset of the voyage. Cook had seen for himself the impact of venereal disease on the Tahitians, and hoped that no more Pacific populations would be infected. In addition, almost all of the scientists (and most of the scientific instruments) were on board the *Resolution* – the senior astronomer William Wales, a thoughtful observer of people as well as planets; Johann Reinhold Forster, described by John Elliott as 'a clever but a litigious quarelsom, fellow', trained in theology at Halle and a devoted natural scientist who drove his shipmates mad; his seventeen-year-old son George, 'a clever good young man' who specialised in botany and sketched many of the specimens; Dr Anders Sparrman, a rather prim Swedish naturalist and student of Linnaeus, who joined the expedition at the Cape of Good Hope; and William Anderson, the surgeon's mate, a good linguist and excellent self-taught naturalist, who made an extensive collection of 'curiosities' during the voyage.

It was the *Resolution*, then, that was the main scientific vessel of the expedition. It carried most of the 'experimental gentlemen', supplies of 'experimental beef', machines for making 'experimental water', and juice for brewing 'experimental beer' (which most of the sailors detested). The crew lived alongside the scientists and helped them to collect plants, rocks and animals, to set up the portable observatory, measure the temperature of sea water and construct their 'tide-machine'. Sometimes, however, they stubbornly resisted these activities – according to Johann Forster, the scientists on board the ship were 'cramped and deprived of the means of pursuing knowledge, in a manner which would only become a set of barbarians'.[10] Even the mild-mannered Wales sometimes found it hard to get the crew's co-operation, and complained. There was friction between naval and scientific requirements, and Johann Forster as senior scientist was unrelenting and often

The Resolution, *painted by Henry Roberts (a sailor on the ship) during Cook's second Pacific voyage.*

querulous in his demands. At the end of the voyage, Cook is said to have exclaimed in a moment of utter exasperation, 'Curse the scientists, and all science into the bargain!'[11]

THE VOYAGE

It was no accident, however, that almost all of the expedition's scientists were together on board the *Resolution*.

Experimental science, then as now, required reliable witnesses for its proce-dures. Observations could only be validated if independent observers could repli-cate them or agree upon what had been seen.[12] Hodges, the artist, and George Forster, as natural history draughtsman, were also there for scientific reasons. Natural history required that specimens, whether plant, animal or human, should be described as faithfully as possible; since each species was held (by Linnaeus, for example) to be a unique divine creation, ranked in an order that mirrored the mind and will of God.[13]

Once the scientists and their equipment had been assembled, the main prepa-rations for the voyage were completed. On 13 July 1772, a month after the Forsters had been officially appointed to the expedition, the *Adventure* and the *Resolution* sailed from Plymouth Sound. Ten days later, near Cape Finisterre, three Spanish men of war challenged the British ships, forcing them to bring to. When the Spanish commander was informed that this was Captain Cook's expedition, he remarked, 'Oh, Cook, is it?', wished them a good voyage and sent them on their way.[14] The ships carried on to Madeira and then the Cape Verde Islands, where Johann Forster reflected upon the relationship between the islands' climate and inhabitants. He drew a sharp contrast between the islanders, whom he character-ised as indolent, superstitious and oppressed, and people from more temperate countries, who enjoyed 'the great blessings of liberty, industry, security in regard to property, & of rational & moderate principles in religious matters'.[15]

Forster wrote detailed accounts of both places, their main towns, climate, geography and populations, and he and his son collected and described local plants, insects, fish and birds. At Porto Praya in the Cape Verde Islands, fruit and some domesticated animals (fowls, turkeys, pigs, goats and a bullock) were brought on board the *Resolution*, and the sailors acquired a number of monkeys as pets, which ran around the ship until Cook got sick of them and ordered them thrown over-board. Johann Forster studied these monkeys and compared them with descriptions from his shipboard collection of works on natural history, including Buffon, Linnaeus, Edwards's *Gleanings of Natural History* and Pennant's *Synopsis of Quadrupeds*.[16]

The ships now sailed south towards the Cape of Good Hope while Wales, Cook and the Forsters carried on with their scientific work. They conducted experiments (described by Johann Forster as 'the firmest & only basis possible for getting at truth') on the temperature of sea water at different depths, the direction and speed of currents, the distillation of fresh from sea water with 'Mr. Irwin's apparatus', and observed an eclipse of the moon. Various birds were shot and fish were caught and sketched by George Forster, and just off the Cape they fished up 'animalcules' from a sea shimmering with phosphorescence and studied them under their microscopes. At the Cape, Wales and his fellow astronomer William Bayly set up their instruments and tested the watches by calculating the longitude, while the Forsters made botanical excursions in the surrounding countryside. Here they found many new species of plants and animals, 'though . . . in fields adjacent to a town, from whence the cabinets and repositories of all Europe have been repeatedly supplied with numerous and valuable acquisitions to the science'.[17] They met with Dr Sparrman, and after some negotiations Johann Forster persuaded him to join the expedition to assist in describing the innumerable new species they hoped to discover during their travels.

The *Resolution* took on board some sheep and a water spaniel at the Cape, as well as other supplies. On 23 November 1772, the ships sailed out of the harbour and began their first sweep south towards the Antarctic Circle. They ran into rough weather; shipboard conditions became cold and wet and the stock began to die. On 10 December, the first iceberg was sighted, but Cook pressed on south in search of lands reported by Bouvet and Kerguelen, and the Southern Continent.

For weeks the expedition sailed through icebergs in search of land, with 'the frost and cold so intense as to cover the Rigging with Ice, like compleat christal ropes'.[18] Christmas was celebrated with drunken festivities. Birds were shot from the boats, and Cook, Wales and the Forsters conducted further experiments on the temperature of sea water at different depths, and the use of various antiscorbutics. On 8 February, however, the *Resolution* was separated from the *Adventure* in thick fog, and the two ships lost contact with each other.

After looking for the *Resolution* for several days, the *Adventure* sailed directly to Van Diemen's Land (Tasmania), and from there to their rendezvous at Queen Charlotte Sound, in the north of New Zealand's South Island, where Furneaux and his men settled in to wait for their consort. Over the next month, the *Resolution* continued the search for Terra Australis in high latitudes, in increasingly difficult conditions. As it got colder, the sheep and cattle were shifted below decks. Johann Forster commented miserably:

> I was now beset with cattle & stench on both Sides, having no other but a thin deal partition full of chinks between me & them. The room offered me by Capt Cook, & which the Masters obstinacy deprived me of, was now given to very peaceably bleating creatures, who on a stage raised up as high as my bed, shit & pissed on one side, whilst 5 Goats did the same afore on the other side. My poor Cabin was often penetrated by the wet, & all the many chinks in it admitted the air & the cold from all sides freely; so that my Situation became every day more unfavourable, at the increasingly cold weather.[19]

Finally Cook turned northward to New Zealand. On 25 March 1773, after four months among the icebergs, land was sighted. According to Pickersgill, 'every

Dusky Bay, painted by the ship's artist William Hodges as the ships entered the Sound in March 1773.

body that was able to crawl on the masts and yards got up to satisfy their longing senses of a sight allmost forgot, whilst those who were not able, importuned the others as they came down for a discription'.[20] While the crew were still celebrating, the *Resolution* sailed past the south-western corner of the South Island, tacked off Doubtful Sound, and on 26 March anchored in Tamatea, sighted and named Dusky Sound by Cook on his previous visit to New Zealand. As Cook noted with resignation, they had been at sea for 117 days and sailed 3,660 leagues without any sight of land.[21]

Two

TAMATEA (DUSKY SOUND)

THE *RESOLUTION*'S VISIT TO TAMATEA
26 March – 11 May 1773

At the beginnings of the world, when the Earth Mother Papa-tua-nuku lay undivided in a great sea, the sons of the Sky Father Raki had set off to see her. They explored the coasts of Papa-tua-nuku, and then sailed in their canoe to look for other countries. Although they voyaged across the ocean for a long time, they found only empty stretches of water. Finally, one of Raki's sons began to chant a karakia to lift them back into the sky. In his weariness he chanted the wrong words, and the canoe began to sink beneath the water. As it submerged, it tipped to one side and turned into stone, forming Te Waka-o-Aoraki (The Canoe of Raki's World) – the South Island of New Zealand. The high side of the canoe became the west coast, a formidable wall of rock on which waves continually crashed. Tuu-te-Raki-Whaanoa, another of Raki's sons, set to work to make this coastline habitable. Taking his adze Te Hamo, he chopped a series of channels into the cliffs. Planting his feet on two islands, (Maaui-katau (Left-right) or Resolution Island in Dusky Sound; and Ka-tuu-Waewae-o-Tuu (Tuu's Standing Place) or Secretary Island in Doubtful Sound), he pushed them apart, and as he strained he deposited two large droppings (Te Tuutae-o-Tuu-te-Raki-Whaanoa: Anchor Island in Dusky Sound and Bauza Island in Doubtful Sound, and two meandering streams (Te Mimi-o-Tuu – Tuu's Urine) which formed the channels around them. Now that the land was shaped, Tuu covered it with rain forest and filled the fiords with birds and fish.[1]

Te Waka-o-Aoraki was so remote that it was many generations before people from Hawaiki crossed the ocean and found it. One of the earliest voyaging canoes to make the crossing was *Takitimu*, with its cargo of god-stones and priestly experts. It stopped briefly in Tamatea (Dusky Sound), which took its name from the canoe's captain.[2] According to stories from the area, Tamatea's earliest inhabitants, the Waitaha, were of *Takitimu* descent.[3] After settling the South Island and living there for some time, Waitaha sent a gift of local delicacies across Raukawa-moana (Cook Strait) to Ngaati Mamoe, who had migrated there from Te Matau-a-Maaui

45

(Hawke's Bay).[4] Ngaati Mamoe found these foods so delicious that they invaded Waitaha's northerly hunting and fishing grounds, forcing them south to various places, including Tamatea. A series of invasions by other North Island groups followed, in turn putting pressure on Ngaati Mamoe, who lost most of their northern lands. Despite this, Ngaati Mamoe remained a force to be reckoned with until the migration of Ngaai Tahu (originally from the east coast of the North Island), who attacked and defeated them in a series of battles.

Finally, Ngaati Mamoe sued Ngaai Tahu for peace and invited one of their principal chiefs, Tarawhai, to a paa south of Timaru. When his party arrived at the paa, they were ambushed; Tarawhai was taken prisoner and all of his companions were killed. According to a Ngaai Tahu account, quoted by Alexander Mackay in 1873:

> As Tarawhai had been a great scourge to them, [Ngaati Mamoe] were determined to cut him to pieces alive, he was accordingly laid on his back on the ground, and a [man] commenced to cut him down the breast and the stomach with a sharp stone. The attention of the four [men] who were holding Tarawhai being directed at the moment to the arrival of some visitors at the pah, he sprung to his feet, and succeeded in making his escape into the bush. Being much distressed at the loss of his patu paraoa (whalebone club), he determined to attempt its recovery, he accordingly took advantage of the shades of the evening to approach the camps of the Ngatimamoe. On arriving near the place, he noticed a large number of [warriors] seated round a fire, and on drawing near, saw them examining the weapon, and talking of the bravery of its owner. Noticing the absence of one Ngatimamoe who had a defect in his speech, he walked up to the outer circle, and seating himself on the ground, asked (feigning the voice of the man of defective speech) to be allowed to look at this celebrated patu. It was handed to him by the unsuspecting Ngatimamoe, when jumping suddenly up, he struck the two nearest him over the head, crying the brave Tarawhai has recovered his weapon, which so astonished his enemies that he succeeded in again reaching the cover of the woods in safety . . .
>
> . . . Messengers were at once despatched to other portions of the tribe residing further north, to inform them of the mishap which had befallen the followers of Tarawhai, and requesting them to assemble as quickly as possible, and take revenge for the death of their friends. These divisions of the tribe at once combined with their southern friends, and great was the slaughter of the now doomed Ngatimamoe, who were driven south, and being almost surrounded by the Ngaitahu, they took refuge in the fastnesses of the southern forest. This was the last time the Ngatimamoe made any stand against the conquering Ngaitahu. Weakened by successive defeats, they ceased to build pahs, secreted themselves in caverns, and fled on the approach of strangers.[5]

In consequence of these defeats, Ngaati Mamoe followed the Waitaha's ancient path to Murihiku, the south-west corner of the South Island. They intermarried there with Ngaai Tahu, and by the time of the *Resolution*'s arrival in 1773, Tamatea

Opposite: *Map of Tamatea (Dusky Sound).*

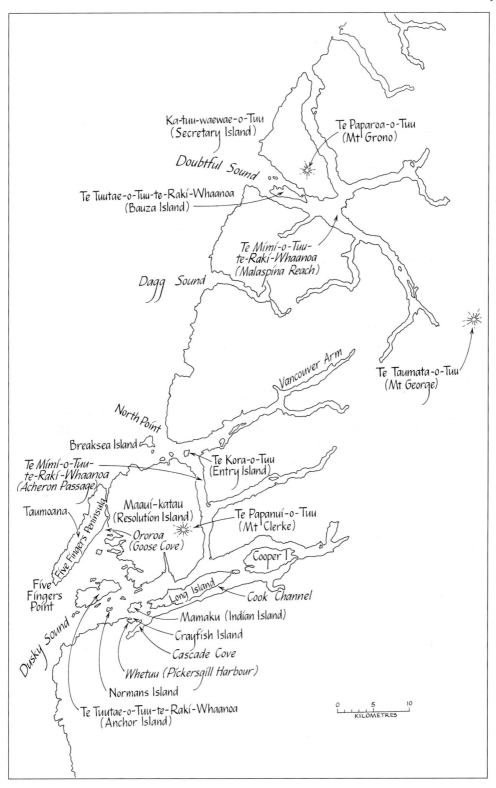

Ka-tuu-waewae-o-Tuu
(Secretary Island)

Te Paparoa-o-Tuu
(Mt Grono)

Doubtful Sound

Te Tuutae-o-Tuu-te-Rakí-Whaanoa
(Bauza Island)

Te Mímí-o-Tuu-
te-Rakí-Whaanoa
(Malaspina Reach)

Dagg Sound

Vancouver Arm

Te Taumata-o-Tuu
(Mt George)

North Point

Breaksea Island

Te Kora-o-Tuu
(Entry Island)

Te Mímí-o-Tuu-
te-Rakí-Whaanoa
(Acheron Passage)

Taumoana

Maauí-katau
(Resolution Island)

Te Papanuí-o-Tuu
(Mt Clerke)

Ororoa
(Goose Cove)

Five Fingers Peninsula

Cooper I.

Five
Fingers
Point

Long Island

Cook Channel

Dusky Sound

Mamaku (Indian Island)

Crayfish Island

Cascade Cove

Whetuu (Pickersgill Harbour)

Normans Island

Te Tuutae-o-Tuu-te-Rakí-Whaanoa
(Anchor Island)

0   5   10
KILOMETRES

had become one of their hunting grounds on their Murihiku lands.

In 1773, the human population of Tamatea was sparse, but the bush was full of birds and the sea teemed with fish and sea mammals. The sound ran thirty miles towards the centre of the island, its waters surrounded by mountains that dropped sheer into the sea. The surrounding countryside was cold, wet and rugged. Fiords, long lakes and rivers wandered inland along waterways and valleys. In an isolated island, this was one of the most hidden corners, protected by difficult seas and dense rain forests.

When the *Resolution* sailed into Tamatea on 26 March 1773, and anchored a hawser's length from the land,[6] it was entering a remote and relatively primeval place. It certainly seemed idyllic to Cook's weary, half-frozen crew. George Forster wrote:

> The weather was delightfully fair, and genially warm, when compared to what we had lately experienced; and we glided along by insensible degrees, wafted by light airs, past numerous rocky islands, each of which was covered with wood and shrubberies, where numerous evergreens were sweetly contrasted and mingled with the various shades of autumnal yellow. Flocks of acquatic birds enlivened the rocky shores, and the whole country resounded with the wild notes of the feathered tribe . . . The sloop was no sooner in safety, than every sailor put his hook and line overboard, and in a few moments numbers of fine fish were hauled up on all parts of the vessel. The view of . . . antediluvian forests which cloathed the rock, and of numerous rills of water, which every where rolled down the steep declivity, altogether conspired to complete our joy. We looked upon the country at that time, as one of the most beautiful which nature unassisted by art could produce.[7]

Shortly after the ship anchored off 'Anchor Island', Cook sent some men out fishing while he and Lieutenant Pickersgill went in opposite directions to look for a more sheltered anchorage. By the time they returned on board, the fishermen had shot a seal for dinner and caught a fine haul of fish, including coalfish, sea mullet, horse mackerel and a number of less familiar species.[8] The next morning they woke to a burst of birdsong, and Pickersgill guided the ship from its anchorage into a cove (Pickersgill Harbour), 'one of the most inchanting little Harbours I ever saw . . . surrounded with high Lands intirely cover'd with tall shady trees rising like an ampitheatre; and with the sweet swelling Notes of a number of Birds made the finest Harmony.'[9] The *Resolution* was backed into a creek and tied with hawsers to the shore. The trunk of a large, almost horizontal tree formed a ready-made gangway, and branches of other trees locked into the yards.

On 28 March, some of Cook's officers went out early to explore the bay. About two miles north of the ship, they noticed smoke from a fire, and soon afterwards heard voices on shore and saw ten or twelve people in the woods with a canoe nearby. It was pouring with rain and they knew that their muskets might

Opposite: *A plan and coastal views of Dusky Bay, drafted by Joseph Gilbert, Master on the* Resolution.

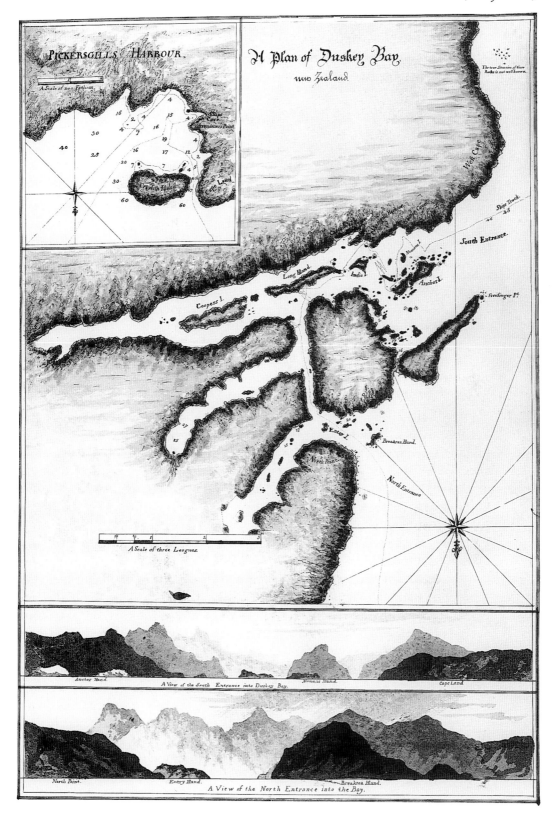

PICKERSGILLS HARBOUR.

A Scale of 200 Fathom.

A Plan of Dusky Bay

new Zealand.

The true Situation of these Rocks is not well known.

West Cape

Ship Track.

South Entrance.

Fivefinger Pt.

Anchor I.

India I.

Long Island

Coopers I.

Breaksea Island.

Entry I.

North Point.

North Entrance

A Scale of three Leagues.

Anchor Island.   *A View of the South Entrance into Dusky Bay.*   Nomans Island.   Cape Land.

North Point.   Entry Island.   *A View of the North Entrance into the Bay.*   Breaksea Island.

misfire, so they decided to return to the *Resolution*. Just as they came back on board, two canoes[10] paddled around a headland about half a mile from the ship. Their crews stared at the *Resolution* for about five minutes, then paddled away again. Cook thought that they were fleeing from a heavy squall of rain, but Wales supposed that they were frightened: 'A sight, so uncommon as our Ship must be to them, would, I suppose, be sufficient to strike terror into the bravest of Mankind!'[11]

This first brief encounter was followed up that afternoon, when a small double canoe came out close to the ship. For half an hour, its crew of eight gazed at the *Resolution* 'with the utmost surprize', while the Europeans tried to entice them on board. Johann Forster described these people in some detail:

> The oldest Man, with a large beard sat at the helm, with his steering paddle, & was of a brownish Complexion, had a redbrown Matt on his back; The rest seemed to be pretty white & had likewise Matts, but of a whiter hue, than the old Mans & had broad paddles to work the canoe with . . . They leaned on the Gunnel of their canoe & stared at the Ship. The Corporal of Marines Gibson, who can talk the Otaheitee Language best, which has an affinity with that of the New-Zealanders, went on the Sprit-Sail-yard-arm, & waved a white cloth to them, calling to them *harre-mai-Tayo* i.e. *come Friend*, & promised them beads or as they call it Pohe: but they either did not understand it or did not chose to come for fear of being over-powered & ill treated. After having satisfied their curiosity, they stood in Shore again & began to paddle & soon came round the point out of sight.[12]

It is not possible to identify this group with any certainty. Various guesses have been made,[13] but none seems authoritative. Tribal histories from the area are fragmented, and stories relating to Cook's visit in 1773 were not collected until about 1910. Very likely these were members of Ngaati Mamoe, but Ngaai Tahu also visited Tamatea from time to time. The tribal records do make it clear, however, that intense intertribal fighting was going on at this time, and it is no wonder that these people were so circumspect.

Cook was eager to make friends with this group, whomever they may have been. That afternoon he and the Forsters, Wales and others went in the pinnace and the cutter to 'Cascade Cove', where these people had first been seen. They found a small double canoe pulled up on a beach, with two dug-out hulls joined by lashed cross-pieces. Each hull had high prow and sternposts, with the prows carved 'like the upper parts of a man and two limpet shells were put for the Eyes'.[14] The canoe was equipped with two carved paddles and contained a basket of tutu berries. Two small shelters were hidden nearby 'about 4 or 5 feet high, and nearly of the same breadth, made of bark and the leaves of [flax]; they were round on top like an arched Vault and were built in the thickest part of the bushes'.[15] One had a mat in front of the door. There were also two small flax nets by these shelters, some fireplaces and some fish, both raw and broiled, lying on the ground or hung in the trees. No-one was to be seen, however, so Cook put ribbons, medals, beads and a looking glass in the canoe bailer, under a paddle. After rowing across the cove, he came back to the hamlet and, taking a small hatchet, chipped some bark off a tree to demonstrate its use then struck it into the trunk. Over the next few days, these gifts lay undisturbed.

On the morning of the 29th, the crew began to build a proper gangway from the ship to the shore. Tents were set up in a clearing for the waterers, the coopers, woodcutters and sailmakers, a forge was established and beer was brewed from rimu and maanuka leaves and molasses. Wales set to work to clear a site for his observatory at 'Astronomer's Point' nearby, and over the next ten days, about a hundred large trees were felled.[16]

The site was levelled around two big stumps, one of which served to fix the astronomical clock, and the other as a base for the quadrant. Wales's task was to calculate the latitude and longitude, and so to fix the exact position of this part of New Zealand. He also set up a thermometer and a barometer, and a 'machine' to measure the tides – 'a long square Tube whose internal side is about 3 Inches: A square float is fitted to this Tube & fixed to the end of a long slender Rod which is divided into feet and Inches from the float upwards.'[17] The first tube was too short, so Wales had one made that was eleven feet long, its base propped in the hollow of a rock just below low-water mark, and its top tied to an overhanging tree. Both he and Cook were surprised to discover that the tides in Tamatea rose and fell almost eight feet at their highest point.

While Wales was measuring temperature, barometric pressure and the tides, and making astronomical calculations, the Forsters began collecting plants and animals. As soon as they stepped ashore, George noted, 'we perceived a new store of animal and vegetable bodies, and among them hardly any that were perfectly similar to the known species, and several not analogous even to the known genera'.[18] Johann found the conditions arduous, however, and grumbled about the difficulties of botanising on shore:

> I found myself quite tantalized with the sight of innumerable plants & Trees, all new ones, none of which had flowers at this Season & the fruits either were quite unripe or allready gone: so that my collection fell short of my Expectation. Tired with disappointment, the continual rain & the bad walking between wet trees, that rained a double portion upon me from their soaked foliage, & between rotten felled trees and heaps of moss, where I frequently fell in with my legs up to my knees & above, I returned on board. Early in the morning I got up, but could take no Excursion on account of the continual rain. We examined therefore several plants, & revised our descriptions & examined the drawings of them.[19]

The Linnaean system for classifying plants, which the Forsters were applying, distinguished different species by counting the pistils and stamens of their flowers and geometrically describing their arrangement.[20] It was almost impossible to use during the autumn months, to Johann's dismay. On board, he complained that:

> My Cabin was a Magazine of all the various kinds of plants, fish, birds, Shells, Seeds etc. hitherto collected: which made it vastly damp, dirty, crammed & caused

very noxious vapours, and an offensive smell, & being just under the Chain-plates and the Ship lying close in Shore under high trees; it was so dark, that I was obliged to light a candle during day, when I wanted to write something. And as it was just opposite the hatchway, there was always a world of lumber before its door: sometimes I was pent in for hours together, or excluded from it during the same time: all the dirt & noise in the whole Ship, was accumulated about it: so that my & my Sons accomodations were the worst in the whole Ship, under all circumstances, in hot & cold climates, in dry & moist weather, at Anchor & at Sea.[21]

Along with the tormenting bites of the local sandflies, such were the sensuous delights of science in Tamatea. Still, the Forsters worked hard in the Sound. They tried to track down a mysterious mouse-coloured quadruped (possibly a Polynesian dog or one of the ship's cats) seen by one of the sailors, and commented on the tameness of the local birds, which hopped onto nearby branches and even perched on the muzzles of their guns.

The quadruped proved elusive, however, and the birds were about to have a rude awakening. Almost every day specimens were shot for description (weka, tuuii, bellbird, kookako, kaakaa; South Island fantails, robins and pipits; gannets, dotterels, oystercatchers, albatrosses, prions and gulls; black, pied and little shags; white herons; saddlebacks, yellowheads, red-crowned parakeets, kingfishers; falcons and blue penguins, according to their records). These were sketched and some preserved in spirits, while others were skinned, and their meat was subsequently eaten. The officers and crew also went out hunting and shot hundreds (or, judging from Johann Forster's tallies, probably thousands) of weka, ducks, shags, oystercatchers and other birds for food. The ship's cats regularly crossed the gangplank and hunted birds,[22] the ship's rats ran ashore, and a dog that ran off into the bush reappeared two weeks later looking fat and sleek after feasting on weka and other game.[23]

The sea was also intensively harvested. Large numbers of seals were shot, and fish, shellfish and crayfish were taken in quantity (four hundred fish in a day was not uncommon), both for specimens and food. According to Johann Forster, 'we had nothing but fish in broath or Chowder, fish boiled & fried, baked & roasted & in a pye; in short we lived like true *Ichthyophagi* & though no Papists we observed the most rigorous Lent'.[24]

The volleys of gunshot must have made the local people afraid of approaching the Europeans, for they avoided them for days. On the evening of 6 April, however, when Cook, Clerke and the Forsters were returning from a duck-shooting expedition, they were hailed by a man on a rocky point jutting out from Mamaku ('Indian Island'), with a 'staff of destruction' in his hand. Since they had seen no locals since their first brief encounter nine days earlier, they responded eagerly. Cook ordered the pinnace rowed towards him, and called out 'Hallema Tayo' (come here, friend); a Tahitian greeting that the man would not have understood, since there is no word 'tayo' (taiao) meaning 'friend' in Maori. According to Johann Forster:

George and Johann Forster, botanising.

He did not stir; now & then he spoke seemingly with violence & threatened with his staff of honour [taiaha or pouwhenua], upon which he leaned. Capt. Cook went to the head of the boat, & called him friendly & threw him his handkerchief & I gave him myne likewise. Capt. Cook took two sheets of white paper & went on the rock, handed it to the Native, who was then trembling; he took it however & laid it on the rock before him. Then Capt. Cook handed both handkerchiefs to him, which he likewise laid down; then Capt. Cook shook hands with him, & lastly went up to him & nosed him [hongi], which is the mark of friendship among these people.[25]

This man was either challenging the Europeans or performing a tapu-raising ritual. White bark cloth was prized by Maori, and seems to have been recognised as a sign of peace,[26] so the gifts of handkerchiefs and white paper were welcome.

Cook's boldness in climbing onto the rock, presenting gifts at close quarters and pressing noses (hongi) with this man was unexpected, for in such situations distance was preserved until all ceremonies were over. The sailors greatly admired their captain's self-possession. Elliott commented:

No man could be better calculated to gain the confidence of Savages than Cap. Cook. He was brave, uncommonly Cool, Humane and Patient. He would land alone unarmed, or lay aside his Arms, and sit down when they threatened with theirs, throwing them Beads, Knives, and other little presents, then by degrees advancing nearer, till by patience and forbearance, he gained their friendship and an intercourse with them which to people in our situation was of the utmost consequence.[27]

Whatever ritual the man had been enacting, it was brought to an abrupt conclusion by these gestures. No early tribal accounts of this meeting have survived, although according to Teone Taare Tikao in the 1920s, South Island Maori called Captain Cook and his crew 'korakorako' (albinos) when they first saw them, and were not sure at first whether they were atua or human beings.[28] It is not surprising, then, that this old man trembled when Captain Cook climbed up to salute him.

Cook now pointed at two young women who stood nearby on the point with long spears[29] in hand, indicating that they should put these weapons down. Instead, the man called them over to meet the Europeans. Elliott described him as 'a very fine old Man of about 60 [and six feet tall] with a Wife something younger, and a daughter about 22, the finest woman we saw in the Country'.[30] The older woman had a huge growth on her upper lip, while the other was pretty and loquacious. Johann Forster commented that she chattered 'like a magpie', during 'half an hours unintelligible conversation at least as edifying as a great many which are usual in the politer circles of civilized nations, & which here at least passed with a great deal more sincerity & cordiality on both sides'.[31] In the course of this discussion, the old man made signs as though he wanted to know where the strangers came from. Cook pointed to the sky 'and gave him to understand that they had sailed more than double the space of all that wide expanse which he saw above him; that they had travelled with the sun, and that they came from that region where the sun lay hid o'nights'[32] – which must have puzzled him extremely. Cook invited these people to the ship, and they invited him to visit them on shore. The younger woman danced for them (provoking 'coarse jests' from the sailors), and her companions gave them gifts of fish and birds, while Cook and his party gave back a medal, a glass bead and a knife, promising to return the next day with more. Cook later commented to his officers that their language was very different from that of people in the North Island of New Zealand.

The next morning Cook, Pickersgill, the Forsters and Hodges visited this family again. They found the man, his two 'wives', a 'daughter' about sixteen years old, a boy of about fourteen and three smaller boys (one of whom was still breast-feeding) living in two bark and flax shelters by a creek in Canoe Harbour on the island. Their double canoe was moored in the creek, tied up to a tree. The old man was anxious and uncertain when they first arrived. Pickersgill commented:

> How shall I describe the agonies of the old man, Hope, Fear, Despair and every other conflict, that was possible to possess the Human brest, was visable in his face . . . but on being convinced of our friendly views he danced and leaped like a frantic man for joy.[33]

He relaxed when Cook presented him with hatchets, spike nails, necklaces, beads and looking glasses in exchange for two 'staffs of honour' (taiaha), although the women would not give up their spears. This was the height of the birding season, when kiwi, kaakaa, kaakaapo and kookako chicks, and pigeon, weka, albatross and muttonbirds were available,[34] and these were bird spears and essential hunting gear. Hodges sketched the old man holding a hatchet, and one of the women carrying a child on her back, causing them to call him 'Toetoe' (tuhituhi; to paint or draw). Hodges was sketching in red chalk, very similar to the red ochre that Maori used to decorate their bodies, carved houses and canoes, which probably explains the use of this term. Before Cook's party left, the old man offered a cloak, a plaited belt, some albatross skins and bird-bone beads in exchange for the Europeans' boat cloaks, which they did not give him, since they had no others. When Cook returned to the ship that afternoon, however, he ordered a boat cloak to be made from red baize. These cloaks were large, hooded semi-circular capes that could be wrapped around the body several times in cold or wet weather – invaluable garments in the Sound, where it rained almost every day.

The next morning Cook, the Forsters and some other officers and crew returned to the small settlement in 'Indian Cove', bringing the new cloak with them. They found the family dressed up in their best clothes, and 'shouting' (i.e. the karanga – cry of welcome, or perhaps the poowhiri – welcoming chant) to greet them. They had put on flax cloaks decorated with parrot feathers, ornaments of albatross skin coloured with red ochre in their ears and bunches or 'fillets' of white feathers on their heads. Their hair (and the women's faces) were anointed with oil and red ochre, and the man wore his hair long and tied up on the crown of his head, while the women's hair was short. Cook put on the red cloak and then gave it to the old man, who was so delighted that he presented the captain with his whalebone patu (hand club) in return. Red was the tapu colour, and a scarlet boat cloak was a magnificent gift. Some of the *Resolution* party had not previously met this family, who pointed out and commented on each of the newcomers in turn. The interpreter on this expedition, Gibson (the corporal of marines who had learned some Maori on the *Endeavour* voyage), could not understand their speech and commented on their 'harshness of pronunciation', although Clerke noted that many of the words seemed to be exactly the same as those used in the North Island and that the variations indicated a distinct South Island dialect rather than a different language.[35]

Over the next twelve days, members of the *Resolution* expedition met this family almost daily. The crew treated them as a great novelty and constantly sought them out. The young girl befriended some of the younger, unbearded Europeans, apparently thinking that they were women. She became fond of one boy in particular, offering him a black silk handkerchief and a piece of plum pudding she had been given, wanting him always nearby. She anointed his hair with strong-smelling seal oil, which made his shipmates laugh, since he was noted on board for his fondness for 'washes and perfumes'. One of the journal accounts said that this boy tried to make love to her, while another claimed that it was when she saw him passing water that she realised that he was male.[36] Probably the first story was true, because one of the officers later offered to shoot the boy for this insult,

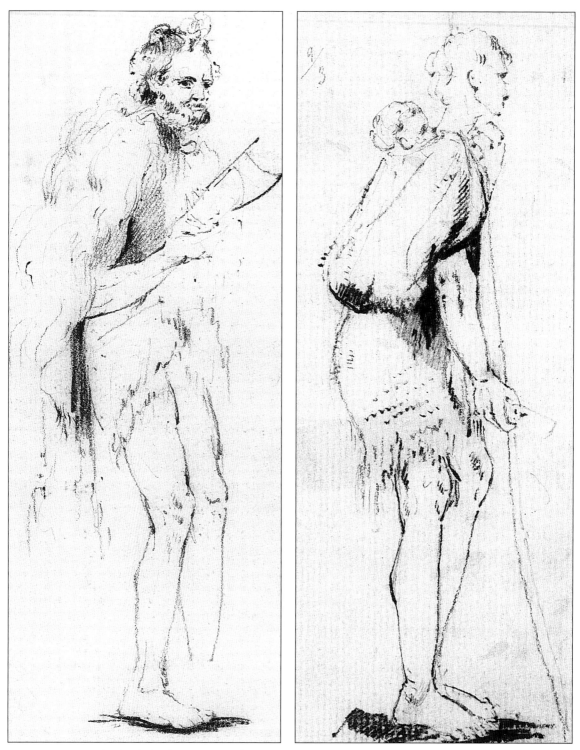

*Sketches by William Hodges of a Tamatea man carrying a European hatchet
he had been given, and a woman with a child on her back.*

causing her to burst into tears.[37] In any case, she avoided him thereafter, staying close to her family and refusing to talk to him.

Cook tried every persuasion to get this family to come on board the *Resolution*, going onto their canoe with them, treating them to a concert of bagpipes, fife and drums (they liked the drumming), and showing them the ship's boats. The old man inspected the boats minutely, examining their construction and particularly the way the rudders worked, but he would not come on board. One day a corporal of marines (probably the Maori-speaking Gibson) asked if he could take the young girl as his 'wife'. He was told that in such a matter of great moment their god would have to be consulted, and almost all that night and the next day the family sang and chanted near the ship, making gestures that seemed to be directed at 'some Being above the Clouds'. For several evenings they camped on the shore near to the *Resolution*'s anchorage. They offered food to the Europeans, making a fire by rubbing two sticks together and cooking fish in a kelp bag over a hardwood grill, but refused to eat any of the food the Europeans offered in return. Their bread was 'the inner bark of a [fern] tree cleansed and bruised' (mamaku), dressed with a seaweed sauce. According to John Marra, some of the crew not only ate with them but slept with them overnight.[38]

Cook kept trying to get this group to visit him on board, and finally, on 18 April, the man agreed that they would come 'abobo' (apoopoo – tomorrow). This provoked a family quarrel; the man hit 'his two wives' and the young girl hit him in return and began to cry.[39] George Forster commented:

> If the young woman was really the man's daughter, it should seem that filial duties are strangely confounded among them; or which is more probable, that this secluded family acted in every respect, not according to the customs and regulations of a civil society, but from the impulses of nature, which speak loud against every degree of oppression.[40]

Probably the women were reluctant to visit the *Resolution*; in any case, the next morning the old man and the girl (whom the Europeans subsequently discovered was not his daughter at all)[41] came alongside the ship while the rest of the family went out fishing. After Cook had shown them sheep and goats that were penned on a hill nearby, they approached the gangway, where the man put on a white bird-skin ear ornament and broke off a green branch:

> [He] then walked stately over: Just when he reached the Ship he stopped & struck the main shrouds with the branch & began to declame or scan a kind of poem or *carmen* [karakia], his eyes fixed to the place he touched & his voice elevated, the whole behaviour grave & solemn: his daughter [sic] pressing to pass by other people in order to come near [him] & seemed all the time over serious. This lasted for about 2 or three minutes.[42]

When this tapu-raising ceremony was over, the man and the girl walked carefully across the tree trunk that hung from the shore to the ship's gunwhale, avoiding the crosspieces that the Europeans had fixed onto it. The old man struck the ship again with his bough before throwing it into the main chains and venturing on deck. They stamped on the deck several times, most likely enacting the 'trampling' (takahi) ceremony used to drive spirits away from a place, then Cook took them below decks to his cabin for breakfast. Neither the man nor the girl would eat, presumably because they were still tapu, but they looked at everything including Cook's bed, sat on his chairs and marvelled at the number and strength of the ship's decks. The old man gave Cook a parrot-feather cloak and a greenstone adze, and offered to anoint his hair with oil from a sealskin pouch. He pressed noses with Forster and presented him with another feather cloak, while the girl threw a cloak around Hodges' shoulders, tried to tie his hair up on his head and hung a tuft of feathers dipped in oil on a string around his neck. In return they were given several hatchets, nails and tufts of feathers, which they valued highly. They liked the geese, sheep and goats, and the girl kept stroking the ship's cat, rubbing its fur the wrong way, probably to see how long it was. They were less surprised by the dogs, but rather afraid of them. It is not clear whether they saw any of the African animals on board collected by the Forsters at the Cape of Good Hope.[43]

The girl received many gifts from the sailors, for she was the first woman they had seen for many months. Clerke remarked that 'the Young Gypsey did not seem at all inclin'd to repay them in the Kind Indian Women in general trade in, and indeed the Kind that's most esteem'd I believe by all men after so long an absence from the Sex'.[44] The man, on the other hand, was fascinated by the sawyers and the carpenters. He took his place in the sawpit for a while, but gave up when he realised the difficulty and unpleasantness of the job. The officers also took him on deck and fired some muskets for him. He wanted to fire one himself, and although the girl threw herself on the deck in fear, resolutely fired it several times.

During this visit the man was told that a hatchet and other gifts had been left for him at Cascade Cove, and at about midday he and the girl left the ship. He returned that evening with his family, having retrieved the gifts, and the next day they went away. As he left, the man indicated that he was going to use his hatchets for killing people. Johann Forster expostulated: 'Thus we see that the Natural depravity of mankind immediately applies things, which are intended for relieving him from labour & tedious toils, to wicked purposes & makes the instruments invented for shortening labour, the tools of cruelty and bloodshed!'[45] This was the last contact between this family and the Europeans. Cook was surprised at their departure, because he calculated that they had received at least nine or ten hatchets, thirty to forty large spike nails and other gifts during their various meetings with the *Resolution*'s crew. Such access to European goods was unprecedented, and Cook was puzzled that they would leave while gifts were still being exchanged.

Their abrupt departure, however, may have been provoked by another group's arrival. The next morning (20 April), while Cook and Johann Forster were hunting ducks south of Long Island, they were surprised by an uproar from two or three places in the bush around them. According to Forster, Cook said to him, 'the best is to retire, the Indians seem to be quarrelsome'. Their boat was half a mile away, so they charged their guns and in their turn set up a clamour and retreated to shore. Their companions hurried to meet them, and once they had regrouped, Cook took both of the ship's boats up a nearby river (the Seaforth), shooting ducks. An unknown man, a woman and a child came out of the bush, the woman waving a white birdskin in a gesture of friendship. Two more people appeared on the opposite bank upriver, but Cook could not reach them. The tide was dropping so he turned back to the coast, where two other men armed with spears hailed him. This time Cook decided to meet with them. He stripped off his shoes and stockings, climbed out of the boat with two of the crew and waded across the shallows towards them, unarmed. They retreated, but Cook ordered his companions to fall back, advancing alone while the two men waited. Cook wrote in his journal that night:

> At length one of them laid down his spear, pulled up a grass plant and came to me with it in his hand giving me hold of one end while he held the other, standing in this manner he made a speach not one word of which I understood, in it were some long pauses waiting as I thought for me to make answer, for when I spoke he proceeded; as soon as this ceremony was over, which was but short we saluted each other, he then took his hahou [kahu, cloak] or coat from off his back and put it upon mine after which peace seemed firmly established, more of our people joining us did not in the least allarm them [on the contrary they saluted every one as he came up], we could see more people in the skirts of the Woods, none of them however joined us, probably these were their women and children.[46]

The gift of a cloak was a sign of peace, and the strands of grass were probably being used as a spiritual pathway of some kind in a ceremony of peaceful greeting.[47] These people (who numbered perhaps three families) had not previously met the Europeans but seemed to have heard about them.

They had no canoes, just rafts of two or three logs of wood lashed together, and their dwellings were nearby. They were frightened of the muskets and would not touch them, yet handled everything else on the boats and wanted to take some things away. George Forster remarked that 'the courage of these people has something singular in it, for it should seem, that in spight of their inferiority of force, they cannot brook the thought of hiding themselves, at least not till they have made an attempt to establish an intercourse, or prove the principles of the strangers who approach them . . . A certain openness and honesty, appear strongly to mark their character. . . as they could not have failed of meeting with frequent opportunities of cutting off our numerous small parties, when dispersed in different parts of the woods.'[48] Cook gave each of these men a hatchet and a knife, declined an invitation to eat with them at their campsite, and returned to the *Resolution*.

For the next three weeks the expedition stayed on in Tamatea, gathering wood, water, birds, fish and seals, and refitting the ship. Cook, Pickersgill and Gilbert, the master, completed a meticulous survey of the Sound, but despite their extensive explorations they met no more local people. One day they saw two shelters

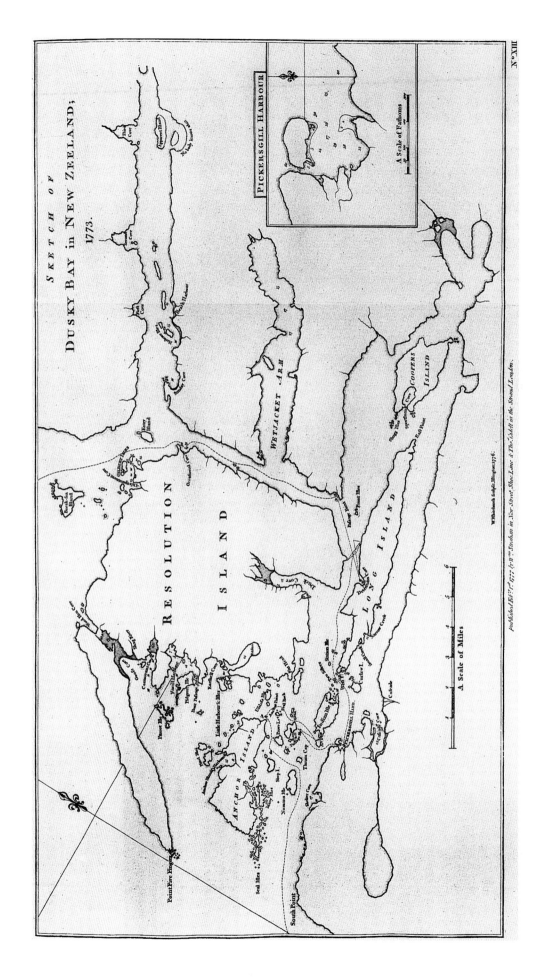

SKETCH OF

DUSKY BAY in NEW ZEELAND;
1773.

PICKERSGILL HARBOUR

A Scale of Fathoms

A Scale of Miles

RESOLUTION ISLAND

WETJACKET ARM

LONG ISLAND

COOPERS ISLAND

ANCHOR ISLAND

South Point

Point Five Fingers

Published Febry 1st 1777 by Wm Strahan in New Street Shoe-Lane & Tho. Cadell in the Strand London.

W. Whitchurch Sculpsit. Islington 1776.

in Detention Cove that had recently been occupied, and one evening there were fires on shore, but the people stayed hidden in the bush. The Forsters and Sparrman carried on collecting plants, fish, birds, shells and rocks, and by the time they left Tamatea they had described at least seventy specimens in text and sketches. Hodges sketched and painted local scenes, including coastal views and various waterfalls. George Forster described the waterfall in Cascade Cove in a long, flowery passage, while Wales was inspired by another such 'romantic scene' to quote (with some inaccuracies) from Thomson's *Seasons*:

> Smooth to the shelving brink a copious flood
> Roll'd fair, and placid; where collected all,
> In one impetuous torrent, down the Steep
> It thundering shot, and shook the country round . . .

Several days later he saw an even more impressive cascade, and self-mockingly wrote in his journal: 'Young Travellers, like young Wits, and young Girls too for that matter, are apt to let their imaginations run riot, and ever think the first that offers a Phoenix: whereas could they but have patience, another infinitely its superior would present itself!'[49]

The officers, gentlemen and crew entertained themselves with hunting expeditions, or 'marooning parties' as they called them, one of which was vividly described by George Forster:

> Having found a beach to land on, with a brook, and a wood close to it, our first care was to bring on shore the oars, sails, cloaks, guns, hatchets and not forgetting a little keg of spruce beer, and perhaps a bottle of strong liquor. The boats were next secured at a grappling, and with a rope made fast to a tree on shore. Some of us were then busied in collecting dry pieces of wood for fuel, which in such a wet country as New Zeeland, was sometimes very difficult; some erected a tent or wigwam, made of the oars and sails together with strong branches of trees, in a convenient dry spot, sheltered as much as possible, in case of wind and rain. Others lighted the fire in front of the tent, by burning some oakum, in which they had previously rubbed a quantity of gunpowder. The preparations for supper were very short; some of the sailors cleaned our fishes, skinned the waterfowl, split, and lastly broiled them; when they were dressed, one of the boat's gang-boards, washed clean, answered the several purposes of a table, of dishes, and plates; and our fingers and teeth did yeoman's service, instead of knives and forks . . . After supper we listened a while to the original comic vein of our boat's crew, who huddled round the fire, made their meal, and recited a number of droll stories, intermingled with hearty curses, oaths, and indecent expressions, but seldom without real humour. Then strewing our tent with heaps of fern leaves, and wrapping ourselves in our boat-cloaks, with our guns and shooting-bags for our pillows, we composed ourselves to sleep.[50]

Opposite: *Cook's 1773 survey of Dusky Bay.*

After a month of such activities the officers and crew were fit and rested, and the ship was cleaned, rerigged and repaired. On 28 April, Cook ordered all the shore tents struck and brought on board. Five geese were liberated for breeding in Ororoa ('Goose Cove'), and a patch of ground near the anchorage was burned off and planted with peas, mustard, parsley and strawberries, while the *Resolution* waited for a favourable wind. On 11 May, after enduring contrary breezes, snow, hail and violent storms, she sailed out of Tamatea and set off towards Totara-nui (Queen Charlotte Sound) to meet with the *Adventure*.

Summary
THE *RESOLUTION*'S VISIT TO TAMATEA

The *Resolution*'s visit to Tamatea amounted to a massive, if short-term, occupation of the Sound. Small migratory populations of Ngaati Mamoe and Ngaai Tahu existed in fragile equilibrium with the local landscape, and the visit by the *Resolution*, with its crew of 114 European men and its cargo of European and other plants, seeds and animals was an unprecedented arrival. Some of the men and animals on board had scurvy, all needed fresh food, and they took large quantities of fish, birds, seals, wood and water. The Europeans had no sense that their presence might be disruptive. For them, Tamatea was simply 'one of the finest Harbours in the World'.[51] As Clerke remarked:

> You Wood and Water here with the utmost facility; the Wood may be cut down close alongside your Ship, and the Water may be fill'd by a fine running Brook about a 100 yards from the Stern – in the next place it abounds most plentifully in Fish – principally Cold Fish with some Cavally's – Gurnets and Mackarel all large, firm and exceedingly well tasted: there are likewise great abundance of very large and very good Crawfish. I believe take one day with another our supply of Fish had been about a Hundred Pr Diem and those I'm sure at an average 2 pounds apiece: so that for near these 7 weeks past our constant consumption of Fish has been 200lb every 24 hours, and as many Craw Fish besides as we know what to do with. The Water Fowl here too, I think may justly claim some mention in this Account . . . I was one of a party of four that in a days shooting kill'd 41 Ducks and Curlews and did not deem it a very extraordinary days sport – there are many Seals about too which are easily come at, whose Haslets . . . make steaks very little inferior (some of our Gentry sware, far superior) to Beefsteak, and the Blubber renders very good Oil for lamps.[52]

Many of the sea mammals, fish and birds (like Ngaati Mamoe and Ngaai Tahu) were, however, seasonal visitors to Tamatea, and their numbers were unpredictable.[53] Maori hunters and gatherers grazed lightly on local animal populations; birds, for instance, were tame and easily taken, yet they were very numerous at this time. The Europeans, on the other hand, hunted with guns and gathered on a hitherto unknown scale, and in addition they introduced new life forms (including plants and animals) into the landscape.

All of this was understood as virtuous, for as George Forster commented in his *Voyage*:

> The superiority of a state of civilization over that of barbarism could not be more clearly stated, than by the alterations and improvements we had made in this place. In the course of a few days, a small part of us had cleared away the wood from a surface of more than an acre, which fifty New Zealanders, with their tools of stone, could not have performed in three months. This spot, where immense numbers of plants left to themselves lived and decayed by turns ... we had converted into an active scene, where a hundred and twenty men pursued various branches of employment with unremitted ardour . . .
>
> We felled tall timber trees, which, but for ourselves, had crumbled to dust with age; our sawyers cut them into planks, or we split them into billets for fuel. By the side of a murmuring rivulet, whose passage into the sea we facilitated, a long range of casks . . . stood ready to be filled with water. Here ascended the steam of a large cauldron, in which we brewed, from neglected indigenous plants, a salutary and palatable potion . . . In the offing, some of our crew appeared providing a meal of delicious fish for the refreshment of their fellows. Our caulkers and riggers were stationed on the sides and masts of the vessel, and their occupations gave life to the scene, and struck the ear with various noises, whilst the anvil on the hill resounded with the strokes of the weighty hammer. Already the polite arts began to flourish in this new settlement; the various tribes of animals and vegetables, which dwelt in the unfrequented woods, were imitated by an artist; and the romantic prospects of this shaggy country lived on the canvas in the glowing tints of nature, who was amazed to see herself so closely copied. Nor had science disdained to visit us in this solitary spot: an observatory arose in the centre of our works, filled with the most accurate instruments, where the attentive eye of the astronomer contemplated the motions of the celestial bodies. The plants which clothed the ground, and the wonders of the animal creation, both in the forests and the seas, likewise attracted the notice of philosophers, whose time was devoted to mark their differences and uses. In a word, all around us we perceived the rise of arts, and the dawn of science, in a country which had hitherto lain plunged in one long night of ignorance and barbarism![54]

The European argument for 'progress' can seldom have been so clearly stated. Its essence was to act upon, and transform a wild 'neglected' nature. Woods, once cleared, became a site for work. Trees were turned into firewood or planks. Water was diverted and stored in casks for drinking. Plants and animals became food, or specimens scrutinised by scientists, and landscapes and seascapes were converted into works of art or charts. Even the stars, the weather and the tides were measured against instruments to make calculations of various kinds. 'This shaggy country' was romanticised in prose and paint, and then controlled. Superiority was asserted by production, and by the observer's measuring, describing eye.

In this process the local people were largely set aside. George Forster described the bush around the Sound as 'unfrequented' and the people as 'ignorant', 'barbaric',[55] and 'in a state of nature'. Like Tamatea's landscapes, they required 'civilization' and 'improvement'. Sparrman, the assistant natural historian, called them 'man-eaters' with 'a deep-seated and filthy taste for bloodshed and the eating of human flesh' (although there was no evidence for cannibalism in Tamatea). He commented that 'many fertile farms might be brought into cultivation by an extensive settlement from Europe; thousands of people could be fed on fish alone in these wild places, now only inhabited by a few households'.[56]

On the other hand, like the indigenous 'tribes of plants and animals', the local people were 'curiosities' that attracted the attention of European philosophers. Accurate, detailed descriptions of them were wanted, and the journal-writers did their best to meet this requirement. Pickersgill, for instance, observed that small family groups wandered from place to place within the sound. In the Indian Island family, the older women (who may have been war captives, or slave wives) did all the work, fishing, cooking and making shelters while the old man and the younger girl 'took their diversions'.[57] The astronomer William Wales gave detailed accounts of this family's clothing (a combination of feather cloak and 'buggybuggy' (pakepake, or rain cape), their double canoe (with its hulls, one eighteen feet and the other fourteen feet long, set one foot apart and slightly converging at the prow, and raised by washboards), and their tools (greenstone chisels, adzes and axes, variously lashed to wooden handles; wood, bone and two-piece fish-hooks; and two-, three- and four-plait flax lines). One can deduce from various details in the journal entries that there were probably five or six families in the Sound, who came there periodically to harvest berries, seafood, pigeons, muttonbirds, albatross, weka and other birds.

For Tamatea, however, there is no good means of balancing the material focus of these 'objective' accounts. In the absence of tribal records and reliable ident-ifications of the people who met the *Resolution* expedition, local understandings of what happened there in 1773 are silent. It is impossible to tell (despite subse-quent European and Maori speculation)[58] what happened to the Indian Island family and their wealth of hatchets and nails, or to the other groups that the Europeans briefly met. Infectious diseases may have been transmitted by contact with the Europeans, or newly acquired goods may have provoked attacks, but if so, all memories of such happenings are lost. George Forster was probably prescient when he remarked that in Tamatea, impressions of the European visit would vanish 'like a meteor'.[59] Only the stumps of trees on Astronomers Point remained.

Three

TOTARA-NUI (QUEEN CHARLOTTE SOUND)
I

THE *ADVENTURE*'S FIRST VISIT TO TOTARA-NUI
6 April – 7 June 1773

On board the *Adventure*, Tobias Furneaux had lost contact with the *Resolution* in fog and dirty weather off the Kerguelen Islands. He spent three days searching for the *Resolution*, then turned his ship towards New Zealand, stopping briefly at Van Diemen's Land on the way. On 2 April, they had sighted 'a confused jumble of Hills and Mountains', the north-western end of the South Island, and that night in bright moonlight sailed into Raukawa-moana (Cook Strait). On 6 April, after firing several guns off Point Jackson, the *Adventure* came to an anchor at Meretoto (Ship Cove) in Totara-nui.

Totara-nui was a maze of deep inlets on the north-eastern tip of the South Island. Cook had stayed in the Sound for three weeks during January and February 1770, naming it Queen Charlotte Sound and describing it as a 'Collection of some of the finest harbours in the world', a perfect place to refit a ship and rest a weary crew.

Like Tamatea, Totara-nui was best suited for hunting and gathering, although its climate was milder, and during the 1770s it was populated by a number of semi-nomadic groups. Unlike Tamatea, however, Totara-nui was centrally located. It was a key staging point for journeys across Raukawa-moana, with argillite quarries for adzes at Nelson and on Rangitoto (D'Urville Island) nearby. Pounamu (greenstone) from the lakes and rivers, and other southern products passed through the Sound, and no group dominated it for long. In the generations preceding the Europeans' arrival, successive northern migrants – Ngaati Mamoe, Ngaati Tuumatakokiri, Ngaai Tarapounamu, Ngaati Kurii of Ngaai Tahu, Ngaati Kuia and Ngaati Apa – had briefly occupied Totara-nui, leaving small groups of descendants behind. By the 1770s, according to some accounts,[1] Totara-nui was dominated by the latest arrivals, Rangitaane, brought from the Wairarapa by their chief Te Rerewa, while Ngaati Apa controlled the outer reaches of the Sound. Like most of the previous migrants (except Ngaai Tahu), they traced their descent from the *Kurahaupo* canoe, and this common kinship enabled them to co-exist with their neighbours. Relations between these groups were precarious, however, and fighting was never far away.

During Cook's visit to the Sound in 1770, the Totara-nui people had congregated in two main paa , one at the southern end of Motuara Island and the other in East Bay (which may have been Rangitaane's stronghold), before dispersing to their hunting camps around the coastline. Banks had described the occupants of these 'towns' as 'two different societies', and it seems that the local population was organised into two main confederations at that time (probably Ngaati Apa and Rangitaane). They had already heard about the *Endeavour*'s arrival on the coast from their neighbours to the north, and there may also have been an earlier

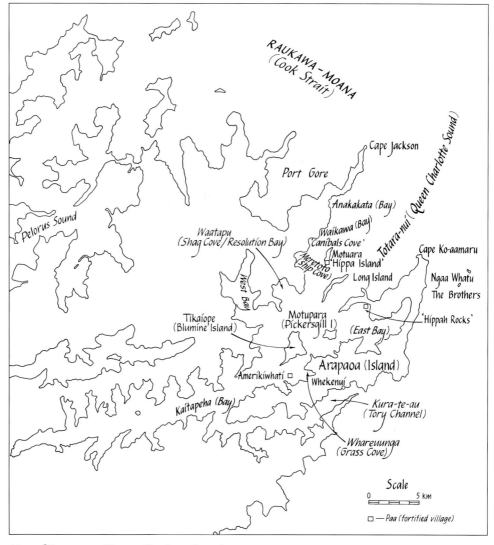

Map of Totara-nui (Queen Charlotte Sound).

European visit to the Sound. Topaa, the leader of the people at Motuara, told Tupaia (the Raiatean high priest who had travelled from Tahiti on board the *Endeavour*) about '2 large vessels, much larger than theirs, which some time or other came here and were totaly destroyd by the inhabitants and all the people belonging to them killd'.[2] This was probably an exaggerated version of Tasman's visit to Taitapu in 1642, however, further west along the strait.[3]

In 1770, Totara-nui had been in turmoil. The people were being raided by their neighbours from the west (possibly Ngaati Kuia, who controlled Pelorus Sound at about this time[4]). The Europeans were horrified to find human body parts beside an earth oven in one of the bays, and chewed human bones. Tupaia questioned people repeatedly about their cannibalistic practices, a preserved human head was acquired, and the *Endeavour*'s crew set up a trade in human hair and bones. A boat's crew including a sailor who had taken human hair from a ritual site was confronted, and a local man was shot and killed. By the end of three weeks, the elders were anxious for the Europeans to leave. Local people had been harmed, and local stocks of dried fish and other foods were being depleted.

Cook, however, had been greatly impressed by Totara-nui as a resting place for European voyagers, and nominated it as a central port for Pacific explorations. Compared with most harbours in the North Island of New Zealand, the Sound had many safe anchorages, the population was small and friendly, and there were excellent supplies of fresh water, wood, fish and anti-scorbutic plants. Cook's charts and descriptions from this first visit were to bring many European vessels (including his own ships) back to the Sound. Over the next few years, Totara-nui became the first place in New Zealand to experience sustained contact with Europeans.

When the *Adventure* sailed into the Sound in April 1773, three years after the *Endeavour*'s visit, therefore, the local people were apprehensive but not entirely surprised. Furneaux moored his vessel in Meretoto, the place where the *Endeavour* had also anchored, and sent men ashore that evening to look for a watering place. They discovered names of some of *Endeavour*'s men carved into tree trunks in the cove, but no signs of the *Resolution*. The shore party caught many fish and shot some birds, and as darkness fell, they heard 'the howling of Dogs and People hollowing on the East Shore'.[5]

The next morning Furneaux's men began to explore the Sound, but found it virtually deserted. James Burney reported:

> Have seen no inhabitants as yet, nor signs of any – there are a great many empty houses in every beach along shore & some deserted towns. one of them is on a small Isld. called the Hippa [he paa – a fortified village] & seems designd for a strong hold – the shore is so steep that it is almost inaccessible except at one place & that none of the Easiest. at the top is a wall about 5 feet high made of brambles between 2 Rows of Stakes – very neat. on this spot our Astronomer fixed his observatory.[6]

This was the paa off the southern end of Motuara Island, visited and named by Cook in 1770, which at that time had been inhabited by up to two hundred people.[7] Over the next few weeks the *Adventure*'s astronomer, William Bayly, stayed there, working in his observatory. He described it as containing thirty-three houses, scattered around a flattened, palisaded summit a hundred yards long by eight to ten yards wide. Access to the paa was difficult, so Bayly made steps up to the summit. The houses on top had no walls, only roofs of woven sticks covered with bark and then untreated flax. The palisade was about five feet high and made of horizontal sticks woven through two rows of upright posts and packed with bundles of brushwood, with a low wooden door in one place, about two feet square. Physically nothing much had changed since 1770, but the paa had been abandoned and overrun with rats. Possibly these were European rats introduced by the *Endeavour*, although the indigenous kiore (Polynesian rat) are also known to have occupied these islands in some numbers.[8]

Over the next few days Furneaux's men set up tents on Motuara for the sailmakers, coopers and the sick, and settled into the houses. They found the carved post that Cook had ceremoniously erected on the island's highest point in 1770 to commemorate the *Endeavour*'s departure from the Sound. He had hoisted the Union Jack in the presence of Topaa and other (Ngaati Apa?) elders, taken possession of the land for the King, named the Sound after Queen Charlotte and toasted her health with a bottle of wine. The local people probably thought that this was a raahui pole, planting Cook's mana (ancestral power) on the island and extended it over its resources, making them tapu (inaccessible to those without appropriate ancestral powers). These two islands may have been left empty since that time.

The *Adventure* was in the Sound for three days before any of the local people showed themselves to the Europeans. On 9 April, a double canoe and a single canoe with an outrigger, carrying sixteen people in all, came out to the ship. They stopped about twenty yards from the *Adventure* where a man stood up with a green bough and made 'a long speech' – probably a protective karakia (incantation). The people called out 'Tobia Tobia', a cry of welcome to Tupaia (the Raiatean high priest-navigator who visited on the *Endeavour*), and came on board to ask after him. Tupaia had died of a fever at Batavia on the homeward voyage, and when they heard that he was dead these people were very concerned, asking if the Europeans had killed him. Furneaux's men tried to reassure them, offering medals, looking glasses, nails, gimlets, beads, old shirts, waistcoats and breeches in exchange for weapons and cloaks. These exchanges proceeded peacefully until one young officer discovered a freshly severed head and neck in one of the canoes, wrapped up carefully in a cloak. Fascinated by what he took as evidence of an 'unnatural act' (in other words, cannibalism), he tried to take a closer look, but the people in the canoe hid the head, passing it among themselves and denying that they had any such thing. After this they quickly left the ship. This was either the head of an enemy or a kinsman, but in any case it was intensely tapu; an embodiment of ancestral power. The man and the woman who had it in their keeping 'trembled from Head to foot' while it was being handled, and did not come out again to see the Europeans. That afternoon the sailors brought six carriage guns up from the ship's hold and mounted them ready for a possible attack.

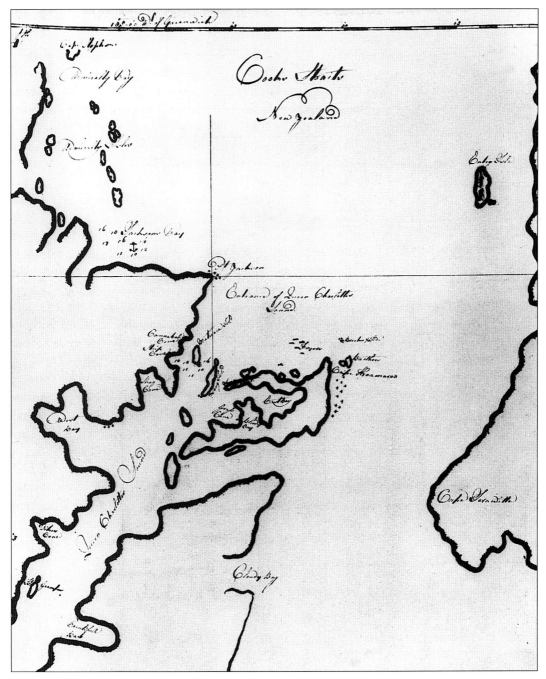

A sketch of 'Cooks Straits' by Peter Fannin, Master on the Adventure, *in 1773.*

When they left the *Adventure*, some of these visitors went off fishing, and later returned to the ship with gifts of fish and fernroot. The *Adventure*'s officers had been given a Maori vocabulary compiled during the *Endeavour* voyage, and when the officers read out words from it and named particular items, these people 'wanted it much and offered a great quantity of fish for it'. They exchanged some small items with the Europeans and went off that evening to a bay about a mile and a half away – probably Waatapu (now Resolution Bay). The next morning five double canoes carrying a group of fifty or sixty including women, two children and their chief came back to the ship. The men helped the seamen to pull casks up from the hold, and enthusiastically bartered weapons, tools and cloaks for nails and old bottles. One man tried to barter the frame of a looking glass he had acquired the previous day, in return for a large nail. The local people were so entranced by these exchanges that it was only when muskets with fixed bayonets were pointed at them that they would leave the ship.

Over the next few days Bayly set up his observatory on Hippa Island, helped by his servant and a good-natured Welshman, 'who would always work if I gave him Brandy'. The first lieutenant gave him a guard of two marines and a Highland piper, all suffering from scurvy, and three fit young midshipmen. During this time they planted a garden of cabbages, peas and wheat on the island, and Furneaux's men planted gardens of root crops (including carrots, parsnips, potatoes and turnips), mustards, cresses and radishes on shore for their own use over the winter and for later European visitors.

News of the Europeans' arrival was spreading. On 12 April, a flotilla of eight or nine canoes (some double and some single, with outriggers) carrying 109 people came out to visit the *Adventure*. Bayly described these people as lusty and strong, although their knees were enlarged and stiffened from constant squatting, with some 'fine jolly girls' among them. Most had black hair, the men's tied up on the crown of their heads and decorated with a large bone comb, while a few had 'sandy'-coloured hair, perhaps the blond-tipped hair described by later authorities. One of these canoes was well carved and much longer than the others, with a 'venerable old man with his hair white as snow' sitting in the stern with an attendant. These people came freely on board and offered women to the Europeans in exchange for spike nails. The carpenter was using vermillion paint that day, and over half the people who came alongside had their faces painted scarlet. Red was the tapu colour, and red ochre mixed with oil was often used as a face paint – hence their enthusiasm. According to Bayly:

> They seem to be in great fear of us, dealing very honestly with us, not offering to deviate the agreement you made with them & very often laugh very heartily when they thought they had a good bargain. But would dextrously pick our Pockets of our handkerchiefs or steal anything they could. They are extremely fond of anything that is red or spike nails, & on other things they put little or no value at present.[9]

These people may have been from Totara-nui or from elsewhere in the region. There were many specialist traders located around Raukawa-moana who acted as middlemen in the exchange of greenstone, argillite and other South Island products for North Island goods, and European nails and other items offered exciting new opportunities.

Exchange with Europeans had hidden hazards, however. At the time of the *Adventure*'s arrival, there were four men on board the ship with long-standing venereal infections. During their stay in the Sound, the muster rolls record that at least five more of the *Adventure*'s crew began to show symptoms, and Bayly speculated that local women had been infected during the *Endeavour*'s earlier visit to the Sound:

> Whether the Endeavours people gave it them or whether the disease was among them before, is a point not easily determined, but 'tis highly probable the Endeavours people left it there as there was more than 40 on the venerial list quickly after they left Otahiti and the run to New Zealand is but short.[10]

If the exchange of sex for spike nails was dangerous, gifts of old European clothing, which had been bought for barter before the voyage, may also have transmitted infectious diseases. It is possible that people in the Sound were afraid to approach the *Adventure* at first because they had already suffered strange maladies from the *Endeavour*'s 1770 visit.

Over the next week the weather was stormy, and the local people (who had told the Europeans that the weather was about to change) 'went up the Harbour' and stayed away from the *Adventure*. On 21 April, three small canoes returned to Meretoto. Their crews camped there for several days, supplying the ship and the shore camp with fish, 'of which the Captain for 3 or 4 nails would purchase a sufficient quantity to serve the whole Ships Company'.[11]

About this time some of the Sound's people decided to test the strength of the Europeans. On 24 April, at about ten o'clock at night, several canoes came surreptitiously to the astronomer's encampment on Hippa Island and were driven off by musket fire. The next day the ship's jollyboat, with a couple of midshipmen and the surgeon's second mate on board, was chased by two carved canoes carrying about thirty people, and was almost intercepted. One of the *Adventure*'s cannons was fired in response, and the shot fell between the jollyboat and the canoes. Their crews (who according to Burney were 'from the Northward', and darker than the Totara-nui people) were frightened and called off the chase, and later came peacefully to visit the encampment on Motuara Island. After this encounter Furneaux sent two fit marines with wall-guns as reinforcements to the astronomer's camp, then, on 28 April, ordered the tents shifted off Motuara to Meretoto, closer to the ship.

These incidents did not much trouble him, however. At the beginning of May, Furneaux wrote in his journal:

> We were daily visted by more or less, who brought us Fish in great plenty, for

Nails, beads and other triffles, and behaved very peaceably. I believe they don't stay long in any particular place or have any settled habitation but wander up and down in different Parties, particularly in the summer season, Sometimes laying in the Canoes and sometimes on shore, As there is a number of Hutts in every Cove you meet with.[12]

THE *RESOLUTION*'S FIRST VISIT TO TOTARA-NUI
18 May – 7 June 1773

During the first weeks of May, Furneaux ordered the *Adventure* shifted further into the cove and moored for winter. The decks were cleared for caulking and the hull and rigging given a winter coating to preserve them from the weather. On 11 May, there were two earth tremors, and that night a large meteor streaked across the sky. On the morning of 18 May, they heard cannonfire out at sea and the guns on Hippa Island fired in answer, and to the sailors' great delight they saw the *Resolution* sailing in to the Sound. 'Both Ships,' Furneaux wrote in his journal that night, 'felt an uncommon joy at our meeting after an absence of fourteen Weeks.'[13] The *Resolution* had had an uneventful journey up the west coast of the South Island and into Cook Strait, except that as they approached the western entrance to the Sound, they experienced a 'strange purterbation' in the atmosphere and the *Resolution* was surrounded by six towering waterspouts, one of which drove straight for the ship and came as close as a pistol shot before it spun away. The local people would have taken the earthquakes, the meteor and the waterspouts as portents, for these were understood as signs of supernatural power. As soon as the *Resolution* had anchored, the ships exchanged eleven-gun salutes, which must also have impressed local Maori. There were now more than two hundred Europeans in the Sound. The Totara-nui people gave up thoughts of fighting (at least for the time being) and turned their minds to trade.

Cook, who had previously visited Totara-nui in the *Endeavour*, was eager to continue his exploration of the south-east Pacific before proceeding to Tahiti for the winter. He asked Furneaux to prepare his ship for sea as quickly as possible. Anti-scorbutics were collected in quantity and fed to the *Resolution*'s crew to get them ready for the voyage. Beer was brewed, celery and scurvy grass were boiled with oatmeal or wheat and portable soup for breakfast, or with pea soup for dinner, and sowthistle and 'lambs quarters' (*Apium australe*) were served as salads with their meals.

More seeds were planted, and the two surviving sheep were put out to graze. Not long after this they died, to Cook's intense annoyance, as a result of eating poisonous plants (probably tutu). The Forsters and Sparrman set to work to survey the local flora and fauna, collecting and describing fish, shells, birds, bats and plants, including a small prostrate species of a new genus they had named *Banksia*, 'in honour of *Joseph Banks* Esqr . . . the first Naturalist, that ever searched the

South-Seas & especially New-Zeeland, & enriched Natural History with more than 800 new plants & 200 or 300 new Animals: an Addition which never one single Man made to this branch of Learning'.[14] George also described local rock types, including strata of argillite and loose pieces of basalt and pumice on the beaches.

On 21 May, the *Resolution*'s quartermaster was punished with six lashes for 'insolence to the boatswain'. It is not clear whether any of the local people witnessed this flogging. The next day Bayly dismantled his observatory on Hippa Island and the Forsters visited Long Island, where they cleared some patches of ground and planted garden seeds near a group of abandoned houses beside a beach on its north-west coast. After this they climbed to the top of the island's central ridge, where George described the scene:

> We found [the ridge] covered with dry grasses, intermixed with some low, shrubby plants; and among them a number of quails exactly like those of Europe, had their residence. Several deep and narrow glens which ran down the sides of the ridge to the sea, were filled with trees, shrubs and climbers, the haunt of numerous small birds, and of several falcons; but where the cliffs were perpendicular, or hanging over the water, great flocks of a beautiful sort of shags built their nests on every little broken rock, or if possible in small cavities about a foot square, which seemed in a few instances to be enlarged by the birds themselves.[15]

On 23 May, local people ventured out to the *Resolution* for the first time. The *Resolution* was a much bigger ship than the *Adventure*, and according to Furneaux they marvelled at its size. Two small canoes carrying five men came alongside, and Cook fed their crews and gave them presents. Despite this there was petty pilfering, which had never happened in Tamatea. Johann Forster reported that these people liked sugared water but not spirits, and were particularly fond of nails, hatchets and glass bottles, calling these 'taha' (tahaa, or calabash). When they wanted something, they pointed to it and then moved that hand towards their chest and said, 'Moke' (mooku – for me). They asked after Tupaia, and seemed to think that the Europeans came from his homeland and that everything they had also came from Tahiti. One of these people, a 'well-looking' young man called 'Koogooaa' (ko Koa?), became very friendly with the Europeans.[16] These people soon worked out who was in command of the expedition. When some of the sailors took their canoes without permission to go on shore, they went immediately to Cook's cabin and complained. He had the canoes returned to them and they went away 'highly pleased'.

Early the next morning, these men came back to the ship with a woman and several children. Cook, Furneaux and Forster left them after breakfast to go on a shooting expedition, and on the way to West Bay they met a double canoe carrying fourteen or fifteen strangers, who asked after Tupaia and seemed distressed to hear that he was dead (mate noa), pronouncing some words 'in a plaintive tone' (probably a tangi, or lament). Later that day a canoe full of strangers from 'the northward' (perhaps the same canoe) visited the *Resolution*, exchanging stone tools, weapons and paddles with the sailors and also asking about Tupaia. Memories of

Tupaia's 1770 visit were still vivid, and his fame as a voyager on a strange vessel from Tahiti had spread throughout the region. In many parts of New Zealand, it seems, the *Endeavour* was remembered as Tupaia's ship.

The *Resolution*'s launch went with twelve men on board that morning to cut greens for the crew and grass for the animals, and when they did not return that evening or during the next day, Cook became worried. They arrived back on the 26th, however, having been caught in squalls (which also blew the *Resolution* loose from its shore mooring). They had camped overnight in some deserted huts in a cove, where they fed themselves with mussels from the rocks. Over the next few days large numbers of local people came out to visit the ships. According to Wales, two of their visitors seemed determined to join the *Resolution* when she left the Sound:

> One of them ventured up to our Top-Gallt Mast head; and, if we did not misunderstand him told us he could wish to go with us. He and three others refused to go away with the rest, and were left on board: In the Evening they had something given them to eat and had a clean dry sail spread for them under one of the Gangways where they lay down and slept 'till about 10 o'clock when two old men came alongside in a Canoe to enquire for them.
>
> The Officer then on deck shewed them where they were & waked them: Two were preswaded by the Seniors to go with them, but the others absolutely refused, and lay themselves down & slept untill Morning seemingly without the least dread; notwithstanding it was afterwards discovered that one of them was in possession of a Vol. of *Tom Jones*, which he had stole out of an Officers Cabbin, who had done every thing he could to entertain them; and the other of a hand lead which he had *found* on the Quarter Deck.[17]

These would-be mariners were deprived of their acquisitions, and soon sent off the ship. Words from the *Endeavour*'s Maori vocabulary had been read out in front of local people, and texts appeared powerful sources of magic. *Tom Jones* (Henry Fielding's famous novel) must have seemed an irresistible treasure.

Johann Forster now began to collect Maori words for a vocabulary of his own, and he and his son wrote down the names of people who came on board the ship. On 25 May, for instance, George recorded the names of the family who first visited them on the 23rd as 'Koghoaa' (ko Koa, the young man whose name they had learned that day), 'Towahangha' (Te Wahanga?) and his little boy 'Khoaa' (Koa?), who may have been the young man's namesake, 'Kollakh' (probably ko Raki or Koraki[18]) or 'Koalleka' (ko Reka?), and an old man called 'Kutughaa' (ko Toka?) and his young son 'Taywaherua' (Te Weherua?[19]). Several days later, Te Weherua, whom George described as 'twelve or fourteen years of age, [with] a very promising countenance, and seemed to be the liveliest and most intelligent among them',[20] came back on board with his father, and was invited to the cabin for a meal. He liked shag pie, especially the crust, but began to sulk when he asked for Cook's boat cloak and some bottles, and was refused. Johann Forster gave him a glass of Madeira to cheer him up. At first he made wry faces, but then began to

enjoy it, licking his lips, so Johann brought him two glasses of sweet Cape mus-
catel, which made him drunk. His father, Toka, went up onto the deck, where he
fired off a gun that one of the officers had handed to him. When he saw a table-
cloth hung up there to dry and asked for it, however, he was refused, and 'grew
almost distracted with disappointment, grunted first & lastly became so sulky,
that he would not speak a word & went away in a pet'. Johann commented that
such reactions were 'chiefly caused by the readiness with which many young
Gentlemen part with their nails, with Shirts and other things the Natives long for;
if therefore they are refused a thing afterwards they cannot bear the disappointment'.[21] In the protocol of Maori gift exchange, if something was asked for it was
generally given, although a generous return gift was expected later on.

It seems probable that Te Wahanga's family were visitors to the Sound, and
they may have been of Ngaai Tahu descent.[22] They had not been in Totara-nui
when Cook first arrived there in 1770, and in 1773 were probably there on a
trading visit (for, as it emerged later, Te Wahanga was an entrepreneurial and
expert trader).

The goods that various people offered to the Europeans during this visit included fish, 'curiosities' (weapons, fishing gear and cloaks) and sex with women,
in exchange for nails, beads, hatchets and old European clothes. Often they simply took things, including a lamp, a four-hour glass, and the volume of *Tom Jones*
and the hand lead mentioned earlier. Perhaps they intended to give return gifts
later for these items, but it seems unlikely. They may have understood what they
were doing as muru – taking goods in exchange for breaches of proper behaviour.
The Europeans were casual in their approach to local resources; as John Marra
later reflected in Tahiti:

> Is it not very natural, when a people see a company of strangers come among
> them, and without ceremony cut down their trees, gather their fruits, seize their
> animals, and, in short, take whatever they want, that such a people should use as
> little ceremony with the strangers, as the strangers do with them; if so, against
> whom is the criminality to be charged, the christian or the savage?[23]

Stealing was uncommon in Maori communities, because household goods
were protected by the owner's ancestor gods, and theft was sharply punished.
Still, the Europeans were a puzzle. Perhaps their goods gave access to new kinds
of power, which provoked a pure desire for acquisition. The ships, with their hoards
of European wealth, were irresistible; and the more prized and private the goods,
the more coveted they became. In return, the most prized and private goods
desired by the sailors involved access to women. Cook commented with regret
on the impact this was having on local behaviour:

> This Second Visit of ours hath not mended the morals of the Natives of either Sex,
> the Women of this Country I always looked upon to be more chaste than the
> generality of Indian Women, whatever favours a few of them might have granted
> to the crew of the *Endeavour* it was generally done in a private manner and without

the men seeming to intrest themselves in it, but now we find the men are the chief promoters of this Vice, and for a spike nail or any other thing they value will oblige their Wives and Daughters to prostitute themselves whether they will or no and that not with the privicy decency seems to require, such are the concequences of a commerce with Europeans and what is still more to our Shame civilized Christians, we debauch their Morals already too prone to vice and we interduce among them wants and perhaps diseases which they never before knew and which serves only to disturb the happy tranquillity they and their fore Fathers had injoy'd. If any one denies the truth of this assertion let him tell me what the Natives of the whole extent of America have gained by the commerce they have had with Europeans.[24]

These sexual exchanges began shortly after the *Adventure*'s arrival, and were quickly extended to the *Resolution* when that ship came into the Sound. On 29 May, for instance, a group of about thirty people came out to the *Resolution*. After exchanging tools and weapons for iron nails and tools, the men went through the ship, offering their 'sisters' and 'daughters' (despite tears and protests from some of the women) to the crew. George Forster tried to work out the implications for local kinship in this new form of exchange:

> It does not appear that their married women were ever suffered to have this kind of intercourse with our people. Their ideas of female chastity are, in this respect, so different from ours, that a girl may favour a number of lovers without any detriment to her character; but if she marries, conjugal fidelity is exacted from her with the greatest rigour. It may therefore be alledged, that as the New Zeelanders, place no value on the continence of their unmarried women, the arrival of Europeans among them, did not injure their moral character in this respect; but we doubt whether they ever debased themselves so much as to make a trade of their women, before we created new wants by shewing them iron-tools.[25]

The Europeans had difficulties in understanding Maori kinship; men could be polygamous and their secondary 'wives' were often war captives, while 'fathers' and 'mothers' could be any close relative of the first ascending generation; 'brothers' or 'sisters' any close relative of the same generation; and 'sons' or 'daughters' any close relative of the next descending generation. Women could take lovers before marriage, although too many lovers were frowned on. Adultery, on the other hand, which raised doubts about paternity, might be punished by death or exile. Although the Europeans routinely misread Maori kin relations, tending to project their own ideas of kinship (monogamous marriage, the nuclear family and European kin terms) on to Maori behaviour, local sexual mores were still being altered, children were being conceived,[26] and venereal diseases were introduced and spread.

During this visit, George Forster observed the people closely, noting that some of the women had tattooed lips and others wore the brown feather hats first depicted during the *Endeavour*'s visit to the Sound. He described old men with grey or white hair and beards, and young men with 'amazing bushy hair, which hung wildly over their faces and increased their natural savage looks', whom Hodges

Red chalk sketches by William Hodges at Totara-nui in 1773.

Above left: *A young man with 'amazing bushy hair'.*

Above: *An old man with a grey beard and hair.*

Left: *The young woman who mistook the nature of Hodges' invitation (see page 78).*

sketched in the ship's cabin. At first one of the women mistook the nature of Hodges' invitation:

> Language difficulties at first gave rise to a misunderstanding between the girl and the painter, for she, having been paid well to go down into the saloon, imagined that she ought to give satisfaction, in the way she understood it, as soon as possible in return for her gift; perhaps she had had previous experience with our sailors? She was astonished when signs were made for her to sit on a chair; such a novel way of doing things struck her as absurd, but she promptly volunteered a prone position on the chair for the painter and his companion. To her further surprise she was eventually put in a correct position, just sitting on the chair with nothing to do; whereupon, to the wonderment and entertainment of herself and the two savages with her, she quickly saw her likeness appearing in a red crayon drawing.[27]

'Language difficulties' were a feature of these visits. Although some of the men spoke some Tahitian, it was not the same as Maori. Vocabularies were a help but no substitute for linguistic mastery. Ironically, communications with Maori were probably best on Cook's first voyage, when the priest-navigator Tupaia had acted as interpreter. Perhaps because he was a traveller, Tupaia had been able to adapt to new dialects, and spoke with the Europeans in a mixture of English and Tahitian.

After the exchange with Hodges these new arrivals camped on shore by the ships, cooking fish for supper that they had caught with hoop nets from their canoes, and sleeping in temporary shelters, where sexual barter continued the next morning.

Although Cook deplored the long-term effects of sexual exchanges with local people, he was convinced that the introduction of European animals and crops was useful to them, as well as to visiting mariners. On 29 May, while his ship was being turned into a floating brothel (which he said that he only allowed because he could not stop it), he took one of the local elders over to Motuara to show him a plot of potatoes planted by the *Adventure*'s master, Peter Fannin. Cook called them 'coumalla' (kuumara – sweet potato), and the man was so delighted with the garden that he immediately began to pick stones out of the beds and hoe the earth around the plants. Cook showed him another garden, planted by the *Adventure*'s men with turnips, carrots and parsnips (which he called 'tara', or taro), and over the next few days ordered more ground cleared on Motuara and Hippa Island, and planted with wheat, peas, French beans, celery, carrots, parsnips and strawberries.[28]

About this time a number of quarrels erupted. A local woman had taken a sailor's jacket and gave it to 'Kogooah' (Koa), the 'well-looking' young man who had first come on board on the 23rd. When the sailor took the jacket from Koa, he retaliated, striking out. At first the sailor was amused, but when Koa threw large stones at him, he punched the man, giving him a black eye and a bloody nose. Several days later there was another fight on shore. Two of the local men began to argue, and eventually stripped off naked, picked up sticks and began to beat each other while their companions watched the fight. In the end one of them gave up, which resolved the argument, at least for the time being. Competing kin groups were being brought together in unaccustomed proximity, and new wealth and other interventions by the Europeans were creating new causes for tension and trouble. There was also trouble on board the ships; on 30 May a seaman and a marine were tied to the gratings and flogged on board the *Adventure* for 'Drunkeness and Rioting & being Insolent', while the crews of several canoes watched alongside.

The presence of the European ships attracted increasing numbers of visitors into the Sound. Canoes came almost every day to the *Adventure*, and on 1 June a party of strangers in a flotilla of canoes came out to the *Resolution*. These canoes were uncarved and seemed quite old, and three of them had sails, which were uncommon in the Sound. The leader of these people, 'Tringho-Waya' (identified by Mitchell as Te Rangihouhia, a man of Rangitaane/Ngaati Kuia descent[29]) was described by Johann Forster as 'a tall and strong man, nearly middle-aged', with deeply incised spiral tattoos on his chin, cheeks, forehead and nose, who was sketched by Hodges during this visit.

The crews of these canoes quickly boarded the *Resolution* and began to trade 'curiosities' including fish-hooks; necklaces made with several rows of human teeth; a woman's dancing-apron or 'awirookoora' (awe tuu kura?) made of closely woven cloth decorated with red feathers, white dogskin and pieces of paaua shell; and greenstone tools and ornaments, which Johann Forster commented 'were new to us', in exchange for shirts and bottles. These included greenstone adzes, small hafted chisels, ear ornaments and 'e teeghee' (hei tiki, described as 'a contorted and squatted figure, something resembling the carricature of a man, in which a pair of monstrous eyes were inserted, made of the mother of pearl of an ear-shell [paaua]'[30]), worn as chest ornaments by both men and women. They had also brought a number of dogs with them, which they traded with the Europeans. George Forster described these kurii (Polynesian dogs) as 'a rough long-haired sort, with pricked ears . . . of different colours, some spotted, some quite black, and others perfectly white'.[31] They seemed very fond of these animals, which they fed on fish and kept restrained by a string around their middles. When they were taken on board the *Resolution*, the older dogs sulked and would not eat, but the pups soon settled down and ate the food that the Europeans gave them.

Before they left the ship, Te Rangihouhia and his party performed a dance on the quarterdeck, throwing off their rough mats, standing in a row, and 'one sung some words & all the rest followed him in his motions, extending one hand or the other & stamping with the legs, & lastly they repeated the last words of the Song, or the burden'.[32] According to James Burney, a young officer on the *Adventure* who had become interested in Maori music, 'they keep singing the 2 first Bars till their words are expended & then close with the last – Sometimes they Sing an underpart which is a third lower except the 2 last notes which are the same'[33] – an interesting observation, which suggests that they were singing in harmony.

By now the two ships were almost ready to leave the Sound. Furneaux put a boar and two sows ashore in 'Canibals Cove', while Cook landed a male and a female goat in East Bay, hoping that they would go off into the bush and breed. On 2 June, Te Wahanga came back to the *Resolution* with his daughter 'Ko-parree' (Pari) and his small son Koa, who had an unhappy encounter with one of the billy goats left on board. Cook had given Koa a shirt, and he was so proud of his new garment that he went around the ship, showing it off to everybody who would look. As Cook wrote in his journal that night:

> This liberty of the Boy offended old Will the Ram Goat who up with his head and knock'd the boy backwards on the Deck, Will would have repeated his blow had not some of the people got to the boys assistance, this missfortune seem'd to him irreparable, the Shirt was dirted and he was afraid to appear in the Cabbin before his father untill brought in by Mr. Forster, when he told a very lamentable story against Goure [kurii] the great Dog, for so they call all the quadrupeds we have aboard, nor could he be pacified till his shirt was wash'd and dry'd.[34]

One of this family (possibly Te Weherua, who with Koa subsequently became the first Maori to travel from New Zealand in a European ship) offered to go away with Cook on the *Resolution*, but later changed his mind.

The next day, as part of last-minute preparations for departure, one of the *Resolution*'s boats went across to Long Island to fetch some hay that had been cut and dried. On their way back they saw two large canoes full of 'strange Natives' coming from East Bay, and one of these canoes (which carried a crew of about fifty people) chased them back to the ship. At about the same time, a boat that had been sent to cut spars on the east side of the Sound was chased by another large canoe. This was a repeat of the pattern of seaborne challenges directed at the *Adventure*'s boats in late April, just before the *Resolution* had arrived. Very likely the local people had realised that the Europeans were about to leave the Sound and were trying some final tests of strength, either with an eye to plunder or revenge for harms that they had suffered.

June the 4th was the King's birthday, a festive day for the Europeans. That morning a carved double canoe about fifty feet long and carrying about twenty-eight strong, well-dressed strangers (all men) from the 'north-east' came out to the ship from Motuara. There were two 'chiefs' on board, both with full facial tattoos, and as they approached the vessel the younger of them began a long, cadenced chant (probably a tapu-raising karakia). Te Wahanga's family, who were already on board, were terrified. According to Wales, the men began to tremble and some of the women wailed, saying that these were enemies who would kill them if the Europeans did not shoot them first. When Cook refused, Te Wahanga and another man 'jumped on the Arm-Chest got hold of Staffs & made a kind of warlike motion towards them, which they accompanied with a few solemn words'.[35] After this Te Wahanga pulled out a greenstone hatchet (which he had never before shown the Europeans) and continued the challenge, diverting the visitors' attention while the rest of his family left the ship.

The senior chief on the visiting canoe was an impressive, white-haired old man 'who might have stood to a Statuary for the Model of a Hercules'.[36] He wore a fine black dogskin cloak, while the younger chief wore a woven cloak dyed black and decorated with white dogskin stripes (a 'taigook' [possibly a tieke or black flax cloak], according to Johann Forster). The senior chief held a green flax leaf in his hand, and every now and then spoke a few brief words in counterpoint to his companion's chanting. The younger man, whom George Forster identified as 'Teiratu' (Te Ratu), brandished his patu (hand club) and 'pronounced a long speech well articulated, loud and very solemn, and gave his voice great variety of falls and elevations. From the various tones in which he spoke, and a few gestures with which he accompanied his words, he appeared by turns to question, to boast, to threaten, to challenge, and to persuade us; he was sometimes running on in a moderate tone, then all at once breaking out into violent exclamations; after which he made short pauses in order to recover his breath.'[37] It seems likely that Te Ratu was the man standing up in the canoe that Hodges sketched and later painted.

When this long speech was over, Cook invited his visitors on board and asked Te Wahanga and his people to come back to the ship. He persuaded Te Wahanga to hongi (press noses) with the 'old king', and after this he ceased to be afraid. According to William Bayly, the 'old man received him on the gang way squat on his hams & as soon as the old king was got up the Ship's side he squat before him & in this

The double canoe alongside the Resolution *on 4 June 1773; the young chief chanting.*

position they joined noses . . . muttering some words all the time & then he joined noses with every one of us & presently we began trade with them & were all Friends'.[38]

The strangers said they came from Te Raawhiti (on the other side of Raukawa-moana), asked after Tupaia, and wept when they heard that he had died. George Forster commented:

> So much had [Tupaia's] superior knowledge, and his ability to converse in their language rendered him valuable, and beloved even among a nation in a state of barbarism. Perhaps with the capacity which Providence had alloted to him, and which had been cultivated no farther than the simplicity of his education would permit, he was more adapted to raise the New Zeelanders to a state of civilization similar to that of his own islands, than ourselves, to whom the want of the inter-mediate links, which connect their narrow views to our extended sphere of knowl-edge, must prove an obstacle in such an undertaking.[39]

News of the *Endeavour*'s visit to New Zealand had travelled widely, and so had trade goods from the ship. One of these people gave Cook an ear ornament made from glass, probably acquired during the 1769–70 visit. Cook took the chiefs to his cabin, presenting them with gifts and receiving the young chief's striped cloak in return, while their companions exchanged goods on deck with the sailors. These people were tall and elegantly dressed, with new cloaks including some ornamented with dogskin and others with red, white and black woven borders (taaniko), fastened around the neck with string ties and pins of greenstone, whale-bone or bone. Their hair was tied up, greased and ornamented with white feathers, and several of them wore large whalebone combs. Some had spiral facial tattoos, while the faces of others were smeared with red ochre and oil, and they had brought with them a greenstone adze hafted on a carved handle (toki pou tangata) and musical instruments including flutes, a shell trumpet with a carved mouth-piece (puu taatara), which made a 'hideous bellowing', and another trumpet about four feet long (puu kaea), with which they made 'a very uncouth kind of bray-ing'.[40] George Forster commented that 'their dress, ornaments and arms were richer than any we had observed among the inhabitants of Queen Charlotte's Sound, and seemed to speak a kind of affluence, which was entirely new to us'.[41]

This group stayed only a short time on the ship before returning to Motuara. Cook, Forster, Pickersgill and others followed them to the island, showed them the gardens they had planted there and presented them with beads, brass medals (engraved with the inscription 'George II, King of Great Britain, France, and Ireland' on one side and 'Resolution, Adventure, Sailed from England March MDCCLXXII' on the other) and other items in exchange for 'curiosities'. They had brought six canoes to the island filled with portable property, and a party of about ninety men, women and children. According to George Forster:

> The captain and his company perceived that Teiratu seemed to be the principal or chief among them, by a certain degree of regard which the rest paid to him: they

could not, however, determine any thing with precision on this subject. Respect is always paid to the old men among them, who may be supposed to owe their consequence to the long experience they have gained. But their chiefs, such as we believed this Teiratu to be, are strong, active young men, in the prime and flower of their age. These are perhaps elected, as among the North American savages; being men of avowed courage, strength, and military sagacity . . . The more we consider the war-like disposition of the New Zeelanders, and the numerous small parties into which they are divided, this form of government will appear indispensible; for it must be evident to them that the qualifications of a chief are not to be inherited, or propagated from father to son; and it is likewise probable, that this free people may have had opportunities of making the obvious reflection, that hereditary government has a natural tendency towards despotism.[42]

Leadership in Maori kin groups was in fact a combination of acquired and inherited status, and Forster's republican sympathies (which later led him to become an ardent supporter of the French Revolution) are obvious in this description. Mana came from the ancestors, but was kept alive by personal effort, and a high-born person without abilities for leadership might retain a certain prestige but little real power. Te Ratu was probably both war leader and 'talking chief' for these people, who may have come from Rangitaane territories on the other side of the strait, but 'the old king' in the black dogskin cloak was almost certainly his senior in status as well as age.

After this encounter with Te Ratu and his Te Raawhiti people, the Europeans returned to the *Resolution* for a dinner hosted by Cook for the officers of both ships, in honour of the King's birthday. The marines lined up on the shore and fired a twenty-one-gun salute, and that evening bonfires were lighted on the beach and fireworks were set off, 'to the great astonishment of the Indian beholders'.[43]

During the next two days the weather was foul, so no further contact with the local people was possible. On 7 April, the ships hauled up their anchors and sailed out of the Sound. A canoe carrying four of Te Wahanga's family passed close by them, but 'they took little notice, paddl[ing] on without any attention'.[44] According to Cook, during this stay in Totara-nui they met nobody whom they had known during the *Endeavour*'s visit, although the fact of that visit was well known to local people, and many of them asked about Tupaia and showed signs of grief when they heard of his death. Topaa and his people, who had spent so much time with the *Endeavour* party in 1770, were nowhere to be seen, and their settlements at Motuara and Hippa Island had been abandoned.

As they left the Sound, William Wales reflected upon the Maori reputation for violence and cannibalism:

Before going to leave this land of Canibals, as it is now generally thought to be, it may be expected that I should record what bloody Massacres I have been a witness of; how many human Carcases I have seen roasted and eaten; or at least relate such Facts as have fallen within the Compass of my Observation tending to confirm the Opinion, now almost universally believed, that the New Zeelanders are guilty of this most detestable Practice. Truth, notwithstanding, obliges me to declare, how-ever unpopular it may be, that I have not seen the least signs of any such custom being amongst them, either in Dusky Bay or Charlotte sound; although the latter place is that where the only Instance of it was *seen* in the *Endeavour's* Voyage. I know it is urged as a proof positive against them, that in the representation of their War-Exercise, which they were very fond of shewing us, they confessed the Fact. The real state of the Case is this.

They first began with shewing us how they handled their Weapons, how they defyed the Enemy to Battle, how they killed him; they then proceeded to cut of his head, legs & arms; they afterwards took out his Bowels & threw them away, and lastly shewed us that they went to eating. But it ought by all means to be remarked that all this was shewn by signs which every one will allow are easily misunderstood, and for any thing that I know to the contrary they might mean they Eat the Man they had just killed; but is it not as likely that after the Engage-ment they refreshed themselves with some other Victuals which they might have with them?[45]

Wales, the scrupulous scientist, would not accept as fact any circumstance that had not been witnessed by reliable observers, and he made it plain that he did not regard the sailors as invariably accurate in their accounts. On the contrary, he reported at least two instances in which sailors had proved unreliable witnesses. One sailor, for example, had given a detailed account of seeing a particular 'In-dian' being killed, which was discredited when this same man was seen walking about, alive and well. Elliott, one of the midshipmen on board the *Resolution*, had no such scruples, and reported:

They are desperate, fearless, ferocious Cannibals, the Men generaly about six feet high, with Limbs and sinews like an Ox, dark copper coloured faces, fine white teeth, and eyes that strike fire, when angry, and I declare that I have seen a couple of them, in giving us the War Song on the Quarter deck, work themselves into a frenzey, foaming at the mouth, and perfectly shaking the whole Quarter deck with their feet . . . And in this state they attack their Enemies, and will rush upon Bayonets or anything else.[46]

Interlude

TO THE SOUTH-EAST ACROSS THE PACIFIC, THEN NORTH TO TAHITI AND TONGA

After leaving Queen Charlotte Sound on 7 June, the expedition's ships sailed south-east to latitude 47° 40' and then turned northward, crossing the Pacific between the courses that Cook had sailed to and from Tahiti in 1769. After several days at sea a black dog from the Cape of Good Hope was cooked and eaten in the gun-room; it tasted like mutton. This made Johann Forster muse upon the Euro-pean prejudice that regarded dogs, cats, and horses as unclean animals, unfit to eat.[47] Weeks later, when another of the dogs from the Cape gave birth to a litter

A painting from the east side of Point Venus, Tahiti, with Motu Au islet to the left,
by William Hodges.

of pups, one was stillborn, and a kurii from New Zealand ate it avidly. On this
occasion George Forster speculated that cannibalism could become habitual with
dogs as well as with people: 'The New Zeeland dogs, in all likelihood, are trained up
from their earliest age to eat the remains of their master's meals; they are therefore
used to feed upon fish, their own species, and perhaps human flesh; and what was
only owing to habit at first, may have become instinct by length of time.'[48]

In other respects, this section of the voyage was uneventful. No continent
loomed over the horizon, and after six weeks at sea the crews began to suffer
from scurvy, the sailor's malady. The ships now headed for Tahiti, where they
found that there had been fighting on the island since 1769. Some of Cook's old
friends were dead, while others had been deposed from power. Crops and pigs
had been destroyed, and it was much more difficult to get provisions there than it
had been during the *Endeavour* voyage. After two weeks at Tahiti, the ships sailed
west to Huahine, where pigs, chickens and fruit were more readily available, and
a young refugee from Raiatea called Mai (named 'Omai' by the Europeans – 'o',
the nominative particle, plus 'Mai') came on board the *Adventure* with his attendant Poetata. Several days later they proceeded to Raiatea, which had recently been
invaded by people from Borabora. Raiatea was Tupaia's (as well as Mai's) home
island, and everyone asked after him and mourned when they heard of his death.
There were feasts and entertainments, and so many pigs were brought on board
the ships that the captains eventually refused to take any more. One of the Borabora

people, a young man about seventeen years old named 'Oedidee' (Hitihiti, also known as Mahine), expressed his wish to visit Britain, and Cook allowed him to join the *Resolution*'s crew. According to Cook, venereal diseases were already well established in each of these places, although the people claimed to have found a cure for at least some cases. They also reported an infectious disease left behind by a ship commanded by one 'Opep-pe' (the Spanish voyager Boenechea), which attacked the nose and throat and then afflicted the body with sores (probably syphilis), killing a number of people on the island. For this they had found no cure.

The English sailors thought that the Society Islands were Paradise, and wrote ecstatically about the islanders. According to John Elliott, 'the Men [were] all fine, tall, well-made, with humane open countenances; the Women beautiful, compaired with all those that we had seen, of the Middle Size, zingy, suple figures, fine teeth and Eyes, and the finest formed Hands, fingers, and Arms that I ever saw with lively dispositions'.[49] His description of Tahitian 'noble savages' was in sharp contrast with his earlier accounts of fierce, cannibalistic, ignoble Maori – images that say more about Europeans' ideas of good and evil in a state of nature than about the actual Polynesian peoples that they encountered.

The expedition stayed about a month in the Society Islands, then sailed via the Cook Islands to Tonga. During the week they spent in Tonga both Cook and the Forsters produced detailed descriptions of local houses, burial grounds, people and their practices, including music, religious ceremonies and kava drinking, honing their ethnographic skills. Their visit began with tumultuous welcomes at Eua and Tongatapu, and ended with violence. On 7 October, after muted farewells from the local people, the ships left Tongatapu and headed southwards back to New Zealand.

THE *RESOLUTION* AND *ADVENTURE* OFF
TE MATAU-A-MAAUI AND PORT NICHOLSON
21 October – 2 November 1773

On 21 October, land was sighted and Cook hauled in to Te Matau-a-Maaui (Hawke's Bay), where he intended to leave pigs, chickens, root crops and seeds. The wind was blowing off the land, however, and no-one came out to the ships, although fires could be seen flaring up on the hills and people moving about on the ridgetops above the houses on Waikawa (Portland Island). According to George Forster, 'The shores were white and steep towards the sea, and we could perceive the huts and strong holds of the natives, like eagles airies on the top of the cliffs. A great number of natives ran along the rocks, in order to gaze at us, as we passed by them, and many seated themselves at the point which extends to the southward, but did not care to come off to us in their canoes.'[50] During the next day three canoes carrying about eighteen men ventured out from Te Matau (Cape Kidnappers), at the south end of the bay.

The first canoe was crewed by fishermen, who exchanged fish for cloth and nails, but the second canoe was richly carved and carried two chiefs whom Cook invited on board the *Resolution*. According to William Colenso, a missionary who was later to live in Hawke's Bay, the principal of these two chiefs was Tuanui (ancestor of Henare Matua).[51] These men were obviously well aware of the fracas during the *Endeavour*'s visit to Te Matau four years earlier, when some local people had tried to kidnap Tupaia's boy and several were shot. The first thing that they said when they came on board the *Resolution* was 'Mataou no te poupou!' (Mataku no te puupuu – We are afraid of guns!). Marra gave a vivid account of Tuanui's brief visit:

> The head of this Chief was curiously tatowed, and his hair was finely ornamented with feathers; it was tied, as their custom is, in a knot on the top of his head; and the feathers of various colours were plaited all round in a very neat and elegant manner . . . [Sparrman added that he wore a kind of 'powder puff' made of white birdskin on his ears.] After admiring the wonderful structure of the ship, being shewn the cabin, the hold, the gun-room, and the other conveniences between decks, he next took a survey of the rigging, the masts, sails, and ropes, and the dexterous manner of handling them. On being shewn so many novelties, he could not help expressing his astonishment by a variety of gestures.[52]

Hodges sketched Tuanui in the great cabin, and Cook gave him several large spike nails, a looking glass and a piece of red baize cloth. He was delighted with the nails, which had him in such raptures that Cook's other gifts – two boars, two sows, two cocks and four hens, and roots and seeds including wheat, beans, peas, cabbages, turnips, onions, carrots, parsnips and yams[53] – seemed an anti-climax. Cook made him promise not to kill any of the animals, and noticed that he counted them carefully before he left the ship.

Hitihiti, the young man from Borabora who had joined the ship at Raiatea, gave Tuanui gifts of coconuts and yams and tried to talk to him, but could not make himself understood. Hitihiti was an ordinary, if amiable, young man, and Tuanui largely ignored him, while presenting Cook with his finely carved 'maheepeh' (maipi), or battle-axe, with its decoration of red parrots' feathers and white dogs' hair. Before he left the ship he and his companions performed a 'war-song' of appreciation, 'which consisted of stamping with the feet, brandishing short clubs, spears, &c. making frightful contortions of the face, lolling out the tongue, and bellowing wildly, but in tune with each motion'.[54] According to Colenso, the gifts presented on this occasion were long remembered by Tuanui's descendants, including 'the "Maori cabbage" of the coast', which later grew wild from Te Matau to Palliser Bay.[55]

That afternoon a gale blew up, which lasted for days. 'We are rolled about in an agitated & tempestuous Sea,' wrote Johann Forster, 'the storm roaring in our rigging, & breaking against our Ship. The storm raises the Sea, & when she breaks over at the top of the wave, the wind entirely dissolves the Sea into Atoms of vapour & carries them off into the Air, like smoke.'[56] During the storm the ships

Two portraits sketched by William Hodges on board the Resolution.
Left: *Tuanui, a chief from Te Matau-a-Maaui (Hawke's Bay). Note the feather ear and head ornaments.*
Right: *'Oedidee' (Hitihiti), a young man from Borabora.*

found themselves separated once again. Cook supposed that Furneaux would go ahead to meet him at the pre-arranged rendezvous in Queen Charlotte Sound, and sailed south in rough weather to find him. When they reached Cook Strait, the *Resolution* anchored off Te Whanganui-a-Tara (Wellington Harbour), where Wales observed 'the appearance of a very good Harbour beyond some Islands which form the bottom of the Bay'.[57] Three canoes came out to the ship, and their crews (who were 'very despicably habited in old shaggy cloaks') were given medals, Tahitian cloth, nails, yams from Tahiti, two cocks and two hens in exchange for fish-hooks and a few dried crayfish tails. They were 'extravigantly fond of Iron' but received the livestock with relative indifference. The next morning the ship sailed through gales into Totara-nui and anchored in Meretoto. To their dismay, there was no sign of the *Adventure* in the Sound.

Four

TOTARA-NUI
II

THE *RESOLUTION*'S SECOND VISIT TO TOTARA-NUI
3–25 November 1773

Almost as soon as the *Resolution* anchored in Meretoto, some people whom Cook recognised from his first visit in 1770, including 'one old Man [named 'Goobaia' (Kupaia?)] who was chief at this place, and resident in it all the time that the *Endeavour* lay here', came out to the ship. They brought fish, which they exchanged eagerly for white Tahitian bark cloth. The *Endeavour* men on board were delighted to see these people and greeted them by name. The local people told the Europeans what had happened during their brief absence from the Sound since June, and several of them blamed Kupaia for killing and eating two goats left during Cook's last visit. They also reported that Te Wahanga and his family had been killed and eaten by enemies during their absence, but this turned out to be mistaken – probably a garbled mixture of the story about the goats and news of Te Wahanga's family.

That afternoon William Wales pitched his tent at the bottom of the cove, alongside the woodcutters and the waterers. He prepared to put up his observatory while the usual business of repairing the sails, overhauling the rigging, drying out the bread, cleaning and mending water casks, and refitting the battered ship went on. The gardens planted earlier in the voyage at Ship Cove, on Motuara and Hippa Island were flourishing (especially the cabbages, carrots, onions and parsley), although the radishes and turnips had run to seed, the peas and beans had been chewed by rats and local people had dug up the potatoes. It was late spring and the Forsters found flax plants in flower and collected other specimens, which they described and sketched when they returned to the *Resolution*. Johann was delighted, because Linnaeus's taxonomic system depended upon the collection of flowering specimens so that the pistils and stamens of each species could be counted and their arrangement noted and thus classified. His last visit to New Zealand had been in autumn, when most of the plants had finished flowering, and he now hoped to complete his botanical descriptions.

The next morning Te Ratu, the young orator from Te Raawhiti who had so impressed them during their last visit to the Sound, came out to the *Resolution*. All his finery had gone, his hair and dress were bedraggled, and according to George Forster, 'he seemed to be degraded to a simple fish-monger'.[1] The Europeans gave him nails, and Te Ratu told them that he and his people proposed to camp in the Sound for the duration of their stay. That afternoon Hitihiti ventured out into the bush, where he marvelled at the different kinds of birds, 'their sweet melody and their beautiful plumage'. A flock of small birds was feeding on radish and turnip flowers in one of the gardens they had planted, and Hitihiti shot a shining cuckoo in his first attempt at firing a gun. Johann Forster remarked of this feat: 'It is amazing how acute senses these Nations have: in Otahaitee the Natives often shewed Me Ducks or Snipes or other birds, where none of us could distinguish any.'[2]

Early on 5 November, the people from the shore camp reported that a watch coat and a bag of dirty linen had been taken from the waterers' tent during the night. Cook went to Te Ratu's hamlet in Indian Cove to demand their return, and after a while the goods were found and handed back. During his visit he spotted one of the sows that Furneaux had left behind. Apart from a lame hind leg, the pig was in good condition, so Cook came back the next day with a boar, a sow, two cocks and two hens (all from Tahiti), and left them with these people, asking them to take care of them. Te Ratu told him that the other sow and the boar left by Furneaux had been taken off in different directions, one to the east and the other to the west. George Forster commented with exasperation: 'Thus by separating the animals, and dividing them as a spoil, these barbarians effectually destroy the possibility of propagating the species. Too preoccupied with the wants of the present moment, they overlook the only means of securing a certain livelihood to themselves, and reject every attempt to civilize them.'[3]

On the 6th, Te Ratu's people came as usual to barter fish for Tahitian cloth (giving three hundredweight of fish for a piece of cloth that cost just one nail in the Islands), but soon began to play games with the Europeans, taking fish away with one hand that had just been given with the other, and trying to pick their pockets. When Cook protested, one of the chiefs 'with fury in his eyes, made a shew of keeping the people at a proper distance', but according to Cook this was mere pretence:

> I apploaded his conduct but at the same time kept so good a lookout as to detect him in picking my Pocket of a handkerchief, which I suffered him to put in his bosom before I seem'd to know any thing of the matter and then told him what I had lost, he seemed quite ignorant and inicent, till I took it from him, and then he put it of with a laugh, and he had acted his part with so much address that it was hardly possible for me to be angery with him, so that we remained good friends and he accompanied me on board to dinner.[4]

During that afternoon four or five more canoes arrived in the cove, bringing fish and weapons ('imetti', or mere [hand club]; 'mahepeh', or maipi [battle-axe]; and 'taigook', or tokotoko?) to exchange for European (and Tahitian) goods. There were now about a hundred and fifty people in the neighbourhood, including Te Ratu's group and the newcomers (possibly also from Te Raawhiti), who camped overnight on a beach by the *Resolution*. In the morning when the Europeans woke up, however, they found that all of these people had gone, taking six of the ship's small water casks with them. Te Ratu's group left behind some dogs and the pigs that Cook had given them, and these were brought back to the ship.

For the next two days the Europeans were left to fend for themselves, collecting greens and catching fish with indifferent success. The weather was wet and miserable, as the work of refitting the ship went on. On 9 November, three canoes (one with a carved sternpost) came into the cove, where their crews exchanged fish and curiosities with the Europeans. The next day they were joined by Te Wahanga and his family (including his daughter Pari and his small son Koa) in 'two wretched canoes', bringing quantities of greenstone chisels and hatchets with them, very likely from the south. Cook recorded that although 'poenammoo [greenstone] is a thing of no sort of Value, nevertheless it is so much sought after by our people that there is hardly any thing that they would not give for a piece'.[5] Te Wahanga, whose family had supplied the *Resolution* with fish during their previous visit, had evidently calculated that the Europeans would give much more for greenstone than for fish, and that they would probably return to the Sound. He was an expert and enterprising trader who had found ways of acquiring quantities of greenstone for barter, although it had taken him six days from the ship's arrival to get back to the Sound.

From this time onwards Te Wahanga's family and others camped near the ship, supplying the crew with 'curiosities' and fish. Hitihiti joined the sailors in sleeping with local women, although like Tupaia he tended to patronise Maori, commenting adversely on their customs. Tupaia had been a high priest who had travelled widely in Polynesia and was an accomplished linguist and philosopher, who had made a great impression on the Maori people that he met in 1770. Hitihiti, on the other hand, although entertaining (he became an arioi, or travelling performer, after his return to Tahiti), was relatively ordinary and much less admired. All the same, he could communicate better with the local people than could any of the Europeans. He accompanied Cook on his planting expeditions and gave the local people yams from Raiatea, telling them to plant them; but yams were out of their climatic range in Totara-nui, and all of Hitihiti's urgings were in vain.

During this time a 'soft and feminine' young woman called 'Togheeree' (Tokiri?) among the local people formed an attachment with one of the *Resolution*'s crew. According to George Forster:

> She was regularly given in marriage by her parents to one of our shipmates, who was particularly beloved by this nation, for devoting much of his time to them, and treating them with those marks of affection which, even among a savage race, endear mankind to each other. Togheeree . . . proved as faithful to her husband as if he had been a New Zeelander, and constantly rejected the addresses of other seamen, professing herself a married woman (tirra-tane).[6]

The name of Tokiri's 'husband' was not recorded, but it may have been the Pacific veteran Gibson, the corporal of marines, who had learned some Maori during the *Endeavour*'s visit and had a reputation among his shipmates for his rapport with Polynesians. George did not approve of this liaison, however, commenting sarcastically upon Tokiri's standards of cleanliness and her fondness (shared by her compatriots) for eating rotten biscuits discarded from the ship.

By now Cook was seriously concerned about the *Adventure*'s continuing absence from the Sound. He hoped that she had ridden out the storm in some nearby harbour and would join the *Resolution* when the weather improved, but after more than a week's separation this began to seem unlikely. On 15 November, he and the Forsters climbed a high hill in East Bay, where a cairn had been built during the *Endeavour*'s visit, to look out for the *Adventure*. It was misty and there was no sign of the ship, and the cairn had been demolished, probably by local people looking to see whether anything was buried beneath. When they came back down to the boat they visited three settlements nearby, where the people exchanged fish, hoop nets, weapons, cloaks and utensils for iron tools and bark cloth, but no-one had seen or heard anything of the *Adventure*.

Over the next few days Sparrman and the Forsters continued collecting birds and plants, exploring the Sound in many directions. They had already discovered a footpath carved into the hillside behind Indian Cove, paved with slate or shingle in the steepest parts and made for collecting fernroot; and colonies of petrels in the hills on Long Island, nesting in 'some holes under ground like Rabbits, & there they all together make a great noise, like to the croaking of Frogs at a Distance, & sometimes to the cackling of Hens'.[7] They tried fishing with a local hoop net with some success and helped Wales with his astronomical observations, and when the weather was wet they stayed on board, describing their new collections.

On 21 November, a group of women came out to the ship. They were frightened and distressed, saying that their menfolk had gone off to fight their enemies to the west. There had been reports of enemies in that direction (possibly Ngaati Kuia of Pelorus) when Cook visited Totara-nui in the *Endeavour* in 1770, and the first direct evidence of cannibalism that Europeans had seen (chewed human bones in food baskets) had come from a canoe-load of those enemies who had been killed and eaten by people in 'Canibals Cove'.[8]

The next morning seven or eight canoes arrived in a triumphant flotilla back into the Sound. Their crews were dressed finely, their hair tied up and their faces painted with red ochre, and their canoes were loaded with cloaks, weapons and ornaments, spoils of a plundering expedition. Some of these canoes went off to Indian Cove, while others came out to the ship where their crews bartered curiosities for bark cloth and red baize. The Europeans were doing very well in the trade until one old man who had spent a good deal of time on board (probably Te Wahanga) 'came and assisted his countrymen with his advice and in a moment turned the exchanges above a thousand per cent in their favour'.[9] George Forster speculated that these people (who seem to have been Totara-nui locals, possibly

Ngaati Kurii from Tory Channel) had gone raiding especially to get goods to exchange with the Europeans:

> I am much afraid that their unhappy differences with other tribes, were revived on our account. Our people not satisfied with purchasing all the hatchets of stone, patoo-patoos; battle-axes, clothes, green jaddes, fish-hooks, &c. of which the natives of our acquaintance were possessed, continually enquired for more, and shewed them such large and valuable pieces of Taheitee cloath, as would not fail to excite their desires.
>
> It is not improbable that as soon as this appetite prevailed among the New Zeelanders, they would reflect that the shortest way to gratify it would be to rob their neighbours of such goods, as the Europeans coveted. The great store of arms, ornaments and clothes they produced at this time seemed to prove that such a daring and villainous design had really been put into execution; nor was it to be supposed that this could have been accomplished without bloodshed.[10]

By now Cook was ready to leave the Sound. That afternoon he left four hogs (three sows and a boar), two hens and three cocks in the bush at the end of West Bay, with food for a week or more. When he returned on board, he heard that some of his men had found chewed thigh bones at one of the hamlets on shore. He ordered the tents to be struck and everything brought on board, and a sailor who had taken hatchets and other items from 'a private hut' was punished with a flogging. That night Cook wrote in his journal:

> It has ever been a maxim with me to punish the least crimes any of my people have commited against these uncivilized Nations, their robing us with impunity is by no means a sufficient reason why we should treat them in the same manner . . . The best method in my opinion to preserve a good understanding with such people is first to shew them the use of fire arms and to convince them of the Superiority they give you over them and to be always upon your guard; when once they are sencible of these things, a regard for their own safety will deter them from disturbing you or being unanimous in forming any plan to attack you, and Strict honisty and gentle treatment on your part will make it their intrest not to do it.[11]

The next morning, during a last-minute visit to the watering place to identify large baked pieces of an edible root (it proved to be the mamaku, or tree fern) that had been brought on board the *Resolution*, Johann Forster witnessed a family quarrel on shore. According to Forster, 'the natives give their Children a very bad Education; a child desired his Mother to give him a piece of broiled Pinguin & as she did not immediately comply & refused to do it, it threw a large stone at her, whereupon she beat the Child, but her Husband beat the woman unmercifully for it'.[12] Hitting children was disapproved of because it was thought to harm their wairua, or spirit,[13] but hitting wives was also likely to invite reprisal (unless this was not a principal wife but one taken in war, whose relatives were no longer able to protect her).

Forster returned to the ship, and that afternoon he, Cook and Wales went with Hitihiti to Motuaro to make a final check on the gardens they had planted. At the same time Pickersgill and some of the other officers went across to Indian Cove, where they found several women sitting together weeping and cutting their foreheads with sharp stones (haehae – a sign of grief). Nearby a group of warriors was cutting up the body of a young man whom they had killed during the plundering raid to the west. His heart was stuck on a forked stick and fixed to the prow of their largest war canoe, while his head (with its jawbone removed and placed inside the canoe), intestines, liver and lungs were lying on the ground. The warriors explained that they had killed several of their enemies in the raid, but some of their companions had been killed and they had only been able to bring one enemy body away. One of them skewered the discarded lungs with his spear and 'with great gayety' (no doubt teasing the Europeans) brought them up to Pickersgill's mouth, offering him a taste. Pickersgill refused but bartered two nails for the head, which he carried back on board the *Resolution* to show to his shipmates. The victim was a young man about fifteen years old, who had been killed by a blow to the temple.

Back on board the *Resolution*, the head was put on the ship's taffrail. Clerke cut a piece of flesh from its cheek and took it to the galley, where he grilled the 'steak' on a grid-iron, then offered it to one of the men on the quarterdeck (who had not been on the raid and was from another part of the Sound). This man ate it with evident pleasure, 'suck[ing] his fingers half a dozen times over in raptures'.[14]

When Cook, Hitihiti, Wales and Forster arrived back on board, Clerke repeated the demonstration for his captain, the 'experimental gentlemen' and all of the crew. Some of the sailors laughed, saying that the warriors had 'been on a hunting party & got a buck', while others exclaimed in disgust or vomited. Hitihiti stood transfixed, 'as if Metamorphosed into the Statue of Horror', then burst into tears, telling both Clerke and the warriors that 'they were Vile men and he was no longer their friend',[15] while the local people laughed at him.

Charles Clerke was the English officer whose straight-faced account of 'giants' at Patagonia had been published in the Royal Society's *Philosophical Transactions* in 1767, to the great joy of his shipmates. This latest demonstration also sent up the idea of 'witnessing' and scientific 'truth'. Clerke's impromptu barbecue mocked both experiments and cannibals, while in their finger-licking responses, Maori were mocking both Hitihiti and the Europeans. For most of his witnesses, though, cannibalism was a cause for horror, and only some of the sailors and the Maori on board laughed. Their reflections on this episode say much about the attitudes of particular European observers towards 'savages', and their philosophical bent. Cook, for instance, commented:

> That the New Zealanders are Canibals can now no longer be doubted, the account I gave of it in my former Voyage was partly founded on circumstances and was, as I afterwards found, discredited by many people . . . The New Zealanders are certainly in a state of civilization, their behaviour to us has been Manly and Mild, shewing allways a readiness to oblige us; they have some arts a mong them which they execute with great judgement and unweared patience; they are far less

Anders Sparrman.

addicted to thieving than the other Islanders and are I believe strictly honist among them-selves. This custom of eating their enimies slain in battle (for I firmly beleive they eat the flesh of no others) has undoubtedly been handed down to them from the earliest times and we know that it is not an easy matter to break a nation of its ancient customs . . . As they become more united they will of concequence have fewer Enemies and become more civilized and then and not till then this custom may be forgot . . .[16]

George Forster, the young European philosopher who was later to become a passionate supporter of the French Revolution, compared Maori cannibalism with contemporary practices in Europe, and asked why civilised cruelty should seem virtuous for being detached:

Though we are too much polished to be canibals, we do not find it unnaturally and savagely cruel to take the field, and to cut one another's throats by thousands, without a single motive, besides the ambition of a prince, or the caprice of his mistress! Is it not from prejudice that we are disgusted with the idea of eating a dead man, when we feel no remorse in depriving him of life? . . . A New Zeelander, who kills and eats his enemy, is a very different being from a European, who, for his amusement, tears an infant from the mother's breast, in cool blood, and throws it on the earth to feed his hounds.[17]

Anders Sparrman, the Swedish naturalist, cited examples of European cannibalism to make a similar point:

During a famine throughout Germany in 1772, a man was imprisoned on Baron Boyneburg's estate in Hess, a herdsman, whose hunger first compelled him to eat a young boy, after which he continued man-eating for many months. That famine, during the Thirty Year's War, gave rise here and there to man-eating, is recorded in history, and shows that the fury of war, in Europe as well as the siege of Jerusalem, may well give rise to cannibalism.

The Catholic persecutions, particularly those which took place under Ludwig XIII, caused cannibalism even in Paris itself, in so far that when Laines and the Marquis Vitri, with the monkish disciples and the rest of the Catholic populace, murdered the Marshal Ancre, some of the murderers devoured his heart. In Castes one barbarian ate the livers of five Protestants who were murdered during the persecutions instigated by the Jesuit families. An Italian, Antonia, and Catharine de Medici, behaved in their time far more barbarously than most of the cannibals in New Zealand . . .[18]

And William Wales, the empirically minded British astronomer, wrote it up as though he had been witnessing a Royal Society experiment (as perhaps he had, at least in parody):

From this Transaction the following Corollaries are evidently deducible, viz.

1st) They do not, as I supposed might be the Case, eat them only on the spot whilst under the Impulse of that wild Frenzy into which they have shewn us they can & do work themselves in their Engagements; but in cool Blood: For it was now many Days since the Battle could have happened.

2d) That it is not their Enemies only whom they may chance to kill in War; but even any whom they meet with who are not known Friends: since those who eat the part of the head on board, could not know whether it belonged to a friend or Enemy. [Here he underestimated the efficiency of local communications.]

3d) It cannot be through want of Annimal food; because they every day caught as much Fish as served both themselves and us: they have moreover plenty of fine Dogs which they were at the same time selling us for mere trifles; nor is there any want of various sorts of fowl, which they can readily kill if they please.

4th) It seems therefore to follow of course, that their practice of this horrid Action is from Choice, and the liking which they have for this kind of Food; and this was but too visibly shewn in their eagerness for, and the satisfaction which they testified in eating, those inconsiderable scrapts, of the worst part on board the Ship.[19]

It is true that European warfare in this period was extremely destructive, and that cannibalism sometimes occurred in Europe during outbreaks of popular fury.[20] The use of muskets and artillery in battle caused very high casualty rates (for instance, during the Battle of Leuthen during the Seven Years' War, the Austrian army alone suffered thirty-eight thousand casualties[21]), and sailors were used to the impact of both cannons and hand-to-hand combat. The physical results of battle were bloody and unmediated,[22] which probably helps to explain Cook's phlegmatic response to all forms of violence (both Polynesian and European). Cannibalism, however, was much feared by sailors as a fate that sometimes happened in times of fire or shipwreck, when boats were cast adrift without provisions and shipmates were forced to cast lots to see who should be killed and eaten so that the others might survive. This helps to explain why, in response to Clerke's burlesque barbecue, some of the sailors vomited in visceral disgust.[23]

From a local viewpoint, on the other hand, when the warriors cut off the head of their victim, stuck his heart on a forked stick and fixed it to the prow of their canoe, they were completing a victory. In war, the mana of both gods and their descendants was at stake. After winning a battle, the victorious warriors fed the hau (life force) of the victims to their ancestor gods in the whaangai hau (literally 'feeding hau') ceremony, offering up those body parts where hau was concentrated (especially the heart, liver and head), or ritually eating them. This at once avenged the insult that had sparked off the conflict, and nullified the power of the enemy atua, who might otherwise engage in spiritual reprisals. Thus when Clerke cut flesh from the cheek of the hapless dead warrior on the deck of the *Resolution* and grilled it on a grid-iron, he was joining the power of his ancestors to that of the victorious group. This complicity would not soon have been forgotten by the dead man's friends and relations.

Very early the next morning, a boat was sent on shore to bury a message in a bottle beneath a tree marked for Furneaux, in case the *Adventure* should follow them into the Sound. The *Resolution* was unmoored to put to sea, but the winds were so contrary that she could not leave the cove. Wales and some of the ship's officers took this opportunity to go to Indian Cove, where they saw the entrails of the dead man still on the ground and his heart still stuck on the forked stick tied to the prow of the largest canoe. Some of their friends came on board to say goodbye to them, a few last curiosities were bought, greens were loaded on board, and on 24 November the *Resolution* weighed anchor and sailed out of the Sound. As they passed Palliser Bay on their way out of Cook Strait, Johann Forster reflected that it would make a fine place for a European settlement. It had a large river that seemed navigable and flat land for cultivation, and if the 'natives could be but taught to manufacture Canvas & Rope with their Flax for the East Indies', a two-way trade between New Zealand and the East Indies might be set up to exchange local products for European woollen and iron goods.[24] George Forster, however, added a prophetic note of caution:

> Perhaps in future ages, when the maritime powers of Europe lose their American colonies, they may think of making new establishments in more distant regions; and if it were ever possible for Europeans to have humanity enough to acknowledge the indigenous tribes of the South Seas as their brethren, we might have settlements which would not be defiled with the blood of innocent nations.[25]

Interlude

THE *ADVENTURE* OFF CAPE PALLISER AND IN UAWA
30 October – 29 November 1773

In late October, while the two ships were sailing down the east coast of the North Island, the *Adventure* had lost sight of the *Resolution* off Cape Palliser, in gales and high seas. At first Mai, the young man who had joined the ship at Huahine, was frightened, but as the *Adventure* rolled with the waves 'he cryed out with rapture that . . . it was a good ship & the sea could not sink her'. They approached Cape Palliser again on 4 November, where several canoes came out and exchanged fish and about two hundred crayfish for bark cloth and nails. Two of these canoes were finely carved and their crews seemed affluent. According to William Bayly, 'the principal man in each Canoe was very fine-looking old men with their beards very gray, these sat in the starn of the Canoes & just before each was a robust middle aged man, these stood up & made long speeches frequently pointing to the shore, but whether they proposed friendship or war we could not tell'.[26] This combination of a ranking elder and a younger 'talking chief' had been seen before by the *Resolution* observers when Te Ratu's people from Te Raawhiti came into Totara-nui, so possibly it was customary on the northern side of the strait. Mai tried to act as an interpreter on this occasion, but could understand nothing that these people said. The wind blew up again, and once again the ship was forced to tack away from Cape Palliser (which the sailors now named 'Cape Turn and be damnd'). The rigging and sails had been damaged, conditions on board were miserable and they began to run out of water. After two more days of stormy weather Furneaux turned the ship north and ran for Uawa (Tolaga Bay), where the *Endeavour* had spent a week in 1769.

The *Adventure* stayed in Uawa over 9–10 November while the crew carried out hasty repairs and collected wood and water. As in 1769, the inhabitants were friendly, supplying them with crayfish in exchange for nails and red cloth. They were more numerous and settled than the people at Totara-nui. Once again, local memories of Tupaia were vivid. When they heard that he was dead, the local people sang a lament in his memory, which Burney, the ship's second lieutenant, carefully transcribed: 'Aghee matte awhay Tupaya!' (Aki? mate aue Tupaia – Departed, dead, alas Tupaia!)[27]

A-ghee mat-te a-whay Tu-pa-ya!

Mai may have basked in some of Tupaia's posthumous glory, but unlike Tupaia (and like Hitihiti) he was just a commoner. He gained no place in local tribal memory, although Uawa people continued to talk about Tupaia for generations.

Burney described the people as 'Cleanly and Sociable', and remarked how fond the local girls were of one another. The watering place was behind a high rock with a paa on top of it, and many 'very good' gardens of kuumara and other root crops near the houses were scattered around the bay. Furneaux was anxious to rejoin the *Resolution*, and on 11 November the *Adventure* sailed south to Pari-nui-te-raa (Gable End Foreland), where they exchanged shellfish, kuumara and greens with local people for nails and beads. Again a contrary gale blew up, however, and Furneaux was forced to turn back to Uawa.

Over the next few days the officers explored the bay. Bayly went ashore one day for a ramble and described the crops in the scattered gardens as 'pompion plants' (taro), grown in holes like cucumbers in England, and 'long, small' sweet potatoes. The ground had been cleared by firing the bush, cutting it about knee-high, then tilling the soil with sticks. The plants were about two inches above ground and had probably been planted a month or so before, in August or September. He also noticed many birds – quails, wood pigeons, parrakeets, grey parrots and tuuii (poey birds), but no fruit trees or quadrupeds. Fishing was good in the bay, and the people freely supplied the Europeans with crayfish and other fish for nails and beads. They placed a very high value on iron and would exchange almost anything for it (including kuumara, fine cloaks and flax), except greenstone adzes and tiki.

During one of their excursions some officers found a canoe that held the head of a woman lying in state, decorated with feathers and ornaments. At first they thought that this woman was alive, but on closer inspection they realised that this was 'the Relict of some deceased relation'. Heads were a focus of ancestral power, and preserved heads were kept as a means of communication with dead kinsfolk, or mocked and degraded if they were those of enemies.

In yet another incident (which may have been linked if anyone had seen them handling the head, and thus breaching tapu), the local people purloined a gallon keg of brandy that had been sent ashore for the wooding and watering party. Jack Rowe, the master's mate, wanted to seize some hostages until the brandy was brought back, but Burney refused to allow this. As he remarked unsympathetically in his log: 'this I thought dangerous as the Zealanders were too numerous – and all our Empty casks ashore – if Sailors won't take care of their Grogg, they deserve to lose it'.[28]

By 16 November, the sails and rigging had been repaired and sufficient wood and water had been brought on board. The *Adventure* weighed anchor and left Uawa, followed by numerous canoes, heading south towards Raukawa-moana. They had a quick passage down the east coast, but off Cape Palliser they were forced to tack until 30 November, when at last the *Adventure* caught a favourable wind and sailed back into Totara-nui.

THE *ADVENTURE*'S SECOND VISIT TO TOTARA-NUI
30 November– 22 December 1773

Furneaux was bitterly disappointed not to find the *Resolution* at anchor in Meretoto (Ship Cove). As soon as the *Adventure* was moored, he sent his men ashore, and they soon came back with a note they had found in the garden at the watering place, buried in a bottle under a stump carved with the message 'LOOK UNDER-NEATH'. Cook's note was dated 24 November, the day that the *Resolution* had left the Sound. It was curt and scrawled in haste:

> As Captain Cook has not the least hopes of meeting with Captain Furneaux he will not take upon him to name any place for a Rendezvous, he however thinks of retiring to Easter Island . . . about the latter end of next March – it is even probable that he may go to Otaheite or one of the Society Isles but this will depend so much on Circumstances, that nothing with any degree of certainty can be depended upon – James Cook

When the message was unearthed, Mai was present. He was so struck by this method of communication that he immediately made up his mind to learn to write. According to Burney, however, 'so many people gave him paper, pens etc and set him copies & tasks that in a weeks time the poor fellow's head was bothered – too many Cooks spoilt the Broth'.[29]

Furneaux decided to get back to sea as soon as possible. He sent the casks ashore for mending and set up the copper oven on the beach to rebake the ship's bread. The waterers and woodcutters pitched their tent next to Bayly's observatory, and Mai went on shore to join them. When they looked for the pigs and chickens that they had earlier released in the cove, they found that the chickens in the bush were laying eggs, but there was no sign of the pigs. The local people came to the shore camp as soon as the tents were up, and began to barter fish and curiosities for nails and other items. Burney was in charge of the camp and allowed them to stay there during the day, but told them that they could not sleep in the cove at night.

On 9 December at midnight, the sentry at the shore camp left his post to fetch some tobacco from the ship's tent. When he returned, he saw 'an Indian' sitting by the fire, who crept back into the bush as soon as he was observed. The sentry raised the alarm and woke everybody up. They searched the surrounding area but found nothing, and eventually went back to bed.

Bayly told the sentry to wake him if he saw anything else, and before long the sentry roused him again, saying that he had just seen a canoe crossing the bay. It was a bright, moonlit night, and they soon spotted two more canoes sliding across the bay to join the first canoe, now hidden under some bushes overhanging the rocky shore. Bayly sent the sentry to wake the others and went down to the beach. The canoes came round the rocks, hugging the shoreline in the darkness. Bayly called out in Maori to their crews, saying that he would kill them if they came any closer. They talked with each other for a moment, and then one canoe came slowly forward. Bayly fired a shot just over the crew's heads, as Burney and the others arrived, and the canoes paddled away at high speed. They saw no more of them that night.

On the 12th, Samuel Kemp, Jack Rowe, Mai and Burney had a 'narrow escape' in Shag Cove (which neither Kemp nor Burney explained any further in their logs), and one of the sailors, Thomas Hill, was given a dozen lashes for 'insolence'. Two days later a number of canoes came to the shore camp and seemed to be spying on the Europeans. That night Bayly stayed up late, observing the stars. He took some altitudes of stars to the east and then went to bed, setting his alarm for a later observation of the altitudes to the west. Some time later the lid of his toolbox rattled loudly, jolting him awake. Bayly had put it at the door of his tent to hold down his greatcoat, which acted as an impromptu tent flap. He jumped out of bed and grabbed his gun, calling out, 'Who is there?', but could see and hear nothing. Soon after his alarm went off, so he got up and dressed, but could not find his hat. As Bayly came out of the tent he found the toolbox with its lid off on the ground, and when he felt around in it he found that his hatchet, saw and hammer were gone. The sentry was sitting calmly by the fire, washing his linen. Bayly accused him of taking the tools, but the sentry protested his innocence, so the astronomer lit his lantern and they went along the beach together, looking for people or canoes.

They found nothing, but as they came back to the camp Bayly saw a man coming around the ship's tent, holding something in his hands. He was not sure whether this was one of his shipmates, so he shouted, 'Who are you?' The man started, dropping his load, and ran towards the bush. Bayly chased after him and was about to club him with his gun when he tripped over a rock in the dark. Recovering himself, he took a shot at the man just as he vanished among the trees. By now the camp was in an uproar, with people tumbling out of the tents to find out what was going on. The musket shot also alerted the sentry on the *Adventure*, and Furneaux sent two armed boats to the camp to investigate. Back on shore, Bayly and one of the sailors ran along the bay towards the rocks, hoping to inter-cept the intruders as they escaped along the beach:

> I had not passed far when I heard an Indian cry hist, hist, which I answered, moving forward at the same time & soon discovered an Indian at a considerable distance. I still went forward untill I had the misfortune slip of a stone which made some noise tho' attend with no damage. Then I imagined the Indian was flying for the woods on which I levelled my piece & let fly at him but missed him with a ball & the Indian fled to the woods & when I came to the place there was great quantities of things [including two muskets, a cutlass and several bags of linen] which they had stole from us, part in their canoes & part on the rocks so that we recovered everything & a Canoe. The Indians made their escape thro' the Woods & got clear off.[30]

In the morning they found traces of blood along the beach, indicating that one of the intruders had been wounded, and a canoe was taken in reprisal for the plundering raid. That night there was a large meteor in the sky, and the next morning Bayly packed up his instruments and went back on board the *Adventure*.

On 17 December, some people came to the ship to ask for the return of their canoe, which was given back to them. Furneaux then sent the large cutter off to Whareuunga Bay ('Grass Cove') with the master's mate Jack Rowe in charge, carrying the coxswain, a midshipman, the captain's black servant and six rowers, armed with muskets, fowling pieces and cutlasses, to collect wild greens for the crew and with strict instructions to be back by mid-afternoon at the latest. Bayly, three midshipmen, the cooper and the surgeon took a small boat off in another direction to gather greens and flax while the rest of the crew struck the tents and got everything on board. When Bayly and his men returned to the *Adventure* that night, however, there was no sign of the cutter.

By the next morning Furneaux was worried about the cutter, and sent off Lieutenant Burney in the launch with ten marines equipped with muskets, musketoons and two wall-guns, and a crew of rowers to find it. They hoped that Rowe might have gone into East Bay, or that the boat may have been damaged on the rocks, so the carpenter's mate went along with them, bringing his tools and several sheets of tin. They rowed around Long Island and across to East Bay, searching the shoreline with a spyglass, then stopped at a cove on the northern side of East Bay to cook their dinner. While they ate, Burney saw a man running along the opposite shore towards the head of the bay, no doubt carrying news of their arrival. After dinner they approached a large settlement (probably opposite the paa that Cook had visited at 'Hippa Rocks' in 1770),[31] where many people were gathered and six large canoes were pulled up on the beach. The people tried to wave them away, but when Burney came ashore with an armed guard of six marines, they were friendly enough and allowed him to search the houses. Three or four well-beaten paths from the beach led to more houses among the trees, but Burney decided to stay close to the boat. Burney saw one man carrying a large bundle of long spears to the shore, but as soon as he realised that he was being watched, this man put the weapons down and walked away. Since some of the local people seemed frightened, Burney gave them nails and a looking glass, searched the cove with his spyglass, had the wall-guns fired as a signal and went back to the launch. The search party carried along the east side of the bay, firing off the wall-guns in each of the coves that they entered. They came to another settlement where the people invited them ashore and offered them fish. Burney asked them about the cutter, but they 'pretended ignorance'.

Soon after they left this settlement, they saw a very large double canoe hauled up on a small beach next to Grass Cove. There were two men with a dog standing by it, but they ran off as the launch approached. Burney searched the canoe and, to his dismay, found one of the cutter's rowlock ports in it, a shoe belonging to Woodhouse (the midshipman who had accompanied Rowe the previous day), and a piece of meat, which they thought might be dog's flesh. Nearby on the beach they saw about twenty food baskets tied up. When they cut these open, they found

The Adventure*'s men find remains of their comrades at Grass Cove.*
An engraving from John Marra's account of the voyage.

them packed with roasted meat and fernroot, still warm from the fire. Burney
hoped that this might also be dog's flesh, but soon they found more shoes and a
hand tattooed 'TH'. This was unmistakeably the hand of Thomas Hill (the seaman recently flogged for insolence), who had worn this tattoo since their stay in
Tahiti. Behind the beach they saw a circle of freshly dug ground about four feet in
diameter, almost certainly a haangi, or earth oven. As the marines feverishly began
to dig there with a cutlass, Burney prepared to burn the canoe, but a great plume of
smoke billowed up from one of the nearby hills and they hurried back to the launch.

By now it was almost dusk. They rowed the launch to Grass Cove, where a
single and three double canoes were hauled up on the beach, and a crowd of
hundreds (or according to Furneaux, fifteen hundred to two thousand people)[32]
were gathered on the hillside and the shore. According to Burney, there was a
large fire on the hill behind the cove, and 'the place was throng'd like a Fair'. As
the launch approached the beach, some of these people retreated to a hillock and
began to taunt the Europeans, calling out and gesturing for them to come ashore.
Burney ordered a musketoon to be fired at one of the canoes, where he thought
some warriors might be hiding, then ordered his men to fire muskets and
musketoons at will into the crowd. At the first volley, the people seemed stunned;
at the second, they broke and ran for the trees, howling with fear and pain. Two
'very stout' men (presumably chiefs) stood their ground until everyone else had
fled, then walked towards the bush with 'great composure & deliberation – their

pride not Suffering them to run'. The Europeans shot at them and one was hit and crawled off on all fours, while the other reached the bush unscathed. The wall-guns were then loaded with pistol balls and fired, and the marines kept on shooting until nobody was left in sight.

Burney left Fannin, the ship's master, to guard the boat while he searched the beach with a party of marines. They found two bundles of wild celery gathered by the cutter's crew, one of her oars broken and stuck upright in the ground, and behind the beach 'such a shocking scene of Carnage & Barbarity as can never be mentiond or thought of, but with horror'.[33] Dogs were chewing at the discarded entrails of four or five men, and they found the eyes, hearts, lungs, livers and heads of their comrades, including the head of Furneaux's black servant, various feet and Rowe's left hand (identified by its scarred forefinger) roasting on fires or scattered on the ground. They had evidently interrupted a great whaangai hau ceremony, in which the hau of their comrades (and their ancestors) was being fed to the ancestors. Fannin called out that he could hear people shouting in the valley, perhaps preparing to attack, so they gathered up some of these body parts and hurried back to the launch. They destroyed three of the canoes on the beach, searched again for the cutter, fired one last volley at a large crowd of people gathered on a hillside up the valley, and left the cove in darkness as it began to rain and a huge fire flared up further along the Sound. As John Marra said in his retrospective account, 'our lieutenant, not thinking it safe to trust our crew in the dark, in an open boat, within reach of such cruel barbarians, ordered the canoes to be broken up and destroyed; and, after carefully collecting the remains of our mangled companions, we made the best of our way from this polluted place'.[34]

As the launch passed between Pickersgill and Blumine Islands, Burney thought that he heard someone shouting, so they rested on their oars, calling in reply and hoping that it was not some of their surviving shipmates crying out. Burney concluded in his report to Furneaux:

> The people lost in the Cutter were Mr Rowe, Mr Woodhouse, Francis Murphy Quartermaster. Wm Facey. Thos Hill. Edwd Jones, Michael Bell, Jno Cavenaugh Thos Milton & James Swilley the Captns Man . . . most of these were of our very best Seamen – the Stoutest & most healthy people in the Ship . . .
>
> I am not inclined to think this was any premeditated plan of these Savages, as the morning Mr. Rowe left the Ship he met 2 Canoes who came down & staid all the forenoon in Ship Cove. It might probably happen from Some quarrel, or the fairness of the Opportunity tempted them; our people being so very incautious & thinking themselves too Secure.[35]

Perhaps Burney was remembering Rowe's impetuous behaviour at Uawa, where he had wanted to seize some of the local people and hold them hostage for some brandy that had been taken. Rowe had spent some time in America and thought he knew all about 'Indians'. According to George Forster he was 'an unfortunate youth' whose naval education had 'induced him to look upon all the natives of the South Sea with contempt, and to assume that kind of right over them, with which the Spaniards, in more barbarous ages, disposed of the lives of the American Indians'.[36] Neither Rowe nor his men knew anything about Maori cannibalism, except by word of mouth, for they had been absent from the Sound when the mock barbecue on board the *Resolution* had taken place.

Burney and his men got back to the *Adventure* at about eleven o'clock that night, and told their shipmates (including Mai) what had happened. It is not difficult to imagine the shock and horror on board. Furneaux was already ready to leave the Sound, and now he could not wait. Although he had lost ten of his best men, he decided to carry on into the Pacific, to complete the high southern explorations. Early the next morning the *Adventure* hoisted anchor and sailed out towards the strait, but was forced back by contrary winds. The human remains rescued from Grass Cove were tied in a hammock with ballast and shot, and buried at sea, and that night 'every Body on board [slept] under Arms expecting the Canibals to be down and board us'.[37] The next day the *Adventure* left Totara-nui and headed out to sea. On 22 December, 'the cloaths and the effects of the ten men who were murdered and eaten, were sold before the mast, according to the old sea custom',[38] and the ship sailed south-east across the Pacific, still looking for the Southern Continent.

Interlude
THE *ADVENTURE*'S VOYAGE BACK TO ENGLAND, AND THE *RESOLUTION*'S PACIFIC EXPLORATIONS

As the *Adventure* headed into high Pacific latitudes, the men began to freeze and suffer from scurvy, which had plagued them throughout the voyage. Furneaux struggled on southwards until 56° South, where contrary winds forced him to change course for Cape Horn. The *Adventure* rounded the Cape and sailed on through icebergs until Furneaux turned north towards the Cape of Good Hope, and then carried on to England, where the ship anchored at Spithead on 14 July 1774. Thus Mai arrived in London, and began his adventures in English society.

Perhaps because Mai captivated King George and his court, reaction to the loss of Furneaux's men at Grass Cove was muted. Banks noted in a letter to his mother, 'ten of the Adventure's people have been rosted & Eaten by our freinds in New Zeland',[39] while Fanny Burney (James's sister) wrote: 'I am heartily glad they *are* returned, & I hope that a Country so savage as New Zealand will never more be visited by my Brother.'[40] In the newspapers, though, the *Adventure*'s surgeon Thomas Andrews praised the fertility of the Bay of Plenty and recommended it as a site suitable for British settlers.[41]

Back in November 1773, while the *Adventure* was sailing from Uawa towards Cook Strait, Cook had taken the *Resolution* out of the Sound on a great sweep across the Pacific. After leaving the Sound, he sailed south-east to the edge of the Antarctic ice-fields, looking for land. As sleet and snow froze the rigging and hung the ship with icicles, and waves drenched the ship, Johann Forster penned another of his eloquent passages on the miseries of exploration:

> The Sea is now tempestuous, the Decks are never dry, all the Ship moist & damp; my Cabin cold & open to the piercing winds, full of unwholesome effluvia & vapours, every thing I touch is moist & mouldy & looks more like a subterraneous mansion for the dead than a habitation for the living. In the Captain's Cabin there are broken panes, the apartment full of currents & smoke, a parcel of damp Sails spread, & a couple of Sailmakers at work, now & then discharging the mephitic Air from the pease & Sower-krout they have eaten; if to this we add that there the pitching of the Ship is more felt, than any where else it will clearly appear, that these Expeditions are the most difficult task that could be imposed upon poor mortals.[42]

Hitihiti was astonished by the 'white stones' and 'white rain' (hail and snow) encountered in these latitudes. The 'white land' (or field ice) where the sun scarcely set was even more amazing, and he included this in his tally of new countries, adding one named stick to a bundle for each new land he had visited since leaving the Society Islands. On Christmas Day, the *Resolution* turned to the north and the dangers of sailing in the ice were doubled as the crew became thoroughly drunk. There were volleys of curses as the sailors tried to work the ship, while George Forster described the ice islands that surrounded them as 'the wrecks of a shattered world'.

No continent appeared in the empty ocean, and ten days later Cook turned back south, sailing his ship down to 71° South, an unprecedented achievement. That day (31 January) he wrote in his journal:

> I will not say it was impossible anywhere to get in among this Ice, but I will assert that the bare attempting of it would be a very dangerous enterprise and what I believe no man in my situation would have thought of. I whose ambition leads me not only farther than any other man has been before me, but as far as I think it possible for man to go, was not sorry at meeting this interruption, as it in some measure relieved us from the dangers and hardships, inseperable with the Navigation of the Southern Polar Regions.[43]

It had finally become apparent that there was no Terra Australis in the South Pacific. If there *was* land, it was underneath the ice, and inhabited by penguins, not princes. Having disposed of this section of the chimerical continent, Cook turned back to the tropics in relief.

As the *Resolution* sailed towards Easter Island, Cook became ill. He was seized with terrible pains, and vomited and retched, until the men feared for his life. Johann Forster sacrificed a favourite dog, which was cooked and fed to the captain, aiding his recovery. The ship carried on to the Marquesas and the Society Islands, where the 'savages' pilfered incessantly from the Europeans and began to seem less noble. Hitihiti told his friends about Maori cannibalism, showing them

Opposite: *The* Resolution *in a stream of pack ice, sketched by William Hodges.*

the head that Pickersgill had acquired in Totara-nui, and took leave of his ship-mates in tears; and the arioi performed a skit about a Tahitian girl running away with an English sailor. The *Resolution* visited Niue, Nomuka in Tonga, the New Hebrides and New Caledonia, finally turning eastward to New Zealand, finding Norfolk Island on the way. The *Resolution* had been knocked about by Antarctic ice and tropical gales, and needed major repairs. On 17 October 1774, they sighted Taranaki (Mount Egmont), and two days later the ship, with its crew of seasoned Pacific travellers, sailed back into Totara-nui. As they returned to the Sound, Sparrman commented with resignation, 'we thought we had abandoned forever this nest of cannibals, but fate and the Captain had decided otherwise'.[44]

Five

TOTARA-NUI
III

THE *RESOLUTION*'S THIRD VISIT TO TOTARA-NUI
18 October – 10 November 1774

As soon as the *Resolution* anchored in Meretoto, Cook sent some men on shore to check on the message he had left behind for the *Adventure*. A flock of shags had nested in the cove, which suggested to George Forster that no people (Maori or European) had been there over the winter. The sailors killed the young shags for supper, and then landed, finding that the marker tree had been cut down and the bottle and message were gone.

At first they thought that some of the local people had done this, then one of the crew pointed out that various trees had been felled with saws and axes since their last departure, and that leeks and onions (which the local people did not like) had been taken from the garden. Cook concluded that the *Adventure* must have followed them into the cove, although he was puzzled that Furneaux had left no message for him. The *Resolution*'s sails were unbent and the topmasts unrigged for repairs, the forge was set up on board, tents were pitched by the watering place, greens were gathered and more birds shot, and the laborious work of refitting the ship began once again.

That afternoon Cook went with the Forsters to 'Canibals Cove' to collect specimens and greens. A cannon was fired from the ship that evening to bring local people to the cove with fish and other goods for barter, but nobody came out to the ship. The next few days were cold, stormy and miserable, so the sailors stayed on board. On the 22nd, however, the weather cleared and Cook went exploring with the Forsters along the coastline towards Point Jackson, landing at various coves on the way. They crossed to Motuara to check on the gardens, which they found overgrown with weeds, and lit a fire to let the local people know that they had arrived back in the Sound. Again, nobody came out to the *Resolution*.

The Europeans were puzzled but not dismayed. That night they feasted on birds, fish and fresh greens. The hunting and fishing had been good, and 'contributed to make a kind of general festival in the ship, which the levity of the mariners rendered the more chearful, as every past discomfort was already forgotten'.[1] At daybreak on the 24th, two canoes came sailing past the point of Shag Cove, but as soon as they saw the *Resolution*, the crews struck their sails and paddled off at high speed. Cook and the Forsters now decided it was high time to make contact with the local people, and set out after breakfast to find them.

As they came into Shag Cove, shooting shags and other sea birds from the boat, they heard shouting on the southern shore. Cook ordered the boat to be rowed in that direction, and as they approached the beach he saw several canoes hauled up and houses concealed in the bush. Three or four people dressed in old, shaggy cloaks waited for them on a knoll, while others scrambled away into the hills. As Cook landed, these people seemed very apprehensive (not surprisingly, given the Grass Cove killings – which Cook knew nothing about, however). When he beckoned them over and pressed noses with them, 'Joy took place of fear, they hurried out of the woods, embraced us over and over and skiped about like Mad men'.[2] The air of relief was palpable. Cook and his companions recognised several of these people and asked for news of some of their old friends, but the responses they received were barely intelligible. All that Johann Forster could gather was that there had been a battle and several of their friends had been knocked on the head, while others had gone to Te Raawhiti. The leader of these people, a middle-aged man called 'Peeterre' (nicknamed 'Pedro' by the sailors), seemed delighted when Cook presented him with hatchets, knives, some bark cloth, a piece of red baize and medals. He gave them a large quantity of fish in return, and promised to bring more to the ship the next day.

Early the next morning Pedro and his people came alongside in five canoes, with greenstone 'curiosities' and quantities of fish to exchange for iron tools, English cloth, bark cloth and mouldy biscuits. Over the next few days they camped on a nearby beach and kept the ship and the shore camp supplied with fish, while the sailors collected wood and water, the scientists described new plants, birds and fish, and the work of caulking the ship, carrying out repairs, and the wooding and watering went on. On 26 October, Johann climbed the hill on Motuara to check the post that Cook had set up there during the *Endeavour* visit, but found no marks left by the *Adventure*. Before he left the summit he carved 'Resolution. 1774. Octob' on the post, then climbed down into the valley on the other side of the island.

By 27 October, Pedro's people had become friendly with the sailors, especially several of the marines at the shore camp (no doubt including Gibson), who by now could speak some Maori. According to Johann Forster, these marines were the source of the following story, which soon began to do the rounds of the ship:

> The Natives told, that a Ship arrived on the Coast of the Northern Isle in a great Storm, & was there broke to pieces. The Men in her were safed on shore, & had an Engagement with the Natives, wherein they killed many Natives, but not being able to keep up a Fire, the Natives came up & killed & devoured them all. This our people interpret to have been the fate of the *Adventure*, but the Natives are by no

means constant in their Story, so that there is little to be depended upon this Tale.[3]

When Cook heard this story he tried to check it out with local people, but they flatly denied it and 'seem'd wholy ignorant of the matter'. The rumours continued to circulate, however, and various versions were given by different Maori to different members of the crew. Some said that this affray had happened across the strait near Te Raawhiti, while others pointed to East Bay; and one man said it was two months (in fact eleven months) earlier, while another counted twenty or thirty days off on his fingers. According to Bowles, one of the sailors, 'neither head or tail is to be understood [of this story] & they all contradicting one & the other – occasioned it to be treated fabulous or [about] some of their own Canoes'.[4]

With the rumours largely shrugged off, the exchanges of fish and curiosities continued unabated. According to Charles Clerke, 'the Utmost sociallity subsists between us and the Natives here – numbers of Visits are paid and repaid upon various occasions'.[5] Pedro's people liked large metal fish-hooks, and brought quantities of fish to the *Resolution*. Cook, the Forsters and Sparrman carried on exploring the Sound, shooting birds and looking for new species. During one of these expeditions they went to the end of West Bay, where they found a few families living, and two new species of plants. On 30 October, however, Pedro and his people left the ship and did not come back for days. This departure was probably not due to Cook's questions, but rather to the arrival of another kin group, come to take over the trade with the Europeans.

During the next few days Cook asked his men to look out for the pigs and chickens that had been released in the bush when they last visited the Sound. One of the officers found a fresh hen's egg near the shore camp, and on 31 October, Johann Forster went with some others to Long Island (which he called Tonga-Onga – Te Ongaonga?), where they saw a black boar on the beach. Cook was pleased when he heard this, because he was beginning to think that all of his efforts to establish livestock on shore had failed. Most of the animals that he had brought to New Zealand had either sickened and died, or been killed and eaten by local people.

On 1 November, soon after Pedro's departure, a party of strangers arrived at the ship. They brought large pieces of greenstone, cloaks, bone clubs, and women for sex, and Johann Forster collected new words for his vocabulary. These people controlled the trade for several days but brought no fish on board. The crew had become obsessed with bartering for sex and 'curiosities', and Cook tried to control this by forbidding further barter except for fish, but neither the crew nor their visitors would co-operate. On 3 November, John Marra, the gunner's mate, got drunk and hid in a canoe to go ashore to one of these women, but was caught and punished with twelve lashes. The next day their new visitors abandoned the area, except for one impoverished family who stayed on in Indian Cove, living off fernroot and welcoming sailors to their huts for sexual exchanges.

During this time Cook and the Forsters continued to explore the Sound.

They went on a shooting expedition at Grass Cove, where they killed numerous birds and collected some new plants, but saw no people. Several days later they went to Long Island to drop off a breeding sow, but the 'boar' seen there proved to be female, so they brought their sow back to the *Resolution*. On 5 November, they went up the Sound in the pinnace to discover whether there was any southern outlet to the sea. Several canoes were out fishing, which paddled off as soon as the pinnace appeared. Cook's party chased and overtook them, and found to their surprise that these were Pedro's people. They bartered with them for fish and asked them to come back to visit the ship, then carried on up the Sound. At the mouth of a long inlet that seemed to turn west and then south (Picton Harbour?), they met four or five men in another canoe and asked them if this inlet led to the sea. These people said that it did not, but they would find what they were looking for towards the north-east. Cook had the pinnace turned round, and rowed back to the mouth of the inlet they had indicated (Tory Channel), where the shores were crowded with people who had gathered from both sides of the Sound. These were probably members of the Ngaati Kurii hapuu of Ngaai Tahu, who occupied Tory Channel about this time.[6]

Cook and the Forsters landed on the beach, where they were greeted by the local chief 'Tringo-Boohee' (Te Ringapuhi?) and his son near their large village at 'Koheghe-nooee' (Ko Whekenui). George Forster described Te Ringapuhi as 'a little elderly man, but very active, lively and friendly; his face was punctured all over in scrolls, by which he distinguished himself from every one of his countrymen present, who were much less disfigured by this operation'.[7] Te Ringapuhi seemed very uneasy as his men crowded around the Europeans, exchanging weapons, cloaks and fish for trade goods. Cook commented later that he tried to hold them back and even threw stones at some of them, but they took little notice of his admonitions. These people were clean, well dressed and numerous. Just a quarter of an hour after the Europeans had landed, there were almost two hundred people on the beach, some of whom they had met earlier. Cook was received with great courtesy, but decided to carry on with his explorations. Te Ringapuhi told him that this channel led to the sea, so after a short stay with these people they returned to the pinnace. As they were about to leave, one of the sailors showed Cook a bundle of fish that he had not yet paid for. He pointed out the man who had given it to him, and Cook called out to this man, throwing him a nail that fell at his feet:

> The savage being offended, or thinking himself attacked, picked up a stone, and threw it into the boat with great force, but luckily without hitting any one of us. We now called to him again, and pointed to the nail which we had thrown toward him. As soon as he had seen, and picked it up, he laughed at his own petulance, and seemed highly pleased with our conduct.[8]

Cook's party carried on up the channel in the pinnace, where they found 'many coves and beaches, with greens, and plenty of wild fowl; the water was perfectly smooth, and the mountains formed many romantic prospects, being clothed with fine forests'.⁹ Finally they saw the sea, with the North Island off in the distance. Double-crested shags wheeled over a paa on a rock rising from flat land in a bay (Hiitaua Bay) near the northern heads, with waves crashing out on the rocks.

Although the weather the next day was dull, Pedro and his family returned to the *Resolution*. Cook took him off to the cabin and dressed him in a shirt, stockings, breeches and coat to reward him for supplying them with fish. Pedro accompanied him on a shooting expedition to Long Island, and then ate dinner on board the ship, drinking a good deal of wine. According to George Forster:

> Peeterre partook with peculiar good manners, considering his education. It is scarce to be doubted, that he felt the superiority of our knowledge, of our arts, manufactures, and mode of living, in some degree, especially as he was always in remarkably good spirits when amongst us; but notwithstanding all this, he never once expressed a desire of going with us; and when we proposed it to him, he declined it, preferring the wretched precarious life of his countrymen, to all the advantages of which he saw us possessed.¹⁰

For all the 'wretched precariousness' of their lives, Forster noted that Pedro and his people were always singing, both on the ship and on the shore. After dinner Cook and the Forsters took the opportunity to ask Pedro and another man if any harm had come to the *Adventure*. Like all the others whom Cook had questioned, they flatly denied it, saying, 'Cauery' (Kaore – No!). Cook showed them a large drawing of Totara-nui, taking two pieces of paper to represent the two ships and sliding these over the chart to show the ships' movements, and asked Pedro to indicate what had happened to the *Adventure*. He took the piece of paper and deliberately slid it out of the Sound, to Cook's relief, counting on his fingers the months since the ship had left. In this way Pedro informed Cook that the *Adventure* had been in the Sound about ten months earlier and had gone out to sea again, and was not shipwrecked as some of the Europeans had been told. Clearly, an agreement had been reached amongst the local people that Cook was not to be told about the Grass Cove killings. When one man had mentioned the *Adventure* in front of the Europeans several days earlier, his ears had been roundly boxed by one of his companions.¹¹

Despite the rumours, some of the crew still found Totara-nui and its people alluring. The following day another of the sailors, John Keplin (or Coghlan), was punished with a dozen lashes for leaving the boat and 'declareing he would go with the Indians'.¹² Over the next few days the weather was wet, but the sailors kept on working and finished caulking the ship.

In preparation for the ship's departure, a boar and a sow were put on shore in Waikawa Bay, birds were shot and fish were salted down, and the Forsters completed their collections. During this trip to the Sound they had found ten or twelve new species of plants, and four or five new species of birds. Pedro came on board to say goodbye and presented Cook with a large quantity of fish, receiving in return an empty oil jar, 'which made him as happy as a prince', for glass seemed like pounamu (greenstone), a prized possession.

On 9 November, while the ship was unmoored and rode at a single anchor, Cook and some others spent the afternoon in a cove where two families had camped. Some of these people were sleeping, and others were weaving mats or preparing food. Cook saw one little girl heating some stones over a fire and taking them to an old woman in a hut, who piled them together, put some green 'celery' and a mat over them and squatted over the steaming heap, evidently to treat some ailment. They returned to the ship for supper, and early the next morning they sailed out of the Sound. As the *Resolution* left Totara-nui, Johann Forster quoted Virgil's *Aeneid* in his journal:

> *Idem omnes simul ardor habet, rapiuntque, ruuntque:*
> *Littora deseruere: Latet sub nave aequon.*
> The same frenzy gripped them all at once. They seized the tackle and hurried off.
> They left the shore; the sea lay beneath the ship.[13]

Interlude

THE *RESOLUTION*'S RETURN TO ENGLAND

After leaving Totara-nui this time, Cook crossed the Pacific in a mid-fifties latitude and took the *Resolution* around Cape Horn and south into the high latitudes of the Atlantic, on his way back to England. Here he found islands and more icebergs, but again no habitable continent.

When they reached the Cape of Good Hope, the *Resolution*'s men met some English seamen on a Dutch East Indiaman who told them that the *Adventure* had been at the Cape twelve months earlier, and that one of their boat's crews had been 'Murdered and eat by the People of New Zealand'. Cook's comment on this news was laconic:

> I shall make no reflections on this Melancholy affair untill I hear more about it. I must however observe in favour of the New Zealanders that I have allways found them of a Brave, Noble, Open and benevolent disposition, but they are a people that will never put up with an insult if they have an oppertunity to resent it.[14]

Some days later he met Julien Crozet, who had been Marion du Fresne's second-in-command and was now taking a French East Indiaman to Pondicherry. Crozet dined on board the *Resolution* with his officers, and gave Cook 'many curious particulars' about the killing and eating of Marion and his men by Maori in the Bay of Islands in 1772. He told the officers that when he talked with Rousseau about his experiences in the Bay of Islands, the celebrated philosopher exclaimed, 'Is it possible that the good Children of Nature can really be so wicked?'[15] The two captains exchanged charts of their Pacific discoveries, and in this way Cook learned about Surville's visit to Tokerau (Doubtless Bay) in 1769, 'where it seems he was when I passed it on my former Voyage in the Endeavour'.[16] (In fact they had passed each other in a storm at sea, off North Cape.) When someone at the Cape gave Cook a copy of his first *Voyage*, edited by Hawkesworth, he was morti-fied by its numerous inaccuracies. On 27 April, the *Resolution* left the Cape, and on 30 July anchored in Spithead, off Portsmouth.

Cook's return home from his second voyage was a personal triumph. He was fêted at Court and in the press. The scientific community was enthralled by the cargo of plants and animals he had brought home. Daniel Solander, the Swedish

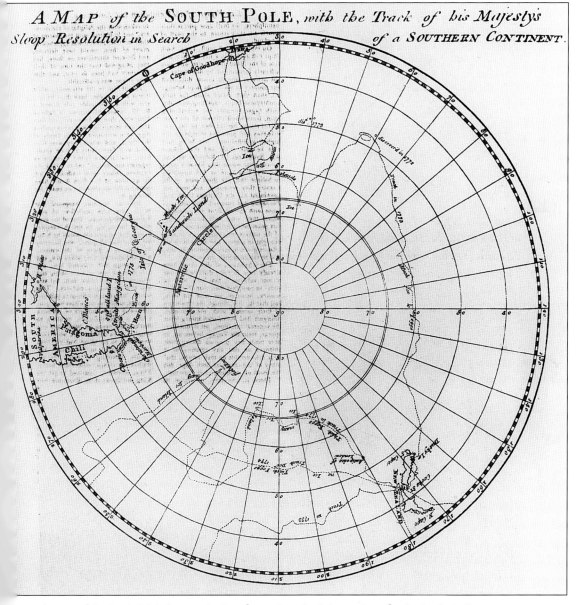

'A Map of the South Pole', showing the Resolution's track while searching for the Southern Continent.

A portrait of Captain James Cook, by John Webber.

scientist who had sailed with him on the *Endeavour,* rushed on board the *Resolution* and reported to Joseph Banks:

> Most of our time, yesterday, was taken up in ceremonies, so I had not much time to see their curious collections. Mr. Clerke show'd me some drawings of Birds, made by a Midshipman, not bad, which I believe he intends for you. I was told that Mr Anderson one of the Surgeons Mates, has made a good Botanical Collection, but I did not see him. There were on board 3 live Otaheite Dogs, the ugliest & most stupid of all the Canine tribe. Forster had on board the following Live Stock: a Springe Bock from the Cape, a Surikate, two Eagles, & several small Birds, all from the Cape. I believe he intends these for the Queen . . . Pickersgill made the Ladies sick by shewing them the New Zealand head of which 2 or 3 slices were broiled and eat on board of the Ship. It is preserved in Spirit and I propose to get it for Hunter, who goes down with me to morrow on purpose.[17]

Cook was tired but not yet exhausted, and when he was appointed to a comfortable position at Greenwich Hospital to reward him for his efforts, he quickly began to feel constrained. On 19 August, he wrote to his old friend and patron Captain John Walker: 'My fate drives me from one extream to a nother; a few Months ago the whole Southern hemisphere was hardly big enough for me and now I am going to be confined within the limits of Greenwich Hospital, which are far too small for an active mind like mine.'[18]

Plans were under way for a new Pacific voyage on the *Resolution* to search for the North-West Passage, and at a dinner party with his principal patrons, only six months after his return to England, Cook volunteered to lead it.

COOK'S THIRD PACIFIC VOYAGE

Within days Cook was back on his beloved ship, ordering in supplies and men. His second-in-command for this expedition was Charles Clerke, who had sailed on both of his previous voyages, and this time would command the *Discovery*, the *Resolution*'s new consort. Clerke's first lieutenant was James Burney, who had sailed with Furneaux on the *Adventure* during the previous voyage and witnessed the ritual feasting on his comrades at Grass Cove; supported by John Rickman as second lieutenant and Thomas Edgar as the *Discovery*'s master. Joseph Banks (who had renewed his old friendship with Cook, and was now director of the Royal Gardens) arranged for a gardener from Kew, David Nelson, to join the *Discovery*. There was also William Bayly, the astronomer from the *Adventure,* and five men from former Cook expeditions. The *Resolution*'s crew included the Pacific veteran John Gore, who had sailed twice to the Pacific before joining the *Endeavour*, as first lieutenant; James King, who had studied science at Paris and Oxford, as second lieutenant; William Bligh (later of *Bounty* fame) as master; William Anderson, the thoughtful Scottish surgeon from the previous voyage, and his second mate David Samwell, a lively Welshman and lover of the 'dear Ladies'; Samuel Gibson, the

Maori-speaking sergeant of marines who had been on two previous voyages with Cook; John Ledyard, a young American who had studied at Dartmouth College and had spent some time among the 'six nations of Indians on the borders of Canada' before joining the expedition as a marine;[19] the landscape painter John Webber as the ship's artist; and a dozen men from Cook's two previous voyages. This time there would be no 'experimental gentlemen'. Johann Forster had caused endless difficulties throughout the second voyage, and Cook was sick of civilian scientists.

He talked instead with James Boswell, Samuel Johnson's biographer, about a plan for the Crown to send 'men of enquiry' to live for several years in key places in the Pacific – perhaps New Zealand, Tahiti and New Caledonia – to learn local languages and conduct systematic enquiries into the lives of local people. Although both Boswell and Johnson thought about going on the voyage, the Admiralty was not interested in this scheme (which anticipated ethnographic field research by more than a century) and nothing came of it.[20] And then there was Mai, the young refugee from Raiatea who had sailed on the *Adventure* and spent a wonderful time in England under the patronage of Banks and Lord Sandwich, meeting the King and the professors at Cambridge (whom he regarded with awe-struck admiration), learning to ice-skate and ride, playing chess, dining with nobility, flirting with women and acquiring a taste for opera and wine. Since Cook's return, both King George and Sandwich had said to him, 'Omai, you go home,' and so Mai was sent on board the *Resolution*, along with household furniture and utensils, clothing, tools and a wheelbarrow for himself, and an array of prestige items for distribution to Pacific leaders – feathers, trousers, swords, cut-glass bowls, knives and forks, iron tools and tool chests, spyglasses, chessboards, jewellery, umbrellas, perfume, silver watches and pictures of the King and Queen.

When Cook sailed from Plymouth on 12 July 1776, the harbour was packed with ships carrying troops to fight the American colonists after the Declaration of Independence. The *Discovery* was delayed because Clerke had been thrown into the King's Bench prison for his brother's debts. Although he managed to get free in time to follow Cook two weeks later, by then he had contracted the tuberculosis that killed both him and Anderson during the voyage. The two ships met at the Cape of Good Hope. From this time on (unlike Cook's previous expedition, when his ships were separated more often than they were together), the *Resolution* and *Discovery* remained together. This offered them greater security in case of shipwreck, but it was also much harder to maintain shipboard discipline. In the various harbours they visited, local people had their own complex protocols and political divisions, and the combined crews of almost two hundred European men were almost impossible to control as they scattered about on shore, whether in European ports or on Pacific islands.

At the Cape, Cook acquired 'two young Bulls, two Heifers, two young stone Horses, two Mares, two Rams, several Ewes and Goats and some Rabbits and Poultry [including turkeys, geese, ducks, guinea fowl and peacocks], all of them intended for New Zealand',[21] to add to the cows and sheep he had brought from England. Somewhat surprisingly, New Zealand had been promoted in the British popular press as the Pacific country best suited for European settlement, despite the fact that its 'sober, civil, tractable and kind' inhabitants had been provoked to the Grass Cove killings,[22] and the animals were intended to prepare the way for later colonisation. From the Cape they sailed south-east to Kerguelen Island, where they shot numerous seals, and from there to Van Diemen's Land and New Zealand.

THE *RESOLUTION*'S LAST AND THE *DISCOVERY*'S FIRST VISIT TO TOTARA-NUI
12–26 February 1777

On 11 February 1777, the *Resolution* and the *Discovery* approached Totara-nui from the west side of Raukawa-moana, and the next day the two ships anchored in Meretoto. As they came into the cove, they saw three or four canoes (including two double ones, one with a carved prow) near the paa on Motuara, approaching the ship, although their crews seemed afraid of coming alongside. According to Samwell:

> In short time having consulted together they came in a body towards the Ship singing the Song of peace & Friendship, & one Man waving a white Ahoo [kahu – cloak] or Cloth & at the same time speaking to us, & he was answered by Omai who kept waving a Handkerchief & assuring them we were their Friends & so they ventured along side of the Ship. This Timidity most probably proceeded from the Affair of the Adventures people which they could not yet have forgot & whose Death they immagined we were come to revenge. However after being informed by Omai who we were and that Toote (as they called Capt Cook) was our Are [ariki] or Chief whom they were well acquainted with, they made no Hesitation at coming on board the Ship & most of them were known to those who had been here before, whom the N.Zealanders immediately recollected & seem'd to express great Joy at seeing them again.[23]

One of these men was 'Tayweherooa' (Te Weherua), now sixteen or seventeen years old, who with his father Toka had spent much time on board the *Resolution* during her first visit to the Sound. They described him then as 'lively and intelligent', and now as 'a good natured honest young fellow'[24] who quickly became a favourite with the crew. Another former acquaintance (probably 'Pedro'), whom Cook had 'treated with remarkable kindness' during their previous visit, came alongside but, despite presents and protestations of friendship, refused to come on board the vessel. Other canoes flocked around, offering fish, clothes and weapons for barter. The sailors were soon busy unloading casks, setting up a guard tent and clearing a place for the two observatories, and after a while the local people went away. That night a number of families camped near the two ships on the shore.

Some of the crew went out fishing the next morning. Wood and grass were collected, spruce beer (made of rimu leaves and other ingredients) was brewed, seal blubber from Kerguelen Island (which the local people eagerly ate) was melted in copper trypots, and Cook's collection of animals was landed. Samwell gave a vivid description of this zoological disembarkation:

> Today our Ship, which for the variety of living Things she contained might be called a second Noah's Ark, poured out the Horses, Cattle, Sheep, Goats &c. with peacocks, Turkeys, Geese & Ducks, to the great Astonishment of the New Zealanders, who had never seen Horses or Horned Cattle before; these being all feeding & diverting themselves about the Tents familiarised the Savage Scene & made us almost forget that we were near the antipodes of old England among a rude & barbarous people.[25]

About two hundred local people came into Meretoto that day to see the Europeans. Anderson, the *Resolution*'s surgeon, observed from the way they greeted each other that they had come from different places, and they later dispersed to set up camps in various coves around the Sound. According to Cook:

> It is curious to see with what facility they build these little temporary habitations: I have seen above twenty of them errected on a spot of ground that not an hour before was covered with shrubs & plants. They generally bring some part of the Materials with them, the rest they find on the spot. I was present when a number of people landed and built one of these Villages: the moment the Canoes landed men leaped out and at once took possession of a spot of ground, by tearing up the plants &c or sticking up some part of the framing of the hut, they then returned to the canoe and secured thier Weapons by seting them up against a tree or in such a manner as they could lay hold of them in an instant, I took particular notice that no one neglected this precaution. While the Men were employed raising the huts the Women were not idle, some were takeing care of the Canoes, some securing the Provisions, and the few utensils they are possess'd of, and others went to gather dry sticks to make a fire to dress their victuals; as to the Children I kept them, as also some of the more aged sufficiently employed in scrambling for beads till I had emptied my pockets and then I left them.[26]

Family groupings, no matter how large, generally seemed to live together. Cook commented that the larger towns and villages were sometimes divided by low palisades to mark out kin-group divisions, adding that Webber's sketch of one of these villages gave an excellent representation of such settlements.

Samwell spent some time talking with Te Weherua (probably with Mai's help) about the 'Courtezans' who were sent out to the ships. Te Weherua told him that they had been especially selected to sleep with the Europeans, and that 'none of the fine Girls were suffered to come near us but were kept with great Care at their Habitations, & that those Girls who came on board the Ships were the mere refuse & outcasts among them'.[27] These women were daubed with red ochre and smelled strongly, unlike (Samwell noted wistfully) the few 'cleanly & handsome' women he had seen. According to Cook, few of the sailors would sleep with these women, and consequently the spread of venereal diseases was limited.

He was glad of this because in his view the sailors were 'selfish without the least mixture of regard or attattchment whatever' in their relations with local women, and neglected their duties when they were chasing them on shore. For all that, the journal-keepers agreed that 'a Brisk Trade For Fish, Curiosities, & The use of Women'[28] was carried on from the beginning of their stay, and Williamson noted:

> The morning after our Arrival we were visited by a number of these greasy brown nymphs who offer'd themselves for sale with as much ease & assurance as the best Strand walker in London would do, and indeed during our Continuance there, we found them the cheapest kind of traffick we could deal in, a Wife . . . was to be had for much less than you could get a fish for your dinner.[29]

During this visit one of the *Discovery*'s sailors formed a close relationship with a young girl, 'Ghowannahe' (Ko Anahe?). According to Rickman, the sailor spent much time with his lover, dressing her hair and engaging in 'a kind of silent conversation, in which, tho' words were wanting, their meaning was perfectly understood'.[30] In an effort to please her, Rickman reported that he allowed himself to be 'tattowed from head to foot' (surely an exaggeration), and that she pleaded with him to stay on with her in Totara-nui as a 'kakikoo' (ariki?) among her people.

On 15 February, many of the canoes went off up the Sound, and Kahura, 'a middle aged Man, very strong, & of a fierce Countenance tattowed after the Manner of the Country',[31] came out to the *Resolution*. Several of the local people on board told the Europeans that he was 'a very bad man' and urged Cook to kill him, but Cook had often been asked to kill the members of opposing kin groups, and always resisted. This man was a key protagonist in the Grass Cove killings, but Cook did not yet know this, and in any case he had no intention of exacting revenge for that affray until he knew precisely what had happened. Kahura was reluctant to come on board at first, but as soon as he realised that he would not be harmed, he came onto the *Resolution*.

Soon after this Cook went off to Motuara to look for grass to feed the stock, and visited Hippa Island on the way. The paa was deserted, although it had been recently occupied. The gardens Bayly had planted there had been rooted up and all the houses and palisades repaired, and as they approached Motuara, an old man stood on the shore waving a green bough. When they landed, this man 'began an oration, accompanied by very significant gestures, and a theatrical display of the passions by various modulations of his voice, till at length he concluded in a plaintive tone, which we interpreted to mean submission'[32] (probably, rather, a waiata, sung at the end of such speeches). After pressing noses with this old man they inspected the gardens, finding them overgrown with weeds, but cabbages, onions, leeks, parsley, radishes, mustard and a few potatoes were still flourishing.

While Cook was away on this expedition, Gibson, the Maori-speaking sergeant of marines, stopped an old chief from entering the *Resolution*'s tent at Meretoto, for fear that he might steal something. The old man was furious and made a fiery speech, challenging the sergeant to fight and promising revenge. He then jumped into his canoe and went to one of the hamlets in a nearby cove, and shortly after this almost all of the canoes in the various coves raced off towards Long Island, where a party of grass-cutters had landed. Everyone in Totara-nui must have been expecting the Europeans to avenge the Grass Cove killings, and the Europeans' foray in that direction had made them apprehensive. An armed boat was sent to warn the grass-cutters, but they were already on their way back to the ships.

The next day (16 February) Cook, Clerke, Anderson, Mai, Te Weherua and and some others set off in five armed boats to cut grass in East Bay. After loading the two launches they carried on to Grass Cove, the scene of the killings three years earlier. Here Cook's 'old friend Pedro', with one companion, confronted them on the beach, armed with patu and spear. This was probably a challenge, provoked by the Europeans' return to the site of the killings. The local people must have been certain that an attack was imminent, but instead Cook presented Pedro and his companion with gifts, to their evident astonishment. Two or three more men joined them on the beach, but most of the people remained hidden in the bush.

When these presentations were over, Cook asked Pedro (whose real name, he now discovered, was 'Matahouah' – Matahoua?), through Mai, to tell him exactly what had happened at Grass Cove. Since Matahoua and his people were not directly implicated, this time he answered freely. According to Anderson:

> He . . . pointed out the spot (which is the corner of the cove on the right hand), where he said they were sitting at dinner except one man who was left in the boat to keep her afloat. Some of the Indians snatch'd up part of the bread they were eating, of which they are very fond, and the others endeavouring to recover it provok'd the Indians to make some resistance which made the person who commanded the boat (Mr Row) fire his musket and kill one of them on the spot. Upon this a chief nam'd Kahoora [the man who had come on board the *Resolution* the previous day] call'd out to some others who were upon a little hill near the middle of the cove amongst their houses to come to his assistance and in the mean time Mr Rowe having loaded his piece again or perhaps taking that of another Gentleman . . . fir'd and kill'd another Indian. By this time having collected to a considerable number and seeing the muskets discharg'd (for though they had two more it appears as if they had been left in the boat) they rush'd in upon them and kill'd some on the spot but the others not immediately. The man in the boat who was a Negroe servant of Captn Furneaux was the last who fell a victim to their rage, and must certainly have felt the most horrid sensations on seeing his companions murder'd before his face without the least hopes of giving them assistance or prolonging his own fate.[33]

Some of the others who were present gave Mai further details about the quarrel. They reported that one of the sailors had taken a hatchet but refused to give anything in return. The owner then seized some bread from him and he retaliated, which began the affray. They said that although several of Kahura's people had been wounded in the fighting, none of them was killed outright.

This was the first time that Cook had been told first-hand about the Grass Cove killings. As he had earlier suspected, the affray was caused by a dispute that had flared up between local people and the Europeans. Many years later, George Clarke, the first Protector of Aborigines, was told an almost identical story by an old man in Blind Bay, which added an interesting elaboration. This old man told Clarke that when the white men sat down to eat that day, one of them took a stone adze he was offered but refused to give anything in return. Its owner snatched some bread from him and ran off, and the sailor ran after him with a tin pan in his hand. When he came back to the beach, fuming with frustration, the sailor up-ended this pan on the head of a chief who was sitting nearby. The pan had contained cooked food, which was noa (the antithesis of tapu). This gesture desecrated the chief's head, destroying his tapu, so he attacked the sailor in a fury, a fight broke out, and all of the Europeans were killed.[34]

When Cook enquired what had happened to the *Adventure*'s cutter, he was told that it had been taken away from the Sound by a party from Te Raawhiti (perhaps Te Ratu's people), who attacked the local people soon after the affray and took the boat, the crew's weapons and other items as utu. This is the most likely source of a story collected by John White in about the 1850s about one 'Rongotute' (Cook's Maori name was 'Toote', a Tahitian version of 'Cook' that had become part of shipboard idiom), whose ship had visited Arapaoa (a large island in the Sound) in earlier generations, and who had given the people there a weapon 'not unlike a mere pounamu in shape'. According to this account, Rongotute's men 'committed evil' on the local people, who were so disgusted with them that they killed, cooked and ate them; plundered their boat (the cutter?) of ropes, nails, iron weapons and other items; and made ornaments from their dinner plates. The nails were sharpened and fixed to the end of long spears, the adzes were given carved handles, and one of these adzes was named 'Kai tangata' (people-eater). Not long after this the people had been afflicted with a sickness that left punctures on the body (venereal disease?), and many of them had died.[35]

The next day Te Weherua added a further detail about the Grass Cove killings, which the marines had also heard during the *Resolution*'s previous visit. According to Te Weherua, when one of the local men had tried to take something (some said it was a sailor's jacket) out of the boat, Furneaux's black servant hit him with a stick and there was fighting. Cook, musing over the matter, thought that probably the bread and the jacket had been snatched at about the same time, and that these accounts were mutually consistent.

One last version of the story came from Anahe, who told her sailor lover that 'Gooboa' (Kahura) was a bad man, who had been chained and beaten for taking things from the ship. In a fury, he had gone to a nearby paa and asked the warriors there to kill the strangers, showing them the marks and bruises of his beating and telling them that the Europeans' 'pow pow', or muskets, could be silenced by throwing water over them. After some hesitation, the warriors agreed to help him, and they attacked the strangers while they were collecting grass in the cove. After killing them, they cut up their bodies, cooked them over fires made by the women, and ate their hearts, livers and heads. Although this version (recorded by Rickman, second lieutenant on board the *Adventure*) makes the attack appear premeditated, it seems more likely that Kahura was the man who was hit for taking things from the cutter, and that Anahe's story had been garbled in the retelling. Anahe added that she was just a child when the Europeans were attacked and killed, but 'she remembered the talk of it, as a gallant action or great achievement, and that they made songs in praise of it'.[36]

With this and Matahoua's account the missing pieces of the puzzle came together. Cook and his companions finally understood (at least in part) what had happened to Furneaux's men.

While Cook was talking with Matahoua, his men loaded up the other boats with grass, celery and scurvy grass, then they set off to Meretoto accompanied by Matahoua's family in their canoe. The wind blew up and Matahoua's canoe put back to shore, and the boats did not arrive back at the ships until one o'clock the next morning. Matahoua and his family joined them a day later, when the storm had finally died down. Over the next few days Anahe gave her lover much information about local life and customs. According to Rickman's journal, she told him that among her people,

> the fathers had the sole care of the boys as soon as they could walk, and that the girls were left wholly at the mother's disposal. She said, it was a crime for a mother to correct her son, after he was once taken under the protection of the father [which might explain the domestic fracas witnessed by Johann Forster during the *Resolution*'s second visit to the Sound]; and that it was always resented by the mother, if the father interfered in the management of the daughters. She said, the boys from their infancy were trained to war, and both boys and girls were taught the art of fishing, to weave their nets, and make their hooks and lines; that their canoes came from a far country [most canoes in the Sound do seem to have come from the North Island], and that they got them in exchange for cloth, which was chiefly manufactured by the women; that their arms and working tools descended from father to son, and that those that were taken in battle supplied the rising generation; that they had no Kings among them, but that they had men [tohunga] who conversed with the dead, who were held in great veneration, and consulted before the people went to the wars; that they were the men who addressed strangers that came upon the coast, first in the language of peace, at the first time denouncing vengeance against them, if they came with any hostile design; that the persons of these men were held sacred, and never killed in the wars, which ever side prevailed; that when the warriors of either nation made prisoners, they were never of the meaner sort, but of some Chief, whom they afterwards killed and eat; but that to the common sort they never gave quarter; that they sometimes tortured an enemy, if they found him singly lurking in the woods, looking upon him as one who came upon no good design; but never otherwise; that they lived chiefly upon fish, which were caught in the Sound in abundance, during the summer, and were

Captain Charles Clerke, commander of the Discovery, *with an unknown chief.*
A portrait by Nathaniel Dance.

dried and preserved for the winter; but that in very severe weather they retired to the North [a fair account of their seasonal migrations].[37]

It is difficult to assess how well the young man understood his lover, but on the whole these statements attributed to Anahe seem reliable.

Over the next few days the Europeans continued to explore the Sound. On 20 February, for instance, Anderson and some others went to Hippa Island, where they visited the deserted paa, noting latrines at each end of the settlement, and then crossed to Motuara, where they climbed to the top of the hill to see the carved post that Cook had raised at the end of his 1770 visit. Anderson speculated that this paa was only used in times of danger, since it had no source of water, and that the rest of the time the people lived dispersed around the Sound. At about this time they were told that there had been a major battle not long before the ships arrived between the people of Totara-nui and those of Pelorus Sound, and that Te Ringapuhi (the chief whom Cook had met in Kura-te-au (Tory Channel) at the end of his last visit) along with fifty of his best men had been killed, and many of their women carried away as captives to Pelorus. During this stay in the Sound the sailors often heard 'the most dismal Cries from different parts of the Cove' at night. They thought that these were the sounds of people being put to death on shore, but more likely it was the karanga and tangi koorero (talking wails), or waiata (chants) sung during ceremonies of mourning for the people who had died.

On 22 February, Lieutenant King walked into the hills behind the cove, accompanied by a chief whom he had met with his family (two 'comely' sons and a daughter) at the shore camp several days before. This man carried the lieutenant's gun, looking for pigeons and other birds, until King turned and headed down the hillside away from the coast. His companion called him back, saying with tears in his eyes that if he went in that direction they would both be killed and eaten. King shouted that his gun would protect them both, but the man would not budge. Finally King had to climb back up the hill and they returned to the ships, where the chief told his friends in consternation about their narrow escape.

Not surprisingly, relations between the Europeans and local people during this visit were complicated and uneasy. Although the Europeans had some friends and allies, there was a measure of contempt on both sides; from Europeans towards Maori for having eaten their countrymen, and from Maori towards Europeans for Cook's failure to take utu. Mai urged Cook to take action against Kahura, but Cook would not listen, so Mai's lack of influence became clear to the local people. Mai's stories about London drew interested audiences, and he slept with some of the women on shore, but he does not seem to have been much respected. Cook himself, while abiding by a policy of avoiding violence wherever possible, must have found it galling to be reproached by Maori, Mai and some of his own people for not punishing the killers of Furneaux's men. Burney, who (like Mai) resented the failure to avenge the deaths of his *Adventure* shipmates, remarked, 'it seemed evident that many of them held us in great contempt and I believe chiefly on account of our not revenging the affair of Grass Cove, so contrary to the principles by which they would have been actuated in the like case'.[38] Some of the sailors felt that justice had not been done, and found their own ways of expressing their feelings; for instance, in a mock trial of a 'cannibal dog', a story recounted years later by the *Discovery*'s master's mate, Alexander Home:

> When we were in New Zealand, Neddy Rhio, one of my messmates had got hold of a New Zealand dog, as savage a devil as the savages from whom he got it, and this same dog he intended to bring home to present to the Marchioness of Townsend, his patroness. But one day, when Neddy was on shore on duty, a court-martial was held on the dog, and it was agreed nem. con. that, as the dog was of cannibal origin, and was completely a cannibal itself, having bit every one of us, and shewn every inclination to eat us alive if he could, that he should be doomed

to death, and eat in his turn, we being short of fresh provisions at the time. The sentence was immediately executed, the dog cooked, dressed and eat . . . but, considering that Neddy had a best right to a share, we put past his portion in a wooden bowl, and by way of having some sport, we cut a hole in the dog's skin, and as Neddy came up the side, I popped his own dog's skin over his head with the tail hanging down behind, and the paws before. He looked the grin horrid, told us all we were a set a d—d cannibals, as bad as the New Zealanders we were amongst, and dived down below quite in the sulks.

I had locked up his share, and went down after him to see if hunger would overcome his delicacy, and sure enough, after growling and grumbling and swearing a reasonable time, he looks at me very woefully and says, 'D—n you, did you not even leave me a share?' – 'That I did', says I, 'Neddy, my boy, and here it is for you'. So poor Rhio munched up his dog, cursing all the while as heartily as we were laughing at him. Ah! those were the glorious days.[39]

In this period, mock trials of animals were one way for subordinates (apprentices, sailors and so on) to express themselves on matters of justice,[40] and the message of this one was clear. Cannibals, especially ones that chewed Europeans, should be 'doomed to death', but Cook was not of a mind to do it. Instead, he ordered his men to be alert and wary, posting sentries at the shore camp to deter would-be raiders and arming the boats. Maori visitors to the ships also took precautions. When the principal chief 'Tomatongeauooranue' (Te Matangi-au-ura-nui?), an 'exceeding lusty well grown man' six feet tall and about forty-five years old with a 'fine cheerfull open countenance', came to visit them on 21 February from the far end of the Sound, for instance, his entourage included about twenty strapping young warriors, all under twenty years of age.

By this time most of the Sound's inhabitants had built temporary hamlets near the ships, close to the Europeans. There were plenty of trade goods on board to exchange for curiosities and fish (including moki, described as 'the most delicious fish in the world',[41] and crayfish). The local people liked seal oil from the trypots, and loaded discarded pieces of blubber into baskets and took them away in canoes. According to Burney, 'they often appeared to have a great deal of friendship for us, speaking sometimes in the most tender, compassionate tone of voice imaginable; but it not a little disgusted one to find all this show of fondness interested and that it constantly ended in begging. If gratified with their first demand, they would immediately fancy something else, their expectations and importunities increasing in proportion as they had been indulged.'[42] John Gore was puzzled by this behaviour, but like Burney he linked it with the Grass Cove killings, saying that the people now seemed 'Confident of their own Power' and expected presents 'in some degree as Tribute for their friendship'.[43]

By 23 February, the water casks and the wood had been stowed on board, along with hay for the animals. That morning the old man who had greeted Cook at Motuara came out to the *Resolution* with some fish and 'a compleat set of their arms' for the captain. In return Cook gave him a brass 'pata-patow, made exactly in their manner', engraved with the royal arms, the names of the ships and the date of their departure from England (like the iron patu made for the second voyage, and referred to in the 'Rongotute' story). That same day, on shore, a local man took an axe that had been laid down by one of the woodcutters, and that evening a captive (probably the culprit) was brought on board the ship and offered to the Europeans. When they refused to accept him, he was bundled back into the canoe, and that night 'a most horrid yelling' was heard in the bush. When a cutter was sent on shore to investigate, however, they found some fires still burning, but the people had all gone and there was no sign that anyone had been killed.[44]

The next day at dawn Cook ordered the tents to be struck and everything brought back on board. As the ships were being unmoored, Te Matangi-au-ura-nui and Matahoua came on board to ask for animals, and Cook gave the first chief a boar and a sow, and the second a breeding pair of goats. He had also intended to leave sheep and cows in the Sound, but considered that there was no local chief powerful enough to prevent them from being killed. According to Te Weherua, the poultry that had been put on shore during earlier visits had established themselves in the bush behind Meretoto, and Te Ratu, the young orator who had camped with his people in Indian Cove during the *Resolution*'s second visit to the Sound, still had a sow and many cocks and hens.

The ships sailed out of the cove, but the winds were unfavourable and they were forced to anchor near Motuara Island. Cook landed and released two breeding pairs of rabbits, then crossed with King to 'Canibals Cove' to plant some more potatoes. Here they found a cluster of half a dozen houses, 'very pleasantly situated', including one 'much superior to the rest' — no doubt a chief's house — which King described in detail:

> It was about 24 feet long, 12 broad, & 5 and a half high, in the shape of a country barn, the inside was both strongly & regularly made of supporters at the sides, alternately large & small, lash'd well together with withs, & painted red & black. The ridge pole was strong & the bull rushes which composed ye thatch were neatly laid & parallel to each other; At one End was a square hole, just large enough to creep in at, & another near it much smaller, perhaps for the smoke to go out at, as there was no other Opening for that purpose; the fire place was in the middle.[45]

The ships' departure from Totara-nui proved to be eventful. Te Weherua, the 'lively and intelligent' young man whom they met during the *Resolution*'s first visit to the Sound, had stayed on board the ship with a younger companion ('Teatea') since its return to Meretoto, and they had accompanied Cook and Mai on most of their excursions. His father (Toka, a leading man) had been killed in the attack on Te Ringapuhi's people, and Te Weherua attached himself to Cook and Mai, saying that he wanted to go with them to Tahiti. Cook was concerned that Mai might have made false promises to Te Weherua, and told him that it was unlikely that he would return from such a voyage, but Te Weherua was adamant. That afternoon his mother 'Tiratoutou' ('Tairatuutuu'?), 'a Woman much respected among them', came on board and 'cryed much & beat her head, & otherwise used every persuasive argument against his going [saying among other things that the Europeans would kill and eat him]'.[46] It was futile. Te Weherua had decided to leave, and even when his younger companion went ashore and did not come back to the ship, he would not change his mind. That evening he parted from his mother with much affection, and she promised that she would cry no more.

That same afternoon, according to John Ledyard, it was discovered that one of the *Discovery*'s crew had run ashore. This was Anahe's lover, who had decided to stay with her. At first he had been reluctant, fearing that he might be killed and eaten, but apparently Anahe assured him that as long as he did not harm them, her relatives would protect him from attack. As soon as his absence was noticed, though, Clerke sent a cutter ashore to bring him back, and late that night they found the lovers 'in a profound sleep locked in each others arms, dreaming no doubt of love, of kingdoms, and of diadems; of being the progenitors of a numerous family of princes to govern the kingdoms of Ea-kei nommauwee [Te Ika no Maui – Maui's fish, the North Island] and T'Avi-Poenammoo [Te Wai Pounamu – the South Island]'.[47] The sailor was seized, tied up and taken to Cook on board the *Resolution* the next morning. Acccording to Ledyard, the sailor was a 'favourite' and Cook forgave him for his folly, but this seems unlikely – twelve lashes was the standard punishment for going ashore without permission.[48]

That afternoon the local people took one last opportunity to barter, and sent out two or three large canoes loaded with dogs, cloaks, greenstone tiki and adzes, which they offered in exchange for hatchets. Kahura, who had led the attack on Furneaux's men, was on board one of these canoes, and came onto the *Resolution*. Infuriated by his impertinence, Mai pointed at Kahura and urged Cook to shoot him, telling Kahura that he would shoot him himself if he dared to return to the ship. Kahura was unimpressed, however, and came back early the next morning with his family, about twenty people in all. Mai took him to Cook's cabin, again saying, 'There is Kahourah kill him,' but Cook preferred to ask Kahura exactly what had happened at Grass Cove. Mai was baffled by Cook's attitude:

> Seeing the chief unhurt, [he] said 'why do not you kill him, you till me if a man kills an other in England he is hanged for it, this Man has killed ten and yet you will not kill him, tho a great many of his countreymen desire it and it would be very good'.
>
> Omais arguments, tho reasonable enough, having no weight with me, I desired him to ask the cheif why he killed Captain Furneaux's people, at this Question he folded his arms hung down his head and looked like one caught in a trap; And I firmly believe expected every moment to be his last, but was no sooner assured of his safety than he became cheerfull, yet did not seem willing to answer the question that had been put to him, till I had again and again assured him that he should not be hurt.
>
> Then he ventured to till us, that on offering a stone hatchet for sale to one of the people, he kept it and would give nothing in return, on which they snatched from them some bread while they were at victuals . . . This man would have been one of those that were shot dead, but hiding himself behind the boat was not seen,

so that a nother man was killed who stood behind him; as soon as the musket was discharged, he instantly seized the oppertunity to attack Mr Rowe, who commanded the party and who defended himself with his Hanger (with which he wounded Kahourah in the Arm) till overpowered by numbers. What became of the boat I never could learn, some said she was pulled to pieces and burnt, others said she was carri'd they knew not where by a party of strangers.[49]

Kahura was so reassured by Cook's promises that, seeing a sketch by Webber of one of his countrymen, he asked whether he could be drawn as well. Webber was called and Kahura was sketched sitting in Cook's cabin. As Mai well knew, this was provocative behaviour. In Grass Cove, hearts had been cut out and no doubt eaten in the whaangai hau ceremony, which destroyed mana and left surviving relatives bereft of ancestral protection. Sitting calmly in Cook's cabin, Kahura was making the captain look like a taurekareka (slave), unable to uphold the mana of his people. It was a bold act of assertion, demonstrating the power of his own ancestors over those of the Europeans.

While all of this was happening, Te Weherua's mother came out again to say goodbye to her son, bringing one of his young relatives Koa (who was about ten years old) to accompany him on the voyage. Koa, who had visited the *Resolution* with Te Weherua during the ship's first visit to the Sound, was reluctant to leave his family, but was given little choice. His father Te Wahanga followed him on board, and presented his son to Cook without visible signs of emotion. At ten o'clock that morning the ships weighed anchor and sailed out of the Sound.

TE WEHERUA AND KOA'S PACIFIC ADVENTURE

As long as the ships were in sight of the land, Te Weherua and Koa were excited and cheerful, but as soon as the *Resolution* set off into open ocean they began to cry, singing a song of mourning for their country and their kinsfolk, whom they knew they might never see again. Cook ordered jackets to be made out of red baize to cheer them up, but this was little consolation. They both suffered from sea-sickness, and over the next four or five days Koa sat crying in the anchor chains for hours, singing his lament, which Samwell, the surgeon's mate on the *Resolution*, laboriously transcribed:

> Nomeira ehiga heramaira acoi tewkitahiti
> *Nau mai ra e hika haramai ra koe, tiu ki Tahiti,*
> Kieiragoi toogieiaw kieretoohagawaw
> *Kei hea ra koe? Tu ki Heiao, ki Heretu, he kawau*
> Ingeriaia kihewhewadoogoi kitetahaw
> *e ngeri ra ia ki'hiwahiwa atu koe. Kei te taha au*
> Oteoomoo away.
> *o te umu. Aue!*

*The portrait of Kahura sketched by John Webber
in the Great Cabin of the* Resolution, *1777.*

Welcome, O sir, come hither, soar to Tahiti.
Where are you? Standing at Heiao, at Heretu, is a
cormorant who is chanting to you to be wary.
I am at the edge of the oven. Alas!

(Modern transcription and translation by J. McEwen.[50])

Whenever Te Weherua heard Koa singing this lament he joined him, and they
sat and cried together.

These two were the first Maori to leave New Zealand in a European ship.
After about a week they began to enjoy their adventure. According to Edgar, 'the
boy Co-co-ah [was] of a very humorous & lively Disposition and he afforded us
much Mirth with his Drolleries. Tay-we-he-rooa was a Sedate sensible Young
fellow, they were both universally liked.'[51] Koa was too young to work full-time as
a sailor, and Te Weherua seems to have spent much of his time with the officers.
The routine rhythms of bells, watches (Cook's ships ran three a day) and meals,
and the tasks of life at sea (working the sails, repairing rigging, cleaning and scrap-
ing) organised their days.

Cook was writing up his 'Observations' on Maori life, and often talked with
them. Among other things, Te Weherua told Cook about a European ship that had

arrived at a port on the north-west coast of Te Raawhiti a few years before the *Endeavour* came to Totara-nui. The captain had had an affair with a local woman, and she had borne a son by him who was now about Koa's age. This ship had been responsible for introducing venereal disease among them, and the symptoms had been terrible at first but had since abated. The only treatment that they knew for this disorder was a herbal steam bath, made by putting certain plants and water on hot stones. Both Koa and Te Weherua assured Cook that everyone around the Strait knew about this visit. Which ship this was, however, is quite unclear.

Te Weherua also told Cook about taniwha, which he sketched for him and described as a giant lizard about eight feet long, which could kill men. These monsters lived in burrows in the ground, and were killed by lighting fires at the mouth of the burrow to smoke them out. It was probably also at this time that Samwell copied out the first texts in Maori from Te Weherua's dictation: a tangi (dirge) and five haka (war chants), including the following:

EHAGA 5

Tehitoo kihicoia wakahi tomonakoo kiahooi
Te Whetu-kihi ko ia whakahi to manako kia hui
Kaietarego caingapooga caria paira caw
Kei Tariko, kei Ngapuka karia a Paerakau
Pariana ketetoogoo ketaga paouri waragi
Pare ana ki te tuku ki Takapouri, whara ki
Tererenga awuaga adema tangigi tehowa
Te Rerenga ou waka e rima. Tangi ki te hauaa
Iete naboora ee eko rerato nghadugi
i tena po ra, e. E kore ratou ngaro ki
Tebooda ikai etiwa niwigi teahi ea
te puta. He kai e tiua ki te ahi, ea!

HAKA NO. 5

It was Te Whetu-kihi who jeered at your wish to assemble.
At Tariko, at Ngapuka, Paerakau was wounded.
Turning aside to the coast at Takapouri,
your five canoes were driven to destruction.
Weep for the coward on that night. They will not be
lost on the battlefield. They are food which will be
turned over and over in the fire, ea!

(Transcription and translation by J. McEwen.[52])

The ships sailed for about a month in fine weather until, on 29 March, land was sighted. This proved to be Mangaia (one of the Cook Islands), hitherto unknown to Europeans. They could not go ashore because of the reef and heavy surf, and so carried on to Atiu. There Mai landed, and it is probable that Te Weherua and Koa went with him. The local people crowded around the visitors, picking their pockets and forcing them to stay ashore. They entertained them with a feast, wrestling matches and dancing. Mai demonstrated the Tahitian war dance and exploded a handful of gunpowder with a live coal, to their evident amazement. According to Samwell, 'they were as much pleased & astonished with looking at [the Europeans] as the rabble rout in England are with seeing a Collection of wild Beasts at a Country Fair'.[53] Mai also met four Tahitians who had been blown south to the island during a voyage from Tahiti to Raiatea. Mai offered them passage in the *Resolution* back to Tahiti, but they were happily settled and refused. Cook commented that Mai, Te Weherua and Koa could all talk easily with the Cook Islanders, who asked them endless questions about the Europeans. At Manuae the people told them that they had previously seen two large ships go past the island, which Cook guessed must have been the *Resolution* and the *Adventure* during his second Pacific voyage.

At the Northern Cooks, Mai, Te Weherua and Koa went fishing, then the ships carried on to Tonga. They anchored at Nomuka and went ashore, and many local people came on board the ships. Mai regaled them with stories about his travels to 'Britannee', which they found riveting, and several important chiefs entertained Cook's party. Te Weherua must have slept with local women, for he contracted a venereal disease at Nomuka, prompting Lieutenant King to comment that 'wherever we go, we spread an incurable distemper which nothing we can do can ever recompence'.[54] At Lifuka they went ashore again, and Cook was received with great hospitality and showered with gifts. Again there were exhibitions of

John Webber's painting of the men dancing at night on Lifuka, 1777.

fighting and dancing, and Cook reciprocated with fireworks and a military display by the marines. Mai exchanged names with Finau, one of the leading chiefs, and, along with Cook and Clerke, was given lavish gifts of food, bark cloth and red feather ornaments. The officers taught Finau to ride, and Cook presented him with two horses. The expedition then moved on to Tongatapu, where they stayed for a month. Te Weherua and Koa became favourites with the people there, 'who paid much attention to them & were very fond of their Company; having once seen the new Zealand Heivah or war dance they frequently desired the Boys to perform it before them which they did & were much caressed & admired for it'.[55] There were more feasts and entertainments, and fireworks and military displays, and at a great inasi ceremony just before his departure, Cook stripped to the waist and let his hair fall loose.

For all the apparent geniality of these exchanges, however, relationships between the Tongans and Europeans were not entirely friendly. Cook had found his encounters with Maori in Totara-nui galling, and he was now in a mood to discipline unruly Polynesians. Urged on by Mai and some of his officers, he became increasingly severe with people who took things from the ships. There were floggings, ears were cropped, people were put in irons, arms were slashed with knives, and Clerke shaved the heads of anyone he caught stealing – punishments that had never been meted out in Totara-nui. Cook even took the Tui Tonga and Finau hostage on one occasion, risking their retribution. The German sailor Zimmerman gave an unforgettable portrait of Cook at about this time: tall, handsome, strong, rather lean, with dark brown hair; very stern, and hot-tempered, so that the least opposition from an officer or a seaman upset him completely. The man of moderation, the 'genius of the matter-of-fact', had become immoderate, burning with rage whenever he was crossed. Since he had learned first-hand what had happened at Grass Cove, Cook's attitudes towards 'Indians' (and his own men) had hardened. He had begun to agree with Clerke, who in Totara-nui had commented:

> Whilst you keep the command in your own hands you are at leisure to act with whatever levity you please, but if you relax so far as to lay yourself open to their machinations, you may be deceiv'd in your expectations. There are few Indians in whom I wou'd wish to put a perfect confidence, but of all I ever met with these shou'd be the last, for I firmly believe them very capable of the most perfidious & most cruel treachery, tho' no People can carry it fairer when the proper superiority is maintain'd.[56]

Polynesians, on the other hand, did not appreciate such assertions of 'proper superiority'. Chiefly dignity was often compromised in these exchanges, venereal diseases were now rife and the floggings, ear croppings and forcible cutting of hair, particularly if chiefs were involved, violated kin-group prestige. Local attitudes towards the Europeans were also hardening, and at Lifuka there was a plot to invite Cook and officers to a great feast in order to kill them all and seize the ships. This was only thwarted because the chiefs could not agree on whether a night or a day attack would be more likely to be successful.[57]

From Tonga the ships sailed to Tahiti, where Mai's more distant relatives greeted him with indifference until they realised that he had come home loaded with red feathers and other treasures. A group of Spanish priests had visited Tahiti on a number of occasions in recent years, taking four volunteers back with them to Lima in Peru, two of whom had returned home in 1774; so Mai was not the only cosmopolitan traveller on the island. His aunt and his sister wept with joy to see him, but the chiefs virtually ignored him. When Cook introduced him to the high chief, he regaled Tuu and his retinue with tales of the glories of 'Pretanne':

> Omai began by magnifying the grandeur of the Great King [of Britain]; he com-
> pared the splendour of his court to the brilliancy of the stars in the firmament; the
> extent of his dominions by the vast expanse of heaven; the greatness of his power,
> by the thunder that shakes the earth. He said, the Great King of Pretanne had
> three hundred thousand warriors every day at his command, clothed like those
> who now attended the Earees of the ships, and more than double that number of
> sailors, who traversed the globe, from the rising of the sun to his setting; that his
> ships of war exceeded those at Mattavai in magnitude, in the same proportion as
> those exceeded the small canoes at Opparree . . . that in one city only on the
> banks of a river far removed from the sea, there were more people than were
> contained in the whole group of islands with which his Majesty was acquainted;
> that the country was full of large populous cities . . . that in the country of the
> Great King, there are more than 100 different kinds of four-footed animals . . .
> [that] the ships of war of Pretanne were furnished with poo-poos (guns) each of
> which would receive the largest poo-poo his Majesty had yet seen within it; that
> some carried 100 and more of those poo-poos, with suitable accommodations for
> a thousand fighting men . . .[58]

Such boasting about Britain was undiplomatic, since it diminished Tuu's prestige by comparison. The chiefs were even less pleased when Mai distributed his new-found wealth to anyone who would befriend him, without regard to their status.

Te Weherua and Koa, as Mai's attendants, must have been taken aback. Mai had appeared a great man in Totara-nui, but in Tahiti the chiefs treated him as a jumped-up commoner. Even when he put on a suit of armour and stood on the stage of a fighting canoe during a naval review, nobody took much notice, although they were amazed when spears bounced off his breastplate. Cook was treated with much greater respect, despite his refusal to assist the local chiefs in an attack on Moorea. They also met Hitihiti, the young man who had travelled on the *Reso-lution* during the second voyage (whom Samwell now described as 'one of the most stupid Fellows on the Island'), and Cook and Mai attended a ceremony in which a human sacrifice was offered to the local war god. There were feasts, plays and fireworks, and Cook, Mai and Clerke rode on horseback around Matavai, to the astonishment of a large crowd of spectators. (Mai, to his chagrin, fell off.) Te Weherua and Koa got on well with the local people in Tahiti, although the boy was inclined to get into fights in which he was often worsted. On one occasion when he teased one of the local girls,

Left: *Cook's taiao, the high chief Tuu.*

Below: *A naval review in Tahiti, showing the fighting canoes.*

Above: *Mai is presented to the King and Queen by Joseph Banks at Kew, July 1774.*

Mai and Cook on horseback at Matavai in August 1777.

[She] reproached him with his Countrymen eating human flesh, at the same time making signs of biting her own Arm, the poor boy was much hurt at it and fell a crying; but presently recovering out of his Confusion and being still insulted by her, he put his fingers to his head as if searching for a louse & made signs of eating it, at the same time telling her that if his Countrymen eat human flesh She eat lice which was almost as bad; by this quick stroke of retaliation our young Zealander got the laugh of his Side & the Girl was obliged to retreat & leave him master of the field.[59]

During his time on Tahiti, Mai made one shrewd exchange for his red feathers. He acquired a double sailing canoe, fully equipped and manned, and had ten or a dozen flags and pendants made up from English cloth. This canoe was named the *Royal George*, and with Mai as its captain it accompanied the European ships to Moorea. Although Cook had refused to join the Tahitian chiefs in an attack on Moorea, when the people there took one of his goats, he and Mai led a punitive rampage across the island, burning houses and breaking up eighteen large war canoes. Planks from these were loaded on board the *Resolution* (and later used to build Mai's house), as well as two sailing canoes for his use. Again Cook's officers were baffled by his behaviour. Williamson commented: 'I doubt not but Captn Cook had good reasons for carrying His punishment of these people to so great a length, but what his reasons were are yet a secret.'[60]

From Moorea they sailed to Huahine, where Mai had first met the Europeans. Cook presented him, along with gifts of Tongan red feathers, to his chief. The priests were in attendance, and in the rituals that followed, Mai mentioned Lord Sandwich, 'Toote' (Cook), 'Tatee' (Clerke), and regaled them with tales of his stay in London. He asked for land for himself and his 'servants' (Te Weherua and Koa), and if that was not possible, said that Cook would go to Raiatea, his home island, to drive out the invaders who had gone there from Borabora. The elders liked this idea, but when they asked Cook to go with them and Mai to Raiatea, Cook flatly refused, destroying Mai's dreams of liberating his homeland. They offered him a place for Mai's house, however, and Cook ordered the carpenters to begin its construction.

Mai's brother and sister joined him, but they were not influential enough to look after what was left of his property. Cook advised him to give most of it to the chiefs in exchange for their protection, which he promised to do. Several days later, when a sextant was taken out of Bayly's observatory, Mai identified a Borabora man as the thief. He denied it and was clapped in irons on the ship, and when the sextant was found the next morning, Cook had this man flogged and his head shaved as a punishment. Two days later the Borabora man raided Mai's garden (which the sailors, helped by Te Weherua and Koa, had planted with vines, vegetables, pineapples, melons and shaddocks), threatening to kill Mai and burn his house as soon as the Europeans had left Huahine. Cook had him seized again, both his ears were cropped and he was clapped in irons on the ship, to be taken away from the island.

138

Mai's settlement on Huahine, painted by John Webber after the voyage.

By now Mai's house was almost finished and his things were brought out of the ship. There were drums, a hand organ he had learned to play, his suit of armour, a jack-in-a-box, an 'electrifying machine' from Banks, a Bible, regiments of lead soldiers, with coaches and horses, a compass, a globe, and maps and charts, as well as dishes, plates, glasses, pots, kettles and other household utensils. Realising that most of the utensils would be of little use on the island, Mai traded them with the sailors for hatchets and other practical items. That night some of his fireworks were let off in front of a great crowd of people, who 'beheld them with a mixture of pleasure and fear'. The next morning Cook landed horses, goats, a monkey and pigs, and gave Mai a musket, two pairs of pistols with ammunition, and swords and cutlasses to protect his household, which now included four or five retainers from Tahiti and his brother and sister, as well as Te Weherua and Koa. Mai's enemy had escaped from the ship overnight, and Cook feared that he might need military support. The next day, 2 November 1777, the ships sailed from Huahine. Mai wept when he said goodbye to Cook on board the *Resolution* that evening, and cried all the way back to the island.

Te Weherua and Koa had learned some broken English, and begged Cook in that language to take them with him to Britain (for according to Samwell, 'it was once universally understood by us as well as by themselves that they were to have gone with us'[61]). When they were taken off the *Resolution*, Koa, who was crying bitterly, jumped twice out of the canoe to swim back to the ship. According to Samwell:

> When he saw his old Ship spreading her sails & leaving him behind [Koa] wept aloud & called to us to take him with us, at the same time endeavoured to jump into the Sea and swim after us, but was held fast by the People on board the Canoe; however with much struggling he disengaged himself, jumped overboard & swum with all his might after the ship, but was soon overtaken & carried back to the Canoe, where soon after he disengaged himself once more & had another hard Trial to reach the Ship, but alass he was too weak to outstrip those who had the Care of him, he was carried back and bound to the Canoe with Ropes, and now the poor little Fellow could do nothing but cry & called to his old shipmates for Assistance which we were so inhuman as to deny him. I was upon Deck & saw all this, and if ever I felt the full force of an honest Heart Ache it was at that time. Captn Cook did not know of it or, he has said afterwards, he would have taken him with him to England.[62]

The sailors farewelled Te Weherua and Koa with real regret; they had become genuinely fond of them. Samwell added:

> Taywe-herooa was a modest sensible young fellow, he always behaved with the greatest Propriety during his Stay with us & was much esteemed by us all. Cocoa was very humorous & lively, by his many Drolleries he used to create no small Diversion on board. He was a favourite with all, & every one of the Jacks took a delight in teaching something either in Speech or Gesture, at which he himself was eminent, and as the sagacious New Zealander perceived that he was caressed and applauded according to his proficiency in this kind of Learning, he became a diligent Student and in a short time was a perfect adept in Monkey-tricks & the witty Sayings of Wapping & St Giles. The two Boys lived with the Captain's Servants, but being fond of Variety they generally used to stroll about at Dinner time, as they found they were welcome to partake with every Mess in the Ship. In short they were both universally liked and we should have been much pleased to have taken them with us to England. The young one was in a fair way of getting a smattering of our Language which he would soon have learnt, and seemed to have some Ambition of being a Seaman as he was never better pleased than when meddling with the Ropes.[63]

According to William Bligh, who visited Huahine in 1789, Te Weherua and Koa lived with Mai for about three years after Cook's departure. Mai often rode his horse around the island, wearing riding boots, and his guns were used to great effect in a battle in which many Borabora and Raiatean men were killed. In about 1780, however, Mai, Te Weherua and Koa all died natural deaths: Mai of an illness, and Te Weherua and Koa of grief that their protector had died. All of the animals except a mare had also died (the monkey from falling out of a coconut tree), and almost all of the European plants had been destroyed. As for Cook, he was killed by Hawaiians at Kealakekua Bay in 1779. So ended the adventures of these Polynesian voyagers.

Six

COOK'S VISITS TO TOTARA-NUI
1770–1777

Totara-nui seems to have been a volatile place, in pre-European as well as in post-contact times. Its location on the crossroads between the two main islands meant that there was constant canoe-borne traffic through the Sound, and fighting seems to have been provoked by local animosities as well as a desire to control inter-island trade. Access to the argillite quarries of the region and the greenstone sources further south was jealously guarded, and life was so turbulent, at least in the period from 1770 to 1777, that people hesitated to plant gardens in case their crops were raided. The population at any time was correspondingly small, numbering in hundreds rather than in thousands, and made up of families who congregated in their paa in times of danger, and at other times lived dispersed around the various coves, hunting and gathering, and frequently travelling for trade. In this respect Totara-nui was different from most North Island coastal communities, whose gardens and fisheries supported larger, more densely settled populations. At the time of the 1770 *Endeavour* visit, the political insecurities of life in Totara-nui and the consequent relative poverty of its people led Pickersgill to remark that they were 'the Poorest and most mizerable sett we saw on New Zealand'.[1]

The arrival of the Europeans provoked new instabilities in the region. The *Endeavour* first visited Totara-nui at a time when the Sound was controlled by two main confederations (probably Ngaati Apa and Rangitaane), centred upon the two main paa (Motuara and East Bay) then occupied in the Sound. Fighting was going on between the Motuara people (led by an elder called Topaa) and their enemies to the west, in Pelorus Sound, and evidence of cannibalism sparked off a trade with the Europeans for souvenirs of human sacrifice, including bones and a human head. It seems likely that venereal disease was first introduced during the *Endeavour* visit, although there was no systematic exchange of sex for European goods at this time. The iron nails, tools, Tahitian cloth and European clothing brought by the Europeans were much sought after, and access to these goods provoked jealousies between the different kin groups in the Sound. Furthermore, when Cook set up a carved pole with much ceremony on the highest point of

Motuara Island early in 1770 as he was preparing to leave the Sound, this may have been taken to be a raahui pole placing a tapu on the island. Certainly when the *Adventure* and then the *Resolution* returned to the Sound in 1773, the island and the paa on the adjoining islet had been abandoned, the paa was overrun with rats (perhaps introduced by the *Endeavour*), and Topaa and his Motuara people were nowhere to be seen.

When the *Adventure* returned to Totara-nui in April, and the *Resolution* in May of 1773, people in the Sound were far from overjoyed. Their memories of the visit of the *Endeavour* (which they called 'Tupaia's ship', after the Raiatean high priest on board) and its aftermath were vivid. Several people had been shot during those few weeks, supplies of dried fish had been depleted and new maladies had been introduced. At first they stayed away from the ships, but the lure of curiosity, and iron nails and tools, gradually brought them back on board. Groups from other places (including a powerful party from Te Raawhiti led by Te Ratu) began to arrive in the Sound, bringing 'curiosities' – weapons, cloaks, musical instruments and greenstone – to exchange with the Europeans. Although venereal diseases were already established on shore, during this stay there were signs that sexual transactions with the sailors, which had formerly been voluntary and private, were being transformed into involuntary and sometimes public acts controlled by men in a new kind of barter. And one of the families in the Sound, headed by Te Wahanga (who were probably visitors from Ngaai Tahu), spent much time on board the *Resolution*, supplying the ship with fish and establishing a relationship with Cook that led to two of its younger members (Koa and Te Weherua) later sailing away with the Europeans.

While the people of Totara-nui sought to profit from the strangers, they also challenged them. The seaborne trials of strength that began during this visit, directed at isolated European boats, were signs that at least some of them, if they could, would attack the strangers. 'Pilfering' of goods, almost unheard of during the *Endeavour* visit, became endemic during this stay, probably as utu or return for the resources (wood, water, greens and fish) taken by the Europeans without permission. Such confiscation of property, known as muru in Maori, was a way of settling conflicts without resource to war. Above all, Europeans were becoming familiar. They and their ships could no longer be taken as bizarre, unprecedented phenomena. Once three such vessels had come into the Sound, local people had to anticipate that more would likely follow.

The *Resolution*'s return to the Sound in November 1773, after a foray to the Society Islands and Tonga, was greeted with resignation and no evident surprise. Some of the people whom Cook had met during the *Endeavour* voyage were back in the Sound by then, and several families who had exchanged goods with the Europeans during their last visit came quickly back to the ship. Te Ratu and his people, who had previously seemed so affluent and powerful, had little to offer this time, and came to Indian Cove primarily to plunder the Europeans, then left. Te Wahanga and his family re-established their connection with Cook, camping nearby and supplying the ship with greenstone curiosities as well as fish. Hitihiti, a young man from Borabora, was on board during this visit to act as an interpreter (although by now some of the marines could speak good Maori), and the first close relationship between a Maori woman and a European man began. Towards the end of the *Resolution*'s second stay, the people (Ngaati Kurii?) who had replaced Te Ratu's group at Indian Cove went raiding their enemies to the west, with some fatalities, and captured 'curiosities' to exchange with the Europeans. They also brought home an enemy body, and when Pickersgill traded for its head, they gave the Europeans 'proof positive' of cannibalism, laughing at Hitihiti's and the Europeans' horror at the sight of humans eating other human beings.

The *Adventure*, which had been separated from the *Resolution* in a storm off Cape Palliser, arrived back in the Sound on 30 November 1773, just a week after the *Resolution* had left. Mai, a young commoner from Huahine, was on board the ship, and like Hitihiti he quickly learned to speak some Maori. Almost as soon as the shore camp was established, people started to prowl around the tents at night. The *Adventure* was a smaller ship than the *Resolution,* with a smaller crew, and must have seemed more vulnerable. A local man was caught taking goods from the tents and was shot and wounded, and a canoe was taken in reprisal. Two days later, as the ship was preparing to leave the Sound, a quarrel flared up in Grass Cove, and a boatload of men commanded by Jack Rowe, who had been sent there to cut grass, were killed.

By this time many people in Totara-nui had good reasons to resent the Europeans. A man had been shot, the succession of visits by European vessels had depleted local resources, and the lure of European goods had sent some groups off to raid their enemies for goods to barter, with unfortunate results. Nor did the Europeans appear to realise that fishing grounds, streams and woods were controlled by particular groups, who ought to be asked for their permission before these were used. In addition, three of the men who were killed that day (Woodhouse, the midshipman, Cavanagh, and Milton, of eleven infected men on the ship at that time) carried venereal diseases. It is unlikely that the local people realised that these men were involved in the new 'mate', or illnesses, that had struck them, but they must certainly have connected these maladies with the Europeans.

Nevertheless, the attack on the Europeans does not appear to have been premeditated. This is a point on which almost all subsequent accounts agree. So far as can be determined, a European took an adze and refused to give anything in return, some bread (or a jacket) was snatched, there was a scuffle followed by shootings, and all ten of the boat's crew, including Furneaux's black servant, were killed. At the feast in Grass Cove that followed, however, when the sailors were cut up and cooked, families for miles around must have been involved. Burney said in his report to Furneaux that he recognised a canoe (which carried a cock) from Shag Cove on the beach, and the numbers at the gathering (although Furneaux's estimate of fifteen hundred to two thousand people was surely exaggerated) were huge.

The *Adventure*'s was the fourth documented stay by a European vessel in Totara-nui. The pattern of rising local tensions, minor trials of strength, raiding for property (known as muru), violent European responses and a final catastrophic attack echoes with uncanny precision the killing of Marion du Fresne and his men in the Bay of Islands, just six months earlier in June 1772. As in that case, it took some weeks for tensions to develop into open conflict, and almost all of the key people of the region became involved in the final ritual feasting on the Europeans.

Cannibalism among Maori was not arbitrary, but a devastating act of retribution. Where there had been hara, or offences against mana, there had to be utu (or some kind of return). If the return gesture brought matters back into balance, the sequence of exchanges could terminate. If the return was too little, or excessive, the exchanges carried on. The illnesses brought by the Europeans to Totara-nui were understood as spiritual attacks, caused by the strangers' ancestor gods. In the case of venereal disease, and perhaps tuberculosis and other diseases that may have been transferred, they attacked others with whom the victim had intimate relations, leading to a series of hara associated with the visitors. There had been many other aggressions, including the shootings at the shore camp and by Rowe in Grass Cove. For such offences the most effective retribution was to cook the offender's body, especially the head, and to eat it, conquering his or her mana by 'biting the head' of their god. This was a ritual procedure and intensely tapu, involving the leaders of all groups whose members had been harmed. When Burney and his men descended on Grass Cove, therefore, they interrupted such a ritual. The shootings that followed were a shocking reassertion of spiritual power by the Europeans, unprecedented in local terms.

It is not surprising that the *Resolution*'s last two visits to the Sound were difficult and uneasy. Everybody knew that the crews of the two ships had been closely connected, and the local people anticipated a devastating revenge. When the *Resolution* returned to the Sound in October 1774, the people tried to stay away from the Europeans; and when that failed, they tried to conceal the fate of the *Adventure*'s men. No-one dared to tell Cook what had happened, although they gossiped to some of the sailors. There was no Polynesian on board this time to talk with the local people, and right to the end of his stay Cook did not believe the rumours. None of the people whom they had previously met seemed to be present in the Sound. The only local kin groups they encountered were those led by Matahoua, and a larger, allied group (probably Ngaati Kurii of Ngaai Tahu) led by Te Ringapuhi, which had its settlements in Tory Channel near the south end of the Sound.

Cook's final visit to Totara-nui in February 1777, during his last Pacific voyage, was difficult for the local people to fathom. Although he knew all about the Grass Cove killings, Cook had no intention of retaliating, despite the fact that he had two large ships and many men and guns. Te Wahanga was back in the Sound, and his young kinsman Te Weherua (whose father Toka had been killed along with many of Te Ringapuhi's people several months earlier) attached himself to Cook and Mai. Matahoua (Te Ringapuhi's son-in-law) was also present, although having lied to Cook about the Grass Cove killings, he did his best to avoid the Europeans. When Cook visited Grass Cove, however, Matahoua and a companion boldly challenged him. Through Mai, Cook was finally told exactly what had happened to Rowe and his companions in Grass Cove. A man called Kahura, who had already been on board the *Resolution* once or twice (and who seems to have been of Rangitaane descent) was named as the ringleader, and on the expedition's last day in the Sound he came back on board the ship. When Mai realised that although Cook knew that this man had killed and eaten his people, he would not retaliate, he was incredulous. And when Kahura asked to have his portrait drawn by Webber, he was surely taunting the Europeans.

Many of Cook's men resented his leniency. In Maori terms, too, he was acting like a man without mana. His ancestor gods had been dishonoured, but he did nothing about it, for all his men and weapons. Although his young friend Te Weherua had realised that he, at least, would not be punished, he must also have been baffled. When Te Weherua and Koa left Totara-nui to travel to Tahiti on board the *Resolution* in February 1777, it was, in every respect, a leap into the unknown.

Te Weherua and Koa never returned to Totara-nui to tell of their Polynesian odyssey, or to explain more about the Europeans. In any case their homeland was forever changed. People had died from venereal disease and shootings, and pigs, chickens, goats and rats had been introduced, as well as a variety of European plants. Women had been used in sexual barter; children had been conceived and born (many years later, a red-headed, bearded man was described as having been fathered by one of Cook's sailors[2]); iron, Tahitian and European cloth and other European items had been obtained; and there had been numerous outbreaks of violence. Some of these strange visitors had been killed and eaten, so they were not invulnerable. And their highest leader, despite his formidable military resources, did nothing to protect their mana or take utu as one might have expected. Totara-nui people had to accept that there was a new kind of tangata (human being) in the landscape, whose behaviour was difficult to fathom. Life in the Sound would never be the same again.

ETHNOGRAPHIC 'ACCOUNTS' OF TOTARA-NUI
1773–1777

Between 1770 and 1777, repeated visits by European ships brought other Maori kin groups to Totara-nui, new wealth, new excitement, new diseases, and new causes for conflict and distress. Yet out of this chaos and consternation, the European scientists produced accounts of Totara-nui that neatly sorted local life into topical headings, placing local people within a global hierarchy of 'savages', 'barbarians' and 'civilisation'. A world patterned by the interactive flows of whakapapa was reinscribed by grids of 'universal' categories; local places, people, animals and plants were renamed; local time and space were reframed in maps and logs and journals. In

New Zealand, as elsewhere, imperial control was rehearsed in the imagination and on paper long before it happened in practical fact.

The scientists realised some of the limits of their 'Accounts'. Johann Forster remarked, for instance, that 'the very short stay we make in all the places we touch at, is so small a portion of time, that if properly divided between Sleep, the time for dining & the other meals, the going ashore, the coming back, the waiting for boats etc., the observing the manners & customs, writing down a few Vocables, looking out for plants, walking over large tracts of Ground, shooting a few birds, etc., it is hardly credible, that we could do so much as we really did'.[3]

In addition, they acknowledged the difficulties of understanding what was going on in communities where they did not speak local languages. Even in the Society Islands, where their contacts were the closest (both on shore, and with the different islanders who travelled with them on the ships), they knew that their understanding of esoteric matters was shaky. As William Wales commented on leaving those islands, 'Such are the Hints which my short stay, and leisure from more important Bussiness have enabled me to give of this Island, and its Inhabitants; in all which I have endeavoured to come at truth, and can safely say that if I deceive, I am deceived, which in deed is very possible, where a person lies under the disadvantages of want of Time, and knowledge of the People's language he has to speak of. . .'[4] Moreover, familiarity had blunted observation. The ethnographic descriptions of Maori life recorded during the second and third Cook voyages were noticeably less detailed than those recorded during the *Endeavour* expedition. The thrill of first encounter had passed, and European observers found it difficult to remain attentive.

For all that, the scientists claimed 'eyewitness' authority for their accounts, and expressed no doubts about ordering their experience of exotic peoples according to Western categories. In the Age of Discovery, new plants, animals and people were 'discovered' simultaneously, and by 1770 the project of systematically sorting them was well under way. The 'Great Chain of Being' had long offered one device for ordering all forms of life, with God ruling over angels, humans, animals, plants and rocks, each in their own 'place', in strict analogy with European social arrangements at the time. Entities were further sorted into 'kingdoms' and 'tribes', for as Linnaeus, the Swedish naturalist, commented in 1760, 'we must pursue the great chain of nature till we arrive at its origin; we should begin to contemplate her operations in the human frame, and from thence continue our researches through the various tribes of quadrupeds, birds, reptiles, fishes, insects and worms, till we arrive at the vegetable creation'.[5]

While European kingdoms were being placed under bureaucratic control, so too were the plant and animal 'kingdoms'. Linnaeus' own taxonomic system was used by the scientists on Cook's voyages, and gave a straightforward means of sorting plant and animal life into species and genera. On the Great Chain of Being, 'primitive' and 'barbaric' peoples (including Highland Scots, the Irish and gypsies[6]) were just one step up from the 'higher' animals, so it was logical to handle them in the same way. As fellow human beings, they might have their own ideas on how their lives were organised, but emergent European anthropology saw this as irrelevant to the classificatory task. At the same time, the application of bureaucratic devices to exotic experience – catalogues, pigeonholes, labels and the like – proved powerful in fact. The use of standard, if 'artificial', categories allowed information to be collected, retrieved, collated and compared in an orderly fashion. The scientists sought out plants, animals, people and practices for systematic description, noticing and recording details that might otherwise be missed; and by collecting type specimens (of artefacts and sometimes people, as well as plants and animals), making sketches, and writing down observations of people and practices, they detached information from its original context, giving it mobility in time and space. Once detached, such information could be taken back to metropolitan clearing houses – museums, botanical gardens, zoos, universities, laboratories, and private cabinets and studies – where it could be collated and compared. Reflection on the results of these comparisons generated new enquiries, which then fed back into 'field' observation and collection. The scientists' accounts of what was available for visual inspection were thus informative and often illuminating, dealing with matters that local kinship histories do not recall. In particular, the journal 'Accounts' by Johann Forster (in the second voyage) and William Anderson (in the third) were quite detailed and form the basis of the topic-by-topic description of material life in Totara-nui that follows, under the standard categories in the approximate order that they used.

Land
At the beginning of his generalised 'Account' of Totara-nui, Anderson gave a vivid description of the landscape around the Sound:

> The land every where about the sound is uncommonly mountainous, rising immediately from the sea into large hills with blunted tops. At considerable distances are valleys or rather impressions on their sides, which are not deep, each terminating towards the sea in a small cove with a pebble or sandy beach, behind which is a small flat where the natives generally build their huts at the same time hauling their Canoes up on the Beach. This situation is the more convenient as in every cove a small brook of very fine water emptys itself, in which are some small trout.[7]

Soil and rocks
According to Forster and Anderson, the hills around Totara-nui were covered with a topsoil of rotted vegetation, lying over a layer of yellowish 'marle' about one to two feet thick, and beneath that, strata of yellowish sandstone that were sometimes divided by thin veins of coarse quartz. Forster noted 'some small black smooth Stones of the Flinty order' lying on the shingly beaches (flinty argillite, often used for making tools), along with large pieces of basalt, which he said was made into hand clubs, and pieces of pumice. Anderson also noted a 'green jasper'

(pounamu) used to make tools and weapons, which 'is not found in the sound and is esteem'd a precious article by these people, who have some superstitious notions about the method of its generation which we could not perfectly understand'.[8] According to Cook, the local people said that it came from the channel of a large river far to the south named 'Tovy Poenammo' (te wai pounamu, or greenstone water), in the form of a fish that turned to stone when it was hauled onto land, and that this stone was then traded all over the country. One of the crew managed to acquire a piece of pounamu eighteen inches long, a foot wide and about two inches thick, which had evidently been taken from a larger rock still. Cook commented that travelling strangers, including those who engaged in this trade, were well treated during their stay in a place, although they were 'expected to be [there] no longer than the business they come upon can be transacted'.[9]

Climate
Anderson described the climate as mild, but sometimes windy with heavy rain. He saw no erosion, noting that 'the only obstacle to this being one of the finest countrys on earth is its great hilliness, which allowing the woods to be clear'd away renders it less proper for pasturage than flat land, and still more improper for cultivation which could never be effected here by the plough'.[10] This preoccupation with the possible uses of a place was characteristic of eighteenth-century British thinking, with its focus on 'improvement' and its utilitarian bent. 'Waste lands' at home were being enclosed and pastured; in the Highlands, for instance, enclosure and pasturage were described at this time as 'the two leading steps of improvement, in the uncultivated parts of Scotland . . . introductory to every sort of polishd Culture'.[11]

Plants
Both Anderson and Forster were interested in botany, and this section of their accounts was quite long. Anderson was impressed with the luxuriance of the local plant life: 'The hills . . . are one continued forest of lofty trees which flourish with a vigour almost superior to any thing imagination can conceive, and afford an august prospect to those who are delighted with the grand and beautiful works of nature.'[12] They noted 'spruce-tree' (rimu), which Cook used for making beer; a kind of 'maple' (perhaps one of the beeches), which was served as firewood, since the wood of both this and the 'spruce' was too heavy for masts or yards; a 'tea-tree' (maanuka), whose leaves were brewed as tea; two berry-bearing trees (karaka and tawa) whose berries were eaten by the 'Indians'; 'sow-thistle' (puuhaa), 'lamb's quarters', 'wild celery' and 'scurvy grass', which the Europeans boiled with ground wheat and portable soup (concentrated meat stock), or ate fresh as anti-scorbutics; ferns, whose roots were eaten by the local people; a supplejack, which carried a red berry; and the indigenous flax (harakeke), which according to Anderson 'deserves particular notice, as the natives make their garments of it and it produces a fine silky flax superior in appearance to any thing we have and probably

at least as strong'.[13] There were also 'common and rough Bind-weed, Nightshade and Nettles . . . a shruby Speedwell found near all the Beeches, Sow thistles, Virgins bower, Vanelloe, French willow, Euphorbia, and Cranes bill: Eyebright and groundsel . . . besides a great number of other plants whose uses are not yet known and only subjects fit for Botanical books'.[14]

Local plants were examined first of all for their utility, in the hope that they might be of value to the home society as well as to mariners. Flax and timber trees, for instance, were essential materials for naval power – flax for making canvas, ropes and rigging; and timber trees for planks, masts and yards. Britain was fighting so many sea battles in this period that an inexhaustible supply of replacement sails, rigging, masts and spars was required. In addition, the local biota was modified by the deliberate introduction of useful European plants. Forster remarked that 'in case the roots & greens in the Gardens we planted succeed there will be plenty of all European Garden-stuff, viz: Strawberries, Garlick, Onions, Sweet Oranges, wheat, Beans, Pease, French beans, Carrots, Parsley, Sellery, Scorzonera & various Sallat herbs & above all, the most precious plant we left here will be the Potatoe, which in length of time will become one of the finest Substitutes for bread, for future Navigators & the Natives'.[15] Potatoes were being planted at home as a substitute for grain crops, in case of harvest failure and famine, and this cheerful shifting around of plants (as well as people) was common-place European imperial practice at the time.

Birds
William Bayly, the astronomer, gave a vivid account of local birdlife. He noted

> great numbers of large grey Parrots that have very beautiful plumage and small Parroquets flying in great plenty so that I frequently killed two or three at one shot. I saw two kinds of small Hawkes, & a small grey owl. There are plenty of large Wood Pigeons much the same as Wood Pigeons in England. There great plenty of a kind of birds much resembling our black birds, except they have a few white feathers in the wings and tail . . . & under the throat are 4 fine curling white feathers growing in a tuff. These are called Poey-birds [tuuii]. They are thought to be the finest eating for delicacy & richness & far to exceed the Otterlin so much esteemed by the Epicureans. There are likewise great variety of Beautiful singing Birds which made the Woods ecco with their different Notes which made the greatest harmony. When we came first into Charlotte Sound we found great plenty of Shel-drakes, Curlues, Ducks & Divers all which we found to be very good eating.[16]

Birds were shot for scientific specimens as well as food, and Anderson added that 'a person by remaining in one place may shoot as many in one day as would serve six or eight others'.[17] He also mentioned two kinds of cuckoo, the saddle-back, the orange-wattled crow, the bellbird, the South Island robin and tomtit, fantail, kingfisher, weka and an array of sea birds.

Fish

The Europeans caught mullet and elephant fish in their seine nets, as well as sole and flounder, while local people supplied them primarily with tarakihi, moki and conger eel. In addition, the sailors caught blue cod (raawaru) and goatfish with hook and line, and sometimes 'small salmon' (kahawai?), gurnard (kumukumu), skate and 'nurses'; while local people occasionally brought them hake, barracouta (makaa), 'small mackerel', parrotfish and butterfish. According to Anderson, 'All these sorts except the last which we did not try are excellent to eat, but the Mogge [moki], small Salmon and Cole-fish [raawaru] are superior to the rest.'[18]

Shellfish

Anderson described rocks covered with quantities of mussels, including one variety more than a foot long. There were cockles in the sandy bays, and small, delicious oysters on the rocks. Other shellfish included periwinkles, whelks, limpets, sea-eggs (kina) and 'sea-ears' (paaua). In addition, 'the indians . . . sometimes brought us Craw fish equal to our largest lobsters, which are very fine, and cuttle fish which they eat themselves'.[19]

Insects and reptiles

Anderson recorded that 'insects are very rare, of which we only saw two sorts of Dragonflies, some Butterflies, small grasshoppers, several sorts of spiders, some small black Ants and vast numbers of Scorpion flies [cicadas] which as we mention'd before fill the woods with their chirping. The only noxious one is the sand flie which are very numerous and almost as troublesome as the Muskitoe, for no reptile is found here except two or three sorts of small harmless Lizards.'[20] Lizards, however, were regarded as harbingers of the spirit world by Maori, and anything but harmless.

Quadrupeds

Quadrupeds were also extremely rare in Totara-nui. Anderson noted only 'a few Rats and a sort of fox Dogs the last of which are a Domesticated Animal with the natives'.

People – their physical appearance

The people in Totara-nui were described as 'stout and nervous' (i.e. robust and sinewy) and not particularly tall by European standards, but active and well limbed in the upper body. Forster, Anderson and others remarked that their legs seemed small and bandy (a feature noted here for the first time by European observers), which was variously ascribed to 'sitting for the most part on their hams', the hilly local environment or being constantly in canoes. Few were 'corpulent', or fat. According to Anderson, they varied in colour from a yellowish tinge, to olive and 'pretty deep black', with strong white teeth and 'the eyes large with a very free motion which seems the effect of habit'. Most people had straight black hair, but some had curly or brown hair. The chiefs, in particular, were impressive. John Ledyard commented that 'among all the savage sons of war I ever saw, [these] are the most formidable. When a New-Zealander stands forth and brandishes his spear the subsequent idea is (and nature makes the confession) there stands a man.'[21]

'There stands a man'. Engraving of an unknown rangatira, after Sydney Parkinson.

Ornaments

In his second voyage 'Account', Furneaux gave a good description of styles of ornamentation in the Sound:

> Their hair [is] strong and tied on the top of their head with a Comb or feather stuck in it. All the men that have distinguished themselves in war, are marked with spiral circles which is done by pricking or cuting the skin 'till it bleeds and rubbing the dye on the wounds, this mark continues for life and is called tattowing; they likewise scratch the forehead with a sharp stone for that purpose, after the death of a friend or parent, making a most lamentable noise. They are very fond of red paint and esteem it a great ornament. One of our gentlemen painted upwards of thirty of them one morning with vermilion, they gave him several things and insisted on him taking them. The Ladies go always painted with a dark greasy red of their own making out of Earth mixed with their oil, and have small pieces of it tied up in a piece of cloath round their necks in the manner of a Locket, and often smell to it; their heads decorated with bunches of feathers of different colours. Their necklaces of Paroquets' bills, birds bones or other such triffles, at which they hang several ornaments down their breast, they have holes in their ears, at which hangs several bunches of human teeth preserved as relicts of a deceased friend, and are in great subjection to the men.[22]

'The thin inner skin of some leaf' was sometimes worn on the head, and some head combs were decorated with 'pearlshell' (presumably paaua). Ear ornaments included bunches of white feathers, dogskin, an oblong piece of greenstone or beads; and a few people had holes bored through the septum of their noses, to carry ornaments on occasion. Neck ornaments included strings of human teeth, and 'a green Stone carved in the Shape of a Mans face, with Eyes of Mother of Pearl, & various spirals' (the tiki). Long beards were common, although people liked to be shaved, and most people had one lip tattooed blue, while women might have a small spot tattooed on the chin, while men's facial tattoos were often incomplete – say, just on one side of the face.

Clothing

Forster gave an excellent description of local clothing:

> Their bodies are covered with a kind of Mat, made of their Flax, wove in a very regular manner, & which often have a fine border worked in black red & white [taaniko] with so great symmetry, taste & elegance that it deserves really the Attention even of polished Nations, who have the Arts among themselves. Some of these Mats are only wove losely, others quite close, & some I saw quite black, others black & white. The black is strongly fixed upon the Flax & would therefore deserve the Attention of our Manufacturers, for we want very much a good lasting black dye, which might be fixed on flax & cotton. This Mat is fixed before by a string about the Neck, with a bodkin ['haroee' – aurii] of bone or whalebone, & below the loins fastened by a belt ['tatooa' – tatua] made of their cloth or a kind of Matting. The Arms & legs are naked. Over this mat which they call Taigook [tieke] they wear in winter another, which is of a loose texture & is on the outside quite

shaggy, which they tie round their Necks & let it hang round the body, it is called kagheeoe [kaakahu] . . . When [the women] dance among themselves they have a kind of small apron to cover their nudities made of their cloath, covered with fine red Parrot feathers, surrounded with white Dogskin & ornamented with a few Pieces of Mother of Pearl. They call this kind of Figleaf Koora [kura – red]. Sometimes they have bunches of feathers on their heads called by them Epoohee [he puhi], which is wove on a kind of stuff, & tied by strings under the Chin.[23]

Anderson added that the fine capes were about five feet long by four broad, and often ornamented with dogskin or chequered at the corners. Some were entirely covered with dogskin, while others had large feathers of birds woven into them.

Weapons
Forster described local weapons as including a long wooden spear ('ahhoat' – huata) about twenty to thirty feet long; short darts about five or six feet long called 'togho-togho' (tokotoko); the 'maheepehh' (maipi), or wooden battle-axe with a curved point and below that the shape of a paddle, which men wielded with great dexterity and elegance; and the 'emetee' (mere) or 'petepetow' (patupatu) – hand clubs of stone, wood or bone. According to Bayly, 'this weapon . . . is always carried under the girdle. There is a hole made thro' its small end or handle & a string tied to it that goes over the hand in time of action to prevent its being lost on their being disarmed as it might prove fatal to them for they depend greatly on these when fighting at close quarters.'[24]

Canoes
Small canoes in the south were commonly fitted with outriggers in this period. All of the observers mention them in Totara-nui. The largest canoes were about fifty feet long (appreciably shorter than those further north) and five feet wide, with a dugout hull built up with planks bored with small holes along the edges, through which flax rope was threaded to tie the planks together. The same rope held long battens tightly in place over the seams, which were caulked with raupoo (bullrush) to make the canoes waterproof. Double canoes were also common. Canoe crews ranged between five and thirty men, who paddled in unison with narrow, pointed paddles about five feet long, which moved the canoes swiftly along. The tall, triangular sails were infrequently used, although on one occasion, three canoes were seen sailing in the Sound. Forster described the sail as having 'on its extremity five tufts of brown feathers, it is fixed to a kind of mast & folds out, so that the other beam below forms an acute angle with the mast & the sail is in a triangular shape or nearly, tapering towards the bottom & having the broadest side uppermost with the abovementioned feathers'.[25]

Larger and double canoes had finely carved prows and sternposts. A human figure with its tongue lolling out and paaua eyes was often carved at the prow, surrounded by interlocked open spirals. The paddles, sideboards and bailers were also sometimes carved, and carved canoes were painted red (the tapu colour).

Tools
According to Anderson, the Totara-nui people 'make every thing by which they procure their subsistance, cloathing and warlike weapons with a great degree of neatness, strength, and convenience for accomplishing their several purposes'.[26] Adzes, chisels and gouges were made of greenstone or basalt, and adzes were hafted and lashed to wooden handles. Knives were made from shells, pieces of flint or greenstone. Augers were made with a shark's tooth fixed into the end of a piece of wood. A small saw made with sharp fish teeth attached to a carved wooden handle was used only to cut up the bodies of enemies killed in war.

Weaving
Forster commented enthusiastically on the local flax, which he said 'would on account of its gloss, fineness, strength & perennial growth deserve to be transplanted into Europe & soon become one of the most usefull materials for manufactories in Linnen, Canvas, & rope'.[27] He thought that it would be difficult to transplant, however, for the seeds were fine and would probably be ruined during the northward passage through the tropics. Blades of flax, or 'Arakeke' (harakeke), were split and woven into hoop nets, beaten roughly for rope, plaited into mats and little baskets for fernroot, fish, and berries, or worked into fine silky fibre (muka) for clothing. Garments were woven by the women, who worked from four weaving sticks stuck in the ground.

Fishing and birding
Large quantities of fish were caught in the Sound with hoop nets or by well-plaited lines, with wooden hooks pointed with bone. In addition, the local people used long spears to kill birds while waiting beneath trees frequented by particular species.

Cooking and eating
Fish, birds and roots of the mamaku (which yielded a substance like boiled sago powder) were wrapped in flax leaves and cooked in earth ovens. These were made by digging a hole, making a fire and heating stones until they were red hot. The oven was then emptied of the fire materials and the food parcels were put in and covered with hot stones or embers. Birds and fish might also be spitted and roasted, but only when the cooks were in a hurry. Fernroot was dried and then roasted over a fire and eaten, or beaten until soft with a stick, when the soft meal was extracted and formed into small cakes that were roasted over the embers. Paaua, mussels, penguins, shags, rails and, sometimes, dogs were also eaten. The people loved blubber and train oil, and mouldy biscuits, and eagerly sought these foods from the Europeans – probably because of their similarity to local delicacies such as shark oil, whale meat, muttonbirds, fernroot and raupo pollen cakes. Head lice

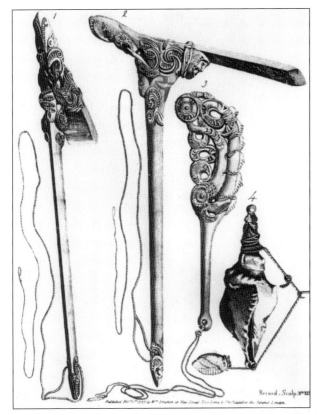

Above left: *A hafted greenstone adze, a carving knife and a shell trumpet, sketched after the second voyage in London.*

Above: *New Zealand flax, engraved in London in 1777, from a sketch by one of the Forsters.*

Left: *The tuuii, engraved in London in 1777, from a sketch by Johann Forster.*

155

were also cracked and eaten, a habit that disgusted the sailors. Anderson noted, however, that their taste for some foods that Europeans found disgusting 'must not be imputed to any defect in their sensations for I have observ'd them throw away things which we eat, with evident disgust, after only smelling to it'.[28]

The local people drank only cold fresh water, and there was no local form of liquor. The Europeans reported no great enthusiasm for the alcohol (rum, arrack, wine, etc.) that was freely available on board the ships. During all of their visits to Totara-nui, only one young boy is reported to have got drunk.

Settlements

The Totara-nui people lived in small coves, in groups of forty or fifty, or some-times in single families with no more than three or four children. Anderson gave a detailed description of their dwellings:

> The best I ever saw was about thirty feet long, fifteen broad and six high, built exactly in the manner of one of our country barns. The inside was both strongly and regularly made of supporters at the sides, alternately large and small, well fastend with withs and painted red and black. The ridge pole was strong and the large Bull rushes which compos'd the inner part of the thatching laid with great exactness parallel to each other. At one end was a small square hole which serv'd as a door to creep in at, and near it another much smaller whose use seem'd to be for letting out the smoke as no other vent for it could be seen. This however ought to be considerd as one of the best and probably the residence of some principal person; for the greatest part of them are not half the size and seldom exceed four feet in heighth . . . No other furniture is to be seen in them than a few small baskets or bags in which they put their fishing hooks and other triffles, and they sit down in the middle round a small fire where they also probably sleep, without any other covering than what they wear in the day or perhaps without that, as such small places must be very warm with but a few persons.[29]

Furneaux added that there was one fire near the door of such houses and another inside, and 'their bed places are raised about Six Inches above the Ground

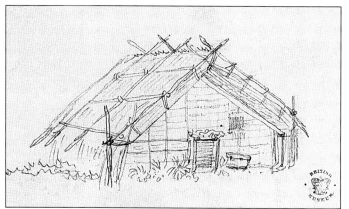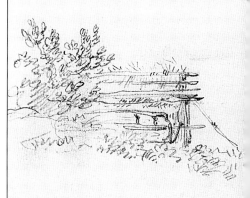

Two Maori houses, one with a carved door lintel, sketched by John Webber in Totara-nui, 1777.

with dry rushes and Grass, and freathed [wattled] round of the same height'.[30] No carving was mentioned on Totara-nui houses, although one of John Webber's sketches seems to show a carved door lintel on the front wall of a house.

Population, migrations and origins

Johann Forster noted that while the South Island had relatively few inhabitants, the North Island was more densely populated. The *Resolution* visited only Dusky and Queen Charlotte Sounds in New Zealand, so he and George had little basis for arriving at a reliable estimate of the overall population of both islands. Nevertheless, they offered a tentative figure of a hundred thousand, while commenting that 'we rather think our estimate to fall short of the true population'.[31] Indeed, later estimates of Maori population given by Europeans visiting the upper North Island were generally much higher.[32] In trying to deduce the original homeland of the populations of New Zealand and Tahiti, Forster dismissed the Americas on the grounds that there were no discernible similarities between Maori, Tahitian, and American languages. Rather, he inferred after comparing various Pacific vocabularies that 'these islanders came originally from the Indian Asiatic isles'.[33]

Marriage and morality

According to Anderson,

> Polygamy is an establish'd custom amongst them, some having two or three wives, and though the young women grant all the freedoms that can be desir'd to strangers and are even encourag'd to it by the men, yet those in a married state are punishd by the husband with a severe beating if guilty of Adultery. Indeed the women seem to be totally at their devotion, on whom they sometimes impose very disagreeable commands which they dare not refuse to comply with, and it is in consequence of this they suffer much from a loathsome disease which we have communicated without as yet giving them any real advantage as a recompence.[34]

The Europeans were aware, however, that the 'fine girls' were kept from them in Totara-nui, and that some of the women who were being brought to the ships (probably mostly war captives) were being forced to sleep with them in exchange for European goods. Prostitution (sex for barter) was a new practice, which had not been reported during previous European voyages to New Zealand. Like Cook and the Forsters, Anderson deplored the spread of venereal diseases, which was a by-product of such traffic with Europeans:

> If civilis'd nations entail misery on any part of mankind more ignorant than themselves, both justice and humanity requires that they should alleviate them as far as lyes in their power by every possible means; yet this is so far from being the case that we often add one to another till we have almost destroy'd whole nations from avaricious motives, to the great disgrace of those whose superior knowledge ought only to be employ'd in relieving the distresses of others.[35]

Expressions of remorse, however, made little practical difference to the conduct of most Europeans on such expeditions.

Child-rearing
Both boys and girls could perform the haka, play the flute and sing chants about their ancestors and their feats in war. At a certain age, the foreskin of many boys was tied over the end of the penis by a string fastened to their belts, while according to Anderson, some of the girls used 'a stopper of dried grass for their chastity'. They became sexually active with each other at an age that in Europe was thought 'detrimental to propogation by impairing the strength of the man while a boy', although Anderson observed drily that 'it appears to have no such effect here'.[36]

Religion
A young boy who accompanied Te Weherua onto the *Resolution* refused to eat after he had had his hair cut one day. He said that 'his god would be angry' if he took food, although by evening he had been persuaded to change his mind. The European observers thought that Totara-nui people believed in a supreme being, whom they (and their priests) often addressed, and King saw hanks of hair tied to trees near their dwellings, which seemed to have some religious significance. Hair was indeed very tapu, a medium of communication with ancestor gods, but as Johann Forster admitted, 'we knew too little of their language for to converse with them. We know therefore but little of their Government, religion and manners.'[37]

Mourning
According to Burney, people often shed tears at parting, and never left each other without joining noses (hongi), even if their absence was to be brief. They slashed themselves and wept when friends returned and in times of mourning, and buried the bodies, but if they had killed more enemies than they could eat, bodies were thrown into the sea.

Leadership and disputes
Anderson commented that:

> There appears to be little subordination and consequently few if any laws to punish transgressions; for no mans authority seems to extend farther than his own family, and when at any time they join for their mutual defence or other purpose those eminent for courage or prudence are directors. How their private quarrels are terminated is uncertain, but in the few we saw, which were of little consequence, they were clamorous and disorderly.[38]

Language
Both Anderson and the Forsters collected vocabularies of Maori, which Johann Forster later used for comparative purposes, while Samwell collected texts of chants and songs. Anderson considered the language melodious and 'sufficiently comprehensive, though in many respects deficient if compar'd with our European languages which owe their perfection to long improvement'[39] – an illuminating remark.

158

Character

Cook repeatedly described Maori as a 'brave, open and honest' people after his first and second voyages to New Zealand. By the end of the third voyage, however, with its revelations about the killings at Grass Cove, he and his companions changed their minds about Maori. Anderson described the local people as 'insolent', 'dishonest' and 'mistrustful', and Cook himself now portrayed them as violent and often treacherous:

> The New Zealanders must live under perpetual apprehinsions of being distroyed by each other. There being few Tribes that have not received some injury or a nother from some other, which they are continually upon the watch to revenge and perhaps the idea of a good meal may be no small incitement. I am told that many years will sometimes elapse before a favourable oppertunity happens, and that the Son never losses sight of an injury that has been done his Father. There method of executing these horrible designs is by stealing upon the party in the night, and if they find them unguarded (which however I beleive is very seldom the case) they kill every soul that falls in their way, not even sparing the Women and Children, and then either feast and gorge themselves on the spot or carry off as many of the dead as they can and do it at home with acts of brutality horrible to relate. If they are discovered before they can put their design into execution, they generally steal off again, some times they are persued and attacked by the other party; they neither give quarter nor take prisoners [which was quite untrue], so that the Vanquish'd can only save their lives by flight. This method of makeing War keeps them continually upon their guard so that one hardly ever finds a New Zealander of his guard either day or night.[40]

Cook's portrait of local life, to judge from Totara-nui kinship histories, was accurate in part. Utu (some kind of return) was sought for hara, or offences, over generations if necessary; ambushes and night attacks were not uncommon; women and children were sometimes (but by no means always) killed in utu attacks; and enemies were certainly eaten. At the same time, his comments were also inaccurate in part. Women, children and some men were often taken captive, and disputes could be settled by strategic marriages, gifts of land or other reparation, or raids (muru) in which property was taken but nobody was killed.

Cook (who after all had known incessant warfare in Europe in his own lifetime, and who had been responsible for a number of local killings) had been moved to bitter reflection by his first-hand knowledge about what had happened in Grass Cove, and in consequence had changed his mind about the 'New Zealanders'. Others of his officers made sharp-edged comments of their own. Anderson, for instance, claimed that the local people 'destroy their prisoners one after the other and never spare any, even murdering the women whom they cohabit with untill their fate is determin'd. They do not eat the heads but keep them and fix the eyes in the same staring manner as when they advance to fight, and in that manner sometimes dry them, at other time throwing away both that and the entrails, but of the Penis of the men they commonly make a musical pipe [a very curious claim]'.[41] He described them in the haka (or war dance) as 'more like infernal daemons than men and would almost chill the boldest with fear'. In these and other comments, an image of Maori as ferocious cannibals was being dramatically constructed.

The ambush of Tasman's cockboat, the killing of Marion du Fresne in the Bay of Islands and the deaths at Grass Cove were iconic 'massacres' for Europeans, proofs of the power of wild savages, markers that, in the end, the 'other' could never be trusted. In dealing with such people, violence was not only prudent but proper. It is no accident that after finding out first-hand what had happened at Grass Cove, Cook and Clerke (urged on by Mai) turned to extreme violence elsewhere in the Pacific (shooting, flogging, ear cropping, the shaving of heads, burning houses and canoes, taking chiefs hostage) to assert their 'proper superiority' over Polynesians.

Maori, however, to judge from various oral accounts recorded last century, understood matters quite differently. In Taitapu, the Bay of Islands and Totara-nui, Europeans were seen as strangers who had breached local mana. Their hara (or offences) – capturing or striking chiefs, fishing in a tapu bay – were offences against ancestor gods as well as people, which required utu if further disasters were to be avoided. The killings were seen as reparation, and the ritual cannibalism that so horrified the Europeans was part of local protocols of punishment.

In the 1770s, both Europeans and Maori could, and did, claim virtue for their actions, although on very different grounds and not without difficulty (as local criticisms of Kahura, and European criticisms of Jack Rowe for their part in the Grass Cove killings attest). And both sides were violent: Maori fought often (although rather less so than popular mythology suggests) at that time, and punishment was physically harsh (including killing, captivity and torture); while in eighteenth-century Europe there were endless wars, and punishment included flogging, hangings, the cropping of ears, slavery in the galleys and judicial torture. Claiming 'proper superiority' (for one side or the other, or ourselves, for that matter) is a perilous act of politics, for scholars as well as for the protagonists whose lives they try to understand.

William Hodges's painting of the Resolution *at anchor in Pickersgill Harbour, with its ready-made gangway.*

Capt.ᵗ James Cook of the Endeavour.

Right: *Captain James Cook, painted by William Hodges during his second Pacific voyage.*

Left above: *A view of the man with his taiaha (here painted over-size) and his female companions carrying spears in Cascade Cove.*

Left below: *Waterspouts off Cape Stephens, as the* Resolution *entered Totara-nui in 1773.*

Below: *Cook meets Totara-nui men on the beach in 1777 — perhaps a depiction of his meeting with 'Pedro' in Grass Cove.*

Above: *The paa on 'Hippa Island', painted by John Webber in 1777.*

Below: *The tents set up in Meretoto (Ship Cove), 1777.*

Seven

LATER SCIENTIFIC VOYAGES
MALASPINA AND D'ENTRECASTEAUX

At the same moment that Maori were being brought under European hierarchies, other groups within and outside Europe were shaking off their chains. In America it was asserted that all men were created equal, with an inalienable right to liberty, and that legitimate governments must be based upon consent by the governed – a sharp attack on subordination and the theories that propped it up. In Russia and the Netherlands there were uprisings, and in Sweden the King was shot. The American war eventually involved France, Spain and the Netherlands (on the colonists' side) against Britain, and people in those countries listened as American colonists invoked the Rights of Man. In Ireland the Protestants claimed legislative independence, and in London the Gordon riots broke out. All over Europe, rulers who had sponsored wars found their subjects restless, and recalcitrant about paying the costs in duties and taxes. In France, where their part in the American war had cost a hundred million livres, Louis XVI's ministers proposed sweeping reforms underpinned by universal taxes, which outraged both nobles and the clergy. Their angry protests, supported by many bourgeois, provoked the King into asserting his authority. Nobles and episcopal clergy banded together to resist the King and bourgeois interests; crop failures and famine in 1788–89 provoked riots in Paris; the French guards joined the insurgents, and the King's agents were lynched. Just as Te Ao Tawhito (the ancient world) in the South Pacific was jittering on its foundations, so too in Europe was the *ancien régime*.

For all that, the scientific voyages carried on. The next expedition to visit New Zealand was headed by George Vancouver, a British naval officer who had sailed with Cook during his second voyage on the *Resolution*. In 1790, Vancouver was ordered to receive back properties at Nootka Sound on the north-west coast of Canada from the Spanish, to return a Hawaiian to his home island, and to complete Cook's survey of that coast in a final search for the North-West Passage. The story of this expedition's encounters with Moriori and Maori in 1791 and 1793 is so entangled with the establishment of the British penal colony in Australia (which

was shifted from Botany Bay to Port Jackson, and grew into the town of Sydney)
that it will be discussed under that heading in the next section of this work.

MALASPINA'S VISIT TO DOUBTFUL SOUND
25 February 1793

After Vancouver, the next visit to New Zealand was by a Spanish expedition headed by
Alejandro Malaspina, an Italian nobleman commanding two Spanish ships. This voyage
had been proposed by Malaspina to Carlos III of Spain as a survey of his imperial
possessions and a demonstration of Spanish scientific and navigational prowess:

> For the past twenty years, the two nations of England and France with a noble
> rivalry have undertaken voyages in which navigation, geography and the knowl-
> edge of humanity have made very rapid progress. The history of human society
> has laid the foundation for more general investigations; natural history has been
> enriched with an almost infinite number of discoveries; and finally the preserva-
> tion of man in different climates, in extensive journeys, and among some almost
> incredible tasks and risks, has been the most interesting acquisition which naviga-
> tion has made. The voyage which is being proposed is particularly directed toward
> the completion of these objects; and the aspect which is being called the Scientific
> Part will certainly be carried out with much care, continuing with effectiveness
> the paths of Cook and La Pérouse.[1]

Carlos agreed to Malaspina's proposals, and the expedition left Cadiz in mid-
1789 for South America, just two weeks after the fall of the Bastille in Paris.
During 1790 and 1791, the *Descubierta* and the *Atrevida* sailed up the west coast of
America to the far north beyond Nootka, where two small schooners attached to
the expedition met up with Vancouver and spent three weeks in his company.
Malaspina had scientists and artists with him, lavishly equipped with scientific
instruments and even a harmonium. As they mapped American harbours and coasts,
the scientists conducted experiments and collected numerous specimens of plants
and animals. Late in 1791, the expedition left the west coast from Acapulco, crossing
the Pacific on the path of the Manila Galleon to Guam, Macao and Mindanao,
where a number of scurvy-stricken sailors were replaced by Filipinos. From
Mindanao, Malaspina headed east back into the Pacific, sighting Erromango in
Vanuatu before turning south for New Zealand. His orders directed him to examine Doubtful and Dusky Sounds at the south-west end of the South Island, where
the scientists had been instructed to carry out 'some experiments in gravity', but
'not at any danger to the security of the crew and ships', and to make their findings 'available to all European nations'.[2]

On 25 February 1793, the ships made a good landfall, arriving to the leeward
of Doubtful Sound. At about midday, Malaspina sent one of his officers, Don Felipe
Bauza, in an armed boat to explore and chart the Sound. Bauza spent the rest of
the day on this mission while the two corvettes tacked off the coast. He landed

briefly on Bauza Island, where he noted only 'a few birds, not a single seal, no shell fish save a few small limpets, and not a sign, however remote, of inhabitants'.[3] The boat arrived back at the ship at nine o'clock, and during the night the weather took a turn for the worse, becalming the vessels, shrouding them in fog and finally driving them in high gales off the coast. After several attempts to tack back to Dusky Bay, Malaspina decided to cut his losses, abandon the experiments

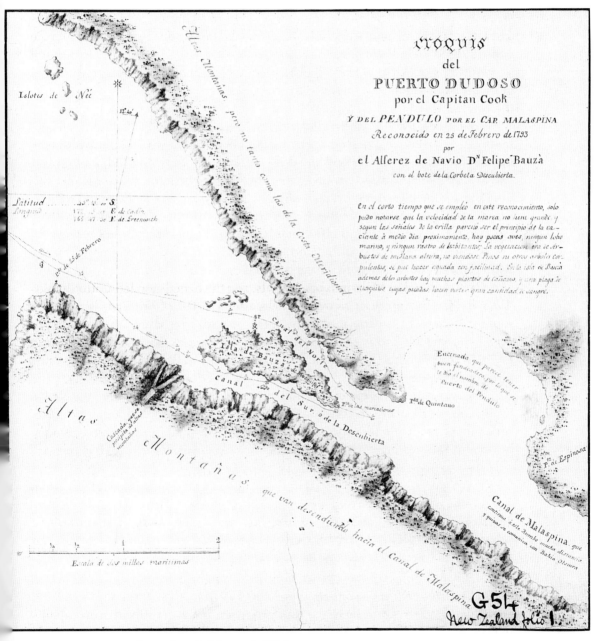

Don Felipe Bauza's chart of Doubtful Sound, 1793.

in gravity and head his battered vessels westward to Port Jackson. So far as Maori life is concerned, the brief visit by this expedition – despite its superb scientific and artistic capacities – offers no revelation, not even of the remotest kind.

D'ENTRECASTEAUX'S VISIT TO MURIWHENUA
11 March 1793

The last scientific expedition to visit New Zealand during this period was a French expedition, searching for Jean-François Galaup de La Pérouse.

In 1785, Louis XVI of France, a keen geographer, had sponsored a great voyage of Pacific exploration, also intended to rival Cook's achievements. The *Astrolabe* and the *Boussole* sailed for the Pacific under the command of La Pérouse, loaded with scientists, trade goods and scientific instruments (including fifty-two plumed helmets and 'aerostatic balloons'). Louis and his advisors had worked out a plan that included visits to New Holland and New Zealand. At New Zealand, La Pérouse was to visit Queen Charlotte Sound, where he was 'to gain intelligence whether the English have formed, or entertain the project of forming, any settlement on these islands; and if he should hear that they have actually formed a settlement, he will endeavour to repair thither in order to learn its condition, strength and object'.[4]

Rumours soon reached England that the French were intending to take a small party of convicts to New Zealand, 'to take possession of that lately discover'd Country'.[5] Although the rumours proved incorrect, and the expedition never visited New Zealand (as far as we know), the ships did head for Botany Bay on the south-east coast of Australia, arriving there just six days after the first convict ships from England had anchored. After cordial exchanges between explorers and the new colonists, the French ships sailed off into the Pacific, never to be seen again by Europeans.

The expedition was expected back in France by 1789, but by then the Revolution was in full swing. In July, the Bastille had fallen and the National Assembly began to write a national constitution. Reformers around Europe were ecstatic: in Britain, Richard Price wrote in his famous *Discourse on the Love of our Country*:

> THIRTY MILLIONS of people, indignant and resolute, spurning at slavery, demanding liberty with an irresistible voice; their king led in triumph, and surrendering himself to his subjects . . . Behold kingdoms . . . starting from sleep, breaking their fetters, and claiming justice from their oppressors! Behold the light, after setting AMERICA free, reflected to FRANCE, and there kindled a blaze that lays despotism in ashes, and warms and illuminates Europe![6]

In the midst of all of this uproar, concerns were raised about the possible loss of the French scientists and their vessels. In 1791, an appeal was sent from the Société d'Histoire Naturelle to the National Assembly, requesting that an expedition should be sent to find them. It ended with a fervent exclamation: 'May they return to our shores, even though they die of joy in embracing this free land!'[7]

The Assembly was receptive, and in 1791 Antoine-Raymond-Joseph de Bruni d'Entrecasteaux, a senior naval officer and experienced Far East navigator, was appointed to take two ships to the Pacific to look for La Pérouse. Again, this was to be a scientific expedition, carrying astronomers, an artist, a hydrographer, and two surgeon-botanists in addition to naval crews. The *Recherche* and *Espérance* sailed from Brest on 29 September 1791 towards Cape Horn, via the Canary Islands. At the Cape, d'Entrecasteaux was handed a letter and reports that claimed that 'natives' wearing French uniforms had been sighted on one of the Admiralty Islands off New Guinea. He headed east across the Indian Ocean towards the Admiralties in his slow and cranky ships, but was forced by adverse winds to turn south towards Van Diemen's Land, where they charted the Derwent River. There were brief meetings with the local people, who soon ran off into the bush, and plants and large numbers of molluscs were collected. As usual there was friction between the scientists and sailors; the sailors persisted in eating the scientists' specimens, while the scientists' collections of shellfish soon stank out the ships. From Van Diemen's Land they sailed on to New Caledonia, the Solomon Islands and New Ireland before arriving at the Admiralties, where local people were spotted on the beaches wearing belts and bracelets that might, at a distance, have been mistaken for uniforms. D'Entrecasteaux sailed his ships slowly right along the archipelago without detecting any sign of the missing vessels.

After this disappointment the expedition briefly visited Amboina in the Dutch East Indies. The Governor there regarded d'Entrecasteaux's papers as suspect, since war had broken out again in Europe, and only reluctantly allowed them to take on food and water. The ships carried on to the southern coast of Australia and back to Van Diemen's Land, where this time local people made friendly overtures, vocabularies were collected and extensive notes written by the scientists about local ways of life. On 27 February 1793, the ships set off for Tonga, but d'Entrecasteaux decided to visit the northern tip of New Zealand on the way. His instructions had advised him to use Cook's observations of the longitude of Cape Maria van Diemen (made during the first voyage and corrected on the second) to check his chronometers and clocks.

There was an extensive library on board the *Recherche*, which had been delivered to d'Entrecasteaux at the beginning of the voyage, and it included accounts, charts and astronomical observations from all three of Cook's Pacific voyages, as well as an account of the voyage of Marion du Fresne.[8] The officers and scientists consulted these accounts of New Zealand as they sailed across the Tasman, which gave ample excuse and motivation for the brevity of their stay. D'Entrecasteaux wrote, for instance, that 'the natives of the islands have been visited so often, their customs and their manners are so well known and described, that there would be nothing to be gained from seeing them at closer quarters'.[9] His motive for avoiding a landing, however, probably had more to do with the Maori reputation for cannibalism – 'the horrible custom they have of eating their enemies'[10] – to which all of the ships' journalists refer.

The ships approached the Three Kings Islands on the morning of 11 March 1793. As the sun rose, a plume of smoke went up from the hill in the middle of Oo-hau (Great Island) – no doubt a fire lit by a sentry raising the alarm. D'Auribeau, lieutenant aboard the *Recherche*, commented querulously that 'nothing [on Oo-hau] gave the impression of fertility or of an agreeable aspect which Mr. Marion seems to signal in his Voyage to New Zealand'.[11] This comment echoed Marion's impatience with Tasman's journal, which had first described a river and gardens in this location.[12]

As they sailed along the islands, coastal profiles were sketched, first of the islands and then of the mainland opposite, while several of the officers checked the ships' watches and chronometers. At five o'clock that evening two canoes came out from the mainland, and the *Recherche* shortened sails to let them catch up with her. The canoes (one with a crew of eighteen men and the other with ten) approached the ship cautiously from the stern, keeping out of range of her cannons. One man at the back of each canoe stood up, waving 'a small piece of linen matting' in welcome and gesturing towards the shore. Four small boys sat on the bottom of the bigger canoe, whom at first the Europeans mistook for women, since 'their physiognomy was softer and their features were more agreeable than those of the men'.[13] When the sailors crowded onto the orlop deck, their visitors seemed terrified to see them. According to d'Auribeau, they were trembling with an anxiety and indecision that 'brought out something hard and wild in their faces', and some of them spoke loudly to the Europeans (probably a karakia of some kind), but 'none of us understood them'.

These must have been people from Ngaati Kurii settlements on shore, sent out to invite the visitors to land. D'Auribeau said that several of the elders in this party had spiral tattoos on their buttocks, while others had tattooed lips. Otherwise, these people were about the same height as Europeans:

> Their complexion is generally brown, or of a light coppery colour, very like the inhabitants of the South of Europe who are obliged to be in the sun; their hair is black, as are their beards; some wear their hair in a knot on their heads, with several white feathers planted upright in it (which one of them didn't mind parting with in our favour), others wear their hair loose and it does not reach beyond their shoulders; some were wearing quite long beards under their chins; others were clean-shaven. Their teeth seemed to me rather fine, their faces have large features but they are generally handsome and expressive. Their limbs are strong, fleshy, well-proportioned and very vigorous, very different in this respect from the inhabitants of Van Diemens Land. It is true that their state of civilisation means that they do not have to suffer all the miseries that the natives of New Holland have to bear.[14]

The sailors threw some pieces of cloth down to these people, and they soon began to exchange goods with the Europeans. They were very keen on iron – axes, knives and nails – recognising it from the metallic sound of two pieces struck together, but also sought cloth and ships' biscuits. According to the scientist de Labillardière, once barter began, the local people

Heroic images of a woman and man of Ngaati Kurii, sketched by the expedition's artist, Piron.

approached with confidence, showing us bundles of New Zealand flax, shaking them so that we might observe all their beauty . . . The stuffs of different colours we gave them were received with marks of great satisfaction, and they always delivered to us with the most scrupulous exactness the price on which we agreed.[15]

In exchange for European goods the local people offered fish; some hanks of fishing line, which d'Entrecasteaux considered 'much better woven than our finest cords'; bundles of fish-hooks made from shells and dog's teeth, some decorated with feather lures; a greenstone fishing sinker about the size of an apple, finely polished and with a hole bored through a small protruberance to hold the line; and some paddles. The French commented on the large quantities of fish that were offered, and the 'numerous shoals which, rising to the surface of the sea, agitated it for a considerable space at different times . . . during the short time we lay to'.[16] The local people also offered pieces of bark cloth; calabashes; several fine mats that were 'skilfully woven, and at their edges they put borders or fringes of various colours' (taaniko); woven belts with different coloured patterns; rain cloaks, with their shaggy surface of exposed flax ends; a number of spears including 'a very beautiful lance' about sixteen feet long, fashioned from a hard red wood and pointed at both ends; several stone war clubs; ear and chest pendants of greenstone, and some of human bone, which provoked d'Auribeau to remark that 'after reading Mr Cook on the habits and manners of these people, one will not be so astonished by this custom, as revolting as it is barbarous'.[17]

After reading the Cook and Marion accounts, the French were obsessed with cannibalism. One of the crew, while offering a knife for barter, showed its use to its intended recipient by pretending to cut off his finger, which he put in his mouth, miming the act of eating it. The man laughed heartily, rubbing his hands together, and d'Entrecasteaux remarked that 'this gesture afforded that ferocious savage infinite pleasure' – although he was probably simply being amiable. All the Europeans were impressed, though, with the fairness of these good-humoured exchanges. According to Raoul, the *Recherche*'s chief quartermaster:

> The reknown those unhappy cannibals have, added to their natural state an air which struck us at first but we were soon disabused. Their good and gentle manner towards us soon effaced all notions of the savage, leaving us with practical men . . . It is true that they are familiar with European strength and that here they were not the stronger party, but in spite of that I will never believe them as bad as we have been told.[18]

After about an hour and a half of friendly barter, the canoes left the *Recherche* at dusk, returning shortly afterwards with another, smaller canoe, which had brought new 'curiosities' to exchange. The twelve men in this canoe wanted axes in exchange for their goods, and one of them shouted out, 'E toki!' (an adze!) in a very loud voice, refusing to be silent until he had one in his hand. D'Auribeau described the canoes as twenty-five to thirty feet long by three to four feet wide, carefully made, with a single hull and sideboards about eighteen inches high. They were painted in various colours, with upright sternpieces, one of which was decorated with 'a sort of flower painted in red'. The paddles were well shaped and very light, and the canoes moved quickly through the water. Their crews did not appear to be at all intimidated when several flares were fired off as a signal to the *Espérance*. It was long after nightfall when they finally paddled back to land.

De Labillardière ruefully commented that

> it would have been easy to go and anchor in Lauriston Bay [Doubtless Bay, where Surville had been]; but the sad events which befell Captain Marion, and later Furneaux, made the Admiral decide to forgo this. However, I felt it was my duty to represent to him how important it would be to collect in New Zealand the lilaceous plant known by the name of *phormium tenax* [harakeke, or New Zealand flax], to carry it back to Europe, where it would thrive. The fibres obtained from its leaves have a strength vastly superior to all the other vegetable products used to make ropes; the cable that could be made of it would stand the greatest strains. No-one should have been better able than the Commander of our expedition to appreciate to the full the usefulness of this plant for our navy. However, we continued on our course for the Friendly Islands, steering North-east.[19]

For all that, de Labillardière later managed to carry out tests in France on the flax samples he had collected, assessing harakeke as second only to silk among rope fibres for durability and strength.[20]

In the event, d'Entrecasteaux's expedition never found La Pérouse. They carried on into the Pacific, finding the Kermadec Islands (named after the captain of the *Espérance*) and visiting Tonga, the Loyalty Islands, New Caledonia and Santa Cruz. At Santa Cruz they sailed past Vanikoro, which they called 'Île de Recherche', without realising that it was there that their compatriot's ships had been wrecked. D'Entrecasteaux died at the Admiralties, the crews were wracked with dysentery and scurvy, and when the ships returned to the Dutch East Indies they were told that France was at war and the King and Queen had been guillotined. The expedition collapsed, and the acting commander arrested the Republicans among the crew, the Royalists made their way back to Europe, and the Dutch eventually took over the two ships.

Conclusion

SCIENCE AND WHAKAPAPA

'Liberty, Equality, Fraternity', the catch-cry of this period, had a limited application. As human beings, 'savages' and 'barbarians' (along with slaves, peasants,
women and children) were thought in principle to be equal to Europeans but, as
beings close to nature, to require guidance and control. Emergent modern science
was preoccupied with achieving dominion over nature, in its human and non-
human guises. Robert Hooke, the great naturalist and instrument-maker, explained
how his devices assisted in this process:

> His design was . . . to improve and increase the distinguishing faculty of the senses,
> not only to reduce these things, which are already sensible to our organs unassisted,
> to number, weight and measure, but also in order to the inlarging the limits of their
> power, so as to be able to do the same things in regions of matter hitherto inaccessi-
> ble, impenetrable, and imperceptible by the senses unassisted. Because this, as it
> inlarges the empire of the senses, so it beseiges and straitens the recesses of nature:
> and the use of these, well plied, though but by the hands of the common soldier, will
> in short time force nature to yield even the most inaccessible fortress.[1]

The senses were ruled by reason, and discoveries came by access to previously unknown places, by instruments or travel, and recorded by description,
sketching, classification and collecting, all 'inlarg[ing] the limits' of reason's power.

Reality was seen as territory to be conquered, and the mythic leap of emergent modern science was to imagine it as a great continuum, flat, featureless and
homogeneous. Across this cosmic expanse, various standard grids were plotted,
registering differences that could then be measured and described. Space, for
instance, was gridded into miles and inches, degrees, minutes and seconds of
arc, latitude and longitude, measured out by rules and instruments, and given
numerical names. The spatial grid, imagined from above, mapped the line between
land and water, along coastlines, lakes and rivers, naming all these features. When it
was imagined from eyelevel, the line between land and sky was drawn, in coastal
views and topographical maps.

Time was gridded out in centuries, months and minutes, calibrated by clocks
and recorded in journals, logs, almanacs and histories. Events were named and

plotted on the continuum – wars, the reigns of kings and queens, 'discoveries', the rise and fall of empires.

Phenomenal life was structured by space and time, and sorted into named categories (rocks and minerals, atmosphere, water, animals, plants and people; elements; genera and species), epitomised in disciplines (intellectual 'fields'), and places such as zoos, museums and libraries, where things were labelled and stored in enclosures, cabinets and cupboards. In 'rational administration', people were categorised, recorded and counted, and their records stored in files and pigeon-holes. Once sorted on such standard grids, the cosmic continuum could be measured (hence the mathematisation of the world) and its distinctive features systematically observed, described and compared. Even the thinking self came under such procedures. Mind was split from matter, subject from object, self from other, people from nature. Mind worked to master matter. On the other side of equality was this meticulous matrix of control.

The mythic leap of whakapapa was not into chaos but into order of a very different kind. One of the great cosmological chants, recorded by Te Kohuora of Rongoroa in 1854, begins the story:

Naa te kune te pupuke	From the source of growth the rising
Naa te pupuke te hihiri	From rising the thought
Naa te hihiri te mahara	From rising thought the memory
Naa te mahara te hinengaro	From memory the mind-heart
Naa te hinengaro te manako	From the mind-heart, desire
Ka hua te waananga	Knowledge became conscious
Ka noho i a rikoriko	It dwelt in dim light
Ka puta ki waho ko te poo	And Poo (darkness) emerged
Ko te poo i tuturi, te poo i pepeke	The dark for kneeling, the dark for leaping
Te poo uriuri, to poo tangotango	The intense dark, to be felt
Te poo wawaa, te poo tee kitea	The dark to be touched, unseen
Te poo i oti atu ki te mate	The dark that ends in death
Naa te kore i ai	From nothingness came the first cause
Te kore tee whiwhia	Unpossessed nothingness
Te kore tee rawea	Unbound nothingness
Ko hau tupu, ko hau ora	The wind of growth, the wind of life
Ka noho i te atea	Stayed in clear space
Ka puta ki waho ko te rangi e tuu nei	And the atmosphere emerged
Te rangi e teretere nei	The sky which floats
I runga o te whenua	Above the earth
Ka noho te rangi nui e tuu nei	The great sky above us
Ka noho i a ata tuhi	Stayed in red light
Ka puta ki waho ko te marama	And the moon emerged
Ka noho te rangi e tuu nei	The sky above us
Ka noho i a te werowero	Stayed in shooting light
Ka puta ki waho ko te raa	And the sun emerged
Kokiritia ana ki runga	Flashing up
Hei pukanohi moo te rangi	To light the sky

171

Te ata rapa, te ata ka mahina	The early dawn, the early day, the midday
Ka mahina te ata i hikurangi!	The blaze of day from the sky!

. . . and then the land emerged, then the gods, then people.[2]

As in the cosmology of European science, order began with thought, but here the characteristic pattern was not the grid, but nets of interactive links, spoken in a genealogical language, spiralling the cosmos. The world began with a surge of primal energy, generating thought and memory, darkness, nothingness and the hau, or wind of life, which brought different kinds of being together. Out of these conjunctions, new forms of life were created. In this form of order, the focus was not on binary divisions (the characteristic act of analytic thinking), but on dual aspects of the world, and what went on between them. Categories for describing relationships were complementary and relative (former/later, dark/light, male/female, up/down, inside/outside[3]). Links between named ancestors and descendants, Poo and Ao ('worlds' of darkness and light), men and women, Earth Mother and Sky Father, older and younger siblings, taangata whenua (land people) and strangers were discussed in relational terms – tapu, mana, utu, hara and the like. They were remembered in genealogies, chants, oral histories; epitomised in whare whakairo (carved houses) and marae; laid down in layers (whakapapa) – each generation upon the last, layered sky on layered earth, in a stratigraphy of being. Relations between such pairs were not always positive, they could be negative (hoa is a friend or companion; hoariri – literally 'angry companion' – an enemy), but when they came together there was power, and either destruction or new being in the world. The leaders of Maori kin groups had direct access to this power (mana), but were expected to use it in the interests of their people.

Once Europeans were bound, by karakia or exchanges of names and gifts or violence, into 'the knot of humankind' (te here tangata), they too were remembered. Characteristically, those memories focused on the qualities of their relations with local people, in terms of tapu, mana, hara, utu, etc., rather than the question of control.

For all that emergent science and whakapapa were very different ways of knowing – one focusing on objectivity, the other on reciprocity – they had something deep in common. Foucault's description of early modern science applies equally to whakapapa: 'a fundamental arrangement of knowledge, which orders the knowledge of beings so as to make it possible to represent them in a system of names'.[4] Their patterns were not entirely incommensurable; learning could happen, some kind of understanding was not impossible.[5] Such thinking allowed for mutual respect, and a variety of possible futures. Mana and honour, justice and tika, revenge and utu, crime and hara all had points of coincidence, out of which future working relationships could be constructed. They were not the same, though, and this otherness required careful consideration. Its dismissal (whether from ignorance or contempt) has always been a potent act of politics, and a perilous strategy.

172

UTU, LAW
AND
COMMERCE

THE TRADING VOYAGES

REFLECTIONS ON UTU, LAW AND COMMERCE

Once the scientific explorers had surveyed various places in the Pacific for European uses, a period of closer exchange between Europeans and Pacific Islanders began. In 1788, British penal settlements were established at New South Wales and Norfolk Island, and increasing numbers of European ships entered the South Pacific. They carried convicts or supplies to the new colonies, and searched for cargoes for the homeward journey. Seals, whales, flax and timber soon attracted a series of trading vessels to New Zealand. These were commercial voyages, intended to collect commodities for sale in the markets of Europe, America, India or China. In return, they offered European goods and skills to local suppliers of goods and labour.

These were not understood as exchanges between equals, however. During the Age of Enlightenment, European science had placed Western thought at the apex of human achievement. Western knowledge and commodities were seen as civilised gifts that justified imperial expansion. Everything apart from the thinking self was subject matter to be put to rational uses, thus creating the preconditions for private property at home, and for European colonisation.[1]

According to Thomas Hobbes in his great treatise *Leviathan*, selves were essentially self-interested, locked in a constant struggle with others for dominion. In the state of nature, where there was no sovereign, they lapsed into 'warre, as is of every man, against every man', threatening their own lives and possessions. Such a state was contrary to self-interest, however, so a rational response was to establish a sovereign power, allowing laws protecting persons and property to be made and civilisation to emerge.[2] John Locke added labour to the equation, arguing that the productive control of property was not only rational, but virtuous:

> He who appropriates land to himself by his labour, does not lessen but increases the common stock of mankind. For the provisions serving to the support of human life, produced by one acre of inclosed and cultivated land, are . . . ten times more, than those, which are yeilded by an acre of Land, of an equal richnesse, lyeing wast in common. And therfor he, that incloses Land and has a greater plenty of

the conveniencys of life from ten acres, than he could have from a hundred left to Nature, may truly be said, to give ninety acres to Mankind. For his labour now supplys him with provisions out of ten acres, which were but the product of an hundred lying in common.[3]

This formulation justified the propertied classes in taking lands held in common by peasants at home or savages abroad. People in a state of nature required the introduction of a sovereign power if they were to become 'civilised', and imperial trade and commerce was thought to be good for barbarian peoples, bringing them into contact with other populations, allowing them to improve their ways of living and to 'polish' their rational powers.

Pacific Islanders did not share these views of their condition, however. In New Zealand, for example, Maori had their own ideas on how relationships between people, and between people, earth and sea, ought to be conducted. The cosmological chant quoted above described a world ordered by reciprocal exchanges. Mind and heart were not split, nor mind and matter – they had a generative relation. From them came the hau, the wind of life, producing the forms of the everyday world through genealogical engagement. Thus all forms of life had hau, including things and people ('ahau' means 'I', 'myself' in Maori). In the case of people, this included the hau of their ancestor gods, called up by the tohunga (priests) at their birth and bound in them. With this hau went tapu, or the presence and power of ancestral gods, and mana, ancestral efficacy.

Rangatira and ariki, or chiefs, through their lines of descent, embodied the ancestors. They were at the heart of their kin groups, bound there by genealogical ties with ancestor gods and the people. When rangatira spoke of their ancestors as 'ahau', or 'I', it was because they were the 'living face' of those ancestors; and when they spoke of their kin groups in the same way, it was because they shared ancestral hau together. The hau, like the tapu and mana of the ancestors, was at once dispersed throughout the kin group and exemplified in its aristocratic leaders. Gifts or insults to any part of the group thus affected the hau of the entire kin group – especially if directed at the ariki or rangatira.

In this way utu, or reciprocal exchange, required the return of hau, whether by gifts or insults. Insults diminished the rangatira's hau and had to be requited. Gifts, by embodying mana and carrying the donor's hau, created an obligation for return gifting. As Tamati Ranaipiri explained at the turn of this century:

I will speak to you about the *hau* . . . The *hau* is not the wind that blows – not at all. Let us suppose that you possess a certain article (*taonga*) and that you give me this article. You give it to me without setting a price on it. We strike no bargain about it. Now, I give this article to a third person who, after a certain lapse of time, decides to give me something as payment in return (*utu*). He makes a present to me of something (*taonga*). Now, this gift that he gives me is the spirit (*hau*) of the *taonga* that I had received from you and that I had given to him. It would not be fair (*tika*) on my part to keep this gift for myself . . . If I kept this other *taonga* for myself, serious harm might befall me, even death.

This is the nature of the *hau*, the *hau* of personal property, the *hau* of the gift, the *hau* of the forest. *Kaati ena.*[4]

If gifts and insults were not requited, this was hau whitia, or 'hau turned aside'. In such a situation, the source of life was weakened, causing misfortune, even dying. Utu was thus sought after in group or individual exchanges, producing constant movement in the network of cosmic relations.

Within this philosophy of utu, impositions of superiority (or whakahiihii) were vigorously resented. Cook observed of Maori in his first reflections on the killings at Grass Cove: 'I have allways found them of a Brave, Noble, Open and benevolent disposition, but they are a people that will never put up with an insult if they have an oppertunity to resent it.'[5] Just as gifts were reciprocated with open-handed generosity, attacks upon mana invited retaliation. Serious attacks (termed 'hauhau aitu') threatened the life force of the group and demanded reciprocal action. As at Grass Cove, this could include the practice of kai tangata, or cannibalism, in the whaangai hau rite, when the hau of aggrieved ancestors was ritually fed and the hau of enemies ritually eaten.

European scientists and their companions spoke often about Maori cannibalism during their Pacific voyages of discovery. The extreme physicality of punishment in eighteenth-century Europe must also be remembered if the patterns of utu, law and property are to be compared. During the *ancien régime* in Europe, authority was upheld by the imposition of pain, and judicial torture was carefully calibrated to the severity of the offence. Regicides and parricides, who struck at the very heart of authority, suffered the most terrible torments. In 1757, for instance, the regicide Damien, who had tried to kill Louis XV, was condemned

> to make the *amende honorable* before the main door of the Church of Paris . . . where he was to be taken and conveyed in a cart, wearing nothing but a shirt, holding a torch of burning wax weighing two pounds . . . then, in the said cart, to the Place de Grève, where, on a scaffold that will be erected there, the flesh will be torn from his breasts, arms, thighs and calves with red-hot pincers, his right hand, holding the knife with which he committed the said parricide, burnt with sulphur, and, on those places where the flesh will be torn away, poured molten lead, boiling oil, burning resin, wax and sulphur melted together and then his body drawn and quartered by four horses and his limbs and body consumed by fire, reduced to ashes and his ashes thrown to the winds.[6]

Such excesses did not pass without protest. Enlightenment thinkers condemned contemporary forms of punishment, describing judicial torture as barbaric and public ordeals (such as hangings and the stocks) as inhumane. Punishments that brought the power of the monarch to bear directly on the body of the criminal, expiating his offence through torture, were disputed in the name of reason, and new, reformative regimes of punishment were being proposed. The French Revolution, though, produced a civic paroxysm so bloody that it cast doubt upon the new philosophies, and in England and many other European countries radical thinkers were imprisoned or exiled.

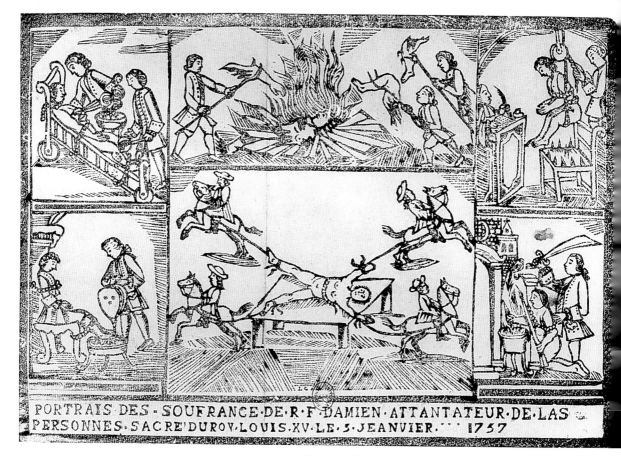

PORTRAIS·DES·SOUFRANCE·DE·R·F·DAMIEN·ATTANTATEUR·DE·LAS
PERSONNES·SACRE'DUROY·LOUIS·XV·LE·5·JEANVIER.···1757

An anonymous artist's portrayal of the sufferings of Robert-François Damien, punished for trying to kill Louis XV in 1757.

At the same time, war was reformed in eighteenth-century Europe largely to make it more efficient. In the name of discipline and military strategy, the sufferings endured by fighting men remained acute. Floggings of up to a thousand lashes or more, and punishments such as running the gauntlet or keelhauling[7] were thought to be essential for maintaining order in armed services where many of the men were recruited from gaols or prison ships,[8] and wounds suffered from musket or cannon balls, grapeshot or the weapons of hand-to-hand combat could be horrific. During 1773–1815, the nation states of Europe were almost continuously fighting (including the American War of Independence, and the French Revolutionary and Napoleonic Wars in Europe). Casualty lists grew exponentially as weaponry improved and the scale of European armies and navies expanded (for instance, it has been estimated that of two million Frenchman called to arms between 1800 and 1815, four hundred thousand died as a result of their military service[9]).

If French and British observers were horrified by Maori cannibalism, therefore, it was probably not primarily because of its violence. It was more likely because of its directness, its appalling intimacy. In Europe, judgement and punishment were independently administered, and criminals were separated from their fellows in hulks, gaols, the galleys and in death. Cannibalism followed an opposite logic, amending wrongdoing (hara) by bringing offender and offended together in acts of ritual eating, destroying the offender's tapu by consuming his body, the 'living face' of his or her ancestors. For Europeans, such a strategy was almost unthinkable, breaching their understandings of human nature. Few scientific observers thought to compare cannibalism with judicial torture or military discipline, the equally violent but impersonally administered representations of the power of the European state.

Eight

INTRODUCING LAW AND COMMERCE

THE PENAL COLONY AT PORT JACKSON

At the time that the penal colony in Port Jackson was being planned, memories of Grass Cove deterred the British from considering New Zealand as a site for a convict settlement. The first Governor of New South Wales, Arthur Phillip, suggested that New Zealand might be used as a place of ultimate punishment instead. If any convict committed murder or sodomy in the new colony, he considered it advisable 'to confine the criminal till an opportunity offered of delivering him as a prisoner to the natives of New Zealand, and let them eat him. The dread of this will operate much stronger than the fear of death.'[1]

But what could be worse than dying? Cannibalism aroused fears of torture, before or after death. Hell was everlasting torture in the afterlife, and at public hangings in England, the condemned person and the crowd sang the 'Hanging Song' (Psalm 51) together, which suggests that salvation was still central in popular ideas of punishment:

> Create in me a clean heart, O God; and renew a right spirit within me.
> Cast me not away from thy presence; and take not thy holy spirit from me.
> Restore unto me the joy of thy salvation; and uphold me with thy free spirit
>
> . . .
>
> Deliver me from blood guiltiness, O God, thou God of my salvation; and my
>   tongue shall sing aloud of thy righteousness.
> O Lord, open thou my lips; and my mouth shall shew forth thy praise.
> The sacrifices of God are a broken spirit: a broken and a contrite heart, O God,
>   thou wilt not despise.
> Do good in thy good pleasure unto Zion: build thou the walls of Jerusalem.
>   Then shalt thou be pleased with the sacrifices of righteousness, with burnt offer-
>   ing and whole burnt offering: then shall they offer bullocks upon thine altar.

The bodies of murderers were delivered to the surgeons for dissection, and denied a Christian burial with its promise of a peaceful passage for the soul from one life to the next.[2] This practice was much hated, and it is possible that cannibalism was proposed by Phillip as an even worse form of post-mortem desecration. To be eaten by pagans must have seemed the antithesis of Christian sacrifice, adding the fear of eternal suffering to the dread of violent death.

At this time in Britain, the defence of private property was increasingly draconian. The number of capital statutes grew from about fifty in 1688 to over two hundred in 1820, and most of these involved offences against property, including arson, forgery, piracy, embezzlement, stealing an heiress, shoplifting above five shillings, stealing or destroying linen, cutting down trees in an avenue or garden, setting fire to coal mines, rioting, cutting hop binds, destroying turnpikes or bridges, and sending threatening letters.[3] Some of these acts occurred when working people were demonstrating their displeasure with employers or land owners, and the statutes were often passed hot on the heels of particular protests or riots.[4] Juries became reluctant to convict people of capital offences, and those who had links of kinship or patronage with nobles or the gentry might be forgiven capital punishment, and sentenced to imprisonment or transportation instead. Because of this, and a fear that punishment might lose its terror if hangings became too common, the numbers of people executed for offences against property remained fairly stable or even fell during this period. This resulted in a very large population of living criminals, who had to be accommodated by the state.

This engraving by William Hogarth shows a public hanging in England in 1747.

By and large, they were accommodated very badly. There was no wish to spend public resources on those who had offended against property and the state. Whenever possible, convicts were set to labour, in the mines or on the docks at home, or on galleys or in plantations in the American colonies. Otherwise they sat and rotted in over-crowded and filthy hulks or prisons, harassed by their jailers and other prisoners; cold, wet, ill fed and loaded down with chains. According to John Howard in his 1777 report on English prisons, for instance, the county jail at Warwick was 'sadly crowded. Only one small day-room for the men; and I saw thirty-two lay chained in a dungeon of twenty-two feet diameter, down thirty-one steps, two of which were ill of a slow fever. There were three others in a room, very ill and in irons. In two rooms (seven feet and a half by six and a half) with apertures only in the doors, there lay fourteen women almost suffocated.'[5] Newgate Prison in London was even worse, sending up a stench that harmed local businesses and 'polluted what little food and water the prisoners could get hold of . . . It was everywhere and it was inescapable; revolting their nostrils and clogging their lungs, pervading their whole existence.' Most other jails in England were as dirty and as dangerous. It was no wonder that many prisoners died before their sentences expired.

These problems in English prisons were soon to overflow into the Pacific. The first sizeable populations of Europeans in the South Pacific came out of British jails. Rapid population growth in England, the enclosure movement, the slave trade, industrialisation, penal reform and the American Revolution all had impacts on Pacific peoples. England was mass-producing convicts, and when the American colonists would no longer take them as workers on their plantations, preferring slaves from Africa, a series of committees was set up to investigate new schemes for transportation.

Sir Joseph Banks and James Matra, who had visited Australia with James Cook on the *Endeavour*, began to suggest that a penal colony should be established in New South Wales. When others mentioned New Zealand as a possible location,[6] this idea was dismissed because Maori were thought to be too numerous and too unruly. Like Australia, New Zealand was so far away from England that this would be a very expensive option, and an expedition was despatched instead to check out a site in Das Voltas Bay in Africa. When the expedition returned to England in 1786, reporting that the coastline was bare and rocky, the government returned to Banks's and Matra's suggestions. A decision was made to send a fleet of transports to Australia, the 'Heads of a Plan' for transporting seven hundred to eight hundred convicts to Botany Bay were drafted, and Arthur Phillip was appointed as the first Governor of New South Wales.[7]

Opposite above: *An engraving of transportees from Newgate Prison being taken to Blackfriars; possibly by Rowlandson.*

Opposite below: *Convicts being delivered to one of the prison hulks in Portsmouth Harbour. An etching by William Cooke, 1828.*

Botany Bay Song.

As sung at the Crown and Anchor Tavern in the *Strand*.

YOU have read of Captain Cook, our late worthy
    commander,
The great Sir Joseph Banks, and Dr Solander?
They fail'd round the world, were perp'ex'd and teiz'd
    too,
To find out a place where the King might send the
    thieves too.
    CHORUS. Row dow' dow, row dow de rouds
    dowdy, row dow dow.

Now Botany Bay is the place that's intendeded,
To send the whole gang to that their morals might
    be mended,
When the plan was made publick it astonish'd all
    beholders,
To part savages from savages by transporting soldiers.

All things are prepar'd, and there's no alteration,
Besides it is done for the good of the nation,
But instead of box and dice they hear the rattling of
    the drums, fir,
And the natives will be kill'd by the firing of their
    guns, fir.

I have an old friend who is no ways cenforious,
He has given me a lift of the names moft notorious,
The firft is flender Billy, a noted knowing prig,
Who employ'd fuch a fquad at a fhop taxing rig.

Surly Ned he demurr'd, for a moment they waited,
Tho' his caufe was not heard, being fo adulterated,
From the paffing of his fentence all his law could not
    hinder,
For he helpt Billy in at the back chamber window.

Squinting Jack thought it hard, fat Charley thought
    it harder,
To think he muft bundle for the fins of his father,
Then looking down the lift I efpy'd Kyam A—,
Likewife Sir Cecil Keg, fo well known in Covent
    Garden.

I took notice of a n ft all caft at one time too,
When looking into facts it was for the fame crime too,
I thoaght to myfelf they had met with their rewards,
Twas for making too free with a houfe beyond the
    Horfe Guards.

One name I obferv'd that was quite early dated,
Tho' his crimes they were black, twas quite oblit rated,
But examining more clofely, twas the noted Warren
    Gre n Peafe,
So lately is a mefs for his villainies beyond feas.

A great number more whofe crimes were fo henous,
But thinking on the fubject it made me grow quite
    ferious,
I examin'd them all round, found them birds of a
    feather,
Then I threw the paper down, and I lump'd them
    all together.

Of females I have faid ne'er a word all the while,
But no doubt they will be fupply'd from this tav'rite
    ifle,
Then Britons fill your bumpers, rejoice now and fing,
What a glorious fet fhall we have from their offspring.

A text of the 'Botany Bay Song', referring to Captain Cook, Sir Joseph Banks
and Dr Solander, as sung in the Crown and Anchor Tavern in London.

In his 1812 critique of the 'thief colony', Jeremy Bentham claimed that Port Jackson had been conceived of as a sewer, to take 'a set of *animae viles* (the convicts), a sort of excrementitious mass, that could be projected, and accordingly was projected – projected, and as it should seem purposely – as far out of sight as possible'.[8] Given contemporary attitudes to 'miscreants', this was not too far wrong. It was reckless to send a flotilla of prison ships around the world to a place that had been barely visited by Europeans, on the say-so of two members of Cook's 1770 expedition. Banks and Matra spoke of fertile soils, luxuriant grass and abundant water, wood and fisheries to the Beauchamp committee, but their autumnal memories of Botany Bay proved to be misleading.[9] They also characterised the place as largely empty; according to Matra it was 'peopled only by a few black inhabitants, who, in the rudest state of society, knew no other arts than such as were necessary to their mere animal existence'.[10] New South Wales was to be colonised in defence of English property, and Australian Aboriginals and English criminals would primarily pay the price.

Various Pacific islands were also implicated, however. Tonga, Tahiti and New Caledonia were suggested as potential sources of women for the settlers, and New Zealand and Norfolk Island as sources of flax and timber for the British navy. Hemp and masting timber were in short supply in Europe, and these commodities were among the keys to naval power. In addition, the convicts for the proposed colony would need clothing, which could be woven out of flax. In his proposal for a settlement at Botany Bay, James Matra had urged:

> The New Zealand hemp or flax-plant [is] an object equally of curiosity and utility. By proper operations it would serve the various purposes of hemp, flax and silk, and it is more easily manufactured than any one of them. In naval equipments it would be of the greatest importance: a cable of the circumference of ten inches would be equal in strength to one of eighteen inches made of European hemp. Our manufacturers are of opinion that canvas made of it would be superior in strength and beauty to any canvas of our own country. The threads or filaments of this plant are formed by nature with the most exquisite delicacy, and they may be so minutely divided as to be small enough to make the finest cambrick; in color and gloss it resembles silk . . .
>
> It may be seen by Captain Cook's voyage that New Zealand is covered with timber of size and every quality that indicates long duration; it grows close to the water's edge, and may be easily obtained. Would it not be worthwhile for such as may be dispatched to New South Wales to take in some of this timber on their return, for the use of the King's yards? As the two countries are within a fortnight's run of each other, and as we might be of the utmost service to the New Zealanders, I think it highly probable that this plan might become eminently useful to us as a naval power, especially as we might thus procure masts, a single tree of which would be large enough for a first-rate ship, and planks superior to any that Europe possesses.[11]

Both of these suggestions were picked up in the official 'Heads of a Plan' for the penal colony,[12] and when Governor Phillip left with the First Fleet for the Pacific in 1787, he had these ideas in mind.[13]

The first few years of the penal colony at Port Jackson were stark and miserable. Phillip found Botany Bay barren and unwelcoming, and founded his settlement at nearby Sydney Cove instead. The tools provided by the British government broke and buckled, rats and grubs ate the crops, the convicts thieved and brawled while the officers quarrelled and despaired. When the local people realised that the Europeans had come to occupy their lands, they began to resist their presence, stoning and spearing settlers and taking their animals and food. Phillip authorised retaliatory raids and handed out grants of their land to freed convicts, officers and marines. Most of the convicts who were assigned to break in the land knew nothing about farming and were either work-shy or too weak. Subsequent fleets had landed their human cargoes in dreadful condition. According to one of the officers who came with the Second Fleet to Port Jackson:

The bark I was on board of was unfit . . . to be sent so great a distance; if it blew but the most trifling gale she was lost in the waters, of which she shipped so much that the unhappy wretches, the convicts were considerably above their waists in water . . . In this situation they were obliged, for the safety of the ship, to be pen'd down; but when the gales abated no means were used to purify the air by fumigations, no vinegar was applied to rectify the nauseous steams issuing from their miserable dungeon. Humanity shudders to think that of nine hundred male convicts embarked in this fleet, three hundred and seventy are already dead, and four hundred and fifty are landed sick and so emaciated and helpless that very few,

An early image of the founding of Port Jackson, by Thomas Gosse.

if any of them, can be saved by care or medecine. The irons used upon these unhappy wretches were barbarous. The contractors had been in the Guinea trade, and had put on board the same shackles used by them in that trade, which are made with a short bolt; thus fettered, it was impossible for them to move but at the risk of both their legs being broken . . . The slave trade is merciful compared with what I have seen on this fleet.[14]

Gradually, however, conditions in the colony improved, at least for some of its inhabitants. More arable land was found and cultivated, people learned to work with local materials, the numbers of animals increased, and ships from the United States and Britain began to arrive with tools, spirits, livestock and supplies for trade. During their journeys to Port Jackson, convict transports and other ships reported whales and seals in nearby waters, and whaling and sealing began. Phillip was succeeded by Acting Governor Francis Grose, who privileged his officers in trade and access to fertile land, and they began to pay the convicts (often in rum) for their labour. By 1793, the year when France declared war on England, Malaspina's expedition visited New South Wales and the first Maori came to Port Jackson, most of the local Aboriginals had died in an epidemic (possibly of smallpox), and their resistance was now muted. The 'thief colony' was beginning to show real commercial possibilities as Europeans secured their first foothold in the Great South Land.[15]

VANCOUVER'S VISITS TO NEW ZEALAND AND THE CHATHAM ISLANDS
1791–1793

By 1790, Sir Joseph Banks was well known in Britain as president of the Royal Society and an influential advisor to the government on exploration and imperial expansion. Banks acted as a kind of ecological impresario, using a worldwide network of contacts to shift useful plant and animal species around the globe. He kept a paternal eye on British ventures into the Pacific, maintaining an active correspondence with colonial agents. In British policy, patriotism went hand in hand with profit, and Banks encouraged government agencies (the Admiralty, the Board of Trade) and commercial and imperial authorities (the East India Company, as well as successive governors at Port Jackson) to protect British interests and to search for useful resources in the South Pacific. After the penal colony was established, Banks spoke of Port Jackson as a child, elaborating this image in an eloquent passage:

> The colony of Sidney at its first Establishment may not inaptly be compared to a new-born Infant hanging on its Mother's Breast. It deriv'd its whole Nourishment from the Vitals of its parent, and the Exhaustion it occasioned was not unfelt . . . Its present state may be compar'd to that of a young Lad beginning to attain some

A portrait of Sir Joseph Banks in later life, as president of the Royal Society and distinguished Admiralty and Board of Trade advisor.

Learning, but, between the Intervals of his Schooling, gaining by his Industry part of his necessary maintenance . . . if a little attention only is given to the Directions of his Talents, and the advancement of his worldly Interest.

In this stage he submits without a symptom of Dissatisfaction to the will of his Parents. The Laws by which he is govern'd are ordinances . . . emanating from the will of his Great Father, the King, or in Proclamations issuing from the Governor himself, as the King's Representative. These he obeys cheerfully, from a sense of the great Benefits he yet continues to receive in supplies of Provisions, clothes &c., sent to him from Home at no small Expence. He will, however, soon be in a situation to provide for himself; and when that time comes he will listen with avidity to the first person who reads to him that chapter in Blackstone which declares that a Briton inherits as his birthright the Constitution of England, and carries this Inheritance with him to every new Country he may think fit to settle in.[16]

This idea of colonies as immature creatures, like women, slaves and savages, requiring guidance and control, was central to imperial power relations. Sometimes it was also satirised, for instance in this *London Chronicle* comment on Banks's relationship with the 'thief colony':

The Botany Bay Scheme originated with the President of the Royal Society; and our Saving Minister readily acquiesced in the plan, from the economy which it presented . . . Sir Joseph Banks is so extremely delighted with his new settlement, that he has already solicited his Royal Patron for the reversion of the Governorship.

The King has but one objection to the Solomon of the Royal Society going to Botany Bay, which is, that this truly great man, with all his sagacity, has not found out the art of multipying his species, although married to a beautiful young woman, and this faculty his Majesty deems necessary to colonisation.[17]

This assumption that imperial expansion was a virtuous necessity for human progress was widely shared. The 'Introduction' to the account of George Vancouver's 1791–93 voyage to the Pacific began:

> In contemplating the rapid progress of improvement in the sciences, and the general diffusion of knowledge since the commencement of the eighteenth century, we are unavoidably led to observe, with admiration, that active spirit of discovery by means of which the remotest regions of the earth have been explored; a friendly communication opened with their inhabitants; and various commodities, of a most valuable nature, contributing either to relieve their necessities, or augment their comforts, introduced among the less-enlightened part of our species. A mutual intercourse has been also established, in many instances, on the solid basis of a reciprocity of benefits; and the productive labour of the civilized world has found new markets for the disposal of its manufactures.
>
> It should seem, that the reign of George the Third had been reserved by the Great Disposer of all things, for the glorious task of establishing the grand keystone to that expansive arch, over which the arts and sciences should pass to the furthermost corners of the earth, for the instruction and happiness of the most lowly children of nature.[18]

Vancouver had sailed as a young man with Cook on his second and third Pacific expeditions. In this voyage, he was ordered to complete Cook's survey of the north-west coast of America, searching again for the North-West Passage, and to chart the Hawaiian Islands, which were to be used as a winter base by the expedition. A British fur-trading base at Nootka Sound and three ships had been seized by the Spanish on the north-west coast, almost provoking another war between Britain and Spain. In the aftermath an agreement was signed between the two governments that they would not 'disturb or molest' the other's subjects,

> Either in navigating or carrying on their fisheries in the Pacific Ocean or in the South Seas, or in landing on the coasts of those seas in places not already occupied, for the purpose of carrying on their commerce with the natives of the country or of making settlements there.[19]

In a secondary set of instructions, given to Lieutenant Hergest of his supply ship the *Daedalus*, Vancouver was ordered to send the transport to Port Jackson with livestock and other goods for the convicts, and 'to touch on New Zealand in his way, from whence he is to use his best endeavours to take with him one or two flax-dressers, in order that the new settlers at Port Jackson may, if possible, be properly instructed in the management of that valuable plant'.[20] The Pacific had become a place over which European governments wrangled; Polynesian peoples had become pawns in a European strategic game.

Vancouver's two ships, the *Discovery* and *Chatham*, left England in April 1791, heading for Nootka Sound via the Cape of Good Hope. There was a botanist on board the *Discovery*, appointed by Sir Joseph Banks, but this was primarily a hydrographic expedition, with no other trained scientists along. The *Discovery* had a crew of a hundred men and the *Chatham* forty-five, including marines. The ships were loaded with lavish supplies of trade goods – sheet copper, cloth, beads, iron frying pans and kettles, pewter pots and basins, red caps, earrings, tartan blankets, feathers, commemorative medals and all kinds of iron tools; and fireworks.[21] Sky rockets, water rockets, Roman candles, Bengal lights and Catherine wheels were used to bedazzle 'Indians' all over the Pacific at this time; pyrotechnics of one kind or another (including, of course, cannons and muskets) were prized items of imperial display. After a short stay at the Cape of Good Hope, where many of the crew contracted dysentery from a ship that had arrived from Batavia, the ships sailed to Australia and charted part of the south-western coastline. After this they sailed straight to Tamatea (Dusky Sound), where Vancouver had spent six pleasant weeks with Cook on the *Resolution* in 1773.[22]

DISCOVERY AND *CHATHAM'*S VISIT TO TAMATEA
2–22 November 1791

After James Cook's 1773 visit to Tamatea in the *Resolution*, we know of no other European visits to the Sound before Vancouver's arrival. Sir Joseph Banks had suggested that when the convicts arrived in Botany Bay in 1787, Governor Phillip should send one of the convict transports to New Zealand to collect flax plants, and then to Tahiti for breadfruit. Phillip was instructed to set about cultivating flax in the new colony, both to make linen for clothing for the convicts and canvas and rope for export.[23] In the event, though, Phillip turned his attention to another source for the flax plant. Only five days after the First Fleet arrived at Port Jackson, he sent Lieutenant Philip Gidley King to Norfolk Island, where Cook had reported *Phormium tenax* growing wild in 1774.

Tamatea thus preserved its isolation for a few years longer. Its reputation as a Pacific port of call was well established, however, and Vancouver knew that he would find supplies of fish, birds, greens and fresh water there, as well as timber for firewood, planks and spars. On 2 November 1791, he approached the south-western coast of New Zealand in a 'thick dirty haze' and lowered the boats, which towed the ships straight into the Sound. As they passed Five Fingers Point, Archibald Menzies, the botanist, described 'its wild & romantic appearance':

> It is formed by a group of high peaked insulated Rocks perforated with holes & hideous caverns & furnishd with projecting rocks & steep cliffs that in many places overhung their base yet afforded a scanty nourishment to some trees & bushes which here & there issued from crevices & adorned their craggy sides. A little

Coastal view of Five Fingers Point, off Tamatea, by an unknown artist from Vancouver's voyage in 1791.

behind these a very steep rocky shore rose to a moderate height, & was covered towards the summit with trees of different kinds, forming, on the whole, a prospect truly picturesque, & which at this time was certainly heightened by the novelty of our situation – the calm serenity of the evening & the wild hideous noise of a heavy surf dashing incessantly against the rocks & cavernous shore.[24]

Early the next morning the two captains, Vancouver and Lieutenant William Broughton, went off to look at Facile Harbour, on the outer coast of Resolution Island, while some of the crew went fishing. When a gale blew up, the *Discovery* was blown off her mooring and forced to run into Anchor Island Harbour. The ships lowered their topmasts and yards to ride out the storm for the next day and night, battered by violent squalls and drenched by driving sheets of rain.

Coastal view from Tempest Roads showing the steep cliffs of Tamatea, also from Vancouver's visit.

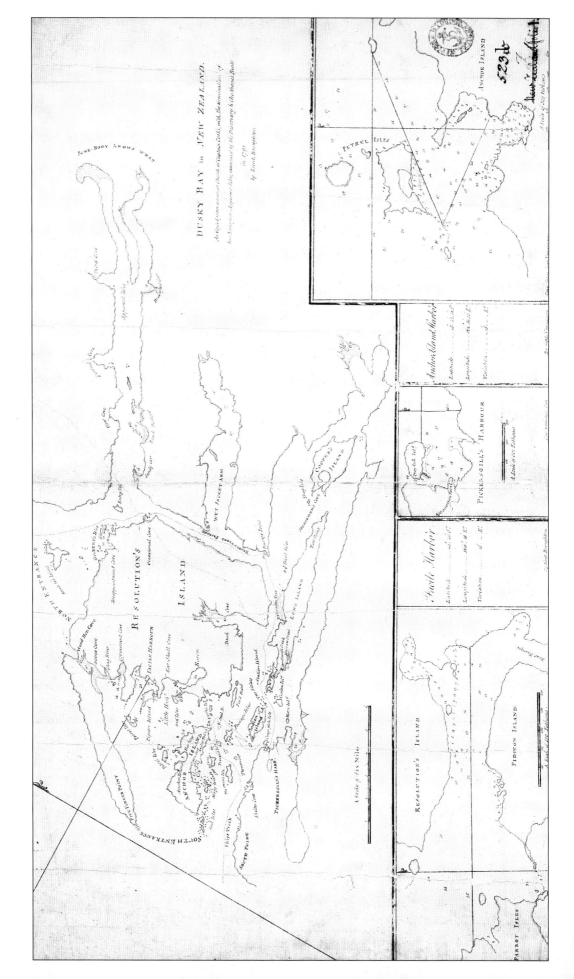

DUSKY BAY in NEW ZEALAND.

As Copied from several Sketch, or Captain Cook's, with the termination, of
their Amours in Appearance: laid open, near to the Discovery & Chatham's Banks
in 1791
by Lieut. Broughton

SOME-BODY KNOWS WHAT

RESOLUTION'S ISLAND

NORTH ENTRANCE

SOUTH ENTRANCE

A Scale of Six Mile

PETREL ISLES

ANCHOR ISLAND

Anchor Island Harbour
Latitude
Longitude
Variation

Pickersgill's Harbour
A Scale of 20 Fathoms

Facile Harbor
Latitude
Longitude
Variation

RESOLUTION'S ISLAND

PIDGEON ISLAND
A Scale of 200 Fathoms

PARROT ISLES

As soon as the weather cleared, on 5 November, parties of sailors went out fishing, cutting wood, collecting water, brewing spruce beer from rimu and repairing the casks, sails and rigging. Although Cook had previously reported only a small population in the Sound, the sailors were warned not to stray too far from the ship 'in case of meeting Inhabitants'. The *Chatham* anchored in Facile Harbour, which one of her crew described as 'the pleasantest, snugest and most convenient harbour I ever beheld, never was a place more properly nam'd'.[25] This same anonymous sailor described their landing and activities on shore:

> Most of [the sailors] went on shore but finding nothing to amuse them, and no Grog shops to prolong their stay came on bd. in an hours time. The Next day Monday of course was a busy one The spot having been fixt upon the preceding day a party was sent to clear it . . . This was done with the utmost Expedition and Alacrity & as business might be forwarded the more, no body was Idle on board, the seperate parties preparing their different utensils to take with them – In the Evening the brewers – The Carpenters – The Armourer – a party splitting wood – two marines washing – The Cooper to repair Casks &c &c all went on shore, Each having their Allottd spot for their different Occupations. The remaining part of our crew that were on board, Altho few, workd hard and did much all being Employd in clearing the hold &c Except two or three that went for water.[26]

Menzies went botanising and came back loaded with ferns and mosses – 'two tribes of plants of which I am particularly fond'.[27] He collected maanuka for brew-ing tea and transplanted several plants, including New Zealand flax, into the frame on the quarterdeck for Sir Joseph Banks at Kew Gardens. During one of these expeditions he noted an abandoned hut on shore, which he described as of 'an obtuse conic form, about 4 feet high & 6 in diameter at the bottom, composed of slender sticks crossing eachother, & fastened together with twigs, closely thatched over all with grass & ferns, with the marks of a fire place before the door of it which faced towards the wood'.[28] On 10 November, he went with a party of officers to shoot birds in Goose Cove. They found another abandoned hut on the east side of the bay, with a few old baskets of 'neat workmanship' nearby:

> This hut was the same form & size as the one in Facile Harbour, but it was much fresher, & seemed to have been later inhabited by some of the Natives, perhaps within the last twelve months. There was a fire place before it with a great number of ear shells [paaua] & limpets scattered round it, the contents of which I dare say had been used as food. There were likewise the remains of two rude baskets formd of the bark of a Tree laying close to it. We immediately set about giving this hut a fresh coat of thatch, & had the bottom of it spread over with a thick layer of Ferns for our beds. We kindled a large fire before the entrance which was kept up by a Centinel all night to keep off the sand-flys, which were very troublesome, & after dressing some of our game, on which we made a hearty Meal, we retird to sleep on our comfortable fern beds, & being pleasantly situated at the foot of high steep romantic mountains clothed with trees the habitation of a numerous variety of

Opposite: *William Broughton's chart of Dusky Bay in New Zealand.*

birds whose warbling cadence lulled us to rest & in the morning entertained us with their wild heterogeneous concert.[29]

The geese that Cook had liberated in the cove were nowhere to be seen, and the local inhabitants were as elusive. Like Malaspina's crew a year or so later, the Europeans saw no Maori in Tamatea. Although Vancouver's men were in the Sound for almost three weeks and explored it to its farthest reaches, they found only abandoned houses (including several more in Ear-shell Cove). One night there was an alarm on board the *Chatham*, provoked by a report that some canoes were paddling towards the ship. As the crew scrambled to their stations and prepared for an attack, however, 'the Farce soon concluded for these Formidable Canoes prov'd to be nothing more or less than Dry Rocks'.[30] Menzies later remarked ruefully:

> As this place was found inhabited by several families when Capt Cook was here it may appear singular that we did not meet with any of the Natives in our various excursions. Indeed, I am much afraid that his liberality towards them has been in some measure the cause of this apparent depopulation, by affording a pretext for war to a more powerful tribe, ambitious to possess the riches he left them, which in all probability has ended in their total destruction, for if we except the few old huts we saw in & about Facile Harbour, we met with no other traces of them anywhere in the Sound, & these to all appearance were formd only for temporary shelter, & bore no marks of being very recently inhabited.[31]

Equally, however, the families that used Tamatea as a seasonal hunting ground may have been elsewhere, and the abandoned huts seen by Vancouver's men were probably their campsites from previous seasons.

While Vancouver's expedition was in Tamatea, numerous birds were shot, including weka, tuuii (or Poe birds), parrakeets and parrots. When one parrot was wounded, its cries brought others to the same tree, and these were killed in their turn until 'two or three surviving ones went away with a pitiful noise, seeming to bemoan the fate of their fellow-companions'.[32] Vancouver's men visited Cook's old anchorage in Pickersgill Cove, noting that undergrowth had already covered the clearing and garden, although stumps from the trees Cook's men had felled were easily found. According to Menzies, 'we drank a cheerful glass to the memory of Capt Cook, whose steps we were now pursuing, & as far as we had opportunity to trace them, we could not help reflecting with peculiar pleasure & admiration on the justness of his observations & the accuracy of his delineations throughout every part of the complicated survey of this extensive Sound, where he had left so little for us to finish'.[33] Vancouver took two boats to the far end of the Sound and surveyed the upper part of the northern arm, which Cook had labelled on his chart: 'No body knows what'. Having completed the survey and dispelled any remaining mysteries, he named the heads of these arms with cheerful satisfaction: 'Some Body knows what'.

By now Vancouver's men were rested and the ships were repaired and refitted. Fresh stocks of water, wood, greens and fish had been brought on board, and

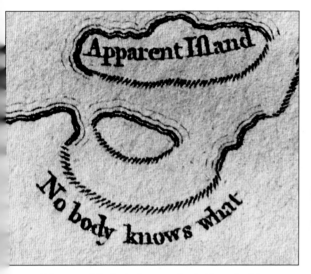

Above: *'No body knows what', from Cook's engraved chart of Dusky Sound.*

Right: *'Some Body knows what', from Vancouver's atlas of his voyage.*

they were ready to continue across the Pacific. As one of the crew remarked in his journal, 'with Fish Fowl &c. it may be reasonably concluded we lived high like Fighting Cocks during our stay here which was pretty much the Case'.[34] Like Cook, they thought Tamatea a perfect port for ships on voyages of Pacific exploration, but not much use for anything else. Menzies thought that it might serve as a flax plantation, while Puget considered that it might become a valuable fishery, supplying Port Jackson and even Bengal with fish. According to Manby, the *Discovery*'s master's mate, however, 'this part of New Zeland, does not appear likely to prove of any material advantage to Navigation, as it is intirely out of the way of all Commercial Vessels'.[35]

On 22 November, the expedition sailed out of the Sound, south-east into the teeth of a violent storm that separated the two ships. In the wake of the gale Vancouver found the Snares and charted them, while Broughton on the *Chatham* followed a different track and encountered first the Snares and then Rekohu, naming its archipelago the Chatham Islands.

THE *CHATHAM* AT REKOHU
29 November 1791

Rekohu is one of a rugged cluster of islands 870 kilometres to the east of New Zealand. The two main islands, Rekohu (Chatham) and Rangiauria (Pitt), total almost a thousand square kilometres of volcanic rock, rising out of turbulent seas. In 1791, there were extensive areas of broadleaf and nikau forests, with ferny

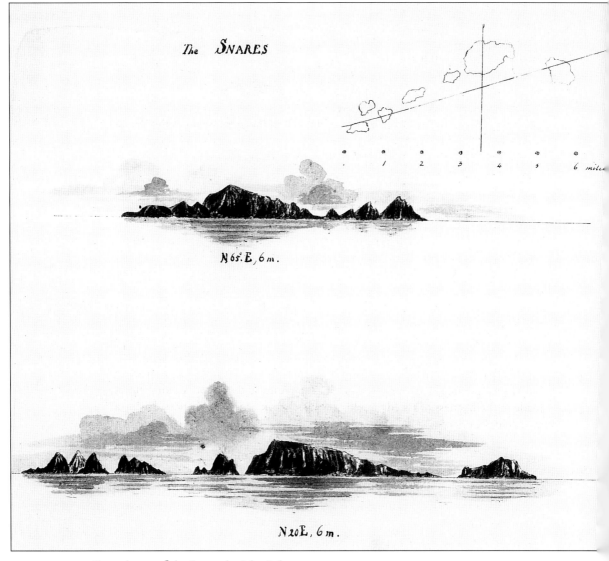

Coastal view of the Snares, by John Sykes.

undergrowth, and groves of kopi, akeake and coprosma trees on the flats. The population of about two thousand lived on kopi berries, fernroot, forest and sea birds, and eels, shellfish, fish and sea mammals. They had no gardens of kuumara or other land crops, but relied mainly on the ocean, which had brought them there from a distant homeland. According to some of their stories, the first people on the islands lived on Rangiauria and were known as the Tuiti:

> How the first pair came is unknown; whether brought by the Spirit from above, or created on the mountain . . . They lived upon the top of the mountain, from whence they caught and worshipped the first ray of the morning sun, and bowed in adoration to that luminary as he sank beneath the western wave . . .

One day, a youth wandered down to the sea-shore among the birds that lined the rocks, and, seating himself near where a [sea] eagle was perched pluming his wing, they fell into conversation. The eagle complained that they could no longer soar into the high air, by reason of a spell cast over his tribe . . . by the Tuiti . . .

The youth answered that the blood of the honey-eater . . . had cried down to the Creator, and brought down upon the eagle his banishment. The Tuiti warred [with no one], they fed on fruit and shed no blood: the eagle had banished himself. The king of birds, avoiding the issue, replied that in the great island to the north-west [Rekohu], which his friend had doubtless seen from the mountain, the woods were filled with beautiful birds, and fruit of every colour, hanging over the dark, transparent waters of many lakes . . .

The youth listened to the tempter, and ambition elated his soul; he arose from the rock and asked to be shown the path that led over the water. The eagle, looking at him askance, promised him wings to fly over, providing he would first render an easy service by taking him to the top of the mountain . . . Taking the eagle on his wrist, [he] ascended the mountain, and in the dark cast him loose . . . All night long the flutter and death-cry of birds smote upon his ear, and, when the morning dawned, the song of the mako was mute and the tuis had ceased to mock.

The people assembled in alarm. A child to whom its mother had given fruit fell dead; they gathered about its body in terror. The eagle hovered over them, and uttered his war-cry. The conscience-stricken youth confessed. The day was passed in penitence and sorrow about the body of the child in the lap of its wailing mother . . . The youth wandered by the shore, alone, stung with remorse, and, meeting the eagle, was taught by him to construct the korari, the model of all canoes, made in the likeness of a sledge, with a wicker-work of tough creepers, having a false bottom filled with buoyant kelp.

He put to sea with his family, and landed on [Rekohu], which he found, as the eagle had said, uninhabited by man, a continent in size compared to [Rangiauria]; with undulating, fertile plains south and lofty mountains in the north, sparkling with lakes of dark transparent water, and vocal with the song and bright with the plumage of birds. Filled with new joy, he sent back tidings to his kinsmen, and was followed by successive emigrations, until [Rangiauria] was deserted save by a timid few who feared the sea. Thus came about the settlement of Warekauri [Rekohu]: and to this extent is the tradition of the people.[36]

Archaeological and linguistic evidence suggests that these first people had originally come from New Zealand. They may have been on a trading expedition along its south-eastern coast and were swept out to sea in a storm.[37] This was about four or five hundred years before the *Chatham* appeared over the horizon. For long generations, the tchakat Moriori (i.e. taangata Maori – ordinary people) of these islands had seen only each other, an occasional canoe-load of storm-bound travellers from New Zealand,[38] and the animals around them. On 29 November 1791, therefore, when the lookout on the *Chatham* saw land looming up in the moonlight, he had found a very isolated place.

As the ship rounded Te Raki on the island's north-western extremity that morning, and sailed along Rekohu's northern coast, fires flared up on the hilltops (which must have been signals of warning) and people ran along the beaches. According to Edward Bell, the ship's clerk:

> The Land was low in general, but some Hills gradually rose up to a very moderate height, whose sides were beautifully cloathed with Wood up to the Tops, and the verdure on the rising grounds was exceedingly gratifying to the view. We ran along shore about 14 miles, but observed nothing like a Bay or Harbour. The depth of the water was moderate & gradual, and the ground good for Anchorage, being fine sand & shells. We saw smokes in several parts, particularly on the high land, but did not see any Inhabitants till we had run a good way, when a few Indians were observed running along the Beach, who were join'd by more as we proceeded.[39]

At 11 a.m. they anchored off Kaingaroa Harbour, towards the east end of the north coast. An armed cutter rowed ashore, with Lieutenant Broughton and James Johnstone, the *Chatham*'s master, on board. Some people had been seen earlier near the east point of the bay, hauling a canoe up on the beach. As soon as the Europeans landed, they examined this and another canoe. Although the local people had retreated to the other end of the beach, according to Broughton, they soon decided to approach the party of strangers:

> Seeing us examine their canoes, they hastily ran round the bay; on which we retired to the boat, to wait their arrival. As they approached they made much noise, and having soon joined us, we entered into a conversation by signs, gestures, and speech, without understanding what each other meant. We presented them with several articles, which they received with great eagerness, and seemed pleased with whatever was given them; but would make no exchanges. Yet as we had reason to believe they were very solicitous that we should land, Mr. Sheriff, leaving his arms in the boat, went on shore; but he seemed to excite the attention of two or three of them only, who attended him towards the canoes on the beach, whilst the rest, amounting to forty or thereabouts, remained on the rocks talking with us, and whenever the boat backed in, to deliver them any thing, they made no scruple of attempting to take whatever came within their reach. Having repeatedly beckoned us to follow them round to where their habitations were supposed to be, as soon as Mr Sheriff returned, we proceeded to comply with their wishes.
>
> They had been very curious in their examination of Mr. Sheriff's person, and seemed very desirous of keeping him, as they frequently pulled him towards the wood, where we imagined some of them resided. On meeting them on the other side, they seated themselves on the beach, and seemed very anxious to receive us on shore; but as all our intreaties were ineffectual in obtaining anything in return for our presents, perceiving many of them to be armed with long spears, and the situation being unfavorable to us, in case they should be disposed to treat us with hostility, we did not think it prudent to venture amongst them; and finding our negociation was not likely to be attended with success, we took our leave.[40]

Johnstone's account of this same episode made the Moriori seem more hostile than curious, but perhaps he was over-reacting. Moriori stories of this meeting report that they were amazed by the ship and its people. When they saw some of the sailors in the cutter smoking, they exclaimed, 'See Mahuika's [the fire god] fire proceeding from their throats!' They also thought that the ship's rigging was nets. They touched and handled the visitors (presumably Sheriff), some concluding that they were women, and tried to drag them off to their houses in the woods.[41] According to Broughton, 'our conversation frequently excit[ed] violent bursts of laughter amongst them. On our first landing their surprize and exclamations can hardly be imagined; they pointed to the sun, and then to us, as if to ask, whether we had come from thence.'[42]

This first meeting was brief and tentative; the Europeans were cautious, and the local people were armed. They sat quietly, though, when Broughton and his men went back along the beach and ritually took possession of Rekohu for Britain. The Europeans turned a turf, displayed the Union Jack, named the place 'Chatham Island' and drank a toast to His Majesty King George the Third. Then they nailed a lead plaque to a tree, inscribed: 'His Britannick Majesty's Brig Chatham, Lieutenant William Robert Broughton commander, the 29th November 1791.' After this ceremony they buried a Latin inscription to the same effect in a bottle in the tree's roots, claiming sovereignty 'on the presumption of our being the first discoverers'. Broughton then went to examine the canoes and nets on the beach:

> The canoes we examined were more in form of a small hand-barrow without legs, than any other thing to which they can be compared, decreasing in width from the after to the fore part. They were made of a light substance resembling bamboo, though not hollow, placed fore and aft on each side, and secured together by pieces of the same wood, up and down, very neatly fastened with the fibres of some plant in the manner of basket work. Their bottoms flat and constructed in the same way, were two feet deep and eighteen inches in breadth; the opening of the seams on the inside and bottoms were stuffed with long sea weed; their sides meet not abaft, nor forward, their extreme breadth aft is three, and forward, two feet; length eight and nine feet. In the stern is a seat very neatly made of the same material; which is moveable. They appeared calculated alone for fishing amongst the rocks near the shore; were capable of carrying two or three persons, and were so light that two men could convey them any where with ease, and one could haul them into safety on the beach. Their grapnels were stones, and the ropes to which these were made fast, were formed of matting, worked up in a similar way with that which is called French sinnet. The paddles were of hard wood, the blades very broad, and gradually increasing from the handle.[43]

There were also nets nearby, including two scoop nets and several with supplejack hoops at the mouth six feet wide, weighed down by stone sinkers, and tapering down eight to ten feet to a closely netted endpiece, which Broughton and Johnstone also described.

Broughton and his men went a little way into the bush, where they found a number of arbours among the low trees, made 'by bending the branches when young, and closing them round with smaller trees'. Some of these arbours, which had been recently slept in, had small palisades around them, and fireplaces and

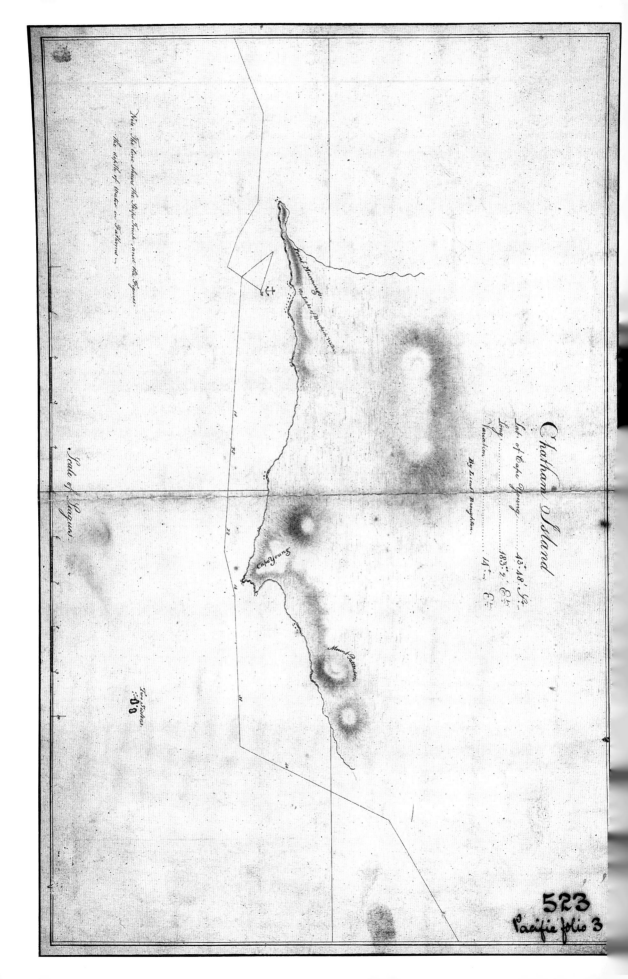

Chatham Island

Lat. of Cape Young .... 43° 48' 9"
Long .... 183° 2' E"
Variation .... 14° E"

By Lieut Broughton.

Cape Young

Mount Patterson

Scale of Leagues.

Ten Leagues.

Note. The tint shows the High Land, and the
depth of water in Fathoms.

heaps of shells. The birds flew around them and seemed quite tame, as if they had never been hunted. As the Europeans came out of the grove of trees, they were approached by a small group of Moriori, who greeted them by pressing noses. The Europeans gave them pieces of red cloth, helmets, nails and beads, but they seemed to have no idea of barter, taking goods without offering anything in return. One man gave his spear, but when he was offered looking glasses for his sea-bear cloak, he was so entranced with his reflection that he ran off with the mirrors into the bush. Broughton now shot a bird 'to shew them the superior effect of our fire-arms', which made them all retreat, except for one old man 'who maintained his ground; and presenting his spear side-ways, beat time with his feet'.[44] Trying to calm him, Broughton shook his hand and talked with him, noticing at the same time that he was holding a patu (stone hand club) rolled up in matting in his hand. He and others were anxious to examine Broughton's gun and shot belt, exclaiming, 'Tohoua' (or 'Toohata') as they looked at them. Their spears were between six and ten feet long, some with carved handles. Broughton described these people in some detail:

> The men were of a middling size, some stoutly made, well limbed and fleshy; their hair, both of the head and beard, was black, and by some was worn long. The young men had it tied up in a knot on the crown of their heads, intermixed with black and white feathers. Some had their beards plucked out; their complexion and general colour is dark brown, with plain features, and in general bad teeth. Their skins were destitute of any marks, and they had the appearance of being cleanly in their persons. Their dress was either a seal or bear-skin tied with sinnet, inside outwards, round their necks, which fell below their hips; or mats neatly made, tied in the same manner which covered their backs and shoulders. Some were naked, excepting a well woven matt of fine texture, which, being fastened at each end by a string round their waists, made a sort of decent garment.
>
> We did not observe that their ears were bored, or that they wore any ornaments about their persons, excepting a few who had a sort of necklace made of mother of pearl shells [while others, according to Johnstone, wore a small piece of bone round their necks on a strand of twisted hair]. Several of them had their fishing lines, made of the same sort of hemp with their nets, fastened round them; but we did not see any of their hooks. We noticed two or three old men, but they did not appear to have any power or authority over the others.[45]

Broughton gestured to the Moriori that his men needed food and drink, and a small group of them set off with the Europeans down the beach. Some collected large sticks, which they swung round their heads, while one man fastened two shaped stones to each end of a stick about two feet long, as a temporary weapon. The Europeans became uneasy at this and decided to go back to the cutter, but as they moved towards the sea their Moriori companions left them and went to a fire one of them had just made near the woods. When Johnstone approached this group, they did not seem to welcome his presence, so he and the others walked

Opposite: *Broughton's chart of the north-east coast of Chatham Island.*

down the beach to a lake they could see in the distance (probably Te Wapu). Four-teen Moriori went with them while the rest remained by the fire. On reaching the lake they discovered that its water was too brackish for drinking, and returned to the cutter, which had been following them along the shore. As soon as they got to the sea's edge, however, their uncertain truce with the local people abruptly ended:

> Abreast of the boat, they became very clamorous, talked extremely loud to each other, and divided so as nearly to surround us. A young man strutted towards me in a very menacing attitude; he distorted his person, turned up his eyes, made hideous faces, and created a wonderful fierceness in his appearance by his gestures [a classic display of the ceremonial challenge]. On pointing my double-barrelled gun towards him he desisted. Their hostile intentions were now too evident to be mistaken, and therefore, to avoid the necessity of resorting to extremities, the boat was immediately ordered in to take us on board.[46]

As the cutter rowed in, the Moriori advanced towards the Europeans. Broughton fired one barrel of small-shot, hoping to drive them off, but one man clubbed Johnstone's gun out of his hand and was shot. A marine and a sailor were forced into the water and also fired, as did the sailor in charge of the boat. Broughton ordered his men to stop shooting as the Moriori ran off, and at first they thought that no one had been wounded. One man, however, fell before he reached the woods and lay on the beach. Johnstone ran after him and examined the body, finding 'to [his] utter grief' that the man was quite dead, with a musket ball shot through his heart. He returned to the cutter, and while they were rowing away a man came out of the woods and knelt by the dead body, where 'he was distinctly heard in a sort of dismal howl to utter his lamentations'.[47]

According to Moriori accounts of the clash, the dead man was Tamakaroro of Kaingaroa. When the Europeans fired, the Moriori had remarked to each other, 'Hear the crack of the kelp of Hauoro [a war god]!' – the muskets sounded like kelp pods, exploding on the beach in the sun.[48] Moriori told Percy Smith many years later that a sailor had tried to take a net from the beach, its owner resisted and fighting broke out; whereas Thomas Ritchie was told that Tamakaroro had tried to take Broughton's jacket and was shot.[49] Koche, a Moriori who had escaped on an American ship after his homeland was invaded by Maori, reported that his father told him that 'as the ship was leaving the shore the atmosphere became dark, sultry and gloomy, and thunder and lightning descended the mountain and pursued the retreating strangers into the sea'.[50]

Broughton was appalled by what had happened, although he blamed the Moriori for their 'unprovoked, unmerited hostility'. He took the cutter back to their first landing place, where they left gifts in the canoes as a peace offering. According to Koche's father, as soon as the European ship had departed the island, a council was held. 'The fact that the slain was not carried off was considered proof that the "children of the sun" were not cannibals, and by some doubts were expressed as to their intent in landing. It was concluded, in the event of their return, to meet them with an emblem of peace.'[51] The irony was that, according to their own traditions, the tchakat Moriori were a peaceable people who had made a pact to avoid warfare among themselves on the island. Koche reported that:

> From the earliest period [his people] were inclined to peaceful pursuits, and sub-sisted chiefly upon fish and seal; that they enjoyed a democracy, and conducted their simple affairs by a council of notable men. He did not hesitate, however, to acknowledge that when at long intervals . . . a high and prolonged west wind drove a canoe-load of New Zealanders upon their shores, they forthwith and with-out ceremony slew them. But he justified this departure from their ordinary hab-its on the ground of public policy; as, had they received them in charity, and pursued the peaceful tenor of their way, their involuntary visitors would have ended by slaying and, moreover, devouring them; the first party of this sort who landed on the island having made it distinctly understood that men and women were their favorite articles of diet. But among themselves, the taking of life, he said, was unknown . . .
>
> They lived in single families, or in companies . . . moving from place to place as food became less plentiful, or as fancy or a love of change dictated; being care-ful, in pitching their new and fragile habitations, not to crowd upon established groups. In the sealing season, the families of the interior came down to the coast, and laid in from the rocks and reefs a supply of meat and skins; and when fishing on the shore became dull, or the birds wild with much hunting, the people of the sea bundled up their effects, and moved to the interior lakes, chiefly to the great Tewanga, filled with fish, and covered with wild fowl . . . Their only weapon of offence or defence was a club, seldom used except in killing a seal. Tattooing was unknown. No ornaments were in use. The Tuiti burned their dead to avoid the fearful idea of prolonged decay. Man springs from the earth as the flower springs: they return him to his mother, as the fall fires, sweeping over the plain, return the flower.[52]

In the aftermath of the council, it was said that those who had threatened the Europeans were thrashed for their misdeeds. On board the *Chatham*, Broughton also regretted their meeting, describing Tamakaroro's killing as 'a melancholy fate' and naming Kaingaroa 'Skirmish Bay'. He gave the bearings of Rekohu in his journal and charted the 'Chatham Islands'. The long isolation and the time of peace for the tchakat Moriori was over. The 'children of the sun' had arrived.[53]

After leaving Rekohu, the *Chatham* carried on to Tahiti, where they rejoined the *Discovery*. After a short stay there, the expedition sailed for Hawai'i, where Vancouver hoped to find the *Daedalus*. The supply ship had left England in late August and sailed via Cape Horn to the Marquesas, but was delayed by a fire caused by spontaneous combustion in the cargo, and did not reach Hawai'i until May 1792, almost two months after the *Discovery* and *Chatham* had left the islands. On their first landing at Oahu, Lieutenant Hergest, the astronomer William Gooch and a sailor were killed by the Hawaiians. After this disaster, the *Daedalus* left Hawai'i and sailed for Nootka, finally meeting Vancouver on 28 August 1792. There the supply ship's stores were replenished and Lieutenant James Hanson, second in command of the *Chatham*, was appointed to succeed Hergest as her commander.

Negotiations began at Nootka Sound between Vancouver and Bodega y Quadra, the Spanish commandant of San Blas and California, for the return of the British base in the Sound. Diplomatic courtesies included an exchange of charts, which may have included a version of Surville's 1769 chart of Tokerau (Doubtless Bay) in New Zealand. Quadra also offered cattle and sheep for transport to Port Jackson, and Spanish sailors to make up the crew of the *Daedalus*, which had been depleted by death and desertion. The *Daedalus* was partly unloaded at Monterey, where some sick sailors from the expedition were discharged into the ship for passage to Port Jackson, and twelve cows, six bulls, twelve ewes and six rams were loaded into stalls that had been built on board.

On 29 December, Hanson received his orders from Vancouver, with letters for Governor Phillip at Port Jackson, instructing him to proceed to the Marquesas for food, water and refreshments and, from there, to Tahiti to pick up pigs, hens and twenty-one English sailors who had been stranded there when their ship had been wrecked on a reef. After this he was to proceed to

a bay lately visited and surveyed by the French in the northern part of New Zealand, called by Captain Cook, Doubtless Bay . . . a sketch of which is herewith inclosed for your information . . . At [Doubtless] or any port near the north extremity of New Zealand . . . you are from thence to use your best endeavours to take with you one or two of the natives of that country versed in the operations necessary for the manufacture of the flax-plant of which their garments are mostly made, for the purpose, if possible, of instructing the new settlers at Port Jackson in the management of that very valuable plant, and this being a subject of no small importance you are to pay particular attention to the effecting it, in the execution whereof the native of the Sandwich Islands you have on board may be essentially serviceable from his speaking nearly the same language.[54]

Nine

THE HUNT FOR FLAX

TUKI AND HURU'S VISIT TO NORFOLK ISLAND
1793

Flax was thus the first of New Zealand's resources to attract serious European attention. The person responsible for the plan to fetch flax-dressers from New Zealand was Philip Gidley King, a naval officer who in 1788 had been sent as the first Commandant of Norfolk Island. From the beginning, Norfolk had been thought of as a place where timber and flax might be procured for the British naval forces in India. In 1785, Sir George Young and Sir John Call had asked the East India Company for permission to establish a colony there to supply 'those valuable Articles of Cordage and Masts for your shipping in India, which are now obtain'd at a most enormous Expence; and from their Scarcity have often reduced the maritime Force employed in the East Indies, to great Inconvenience and even Distress'.[1] They did not succeed, but the idea of a settlement at Norfolk became part of the plan for a penal colony in New South Wales.[2]

Soon after the First Fleet arrived at Botany Bay in 1788, King had been despatched to Norfolk to establish an outpost on the island. He immediately inspected the local timber and set some convicts to work the Norfolk flax. This proved to be by no means simple. When European flax is immersed in water for several weeks, the outer layer of the leaves becomes soft and can be beaten off, leaving the fibres, but this method failed with the local species. King began to send off urgent requests for convict flax-dressers to be sent to New Zealand to study Maori weaving and brought back to Norfolk to teach the convicts the appropriate techniques. The authorities considered this approach to be impractical and probably too dangerous, but King was persistent. In December 1790, he arrived in London on leave, and in January 1791 wrote a report (backed by discussions with Lord Grenville, the Secretary of State, and Sir Joseph Banks, president of the Royal Society and the Admiralty's trusted advisor on Pacific exploration) that put forward another suggestion:

> The Flax Plant of New Zealand, grows spontaneously, in many Parts of [Norfolk] Island, but mostly abounds on the Sea Coast, where there is a very great Quantity

205

A portrait of Philip Gidley King.

Flax plant of Norfolk Island,
sketched by John Hunter.

of it . . . Every Method has been tried to work it, but, I much fear that, until a Native of New Zealand, can be carried to Norfolk Island, the Method of dressing that valuable Commodity will not be known. Could that be obtained, I have no doubt but Norfolk Island would soon clothe the inhabitants of New South Wales.[3]

In April 1791 at Tenerife, on his way back to Norfolk Island on the *Gorgon*, King wrote a letter to Under-Secretary Evan Nepean, spelling out the precise, practical nature of the problem:

Should the manufacturing of the flax-plant on Norfolk Island be thought an object, which it must be, were it only to cloath those who are now there, two or three New Zealanders would be necessary, to show how the operation of separating the flaxy from the vegetable part of the flax is performed . . . Without that assistance I do not think we shall succeed, as every method we could devise has been tried already, but without success.[4]

Later in the voyage, King met George Vancouver at the Cape of Good Hope on his way to the Pacific and asked him 'if it should be in his power during his Stay in these Seas, to procure Two or three New Zealanders of that Country, that it would be an Act of Publick Utility to send them hither'.[5] One way or another, King's persistence finally paid off. Orders for Vancouver to send his supply ship *Daedalus* to New Zealand for this purpose were drafted in London in November 1791, reaching him nine months later.

The *Daedalus* finally sailed from Monterey in late December 1792 with Spanish as well as English sailors on board, and Kalehua (or 'Jack') from Kauai, a bilingual Hawaiian sailor who had spent six months crewing on an American fur-trading ship before joining the *Discovery*.[6] After visiting the Marquesas and Tahiti (where one hundred pigs, four goats and six dozen fowl were purchased and one of the shipwrecked British sailors came on board), Hanson set sail for New Zealand to fetch some flax-dressers. By the time the ship arrived off the Cavalli Islands, it was a floating piggery.

Maori would have been fascinated by the pigs, goats and fowl on board the *Daedalus*, but unsurprised to find that the first link to bind them closely to Europeans was made of flax. 'Muka tangata' (literally 'human flax fibre') is a phrase often used in Maori to refer to ties between people. The silky inner threads, or muka, stripped out of flax leaves represent genealogical lines. Flax strands, lines and ropes, and the threads for weaving garments are persistently linked in Maori language with talk of relationship and ancestral power:

kaha	• rope	• hill ridge
	• navel string	• line of ancestry
	• lineage	• line on which niu rods were placed for divination
	• boundary line of land	• file of an army
	• strength	
aho	• string	• line
	• woof of a mat	• line of descent
	• radiant light	• medium for an atua in divination
kanoi	• strand of a cord or rope	• weave the aho taahuhu (main thread) of a garment
	• trace one's descent	• authority, position

Exchanges of cloaks acted as exchanges of mana and a way of ratifying alliances, while links with ancestors and land were spoken of in the language of weaving. In a fine mat, the line where one panel joined another was called whakapapa – the word for genealogy, the weaving of the world.[7]

Hanson's way of negotiating with Maori must have aroused resentment rather than amity, however. Shortly after arriving off the Cavalli Islands early in 1793, he lured two Maori on board his ship and unceremoniously kidnapped them. Furthermore, they were both high-born men, who knew little enough of weaving (a woman's art) – a strange way to create an alliance. Hanson's own report of the episode to the Admiralty was cursory:

I beg leave to inform you Sir, I proceeded on to New Zealand in the Bay of Islands obtained two Natives of that Country; and proceeded on to Port Jackson and delivered to His Honor Lieut. Governor Grose, Capt. Vancouvers despatches, the two Natives are sent to Norfolk Island by his Order.[8]

A more detailed account of what happened came from the two young men themselves, who told their story to Lieutenant-Governor King on Norfolk Island some months later. According to their account, 'Tooke' (Tuki-tahua) had been visiting his friend 'Woodoo' (Huru-kokoti) at his home near the Bay of Islands when a European vessel was sighted far out at sea. The ship was close to two inhabited islands, 'Ko-mootu-kowa' (Motukawanui) and 'Opnake' (Panaaki), of the Cavalli group north of the Bay of Islands. Seized with curiosity, Huru's chief 'Povoreck' (Pohoreka?) took Tuki, Huru, one of Huru's wives and his brother, and a priest out in several canoes to the largest island, Motu-kawanui, where they were joined by the local chief 'Tee-ah-wor-rock' (Te Awaroki?), Huru's father-in-law; and Te Awaroki's son (who controlled Panaaki at that time). They all went out to look at the ship:

> They were some time about the Ship, before the Canoe in which Tooke and Woodoo were, ventured alongside; when a number of Iron Tools and other Articles were given into the Canoe, the Agent Lieutenant Hanson (of whose kindness to them they speak in the highest terms) Invited and pressed them, to go on board, which Tooke and Woodoo were anxious to do immediately, but were prevented by the persuasion of the Countrymen; at length [they] went on Board, & according to their Expression, they were blinded by the Curious things they saw; Lieutenant Hanson prevailed on them to go below, where they Eat some meat; At this time the Ship made sail, One of them saw the Canoes astern, and perceiving the Ship was leaving them, they both became frantic with Grief, & broke the Cabbin Windows, with an intention of leaping Over Board, but were prevented; whilst the Canoes were in hearing, they advised Povoreek to make the best of his way home for fear of his being taken also.[9]

In his *Chatham* journal, Edward Bell gave a similar description of their capture, based on a conversation at dinner on the *Discovery* between Mr Puget and Lieutenant Hanson in Nootka in October 1793. According to Bell:

> At New Zealand they did not anchor, their business at this place was to endeavour to get two or three of the Natives to go with them to Botany Bay, for the purpose of cultivating the Flax plant, but as the Natives came off to the vessel in great numbers, and knowing them to have the character of a very troublesome, daring, insolent people, Lieut. Hanson did not think it prudent to stop to make a strict scrutiny into the abilities of any particular people, more especially as the crew of the *Daedalus*, at all times weak, but then were much more so, from a number of sick among them, he therefore by presents inveigled two young men out of a Canoe, and taking them below, under pretence of giving them something more, he instantly made all sail; Victuals were given to these poor fellows, and different methods used to keep their attention alive below for a couple of hours, when

going on Deck, instead of finding themselves in the same place as when they
Came on board, and their canoe alongside, into which they were ready to jump –
to their inexpressible grief and astonishment they found themselves some Leagues
from the Land, and no Canoe to get on shore in; In a little time they appeared
contented.[10]

When he wrote this journal entry, Bell argued that what had been done was
justified, because 'a large ship, valuably laden, poorly manned, and with the best
part of the crew sick, must act with prudence', even though this might not meet
with 'the feelings of these people, who . . . Philosophise by the Fireside'. In 1815,
though, he wrote a marginal note to this entry, 'I dont think so now 1815, I am
20 years older.'[11]

Lieutenant Hanson was probably wise not to land in the Bay of Islands. At the
time of the *Daedalus*'s arrival, the Bay was densely populated, with perhaps fifteen
thousand people living in fortified and open villages, supported by productive
fisheries and fertile inland gardens. Cook and other members of the *Endeavour*
expedition had almost been cut off there in 1769, in an affray where a number of
local people were shot. There had also been shootings off the Cavallis, when the
local people attacked the *Endeavour* with a barrage of sticks and stones. Three
years later, in 1772, after a month spent anchored in the Bay in relative tranquillity, Marion du Fresne and a number of his men had been killed for violating a
death tapu and for interfering (disastrously if unwittingly) in local politics. The
rest of his expedition retaliated with musket- and cannon-fire, and scores of local
people (including old people and women) were shot. The inhabitants of the Bay of
Islands may have learned to covet iron by 1793, but they also had long memories.
It was scarcely surprising that they treated the *Daedalus* with extreme caution.

Nor was it surprising that Tuki and Huru's countrymen tried to dissuade them
from going on board the *Daedalus*. In 1769, after a two-week visit to Tokerau, the
French explorer Surville had retaliated for the loss of his ship's yawl (which was
washed up on Tokerau Beach by a storm and claimed according to local custom by
the residents) by burning houses, canoes and nets, and kidnapping a local chief.
This chief, Ranginui, had earlier offered food and shelter to a group of Surville's
sick sailors when they were marooned below his paa during the same storm. A
later tribal account showed the extent of local mystification and anger at Surville's
behaviour:

> A gale came on and the sick people of these salts (maitai) from the other side of
> the sea were on shore, and the people of Patuu tribe attended to and fed these sick
> people, and they were kind to these white skins [Pakeha in the original] till the
> gale subsided . . . [Then] the chief who was called Ranginui was tied by orders of
> the chief of those salts, and the ship sailed away with Te Ranginui on board, and
> the vessel was lost to sight out far on the sea and sailed away no one knew where.
> There was not any cause given for which Ranginui was made prisoner by these
> salts, nor was there any reason for his being taken out to sea, but for such acts as
> this the Maori retaliated on the salts, who might come to these islands, that the

Maori might have revenge for the evil bought on them by the salts, or those from over the sea.[12]

Tuki was from Oruru in Tokerau and must have known of that earlier kidnapping. The two young men, however, 'blinded by the curious things they saw' and perhaps reassured by Kalehua, the Hawaiian sailor on board, were impetuously inquisitive. They went aboard the *Daedalus*, which, like Surville's ship more than twenty years earlier, 'sailed away . . . and was lost to sight out far on the sea'. Another tribal account, recorded by John White in about the 1850s, recorded their kidnapping:

> Two of our people were taken by the European on board of a ship to teach the European to make the tow from the flax leaf. These two men went out in a canoe to fish for kahawai, they were called Tuki and Huru-kokoti, or Toha-mahue who were one a priest and his friend, who was a warrior. They were occupied in fishing when a ship made her appearance and they two went on board of her, and the canoe was lifted on board also, and the ship sailed way on the sea for many days and then she came to an Island, where there were many Europeans . . .[13]

From their own and other reports, it seems that Tuki and Huru were well treated on board the *Daedalus*, despite their grief at being so unceremoniously snatched from their families and their consternation at being on board a European vessel (with its cargo of peculiar animals and European goods).

On 20 April 1793, the *Daedalus* arrived in Port Jackson with its cargo of sick sailors, Vancouver's supplies, Tuki and Huru, seventy squealing pigs, one calf and four sheep. Almost as soon as the ship anchored, Acting Governor Grose ordered Tuki and Huru to be transferred to the *Shaw Hormuzear*, a Calcutta merchantman crewed by Lascars and Chinese,[14] which had arrived at Port Jackson from India several months earlier. Its commander, William Wright Bampton, and his wife had embarked on the voyage to bring a cargo of livestock, meat, dried goods and a large quantity of spirits[15] to Port Jackson as a private speculation. Several weeks after their arrival, Malaspina's exploring expedition appeared off the heads at Port Jackson, and about a month later, on 20 April, the *Daedalus* anchored in the harbour.

By that time Arthur Phillip had returned to England and Grose was in charge at the penal colony. When the *Daedalus* was sighted, the *Shaw Hormuzear* had off-loaded its cargo and was about to sail for Calcutta. Grose persuaded Bampton to delay for a few days so that he could send a despatch to England confirming the storeship's arrival. In his letter to the Secretary of State, Henry Dundas, Grose reported that 'Captain Vancouver has sent here two natives of New Zealand, for the purpose of teaching us their manner of manufacturing the flax-plant'.[16] Remembering King's continual requests for New Zealanders to instruct the convicts at Norfolk Island in flax-working, Grose ordered Tuki and Huru to be transferred to the *Shaw Hormuzear*, accompanied by Lieutenant Hanson, who stayed with them until the ship sailed past the Port Jackson Heads. On 24 April, after three days in port during which they had seen little or nothing of the town, Tuki and Huru sailed on the *Shaw Hormuzear*, with its crew of shivering Lascars, five freed convicts and a cargo of 220 tons of provisions, six Bengal ewes and two rams, for Norfolk Island.

TUKI AND HURI ON NORFOLK ISLAND
May–November 1793

Norfolk had been chosen as an outpost for the main penal colony at Port Jackson. It was small (about three by six miles), rugged, and extremely isolated, surrounded by a thousand-mile moat. Its cliffs dropped straight into the sea, and its one good landing place was guarded by a rocky reef, making access difficult for seaborne travellers. Two high hills covered with dense sub-tropical rainforest dominated the skyline, and the ridges and coastal cliffs bristled with the island's characteristic pines. Norfolk's pines, the flax that grew on many of its cliffs, and its strategic location in the Pacific sea lanes (reported by Cook on his second voyage) had recommended it to the Admiralty planners. Furthermore, it was uninhabited. When the first party of convicts landed on Norfolk in 1788, they found Polynesian rats, two canoes (which had suggested to Governor Phillip a recent visit from New Zealand), a carving, cultivated banana trees, stone adzes and artifacts on shore, but the Polynesians had gone again and the island was abandoned.[17]

Norfolk's valleys and coastal flats proved to be fertile, so a convict farm and flax factory was established on the island. After his return to Norfolk in late 1791, Philip Gidley King had continued to plead for New Zealanders to be brought to the island to instruct the convicts in flax-working. The Admiralty eventually responded to his arguments, but King did not know this, so his letters to Grose and others often repeated the request. On 15 January 1792, for instance, he wrote to Lord Grenville:

> The Piece of Canvas that covers these Letters I have sent as a Specimen of the very imperfect State that the Flax is brought to, nor do I imagine that it can be meliorated without some of the New Zealanders to point out the Manner of their dressing that valuable Article. As every Method has been unsuccessfully tried to attain that desirable Perfection which the New Zealanders give it (many Specimens of which are in the Possession of Sir Joseph Banks, which he obtained from these Natives when there) and the very great Quantity they gave in Return for trifling things, may be a Reason to suppose that the Manufacturing of it is not tedious, but very simple.[18]

King also reported that he had asked Eber Bunker, the American master of the *William and Ann*, a convict transport on a whaling expedition, 'who is going to fish on that coast, to get 2 of them, and to return here with them'. When Bunker made difficulties about the proposal, a £100 reward had been offered if he were successful.[19] Subsequently, King noted that Bunker had agreed to go to the Bay of Islands or thereabouts to fetch samples of the flax plant in various stages of manufacture, and to try to persuade, with gifts of axes and kind treatment, 'two healthy

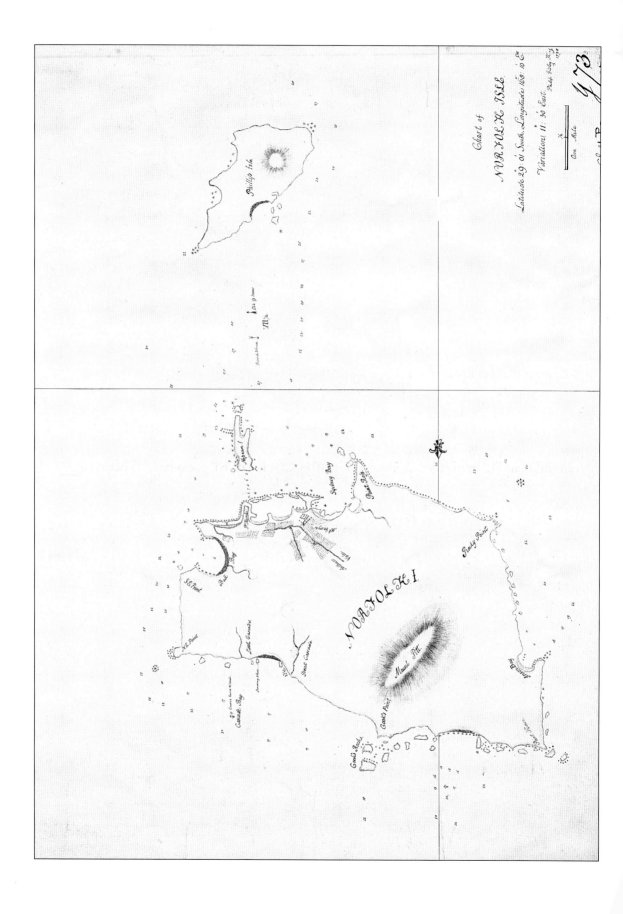

Phillip Isle

Chart of
NORFOLK ISLE.
Latitude 29° 01' South, Longitude 168° 10' East.
Variation 11° 30' East.

One Mile

NORFOLK I.

Mount Pitt

Sydney Bay

Point Ross

Rocky Point

Nepean I.

Ball Bay

Cascade Bay

Great Cascade

Little Cascade

S.E. Point

N.W. Point

Cook's Point

Cook's Rock

4/3

Men, of between Thirty and Fifty Years of Age, & . . . [who] understand the Method used in that Country of manufacturing the Flax Plant'[20] to come back to Norfolk. On 19 January, Bunker sailed for the north-east coast of New Zealand.

On 29 March, however, King reported that the *William and Ann* had not returned to Norfolk (a later marginal note in his journal added, 'The Ship went to Doubtless Bay but could not prevail on any of the Inhabitants to go with him.'[21]). Again he asked the government to arrange for New Zealanders to be brought to the island. He repeated this request once more to Governor Phillip in September. Finally, in April 1793, his two 'flax-dressers' arrived, accompanied by the following letter from David Collins, Secretary to the Governor:

> . . . Since writing the above, the *Daedalus*, Store Ship has arrived from the North-West Coast of America. The Agent, Lieut. Hanson (Lieut. Hergest having been killed by the Natives of one of the Sandwich Islands), according to Instructions he received from Captain Vancouver, has brought with him two men, Natives of New Zealand, and the Lieut. Governor [now Grose] has sent them to you by Captain Bampton for the purpose of giving such Information as they possess respecting the Manufacture of the Flax Plant. The Lieut. Governor thinking it perfectly unnecessary to recommend them to your care, desires me only to add that, he hopes much Benefit may be derived from their Introduction among us. You will of course victual and clothe them.[22]

At the time of Tuki and Huru's arrival at Norfolk in 1793, the island community was in many ways extraordinary. Its population of 1,026 numbered 495 convicts, 126 children, 318 free settlers, seventy-six military and eleven civil personnel.[23] There were only 126 women on the island (of whom all but the Governor's wife were convicts), and three 'Natives' (presumably Aboriginals).[24] Almost half of these people were convicts, from England's hulks and jails. Many of them had suffered greatly on their voyages from England, and recurrent food shortages and the lack of adequate clothing in the 'thief colonies' had worsened their condition. In March 1792, Governor Phillip was forced to report to the Admiralty from Port Jackson:

> I am very sorry to say that most of the convicts who were received by the last ships still continue in the same debilitated state in which they were landed, and of whom, in less than seven months, two hundred and eighty-eight men have died . . . The returns of sick this day is – civil and military, eighteen; male convicts, three hundred and ninety-four; and females, seventeen . . . The cloathing that has been rec'd for the use of the convicts is so very slight that most of the people are naked a few weeks after they have been cloathed.[25]

Rations were also in short supply on Norfolk at this time, and many of the convicts were so weak and emaciated that they were unable to do much work, and they were often harshly punished.[26]

By May 1793, however, the situation had improved somewhat. King reduced the hours of public labour required of the convicts to forty hours a week, allowing

Opposite: *A chart of Norfolk Island, sketched by Philip Gidley King in 1790.*

'those who were industrious' to work on the government lands to supplement their rations. Convict labourers were allocated to help the free settlers (who included some convicts whose sentences had expired), and as a result the 1792–93 harvest increased fivefold.[27] Fruit trees, pineapples, strawberries, melons, sugar cane, bananas, grapes, figs, indigo, coffee and cotton plants, potatoes and yams were planted; and the numbers of animals on the island increased to fifteen hundred pigs, eighty goats, thirty sheep and large numbers of ducks, geese and chickens,[28] supplemented by muttonbirds caught on Mount Pitt, eels from the creeks and fish caught out at sea.

From the time of their first arrival at Norfolk, Tuki and Huru's position on the island was paradoxical. Although they were captives, and 'savages' to boot, they lived in Government House with Lieutenant-Governor King, ate at his table and were excused from manual labour. Acting Governor Grose had instructed that they should be treated kindly, and so they were. They were issued clothing and rations from the public store,[29] and lived in friendship with King's family at the pinnacle of Norfolk society.

At first, King's interest in Tuki and Huru was pragmatic. Almost as soon as they came on shore he tried to get them to show the convicts how to work the local flax. He sent a report to the Secretary of State by the *Shaw Hormuzear*, which commented:

> The New Zealanders method of dressing the flax has a present appearance of being very tedious, perhaps when they have been longer with us, we shall mutually improve. A Flax dresser & Three Women attend them as often as we can prevail on them to instruct; As yet it requires entreaty, to persuade them to give us the least information.[30]

Their reluctance to instruct the convicts was not surprising, however, for during their first few days on the island Tuki and Huru were grief-stricken and in shock. The experience of being snatched onto the *Daedalus*, with its cargo of pigs, sheep and cattle, then transferred to the *Shaw Hormuzear*, with its Lascar crew, and taken to Norfolk Island must have seemed a nightmare; and King's urgent enquiries about flax-working only added to their confusion. All of the Governor's planning and effort to bring them to Norfolk for this purpose proved largely futile, for as he later reported:

> Every information that could be got from them, respecting their mode of manufacturing the Flax plant, was obtained in One day . . . and which turned out to be very little, as this operation is the peculiar Occupation of the Women, & as Woodoo is a Warrior, & Tookee a Priest, they gave us to understand, that Dressing of Flax, never made any part of their studies.

Opposite above: *A sketch of the settlement of Sydney on Norfolk Island, by the convict artist George Raper.*

Opposite below: *A plan of the settlers' lots on Norfolk Island, drawn by Deputy Surveyor Charles Grimes in 1793.*

Such little information as he could immediately obtain, King reported in a letter to Sir Joseph Banks on 24 May 1793, along with a jar containing processed flax.[31] King added that Tuki and Huru seemed very familiar with the local vegetation and had already taught the Europeans on Norfolk to eat some things they had previously thought poisonous. They had joyfully recognised some stone axes that had been dug up on the island as 'Etoki' of 'Eaheinomawe' (He toki [adzes] of 'He ahi no Maui [literally 'Maui's fire' – the term collected by Cook for the North island of New Zealand]).[32]

When the *Shaw Hormuzear* left the island in May 1793, King hoped that he still might learn more about flax-working from Tuki and Huru. Taking a 'coloured general chart' of the Pacific, he showed them the relative positions of Norfolk Island, Port Jackson and New Zealand, and promised them that if they would teach the women on Norfolk everything that they knew about flax-work, he would send them home in five or six months' time. Then he gave them a choice: either leave Norfolk Island and go to England on the *Shaw Hormuzear* or stay with him pending their return home. Without hesitation, Tuki and Huru chose to stay, but when Captain Bampton and his wife 'took their leave, they were sensibly affected, and cryed bitterly, however kind treatment soon made [them] Chearful'.[33]

Tuki and Huru were the first Maori to spend any time in a European community. The Europeans on Norfolk Island knew of the inhabitants of New Zealand by reputation as ferocious cannibals, and were surprised and disarmed by their genial guests. In November 1793, Thomas Jamison, assistant surgeon on the island, wrote to a friend in England: 'The New Zealanders are pleasant and good-natured beyond anything one could expect to meet with amongst so barbarous a people as they have always been considered to be. One of them is called Odoo [Huru], the other Tugee [Tuki]. The former is son to one of the princes of that country; the other is son to one of their priests.'[34]

Lieutenant-Governor King knew Tuki and Huru better than anybody else on the island, and his description of his two visitors is worth quoting in detail:

> Hoo-doo Co-co-ty To-wai-ma-how-ey [Huru Kokoti Te Waimahoe?] is about twenty four years of age; five feet eight inches high; of an athletic make; his features like those of a European, and very interesting. He is of the district of Teer-a-Witte [Te Raawhiti] . . . about the Bay of Islands. Both [Tuki and Huru] agree that the distance between their dwellings is only two days journey by land, and one day by water . . .
>
> Hoo-doo is nearly related to Po-vo-reek, who is the principal chief of Teer-a-Witte. [In a letter to Banks, King added that Huru was 'a warrior, and a Superior Rank to Tookee, he is always treated by great deference and respect by the latter . . . Five years ago his Father was killed in battle and he says Eat by the Natives of T'Sou duckey (Hauraki)'.[35]] He has two wives and one child, about whose safety he seemed very apprehensive; and almost every evening at the close of day, he, as well as Too-gee, lamented their separation in a sort of half-crying and half-singing, expressive of grief, and which was at times very affecting.
>
> Too-gee Te-ter-re-nu-e Warri-pe-do [Tuki Te Terenui Whare pirau?] is of the

same age as Hoo-doo; but about three inches shorter, he is stout and well made and like Hoo-doo of an olive complexion, with strong black hair. Both are tattowed on the hips. Too-gee's features are rather handsome and interesting; his nose is aquiline, and he has good teeth. He is a native of the district of Ho-do-doe [Oruru] (which is in Doubtless Bay) of which district Toogee's father is the Etang-a-roa [He Tangaroa – god of the sea, or maybe 'tohunga'], or chief priest; and to that office the son succeeds on his father's death. Beside his father, who is a very old man, he has left a wife and child; about all of whom he is very anxious and uneasy, as well as about the chief (Moo-de-wy [Muriwai]) whom he represents as a very worthy character.

Too-gee has a decided preference to Hoo-doo both in disposition and manners; although the latter is not wanting in a certain degree of good nature, but he can at times be very much of the savage. Hoo-doo, like a true patriot, thinks there is no country, people, nor customs equal to his own; on which account he is much less curious as to what he sees about him than his companion Too-gee, who has the happy art of insinuating himself into every person's esteem. Except at times, when he is lamenting the absence of his family and friends, he is cheerful, often facetious, and very intelligent . . . It is not, however, meant to be said that if Too-gee were not present, an indifferent opinion would have been formed of Hoo-doo; on the contrary, the manners and disposition of the latter are far more pleasing than could have been expected to be found in a native of that country.[36]

King was a conservative and dutiful officer with a conventional faith in God, King and Empire, who had some liberal leanings. He later expressed sympathy for the Australian Aboriginals in their conflicts with the colonists in New South Wales.[37] On Norfolk, while he was struggling to establish the island as a self-sufficient colony, he gave land and stock to some freed convicts, commuted many sentences for offences committed on the island and tried to protect the convicts against arbitrary violence. King had some capacity for fellow feeling, and Tuki and Huru's misery over their captivity moved him:

> The daily lamentations of Two sensible men, who were continually reminding me of my Promise, & repeating their anxious fears, respecting the safety of their Familys, from whom they were separated in a sudden manner made me feel for them as a Father & a Husband.[38]

King's sympathy for Tuki and Huru was shared by his wife, Anna Josepha. Anna was King's cousin, whom he had married in haste during his leave in England, when he was ill with the gout that often plagued him, and under orders to return to Norfolk. When they arrived back on the island in late 1791, Anna was heavily pregnant and in addition had in her care Norfolk, one of King's two illegitimate sons by a convict woman, born during his previous term of duty on the island. William Neate Chapman, King's twenty-year-old secretary and protégé, said of Anna King, 'She is so good a woman that it is a pleasure for any person to be near her.'[39] By 1793, the King household included Norfolk (four years old), Phillip (two) and a baby daughter, Maria, as well as Chapman, who often stayed with

Lieutenant-Governor Philip Gidley and Anna Josepha King, with their family, by R. Dighton.

them. Family relations were affectionate. Over the months that they lived in Government House, a friendship grew up between the Kings and Tuki and Huru. Just before the Governor left Norfolk to take them back to New Zealand, he wrote to Sir Joseph Banks: 'Our intelligent and worthy friends the two New Zealanders . . . have now been here seven months during which time they have lived with me and we are so much attached to each other that much real concern will be shown by every description of people here when they leave us.'[40] When King finally farewelled Tuki and Huru off the north coast of New Zealand in November, according to William Chapman, 'they cryed terribly and everybody on board was very much affected at the parting particularly the Governor who said he never parted with his mother with more regret than he did with those two men'.[41]

On Norfolk Island, Tuki and Huru mixed mainly with King's family; with the civil and military officers who visited his house – William Chapman, King's secretary and the storekeeper on the Island; the Reverend James Bain, the chaplain; Deputy Surveyor-General Charles Grimes; Assistant Surgeons Thomas Jamison, William Balmain and D'Arcy Wentworth; Lieutenant Abbott and the other officers of the 102nd Regiment (the New South Wales Corps); and with the settlers on the island.

It is difficult to know what Tuki and Huru themselves thought of their situation. Although they were free and well treated, they must have been aware of the condition of the convicts and the regime of trials and punishments on the island. In July 1793, for instance, two men were imprisoned pending transfer to Port

Jackson for stealing a bottle of rum, a dollar and a silk handkerchief; another was sentenced to fifty lashes for harbouring them; a fourth was sentenced to three hundred lashes for stealing tiles from the blacksmith's shop; and a fifth was sentenced to a hundred lashes and six months' imprisonment in the penitentiary for disobeying an overseer. In August, a man was sentenced to fifty lashes, an iron collar and two months in the penitentiary for swearing at a soldier; another to a hundred lashes for striking a convict who was with a soldier; and an inveterate thief was chained to the public grindstone for stealing a watch and twenty dollars, until he could be sent to Port Jackson for trial.[42]

Such punishments were unknown in Maori communities, where offenders were plundered, ostracised and sometimes killed, but never confined. Later Maori visitors to European settlements (for instance, Te Pahi in Port Jackson in 1806[43]) were horrified by the treatment meted out to prisoners for what seemed to them trivial offences, but Tuki's and Huru's reactions to life on Norfolk were not reported. On the one hand, given their aristocratic backgrounds, they may have taken their privileged position on the island for granted and thought of themselves as chiefly visitors, living with the most important family on the island, in a community composed mainly of toa (warriors) and taurekareka (slaves, war captives). On the other hand, it is obvious that their own captivity (and perhaps that of others) grieved them. According to King, they 'often Threatened to Hang themselves on very slight occasions, & sometimes made very serious promises of putting it into execution, if they were not permitted to return to their own Country'.[44]

While they were on Norfolk, Tuki and Huru visited some of the settlers in their houses up the valleys in Phillipsburgh and Queensborough. They, like other people on the island, were subject to the curfew, signalled by a roll of drums at 8 p.m. and policed by the nightwatchman, who patrolled the streets of the main settlement and called the hour each half hour throughout the night.[45] After six months on the island, the rhythms of local life must have dulled their initial sense of dislocation. According to King, they learned to speak some English, and he and some of the officers on Norfolk learned to speak some Maori:

> It may be expected that after a Six Month residence among us, that we should not be entirely ignorant of each others Language. Myself & some of the Officers (to whom I am obliged, for their commmunicating the information they gained from the two New Zealanders) have made such a progress that we could make ourselves well understood, & communicate our ideas to our visitors. They by intermixing what English words they knew ['which is not a little', King added in a letter to Banks[46]], with what we knew of their Language, could make themselves sufficiently understood by us.[47]

King regretted that he had no copy of any of Cook's voyages on the island, 'to compare their language with that of the other I.ds in these Seas', but commented that 'to the New Holland language it has as little affinity as the New Hollanders have to the accomplished manners, amiable disposition & ingenious turn of Tooke and Woodoo'.[48] This was one of the many unflattering comparisons that were to

be made during the early colonial period between Maori and Australian Aboriginals, to the latters' disadvantage.

King and one of the surgeons (Jamison?) eventually produced an extensive
and quite accurate vocabulary of Maori.[49] The development of a mutual linguistic
capacity allowed King to record some quite complex information from Tuki and
Huru about Maori social hierarchies, cosmological ideas and flax-processing.
According to King, for instance, there were four classes of persons in New Zealand:

> E tanga teda E tiketica [He rangatira tiketike – a high chief, or ariki]. A principal
> Chief, or Man in very great authority, his Superior Consequence is signified by a
> repetition of the word Etiketica [tiketike – high?]. This Title appears hereditary.
>
> E tanga roak, or E ta-honga [Tangaroa (the sea god), or he tohunga – a priest].
> A priest whose Authority in many cases is equal, and in some Superior to the E
> tiketika.
>
> E tanga teda Epodi [He rangatira hapori – the rangatira of a hapuu, sub-tribe].
> A subordinate chief or Gentleman.
>
> Te Ane E moki [taane mookai]. A labouring man.[50]

King added:

> the dead are buried in graves; and they believe that the Third day after the Inter-
> ment; the Heart separates itself from the Corpse. This separation is announced by
> a Gentle air of wind, which warns an inferior Ea-tooa [atua] (or Divinity) hover-
> ing over the Grave of its approach and carries it to the Clouds. In Tooke's Chart he
> has marked an imaginary road which goes the length ways of Ea-kei-no-maue [Te
> Ika-a-Maui – the North Island], viz. from Cook's Streight to the North Cape which
> Tooke calls Terry-inga [Te Reinga]; whilst the soul is received by the good Eatooa;
> an evil spirit is also in readiness to carry the impure part of the Corpse to the
> above road, along which it is carried to Terry-inga from whence it is precipitated
> into the Sea.[51] Every undertaking whether it is to fish or any other common
> occupation is preceded by a prayer – E kara kee a [he karakia] addressed to the
> Supreme Ea Tooa.[52]

Here, Tuki was describing the passage of the hau (wind, breath of life) of a
dead person along the spirits' pathway to Te Reinga, in the far north of the North
Island. These are illuminating comments, well supported by later information
about the relative roles of high chiefs, priests, chiefs and commoners in New
Zealand, and the use of karakia (god chants). King also commented that suicide
was very common among the New Zealanders, and that if a woman was beaten by
her husband she would hang herself immediately.

A detailed account of flax-working shows that, with improved communication, better information on this topic was eventually obtained:

> Preparing the Flax from the Plant, weaving it into cloath, or making fishing lines;
> it is all performed by the women; When the leaves are gathered, the hard stalk
> which runs through the centre is taken out with the thumb and nail, the red edges
> of the leaf are also stripped off; the two parts are then separated in the middle,
> making four slips of about three quarters of an inch wide, and the length of the

leaf, which on this Island is about three feet long. Two of these slips are put one over the other, holding them in the centre with the thumb of the left hand, resting on the upper slip; the sharp edge of a muscle shell is then drawn across them, so as to cut through the vegetable covering, but not to touch, or divide, the Fibres (which is the Flax), The slips thus prepared, are taken up singly, the left thumb resting on the upper part of the slip, just above the cut. The muscle shell which is held in the right hand is then placed on the upper part of the slip, just below the cut, with the thumb resting on the upper part. The muscle shell is then drawn to the end of the slip, which effectually separates the vegetable covering from the flaxen filaments, the slip is then turned, and the same operation is performed on the remaining part, which leaves the flax entire: After procuring the Flax by this simple method, if it is designed for fishing lines or any other course work, nothing more is done to it, but if designed to make Eka-kuow [kaakahu] or fine cloth, it is beat a considerable time in a clear stream, and when dried, twisted into such sized thread as the work requires, which finishes the process; until it is wove, which is performed in the same manner as fringe work is made: I have before observed that our visitors knew very little about the Flax or its preparation, but from what little they did know, and communicated to us, considerable improvements have been made.[53]

King reported that, according to Tuki and Huru, flax was sometimes cultivated in New Zealand by separating out the roots and planting them three in a hole, about a foot apart. He then described the improvements that had been achieved in local flax processing, saying that the flax-workers now found it much easier to strip the outer vegetable matter from the fibre. They stored bundles of flax leaves in a closed room for seven days, stripped them with a knife, twisted the fibre into hanks and soaked it in a tub of water, washed and beat it, then dried, hackled and spun it. By November, they had twenty people engaged in flax work on the island who between them produced twenty yards of number seven canvas in a week, although with a proper loom and weavers' tools, he thought that better results might be accomplished.[54] Maori would have been amused by these laborious efforts, because according to the tribal account of Tuki and Huru's kidnapping, Norfolk flax was no good for weaving: 'Ehara hoki te korari o taua motu ra i te Tihore, ara i te takiri kau, koia i motumotu ai te hukahuka' (The flax of the island was not the Tihore [the best flax to make tow out of], and hence the flax tow broke in short lengths).[55]

Tuki told King that his 'father' (matua – male relative of father's generation) still remembered the *Endeavour*'s 1769 visit to the north. Apparently the ship had anchored near his house, and his 'father' still had a red jacket given to him on that occasion. This may have been off Matauri Bay near where Tuki and Huru were taken, because according to the famous Ngaa Puhi chief Patuone, his own father Tapua had visited the *Endeavour* from that place:

> One day, before Patuone and Nene were old enough to bear weapons, Tapua (their father) and his people were out fishing at the sea coast at Matuari. They had caught many fish, when the ship appeared beyond Motukokako . . . They went to see the

vessel because such a ship had never before visited that place. When the canoes were near the ship, the people on board beckoned to them to come closer, So Tapua's men conferred together, and when they had come to a decision, the canoe commanded by Tapua went alongside the ship. Then they threw the fish from the canoe up on the ship, as an offering to these strange sea-goblins. The goblins were pleased with the fish, and shouted with joy as they gathered them up.

After this Tapua went on board the ship, and the leader of the goblins presented him with a red garment and with the salt flesh of an animal . . . Tapua took it and gave it to his son and daughter, Patuone and Tari. Food of this kind had not been previously known to the Maori; they found it to be sweet, and very good.[56]

The most remarkable record of Maori thinking obtained in Norfolk Island, however, and a tribute to the eventual quality of communication between Tuki and the Governor, was Tuki's map of New Zealand, sent by King in November 1793 to the Secretary of State.[57] David Collins, the Judge-Advocate at New South Wales, gave the best account (presumably based on later conversations with King) of the production of this map:

> When they began to understand each other, Too-gee was not only very inquisitive respecting England &c. (the situation of which, as well that of New Zealand, Norfolk Island and Port Jackson, he well knew how to find by means of a coloured general chart); but was also very communicative respecting his own country. Perceiving he was not thoroughly understood, he delineated a sketch of New Zealand with chalk on the floor of a room set apart for that purpose. From a comparison which Governor King made with Captain Cook's plan of those islands,[58] a sufficient similtude to the form of the northern island was discoverable to render this attempt an object of curiosity; and Toogee was persuaded to render his delineation on paper. This being done with a pencil, corrections and additions were occasionally made by him, in the cause of different conversations; and the names of districts and other remarks were written from his information during the six months he remained there.[59]

Entire treatises have been written about Tuki's map of New Zealand.[60] Other maps were produced by Maori in the early contact period,[61] but Tuki's is unique because it includes social, mythical and political information written at his dictation. In effect, Tuki's chart is a socio-political description of the northern part of the North Island, with some brief comments (and inaccurate coastlines) for the southern districts of New Zealand. The key features of Tuki's map included 'Mano-ui-tavai' (Manawatawhi, the largest of the Three Kings Islands), said to have no water on it but inhabited by thirty people; 'Modey-Mootoo, on which Te-ka-pa has an Hippah' – Murimotu, where the chief Te Kapa was said to have had a paa, presumably that described by Cook on this small island off the North Cape; Terry-inga (Te Reinga), the spirits' place for leaping off into the underworld, which was shown at the termination of a spirits' pathway (Te Ara Whaanui) running from the bottom to the top of the North Island, where it terminated at a symbol that represented the tapu tree there; 'Moodo Whenua' (Muriwhenua), whose boundaries on the map extended from around Ahipara on the west coast to north of Tokerau on the east;[62] and 'Ho-do-do' (Oruru), whose boundaries crossed the spirits' path and was said on the map to have two thousand fighting men (although King's journal says a thousand[63]). Within Oruru, Tuki's habitation was marked on the north sea coast of the valley, while the dwelling places of two of his chiefs, 'Moodeewye' (Muriwai) on the south coast and 'Te Wy-te-wi' further south, were marked with symbols that probably represented carved houses, and the habitation of a secondary chief 'Wytoa' (Waitoa) was marked far inland.

Further south on the east coast was the district named 'Wongar-ooa' [Whangaroa], supposed to contain two thousand fighting men, whose chief 'Tu-ko-rawa' (Tukarawa, the brother of Hauraki) was said to be 'inimical to Hododo [Oruru] and Teer-a-witte [Te Raawhiti], but in league with T'sou-duckey [Hauraki] & Moodoo Whenua [Muriwhenua] & Tettua Woodoo [Te Tai Hauauru?]'. 'Tettua Woodoo', to the south of Muriwhenua on the west coast, was said to be governed by 'Whadu' (Wharo) and to have four thousand inhabitants. 'Cho-ke-anga' (Hokianga), further south on the west coast, was described as having a hundred thousand inhabitants, headed by the principal chief 'Toko-ha', who was at peace with Oruru and Te Raawhiti. On the east coast, again, 'Woodoo's' (Huru's) habitation was marked in a district north of Te Raawhiti (at Matauri Bay?), and supposed to contain two thousand fighting men. This district was opposite to 'Motu-cowa' (Motukawa), governed by 'Tea-worock', father-in-law to Woodoo, with a hundred people, very few trees but much flax and water, and 'Pani-ke' (Panaaki) with fifty people, where Tuki and Huru were captured in the seas to the east.

South of all of these districts was 'T'sou ducky' (Hauraki), and then another large island 'Poenammoo' (Te Wai Pounamu – the South Island), with a 'tree about which Tookee and Woodoo tell some wonderful stories', which apparently they had been told by the Hauraki people; and a lake where 'stone for Hatchets are got' – presumably the greenstone waters of that island.

In explanation, Tuki told King that the North Island of New Zealand was divided into eight districts, governed by their respective chiefs, the principal one being Hauraki, which was often at war with other tribes. According to Tuki, on occasion the Hauraki tribes were allied with Muriwhenua, 'Tettua-Whoodoo' [Te Tai Hauauru] and Whangaroa, but at other times those last tribes allied with Hokianga, Te Raawhiti and Oruru against the Hauraki people. This information seems to fit in well with the volatile tribal histories for that period, which tell of numerous raids between various northern and Hauraki tribes. It also suggests that the Forster's 1774 estimate of a contact population of a hundred thousand for the whole of New Zealand (based on visits to Tamatea and Totaranui in the South Island alone) was too conservative.

Overleaf: *Tuki's map of New Zealand, sketched on the floor of King's study in Government House on Norfolk Island, and then transcribed by the Governor; together with a modern reconstruction of the map.*

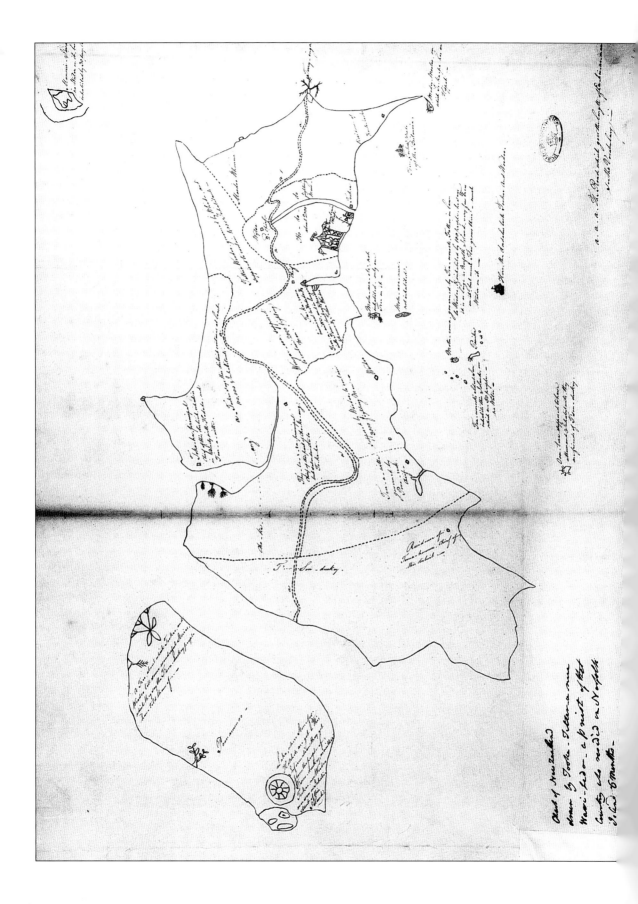

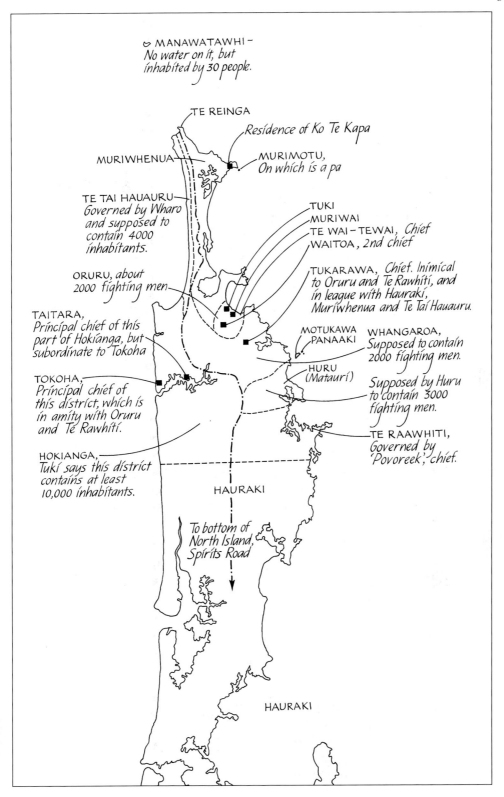

Tuki added that there were long periods of peace, when flax and greenstone for axes and ornaments were exchanged and groups visited one another. He was prepared to concede that all of the inhabitants of the South Island and Hauraki were cannibals, but vehemently denied that all New Zealanders ate people, expressing 'the greatest horror at the idea'.[64] Tuki also described a large freshwater river with a bar on the west coast, which he called 'Choke-han-ga' (Hokianga). The chief here, Tokoha, lived halfway up the river, where the country was covered with immense pine trees. When King obtained a copy of Cook's chart of New Zealand from one of the vessels that visited Norfolk Island during their stay, he pointed out to Tuki that Cook had not noticed a river in that region. Tuki asked if Cook had seen an island covered with birds, and when King pointed to Gannet Island (off Kaawhia Harbour), he suggested that this must be the place. In fact Gannet Island was too far south, but Tuki's description of Hokianga, its bar, its kauri forests and the offshore island was accurate. Tuki identified the chiefs of his own district, Oruru, as 'Te wy-te-wye' (Te wai-te-wai), the principal chief whose house was ornamented with the heads of enemies killed in battle; 'Wy-too-ah' (Waitua), 'Moode-wye' (Muriwai), 'Wa-way' (Wawae), 'To-moco-moco', (Tomo-komoko?), 'Pock-a-roo' (Pakaru?) and 'Tee-koo-ree' (Te Kurii), the principal chief's son. Milligan has attempted to identify all of the chiefs mentioned by Tuki, either on the map or in King's account, but a more detailed study of northern tribal histories is necessary to assess many of his claims.[65]

Tuki's map and commentaries are the best insider information available on northern Maori life in the 1790s. They demonstrate a preoccupation with kin-based geopolitics, linking the names of chiefs and places, and recording the shifting relations between them. Whakapapa (genealogy), and the koorero (talk) associated with it, worked in just this way. Key people and places acted as pivotal points in complex nets of kinship, alliance and enmity, allowing them to be strategically deployed and named. The links between people and places were mobile and dynamic, in a constant state of negotiation. Gifts, insults, magic and war were all part of this process of balancing different forms of ancestral power. Gifts (whether from gods or friends) should be returned and enhanced; insults should be avenged; ancestors and kinsfolk should be cared for; and enemies obliterated. Mana had to be protected if life was to be worth living, and the process by which this was sought was utu, or reciprocal exchange.

It seems that Tuki and Huru managed to convey some of this to Lieutenant-Governor King during their stay on Norfolk Island. King had looked after (manaaki) Tuki and Huru, and in the process a bond emerged between them, which they and their kinsfolk would acknowledge — along with the hara (offence) of their kidnapping. King became a person with whom a relationship existed in the geopolitics of alliance. And once he had given his word to Tuki and Huru that he would return them home, he had to do it, for his honour depended on it. Rangatira were expected to keep their word, and during their six months together, King had also learned something about mana from his friends.

THE RETURN HOME ON THE *BRITANNIA*
8–13 November 1793

On 2 November 1793, the storeship *Britannia* anchored off Norfolk Island.[66] Although two other ships, *Sugar Cane* and *Boddingtons*, had arrived in Norfolk in late May, they were en route to India, and King was not able to fulfill his promise to Tuki and Huru that they could return home on the next vessel. When the *Britannia* arrived, therefore, they redoubled their pleas, begging King with 'hourly lamentations' to keep his promise and send them home. This time King agreed. He drafted orders for the master of the *Britannia* to divert his course southwards to New Zealand, before resuming his trading voyage on behalf of the New South Wales Corps from Port Jackson to Bengal.

The *Britannia*, commanded by Captain William Raven, had arrived in New South Wales with a licence from the East India Company allowing the ship to go sealing in southern waters. Raven had already made one profitable trading voyage for the Corps to the Cape of Good Hope (combined with a sealing expedition south), and he was now on a voyage to India for a similar purpose. He left Port Jackson on 8 September, and soon arrived in Dusky Sound to check on a sealing party left there earlier under the command of his second mate, William Leith – visits that will be discussed in the chapter on sealing. While the *Britannia* was in Dusky, the colonial schooner *Francis* arrived from Port Jackson to assist the sealing party, and Raven carried on to Norfolk Island.

Captain Nepean of the New South Wales Corps (and brother of Evan Nepean, Under-Secretary of State) was on board the *Britannia* for this voyage, returning to England on leave. King asked Nepean to make a thorough survey of Norfolk so that he could report on the colony to the Admiralty, and left him in charge of the island while he took his two friends home. There was an exchange of letters, including instructions for both Captain Nepean and Captain Raven, a report from Raven about his sealing activities in New Zealand and a letter to Under-Secretary Nepean, to be delivered by his brother. In this letter King suggested that enough flax could be got from New Zealand to clothe all the inhabitants of New South Wales. He added, 'If it should be thought necessary to settle New Zealand and I should happen to be the person fixed on, I hope my family, which is now growing numerous, will be considered.'[67]

Several days later, King suggested in a letter to Henry Dundas that New Zealand, with its 'capacious harbours, fertility of the Soil, and [Tuki and Huru's] assurances of the amicable disposition of their Country men' would make 'a very eligible colony'.[68] King was obviously captivated by this idea, because on 9 November he drafted the first detailed plan for settling New Zealand. This involved six hundred convicts, an eighty-ton schooner, two years of supplies, a governor, chaplain, surgeons, a surveyor, commissary, three superintendants, three officers and forty privates. This plan included a full list of the stores that would be needed (including cannons from the wreck of the *Sirius* off Norfolk Island, if the settlement was to be in Dusky; but at least two to four extra brass three-pounder cannons if the settlement was to be in the North Island). In his plan, King suggested that most of the key personnel on Norfolk (including himself and his family) should be relocated in the new colony.[69]

Later that day, King embarked on the *Britannia* with Tuki and Huru and eighteen other passengers, including the Reverend James Bain, Thomas Jamison the assistant surgeon, William Chapman the storekeeper (who had with him a supply of gifts), two non-commissioned officers, twelve privates and one convict,[70] and sailed for New Zealand. If the voyage took only three days, King intended to land 'and make such Cursory Observations (on the Soil and Quantity of Manufactured Flax which could be obtained) as I might be able to make in One Day'. For that reason he had included a contingent of soldiers in his party.

The winds were favourable but light, and it was not until 12 November that North Cape was sighted. A number of houses and a paa were sighted on Murimotu, and then a very large paa on a hill 'just within the Cape [Tokatoka Point]'. At four o'clock in the afternoon, six large canoes (according to Chapman, forty to sixty feet long), each carrying about thirty men, came out from this paa to the *Britannia*. They recognised Tuki immediately, and as another canoe joined the fleet, some of these men boarded the *Britannia*, where the chiefs:

> Embrac[ed] and shed Tears of joy over Tooke, whose first, & earnest Enquiry was after his Family, & Chief, on those heads, he got the most satisfactory information from a Woman, who he informed us, is a near relation of his Mothers [according to Chapman, his sister-in-law]. His Father & Chief were still inconsolable for his loss; the latter . . . was about a fortnight ago, on a visit to the Chief of the Hippah above mentioned, where he remained Four days, and Terry-te-wye, the Principal Chief of Tooke's district, was dayly expected; this information pleased him very much.[71]

The people of the far north and those at Oruru were currently on friendly terms, with frequent visits being exchanged between their senior chiefs. One chief told Tuki and Huru that the Muriwhenua people were at present allied with those from Oruru, Whangaroa and Te Raawhiti, and that they had just returned from an attack on the Hauraki tribes.

There were more than a hundred people alongside, but Tuki greeted only his mother's kinswoman and the chiefs, 'who were distinguished from the rest by the Tattowing on their faces; & by the Respectful deference which was shewn them by the Emoki's [mokai – war captives without mana, sometimes described as 'slaves'] (i.e. the Working Men, who paddled the Canoes) who at times were beat most unmercifully'. This last comment is interesting, indicating that war captives could be harshly treated in Maori communities.

King gave gifts of iron tools to the 'Epodis' (or subaltern chiefs) at Tuki's direction, and then scraps of iron were exchanged for prepared flax, cloth, patupatu (hand weapons), spears, greenstone ornaments, fish-hooks and lines, and paddles. Robert Murry, one of the crew, wrote in his journal that night: 'We purchased mats, paddles, patoo-patoos, bracelets etc. Purchased a canoe – it was the smallest we saw, about 40 feet long.'[72] At 7 p.m. the canoes left the *Britannia*, which set sail for the Bay of Islands but was soon becalmed. Two hours later, a canoe with a crew of four men came out to the ship, and they willingly boarded. They traded their canoe to the master of the *Britannia* and stayed for supper. After the meal Tuki and Huru asked them for news of events since they had left New Zealand. In answer,

> [They] began a Song, in which all the Four Men who came in the Canoe took a part, & used some fierce and Savage Gestures, & at other times sunk their voices, according to the different passages and events which they were relating, Woodoo, who was paying great attention to the Subject of their Song, suddenly burst into Tears, which were occasioned by an Account they were giving of the T'Sou duckey [Hauraki] Tribe, having made an irruption into Teer-a-witte, (Woodoo's district) & killed the Son of Povoreek the Chief, and Thirty Warriors. Woodoo was too much affected to hear any more, he retired into a Corner of the Cabbin, where he gave vent to his Grief, which was only interrupted by his vowing Revenge.[73]

At six o'clock the next morning, eight canoes came out from the main paa, led by a canoe with thirty-six men and a chief on board, who stood up and signalled to the *Britannia*. As the canoe came alongside, Tuki recognised 'Koto-ko-kee' (Tokoki?), the senior chief of the paa, an old man dressed in white whose face was heavily tattooed. Tuki greeted him affectionately, and then introduced him to King. They pressed noses, and then the chief put his cloak around King's shoulders. In return, King presented him with a cloak of green baize, decorated with broad arrows. A fleet of seven more canoes, each carrying twenty or more men and women, now approached the *Britannia*, and some of their crews boarded the ship. William Chapman wrote: 'They are the finest set of men I ever beheld, the shortest we saw was at least 5ft 11in & very strong & muscular. The Women are small but have very pleasing countenances. I have heard it remarked that the women of most country's have the greatest flow of spirits, much greater than the male sex & I assure you it is so in New Zealand.'[74] At Tuki's request, King declared the poop 'tapu', so that only 'To-ko-kee' and two other chiefs had access to it.

King had become uneasy about the increasing length of his absence from Norfolk Island. Earlier that morning he asked Tuki and Huru whether they wished to land at Muriwhenua or stay on board and return with him to Norfolk. Tuki was not enthusiastic about disembarking at Muriwhenua, saying that so far only subordinate chiefs had assured him that there was peace between his own people at Oruru and the Muriwhenua people, but nor did he want to return to Norfolk. Rather, he wanted to carry on to Oruru so that he could send 'some Marks of his esteem and love to his Friends at Norfolk Island'.[75] When 'To-ko-kee' came on board, however, all of Tuki's doubts vanished. 'To-ko-kee' assured Tuki that their people were indeed at peace and that he would personally return Tuki to Oruru the next evening. King was still uneasy, fearing that this might be a subterfuge to get hold of Tuki and Huru's gifts from Norfolk, but Tuki assured him 'with an honest Confidence that "E tiketica no E teka" [a pidgin phrase – He tiketike no (kaore) e teka] ie. That an E tiketica [high chief] never deceives, and that he rather wish'd to go with Ko-to-ko-ke than to return to Norfolk Island before he had seen his family & Chief'.[76]

King took the old chief into the cabin and, with Tuki's help, explained that he wanted Tuki and Huru to be taken to Oruru immediately. In three months' time, he added, he would visit Oruru, and if Tuki and Huru had been returned home safely, he would return to Muriwhenua and give the chief many gifts. According to King:

> The only answer Ko-to-ko-ke made was by putting both his Hands to the sides of my Head, (making me perform the same Ceremony) & Joining our Noses, in which position we remained Three Minutes, & the Old Chief muttering in a very earnest manner, what I did not understand; After which he went through the same Ceremony with Tookee & Woodoo, which ended with a dance, when the Two latter joined Noses with me, & said that Kotokoke was now become their Father, & would in Person conduct them to Hododoe.[77]

This ceremonious hongi (nose-pressing) accompanied by karakia (incantations) mingled their hau (breath) together. It was evidently intended to establish an honorary kinship relation among the chief, King, Tuki and Huru, and was thus of deep significance for relations between King and Maori people. Tuki now gathered the people in a circle around 'To-ko-kee', 'recount[ing] to them what he had seen during his absence; at many passages they gave shouts of admiration'. When they refused to believe that Norfolk was only three days' sail from Muriwhenua, he ran to the poop and fetched a cabbage, telling them to their astonishment that it had been cut five days earlier in King's garden.

Tuki and Huru now passed on a request from 'To-ko-kee' that the soldiers should exercise and fire their muskets, and that the great guns should be fired. King assured the gathering that as long as the New Zealanders and his own people remained good friends and neighbours, these weapons would never be used against them, but only if Europeans were ever harmed. The soldiers then paraded in front of the crowd of a hundred and fifty Maori, went through their drill and fired off three rounds. Next they fired a cannon loaded with grapeshot, 'which surprized them greatly, particularly the Chief, who [King] made notice the distance the shot fell from the Ship'.[78]

A wind blew up from the south and a high surf began to run on shore. Tuki and Huru already had with them a bag containing six sets of linen, two green suits faced with orange, three swords, plus needles, thread, knives and looking glasses. Before they left the ship, King also gave them axes, a selection of carpenters' tools, six spades, hoes, knives, scissors, razors, two bushels of seed maize, one of wheat, two of pease, a number of garden seeds, ten young sows and two boars (three goats King had intended to give to them had died on board, and hats, jackets and frock trousers intended for Tuki and Huru were not handed over in the haste of their departure).[79] He also presented the local people with a hundred mirrors and a hundred hundredweight of biscuit. As these gifts were loaded into

A greenstone adze, now in the Auckland Museum, said to have been sent by Lieutenant-Governor King to Under-Secretary Nepean in 1792.

the canoes, Tuki and Huru affectionately farewelled everyone on board, reminding King of his promise to return in two or three months' time, when they and their families would go with him to Norfolk. 'To-ko-kee' pronounced King's name carefully, and taught King to pronounce his name in turn. This was probably a ceremonial exchange of names, to ratify their new relationship. The local people now performed a haka, to Chapman's utter astonishment: 'I never heard such a noise, nor saw such ugly faces as they made in my life in any country.'[80] As the canoes left the *Britannia*, the Europeans saluted them with three cheers, and at Tuki's direction the local people replied in kind.

Upon his return to Norfolk, King wrote a detailed report to Henry Dundas, telling him about the expedition to New Zealand and enclosing a cloak and fishing lines made from New Zealand flax. He also wrote another letter to Under-Secretary Nepean, suggesting that 'much publick good would result to the commerce of Great Britain and these colonies if a settlement was made [in New Zealand] at the Bay of Islands or the River Thames', and offering to spend two months on an expedition to New Zealand to assess its suitability for settlement from Britain.[81] A box of New Zealand curiosities was also sent to Nepean — perhaps including a greenstone adze now in the Auckland Museum, said to have been sent from King to Nepean in 1792. Two basalt hand weapons (patu onewa), now in the museum at Norfolk, are said to have been presented to King by Tuki and Huru, presumably by the good graces of 'To-ko-kee', 'in gratitude for his action in returning them to New Zealand in November 1793 from Norfolk Island, where they had been taken by Lieutenant Hanson in the transport *Daedalus* earlier in the same year for the purpose of showing the methods of treating

New Zealand flax'.[82] These are the last surviving material tokens of Tuki and Huru's stay in Norfolk Island.

When Acting Governor Grose heard that King had diverted the *Britannia* from its trading voyage to India, he was furious. At that time Grose was also the commander of the New South Wales Corps, which had underwritten the voyage as a profit-making venture, and King was a naval officer, technically subordinate to Grose. Shortly after King returned to Norfolk, there had been a mutiny among the Corps contingent there, and Grose may have been looking for a scapegoat. He wrote a very angry letter of rebuke to King, who replied with several lengthy letters to Grose and Dundas in his own defence.

This episode did King's career no lasting harm, however. He was able to argue that in taking Tuki and Huru back to New Zealand, he was simply fulfilling his instructions that they be well treated. The furore over this escapade and the mutiny eventually died down, and King continued to be promoted until eventually he became Governor of New South Wales.

The most lasting consequences of Tuki and Huru's stay with Lieutenant-Governor King in Norfolk proved to be threefold. First, the local manufacture of flax improved markedly. Some garments (including trousers and aprons), and a foretopgallant sail, ropes and a log-line that were tested on the *Daedalus*, were eventually made. This kept alive the hope that a flax industry in Norfolk or New Zealand might eventually prove to be profitable.[83]

Second, the effective introduction of potatoes (and perhaps also maize and pigs) to Northland can be dated to 1793. The one tribal account of Tuki and Huru's adventures ends: 'the Europeans gave them some pigs, male and female, and some Indian corn and potatoes, these increased (tupu) and were distributed to the other tribes of Ngapuhi [in Northland]'.[84] Te Pahi, who later visited Port Jackson in 1806, told King that his father had instructed him to seek out Governor King so that 'his country [might be] benefited by his Visit, as it had been by the great Blessing bestowed on it by the two New Zealanders return from Norfolk Island who introduced the Potatoe which is now in the greatest Abundance'.[85] Furthermore, Joseph Mathews, one of the first missionaries in the north, reported in 1837 that Tuki and Huru had brought with them 'potatoes, and five very large pigs. There were no pigs in New Zealand before this so far as we know, nor potatoes.'[86] Tuki and Huru not only brought the plants and animals with them, but also a fair knowledge of how to care for them, and it may have been this that made the critical difference. In Northland at least, it seems likely that the kidnapping of Tuki and Huru led to a local agricultural revolution.

The third lasting consequence of their stay in Norfolk Island was a close relationship between Northland Maori and 'Kaawana Kiingi' (Governor King) and his family. The old chief in Muriwhenua who had ceremonially established a kind of kinship with King (and possibly assumed his name) would never have forgotten him, and both Tuki and Huru were high-born people with their own wide networks of kinship and alliance in the north. Much of the content of the term

'Kaawana' (Governor) in Northland Maori in the late eighteenth and early nineteenth centuries derived from what people knew about Philip Gidley King. He was the Governor whom Maori people knew best, who had learned some of their language, had treated their kinsfolk with honour and had shown his chiefly prestige with generous hospitality and gifts. The taonga (treasures) that King gave Tuki and Huru were widely redistributed in the north, establishing reciprocal relations between King and his people and a number of ranking chiefs. And when in later years, other Maori went to visit King in Port Jackson, taking return gifts of their own, they were reinforcing those bonds. Utu and the power of mana were shaping history.

On reflection, then, George Vancouver's euphoric account of European exploration in the preface to his 'Voyage' was not entirely mistaken. There was friendship on occasion (as well as considerable mutual violence), and exchanges of useful goods and information. Yet in the context of Tuki and Huru's visit to Norfolk Island, it is difficult to say with any conviction just who were 'the most lowly children of nature'. Lieutenant-Governor King himself, and Assistant Surgeon Jamison, after six months' acquaintance with Tuki and Huru, no longer wished to call them 'savages'. But Vancouver and most other Europeans of that period, despite the savagery of some of their own social practices, would have had no such compunction. Vancouver's 'grand keystone to that expansive arch', linking Euro-peans to other people in the eighteenth century, may prove after all not to have been 'knowledge'. On the contrary, it may turn out to have been a resilient mythology about 'savages' that still survives in various guises, and which even contrary experience – in the end – could not shift.

Ten

THE TIMBER VOYAGES
1794–1797

Phillip Gidley King was not the only person to think that the European settlement of New Zealand might be imminent. In the early 1790s, the idea of establishing a British colony there was in the air. In November 1792, for instance, one John Thomson, AM, wrote to Henry Dundas, the Secretary of State, offering either to serve as a superintendent of agriculture at Botany Bay or to establish a colony in New Zealand. His settlement plan came to nothing, but it does offer interesting insights into the kinds of colonial strategies that were debated at that time. Thomson suggested that a colonising party from British India of 'fifty sober men; one hundred sepoys, & 100 convicts' might be sent to New Zealand, with military supplies and stores sufficient for one year. The people there, he thought, were 'just in that state of civilisation proper to be made useful', and could be persuaded to co-operate with Europeans. His ideas for gaining Maori co-operation were ingenious, and spelled out in some detail:

> By coming upon the coast in a friendly manner, and observing the state of the people, an opportunity may be found to join one Tribe against another; which last, on conquest, would be obliged to submit to your own conditions, which must be to furnish a Town and District, with an engagement to refrain from war unless when in alliance with you. This unheard of clemency in that Country would have a great effect on the neighbours, more might be reduced and Hostages received, who, by being taught and well treated, would introduce civilisation and render the Country, now so inhospitable, then an asylum for distressed mariners & by introducing the European grains & roots &c in addition to those already cultivated it might be an Emporium for many Nations . . .
>
> My method for bringing the Natives under command is this, by the superiority of fire arms, there is no doubt of subduing the most powerful King & bring him under; by confining himself or taking hostage; make *him* give *orders* to his *people* and share his revenues – a fleet of Canoes by no means formidable to armed ships, yet powerful in these seas might be equipped, with stationary shields, prows, awnings, slings, bows and other European machinery quite unknown in that Country and discipline might be introduced (without fire arms) which would make

them superior to their neighbours, thus they would subdue each other and we be the masters hence peace would ensue and subjection; and agriculture . . . almost eradicated by war, would thrive, and the King of England would enjoy a fine Country, from whence he might conquer the greatest part of the South Sea Islands, & conquest would bring peace, hence improvement & civilisation &c. A work worthy of so great a King.[1]

Thomson's language was unvarnished, but the strategies he was suggesting were not unusual. Similar devices had been used by European powers in many other parts of the world.

On the whole, however, the colonial authorities saw no great virtue in settling New Zealand at this time. Maori seemed turbulent and not at all easy to subdue. Since Cook's last visit, European explorers of the Pacific had edged past the New Zealand coastline, visiting only the most remote harbours and barely coming into contact with local people. After the killing of Tasman's men in Taitapu, Marion du Fresne and some of his crew at the Bay of Islands, and Furneaux's men in Grass Cove, Maori had gained a formidable reputation for bellicosity that acted as a deterrent to European imperial ambitions. It was left for commercial interests in Britain, India and Port Jackson to make the next move.

The British East India Company played a key role in the next meetings between Europeans and Maori. Chartered in 1600, the Company was run by a wealthy oligarchy that controlled its own army and marine forces, fighting Indian rulers as well as European rivals. It held a monopoly over British trade and navigation between the Cape of Good Hope and Cape Horn, using fleets of chartered ships crewed by Indian sailors (Lascars), marines (Sepoys) and black slaves as well as by Europeans. East Indiamen crossed the Atlantic, Indian and western Pacific Oceans in a search for profitable cargoes. They carried woollen goods, silver and base metals from Britain to India, and woven cotton, silk, spices, sugar, indigo, saltpetre and other goods from India back to Britain; while the 'country ships', many of which were built in India, carried grain, rice, cowrie shells (for the slave trade) and coir rope between ports on the Indian coast; raw cotton and opium to the East Indies and China; and tea, silk, sugar, mercury, porcelain, spices, gold dust and teak from China and the East Indies back to India.[2] When British penal colonies were established at Port Jackson and Norfolk Island, East India Company ships were chartered as convict transports and supply ships, carrying cattle, rice, dholl (peas), sugar, salted meats and woven cotton to Port Jackson and Norfolk, and New Zealand became a handy place to pick up homeward cargoes. One consequence of this was that in these early contacts Maori met many Lascars and Sepoys, and a few black slaves, as well as Europeans.

Throughout this period, the use of colonies as outposts for the control of trade was being vigorously debated in Britain. In *The Wealth of Nations* (1776), Adam Smith argued against the old mercantilist notion that states were locked in endless struggle with each other for a limited supply of wealth. Wealth, he claimed, was inexhaustible, providing that its production was not stifled by national monopolies, and the duties, embargoes and navigation laws that propped them up. Consequently, it was mistaken to expect colonies to trade exclusively with their mother countries. People in mother countries and colonies alike should exchange their goods freely on a world market, for this would maximise production. Once private property was freed from the tyranny of state controls, progress would necessarily follow:

> Little else is requisite to carry a state to the highest degree of opulence from the lowest barbarism, but peace, easy taxes, and a tolerable administration of justice; all the rest being brought about by the natural course of things. All governments which thwart this natural course, which force things into another channel or which endeavour to arrest the progress of society at a particular point, are unnatural, and to support themselves are obliged to be oppressive and tyrannical.

In his *Essay on the History of Civil Society* (1767), on the other hand, Adam Ferguson argued that the pursuit of private wealth and public liberty were often at cross-purposes, for 'in every commercial state, notwithstanding any pretension to equal rights, the exaltation of the few must depress the many'. He added this sober warning:

> The virtues of men have shone most during their struggles, not after the attainment of their ends. Those ends themselves, though attained by virtue, are frequently the causes of corruption and vice. Mankind, in aspiring to national felicity, have substituted arts which increase their riches, instead of those which improve their nature. They have entertained admiration of themselves, under the titles of *civilized* and of *polished*, where they should have been affected with shame; and even where they have for a while acted on maxims tending to raise, to invigorate, and to preserve the national character, they have, sooner or later, been diverted from their object, and fallen a prey to misfortune, or to the neglects which prosperity itself had encouraged.[3]

Merchants in Britain, India and in Port Jackson all had different interests in this argument. The East India Company merchants were concerned to protect their legal monopoly of British colonial trade in the Indian and western Pacific Oceans, so they favoured unabashed mercantilism. Other merchants in Britain wanted to maximise their access to the China and Indian markets, as well as raw materials from the Pacific, and to secure bounties (for instance, on whale bone and oil) for their imports into Britain, so they veered between seeking mercantile privileges for themselves and trying to free up Pacific commerce. Traders in Port Jackson (the officers of the military establishment, and some emancipated convicts), who were forbidden to build and operate their own ships, hoped to break metropolitan monopolies, and profit from local trade and resources. And, of course, there were the Americans, who wanted free access to the Pacific for their own purposes, and were happy enough to thumb their noses at British attempts at colonial control.

As for Maori, they were neither mercantilists nor free-traders, nor did they subscribe to European ideas of private property – especially when those gave

Europeans the right to take other people's territory and resources. Utu required reciprocity, and all exchanges of goods with Europeans were closely monitored. In some remote parts of the country, this led to a stringent avoidance of European visitors after initial, unsatisfactory contacts. While in more densely populated regions, where this was not possible, local leaders asserted their own ideas about the proper use of resources, and their own forms of control.

THE VOYAGE OF THE *FANCY*
1794–1795

In the economy of European colonialism, gold and silver headed the list of desirable 'goods' to be acquired by imperial expansion. Then came the materials required in warfare – saltpetre for gunpowder, and the timber and flax required for the hulls and rigging of naval vessels, as well as sails and fabric for uniforms. In his proposal for the settlement of Port Jackson, Matra had noted:

> It may be seen by Captain Cook's voyage that New Zealand is covered with timber of size and every quality that indicates long duration; it grows close to the water's edge, and may be easily obtained. Would it not be worth while for such as may be dispatched to New South Wales to take in some of this timber on their return, for the use of the King's yards? As the two countries are within a fortnight's run of each other, and as we might be of the utmost sevice to the New Zealanders, I think it highly probable that this plan might become eminently useful to us as a naval power, especially as we might thus procure masts, a single tree of which would be large enough for a first-rate ship, and planks superior to any that Europe possesses.[4]

Throughout the wars with America and France, the oak groves of England could not meet the demands of the British naval dockyards. During the American War of Independence, the dockyards had access to Baltic pine and a fleet of ships of the line was constructed that gave Britain superiority at sea. When war broke out with Revolutionary France in 1793, however, more timber was urgently needed. During the years of peace, timber stores had been allowed to run down, so that when Napoleon instituted a blockade of Britain, the Royal Navy was starved for timber. British naval vessels were almost constantly at sea, on convoy duty or on blockade, and needed frequent repairs and refitting. The fear of invasion and naval defeat inspired a worldwide search for suitable timber, and the forests of New Zealand, although remote, offered one possible option.[5]

James Matra's suggestion about New Zealand timber had been included in Governor Phillip's instructions and was repeated by official and commercial commentators. The first person to do anything about it, though, was William Wright Bampton, captain of the *Shaw Hormuzear*, a Calcutta merchantman. As we have noted earlier, Bampton had delivered a speculative cargo of stock, spirits and supplies to Port Jackson in 1793, at a time when the colony was in dire need of

Captain William Wright Bampton.

provisions. Acting Governor Grose then engaged him to fetch further cattle and supplies from India for the penal settlement,[6] asking him to drop off Tuki and Huru at Norfolk Island en route to India. Bampton had fulfilled this part of his contract, then headed west to the East Indies, but in Batavia he discovered that war with France had broken out again in Europe and French privateers were attacking British ships in eastern seas.[7] His departure for India was delayed, and by the time he arrived in Bombay in February 1794, no large vessels suitable for shipping livestock were available in the port. British ships were being sunk and battered by the French, and timber was desperately needed for repairs, as well as flax for ropes and rigging.

In May 1794, Bampton finally managed to purchase an ancient 800-ton East Indiaman, the *Endeavour*, to carry cattle and supplies back to Port Jackson. The ship required extensive repairs and refitting, so a 'snow' (a brig with an extra mast for its trysail), the *Fancy*, commanded by his chief mate, Edgar Thomas Dell, was sent ahead to Port Jackson with part of the contracted cargo and a despatch from Bampton to explain his long delay.[8] After delivering their cargoes at Port Jackson, Dell and Bampton were commissioned by the Bombay Marine, the East India Company's naval force, to collect masts, planks and spars in New Zealand.

Dell arrived at Port Jackson in July 1794 and waited for several months for Bampton to arrive, then left the port for an unnamed destination. As Secretary of the Colony David Collins remarked when the *Fancy* sailed on 29 September:

> Mr. Dell, the commander, purposed running to Norfolk Island, but affected a secrecy with respect to his subsequent destination. It was generally surmised, however, that he was bound to some island whereat timber fit for naval purposes was to be procured; and at which whatever ship Mr. Bampton should bring with him might touch and load with a cargo for India. The snow was armed, was about 170 tons burden, had a large and expensive complement of officers and men, a guard of sepoys, and a commission from the Bombay marine. (Mr Dell had likewise on board a much greater number of cross-cut saws than were necessary to procure wood for the mere use of the vessel.) New Zealand was by us supposed to be the place; as force, or at least the appearance of it, was there absolutely requisite.[9]

The *Fancy* called first at Norfolk Island, where Lieutenant-Governor King asked Dell to renew his contacts with Tuki and Huru, and with 'Kotokokee', the chief who had welcomed King so warmly when he returned Tuki and Huru to New Zealand in November 1793. Accordingly, Dell sailed directly from Norfolk to North Cape, where he tried to locate Tokokee. The chief was nowhere to be found, however, so Dell proceeded to Tokerau to try to find 'Our Friend Tookee' instead.

THE *FANCY*'S VISIT TO TOKERAU (DOUBTLESS BAY)
12–14 November 1794

Tokerau, a wide bay on the east coast of Northland, had been visited by Europeans on several previous occasions – by Cook and Surville in 1769, and Eber Bunker in the *William and Mary* in 1792. Surville had kidnapped a local man, and Tuki-tahua, a young man from Oruru, had been kidnapped in the Bay of Islands in 1793 and taken to Norfolk Island. As we have seen, Governor King returned Tuki to Muri-whenua about nine months later, and promised to come back soon to see him. He had not yet kept his promise, but during Dell's visit to Norfolk in October 1794, King had given him messages for Tuki. When the *Fancy* sailed into Doubtless Bay on 12 November, therefore, and fifteen people came out to the ship in a 'very large Canoe', Dell asked them to tell Tuki that a ship had arrived from Norfolk Island. At one o'clock 'our Friend Tookee' came alongside in a canoe with his wife and family and climbed on board. Several of the *Fancy*'s crew had been on the *Shaw Hormuzear* when Tuki sailed on that ship to Norfolk Island the previous year, and he greeted them warmly. According to Dell:

> [He] made great enquiries after Governor & Mrs King, and Family and Several other Gentlemen who resided at Norfolk island during his Stay there, and appeared very happy when I informed him they were all well. I gave him a Small box, Containing a few pieces of Iron beat out in the Shape of Plains or Chizels, which they call Whaw [whau] and informed him it was sent by Gov.r King of

Norfolk Island as a present and with which he appeared highly pleased, saying Mitiy Gov.r King (or Good Gov.r King) repeating it several times; as Tookee seemd very happy and staid with us on Board all the remainder of the night, I was in great hopes he would have accompanied us to the Southward as far as the River Thames . . .[10]

The next morning Dell asked Tuki to accompany him to Hauraki, where Cook's 'Voyage' promised excellent timber, but Tuki insisted that he could not leave Doubtless Bay until Governor King had arrived to see him. Although Dell told him that this was very unlikely, Tuki was adamant. At daybreak, twenty-four canoes surrounded the *Fancy*, bringing a local chief with about five hundred men, women and children to barter flax, fish-hooks, lines, patu and other weapons for metal buttons, beads, glass bottles and pieces of old iron hoops. Tuki asked Dell to have one of the brig's four-pounders fired, which he did, to the astonishment of the local people. After this, Tuki and his family went down with Dell to the cabin for breakfast. When Dell asked after Huru, Tuki's companion on Norfolk Island, he was told that Huru had returned to his home in the south as soon as they arrived back in New Zealand, and they had not seen him since. Tuku remarked in English that Huru was 'very bad' and, brandishing his spear and patu, warned Dell that Huru and his people were cannibals, and that if he went to visit them, Dell and his people would be killed and eaten. He also said that he still had a hog and some hens from the stock that Governor King had given him, and plenty of green peas growing on shore. Dell gave him some cabbages, which he promised to plant as soon as he returned to shore.

After these exchanges, Dell tried again to persuade Tuki to go with him to Hauraki, promising that he would return him home as soon as the *Fancy* was loaded. Again Tuki refused. In frustration, Dell decided that he was wasting his time at Doubtless Bay, so he ordered the anchor to be raised. When the *Fancy* set sail, however, the wind veered around to the east and she could not beat out of the bay. Tuki tried to persuade Dell to stay on at Tokerau, assuring him that there was plenty of timber suitable for large spars to the south of the bay (presumably at Oruru). He added that many of the canoes Dell had seen around the ship were made from these 'pine trees'. The winds were worsening by the minute, so Dell decided to run up the bay for shelter, hoping that he might obtain a cargo of timber there when the storm subsided. The canoes began to go ashore, and eventually Tuki and his family left the brig, saying that they would return when the storm died down in about three days' time. Two of the local men, however, decided to stay on board. Dell noted:

> [They] beg'd to be allowed to stay . . . and [be] taken to Gov.r King at Norfolk Island, being intirely at their own request, I made no Objections, and they accordingly staid, they appeared very happy and immediately went down below, eat a very hearty Meal, and then went to Sleep equally as unconcerned as if they had belonged to the Vessel a long time., there was likewise another young Man, belonging to Tookees Canoe who wished very much to Stay, he very often mentioned the name of Gov.r King, Norfolk Island.[11]

After Tuki's departure, Dell worked the *Fancy* high up the bay, looking for shelter in the lee of the eastern shore. Squalls and high seas buffeted the ship, breaking one of her anchor cables, and that night there was a violent thunderstorm. At daybreak, in a high swell, several canoes packed with men and women came out to the *Fancy* to trade. They exchanged fairly with the sailors until the quartermaster, who was on watch, went off to haul the deep-sea lead. Seizing this opportunity, one man grabbed the half-hour glass from the binnacle, and another managed to get an iron stanchion off one of the pumps and into his canoe. When the sailors challenged them, these people were terrified, asking Dell 'if I was going to Tu them (meaning to shoot them)'. Dell assured them that as long as the goods were returned, he would do them no harm.

The men who had stayed on board the ship that night were desperately seasick, and when several more canoes came alongside they made signs that they no longer wanted to go to Norfolk Island, and went ashore. There was no sign of Tuki, nor of any good anchorage or tall trees at Tokerau, and Dell had begun to mistrust these people. Finally he decided to 'give up all thoughts of succeeding here, and to get under Weigh and proceed to the River Thames with all Expedition'.[12] At 9.30 a.m. on 14 November, the *Fancy* raised her anchor and sailed out of Tokerau, heading south for Hauraki.

THE *FANCY*'S VISIT TO HAURAKI
20 November 1794 – 21 February 1795

Hauraki was a deep, island-studded gulf on the east coast of the North Island.[13] Cook had been there on the *Endeavour* twenty-five years earlier, in November 1769. His stay had been brief but consequential. Shortly after their arrival, Cook, Joseph Banks and a party of sailors took the ship's boats about twelve or fourteen miles up the Waihou River, at the bottom of the gulf. That night, Banks noted in his journal:

A fresh breeze of wind soon carried us to the bottom of the bay, where we found a very fine river broad as the Thames at Greenwich tho not quite so deep, there was however water enough for vessels of more than a midling size and a bottom of mud so soft that nothing could possibly take damage by running ashore. About a mile up this was an Indian town built upon a small bank of Dry sand by totaly surrounded by Deep mud, so much so that I beleive they meant it a defence [now identified as Oruarangi Paa[14]]. The people came out in flocks upon the banks inviting us in . . . After this visit we proceeded and soon met with another town with but few inhabitants. Above this the banks of the river were compleatly clothed with the finest timber my Eyes ever beheld, of a tree we had before seen but only at a distance in Poverty bay and Hawks bay [the kahikatea]; thick woods of it were every where upon the Banks, every tree as streight as a pine and of immense size; still the higher we came the more numerous they were . . . As far as this the river have kept its depth and very little decreasd even in breadth; the Captn was so much pleasd with it that he resolvd to call it the Thames.[15]

The Waihou, with its wide waterways and forests of tall trees, excited Cook's imagination. In his reports to the Admiralty he commended 'The Thames' as a site for a future British colony. Banks added that this was 'indeed in every respect the properest place we have yet seen for establishing a Colony; a ship as large as Ours might be carried several miles up the river, where she would be moord to the trees as safe as alongside a wharf in London river, a safe and sure retreat in case of an attack from the natives . . . The Noble timber, of which there is such an abundance, would furnish plenty of materials either for the building defences, houses or Vessels.'[16]

Cook and Banks, however, were not the first visitors to covet Hauraki's woods and waterways. The region was strategically located between Northland, the Waikato and the Bay of Plenty, all densely populated districts, and parties of traders and warriors often came through the gulf. The inhabitants, a numerous mix of Ngaati Paoa, Ngaati Maru, Ngaati Whanaunga and Ngaati Tamateraa (all descended from Maru-tuaahu, who had migrated there from Kaawhia) with older local kin groups, had a turbulent recent history. Ngaati Maru had attacked and largely displaced the earlier occupants of the district – Ngaati Hako, Te Uri-o-Pou and Ngaati Huarere – in a series of raids dated between about 1650 and 1700.[17] By the 1790s, these internal animosities had become muted, but Hauraki was being attacked by descent groups from outside the district. According to Horeta Te Taniwha, a Ngaati Whanaunga who had met Cook at Whitianga as a child:

> After [Cook's visit in 1769] a war-party came to conquer us; but the tribes of Hauraki were not overpowered by them, and the land from Whitianga even to the Thames was kept by us, as it was claimed and held by our ancestors in days of old. The Waikato people were our most inveterate foes. They are a great and numerous people, and we are few. The Nga puhi fought with Waikato, and Waikato fought with Taranaki, so that war was universal from the North Cape even to the end of the Wai Pounamu (South Island); and our tribe joined in those wars, but we were not driven out of Hauraki, but our lands were held by us by the power of our warriors.
>
> In the days when we were attacked by a war-party from Tauranga we gained the battle, and they fled back to their home. And when the Ngati Whakaue tribe came as a war party on us from Rotorua, we attacked them, and they fled to their home. We ever held firmly to our land, but when the days of extreme evil came we hauled our canoes up on shore; but at other times we paddled our canoes from Whitianga around Moehau (Cape Colville), and hid them in places where they might not be found, and we gave battle to our enemies on the sea-beach . . . And if a war-party of the Nga puhi Tribe came in their double canoes to Hauraki, we attacked and fought them on our islands in the Waihou. They could not say they held possession of any one battlefield, but went disheartened to their home in sorrow, as we had been left in sorrow at our homes. Our people kept our fires burning at all our homes.[18]

242

The region was worth fighting over. Out at sea, the fisheries were productive. The ridges of Te Paeroa-o-Toi (the Coromandel Peninsula), which sheltered the gulf, were covered with forests of rimu, miro, tootara, kahikatea, kauri, tawa and taraire. Many of these trees fruited during the summer, attracting birds (tuuii, bellbirds, huia, kookako, parrots and pigeons) and kiore (Polynesian rats) as well as people. Mosses, shrubs, ferns and climbers tangled in the luxuriant undergrowth, where kiwi scuffled and shrieked at night. Beneath the forest canopy, there were rocky outcrops – obsidian for cutting tools, basalt and greywacke for adzes, andesite for cooking stones, chert for drill points and sandstone for grinding stones. Sloping gardens were dug on the foothills of the ranges, where kuumara and gourds grew in yellow loamy soil.

Down on the plains, the Waihou River and its tributaries ran far inland, winding through kahikatea forests, low-lying raupo swamps and salt marshes. Eels and mullet swarmed in the rivers, and ducks and other waterfowl flocked in the swamps. Occasional ancient beach ridges or places where a river or stream joined the Waihou made favoured sites for settlements. Here, eel weirs were built; taro, karaka, flaxes and cabbage trees were planted; and house sites raised off the wet ground with layers of timber, fossil shells, clay, sand and shell midden. In several places paa had been built on low islands or promontories, their living surfaces raised over generations with layers of flax mats or scrub, staked in place and covered with thick layers of shell. These sites were defended by banks, ditches and palisades against waterborne attack.[19]

The Waihou's wetlands and soaring forests of kahikatea trees were vividly evoked in an 1830s description by the missionary William Yate:

> But the scenery is most lovely on the fresh-water banks of this river: the only drawback to its enjoyment is the difficulty of landing, except at high water, on account of the depth of mud deposited on its banks. It is true, that, for fifty or sixty miles, there is a great sameness in the views, being confined by hills on one side, and an immense flat forest on the other; yet the whole is so peaceful, so well suited for meditation, and fitted to calm the ruffled passions of the soul, that hearts, even the most insensible to the beauties of nature, must feel its influence . . . The copse-wood and flax, with reeds and rushes of every description, flourish most luxuriantly on the banks of this noble river; ducks, and other water-fowl, sail proudly and undisturbedly on its placid bosom, and are so remarkably tame, as to come fearlessly within reach of the paddles, with which our boats are rowed. Nor does the fragrance exhaled from the flowers and shrubs fail to increase the pleasure derived from an excursion on this stream. Indeed, the whole atmosphere seem impregnated with perfumes . . .[20]

On 20 November 1794, when the *Fancy* sailed into Hauraki, there had been no recorded European visits to the gulf during the past twenty-five years. Despite this, two small canoes, each carrying three men, came quickly out to the ship to exchange fish for metal buttons. The next day, when Dell anchored the *Fancy* about eight miles north-west from the mouth of the Waihou River, three canoes

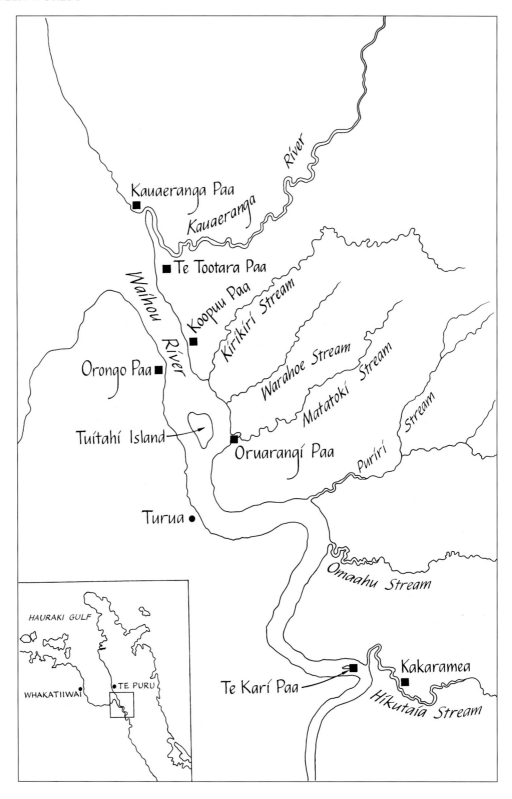

Kauaeranga Paa

Kauaeranga River

Te Tootara Paa

Koopuu Paa

Kirikiri Stream

Warahoe Stream

Matatoki Stream

Waihou River

Orongo Paa

Puriri Stream

Tuitahi Island

Oruarangi Paa

Turua

Omaahu Stream

HAURAKI GULF

TE PURU

WHAKATIIWAI

Te Kari Paa

Kakaramea

Hikutaia Stream

carrying about forty people came alongside. According to Dell's account:

> [They] trafficked with us as before, and with the same Articles, they appeared to place the utmost Confidence in us, as the greatest part of them came unarmed and most of them came aboard, they surveyed every thing with great attention, And seemed very much surprized, when on board they entertained us with One of their Songs and Dances. I made them presents of some Small Knives Looking Glasses Metal Buttons, empty Glass Bottles. In the evening they returned on Shore seemingly highly gratifyed.[21]

The next day the weather turned foul. The *Fancy* stayed at anchor, and no canoes came out to the ship. At 4 a.m. on 23 November, the brig's boats were lowered, and at ten o'clock Dell went off in the longboat accompanied by six Europeans, two Lascars and five Sepoys; and his third officer Alms was in the jolly boat with two Europeans and two Lascars, to take soundings towards the river. When they were within half a mile of the eastern shore, a crowd of people (mostly unarmed) gathered on a sandbank,[22] waving for them to come ashore. Dell signalled the jolly boat to come closer, and the two boats anchored at a safe distance from the shore while their crews ate dinner. Two local people swam out to investigate but would not come near the boats. After dinner, when the crews were refreshed and rested, they rowed up the river on a rising tide.

As they entered the Waihou, Dell noted villages scattered along both sides of the river. The people thronged to these places, inviting the Europeans to come on shore, but as soon as they realised that the strangers were not going to land, they launched their canoes and met them on the water. Before long, the boats were surrounded by twenty-five canoes, each carrying between five and twenty people, who eagerly exchanged goods with the sailors. As they rowed up the river, the boats grounded several times, and their companions in the canoes obligingly pointed out the deeper channels. Further upstream (before the mouth of the Kirikiri Stream, where there was a major paa), all but two canoes turned back, probably because they had reached another kin group's territory. Accompanied by these two canoes, the boats rowed on up the river. At nightfall, as the weather began to worsen with rising winds and dark clouds that threatened rain, Dell noticed a creek opening to the eastern bank (probably the Warahoe or the Matatoki) and ran the boats into it for shelter, followed by the canoes. That night they set up camp beside the stream, in high winds and driving rain. Their Maori companions stayed in their canoes, which were soon beached by the falling tide, although at daylight two of them joined the group of Europeans and Indians at their camp. Dell was impressed by their composure:

> I cannot help remarking how well the Natives in the Canoes behaved, and what implicit Confidence they put in us, they were quite un armed and at day light Two of them Came on Shore amongst us, and eat and drank whatever we gave them without the Least appearance of Fear.[23]

Opposite: *Map of Hauraki.*

Early the next morning the weather had cleared and the tide had turned, floating the boats again. Everything on board was sodden from the night's rain, so Dell thought it unwise to proceed further up the river, 'not knowing the Dispositions of the Natives who appeared very Numerous, although at the same time very Friendly'. The crews embarked and, accompanied by the two canoes, rowed back down the river to a village on the western bank (possibly Orongo Paa), which appeared to be the home of their companions. Canoes flocked out to the boats, packed with men, women and children offering goods for barter. Dell noticed 'a fine Boy about Ten years of age, and who appeared much fairer than any I saw amongst them'. If this child had European as well as Maori parentage, this suggests a European arrival in the region (or perhaps elsewhere in the North Island) in the 1780s.

Various ships may well have visited New Zealand during the decade after Cook's charts and journals were published. European sea traffic in the Pacific was increasing; many vessels travelled between ports in South America, the East Indies, China or India whose records have not been systematically studied by New Zealand historians; and if a voyage was unlicensed by the East India Company, it was wise to avoid official scrutiny. Indeed, tribal accounts tell of an outbreak of a disease similar to dysentery in this district in this period, caused by the visit of an otherwise unknown English ship to Whitianga, just across the Coromandel Peninsula.[24] According to G. F. Angas in 1841, furthermore, seven vessels had arrived in Port Jackson before 1795 with timber from New Zealand.[25]

The rest of the day was occupied with a long, weary haul back to the *Fancy*, against wind and tide. Out in the gulf, high swells almost swamped the jolly boat, leaving the rowers cold and exhausted. Dell took it under tow, and they finally arrived back on board that evening. By and large, Dell was contented with their efforts. That night he commented in his journal:

> I can only say I met with every thing according to [Captain Cook's] description, The Pine Trees which he mentions I saw in great abundance, but at a greater distance from the Banks of the River, than what I expected to find them, being at least a Quarter of a Mile, and that Space over a very Marshy flat Country intirely covered with Reeds and the Flax plant, which grows in great abundance on each side of the River and which would occasion much Labour time, and people to get them near the Banks after they were felled. I have however not the least Doubt but I shall find every thing which Captain Cook describes higher up the River, and shall at this place be able to accomplish the intentions of the voyage. I am already conscious that on the Spring Tides I shall meet with no difficulty in getting the Vessel high up the River.[26]

At daybreak on 25 November, a crowd of canoes loaded with fish came out to the *Fancy* and traded until mid-morning. One man offered a freshly preserved head, its brains scooped out and the skull cavity stuffed with flax, in exchange for a small axe, but Dell would not allow the purchase, and its owner left the ship dismayed. Dell decided to take the brig as high as possible up the Waihou, to act as a safe base for his men while they felled and trimmed the trees. He sent the longboat up the river under the command of the *Fancy*'s first officer William Denniston, with Alms, the third officer, and seven armed Europeans, to take soundings and find a safe channel for the vessel. When the boat returned at 10 p.m., Denniston reported that they had travelled high up the river, past a number of shoals and creeks, accompanied by forty-six canoes. During the day they had seen at least eight or nine hundred people, who behaved very peacefully. Denniston had landed (perhaps by the Puriri Stream), accompanied by two armed Europeans and about fifty local people, who trampled down bushes and flax plants to clear a pathway into the forest. One of Denniston's companions had been a carpenter's mate on HMS *Sirius* when she was wrecked in 1790 at Norfolk Island, and had lived there for several years. When the longboat party felled a tree with a trunk seventy feet high, he judged that it was much superior to the pines on Norfolk, having turpentine in its heart and a much tougher wood. Further up the river the officers reported stands of tall trees growing close to the river banks, but because it was getting dark they did not think it safe to land, and turned back to the ship.

The next morning, 26 November, more canoes loaded with fish flocked around the *Fancy*, exchanging these for European goods. Dell decided to rest his men, not being willing to risk the Lascars on an expedition inland. After a day of relaxation, Denniston, Alms and nine Europeans took the longboat back to the Waihou. Far upstream Denniston landed with four Europeans (probably by the Hikutaia) and felled a tree measuring 122 feet to the branches, thirty-six inches diameter six feet from the ground and sixteen inches diameter near the branches. Denniston returned to the *Fancy* at 4 p.m. the next day, reporting that the river was deep enough for the snow to travel upstream at high water, with a soft muddy bottom so that she would not be damaged if she grounded at low tide.

On 29 November in the evening, Dell ordered the *Fancy*'s anchor raised and the ship was steered up the gulf and anchored overnight to wait for the tide. The next morning he worked his ship towards the mouth of the river, finally mooring her off 'Cockle Shoal', where a number of canoes surrounded her. The local people swarmed on deck, trying to loosen the clamps on the rails of the gun carriages and the chain plates with stone adzes. When they were ordered back on shore, however, they went quietly. The next morning, Dell sent the longboat upriver again to look for a deep-water channel for the brig. More locals came on board and tried to pilfer iron. That night Dell wrote in his journal:

> I would not wish to use harsh means with them if possible; I only recover the stolen articles, when detected, and turn them away from the Vessel with threats of punishment. In future I am in great hopes we shall not be troubled with them higher up the River, as the Officers inform me that there does not appear to be many Inhabitants. This day hawled the sein, and Caught some Salmon, Flounders, Soles and a few Smelts. Several of the natives came from their Village and lent us a hand to hawl it. Thermometer in Cabbin at 72 degrees.[27]

On 2 December, the weather was wet and miserable, so the brig stayed at anchor off 'Cockle Shoal'. The next day at noon, the *Fancy* weighed anchor and set sail up the river in a light breeze, with the boats ahead towing. When they came to 'Shoal Island' (Tuitahi Island), Dell tried to steer his vessel into the western channel, but the tide was running fast up the eastern channel and drove the *Fancy* onto a bank at the north end of the island. Dell ordered his men to take the stream anchor and then the best bower out in the longboat, drop them overboard and try to drag her off the mud by hauling in the cables. When this failed, he had the ship propped off the mud with spars, then waited for the rising tide. Early the next morning at high water, the sailors took each of the anchors out in the longboat in turn and tried to haul the *Fancy* off, again without success. Dell had her propped up once more, and the crew began to off-load water and ballast and to nail copper over the hull where the timbers had been damaged in the grounding.

While all of this was going on, large numbers of local people gathered around, examining the ship, collecting food, helping out the sailors and trying to take their things. As Dell observed:

> When the Vessel was dry on the Flatt a great number of the Indians Men Women and Children came round her and gazed on her with astonishment and seeing our People clearing away the Sand, they assisted by taking our Shovels and likewise with their Paddles, the Women after having satisfied their Curiosity began to Collect Clams and Cockles with which the Flatt abounds; and what appears to me to be their Employment. As I could observe the Men standing up to their necks in water in the River, spearing Salmon and other Fish. They continue to behave very well, excepting there still continuing to thieve but when detected and a musquett is pointed towards them of which they are very much affraid they immediately return the Stolen Article and paddle from the Vessel, with the fear of being fired at.[28]

Finally, at 4 p.m., the *Fancy* floated off at high water and sailed up the river, anchoring south of Tuitahi Island. In the morning Dell weighed anchor and kedged upriver, grounding the *Fancy* by a stream that ran into a grove of kahikatea trees. There he went on shore and met the inhabitants of a small village, who showed him a pathway into the forest. The trees there did not seem suitable, so Dell and his men returned on board. The next day they kedged the *Fancy* further upstream, finally anchoring in four fathoms opposite another stream (either the Puriri or the Hikutaia), by a large village on the western bank, which they called 'Gravesend'.[29] A local man, nicknamed 'Jack Thames' by the sailors, had guided the longboat on several earlier excursions and now was living on board. According to Dell, 'They have found [Jack] of great Service at times. He eats and drinks whatever we offer him, and I hope I shall find him a useful Person towards accomplishing the intention of the Voyage.'[30]

The next morning Dell and Alms went ashore, where the inhabitants of 'Gravesend' welcomed them in a very friendly manner. More canoes came up the river that evening, and their crews landed and set up camp. Early the next morning Denniston and Alms went with the carpenter, the sawyer, six Lascars and two Sepoys in the longboat to begin felling trees, and another large group of canoes came upriver, landing on the western bank. By seven o'clock, 117 canoes had gathered around the *Fancy*. They were full of armed warriors, and when Dell tried to send them away from the ship, they refused to go. Dell identified their leaders as chiefs from the villages at the east entrance of the river, presumably at Kauaeranga, Totara Paa, Kopu Paa and Oruaruangi. After several warnings, Dell fired a musket over their heads, which sent them off to the western bank in confusion. According to his journal:

> [They] joined those who had assembled on the Western Shore, where Number[s] had amounted from Fifteen Hundred to Two Thousand amongst which was several Chiefs, and one in particular who seemed to have Superior authority over the rest – he run from one party to another Haranguing them, and beating his mantle which he had taken off with his Patoo Patoo and shaking it at us and Calling to us . . . to come on Shore. From their behaviour I am sure they meant to attack us, but had not Courage Sufficient to put there design in execution, as they are too well acquainted with the effect of our Fire arms; to make the attempt. [31]

'Jack Thames' may have been sent to report on the Europeans' strength and movements, for he now joined his friends on shore. So far as the Europeans could see, however, the people of 'Gravesend' village took no part in this affair. There may well have been some earlier dispute or breach of tapu committed while the *Fancy* was anchored out in the gulf, and the people of the eastern coastal district decided to seek utu while the ship was up the river. Later that morning several canoes came peaceably alongside, but Dell would not let their crews come on board. He was relieved when the crew of the longboat returned safely that evening, to report that they had felled ten trees of different sizes.

At daybreak the next morning there were still several thousand people camped beside the river, so Dell decided not to send the longboat out that day. Again, several canoes came to barter amiably with the Europeans. At 10 a.m. Dell allowed two old men who had previously visited the ship several times to come on board. There was something particular on the *Fancy* that they were anxious to show their people, but Dell could not work out what it was. Finally he understood that it was a red Indian bedspread on his bunk, and he gave it to them. As soon as the elders carried this up on deck and showed it to the people on the river bank, the principal chief with two subordinates launched his canoe and came alongside. This signal must have invoked the power of tapu, for red was the tapu colour and the bedspread was equivalent to a red feather cloak, an intensely tapu garment used only on ceremonial occasions. All the same, the principal chief (or 'eticatua' [ariki tua? – senior chief [32]) would not come on board until noon. He and his companions seemed afraid of everything at first, but when Dell and his officers gave them gifts and treated them kindly, they relaxed and stayed on board, returning to shore that evening with promises to come back the next day.

By the next morning most of the people at the riverbank camp had left, and those who remained seemed quiet and peaceable. Dell took a party of nine Europeans, a Sepoy and four Lascars up the river, where they cut down two tall trees, and four more at another place where trees had already been felled. Kahikatea trees were prized for their fruit and the birds that flocked to them, and such trees were named and claimed by particular families. Dell had no notion of this, however. So far as he and other Europeans were concerned, trees in a place like New Zealand were simply part of the wilderness, and the question of ownership did not arise.[33] Over the next few days, the longboat went out each day and the crew felled trees – eleven one day, eight the next, while the men on board the *Fancy* dressed and spun flax to make rope and running rigging for the snow. Houses were springing up at the camp on the western shore close to the ship, and the old principal chief came on board several times, asking Dell how long he and his men intended to stay in Hauraki. On 11 December, when a wood axe and a piece of iron from the forge were taken from the wooding place, Dell asked the old chief to get them back. It seems likely that the local people saw these transactions as utu for the trees that were being felled, but Dell knew nothing of this and regarded the appropriations as theft.

Unfortunately, the surviving copy of Dell's journal of his three-month stay at Hauraki ends at this point, just one month after his arrival. When he arrived at Norfolk Island in March 1795 to report to the Lieutenant-Governor, King ordered his clerk to copy Dell's journal for despatch to London, but Dell had to leave the island before the copy was completed.[34] According to David Collins at Port Jackson, however, Dell's men exacted retribution for the missing iron:

> Like other uncivilized people, these islanders saw no crime in theft, and stole some axes from the people employed on shore, gratifying thereby their predeliction for iron, which, strange as it may sound to us, they would have preferred to gold. Unfortunately, iron was too precious even here to part with, unless for an equivalent; and it became necessary to convince them of it. Two men and one woman were killed, the seamen who fired on them declaring (in their usual enlarged style of relation) that they had driven off and pursued upwards of three thousand of these cannibals. They readily parted with any quantity of their flax, bartering it for iron. As the valuable qualities of this flax were well known, it was not uninteresting to us to learn, that so small a vessel as the Fancy had lain at an anchor for three months in the midst of numerous and warlike tribes of savages, without any attempt on their part to become the masters; and that an intercourse might safely and advantageously be opened between them and the colonists of New South Wales, whenever proper materials and persons should be sent out to manufacture the flax, if the governor of that country should ever think it an object worthy of his attention.[35]

According to both Collins and King, Dell's men had felled 213 trees from sixty to 140 feet long, fit for plank or spars for East India Company ships, and collected and dressed a large quantity of flax during their three months at Hauraki. A few axes were not much to take in return. For a sense of proper equivalence to be established, though, Maori and Europeans had to learn something of each other's customs, and merchant sailors on trading expeditions were not much interested in such niceties. All the same, Dell and the old chief had evidently established some kind of understanding. On his arrival at Norfolk, Dell commented to King, 'On the whole the natives were on very good Terms with us and regretted our Departure very much.' The local people promised to take care of the trees that had been felled until they were collected, which Dell expected would be as soon as the *Endeavour* had discharged her cargo at Port Jackson.

On her way back from Thames to Norfolk Island, the *Fancy* stopped at North Cape, perhaps in another attempt to find 'Kotokokee'. This visit may have caused an epidemic that is said to have broken out in the north in 1795, 'spread[ing] like fire through flax' and killing so many people that it was only with difficulty that the living could dispose of the dead.[36] The *Fancy* carried on from North Cape to Norfolk Island, arriving there in early March. Dell reported to Lieutenant-Governor King on his New Zealand visit, and then carried on to Port Jackson, arriving there on 15 March 1795.[37]

Eleven

THE TIMBER VOYAGES
1798–1801

THE *HUNTERS* (I & II), *EL PLUMIER* AND *ROYAL ADMIRAL* AT HAURAKI

By and large, the inhabitants of Hauraki adopted a confident, entrepreneurial approach to the various European ships that arrived in their territory. They were eager to enter into exchanges with their crews, and particular rangatira forged alliances with the leaders of successive expeditions. This may have been due to the numerical strength of local populations, and the relative geniality of their meetings with both Cook on the *Endeavour* in 1769 and Dell on the *Fancy* in 1794–95.

The next visit by a European vessel further illustrates this attitude. The *Hunter*, a 300-ton Java-built snow, arrived in Port Jackson from Bengal in June 1798, carrying Robert Campbell, a partner in Campbell and Clarke, the Calcutta company that owned her, and a speculative cargo of cattle, horses, spirits and supplies.[1] Campbell had come to the penal colony to assess the prospects for setting up a branch of his company there. When he returned to India in September on another vessel, he left William Smith, one of the missionaries who had recently been evacuated from the London Missionary Society (LMS) mission in Tahiti, in charge of his affairs. The *Hunter* sailed under the command of James Fearn on 20 August 1798 to collect a load of spars from 'the river Thames' (the Waihou) in New Zealand. Unfortunately, no log survives from this voyage, but Campbell later reported that the *Hunter*'s crew (about fifty men[2]) 'cut down a quantity of very fine spars, sufficient to load [Fearn's] vessel; but, being rather short of hands, he could not have shipped them, had not the natives with much alacrity and good humour assisted his people in getting them to the water's side'.[3] The *Hunter* is said to have left for China in mid-October, a fairly brief stay, and most of her cargo may have in fact been the logs felled three years earlier by the *Fancy*'s crew.

Fearn's venture in Hauraki seems to have inspired several traders in Port Jackson to follow suit. In the following year, Simeon Lord (a former convict) formed a partnership with William Hingston, formerly master of the *Hillsborough*,

A miniature of Simeon Lord, the ex-convict shipowner.

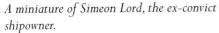

A portrait of Robert Campbell, by Rodius.

and the Norfolk Island dealer Aaron Davies to buy *Nostra Señora de Bethlehem* (a Spanish prize captured by English whalers off Lima).[4] They refitted the ship and renamed her the *Hunter* after the Governor. Once Spain had made peace with France in 1795, Spanish ships off the coast of America were liable to attack or capture by British privateers (including some whaling and sealing vessels). The purchase of Spanish ships that had been captured and brought to Port Jackson was one way of avoiding the local prohibition on building large vessels. Furthermore, such ships could be sailed to India and sold without breaching the East India Company's rights, although the *Hunter*'s draft articles demonstrate that Lord and his partners had no intention of respecting the Company's trading monopoly. Instead, they planned a return voyage from Port Jackson, with a stop to collect a cargo of timber (and possibly also sealskins and whale oil) in New Zealand en route to Bengal, and bringing back a cargo of supplies from India to the colony. By naming the ship the *Hunter*, the same as Campbell's vessel, they may have hoped to confuse the Bengal authorities (as indeed they have confused some scholars[5]) and so escape detection.

As it happened, the plot failed. After conflicts with the authorities in Port Jackson,[6] the *Hunter* sailed in October 1799 under Hingston's command to 'The Thames', where a cargo of spars was collected. Simeon Lord and Aaron Davies had commissioned James Puckey (another former missionary from the LMS mission at Tahiti) to travel on the *Hunter* to look after their interests.[7] When the ship arrived at Calcutta, however, and began loading a cargo of spirits for Port Jackson, the authorities were alerted. The ship was seized, Hingston was thrown into prison, and in the investigation that followed, it was found that he had carried twenty-three other escaped convicts from Port Jackson to India.[8] Hingston pleaded that Governor Hunter had authorised the voyage, and was released, but knowing that a denial from Port Jackson would soon follow, he quickly sold the ship and its cargo and vanished with the proceeds.[9] Not surprisingly under the circumstances, the log of this voyage also disappeared. We do not know how long the second *Hunter* stopped at Hauraki, nor anything much about the circumstances of her stay. We can assume, however, that relationships with the local people were reasonably friendly, because four of the men on board (who were probably escaped convicts) decided to stay on at Waihou rather than risking a voyage to India in a leaking vessel. One of these men, Thomas Taylor, formed a relationship with a local woman and intended to live there until the war in Europe was over – or so he told the Europeans on the *Royal Admiral*, a large East Indiaman that visited Hauraki several years later.

The next ship to arrive at Hauraki was the *Betsey*, a British whaler that visited briefly in May 1800. The *Betsey* had been raiding Spanish shipping on the west coast of America, where she sacked Spanish settlements, pillaged and destroyed nine Spanish ships, and sent two prizes, *El Plumier* and *Euphemia*, loaded with wine and spirits to Port Jackson.[10] The ships sailed in convoy across the Pacific to Tahiti, where a young local man named 'Tapeooe' enlisted on board the *Betsey* as a sailor.[11] The vessels carried on to Tongatapu, where another beleagured party of LMS missionaries was rescued,[12] and then sailed to Port Jackson for repairs. There, 'Tapeooe' was fêted by Governor King and the Reverend Samuel Marsden, and the ship's captain suffered 'a fit of insanity'. He was replaced by John Myers, formerly the *Betsey*'s third officer, and 'other competent Navigators belonging to the ship'. *El Plumier* was left in Port Jackson to be sold, and in May 1800 the *Betsey* sailed from Port Jackson with a crew of fifty (including 'Tapeooe') and two women passengers, heading for the west coast of South America. En route, the ship called at 'The Thames' for just three days, to collect some spars to complete the refitting. This was the first time that a Tahitian had visited New Zealand since Tupaia, Hitihiti and Mai had arrived with Cook's ships, and the first visit by European women to the North Island.

Myers reported that 'the Natives are of a copper colour, stout made, and of a very savage disposition. They differ in many respects from the inhabitants of New South Wales, and are reported to be cannibals.'[13] He added, though, that they were 'artful', making canoes that were 'very handsomely executed, and . . . ingeniously carved', also noting the prodigal local fisheries, which were harvested by lines and nets. It may have been either this ship or one of the two *Hunters* to which Horeta Te Taniwha referred when he said that long after Cook had arrived in the gulf, 'another ship of goblins (tupua) came to Hauraki, and the goblins of this ship worked the kahikatea of Wai-hou, and took them away'.[14]

In January 1801, *El Plumier* (also called 'Ploomer', 'Pluma' or 'Plumo'), one of the Spanish prizes captured by the *Betsey*,[15] left Port Jackson, arriving at Hauraki in March. *El Plumier* had been bought by a syndicate that included one of the 'Scottish Martyrs', Thomas Fyshe Palmer.[16] Palmer was an old Etonian who, after graduating from Cambridge University, had become first an Anglican, then a Unitarian minister. During a period of unrest in Britain, inspired by the American and French Revolutions and the writings of Tom Paine, Palmer along with his colleagues Muir, Gerrald, Margarot and Skirving had become radical enthusiasts, advocating universal suffrage and parliamentary reform. These 'Martyrs' were tried for sedition by the Scottish authorities and sentenced to transportation.[17] The trials were widely criticised in Britain, America and France as a miscarriage of

'Transported for Sedition' – portraits of the 'Scottish Martyrs', Palmer, Margarot, Skirving, Muir and Gerrald, transported to Botany Bay for sedition. A woodcut on a linen handkerchief.

justice,[18] and instructions were sent to Port Jackson that the Scottish transportees should be watched but leniently handled.[19] Palmer had established a farm in the penal colony and, among other things, lived for a time with a group of Aboriginals, writing a sympathetic account of their way of life and vehemently protesting their ill-treatment by soldiers and convicts. He was a learned and genial man who had built several small sealing boats (with the aid of an encyclopaedia he had brought from Scotland) with his friends, the free settler James Ellis and the surgeon John Boston, who sailed with him to Port Jackson.[20] Although he had prospered in the colony, Palmer openly criticised Governor Hunter's administration, and when his sentence expired, he was anxious to return to Britain.[21] Along with Boston and Ellis, he purchased *El Plumier* and hired William Reid, formerly a sailor on the *Sirius* (but an incompetent mariner), as the ship's captain.

On 5 January 1801, after a short-lived mutiny by the crew,[22] *El Plumier* sailed for England via 'The Thames'. The former missionary James Puckey (who had made his way back to Port Jackson after the *Hunter*'s abortive voyage) was on board as second officer,[23] with a number of passengers, including Palmer, Ellis, Boston with his wife and two children, Mrs Butler (the wife of the mate) and a father and son by the name of Harris.[24]

The ship was in poor condition, with only two guns and a scratch crew of thirteen men,[25] and no more than six months' provisions. *El Plumier* arrived at Hauraki on 2 March 1801,[26] looking for fresh supplies. Shortly after her arrival, Reid attempted to take the ship up the Waihou River, where, just like the *Fancy*, she grounded on a shoal, shivering her larboard timbers in the process. The crew were in the process of trying to repair their ship when, on 20 April 1801, the *Royal Admiral* sailed into Hauraki.

This old East Indiaman (923 tons), heavily armed and manned by a crew of eighty-three European sailors and fifteen Lascars,[27] was on its way from London to China via Port Jackson, where it had landed a small detachment of soldiers with their wives and families, 250 male convicts and a group of London Missionary Society missionaries and their families.[28] The *Royal Admiral* also carried clothing and supplies (including spirits and copper coinage) for the penal colony.[29] During the voyage forty-three convicts had died of 'jail fever' (typhus), and many other convicts and passengers had been landed in a weak and debilitated state. Although none made complaints about ill-treatment on board, it was by now unusual for convicts to arrive in Port Jackson in such dreadful condition.[30]

The *Royal Admiral* remained for four months at Port Jackson, where the crew cleaned and refitted her, loading ballast and fresh supplies. The remaining missionaries, Brothers Youl, Elder, Wilson, Hayward, Davies, Scott, Watters, Tessier, Mitchell and Read, were on their way to Tahiti, and during this delay they studied the Tahitian vocabulary supplied to them by the LMS,[31] visited and took services on shore, and went to hear the Reverend Samuel Marsden preach in Sydney Church. They had embarked upon this journey with evangelical zeal. As one of the founders of the LMS urged:

Modern discoveries in geography have . . . contributed to enlarge the desires of Christians in this respect. Captain Cook and others have traversed the globe, almost from pole to pole, and have presented to us, as it were, a new world, a world of islands in the vast Pacific Ocean – some of them as promising in the disposition of the people as in the appearance of the country. May we not reasonably hope that a well-planned and well-conducted mission to one or more of these, seconded with the earnest prayers of thousands of British Christians, will be attended with the blessing of God, and issue in the conversion of many souls?[32]

Unfortunately, the LMS missions in Tahiti and Tonga were neither well planned nor well conducted. In 1799, when one of the leaders of the Society wrote to Sir Joseph Banks, asking for his help in gaining government support for their enter-prise, he pointed this out with some asperity.[33] By 1800, the Tongan mission had been evacuated by the *Betsey* and the Tahitian mission was in disarray. Both the languages and the people had proved difficult to master, as one of the missionaries at Tahiti lamented:

The poor heathen around us . . . do not discover the smallest desire to know aught of the things of God; nor have they any curiosity to know why we so frequently meet together, to read, sing, and pray; or why we so particularly honour every seventh day, in setting it apart for the worship of God, and refraining from labour theron. The poor Otaheiteans are deeply prejudiced in favour of their idolatrous worship, though they do not scruple frequently to say, *their gods are good for nothing*. Nor are they less attached to their manners and customs in civil life. Not-withstanding their rude uncultivated state, they seem to hold themselves as civi-lized a people as any beneath the sun, and treat the arts and sciences, customs, and manners of Europeans with great indifference and contempt.[34]

After a fracas in Tahiti in 1798, a number of missionaries (including James Puckey and William Smith, who joined the *Royal Admiral* as ship's purser in Sydney) had fled the island for Port Jackson, just one year after their arrival. The Tongatapu mission suffered even worse disasters, and in 1799 the last of the missionaries left that island. A further party of evangelists left England on the *Duff* for Tahiti at the end of 1798, but they were captured by a French privateer and straggled home, where many of them left the Society. Some of this group – Youl, Watters, Hay-ward, Mitchell, Wilson and Turner – had joined the *Royal Admiral* party in England with their captain William Wilson (nephew of Captain James Wilson, the pious commander of the *Duff*, and formerly his first mate), and in May 1800 sailed for Tahiti via Port Jackson with letters, supplies and encouragement to reinforce the mission.[35]

They found considerable sympathy and support for their venture in the penal colony. Various local settlers offered the missionaries hospitality. One evening Philip Gidley King (recently appointed the new Governor of New South Wales), his wife Anna and some of the local ladies dined on board the *Royal Admiral*, and King promised to order that any visiting sailors who harmed their mission or the Tahitians would be severely punished. William Wilson set up a subscription fund for Smith to pay his debts and free him from imprisonment, and many of the colonists contributed.[36] They also spent time with Rowland Hassall and Francis Oakes, both of whom had escaped to Port Jackson from the Tahitian mission; as well as Mr Shelley, who had left the Tongatapu mission and now joined their party; and Samuel Marsden, a strong supporter of the LMS's Pacific mission. Their living allowances were not generous, however, and they fretted about the impression they were making on Port Jackson society, and on Marsden in particular:

> If you had been amongst us, and dressed like us, Mr. Marsden would have thought of you, as he has insinuated of us, in his Letter addressed to Captain Wilson (which he showed to Governor King and I suppose to the principal, if not to all of the Gentlemen of New South Wales), that you had received no education, that you was a Clown in your Manners, and that you belonged to the dregs of the Common People, unless he had been told, that you was a minister . . .[37]

They must have seen Marsden's letter to Captain Wilson. In expounding on the qualities of a good missionary, he had written:

> A missionary was I to define his character should be a pious good man should be well acquainted with mankind should possess some education should be easy in address and of an active mind. Some of the missionaries which have come to this colony are the opposite characters they are profane in their lives and conduct, they are totally ignorant of mankind, they possess no education they are clowns in their manners.[38]

Mitchell, whose 'vain and frivolous conduct' troubled his brethren throughout the voyage, was one of the men to whom Marsden was referring. He decided to stay behind in Port Jackson, to give up his mission and to work instead for Simeon Lord. On 30 March, their last day in Port Jackson, when Marsden came on board to farewell the Brothers, he asked them to write to him as often as possible. As the ship set sail, the secretary of the missionary group wrote bravely in their collective journal:

> Thus we leave this place, after being detained here from Novr. 20 to March 30th and again venture once more on the face of the Mighty deep. May he who has the Governing the Wind and Waves conduct us safe to our Journey's end . . . But whether we shall meet Prosperity or Adversity the remaining part of our Voyage we know not, but desire to leave ourselves to Divine Providence, hoping all Things are working together for our good. About Four in the afternoon we were out of sight of Land, directing our course, with a fair wind for New Zealand.[39]

Although the missionaries were anxious to get to Tahiti, Wilson decided to make a detour to pick up a cargo of New Zealand timber, some for the mission station at Tahiti, but mainly for sale on the China market. The voyage across the Tasman was uneventful, except for the discovery of four stowaways. The Brothers held prayer meetings and occupied themselves with sawing timber for their mission compound in Tahiti.

Cape Maria van Diemen was sighted on 13 April, and three fires were seen on shore, but no people. After a quick passage down the east coast, the *Royal Admiral* came to the Poor Knights Islands on 18 April, where she struck 'hard squalls with very high seas'. That night the ship was moored, but during the next morning she was battered by a hurricane, losing an anchor and splitting the fore and main sails, and narrowly escaping shipwreck on the rocks.[40] The ship's log was matter-of-fact about this episode, but the missionaries recorded it in dramatic detail, adding, 'Then they cry unto the Lord in their trouble, and he bringeth them out of their distresses. He maketh the storm a calm, so that the waves thereof are still. Then are they glad because they be quiet, so he bringeth them unto their desired haven.'[41] When the storm died down, the *Royal Admiral* sailed into Hauraki, anchoring in mid-channel on 20 April at 11 p.m.

At eight the next morning several canoes came out to the ship. Their crews were the first Maori that the *Royal Admiral* party had met. Captain Wilson invited them on board, calling out in Tahitian, 'Harree Mai, Harre Mai te Pahhii' (Welcome to the canoe). Although the Tahitian word 'pahii' (canoe) had no close equivalent in Maori, the words of welcome were clear enough, and the crews came confidently on board. The *Royal Admiral* was a very large ship, three times the size of any European vessel that had so far visited Hauraki, with many more guns, but the local people were not intimidated. They pointed out their leader, a 'warreekee' (ariki) named 'Towtowa' (Tautaua?)[42], and he accompanied Wilson to the ship's cabin with one of his friends, while eighteen canoes carrying about 140 people gathered around the ship. Many of these people came on board, where they soon began to exchange fish, raw and cooked sweet and English potatoes, raw turnips, fishing lines and 'wooden axes' (probably patu) for gilt buttons, nails, fish-hooks and 'any kind of old iron'. The missionaries were fascinated to see that English crops (potatoes and turnips), which they supposed had been left by Captain Cook, were now being grown on shore. Their visitors told them that there was an English ship already anchored upriver. They guessed that this must be *El Plumier*, since they knew that Palmer and his companions had also sailed for Hauraki. Late that afternoon the longboat and the yawl went up the Waihou to investigate, carrying the captain, the second and third officers (Lloyd and Keller), the former missionary and now ship's purser William Smith, two of the Brothers (Read and Youl), about forty-four sailors, and woodcutting tools and supplies. At 10 p.m. an English boat came alongside the ship, carrying Captain Reid, and Messrs Boston and Ellis from the 'Pluma', who reported that they had been at the Thames for the past six weeks, where they had 'experienced every kindness from the natives', and that their ship was up the river about twenty-five miles (probably this was measured from out in the gulf, since the *Plumier* was anchored near the Puriri Stream, seven miles up the Waihou River).

That night, the old chief Tautaua and about twenty companions, along with the party from *El Plumier,* slept on board. Tautaua slept in the cabin, and the missionaries were quickly told that he and four of his party were 'ta'bued' and that it was a great transgression to touch their heads. The head of a chief was the resting place of his ancestor gods, and intensely tapu; and if this tapu was defiled, it was a terrible insult. The local people had already learned that Europeans had no notion of such matters and thought it best to take precautionary measures, making certain that they learned the proper protocols as quickly as possible.

Over the next two days the remaining crew and passengers stayed on board, waiting for the yawl to return and engaging in amiable exchanges with local people. A number of their visitors helped the sailors to haul the cables and slept on board, and their friends brought out cooked food for them and the officers in return for the ship's hospitality. More canoes came out with fish, potatoes and turnips, and on 24 April the yawl returned to the ship with Lloyd and Brother Youl to report on their expedition up the Waihou River. The longboat and yawl had been piloted by local people, who took them seven or eight miles up the gulf towards the eastern coast, where they anchored overnight, landing all but three of their guides. At daybreak Captain Wilson wanted to go ashore to look at the trees, but a canoe came alongside with four or five people who persuaded him to carry on up the river, where there was a European ship. The two boats set sail and soon entered the river mouth, where they saw marshes and mangroves at the western entrance, and some houses and a 'town' on the opposite shore (either Tootara or Kopu Paa), whose inhabitants waved out to them in welcome. As they sailed upstream, several acres of gardens and more towns appeared, one very large, which their guides told them was 'the principal town in this part, and the residence of the greatest chief on this side of the water [later identified as an old priest named 'Taurangi']'. This was Oruarangi Paa, described earlier by Cook and now sketched in Wilson's chart of the river and labelled 'Howrok? Hippa' (Hauraki Paa). Large numbers of canoes surrounded them, and soon they saw *El Plumier*, apparently wrecked on a shoal near the Puriri Stream, with several Maori on board. Fearing that she had been captured, they took up their muskets, and their guides, afraid that they were in danger, drew out their weapons and twisted the thongs around their wrists ready for combat.

As they approached *El Plumier*, however, a canoe carrying her chief mate came out to meet them. He told them that all was well. The local people were peaceful and friendly, and were helping them to repair the ship and cut down trees in the forest. Wilson went to see some trees opposite the grounded vessel, which he later described on his chart as 'Good Timber'. He then accompanied William Smith on board the *Plumier*, where they met James Puckey and Patrick Riley (Puckey was Smith's former colleague from the Tahitian mission, while Riley had been his servant at Port Jackson[43]), finding them well and in good spirits. After breakfast on board they carried on ten or twelve miles upstream, guided by some local people in a canoe, now and then landing to look at the trees. They rowed past a creek (the Hikutaia), noting a burial ground on the opposite bank marked by a few huts with an image in the shape of a man in front of them. This was almost certainly Te Kari Island, a sacred site. About half a mile further on they saw a village, and about two miles from the creek Wilson landed to look at the forest and to take some refreshment. The trees were not suitable for his purposes, so he ordered the yawl to turn back downriver.

Shortly after this, a canoe came alongside carrying two Englishmen, one of whom told Wilson that there was better timber up the Hikutaia. This man, Thomas Taylor, said that he had arrived on Simeon Lord's *Hunter* and had been living in Hauraki for the past two years. Wilson ordered his boat to anchor at the mouth of the Hikutaia, then joined Taylor in the canoe. With the yawl following, they paddled up the stream, passing several canoes, many houses, several large tracts of cultivated land, enclosed and divided into small plots, and 'a multitude of natives'. Further upstream they came to a large town called 'Kokramea' (in the missionaries' journal) or 'Kakrama' (on Wilson's chart) containing a number of fine houses, where they were welcomed by the chief 'Hupa' (Te Haupa, an important Ngaati Paoa leader), his brother and about three hundred others. Kakaramea was built on a low rise, and the people told them that this was the second largest town on the river. Wilson went to look at a forest about three-quarters of a mile away, where he found excellent trees, so he sent for the longboat to join them. The tide had ebbed, however, and the longboat could not get up the creek. Wilson returned to the long boat and slept there while the rest of his party spent the night at Kakaramea Paa, some sleeping in a house occupied by the *Plumier*'s people, and others in the yawl.

Early the next morning Wilson gave a gift of axes and red cloth to Te Haupa in exchange for assistance from his people. He and his crew felled some trees and began building a pair of thatched conical huts in a palisaded enclosure, one for the officers, the stores and the missionaries, and the other for the crew. On 24 April, however, two axes were taken by people from the eastern coast opposite the *Royal Admiral*, and Wilson detained four of their chiefs. The sentinels were careless, and the prisoners escaped without harm, although three muskets were fired after them as they fled. These were probably people who were challenging Te Haupa's right to monopolise the Europeans. Iron was prized for weapons as well as tools, and the Europeans' gifts to Te Haupa and others were disrupting local balances of wealth and power.

That same day, out in the gulf, James Elder and Charles Wilson crossed by canoe to the 'east side of the river' (probably to Te Puru, since the *Royal Admiral* party often used 'river' to describe the upper gulf). Their account of this expedition was vivid:

> On Landing on the Beach we were met by a number of Natives, who seemed overjoyed at our unexpected visit. They took hold of our hands and led us towards their Huts. About 20 yards from the water side we saw a fence, or Pailing 5 feet high with an opening in the Middle to enter in, within were their Huts. The Generality of their Huts are about 5 feet square and six feet high, made of Reeds and Flax Leaf.
>
> We were soon introduced to an old Man, and his Wife. the old Man appeared to be a Chief, and had a Brass weapon with the name of Joseph Banks, Esq.r

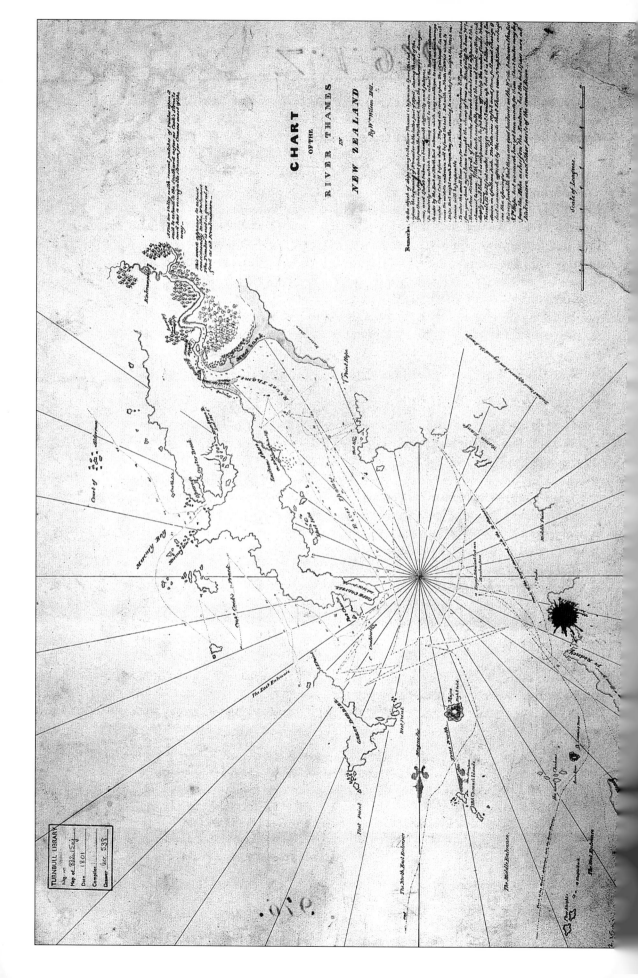

CHART
OF THE
RIVER THAMES
IN
NEW ZEALAND

By Wm. Wilson 1801.

Remarks.

Scale of Leagues.

engraved on it [this weapon must have come from either Uawa on the East Coast or from the South Island, for these brass patu were given as gifts only during Cook's second and third voyages]. At another place we saw another old man, who had been a Chief, but was so far advanced in years that he could not walk, and was blind; but being informed that some strangers were near, he crawled out of his hut and shook hands with us, and then began to shew how expert he was in their songs – After singing awhile he gave it up, being quite fatigued.

After sitting here refreshing ourselves, surrounded by about 100 Natives, who quietly collected together, we asked them to Eat and Drink with us, but they would not, for fear we should not have enough for ourselves (this could be their only reason), as they eat when on Board, and are very fond of our Biscuit.

We left the rest of our provender with them, and went to look around the place, at the foot of an hill, we saw about an Acre of Land cultivated, part of it appeared as if English Potatoes had been Dug out, and the other part seemed to be Sweet Potatoes not taken out of the ground. Saw also several huts larger than the former, which seemed to be Potato Houses.

Besides these saw several Tabu'd places, or sacred Houses where their dead, were deposited – these being shut up, we could not see what were in them, and the Natives warned us not to approach these places, because they were Eta'bu [the first European record of the term 'tapu' in New Zealand]. However one of us Transgressed in going too near, they on seeing it, gave him Leaves of two different sorts of Trees – and by that means to be Purified (as we supposed) from the defilement. Passing a small brook in a valley being carried over by the Natives we saw some more cultivated Land, where several were digging the ground with a spade (or a resemblance to one) having a step on one side, to press it down to the ground with the foot [a good description of a koo, or digging stick, in use].

On their return to the beach, Elder and Wilson shared a meal of roasted fish and potatoes with local people. No canoes were free to take them back to the *Royal Admiral*, so they stayed in a hut overnight, with the son of the ariki Tautaua guarding the door. The missionaries knew nothing of the capture inland of the 'chiefs belonging to the party on the east shore near the ship', but Tautaua was better informed, and unwilling to risk a surprise attack.

On 25 April, when a canoe came alongside the *Royal Admiral* and evacuated all of the local people, the missionaries became worried about the safety of their friends on shore. Shortly afterwards, though, another canoe arrived, bringing Elder and Wilson back to the ship. The next morning Mr Shelley came out in one of *El Plumier*'s boats to tell them that the upriver tribes were expecting an attack from the Waikato people and were preparing for war. That night the four escaped convicts who had stowed away on the ship chose this moment to free themselves from their chains and escape in *El Plumier*'s boat.

Early the next day the chief mate, Mr Skeene, went ashore in the yawl to search for the escaped convicts. He told the local people that he was going to hold some of them hostage until the convicts were captured and returned, but that as

Opposite: *William Wilson's 'Chart of the River Thames in New Zealand', 1801.*

soon as this was done he would let them go and give them a reward. At the same time, Brother Davies and Shelley went in *El Plumier*'s boat to 'the principal chief of Warreekee's village' with gifts of two hens and a cock for the chief. The recipient of this gift was later identified as 'Taurange' [Taurangi?], 'the greatest chief in these parts . . . and probably he is also an High Priest – he is an aged man of sober and mild aspect and has not that ferocious appearance as some of them have'.[44] Taurangi had visited the *Plumier* but never came out to the *Royal Admiral*. He may have been the ariki who, according to tribal tradition, took Te Haupa of Ngaati Paoa as an ally and invited him and his hapuu Te Urikaraka to come and live at Kakaramea.[45] It was quite common for the senior in a chiefly line of descent to act as ariki and 'high priest', controlling communications with the ancestor gods, while a rangatira led the people in war.[46]

This same day Brother Scott took the yawl upriver to see Captain Wilson, taking seeds with him to give to Thomas Taylor, who was referred to seventy years later in the Native Land Court as 'Tararoki . . . the Pakeha who first discovered this island, who gave the stone from which grew the first peach tree at Kakaramea'.[47] It is quite likely that this peach stone came into Taylor's possession on that occasion.

The next day, 28 April, a messenger came alongside in a large canoe to report that the escaped convicts had been located, and asking for an armed party to come and get them. When the seamen went ashore, the convicts were led to them by a ruse, and captured. They were brought by canoe back to the *Royal Admiral*, where the hostages were released and the people given the promised reward. That night a strong gale and high seas buffeted the ship, and when the anchor cable was raised, the people who remained on board began to cry, thinking that the ship was about to sail and carry them away from their homes and families. It was only with difficulty that they were reassured.

Over the next several days, not surprisingly, few people visited the *Royal Admiral*. On 2 May, however, Thomas Taylor came on board and had a long conversation with the Brothers. According to Taylor's account:

> He came in the Hunter belonging Mr. Simon Lord of Port Jackson, and that he with three others left the Ship because she was Leakey . . . He further said he meant to remain on the Island till he heard that the War [in Europe] was over – and the 3 others meant to leave and go in the Pluma.
>
> We asked him if he was Married to any of the Women, he said in answer that he lived with one, but was not Married, on account of some bad customs which prevailed, as the Woman went with 4 or 5 men at the time she takes her husband. It was very rare to find any man have more than one Wife and that after Marriage she would rather suffer Death than be unfaithful.
>
> He said that he had been 300 Miles up the country, and in the interior it was more populous and that there were wars among the different tribes. The Captives taken in War and their Progeny are doomed to perpetual Slavery, Men and Women. That the conquered are never Killed when taken in war. Also that the ultimate

object of their Worship and Adoration is said to be the Sun, Moon and Stars, and their Priest meet them two or three times a Month, especially before and after War. Their manner of Worship is to fall on their faces to the Earth, but have no set times for Worship. Many things are made sacred. Potatoes of each kind when Planted are Tabue'd and every Morning and Evening an Old Man is set to Pray over them, and no one suffered to go near them. They punish offenders by rooting and destroying his Potatoes as each has a portion of ground allotted to him to cultivate Potatoes for his and his family support.[48]

The missionaries also learned that Taylor was illiterate and had been acting as an interpreter and river pilot for the *El Plumier* party. His journey far inland up the Waihou River had been carried out in the company of Te Haupa, who was travelling to visit his sister. The inland people were friendly and very numerous, and had large stretches of land under cultivation. He claimed to have travelled a hundred miles westward from the river (probably to the Taamaki district), where the language and customs were the same as at Hauraki.[49]

By and large, Taylor's account seems accurate enough, although tribal histories are full of accounts of conquered peoples being killed in war, and his comments about people prostrating themselves in worship are not echoed in any other account. Prostration in the presence of high chiefs and the ancestor gods was commonplace in Polynesia, however, and it is possible that this custom had continued to be practised among the Hauraki and Tainui tribes. Later sources agree with Taylor that women had multiple sexual partners before marriage, and that adultery by women was harshly sanctioned. When the 'worship' of the sun, moon and stars is mentioned in other early accounts,[50] it seems to refer to a regular scrutiny of the night sky by tohunga, who found 'tohu', or signs in the heavens, to guide them in planting, fishing and war as well as in navigation.[51] According to Taylor, English as well as sweet potatoes (kuumara) were being grown under tapu conditions, with karakia to the gods twice daily, and the practice of punishing offenders by rooting up their gardens was often referred to in later descriptions of Maori life as muru, or the just confiscation of resources. While conquered peoples may have been killed, undoubtedly others became taurekareka, or 'slaves', who had been deprived of their mana.

Most importantly, perhaps, Taylor had travelled inland and to the west, and from his reports and their own observations the *Royal Admiral* party began to suppose that there must be 'many hundred thousand of natives at New Zealand'. This supposition is in striking contrast with George Forster's estimate of a total population of one hundred thousand people in New Zealand upon contact, based on Cook's *Endeavour* experience and his own voyage on the *Resolution*, both limited to coastal observations.[52] Archaeological and early historical evidence show that inland populations were dense, and Taylor's estimate, along with material from the early Hauraki visits, the estimates of warrior numbers on Tuki-tahua's map of the north, as well as the missionary William Ellis's 1816 estimate,[53] suggest that Forster's estimate was far too low.

By now the wooding party at Kakaramea was felling trees for spars and masts – 'of the spruce kind, running upon an average from 90 to 120 feet in height, very straight, and without a branch'.[54] Wilson thought that this timber would not be suitable for naval use (an accurate judgement, since experience soon showed that kahikatea rotted in the damp), but seemed useful for other purposes, so they persisted. At first the men tried to shift logs across the marshlands along the river with a timber carriage, and then by rollers over a slab road, but when these methods failed, Wilson presented Te Haupa with gifts and asked for his people's assistance. For payments of axes and red cloth, the people hauled large logs to the river's edge and helped to make rafts to send out to the ship. It is evidently these gifts that were referred to by Te Karamu Kahukoti in his address to Sir George Grey in 1854:

> Do you hearken – the captains of the ships that arrived in New Zealand in olden time sought out my fathers. They left them as presents scarlet garments, some with fringes, axes also, peaches and potatoes. At this time we first saw European axes. Our own axes were made of greenstone. With these we used to fell trees, and dub the canoes, but the trees were split with ordinary stones.
>
> When my ancestors and fathers received these axes, the news was heard at the Bay of Islands, it was heard at Waikato, it was heard at Tauranga, at Rotorua and Taupo; and the chiefs of those places came to get axes, for Te Haupa alone possessed those treasures.
>
> It was then Te Rauangaanga (the father of Potatau [high priest of Tainui]) came to my mother, who was his sister, and axes and red garments were given to him, which he took to his place – potatoes also, and peach stones.[55]

Te Haupa's peaches are often referred to in tribal accounts, and it seems they originated from Samuel Marsden's farm at Parramatta. The missionaries had with them young peach and fig plants in soil, and very likely also peach stones, supplied by Marsden from his farm.[56] These peaches, and potatoes, were soon growing inland.

By now, shipboard life was settling down to a steady routine. Every now and then canoes, some of them filled with strangers, arrived alongside to trade fish, fishing lines and woven garments for iron 'toges' (toki, or adzes), and to pilfer odd pieces of iron. There were prayer meetings and services on board, and rafts of squared logs began to arrive from the river, to be hauled up one by one onto the ship's orlop deck.

The people from the eastern coast opposite the ship were also beginning to establish exchange relationships with the visitors. According to the missionaries, the main rangatira in this district were Heke,[57] whose town was marked on Wilson's chart near the site of present-day Tapu, and Tautaua, whose settlement (probably Te Puru Paa) was on the eastern side of the gulf. On 3 May, one of these chiefs sent a sample spar across to the ship, and on the 6th the ship's steward Edward Marshall and two of the Brothers (Watters and Tessier) slept on shore (probably at Heke's village). Watters had been spending much of his time with the people on the coast, who asked him to live with them permanently, and that night he and Tessier were given a meal of fish and potatoes, and a mat to sleep on. At about 3 a.m. a woman came weeping into their hut and begged the captain's steward to go with her. Soon afterwards the Brothers were also roused up and taken to a hut about half a mile away, where a young man lay 'crying and Groaning as if he was exceedingly ill. Two men were holding him in their laps and about 100 people were collected together with the Father of the young man weeping, crying and making a great noise about him, and one man whom they supposed to be a Priest sitting near the sick man repeating some words probably a kind of prayer.'[58] Watters and Tessier thought that this was 'a fit of the cholick', and when the young man had recovered somewhat, they went back to bed. Probably his family feared his illness was of European origin, and hoped that the Brothers could help him. The next day they fed their visitors another meal of fish and potatoes, and a canoe took them back to the ship.

On 7 May, a large canoe decorated with feathers brought out some strangers, who said 'they had come from a far place to see the ship', and their chief came on board. At the same time James Elder went in the yawl to Kakaramea, while Skeene and some of the Brothers went ashore to look at trees on the eastern coast. They returned there the next day to cut wood, and the local people dragged the logs down to the beach. That evening the ship was shifted to an anchorage close to the coast, and the Brothers slept on shore. When the pinnace came to collect them the next morning, however, they were happy to leave, for the people had suddenly become unfriendly, appearing to harbour 'some hostile intention, if not to take away their life, [to] rob them of everything they had'. That night Skeene and the Brothers, with a crew of armed sailors, took the pinnace to pick up the spars from the beach. Although Skeene took a cloak and an axe as a present for Heke, the chief of the nearby town, 'after all he nor his men were satisfied'. Obviously Heke and his people were affronted, but the Europeans either did not know or did not admit to the reason.

Elder later claimed on a number of occasions that the local people had many reasons for resenting the Europeans. Some of the *Royal Admiral* party had shot at them for no good cause, both on the coast and inland:

> I was one Day coming down the River Thames [a term the missionaries also applied to the upper gulf] in a boat, in which there was one of our Officers, and Six Men. He stopped at a certain Place for fresh Water, the Natives came to us in a very friendly Manner, expressing their Joy, at our landing, they not only permitted us to take their water, but they brought it to us themselves, and gave us Turnip for nothing. They offered some of their Articles for sale, some of which were purchased by the Officer. As soon as the Boat was afloat, and us coming off, He began without any Cause, and insulted the Natives, and fired two Muskets loaded with Ball amongst them, they showed great Resentment at such ingratitude, and I beheld, not without indignation but said nothing, because I knew that would do no good, but harm.
>
> [When] Capt. Wilson was Cutting Down timber a few Articles were stole by the Natives, some of which were easily recovered. He saw a native one day landing looking at his men while they were at work, he supposed that he was wishing to steal something. He fired at him and lodged small Shot in his Thigh. Mr. Smith

(from Otaheite) observed a native another Day, in the same Situation and he fired at him and he said that he was sure he wounded him for he found blood in the Track, he took when he fled, but neither He, nor the Capt, had any proof, that these Natives ever stole any thing, or that they had a bad intention at the Times they were fired at.[59]

Elder added that *El Plumier*'s crew, having received food and assistance from the local people, also fired upon them and drove them out of the ship.[60] At the same time, the exchange relationship was so valuable to both sides that a good deal of conflict was tolerated, and if one hapuu was insulted, their neighbours were not necessarily displeased. The day after the difficulty with Heke, for instance, 'the old chief' Tautaua came on board with a gift of potatoes for Skeene, and asked for one of the *Royal Admiral*'s nine-pounders to be fired. There was a flash and a loud blast as the cannon went off. Tautaua was astounded and many of his people lay flat on the deck, while others watched the cannon ball streak through the sky and fall with a splash in the sea. At about the same time, four canoes from another district were seen to arrive in the gulf, apparently on a muru expedition. That night, Tautaua slept on board, taking Skeene the next morning to fell trees near his place. A day later Heke was back on the ship, 'entreat[ing] us to go on shore as he had some wood ready'.

While they were on board the *Royal Admiral*, various of the local people watched a sailor being flogged for theft (12 May) and the missionaries holding a prayer meeting (13 May). A man named Taringa, seeing Brother Tessier at prayer, asked what he was doing:

> It was answered, 'Pray, or call on Eatua, or God.' Then he asked what God Bro. Tessier was; meaning, the representative of what God? It was answered he was no God, but was praying to the Great God that dwells on high. We could not explain anything, about God, not having Their Language sufficient. It was asked him the name of their God, he said they called their God Wannugu [Uenuku – the atua represented by a famous carving now in the Te Awamutu District Museum], but that they did not Pray to him, that they heard him in the night time Whistling and were afraid.[61]

Indeed, later accounts agree that spirits were held to whistle when they appeared to human beings.[62]

Although linguistic communications were improving, the temptation for the local people to take iron led to continuing friction. People had quickly learnt the value of iron nails (for carving and fine woodwork) and chisels, adzes and axes (for felling and shaping trees). These tools also made lethal weapons. Upriver, the woodcutters were regularly being attacked in the forest by small groups of men who knocked them over and took away their axes. On one occasion, a man who was carrying an iron kettle for the cooks disappeared with it; and on the night of 18 May a timber carriage was taken from outside the wooding camp enclosure. When Captain Wilson discovered the loss of the carriage, he decided to take stern measures. Three kinsmen of Te Haupa were taken as hostages, and the sailors were sent to Kakaramea to burn down some huts. Eight or nine dwellings were torched, and Wilson threatened to destroy the entire town unless the carriage was immediately returned. Later that afternoon the carriage was brought back, but it had been pulled apart for its iron and was in pieces. Wilson told the chief's relatives that they would be detained until all of the axes and other property taken from the wooding party had been returned, and kept them overnight in one of the huts inside the palisaded enclosure.

There were only thirty Europeans at the camp, so Wilson posted his men in two watches, armed with muskets, cutlasses and two swivel guns, double-shotted and mounted on posts, in case of an attack. He intended to take his prisoners back to the ship the next morning, but by daybreak an army of almost seven hundred men and women armed with patu and spears had gathered around the camp. Te Haupa's brother came forward and told Wilson that if their relatives were killed, he and his men could expect the same fate. If the hostages were released, on the other hand, the lost articles would be returned and he and his people would deliver a certain number of logs to the riverside. Wilson knew that his men were short of ammunition, so he agreed to this ultimatum. When the hostages were released, they were overjoyed. As they left the enclosure one man caught sight of his sister waiting outside, and burst into tears. They joined a group of women who wept for a time, and then stood and 'sang a song with much pleasure'. These were the ceremonial tangi and waiata, performed when kinsfolk were reunited.

The articles that had been taken were collected up and returned, and the logs were delivered to the river's edge and tied into rafts to float out to the ship. During the next few days the weather turned foul, smashing some of the rafts and scattering the logs. The missionaries wrote in their journal: 'The wind blew high therefore the sea ran high, and the rain fell in torrents. The bad weather here at this time of the year (the beginning of winter) made us wish for the time of our departure from this place.'[63]

On 19 May, Mr Shelley went ashore again with the pinnace. As they came close to the river, about twenty canoes carrying some three hundred people formed into a line in front of them. The Europeans feared that they were about to be attacked, but it turned out that this was a friendly group travelling to a feast 'up the River at Warreekee's [ariki's] town (probably Oruarangi, headquarters of the ariki Taurangi). At the same time, out at sea, Tautaua and some of his people came on board the *Royal Admiral*. When one of them was found taking some clothing belonging to one of the sailors, he was seized and tied up to be flogged. Tautaua's people were horrified and, weeping bitterly, begged that he should be released. The goods this man had taken were held up, his offence was explained and his relatives were told that he was about to be beaten for stealing. For ten or fifteen minutes he was left tied up to the gratings, 'all the while crying exceedingly', until finally he was freed. Tautaua's people immediately returned to their canoes and left the ship. No more work was done on preparing the timber for rafting over the next few days, and when some people came back to the ship on 21 May, they bitterly reproached the Europeans, saying that tying up the man had been 'Moggira', or bad (treating him as a taurekareka), and asked for a red garment or something equivalent as compensation (utu). Nothing was given to them, however.

According to James Elder, 'I believe the New Zealanders formed a very bad opinion of the Royal Admiral and I think not without reason. Stealing is the cause of all differences between savages and Europeans and nothing would remove the cause so soon nor so completely as to introduce as many iron tools among them as soon as possible.'[64] In fact, Europeans and Maori had very different ideas about rights to resources. Much (but probably not all) of what the Europeans saw as 'stealing' was, rather, utu for timber, flax, fish and other things taken without proper permission or adequate compensation. Furthermore, according to Maori ways of thinking, trees, fish and other living creatures were the children of founding ancestors (Taane, god of the forests; Tangaroa, god of the ocean; and other creator beings), to be taken only after the correct rituals had been enacted. Muru, or taking utu by seizing the offender's goods (sometimes described as 'stripping', or institutionalised 'plunder'), was a nonviolent form of retribution for such offences. Elder was correct, then, in claiming that 'there is such a thing as justice among the New Zealanders, and . . . they execute it with equity'. He cited as an example a dispute he had witnessed between the runaway convict Thomas Taylor and a local man. Taylor had quarrelled with this man and tried to knock him down, but instead his antagonist seized Taylor, put his head in a hole and sat on him, and when Taylor struggled, punched him hard. Other local men then intervened, releasing Taylor, but when he threatened to kill his opponent, they told him that if he tried he would be killed in turn, 'for they were not afraid of all the sailors in the place. Since they had rescued him from danger they would not allow him to injure their countryman.'

Despite constant misunderstandings, canoes continued to visit the ship almost daily, bringing out 'gumera' (kuumara), fish, mussels and other goods. On 25 May, the chief Heke and his wife came on board, but had the great mortification of losing their canoe when it broke loose from the ship and drifted away. There was no boat or canoe alongside to go after it, so they were forced to stay on board for the next two nights. Heke's wife was distressed because she had left her baby, whom she was breastfeeding, on shore. At breakfast the next morning Heke took some meat and biscuit and went on deck. Looking up to the sky, he threw these into the sea, which the Europeans supposed to be a sacrifice to the sun (although he was probably trying to calm the sea). When he and his wife attended family service after breakfast, they knelt when the Europeans knelt. At the end of the service Heke told the missionaries that they also worshipped their god, who was called Ee-ra, or the sun.

According to Elder, William Smith had shot and wounded a man without provocation, and on 26 May the local people had their revenge. Smith was on board *El Plumier* that morning when a message came from Captain Wilson that a raft had broken loose from the boat and had been washed ashore at the mouth of the river, near the ariki's town. Smith took a canoe and one man to look for it. They sighted the raft grounded near the eastern shore of the river mouth, but rough seas forced them to beach the canoe about two miles upriver. Smith set off overland, leaving his companion in charge of the canoe. Before he had gone very far, he met a large party of people who were going to join the feast that was still going on at the ariki's settlement, before fighting the Waikato tribes. There were no fewer than four or five thousand men in this party, painted and dressed for fighting, and armed with clubs and long spears. It seemed to Smith that most of these people had never seen a European before, and they handled him roughly, treating him in an insulting manner. According to his journal, when he reached the raft:

> I was now surrounded by the multitude, who were shouting and yelling in a most hideous manner, and myself trembling like an aspen leaf; I at length endeavoured to divert them by begging a piece of string to measure the length and diameter of the timber, and, by making some marks, and tying knots on the string, arrested their attention so as to create silence, and for a short time, any further abuse.
>
> But, as it was necessary now to attempt returning, their deportment became more violent and oppressive; some spitting in my face, others throwing sticks and stones, some attempting to throw me down, some to untie my small clothes, and various other modes of insult were used . . . Having arrived beyond the different encampments, and an open beach before me, my fears compelled me to the resolution of trying their agility in running; but as soon as I started, they commenced the most hideous yellings and dreadful noises, and a great majority in full pursuit, like so many hounds after an unprotected and innocent hare; this, together with increasing fears, commanded double exertion; so that I believe I never before, or since, ran so swift. My efforts were crowned with success; for, upon gaining considerably over my pursuers, they shortly after relinquished the chase; which gave me time to breathe and return peaceably to my canoe.[65]

The experience was terrifying, but Smith was probably in no serious danger. So large a crowd of armed men could have killed him at any moment, if that had been their intention. Rather, it seems as though they entertained themselves by frightening him as much as possible, performing haka and challenges, pelting him with sticks and stones, tearing off his clothes and finally chasing him, to see how he would react. Ironically, it was because of an almost identical episode in Tahiti four years earlier, when four of his fellow missionaries were abused and stripped naked by a group of irate Tahitians, that Smith and others had fled the London Missionary Society's Tahitian mission. After Smith returned to the ship, shaken but unhurt, the canoe he had used was swept out to sea in the storm and was lost.

Two days later, on 28 May, there was another fracas. The ship's butcher went ashore to purchase turnips for the cattle on board the ship, and dumped several bags of these vegetables on a sacred place (waahi tapu). The people handled him roughly for this offence, and refused to let him take away the turnips; these were now also tapu and could not be removed. While tensions with the *Royal Admiral* party were rising, war with the Waikato tribes was imminent. Parties of warriors kept arriving at the river, saying they had come to fight the 'Weygate party', and there were reports that two villages on the eastern coast had been burned by the crews of several war canoes. The presence of the Europeans was at once an indispensable source of iron for weapons, and a disconcerting complication.

Rafts of logs kept arriving out at the ship and were loaded on board, despite very unfavourable weather. After the burning of the huts at Kakaramea, Wilson had shifted the main wooding camp downriver five or six miles, where another hut was built for the sailors, while he slept each night on board *El Plumier*. The local people continued to harass the sailors on shore, knocking them over in the forest and taking their axes; and one evening (either 3 or 4 June), when all of the sailors fell asleep instead of posting a sentry, a number of axes and garments were taken from their hut. No one was certain whether the local people or sailors from *El Plumier* were the culprits, but when Captain Wilson and William Smith heard about it the next morning, they took an armed party to a small town nearby and seized two canoes, some cloaks and a number of other items belonging to Te Haupa's people. Some local people tried to resist them and were shot, and one was mortally wounded. Two sailors from *El Plumier* were captured, and Wilson took them on board the *Royal Admiral* where they were questioned about the thefts. When no satisfactory answers were forthcoming, they were each given a dozen lashes. Thomas Taylor was also under suspicion, and he was captured and taken against his will to the *Royal Admiral*, and made to serve as a sailor on board the ship. That night the longboat went ashore for water, but the sea was rough and one of the ship's boys was left behind to guard some casks that could not be loaded.

On 6 June, several large canoes were seen going to the western shore of the gulf (probably to Whakatiiwai), where various tribes were gathering to go to war with the Waikato people, and those on board the *Royal Admiral* were told that Tautaua,[66] Heke, the ariki (Taurangi) and their people had already gone to war. Late that afternoon there was another violent storm, and the longboat was sent from the ship to look for shelter. It was dark and the channel was winding and shoaling, and high seas caught the longboat and beached her high on the mudbank at the western entrance to the river. Captain Wilson took the yawl and accompanied by Smith with eight armed men and supplies in the pinnace, went to rescue the longboat's crew. As they approached the mudbank on a falling tide, they were also grounded and spent the night stuck on a shoal in driving rain, waiting for the tide to rise and float them off again.

Over the next few days the weather was foul, and the people on board the *Royal Admiral* became worried when the ship's boats did not reappear. On the evening of 10 June they fired one of the great guns as a signal, and again the next morning. On the morning of 12 June, the weather was fine and four canoes were seen coming from the west with small crews, to collect more warriors to fight in the war. The *Royal Admiral*'s cutter, their last remaining boat, was sent to look for their shipmates and to collect the ship's boy and the casks that had been left on shore a week earlier. They found that some of Te Haupa's people had looked after the boy, and these people told the cutter's crew that the *Royal Admiral* party were all well and helping to get *El Plumier* afloat again. As soon as the ship's boy and the barrels of water were safely back on board, the cutter, with Lloyd in command, was sent upriver to *El Plumier* to ask the captain and his men to come back immediately to the ship.

The next morning a canoe came out to the *Royal Admiral*. They thought this must be bringing them a message, but it was only two young boys who had come to see their friends, ship's boys who had gone on shore. The wind came up again during the day and the boys asked to be able to sleep on board overnight, rather than risk a passage in their small canoe back to land.

Finally that evening Lloyd came back in the cutter. He had rowed upriver to *El Plumier*, where he was told the saga of the stranded longboat, which Smith and the sailors were still struggling to free from the mudbank at the river's mouth.

On 15 June, Smith made one last desperate effort to drag the longboat off by hauling it across the mud. He became hopelessly mired and had to be rescued by some friendly local people. The sailors brought a raft of spars out to the ship, and when one of them went into the water to tie a rope around a log to lift it up to the orlop deck, a huge shark rose near him and he was pulled out of the sea just in time. Early on 16 June it was decided to abandon the longboat, and Wilson brought the pinnace and the yawl back to the ship, accompanied by *El Plumier*'s boat with Boston, Ellis, Riley and Puckey on board. Palmer did not come out to farewell them; it appears that he did not approve of efforts to evangelise 'the heathen'. The Brothers had decided that 'he was a complete infidel, his conversation was profane and disgusting and missionary business the subject of his contempt',[67] and no doubt their poor opinion was returned in good measure. Nor did the missionaries mention Boston's wife and children, or the mate's wife in their accounts, which suggests less-than-friendly relations.

As they prepared to leave Hauraki, Smith tried to persuade Wilson to give his friend and servant Patrick Riley a passage to India, but because Riley was a convict and HMS *Dolphin* was expected to meet them at Tahiti, Wilson refused. They said their farewells, and at eleven o'clock that day the *Royal Admiral* set sail from the gulf, leaving *El Plumier* still upriver.

Apparently *El Plumier* remained at Hauraki until 20 August 1801 (almost six months in all), during which time her provisions were consumed. The ship's repairs were makeshift, so Palmer and his shipmates decided to head for Macao instead of to the Cape. After limping across the Pacific to Tongatapu and then Fiji, where the ship ran onto a reef, *El Plumier* was taken as a prize by the Spanish in Guam and condemned, and all her crew were imprisoned.[68] Palmer, Ellis, Boston and Captain Reid were treated kindly by the local governor, but when Boston (whose children had died) and Ellis managed to escape on a Spanish ship that called at Guam for a few hours on her way to Manila, Palmer was left behind. He tried to catch up with them in a small boat but suffered from exposure and returned to shore,

A portrait of Thomas Fyshe Palmer.

where he died soon after.[69] No journal of *El Plumier*'s Pacific odyssey, including their stay in Hauraki, is known to have survived. This is a pity, for Boston, the surgeon with radical sympathies, and Palmer, the old Etonian and Cambridge graduate, very likely wrote accounts of the voyage. Palmer was cultivated and humane, and Boston was a trained observer who could draw on his wife's and children's experiences of New Zealand as well as his own. Their accounts of their six months' sojourn in Hauraki would have been fascinating.[70]

THE *ROYAL ADMIRAL* ACCOUNTS OF HAURAKI

In their descriptions of Hauraki, the *Royal Admiral* party often mentioned James Cook's journals and charts. Although they deferred to Cook's descriptions, the missionaries produced a number of informative accounts of life in the district at the time of their visit. I will summarise these according to the topics discussed by Charles Wilson, in a letter home to his cousin on 16 June 1801.[71]

Climate and landscape
The climate at Hauraki was praised as temperate and mild, and healthy for Euro-peans. Charles Wilson noted:

> Much of the land here is high and Mountainous mostly a forest abounding with large timber: these are 120 feet high. The soil is excellent and if it were cultivated

with care, we have reason to believe that it would be exceedingly fruitful. The produce at present is very scanty as there is comparatively little of it Manured.[72]

William Smith added that the soil along the river for many miles was a rich black mould, where good harvests of potatoes grew, and various kinds of trees. One that 'grows as large as an oak, and is distinguished by a red flower; the wood . . . is hard and heavy' was evidently the pohutukawa; while the 'spruce' (or kahikatea) had tall, straight trunks, but the durability and strength of the wood seemed doubtful. Flax grew prolifically. According to Smith:

> The flax-plant is very abundant, and chiefly grows in marshy ground; it is a broad-bladed leaf, of about six feet in height; the fibrous parts constitute the flax; it is very durable and fine in quality, and no doubt cloths of every texture may be manufactured with it. Perhaps in the process of time a colony may be established on this island, in the event of which, the culture of this plant, and manufacturing of it into cloths, will become a staple commodity.[73]

Food and diet

The missionaries described extensive gardens of potatoes, both sweet potatoes and the English variety. These were in high cultivation, and mature tubers were kept in well-constructed communal storehouses, raised on four pillars six feet high (perhaps because underground storage was impractical in the swampy Hauraki floodplain).[74] The people seemed to eat mainly potatoes and fish, as well as turnips, which had also been introduced by Cook, although on occasion they also ate dog. The fish were plentiful, delicious and of many varieties, and were caught in nets staked in the river. No introduced animals (pigs, chickens, sheep) were seen, only Polynesian rats and dogs.

The people – physical appearance

Wilson described the Hauraki people as:

> A tall stout [i.e. strong] made people good features of a brownish colour some-what resembling copper, as agreeable as some Europeans. The higher ranks are tatoo'd or stained on different parts of the Body. Some of those have their lips dyed blue and Both sexes practice the same method as some European ladies who Paint their faces though not with vermillion, but with some thing like Brick Dust [in fact red ochre] mixed with Oil. The women seem to be possessed of a greater degree of Modesty than many other Heathens, I have never seen any of them uncovered. The dress of both sexes are the same being generally an inner garment made of flax of an oblong form 4 feet long and 3 feet wide, and an outer of the same form and size made of grass . . . When they are at work all above the loins is naked. They are hardy and can bear a cold wind without any seeming inconvenience.

Smith added that the fabric of their clothing was 'delightfully soft and regular in its texture', made by stripping the outer layer off the flax with a shell, and twisting the thread on the knee, then knotting it by hand. A number of these garments, and other items including at least one patu had been acquired to be sent back to Britain, although 'the New Zealanders ask an astonishingly high price'. They also made fishing tackle and rigging for their canoes from flax.

The people at Hauraki seemed to be very healthy.[75] According to the missionaries' journal, 'we never saw but two or three instances of any sickness or disease among these natives' (a young man with a wound on his thigh and a greatly swollen knee, with his leg wasted away to skin and bone; and a woman with a swollen head and cancerous face), although it was evident that venereal disease was already established. James Elder added, 'At New Zealand, I have observed . . . few old people, and few young children, but a great number from between 6 to 16 Years of Age, just fit for the school.'

Character of the people

There were two kinds of descriptions of the character of Hauraki people in the *Royal Admiral* accounts. One was positive; for example, in the missionaries' collective journal:

> The inhabitants are very different from the careless Indians of New South Wales, these seem capable and eager to learn any thing from the Europeans, and are careful and diligent observers of everything they see and many of them discover deep penetration and genius.[76]

The other was deeply negative; for instance, these comments by Captain Wilson:

> The New Zealanders are wretches, driven forth from among men; they are below a state of Nature many degrees. The New Zealanders sleep on their Patoo and Spear, to repel or destroy each other, seems chiefly to occupy their thoughts.[77]

There were also equivocal comments. Charles Wilson remarked, for instance:

> The natives here are very susceptible when an injury is done them by us; and they are very sensible of doing wrong to us when their conduct is not agreeable to the law of kindness and honesty. In general their behaviour towards us have been kind and courteous, with this exception that we have had sufficient evidence that they may act according to the dictates of their ferocious nature.[78]

Although there is no evidence that cannibalistic rituals were witnessed, local people had spoken 'with delight' about eating their enemies, and both Captain Wilson and William Smith described the Hauraki people as 'ferocious, and cruel, and uniformly cannibals'.[79] To counter this, the missionaries' journal noted, 'they are very affectionate to one another in the general', while Elder described them as sociable, 'amazingly active' and friendly, making great efforts to get the missionaries to understand them.

Language and music

The local language was identified as a dialect of the language spoken elsewhere in Polynesia, which lacked the letters 'f, j, l, and s'. This may indicate that, as in the north, 'wh' was aspirated rather than pronounced like the fricative 'f'. A vocabulary was collected and sent to the Reverend Buchanan, although this has not been located. John Davies later commented that he found Maori easier to learn than Tahitian, and that it contained more guttural and nasal sounds.[80] Elder added that they often heard the people singing at night.

Housing and settlements

The houses were described as very small, 'hardly fit to hold three people', and often people were seen sleeping outside. These were probably visitors to the area, of whom there were many during the *Royal Admiral*'s stay. At certain places along the river there were twenty or thirty huts together, which the Europeans described as 'towns'. These settlements all seemed to be located on the eastern bank of the Waihou River, although there had been settlements on the western bank just six years earlier, at the time of the *Fancy*'s visit. It is possible that the river served as a tribal boundary, and that when war with the Waikato people was imminent, people retreated to the east side. Indeed, those who visited the ship often warned the Europeans that the people to the west were their enemies, and very bad.

Civil government

Charles Wilson noted that:

> Respecting civil Power or government we have not learned whether there be one principal chief and the others in subjection: or whether all exercise their Power absolutely and independantly, it appears however that the right of government and dominion is Hereditary and runs in succession, not delegated . . . Different chiefs go to war here and lay whole Districts to waste all who are taken prisoners men and women are made slaves and their offspring.

The people spoke of their principal enemies as the 'Weygate' (Waikato) people, and their chief as a man called 'Tugarnarvoa' (Te Kanawa?).

Weapons and tools

According to William Smith, the people armed themselves with lances fifteen feet long, and darts, and stone battle-axes, some made of polished stone and others of 'petrified fish skin' (probably whalebone). A number of tools and ornaments were also made of this material, a specimen adze later being presented to the 'American Museum' in Chatham Street in London. The missionaries also mentioned acquiring some resinous gum that would burn, and seeing some pieces of a glass-like substance (obsidian), which they supposed to be of volcanic origin.

Canoes

Smith added that the Hauraki people had numerous canoes, usually crafted from a single log, hollowed out by fire and neatly shaped with stone adzes and bone chisels, and 'considerably ornamented'. The war canoes were from eighty to a hundred feet long (the *Fancy*, both *Hunter*s and *El Plumier* would have been no longer), and carried between a hundred and two hundred warriors.

Religion and burial of the dead
According to William Smith:

> It is certain that they acknowledge the influence of superior beings, one of whom
> is supreme and the rest subordinate. One of these islanders [probably the ariki
> 'Taurange'] appeared to have a much more deep and extensive knowledge of these
> subjects than any of the other people; and whenever he was disposed to instruct
> them, which he did sometimes in long discourses, he was sure of a numerous
> audience, who listened in profound silence, with much reverence and attention.
>
> What homage they pay to the deities could not be learned no place of public
> worship was visible; but near a plantation of sweet potatoes was seen a small area,
> of a square figure, surrounded with stones, in the middle of which one of the
> sharpened stakes which they use as a spade was set up, and upon it was hung a
> basket of fern-roots, which the natives said was an offering to the gods, by which
> the owner hoped to render them propitious, and obtain a plentiful crop.
>
> Their manner of disposing of the dead varied in different parts of the island. In
> the north, they buried them in the ground; in the south, they threw them into the
> sea [a comment evidently derived from Cook's journals]. No grave was to be seen
> in the country, and the inhabitants affect to conceal every thing relating to the
> dead with a sort of mysterious secrecy [although some of the 'etabu' places seen in
> Heke's village were probably sepulchres[81]]. But whatever may be the sepulchre,
> the living themselves are the monuments; for scarcely a single person is to be seen
> of either sex, whose body is not marked by the scars of wounds which have been
> inflicted, as a testimony of their regret for the loss of a relation or friend.[82]

Taurangi seems to have been a tohunga, like most high chiefs of his period.
The offering of fernroot was probably dedicated to Haumia, the god of edible
wild root plants. The kuumara garden may have been planted in an area formerly
used as a fernroot digging, since both crops grew best in deep, rich soils.

Prospects for a settlement
At Port Jackson, Governor King told the missionaries that he was planning a
colony at New Zealand.[83] They assessed the prospects for a mission settlement at
Hauraki as excellent. James Elder was eloquent about the advantages:

> If you send a Mission, consisting of Two Hundred Families, to the South Seas,
> New Zealand appears to me to be the Place where they may settle with the great-
> est advantage to the Missionary Cause . . . At New Zealand they may get many
> thousands of Acres of land fit for cultivation, not inhabited by a rational Creature.
> Where there are the greatest Number of People, there you are near the extensive
> Island of New Holland, and you are near New South Wales, where you could
> dispose of, and purchase all most everything. You may send one Hundred
> Thousand People to New Zealand, they may all get large possessions, without
> infringing upon the Property or liberty of the natives. Here there are few People,
> very little land fit for Cultivation, and if you send a great number the Native will
> be brought (most likely) in slavery, of which they are already afraid, and I wish
> that missionaries, may never contribute towards bringing the Heathen under a

Foreign Yoke . . . New Zealand is very near the Friendly Islands, from whence Yams, and Hogs can be got over to spread New Zealand.[84]

According to the missionaries' journal, 'the natives seem eager to have some Europeans among them as they expect that they would assist them either in their cultivation or in their Wars'.[85] It is interesting, though, that local people were already worried about being enslaved by Europeans. Thomas Taylor and his companions must often have been questioned about Europe and Port Jackson. Any reasonable description of the penal colony phrased in Maori would have sounded like a community of taurekareka ('slaves' – the convicts) ruled by toa (warriors) and rangatira (the Governor and colonial officials). Perhaps the ex-convicts had also warned them about what was happening to the Aboriginals, and the harsher aspects of British law. In addition, word of Tuki and Huru's sojourn in Norfolk Island had travelled as far as Hauraki, with news of that penal colony. The missionaries reported that according to local people, 'Tongatta Tubua [tangata tupua] or White people took with them two of Tongata Maura [tangata Maori or 'ordinary people'] (New Zealanders) to their own country, and some time after they returned they say they ate well with the white people eating Bunga Bunga (bread, from pungapunga – raupo-pollen bread) and Gure (kurii – dog; flesh of all kinds). These we suppose were the natives taken to Norfolk Island by Governor King and were from thence afterwards brought back to New Zealand.'[86] It is fascinating that by 1801 the term 'Maori' was already being used for local people, in contrast with 'tangata tupua', or 'goblin people', the term used in Hauraki to describe Europeans. Horeta Te Taniwha, a man from this district who had met Cook as a child, also used the term 'tupua' for white people many years later when recounting his memories of the *Endeavour* visit.[87] It seems that the word 'Pakeha' did not quickly come into general circulation. Rather, there were early regional variants ('maitai' in the north, 'tupua' in Hauraki, 'pakeha' on the East Coast and 'tangata pora' in the south) used to describe the Europeans.

Although Elder disliked the idea of 'bringing the heathen under a foreign yoke', his view of how missions might work in New Zealand proved prophetic:

> The missionaries [can] live in their own houses, and never allow the Natives to come within their inclosures except when they please and in such numbers as they please, they will have plenty of opportunities of learning the language. They can take some of the Natives for servants, to assist them in cultivating their land, and making their fences. They should learn some of them to be Carpenters, Smiths, weavers and taylors. The missionaries may go at certain hours, to assist the Natives to erect houses for the Chiefs, and for teaching the Children in . . . and they will have plenty of opportunities of learning the Language.[88]

The local people were to work as servants and artisans, labouring for the Europeans. In return, the Europeans would help to build European-style houses for the chiefs and schools for teaching the children. Elder added, 'the great kindness they have shown, and indeed I think it is astonishing, is surely an evidence that they are waiting for, and ready to receive the Gospel, but still they are but Savages, and at times will prove treacherous'. Although Elder was the most liberal of the *Royal Admiral* contingent, he had no notion that Maori might be his equals. As 'Savages', they were irredeemably lesser human beings.

Summary

EUROPEAN VISITS TO HAURAKI 1794–1801

Like Totara-nui, Hauraki was a crossroads in pre-European as well as in post-contact times. It was sited between the harbours of Northland and those of the Bay of Plenty and the East Coast. Raiding and trading parties frequently stopped at the Waihou River, fighting or exchanging goods with the local people. The Hauraki people were used to engaging with outsiders and defending their resources, and their forests, fisheries and gardens supported a dense population. When a succession of vessels brought European and Indian sailors to their district, they responded with alacrity, helping the strangers to cut and load timber in return for iron tools and other exotic treasures. In these early contacts, Hauraki tribes were unabashed and assertive. Europeans who cut down trees without permission were confronted and made to change their behaviour. Those who treated local people with contempt (William Smith, for instance) were tormented and sent away. Once they decided they were human, Hauraki people had no notion of these strangers as superiors – quite to the contrary.

During this time at least three hundred Europeans and Indians visited the district. Children of mixed Maori–European parentage were born, there was at least one serious epidemic, and intensive exchanges of cross-cultural information began. Local people spent time on board European ships, and some European sailors deserted their vessels and went to live among local people. Thomas Taylor and his three companions, who ran from the second *Hunter* at Hauraki in 1799, are the first Europeans known to have lived for any length of time with Maori. They formed liaisons with local women, travelled extensively within the region and learned a good deal about Maori customs. Taylor, and to a lesser extent his companions, began to act as agents in commercial transactions between European traders and local people. In the process of these visits, European crops, including potatoes and turnips, were established on shore, fruit trees and chickens were introduced, and a number of Hauraki rangatira, including Te Haupa, began to deploy European goods (especially iron tools) to advance their diplomatic and military ambitions.

It seems likely from both the European accounts and tribal historical evidence that the influx of European wealth intensified raiding in the region. Other tribal groups, already envious of Hauraki's sea fisheries, inland waterways, forests and gardens, became jealous of local kin groups' monopoly of barter with the Europeans, and attacked their rivals. Hauraki groups, armed with iron axes and other weapons, could mount formidable military reprisals. In addition, when European sailors took timber without adequate return, rangatira followed local notions of justice and took European goods as utu. This sometimes led to skirmishes and hostile stand-offs, but the exchange of iron for timber was so valuable to both sides, that Maori and European leaders alike made sure that friendly relationships were soon re-established.

Hauraki, then, was the first densely populated region in New Zealand to experience sustained contact with Europeans. Accounts of its towering forests, apparently so suitable for spars and masts, attracted immediate European interest. This soon died down, however, after the first logs were delivered to India and Port Jackson. Kahikatea wood rotted in damp conditions, and the coastal pohutukawa yielded a heavy, dense wood that was not much good for ship-building. Although the 1801 visit of the *Royal Admiral* yielded detailed descriptions of the area, nothing came of the missionaries' idea of a mission to Hauraki. By 1801, Europeans had already turned their attention elsewhere, to seal rookeries in the far south and the whale fisheries to the north of the North Island.

Twelve

SEALING IN THE SOUTH

Seals were another local resource to be exploited by Europeans. At Tamatea, James Cook and George Vancouver had found fur seals on the rocky islands during their visits. Their sailors shot and clubbed them, using the hides for rigging, extracting the oil for lighting, and eating the left-over meat. According to Johann Forster, seal steaks made an excellent meal – 'a most excellent & palatable food; by far more tender, juicy & delicate than beefstakes'.[1] New Zealand fur seals had pelts as soft as beaver hides, and their skins sold for good prices on the European and China markets. Lured by the prospect of high profits, sealing ships followed the explorers to Dusky Sound and the south of the South Island.

As machinery was increasingly used during the Industrial Revolution, quantities of lubricating oil (especially from sea mammals) were needed. Oil was also required to light the cities and towns of Europe and America. Elephant-seal oil burned with a bright pure flame, without smell or smoke, and was used in various manufacturing processes, while fur-seal skins could be dried and sold in China for clothing or felt, or salted and sold in England, where the 'seal wool', or fur, was later used in the manufacture of hats and the leather was used for shoes. Sir Joseph Banks supported Governor King in fostering a local industry, so long as the seal-skins were sent to England, and not to China. As a confirmed mercantilist, Banks argued that 'the whole benefit of the colony, either in consumption or in produce, should be secur'd, as far as possible, to the mother country'. Since the rookeries to the south of Australia and New Zealand produced 'seals of all kinds in Quantities at present almost innumerable . . . and those who visit their Haunts have less trouble in killing them than the servants of the Victualling Office have who kill Hogs in a Pen with Mallets',[2] the southern seals should be harvested by British subjects, not by those of other powers.

Sealing was hard work, carried out by hard men. Gangs of 'sea-rats' (escaped or emancipated convicts, deserters or sailors) were landed on rocky beaches and islands, hunting for seals, sea lions and elephant seals. When they found them,

Note: Details of sealing voyages to New Zealand appear in Appendix I, pages 518–25.

they killed them, extracting oil from their blubber and salting the skins in casks or pegging them out to cure for the China market. Sometimes, ships would lie-to in the lee of a point or island while the boats rowed quietly to the rocks. As Charles Heaphy later explained:

> The sealer's eye seeks for some projecting rock that may conceal the approach of the boat, which, kept carefully in a line, with muffled oars, and not a word spoken, is steered straight for the rock, until the crew can spring to land and commence on the luckless animals with lances and clubs.
>
> An experienced sealer, when approaching a rock on which a seal is basking, knows by which side the animal will take to the water – whether direct to seaward or into the crevice . . .
>
> Some favorite haunt in a narrow rocky bay is watched by the sealer . . . until a sufficient number of the animals are together, and the water be low; the boat then approaches – if possible under sail – and as soon as land is made, a rush takes place up the beach. The seal moves awkwardly upon sand (although better than a man among rough rocks) and becomes an easy prey. A blow on the snout with a club stuns, and a thrust under the flipper despatches the animal, and one after another they succumb, amidst a Babel of swearing and shouting. A man may often get an

Clubbing seals in a cave.

283

A sealer's encampment in this period.

awkward tumble and a severe bite, but the misfortune, like sea-sickness, allows of no commiseration.

In sealing it is essential that much of the hardest work should be performed at night, that a landing should be forced upon the most exposed beaches, and that the most dangerous reefs should be visited; and all this in a high latitude, and without assistance from other vessels, in event of casualty.[3]

More often, gangs were landed on rocky bays or islands and left, for months or even years. When there was no timber or fresh water nearby, they lived in caves, rock shelters, tents or under their upturned boats, drinking rainwater and eating seal meat, fish, muttonbirds and the supplies (usually skimpy) that had been landed with them. Living in miserably cold and wet conditions, sealers were often plagued by thirst, hunger and scurvy. They took the skins of pup seals in about April, and in December female seals were caught as they came to the males. Although sealers were rewarded with 'lays', or proportionate shares of the skins and oil they collected, this usually amounted to no more than a quarter of the cargo in all; and some owners cheated their men or abandoned them if a more profitable cargo for their ships became available. Because of this system of payment, the men were primed to kill as many animals as possible, and bludgeoned, lanced or shot seals without compunction.

BRITANNIA AND *FRANCIS* AT TAMATEA
1792–93

After Vancouver's visit to the Sound in 1791, a series of sealing vessels had arrived in Tamatea. According to Jules de Blosseville, midshipman on the French ship *Coquille*, which later visited New Zealand, once a sealing gang had landed:

> The ship, which may be considered as a floating metropolis, then goes away to distant islands to establish other temporary colonies, separated at times by several thousand leagues. At the end of several months, – sometimes even a year, and longer still, – the men, who compose these little colonies . . . are called for.[4]

The first such mini-colony to be founded in New Zealand was established by the *Britannia* in Tamatea. This storeship, owned by St Barbe of London, later took Governor King with Tuki and Huru to Muriwhenua.[5] Captain Raven had been granted a licence by the East India Company to go sealing in southern waters, and carried an outward cargo of supplies of food and clothing to Port Jackson.[6] In October 1792, just as the ship was about to leave the convict colony for New Zealand waters, a consortium of civil and military officers headed by Major Francis Grose of the New South Wales Corps offered Raven £2,600 to sail to the Cape of Good Hope to get a cargo of cattle, clothing and supplies for the soldiers. Grose announced this arrangement to the Governor, Arthur Phillip, in a peremptory letter:

> The situation of the Soldiers under my Command, who at this Time, have scarcely Shoes to their Feet, & who have no other Comforts than the reduced, & unwhole-some Ration served out from the Stores, has induced me to assemble the Captains of my Corps, for the purpose of consulting what could be done for their Relief, & accommodation. – Amongst us we have raised a sufficient sum, to take up the Britannia, & as all Money matters are already settled with the Master, who is also an owner, I have now to request you will interest yourself in our favour, that you will, by representing the necessities of my Soldiers, protect this Ship from interrup-tion as much as you can – that you will assist us to escape the miseries of that pre-carious existence we have hitherto been so constantly exposed to.[7]

Phillip suspected that, rather than trying to relieve their men, his officers were planning a speculative voyage to purchase goods for sale to the colonists, and replied that the venture might be in breach of the East India Company monopoly, and the terms of Raven's licence. He refused to give the voyage his blessing,[8] but he did not forbid it either.

Raven had planned to go to Dusky Sound to collect a cargo of sealskins to sell in China. He agreed with Grose that he would leave a sealing party there before going on to the Cape of Good Hope to get goods for the Corps, and that he would 'not carry on any private Trade whatsoever at any Port, or Ports, which he may be directed to in India, which might . . . interfere with the Trade carried on by the Servants of the Honorable the United Company of Merchants Trading to India'.[9]

On 23 October 1792, the *Britannia* sailed from Port Jackson. The 'snowey summits' of New Zealand were sighted on 3 November, but adverse winds kept the ship off the coast until three days later, when she moored in Facile Harbour. Raven and his sailors went shooting ducks, then visited Pickersgill Harbour, where they found several logs felled by Cook's men at the site of William Wales's observatory, and tree stumps cut a year earlier by Vancouver's crew. They felled more trees for planking and spars while the ship's boats visited various islands in the Sound, locating colonies of seals. On 10 November, the mates returned from the 'Seal Islands' (off the end of Anchor Island) and 'gave Capt. Raven so good an account of them that It henceforth was determined to leave a party here to collect Skins for the China Market'.[10] Several days later, while Raven was on an expedition towards the mouth of Breaksea Sound, a fire was sighted in a cove on Resolution Island. Raven ordered the boat to row to shore, where they surprised some local people who ran off into the bush. According to one of the boat's crew, Robert Murry:

> I saw a small hut, at a small distance from the edge of the water, at this moment one of our people made a noise which roused the inhabitants who issued from their abode and took to the woods. We landed, and found the hut had been newly erected, every part of the materials of which it was constructed were green; particularly the roof, which was covered, with the leaves of the Flax plant. A fire was at the entrance and within there lay some matts; these appear'd to be their bed. Capt. Raven left an Axe & two knives, upon a log of wood, near the Dwelling place, he laid a small green branch upon the things, and left them, expecting they would return, but in this, was disappointed.[11]

That was the last time that any of the local people were seen. After this, they completely avoided the Europeans.

The *Britannia* stayed in Tamatea for two more weeks while the crew built a shed forty feet long, eighteen broad and fifteen high,[12] and another shelter for the sealing party. The sealers were placed under the command of William Leith (the *Britannia*'s second mate), twelve months' supplies and ironwork, cordage, sails and rigging for a small vessel were landed, and the ship was prepared for sea. As the *Britannia* left Tamatea on 1 December 1792, an earthquake shook the Sound, making the ship 'tremble to a violent degree'. The crew thought they had struck a shoal or a rock, and left the Sound with relief, sailing off across the Pacific, around Cape Horn to the Cape of Good Hope.

At the Cape, Raven fulfilled his contract with Major Grose, loading thirty cows, three mares, twelve goats, a full load of supplies, and some wine and spirits as a private speculation.[13] By the time he returned to Port Jackson in June 1793, Grose had replaced Arthur Phillip as Acting Governor. He was so delighted by the success of their venture (although most of the animals had died at sea) that on behalf of the officers' syndicate he hired the *Britannia* again, this time to fetch provisions from Calcutta.[14] The convict colony was desperately short of grain and meat, and the British settlements in India were the nearest reliable source of supply. The colonial schooner *Francis*, a small vessel that had been brought in frame from

London to Port Jackson, was launched under the command of William House (a boatswain from Vancouver's expedition who had recently arrived in Port Jackson on the *Daedalus*). Raven helped to launch the *Francis*, fitting her with a foremast brought by the *Britannia* from Dusky. He planned to sail the *Britannia* back to Dusky, and to collect Leith's sealing party on his way to India. House was given a crew of seamen and boys left behind by various ships, and ordered to accompany Raven to New Zealand 'to ascertain how far that place . . . may tend to the Benefit of His Majesty's Service, as connected with these Settlements'.[15]

The *Francis* and *Britannia* were provided with Vancouver's bearings for the Snares and the Chatham Islands; and a number of passengers, including Captain Nepean (the senior officer of the New South Wales Corps) and one female and several male ex-convicts came on board. The vessels sailed from Port Jackson on 8 September 1793. They kept in close contact until two weeks after their departure, when they were separated in a storm that drove the *Francis* south. The *Britannia* arrived in Dusky Sound on 27 September, while the *Francis*, which had been repeatedly blown off the New Zealand coast, limped in two weeks later.

As soon as the *Britannia* arrived at Anchor Island harbour, Raven visited the sealing station, and that evening Leith and five of his men came on board. All of the sealing party were healthy, except for Thomas Wilson, who was still suffering from a disease he had contracted at Port Jackson. After ten months in the Sound they had collected only 4,500 sealskins, but had almost finished building a vessel fifty-three feet long and sixteen feet ten inches wide from local timber. According to the ship's carpenter, the local wood was excellent for ship-building, comparing well with 'English oak for durability and strength',[16] while the local flax was good for fishing lines and ropes. Leith's men had lived off fish (which they reported were plentiful and excellent), seals, ducks, weka and other birds, as well as their own supplies; and the animals released by Raven in the bush were thriving.

Although Malaspina's expedition had sailed past Tamatea earlier that year, Leith's people and the Spanish had not seen each other. Nor had Leith's party seen any Maori. Raven later reported:

> [W]e saw three natives the first time we were in Dusky Bay, but notwithstanding our giving them all the signs of Friendship & hospitality we could not procure any intercourse. They took to the woods, & we never saw them again, nor did Mr. Leith see any inhabitants during his residence at Poenammoo he once found a fire but the Natives had fled at his approach.[17]

Leith had left gifts for these people (including nails and 'a few baubles'), but these were left untouched. Other abandoned houses visited by the Europeans were subsequently pulled to pieces by the local people; Leith's men found only ruins when they returned.[18]

On the night of the *Britannia*'s arrival, her crew and the sealing party shared a festive meal of goat's meat, and the next day they began the arduous work of loading stores, firewood and planks on board the ship. They did not have time to finish the vessel that Leith's men had almost completed, however, because Raven's agreement with Grose allowed only a two-week stay in Dusky Sound. On 12 October, the day before they intended to leave Tamatea, a party led by Captains Raven and Nepean (who was returning to England on sick leave) visited an abandoned house in Goose Cove, described here by Robert Murry:

> It was Built about 10 Yards from the High Water mark – in the entrance of the Woods. The materials of which it was constructed were chiefly the Flax plant and a few Sticks stuck in an Upright position, it appeared nearly circular; but wanted a segment of 1/3 of its circumference which was the entrance a man might sit upright, but I think it impossible for one to stand upright in it. They must creep on all fours to enter it – and a family of 5 or 6 persons must lie very warm, the whole reminds me of necessary buildings I have seen at Port Jackson built by the Convicts and designed for the accommodation of a Sow and a litter of Pigs . . .[19]

According to Murry, there were a number of abandoned shelters of this kind scattered around Goose Cove and Wood Hen Cove in the Sound.

Later that afternoon, a boat went off to Luncheon Cove to collect a cat that the sailors had accidentally left behind. To their surprise they found the *Francis* there at anchor, her sails in tatters and the bowsprit and rudder broken by recent storms. Two of the *Britannia*'s boats were sent to tow the schooner into Facile Harbour, where the men began to repair it and load it with firewood and water. This delay kept them two weeks longer in the Sound, but finally on 20 October 1793 the *Francis* and *Britannia* set sail for Norfolk Island. It was at this time that Lieutenant-Governor King received the glowing reports from Raven that made him keen to establish a British colony in New Zealand. He commandeered the *Britannia* and ordered Raven to make a diversion from his voyage to India so that he could take Tuki and Huru back to New Zealand, while the *Francis* under William House's command returned to Port Jackson to report to Acting Governor Grose. House was unenthusiastic about New Zealand's colonial prospects, however. He told Grose that although there were plentiful fresh provisions, including ducks, woodhens and fish at Dusky Sound, it seemed an unpromising place for a European establishment. David Collins, Grose's secretary, concluded:

> Nothing appeared by this information from Dusky Bay, that held out encouragement to us to make any use of that part of New Zealand. So little was said of the soil, or face of the country, that no judgement could be formed of any advantages that might be expected from attempting to cultivate it; a seal fishery there was not an object with us at present, and, beside, it did not seem to promise much. The time, however, that the schooner was absent was not wholly misapplied; as we had the satisfaction of learning the event of a rather uncommon speculation, that of leaving twelve people for ten months on so populous an island, the inhabitants whereof were known to be savages, fierce and warlike. We certainly may suppose that these people were unacquainted with the circumstance of there being any strangers near them; and that consequently they had not had any communication with the few miserable beings who were occasionally seen in the coves of Dusky Bay.[20]

ENDEAVOUR AND *FANCY, PROVIDENCE, ASSISTANCE*
AND *MERCURY* AT TAMATEA
1795–97

The next vessel to arrive at Tamatea was the *Endeavour*, commanded by William Wright Bampton. In 1793, he had carried Tuku and Huru to Norfolk Island on the *Shaw Hormuzear* before sailing to India to collect a cargo of cattle for Port Jackson. Because war had broken out again in Europe, he found it difficult to find a ship big enough to carry his cargo. Finally he purchased a dilapidated old East Indiaman, the *Endeavour,* and, while it was being repaired, loaded some of the contracted cargo onto the *Fancy*, a small brig commanded by his chief mate, Edgar Dell. The *Fancy* sailed to Port Jackson, followed by the *Endeavour* in March 1794, with 132 head of cattle and a load of supplies including quantities of Surat grain.

When Bampton arrived at Port Jackson and delivered his cargo in May 1795,[21] the cattle proved to be in good health but were mostly very old. As Secretary of the Colony Collins acidly observed, 'Of little use could toothless, old, and blind beasts be to us.'[22] Bampton's ship was as old and decrepit as his beasts, and required extensive repairs which delayed her departure on another voyage to India to fetch supplies for the penal colony. Still, Dell (who had visited Hauraki while awaiting Bampton's arrival) was glad to see him. While the *Endeavour* was being refitted, Dell made another brief visit to Norfolk Island in the *Fancy* during June and July, picking up a cargo of dressed flax from the island, and brought it back to Port Jackson. In September 1795, the *Fancy* and the *Endeavour* finally sailed in company for Bengal, carrying about fifty freed convicts (all men, except Elizabeth Heatherly, also known as Elizabeth Bason, who was travelling with her partner James Heatherly and their small son James[23]). En route they visited Dusky Sound, where Bampton planned to hunt seals, finish the half-built schooner left there by the *Britannia*, and load her with spars and planks for the Bombay Marine before proceeding to Hauraki to collect the timber left there by the *Fancy*.

Robert Murry, formerly a crewman on the *Britannia* and now the *Endeavour*'s fourth officer, wrote a vivid journal of this voyage. According to Murry, almost as soon as the vessels had left Port Jackson, forty male convicts and deserters and one female convict, named Ann Carey, were found to have concealed themselves on board.[24] Bampton asked his officers to sign a document, no doubt disclaiming any involvement in this mass escape. 'I did yesterday sign a paper which I will not swear to on a future occasion,' wrote Murry; '. . . it was concerning the prisoners there Mentioned.' The next day, however, he added: 'Of the convicts . . . 4 are Carpenters this may look as if we had conceald them but I am certain it was not the case.'[25]

The *Endeavour* was cranky and seriously overcrowded. After two weeks at sea, a violent storm blew up. The hull began to leak, the pumps were manned day and night, and there were arguments and recriminations on board. The pages recording the events of the following week were cut out from Murry's journal, so we do not know exactly what happened, nor just when the ships arrived in Tamatea. The journal resumes on 12 October 1795, when Captains Bampton and Dell visited Leith's old shipyard at Luncheon Cove. There they found the wharf built by Leith's men, the house with its trypot and the semi-completed vessel still intact, although part of the roof of the house had blown off, some of the ship's planking had split and buckled, and the decking of the wharf was knocked off its posts when the ship's boat came alongside. The local people apparently had not interfered with these structures, which must have seemed mysterious to them, and potent with supernatural power.

The *Endeavour* was a large ship of about 800 tons and, with the *Fancy*, brought almost 250 people to Tamatea. The captains ordered their crews to begin the work of repairing the house and wharf, building a storehouse on a stony beach opposite the ship, killing seals and preparing their skins, and finishing the partly built vessel. The next day Bowell, Bampton's chief officer, asked to be discharged from the *Endeavour*. Bampton called a meeting of the officers in his cabin, and allowed Bowell to resign as first officer but refused to let him leave the ship. It was obvious, though, that the *Endeavour* was no longer fit for sea, and a week later the ship was surveyed and condemned. When the surveying party inspected the hull, they found so many rotten timbers and loose bolts that it seemed a miracle the *Endeavour* had not sunk during their stormy passage from Port Jackson. It was decided to use the ship's sound timbers and fittings to finish off the craft that Raven's party had left behind in Luncheon Cove. This was named the *Providence,* a fifty-ton craft that Bampton estimated could carry about ninety people. In addition, the *Endeavour*'s longboat would be converted into another vessel (named first the *Resource* and then the *Assistance*) that might carry another ninety people. The rest would have to sail on the *Fancy*, or stay behind in Tamatea.

The 244 people who had arrived in the Sound included European ex-convicts, escapees, deserters, passengers, officers and sailors. Like most East Indiamen, the *Endeavour* and the *Fancy* also carried Lascars and Sepoys. Amongst this motley party, discipline was difficult to maintain. Despite their desperate situation, many of the people were reluctant to help with the work of refitting the vessels. They preferred to wander around the Sound, fishing, collecting shellfish or shooting ducks and weka, and avoiding the labour of stripping the *Endeavour* and sending her guns and stores ashore, felling trees, setting up sawpits, cutting planks and firewood, or hauling water. There were thefts of food, which were punished with rough justice, and acts of negligence (two of the *Endeavour*'s guns, for instance, were lost while being rafted ashore). Disputes broke out between crew and passengers, some of which may have been recorded on yet another page (for November) torn out of Murry's journal. So far as we know, there were just two women among more than two hundred men in the Sound,[26] which must also have caused difficulties. In the end, Bampton threatened to leave behind anyone who refused to work or who committed a serious offence.

Some of the sailors, including Murry, had never sealed before, and when they

Killing seals on the rocks.

tried their hand at 'the sport', they found it difficult and dangerous. On 11 December, for example, when Murry was out at the 'Sealing Isles' with his captain:

> [H]appening to see a very large Seal, I begged of Cn. Bampton to permit me to land which he complied with, hardly had I stepped out of the boat before 3 very heavy surfs came about me, I had no club with me; the boathook, which I had thrown on shore for that purpose had been carried out by the send back of the Sea. And had the animal attacked me I was defenceless. My anxiety for the boat was greater than for the event of the Seal. I had, however, some wish to kill him, but the heaviness of the surf prevented my moving from the summit of the rock on which I stood, like 'Patience on a monument, smiling at Grief'.
>
> At last, however, the sea went down, they took me in, and we made the best of our way for the ship.

Others of their party entertained themselves by fighting with one another. On 19 December, for instance, a disagreement flared up between Mr Waine, Bampton's new first officer, and one of the passengers. Waine swore at the passenger, who then challenged him to a duel. Murry was a witness to this argument, recording its finale as follows:

> Mr. A [the passenger] You hear Mr Waine? I now desire you to ask my pardon before Mr. Murry, or give me satisfaction in another manner this instant.
>
> Mr. W[aine] I will not! I cannot think of fighting a man who has been used to practise a Pistol. I don't like to be shot at like a bird.
>
> Mr. Alms. That's nonsense Sir. here are two pistolls, take your choice of them,

load them yourself, you shall have every advantage I can offer, but as you have refused to make attonement for the offence. You must fight me.

Mr. W. I cannot.

Mr. A. Then Sir You are a Coward, a Dastardly Coward! Mr. Murry you hear what I say. I call Mr. Waine a Coward, who would dare affront a gentlemen, and refuse him satisfaction. Mr. W. you are a Coward, I shall publish this in India.

Mr. W. Well, if you call me a Coward I shall act accordingly.

(He then left the Cabin).

Since then the Gentlemen have not spoke to each other.[27]

Despite this drama, Christmas Day was celebrated in relative tranquillity, with a meal of pork and mutton for the crew, seal meat and fish for 'the ragged gang' (the convicts and deserters) and arrack for everyone. New Year's Day, however, was heralded by another loud quarrel, this time between Waine and his captain. Bampton had decided to begin by completing the *Providence*, commanded by Weathrall, the second officer, rather than the longboat commanded by Waine, which upset his first officer. At about this time, too, the *Endeavour* – or what was left of her – was unmoored and allowed to drift onto the rocks in Facile Harbour, where she beached. Finally, on 7 January 1796, the *Fancy* and the *Providence* – the first vessel to be built from New Zealand timbers – sailed out of the Sound. The *Providence* missed stays by Point Five Fingers and only just escaped being wrecked. Bampton took the ships to Norfolk Island,[28] where he begged supplies from Lieutenant-Governor King and left behind several Lascars and Portugese seamen, and forty-eight half-starved passengers (including Elizabeth Heatherly and her son),[29] then carried on to China. His quarrelsome first mate and about ninety other Europeans (including Ann Carey) were left behind in Tamatea. As the vessels left the Sound, Murry summed up what had been learned about Dusky's resources:

> The timber which grows here, would answer very well for plank, for the Ship Builder, Joiner or Cabinet Maker, this is the opinion of our Carpenter in the Britannia. He being as well acquainted with its properties as any man of his profession; and the Joiner preferred it to the wood of Port Jackson or the Brazill wood. But I think it be a task of some trouble, to get a Cargo of spars, sufficiently long for the Masts of Ships.
>
> To procure turpentine, we made several experiments, by tapping, &c. but found no method of extracting any . . . In the Pitch Pine trees, there is no gum of any sort but the bark emits a transparent resin which has a most agreeable smell, but it would take a man a week to get a Pound of it . . . Captain Cook has given so good an description of the Spruce Fir, that it is impossible to mistake it. But he has not taken any notice of the Pitch Pine – Birch – And large Myrtle.
>
> The Pitch Pine is remarkable for its black bark, which when cut and rubbed with the finger smells agreeably. It generally grows from 20 to 40 feet without branches, and the wood is much like Norway Pitch Pine, but whiter.
>
> The Birch is only fit for fuel – Its uncommon whiteness would cause it to be preferred for decks, &c. but it splits with the smallest blow, and, of all the woods at Duskey Bay is the least durable . . .

The Myrtle is not so large . . . it is of use for turners or Cabinet Makers, makes excellent block Pins, and from its hardness may be converted to many uses with which I am unacquainted. There are many other kinds of wood, which, as they scarcely deserve notice, I have not ment'd but the Spruce Pine is best for Naval Purposes, and the Pitch for small spars.[30]

After the departure of the *Providence* and the *Fancy,* Waine and his men felled trees, shaped the wood and laboured to finish off the *Assistance* (as the *Endeavour's* longboat was finally named) with the help of their shipwright, James Heatherly. Two months later this ungainly vessel sailed to Norfolk with a bedraggled crew of sailors and a few convicts. Other convicts and some colonists 'of good character' were still living in Tamatea. Their supplies were almost exhausted, and they were forced to hunt and gather to survive. They were not rescued until 1797, when an

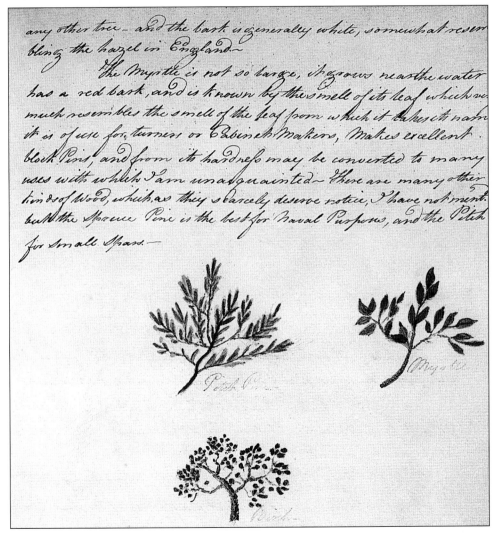

Sketches of 'Pitch Pine', 'Myrtle' and 'Birch' from Robert Murry's journal.

A greenstone tiki (now in Auckland Museum) said to have been taken back to England by one of the men on the Endeavour, *after the ship was wrecked in Tamatea.*

American snow from Rhode Island called the *Mercury*,[31] which was en route from Manila to the north-west coast of America, arrived at Port Jackson and heard of their predicament. American ships were trading with China and South-East Asia during this period, and sometimes called at New Holland. The captain of the *Mercury*, William Barnet, offered to go to Dusky to collect the castaways, provided that he could take materials from the wreck of the *Endeavour*. Governor Hunter refused him salvage rights but authorised him to make terms with the survivors and to land them at Norfolk Island. The *Mercury* sailed in May 1797 (with one female convict on board) and picked up thirty-five half-starved survivors, finally landing them in Norfolk after a stay of more than eighteen months in the Sound.[32] During the whole of this time there was no mention of meetings with local Maori. Quite clearly they wanted to avoid any further encounters with Europeans.

VENUS AT TAMATEA
5–21 December 1801

No European ships are known to have visited the Sound for several years after the last castaways from the *Endeavour* and *Fancy* were rescued in 1797. During that year large seal rookeries were discovered in Bass Strait, and an American ship, untroubled by the East India Company's monopoly, soon collected a rich cargo of sealskins and oil there and took it to the China market. This infuriated the colonists. Both Governor Hunter and Philip Gidley King, when he became Governor of New South Wales in 1800, allowed some craft to be built at Port Jackson in excess of the officially sanctioned tonnages, and fitted out for sealing.[33] For the next few years the Port Jackson sealers ignored New Zealand, turning their attention to the rookeries on the south and western coasts of New Holland instead. The merchants responsible for this growing industry included Robert Campbell of Campbell and Co. in Calcutta (who had sent the Bengal ship *Hunter* to Hauraki in 1798); his partner from 1800, the Commissary-General John Palmer, who established a ship-building yard at Woolloomooloo; the emancipists Henry Kable and James Underwood, whose yard was near Tank Stream; and Simeon Lord (the ex-convict whose ship, also called *Hunter*, had visited Hauraki for spars in 1799). Campbell commented in later years:

> Governor King, anxious to promote the welfare of the Colony, sanction'd several free Inhabitants to fit out Shallops for fishing of Oil and Skins with a view to giving employment to numbers who would otherwise be idle, and this laudable public measure invigorated my infant enterprize and I purchased these articles, the produce of the poor people's industry with an intention of exporting the oil and skins to England by one of my ships employed in bringing the cattle from Bengal, as no return cargo whatever could then be made to that quarter but ballast which subjected me to double freight.[34]

In 1801, however, the *Venus*, a brig licensed by the East India Company and owned by Creighton, Bishop and George Bass (formerly surgeon of HMS *Reliance*) made a brief visit to Tamatea. Bass was an enterprising individual who had already gained a reputation as an explorer in New Holland. In 1797, he and Lieutenant Matthew Flinders had investigated the coastline around Port Jackson in *Tom Thumb*, a tiny boat only eight feet long; in 1798, he took a crew of six sailors in a whaleboat and established the existence of Bass Strait; and in 1798–99, Bass and Flinders sailed through the strait in a small sloop and circumnavigated Van Diemen's Land, collecting plants and animals that they sent back to Sir Joseph Banks in London. In 1799, Bass took a cargo of sealskins to Macao, and in March 1800, during their voyage to England on *Reliance*, he and his friend Captain Henry Waterhouse sighted the Antipodes Islands. It was probably Bass who brought the news of their discovery back to Port Jackson.

The *Venus* stayed at Facile Harbour in Tamatea from 5 to 21 December 1801, while Bass and his crew of about twenty investigated the seal rookeries. They cut

A portrait of George Bass.

planks for chests that they later filled with salted pork for Port Jackson at Tahiti and Hawai'i, and stripped unwrought iron from the beached wreck of the *Endeavour*, which the ship's smith forged into axes to trade with Pacific Islanders. In a letter to Governor King, Bass wrote that after leaving Dusky Sound, the *Venus* sailed south where '[we] discovered some harbours in the southermost part of Tavai Poenammoo, which we call the *Inlets of Venus*'.[35] After returning from this voyage, Bass announced in January 1803 that he intended to return to Dusky, en route to the Spanish ports in South America on a speculative voyage to get supplies of salted beef and livestock for the penal colony. He planned to salvage the *Endeavour*'s two anchors to sell to the Spaniards, and to break out its iron fastenings to rework for trade in the Islands.

Bass's letters on the subject[36] indicate that he hoped to make enough money on this voyage to fund a more extensive sealing expedition. In addition, he applied to Governor King for 'an exclusive privilege or lease of the South part of New Zealand, or that South of Dusky Bay . . . as also of the Bounty Isles, Penantipode Isle, and the Snares, all being English discoveries, together with ten leagues of sea around their coasts' so that he could supply salt fish to the colony's Public Stores. His application urged that 'If I can draw up food from the sea in places which are lying useless to the world, I surely am entitled to make an exclusive property of the fruits of my ingenuity, as much as the man who obtains Letters Patent for a corkscrew or a cake of blacking'.[37]

King encouraged Bass in this enterprise but decided not to grant him a lease until a trial of the fishery had been made. If it succeeded, Bass wrote exuberantly to Captain Waterhouse, he would 'return to old England, when I mean to seize upon my dear Bess [his wife], bring her out here, and make a *poissarde* out of her, where she cannot fail to find plenty of use for her tongue'.[38] Instead, he sailed on the *Venus* from Port Jackson on 5 February 1805, and disappeared. Many of his contemporaries believed that Bass had reached South America (presumably after a second visit to Dusky), where the Spanish seized his vessel and sent him and his crew to labour in the mines.[39]

The only records that remain of Bass's visit(s) to Tamatea are a series of good-humoured letters, which say little about his experiences in the Sound. From these we cannot tell whether he met any Maori there, or the nature of their interactions. It is probable that the local people avoided him, as they had done all other recent European visitors (or had abandoned the place), although inhabitants of the 'Inlets of Venus' (presumably the southern fiords) may have been more welcoming.

ENDEAVOUR, SCORPION, CONTEST AND *INDEPENDENCE* AT TAMATEA
1803–05

By 1803, the Bass Strait rookeries off New Holland were depleted. An anonymous correspondent wrote to the *Sydney Gazette* that year:

> The islands in Bass's Straits might have been a constant source of enterprise and emolument, properly managed, but I at present conceive, that in the course of two years more it will be difficult to clear the expenses of fitting out, without the smallest allowance for risque or damage. There are now a number of parties constantly kept upon the different islands, skinning and boiling; they mostly, if not altogether upon shares, are anxious to procure as many furs as possible; to do which, they indiscriminately hunt down all ages and sexes; the females share in the general massacre with the pupps or young wigs. The impolicy of killing the breeding seals will in time discover itself; the parties already complain of the scarcity occasioned by themselves, and unless new islands are discovered, a new employ must be.[40]

Nor was there any consideration for the interests of local indigenous populations, who had used the seals as long-term supplies of food. In Bass Strait, Aboriginal women were taken from their families, often without consent, as hunters and sexual partners for the sealers. William Stewart, who subsequently worked as a sealer in New Zealand, alleged that the sealers kept Aboriginal women as 'Slaves or Negroes, hunting and foraging for them . . . and, if they do not comply with their desires or orders in hunting, etc., they by way of punishment half hang them, cut their heads with Clubs in a Shocking Manner, or flog them most unmercifully with Cats made of Kangaroo Sinews . . .'[41] In later years, Maori women, along with Tahitians and other Polynesians, were also taken to the Bass Strait sealing grounds, and some Maori men, as well as Tahitians, Hawaiians, Portugese, Lascars and some American blacks, joined the gangs.[42]

As the Bass Strait rookeries became depleted, the sealers began to look elsewhere for their cargoes, and several vessels from Port Jackson soon returned to Tamatea. The first of these was a small schooner called the *Endeavour* (formerly the *Martha*), built by the emancipist shipwright James Underwood, owned by Kable and Underwood and commanded by Joseph Oliphant, a member (along with Daniel Cooper and Samuel Rodman Chace, who both later sealed in New Zealand) of the first gang to go sealing in Bass Strait.[43]

The *Endeavour* sailed from Port Jackson on 19 April 1803, dropping off a gang of sealers in Bass Strait before proceeding to Tamatea, where she arrived on 9 May. During the following months the small craft explored the south-western coast, looking for seals. The animals had largely left the Sound, so Oliphant explored the adjacent coast, visiting Breaksea and Solander Islands. At an islet near Breaksea, one of her six crew drowned when a boat drove onto a ledge of rocks in the surf, and swamped. The *Endeavour* sailed past West Cape, noting Chalky Island and four entrances into the Sounds, and past South Cape at the end of Stewart Island, where they sighted the Snares. After this they put into 'Launching Cove' (Luncheon Cove in Dusky Sound?) and went sealing in miserable weather, with little success. The ship arrived back in Port Jackson in October 1803 with 2,200 salted skins, 'all procured with extreme difficulty and hardship'.[44] During his travels along the south-western coast, Captain Oliphant met local Maori, whom he reported to be 'very friendly, and ready to render every assistance he could possibly require. This peaceable and amicable disposition has manifested itself in several instances . . .'[45] Unfortunately he gave no further description of these encounters.

At the end of 1803, a British ship, the 'South Whaler' *Scorpion*, followed the *Endeavour* to Tamatea. She had sailed from England with Letters of Marque in June 1803[46] under the command of William Dagg. Before reaching St Helena she took two French whalers as prizes, and in December sailed for the coast around Dusky, where she went sealing. The *Scorpion* arrived at Port Jackson in March 1804 with a cargo of 4,759 skins and twenty barrels of sperm oil (presumably from the French whalers).[47] Apart from this, and a clue from the name 'Dagg Sound' that the *Scorpion* landed there, nothing further is known of this voyage. After leaving Port Jackson, the *Scorpion* went whaling off the north of New Zealand, where she was seen by *Hannah and Eliza* off the Three Kings on 14 November 1804.

Such laconic scraps of information are typical of the sealing voyages. Sealing was a competitive business, and the locations of rookeries were kept quiet as long as possible. Uncertainties about the East India Company's monopoly and the legality of sealing ventures (especially after regulations gazetted in 1804 prohibited sealing in latitudes below 43° 59'S[48]) discouraged sealers from reporting their activities in any detail. Furthermore, sealing gangs included men whose behaviour did not always bear close inspection. There was no requirement that masters of sealing vessels should hand in their logs, the Naval Officer at Port Jackson did not report the movements of colonial vessels to the authorities in Britain, and many sealers were illiterate. All of these factors contribute to make research into sealing, despite its key significance in this early period, a frustrating affair. Ironically, the best sources on early southern sealing are the contemporary court records. Breaches of contract by unscrupulous owners or masters often led to litigation, and evidence given by witnesses in court provides some of the most illuminating accounts of the industry.

It seems that by about 1803, the Tamatea rookeries had been devastated. From 1804 onward, the Sound was mainly used as a rendezvous and a harbour for collecting fresh food and water. Since the *Resolution*'s visit in 1773, twelve European vessels had arrived in Tamatea, bringing more than five hundred Europeans (including several women) and some Lascars and Sepoys to the Sound. So far as we know, however, the small bands of Ngaati Mamoe and Ngaai Tahu who frequented Tamatea avoided their strange visitors. From the time of Vancouver's 1791 visit until 1815, there were no recorded contacts with local Maori. Their meetings with Cook and his men had evidently been so traumatic that they were reluctant to risk further encounters. The whole district may have been declared tapu, for fear of supernatural contamination. For whatever reason – introduced diseases or cosmological puzzlement – they took to the bush and refused any further face-to-face meetings with Europeans.

SEALING IN THE FAR SOUTH
1805–15

After 1804, the sealers shifted their attention to Foveaux Strait and the far southern islands. George Bass had reported seal rookeries on the Antipodes Islands, and the wily and increasingly prosperous ex-convict merchant Simeon Lord entered into partnership with an American sealing captain, Isaac Pendleton of the *Union*, to check them out. Pendleton's men built a small craft on Kangaroo Island, the schooner *Independence*, which they decided to send to the Antipodes. When Governor King got wind that Lord was in league with Pendleton, he issued a proclamation in May 1804 that not only prohibited the unauthorised construction of vessels over fourteen feet long in the colony, but declared that any such craft would be confiscated. This was followed by a General Order in August forbidding foreigners from sealing in Bass Strait, southern New Zealand or the sub-Antarctic islands, or from recruiting local crew under any circumstances.[49]

Successive governors at Port Jackson had tried to maintain a British monopoly of trade in Australasian waters, but American ships visited the colony from the beginning, and American captains (particularly men from the small island of Nantucket on the eastern seaboard) often commanded British sealers and whalers. As a former convict, Lord was motivated more by profit than by patriotism, and by working with the Americans he could circumvent the East India Company's monopoly. When the *Union* and *Independence* cleared Port Jackson on 28 August, therefore, he decided on subterfuge. The ships were declared bound for China, and the sealing gangs slipped out of Port Jackson on other craft. These included the *Endeavour*, now commanded by Joseph Higgins (formerly mate during the schooner's previous voyage to Dusky), which carried Owen Folger Smith of Nantucket and his gang to Bass Strait; the *Honduras Packet*, commanded by another Nantucket man, Owen Bunker, which picked up Higgins, Smith and the sealers in Bass Strait and took them to the east coast of Stewart Island; and a newly built schooner, the *Contest*, commanded by Joseph Oliphant (formerly of the *Endeavour*), which slipped out of Port Jackson early in August 1804 and met the *Independence* in Dusky Sound during January 1805, while the *Union* sailed on to the Pacific.

Several of these ships are likely to have met with Maori, so it is worth recounting their movements. The *Honduras Packet* sailed with Lord and Pendleton's sealing party to Rakiura (Stewart Island). It is possible that Bunker had been given information about sealing grounds there by his cousin, the veteran whaler Eber Bunker, who began his adventures in New Zealand waters on the *William and Ann* in 1792. The *Honduras Packet* arrived at Rakiura in December 1804, where Smith drew a rough chart of the western coast from his whaleboat. During this exploration he found Te Moana-ki-Rakiura (which he called 'Smith's Straits'), which Captain Cook had not realised separated Rakiura from the mainland.[50] In the course of this expedition the sealers must have met local people, the first of many such contacts. Before the *Honduras Packet* sailed back to Bass Strait, however, Smith and his gang left the ship, possibly on board the *Independence*, and crossed 'Smith's Straits' to join the *Contest* for a rendezvous in Tamatea.

The voyage of the *Contest* is known from the memoirs of Jorgen Jorgensen, her flamboyant Danish mate.[51] Jorgensen had gone to sea as a young man on an

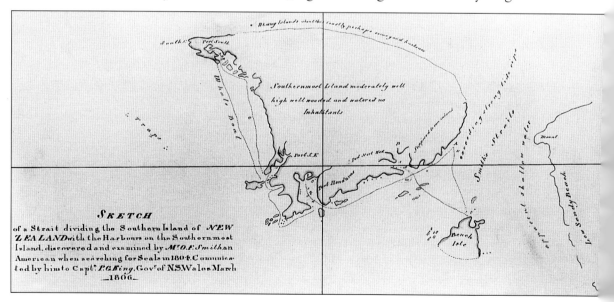

Above: *Owen Folger Smith's sketch chart of 'Smith's Straits' (Foveaux Strait).*

Opposite: *Sealing locations in the sub-Antarctic Islands and Foveaux Strait.*

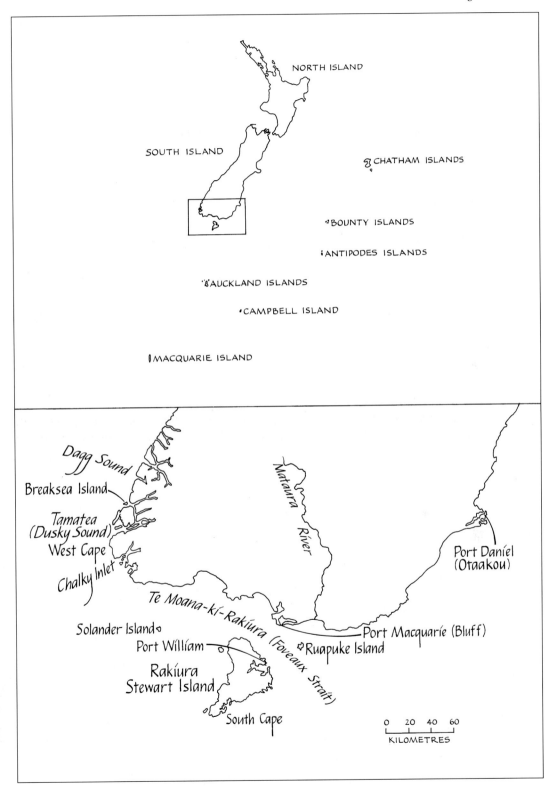

NORTH ISLAND

SOUTH ISLAND

CHATHAM ISLANDS

BOUNTY ISLANDS

ANTIPODES ISLANDS

AUCKLAND ISLANDS

CAMPBELL ISLAND

MACQUARIE ISLAND

Dagg Sound

Breaksea Island

Tamatea
(Dusky Sound)

West Cape

Chalky Inlet

Mataura River

Port Daniel
(Otaakou)

Te Moana-ki-Rakiura (Foveaux Strait)

Solander Island

Port William

Rakiura
Stewart Island

South Cape

Port Macquarie (Bluff)

Ruapuke Island

0 20 40 60
KILOMETRES

English collier and later joined a South Seas whaler, which brought him to the Cape of Good Hope. There he joined a trader bound for Port Jackson, where he was hired as a cabin servant on the colonial brig *Lady Nelson*, rising to become second mate. In a rare pamphlet published and printed in Danish, Jorgensen claimed that the *Contest* arrived at the south coast of New Zealand early in 1805, but the schooner was so leaky that they had to return to Port Jackson after only a short stay, leaving two small boats behind at Dusky. Four new harbours were found, however, and several sealing islands, where 7,000 skins were soon collected.[52] Jorgensen remarked, 'It is indeed astonishing with what eagerness the sailors enter into this pursuit, knocking down the animals with their clubs, stripping them of their skins, and pegging them out to dry, or salting them down in casks, with the greatest zeal and perseverance.'[53] In his pamphlet he added helpful comments on the economics of the southern sealing trade:

> The Americans have much more experience in this trade than the English, and for this one can thank the East-Indian Company who would not permit the sealskins to be imported into China on their European ships, whereas the Americans have brought whole great cargoes – partly sealskins, partly otter furs – to China, and thereby saved a considerable amount of silver . . . not just in this instance, but in many other respects . . . the East-Indian Company does the country more harm than good . . .
>
> A ship which sails in this sealing trade uses many more men than a whaleship, for it usually sets off a gang on several islands, and the more men one has, the more work is performed, and the more islands [can] be occupied at one time. The men . . . are paid . . . in proportion to the number of men employed. If one has, for example, 60 men, then a sailor must have one skin out of 160 and everything else ought to be apportioned accordingly.[54]

The *Contest* seems to have taken most of her skins on the south-west coastline of the South Island, where she left two boats behind. It seems highly likely that during this time, the crew met local people. After keeping the rendezvous with the *Independence* in Dusky Sound, the schooner returned to Port Jackson under Jorgensen's command, arriving there on 9 February 1805. At the same time the *Independence* carried the sealing gangs under the command of Owen Folger Smith, Joseph Oliphant and John Voce south-east to the Antipodes Islands, where they were left for the next two years. On these inhospitable shores they built their huts and landed their rations of meat, flour, biscuit, sugar, rice and tea. The *Independence* returned to Port Jackson via Norfolk Island in April 1805, and the great seal rush to the Antipodes began.[55]

THE SEAL RUSH TO THE ANTIPODES
1805–1807

The Antipodes are a bleak and rocky cluster of islands 975 kilometres south-east of the South Island, home to large rookeries of seals. Over the next two years a series of ships left Port Jackson for the Antipodes (1805 *Independence*, *Favorite*, *Venus*, *Honduras Packet*, *Governor King*; 1806 *Ceres*, *Star* and *Commerce*[56]). Most of these were associated in some way or another with Simeon Lord (whether as owner or contractor), and several had American captains. As Governor King complained in March 1806:

> Under cover of procuring seals and oil about the coasts of this colony . . . American vessels, in defiance of Colonial Regulations on that subject, [have] taken a number of people off the islands of Bass's Strait and carried them to a smaller group of islands being considerably without the limits of this territory, where upwards of 80 people are on those islots, the largest is a bare rock and not six miles round, where seals resort in great numbers. In the course of two years, upwards of 160,000 skins have been taken on these islands.[57]

Many of these vessels probably also visited harbours in New Zealand during their expeditions. A small craft called the *Venus* (not to be confused with George Bass's vessel of the same name), having delivered a cargo from Calcutta to Port Jackson in 1805, then sailed to the Bay of Islands. There her captain, William Stewart, picked up the local chief Te Pahi and his sons and took them to Norfolk Island (an expedition to be discussed later), then carried on to the Antipodes.

In late 1805 a tiny craft, the *Speedwell*, explored the south-west coast of the South Island, while in early 1806 the *Governor King* under Captain Edwards returned to Dusky to pick up more iron from the wreck of the *Endeavour*. In 1806 the American sealer *Favorite* brought Owen Folger Smith and his sealing gang back from the Antipodes with a record cargo of 60,000 skins, and sailed through 'Smith's Straits' (Foveaux Strait), while about the same time the *Star* (Captain Birnie), and then the *Dart* (Captain Smith) in 1807, were probably sealing in the Chatham Islands.[58] According to Koche, a Chatham Islander who joined one of the early sealers that visited Rekohu, his people had decided after their violent clash with George Vancouver's men to greet 'the children of the sun' in peace. Accordingly, when the first sealers arrived at Waitangi Bay in Rekohu:

> A man advanced and placed one end of a grass plant in the hands of the captain, and, holding on to the other, made him a speech of welcome, threw over him his own cloak, and thus established a firm and lasting peace; and from thenceforward the fishermen who frequented the coast found them hospitable, cheerful friends, and willing assistants in their labor, and 'love between them flourished like a palm'.[59]

In 1807, the *Topaz*, commanded by Mayhew Folger of Nantucket, having just visited the Antipodes, also cruised off the Chathams, where many fires were seen on shore. There they spoke (exchanged news with) the *Antipode*, one of Simeon

Lord's small sealers under the command of Captain Scott, who told Folger that he had not dropped off his gangs there because 'almost Every Isle was full of natives'.[60] Folger reported that at the Antipodes he had landed twice and searched the beaches, but found no seals, although there were two sealing gangs in residence, which had taken 4,000 skins during the preceding four months.

These gangs almost wiped out the Antipodes rookeries, and cargoes of skins abruptly declined in numbers.[61] Kerr has estimated that at least 140,000 seals were killed there in less than three years.[62] Interest began to turn to the Bounty Islands, where the *Santa Anna* left a gang before returning to England; and the Auckland Islands, discovered in 1806 by the whaler *Ocean*, owned by Enderby and Sons and commanded by Abraham Bristow.[63]

THE SEAL RUSH TO THE BOUNTY AND AUCKLAND ISLANDS
1808–1809

A rush to the Bounty and Auckland Islands now began. According to Jacky Marmon, a cabin boy on board the *Commerce*, 'Some of the Sydney merchants having heard of the vast numbers of seals that congregated there, determined to fit out a vessel for the trade. The *Commerce* was accordingly chartered, and Captain Sirone [Ceroni], a careful trustworthy sailor, placed in charge over a crew of [thirty] picked men.' Later in his life, Marmon dictated memoirs which gave an unusually graphic portrait of the lives that sealers led.[64] The *Commerce* (which had visited the Antipodes and the Bay of Islands under Captain Birnie the previous year) left Port Jackson in February 1808 and sailed in a sweep around the North Cape of New Zealand past the Bounty Islands and south to the Auckland group, which Marmon vividly described:

> The islands are mountainous throughout, and are of volcanic origin. The soil is rich, throwing out a luxuriant vegetation, although the surface is rather marshy and spongy, but if drained, might be capable of high cultivation. Timber covers all the islands, and a sort of thick brushwood renders the bush very dense. They are chiefly valuable for the immense numbers of seals resorting thither, though since my day I hear the number is very much diminished, through the constant slaughter. Many a good sealing-ground has been ruined in this way, as, for instance, the Antipodes . . . Considerable danger and difficulty attend the approach to the islands, both on account of the precipitous character of the shore and the magnetic attraction of the rocks, which Captain Bristowe warned our skipper was sufficient to render the compass almost useless. I should not be surprised if many an unwary sailor found a grave there yet.[65]

When the *Commerce* arrived at the Aucklands, two sealing gangs were already at work on Enderby Island, where most of the rookeries were located. To avoid a fight, Ceroni invited them on board the *Commerce*. He offered them grog, and once the celebration was under way, Ceroni had some of his men ply the visitors with drugged rum while he landed a sealing party on the island. The next morning the carousers awoke with 'haggard looks and bloodshot eyes' to find the newcomers already busy in the rookeries. After a stay of several weeks, when relations between the rival gangs had settled down, Ceroni left a group of his men on the island and sailed to Rekohu, where he bartered for sealskins. Marmon's memoirs also give a memorable glimpse of the Chathams at this time:

> The islands for the most part present a broken surface, the undulations occasionally attaining to the size of small hills. The soil seems good, and an abundant vegetation was everywhere visible, the native trees and flax, as I afterwards discovered, being much similar to those in New Zealand. Besides several sealing gangs stationed here, we found a considerable number of the natives, called in their own tongue *Moriori*, who seemed in dialect, colour, and customs, to resemble the Maori, as I afterwards found him. One extraordinary thing I observed here, was that in many places the island (Chatham) was on fire; not a mere surface conflagration, but a steady underground combustion. There are large formations of peat, one of the sealers told me, and these, having become ignited, have burned steadily for years and may yet be burning for all I know.[66]

Captain Ceroni left the Chathams after purchasing 300 sealskins, and sailed up the east coast of the North Island to Whitianga (Mercury Bay), where Marmon landed with his captain and 'stood upon the spot which Captain Cook, 28 years previously, had selected as his point of observation during the transit of Mercury'. Ceroni was very cautious in his dealings with local people, and only allowed his men to land in large, heavily armed parties. As Marmon noted in his account, 'The sight of their hideously tattooed faces and bodies steeped in red ochre, was sufficiently terrifying to many of us, especially as they bore in their hands most suspicious looking spears and clubs.' According to Marmon, a Moriori named Hororeka had joined the *Commerce* at the Chathams; indeed, a number of sealing vessels soon recruited Maori as interpreters, negotiators and workers. The seal rush in the Auckland Islands was relatively brief, and by 1808 the sealers' attention was already turning to the shores around Te Moana-ki-Rakiura (Foveaux Strait), found in late 1804 by the *Honduras Packet*.

THE SEAL RUSH TO TE MOANA-KI-RAKIURA
1808–1810

Unlike the Snares, the Antipodes and the Auckland Islands, the shores of Te Moana-ki-Rakiura were inhabited by Maori, and, from about 1808, contact with Europeans in the south intensified. Several thousand Ngaai Tahu and Ngaati Mamoe lived in communities around the strait and on Ruapuke and Rakiura (Stewart Island), travelling to the nearby fiords and small coastal islands where they hunted sea mammals including fur seals (kekeno), hair seals (pakake), elephant seals (ihu puku), sea leopards (toro and rapoka) and sea lions (whakahao); as well as sea birds' eggs, shellfish such as paaua, and tiitii (muttonbirds). Communities in this part of the country were highly mobile, each group owning several large double canoes about seventy to a hundred feet long, which could be sailed or paddled around the coast or to the offshore islands.[67] For skilled sailors such as these, voyages on European ships simply extended their migratory lifestyle.

Maori populations around the strait were semi-nomadic. The people on Ruapuke, for example, lived in villages on the island during January and February, where they made kelp bags in preparation for the movement to the tiitii islands in March. Seals were taken in the western fiords over summer, when they gathered in the rookeries. After moving to the islands in March, people stayed there until May, returning to Ruapuke with large kelp bags full of preserved birds for their own consumption or for exchange with allied kin to the north. In July, they crossed the strait to the plains on the south coast, where weka were caught, and in August, bush birds were taken in the forest. In September, groups camped at Tuturau near the Mataura River falls to catch lamprey, and went eeling in November along the south coast. During December they returned to Ruapuke. All around Te Moana-ki-Rakiura similar complex patterns of travel were going on.[68]

The sea mammals were plentiful, and for some years after European sealers first arrived, relationships with the local people were generally amiable. Some local men were recruited as sealers, and sometimes European sealers married local women. According to a story collected by William Baucke from an elder at Bluff, in about 1805:

> White men came to our coasts to seal . . . and sailed away . . . The ship that satisfied us most, killed her seals and went her way, but left with us a man who said, 'I will not return to my country, nor leave the woman who will be mother of a child to me.' So he stayed and became the father of many children by that wife. Presently they grew to an age when marriage is thought of, and our young men viewed his daughter with a shrewd relish to possess her, but she hid her face; her thoughts were for the tribe of her white father. For she had crossed eyes with a bearded boy who was third mate of a sealer, and from her eyes, how they searched every ship that passed, it was guessed he would return. The eyes of the Maori never forget what they have seen, but the ship of her longing was not among them. At last it came . . . and Riaki – the uplifted – because her father lifted her much to his knee, Riaki knew, and cried, 'He comes!'
>
> Without shame she sat on a headland and watched her ship come in. It anchored. Her captain came ashore. But what omen of evil is this? It is a stranger . . . Shyly she touched his arm, and in the broken language of her father asked 'Charly Thoms – where is he?' We watched our daughter, and how the stranger's eyes . . . consumed her beauty. Barely had he ate enough than he replied, 'At Sydney, in the hospital; I am the new captain; the other's left the sea.' Suddenly she hardened into wood . . . But the strange captain saw no one but her . . . Presently he asked: 'What is your name?' My name is Riaki: I am the daughter of the white man, Thomas Fink. He lies on his back with many aches. Come and speak with him.

'Maa te wahine, maa te whenua, ka ngaro ai te tangata' (By women and land, men are lost) says the proverb, and so it proved in this case. According to Baucke's informant, the visiting captain became infatuated with Riaki, but she remained loyal to her lover, Charly Thoms. In a frustrated fury her new suitor declared that her father was an escaped slave (i.e. a convict), and that unless Riaki would sleep with him, he would seize her father and take him back to Port Jackson. The local people told the visitor to return to the ship, and went to Fink to ask him if he was indeed a slave. 'I was,' he said to them, 'but for no sin of mine. Besides, my days of bondage were ended when I married a daughter of the tribe. Further, I am a rangatira born. I am no slave.' So the people decided not to give him up.

The next day the captain and twenty-four of his men came ashore to ask for Riaki's answer. Once again she refused him, and her elders told them to leave the bay. They expected no trouble, because for years their relationships with the sealers had been friendly. To their horror, however, the captain signalled to his men, who took out muskets that had been hidden in their boat, then rushed to the house where Fink lay sick, followed by Riaki and her people. They shot Riaki's father at his doorway, and then turned and fired on the crowd, shooting seven local people including Riaki, who fell with her left ear shot away. The survivors gathered her up and fled. The story ends: 'As we turned at the gate of the pa, we saw the house aflame, and later, entering their boats, the murderers sailed away.'[69]

Maori attitudes to visiting sailors were generally pragmatic. Europeans were regarded as members of another, if peculiar, kin group, and individually judged on their merits. As Baucke's informant put it crisply, 'If [the Pakeha] be little use, let the vermin go. If he be of value, lash him to a wife. If he be neither, the tomahawk decides.' Over the next few years a series of European vessels brought numerous sealing gangs to the region (1807–08 *Santa Anna* to the Bounty Islands; 1808 *Perseverance*, *Antipode*, *Governor Bligh*, *Pegasus* (when Eber Bunker produced a chart of the region) and *Fox* to Foveaux Strait; 1809 *Adventure*, *Governor Bligh*, *Pegasus*, *Unity*, *Brothers*, *Sydney Cove* and *Antipode* visited the strait and *King George* and *Perseverance* sailed to the Auckland Islands). The newcomers had to be dealt with, and if they gave access to iron and other trade goods as well as work for kinsmen and travel on ships, alliances with them were attractive. People exchanged potatoes, fish and mats with the visitors for iron and other European goods, and some sealing gangs spent months or even years in the region. As Jules de Blosseville later noted, 'a long sojourn and continual exploration make them acquainted with the smallest inlets, the most hidden retreats. No peculiarity of the region escapes their notice.'[70]

In 1808–09, for example, two gangs were landed by the brig *Fox* under Captain William Cox in Foveaux Strait. The first gang was dropped off on Solander Island in 1808, where they were left for more than four years before they were picked up by the *Perseverance* in 1813; while a gang led by Robert Murry was landed by the *Fox* in October 1809 and lived for about nine months in Foveaux Strait, until they were picked up by Captain Chace in the *Governor Bligh*. Murry later reported

Right: *A portrait of Captain Eber Bunker.*

Below: *Bunker's chart of the 'South End of New Zealand', made on the* Pegasus *in 1808.*

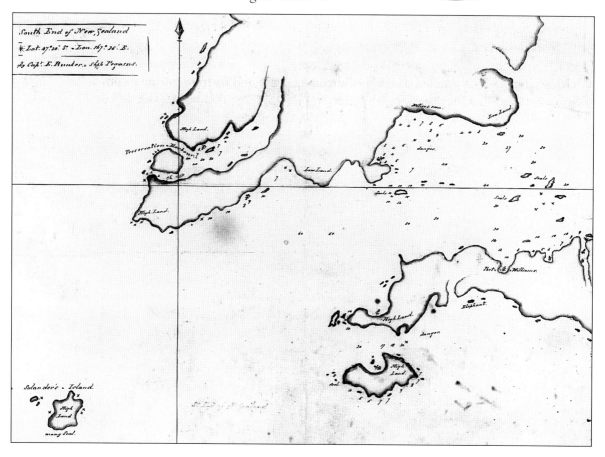

two small towns on the coast, at Port William and 'Murry River', each containing between twenty and thirty houses, and each house accommodating two families. The people had small double canoes fourteen to sixteen feet long, lived by fishing and growing potatoes, and were led by fighting chiefs, or 'Paroroy' (paraeroa), whom they greatly respected.[71] Their dialect was different from that of the Bay of Islands, and Murry reported when they fought, 'two factions take the field, their women are ranked in front of either line, in which posture they attack and defend, the men levelling their weapons at each other over the heads of the unfortunate females, who rend the air with shrieks and lamentations while the conflict lasts, and frequently leave more dead upon the field than do their savage masters'.[72] This casts an interesting light on the part that Maori women played in combat, at least in this part of the country.

Murry learned Maori and was treated as a chief, as was James Caddell, who arrived in the region on the *Sydney Cove*. This vessel landed its sealing gang at 'South Cape' (i.e. Stewart Island) in January 1810. Some of this gang (five men and Caddell, who was then sixteen years old, according to his own account) took a boat and some carpenter's tools, and escaped across Foveaux Strait. There they ran foul of local people and were attacked by a party of warriors led by 'Hunneghi' (Honekai), the chief of 'Oouai' (Oue, a village near Oreti and the present site of Invercargill).[73] During the affray Caddell touched the chief's mat and was saved by its tapu, but his companions were all killed and eaten. As the *Sydney Gazette* reported unsympathetically the following year: '[They] thus sadly atoned for their desertion, under circumstances that intailed a series of inconvenience and distress on their companions, as well as for their temerity in wantonly exposing themselves to the fury of the merciless hordes of savages that infest that barbarous coast.'[74]

Caddell was taken among Honekai's people at Oue and tattooed. He married Honekai's 'daughter' Tokitoki and lived there for many years. According to de Blosseville, who met Caddell in Port Jackson when he arrived there with his wife on the *Snapper* in 1823, he 'had so fallen into the manner of life of these savages that he had become quite as open a cannibal as any of them. He had embraced their ideas and beliefs, accepted with faith their fables, had yielded to all their customs, so much so that one might have believed that New Zealand was his true native country . . . [At first] he had some trouble to make himself understood, and had so greatly forgotten his mother tongue that it was difficult for him to act as interpreter.'[75] The *Sydney Gazette* added that by his marriage to Tokitoki, daughter to one chief and sister to another, 'to whom he appears to be tenderly attached', Caddell had become 'a prince of no small influence among such subjects as those barbarous despots are destined, in the present constitution of things, to have control of'.

Caddell had, in fact, married into one of the key families of Foveaux Strait. Honekai was a son of Te Hau-Tapunui-o-Tuu, a Ngaai Tahu chief who had been responsible for making a lasting truce with Ngaati Mamoe; and grandfather to the notable Ruapuke chief Tuhawaiki.[76] Atholl Anderson reports that Tokotoki was daughter to Honekai's brother Purerehu, and thus Honekai's niece rather than his daughter (the same term, 'tuahine', being used for both daughter and niece in Maori).[77] Caddell was in a privileged position to observe tribal life in the region, and was a key source of de Blosseville's description of the Foveaux Strait people:

> The natives who inhabit the coasts of Foveaux Strait are of medium height, well built, stout and robust. Their colour is darker than that of mulattoes, but its tint is affected by the deep figures on their skin. The women are generally short, and their features are in no way remarkable. They consider tattooing as the prerogative of noble birth . . .
>
> They only attack each other, as a rule, when they believe themselves assured of their superior strength and of a rich booty. In such a case no account is taken of the loss of a few warriors of the inferior class; but if, on the contrary, a chief be killed, his side calls together his friends and his relatives, and when victory attends their efforts, death becomes the inevitable fate of the entire tribe of murderers. If, on the other hand, the tribe does not consider it is strong enough, trickery comes to its aid, and attempt is made to capture, by surprise, a few of its enemies, its wrath being appeased by the latter being devoured. The death of these unlucky ones is rarely avenged. All the prisoners are adopted by the victorious chiefs or they are killed and devoured . . .
>
> The children are full of fun, and show great affection for each other. They display in their games remarkable agility. They amuse themselves by making kites, whips, other playthings, and little canoes. They dance together, and use slings. The young men are not considered grown until they attain the age of 20 years. By that time they have learned to use the lance and the patoupatou [patupatu – hand club], and they have a certain corpulence of body. They are then tattooed all over and are proclaimed warriors. Often the operation of tattooing around the eyes causes them frightful pains, and the result is a loss of sight . . .
>
> Polygamy is permitted. The morals of the natives are not of a high class . . . Old age is the object of the most profound respect. Even a chief will give food to a man of low degree, whom old age has deprived of his faculties . . . The laws of friendship, and the ties of relationship are nowhere more respected. The men live generally to 80, and the women to 85 or 90 . . .
>
> When building their villages, the slope of a hill facing the point of the shore from which they can embark is chosen. Everything which might impede the view of canoes or ships arriving is removed. Their houses are clean and solid. They are 16 ft in height, 10 ft in width, and 30 ft in length; the floor, raised a foot above the ground, is covered with wattle boughs. Small holes are left in the floor in which they light fires when the weather is cold and humid . . .
>
> The men hunt and fish, and build huts, construct canoes, and work in the garden [where potatoes, cabbages and other introduced vegetables were grown]. Gardens are generally placed a certain distance away from the house. They would rather die than carry their provisions themselves. The women always undertake these burdens. During the season they kill albatross, wild hens [weka], seals and rats, &c. They smoke these animals and preserve them whole, enclosed in sacks [kelp bags?] for months. These winter provisions are protected from rats by a

platform built on top of a broad pole, which they mount by means of a movable ladder. They make fire by rapidly rubbing a pointed stick in a groove of the same wood . . .

Their canoes, which are well built and adorned with carvings, offer a feeble resistance to a high sea, but when the water is calm the rowers send them along at a great speed. The war canoes are generally [single] and are from 70ft to 100ft in length. This is also the number of the warriors and rowers. The big fishing nets are of one to two miles in length, and between 10ft and 12ft in height. They are made of flax fibre in its raw state. The sea abounds in fish.

The inhabitants of Tavai-pounamu [Te Wai Pounamu] believe that a Supreme Being has created everything except when it is the work of their own hands, and that He will do them no harm. They call Him Maahoua [Maaui]. Rockou-Noui-Etoua [Raakau-nui-atua] is a good spirit to whom they pray night and day to preserve them from harm. Kowkoula [Ko Kura?] is a spirit, or Etoua, who governs the world during the day from the rising of the sun until its setting. Rockiola [Rakiura] is the Spirit of Night, the cause of death and illness, and of any accidents which may occur during the hour of his reign . . .

The beautiful and curious things which they see in the hands of Europeans make them regard the latter as species of devils or spirits (Etouas). They watch the whites with the greatest attention, and scrutinise all their proceedings . . . If a chief receives a present less important than one given to another chief, the wrath of the former knows no bounds. This susceptibility is the cause of much trouble to the stranger who trades with these people, and he, in everything that he does, must seek to satisfy all. It is to the lack of wise discretion that the deaths of several whites must be attributed.[78]

De Blosseville also described death rituals, and made comments on fighting techniques, health, dress and modesty. Caddell's close knowledge of the people around Te Moana-ki-Rakiura is reflected in this description, which is rivalled up to this point only by the account of northern lifestyles given to Philip Gidley King by Tuki-tahua and Huru-kòkoti in 1793.[79] Foveaux Strait people in this period were evidently affluent, with tattooing, large carved canoes (in addition to the small double canoes described by Murry), and fishing nets on a scale also reported by Captain Cook in the Bay of Islands. They were growing potatoes (which Murry also noted) and cabbages early in the nineteenth century, and venereal disease was established, although the Europeans sometimes mistook its symptoms for yaws. The claims made here for longevity are interesting, in the light of statements by physical anthropologists that Maori had short pre-contact lifespans.[80] These claims are consistent, however, with the accounts of other early European visitors, and with the long lifespans claimed for many Maori individuals in early historic times.[81] Their curiosity about the Europeans, and their uncertainty as to whether or not they were human, were also characteristically Maori.

De Blosseville's cautionary comments about the politics of gifting to chiefs were apposite, because inequalities of generosity caused considerable strife in early relations between Maori and Europeans. Gifts recognised and raised the mana of leaders, and, given mutual ignorance, diplomatic blunders were inevitable. A sudden excess of wealth could be dangerous, for recipients as well as the indiscreet donors. Whether for these or other reasons, there were several attacks on sealers around the strait in the next few years; one at 'Molyneux Harbour' (probably Waikawa) in about January 1811, when four of a sealing gang of eleven men landed by the *Brothers* were killed; and another in 1814, when Captain Fowler of the *Matilda* lost three boats in the far south of the South Island. One of his boats was taken by local people; another was stolen by six of his crew of Indian sailors who deserted at 'Port Daniel', or Otago Harbour (one of these Lascars later took the moko [tattoo] and was still living on Stewart Island with his adopted kin in 1844[82]); and the third under the command of his chief officer Robert Brown, formerly of the *Brothers*, simply disappeared and the crew were later reported killed and eaten.[83]

Despite these clashes, most contacts between Maori and sealers were friendly. When Captain Fowler returned to Otakou (Otago Harbour) in 1815, for example, he and his crew of Lascars were in great want of fresh food and water. The local rangatira 'Papuee' immediately organised a fishing party to supply them with fish and gave them potatoes from the communal store, although the crops were still in the ground under tapu, and the people themselves had few potatoes to eat. The supply of fresh water was a mile away from the anchorage, and when 'Papuee' saw the Lascars struggling to roll the casks across flax-covered terrain, he shouldered one cask and ordered his people to carry the rest to the ship. After that:

> The good chief visited the vessel invariably at sunrise every morning, and was personally attentive on all occasions to the supply of food for the crew. He noticed the running rigging to be in a decayed state, the vessel having suffered a long continuance of very bad weather; and without any prefatory remark sat down on the deck with a number of his people, women and men promiscuously, and commenced rope-making after the manner of the country . . . Captain Fowler speaks of this chief in the highest terms of regard and veneration; his stature of full six feet and a half in height, athletically formed; his countenance as benign as his manners are mild; and commanding obedience more as the father of a family than as the chieftain of a barbarous district. At taking leave he expressed the most friendly concern for the welfare of the captain and his people, and hoped if they should come that way again he would call and acquaint him with their welfare.[84]

From about 1810 onward, when the rookeries were depleted, Foveaux Strait was largely abandoned. When Macquarie Island was discovered in July 1809 by Robert Campbell's *Perseverance* (which included a 'New Zealand boy' among her crew), a new rush to those sealing grounds began. Although both the London and China markets were glutted with sealskins and a punitive duty had been placed in Britain on oil from colonial ships,[85] the Port Jackson merchants still found profit on that bleak, tussock-covered island, and a stream of their vessels headed far south to the freezing, sub-Antarctic waters.[86] Some of these ships (including *Perseverance* and *Star* in 1810) took the safer route around the top of New Zealand, down the east coast of both islands to or from the sealing grounds, and called at the Bay of Islands en route, while many others must have visited the western fiords, Stewart Island or Foveaux Strait for refreshments.

Although a few young Maori went sealing, there is no evidence of extensive Maori participation in the gangs. The seal hunt brought more than thirty vessels to the southern districts during this period, and ex-convicts, runaways and sailors who scoured the coastline for fresh food, wood and water as well as seals, and women. Many sealers (including some Indians as well as Europeans) made their way into local communities, where they married and mated, beginning a 'cross-race' population in the far south and shaping the distinctive cultural history of that region.[87] Their arrival changed local technologies, beliefs and practices, and they themselves were often fundamentally altered. Like James Caddell, such men might 'embrace the ideas and beliefs [of their adopted families], accept with faith their fables, and yield to all their customs, so much so that one might have believed that New Zealand was [their] true native country'. Despite commonplace assumptions to the contrary, cross-cultural history was a two-way process. Europeans as well as Maori were transformed as their lives intermingled. For these early sealers, though, although their impact on the far south was revolutionary, the evidence of the changes they experienced is skimpy. When the documents fall silent, history can be a baffling business.

Thirteen

WHALING VOYAGES
AND MAORI EXPLORERS

Whales also brought European mariners to New Zealand. Whaling, unlike sealing, required specialist equipment and skills, and ships that were built or rebuilt for the purpose. The vessels had to be sturdy enough to hold whales alongside, and large enough to carry four to six whaleboats, the tryworks and other gear, wood for the fires, food and water for the crew of about thirty men, whalebone and tons of oil in barrels. Local traders were forbidden to build ships big enough (two hundred to three hundred tons),[1] and in any case the level of investment required for whaling made it difficult for them to enter the business. From the beginning, the southern whale fishery was dominated by British and American interests.

Whaling produced tough, experienced sailors for the maritime powers, and valuable industrial materials. Whale products were in high demand throughout the Industrial Revolution. Whale oil (especially spermaceti) provided lubricant for machines, an odourless lighting and cooking oil, and a valued ingredient in candles, soaps, processed wool and tanned leather. 'Whalebone', or baleen – flexible strips that hang in the mouths of southern right whales – was used in upholstery, corsets and umbrellas. Ambergris, which is found in their guts, was prized as an aphrodisiac and a base for perfumes. By the 1780s, British ships were hunting whales along the Pacific coast of South America, and some owners contracted to carry convicts to Port Jackson as an outward cargo. Two whaling ships took convicts in the First Fleet, which arrived in Port Jackson in 1788, and in 1791 five whaling ships owned by Enderbys of London brought convicts to New South Wales, en route to the southern fishery. On this occasion as the ships approached Australia, great numbers of whales were sighted.[2] Thomas Melvill, the master of the transport *Britannia* (not to be confused with the storeship *Britannia*, Captain Raven[3]) told Governor Phillip that he had seen 'more Spermaceti whales on this Coast than he had seen in Six years on the Brazil Coast'.[4]

On the South American coast, British whalers ran the risk of attack and

---

Note: Details of whaling voyages to New Zealand appear in Appendix II, pages 525–33.

A sketch of a whaleboat, showing the positions of its crew.

capture by Spanish naval vessels.[5] In Australian waters, where there was no such danger, the sighting of whales was enticing. Governor Phillip hoped that a whale fishery might make the colony self-funding, so he encouraged captains to try their luck in Australian waters. On 8 August 1791, the *Mary Ann* went south to look for seals, while in late October the *Britannia* and the *William and Ann* went whaling. They sighted innumerable whales and seven fish were killed, but a storm blew up and they could only secure two of them. During this expedition the *William and Ann* visited Norfolk Island, where Lieutenant-Governor King asked her captain, Eber Bunker, to go to Doubtless Bay and fetch Maori flax-dressers back to the island.[6] His efforts, we noted earlier, were thwarted. As Phillip reported to Viscount Sydney in London: 'The establishing a spermaceti whale fishery on this Coast will be of infinite advantage to the Colony, but in this, our first attempt has shown that the chapter of accidents does not yet open in our favour.'[7]

Despite this, in 1794 Enderbys sent another whaling ship to New Zealand,[8] and in 1798 the *Cornwall* went whaling in New Zealand waters.[9] The East India Company's control over Australasian waters was lifted that year, and in 1799 another British vessel, the *Albion*, a fast sailing ship commanded by Eber Bunker, was sent to make a 'complete and fair trial' of the fishery.[10] Although the Napoleonic Wars began in 1800, Philip Gidley King, the recently appointed Governor of New South Wales, was able to report six ships whaling 'on the coast and off the north end of New Zealand' in 1801.[11] The British whalers that visited New Zealand at this time included *Speedy*, *Britannia* and *Venus*. In May 1802, King put a series of written questions to the masters of these vessels about whaling in New Zealand waters, and sent the answers to key authorities (including Sir Joseph Banks) in London.[12] The whaling captains reported good conditions and numerous whales, so that by the 1803 season, more British ships, including *Greenwich*, *Harriet*, *Alexander* and

Albion; and the *General Boyd*, an American vessel commanded by Owen Bunker of Nantucket, were whaling off New Zealand. Other American ships may have worked the New Zealand grounds in those first years, although they generally avoided Port Jackson. A number of Maori 'curios' in the Peabody Museum, donated by Salem men in 1802 and 1803, were probably collected during visits to the New Zealand coast en route to or from China, or by American crew on British whalers in New Zealand waters.[13]

Whaling was a cosmopolitan industry. Ships were crewed by men from an exotic mixture of countries. Most were English, with some Scots and Irish, a few Welsh, Scandinavians, Russians and Prussians, Spanish and Portugese, a scattering of sailors from China, India and the Caribbean,[14] and a goodly number of Americans. Many whaling ships had American owners (Samuel Enderby, Alexander Champion, Benjamin Rotch and John St Barbe, for example) who had moved to England at or about the time of the American Revolution.[15] During the fighting the British captured or sank most of the American whaling fleet, forcing men in the industry to move elsewhere to make a living. Their captains and crew were often also American by birth, including a surprising number from Nantucket, a small island off the east coast of North America with a population of only five or six thousand, which had declared itself neutral during the Revolution. Bunker, Gardner, Coffin, Starbuck, Swain, Paddock, Hussey, Folger, Worth, Whippey and Chace are all Nantucket names that recur in the crew lists of southern whaling vessels.[16]

Nantucket played a leading role in American whaling, and the industry ruled life on the island. As William Comstock explained in his 1838 account of Nantucket whaling:

> In the present day, every energy, every thought, & every wish of the Nantucketman is engrossed by Sperm Oil and Candles. No man is entitled to respect among them, who has not struck a whale; or at least, killed a porpoise; and it as necessary for a young man who would be a successful lover, to go a voyage round Cape Horn, as it was for a young knight, in the days of chivalry, to go on a tour of adventures, & soil his maiden arms with blood, before he could aspire to the snowy hand of his mistress.[17]

Most of these Nantucket families were Quakers, frugal, hard-working people with a strong kinship ethic. They often took on kinsmen as crew, and shared knowledge about whaling grounds and sailing directions. Such kinship networks, and the collective expertise they built up, help to explain the Nantucket involvement in South Pacific whaling. On their home island they often used black and native Americans as crew,[18] who were forced to pay their debts at sea as indentured servants, and in the Pacific they soon recruited Maori and other Pacific Islanders as sailors (inspiring the character of Queequeg in Herman Melville's famous novel *Moby Dick*). Some of these men later settled on Nantucket itself, in a mixed neighbourhood of black and native Americans and Islanders called 'New Guiney'.[19] Nantucket, along with Norfolk and Britain, are islands that played an important role in early New Zealand contact history. A shared experience of life surrounded by the sea seems to have served as common ground for people from these places.

'Going down on a whale' took a good deal of courage. Benjamin Doane, an American whaler, described this experience in vivid detail:

'What's up, Mr. Taylor?', the captain asked. 'Sperm whale, by thunder, Captain,' said the mate, who had hopped into the main rigging and made out the low bushy spout of a 'still' whale. 'Larboard and waist boats, lower away!' were the captain's orders, as he started up the fore rigging, bound for the topmast crosstrees, to watch manoeuvres. The mate and I got into the larboard boat, hoisted, swung and lowered, and as she touched the water we unhooked the tackles, and the boat's crew followed down and took their places.

It being calm, we could not use sails, so we rowed until we were within about half a mile of the whale and then peaked our oars and took to paddling. For some reason the whale was suspicious and keeping a pretty good lookout, sounding for a few minutes and coming up . . . The first thing we knew he was broadside on, and then we had to lie still and wait until we were 'off his eye'. After two hours or more of such manoeuvring, the whale went down tail towards us, about a quarter of a mile away, and nobody knew where he would come up. Suddenly the mate, with excitement leaping into his eyes, told me to stand up. I did so, taking in my paddle; and as I turned round, the first thing I saw, perhaps a hundred yards ahead and about twenty feet below the smooth surface, was the whale coming up – rising – rising, not directly towards the boat, but to cross quartering the bows. The mate with the steering-oar laid the boat's head to intercept him, and the men kept paddling, while I stood ready, iron in hand.

Then up came that mighty bulk, not six feet away, the spray of his spouting flying almost into my face, his glistening black skin marked with the white scars of former wounds, while huge parasites upon his body, finding themselves lifted from water to air, wiggled for a moment and then settled down close and still. Let anyone inclined to scepticism in religious matters have that sight presented at close quarters for the first time, and I think he would gladly subscribe, heart and soul to the whole Catechism, for one moment's assurance that he would ever see another day. As the boat's stem touched him with all my strength I let him have both irons – and away he went with them, full dash, the poles sticking up in his back like stray hairs on a bald head.

Oh, such a noise as all hands then set up! We clapped our hands and shouted and hurrahed like children, so that we could have been heard three miles away, if anybody had been there to hear. After putting the lance in the crutch, I went aft and took the steering oar, and the mate went forward. Obeying the mate's orders, the men faced forward on their thwarts and hauled line, and as they pulled, one started a song – short verses which he sang alone, and all came in heavy on the long chorus. As we got nearly up to the whale he sounded, and we had to give him the line again . . . About one hundred and twenty fathoms were run out before we felt the line slacken as the whale turned to come up, and the men tried once more to haul line. At first it came in only inch by inch. Gradually, however, it came in faster, and at last the whale broke water a hundred yards ahead and, exhausted after his deep sound, he lay still and spouted. 'Now, boys, drop the line and take

A boat smashed by the whale.

your oars – pull away!' whispered the mate. And I laid the boat's head toward the whale, about two fathoms off and just aft of his fin. The mate let go his lance, and the instant the whale felt it he struck towards boat, the corner of his flukes reached our bows and knocked a hole through, big enough for a man to crawl out through.

The whale was off again like a flash. As the water rushed into the boat the crew ran aft, which trimmed us so by the stern that the hole was almost out of water. The mate sang out, 'Pull off your shirts, boys, and hats too, and give them to me – quick.' Every man climbed out of his shirt, rolled his hat in it and passed the bundle to the mate, who stuffed the whole wad into the hole and braced it in with his feet. That kept out some of the water, anyway. The whale now showed the effects of the lance. His lungs filled with blood; he stopped in distress, and red jets rose from his spout-holes and coloured the water around him. Now, if we were not a wreck ourselves, we could haul alongside and give him another lance; but before we could do so he spouted clear and started off. We should never be able to kill that whale alone – not even prevent him from going off with our irons and line. We held up a waif – a little flag on a short pole – a signal to those who might see it that we had a stoved boat, [and handed the line to the waist boat as our boat slowly sank].

The captain was spying us from the ship's fore-topsail yard, and in about an hour the bow boat with four men came to us, and the mate and I got into her and put off to help Mr. Thomas kill the whale, leaving the crew of our boat still clinging to their oars. But the captain, seeing that all hands were not taken out of the water, sent the starboard boat after them, which picked them up, took the stoven boat in tow and returned to the ship, in time for a late dinner.[20]

Opposite above: *Boats approaching a whale.*

Opposite below: *The harpooner attacking a whale at close quarters.*

Once a whale had been killed and towed to the ship, one of the crew climbed onto its back and began to 'cut in' the carcass. According to Doane, at this point 'the water [was] swarming with sharks that are darting about as if raving distracted, crazed by the sight and taste of blood, now launching themselves full length out on the whale's back, and now running head on with stunning force into the ship's side, snapping at slivers or anything they can get hold of'.[21] The blubber was peeled off in a long coiling strip from around the whale's body, hauled up on board and boiled in the try works. In the case of a sperm whale, the head was cut off first, and the spermaceti in the head case baled out into special casks. It was hard, risky work, which left the men filthy and exhausted.[22] Their reward, like that of the sealers, depended on their efforts, for they were paid in 'lays', a pre-arranged fraction of the final cargo of oil and whalebone.

For young Maori warriors, the adventure of voyaging in British and American whaling ships, and the challenge of chasing and harpooning whales was often exhilarating. The skills of spear-throwing readily translated into harpooning, and in tribal accounts, whales were cosmological creatures, associated with oceanic voyaging

Bringing the whale alongside the vessel, for 'cutting in'.

and discovery.[23] In addition, beached whales were a prized source of meat, and bone and teeth for the manufacture of weapons and ornaments. Many more young Maori participated in whaling than in the arduous, isolated life of sealing gangs on the far southern coasts and islands.

WHALING VISITS TO THE BAY OF ISLANDS: TEINA AND MAKI'S VOYAGE ON THE *ALEXANDER* 1803–1806

In the earliest days of New Zealand whaling, most vessels headed to grounds north-east of the North Island. The Bay of Islands, with its curving inlets sheltered by a cluster of islands, was one of the finest harbours on the north-eastern coast, and it soon became a popular port of call for British and American whaling vessels. The climate was mild, the fisheries were productive, and extensive gardens were planted on inland volcanic soils. According to tribal accounts, this was one of the first sites of Polynesian settlement in Aotearoa. The people of the area traced their descent from Kupe, the great Polynesian explorer who first circumnavigated the North Island. Kupe had landed at Hokianga on the west coast, leaving behind two taniwha (supernatural guardians) as its headlands. Other founding ancestors included Tuputupuwhenua, in some accounts Kupe's son, a taniwha who had burrowed across the narrow neck of land from Hokianga to the Bay of Islands; Nukutawhiti and Ruaanui, who came from Hawaiki to search for Tuputupuwhenua in the *Maamari* canoe. The kin groups of the Bay also traced lines of descent from Toi through Te Awa-nui-a-rangi and Puhi-moana-ariki of *Mataatua*, linking them to the Bay of Plenty, and from Tamatea of *Takitimu* canoe, linking them to Tauranga and the East Coast.[24]

Not surprisingly, given the wealth of the region, kin groups in the Bay were large and well used to defending their resources. Local politics, which were already volatile, had been further complicated by European arrivals. At the time of Cook's visit to the Bay in late 1769, Ngaa Puhi, the descendants of Puhi-moana-ariki and his grandson Raahiri, were in the process of expanding into the Bay from their strongholds in Hokianga and inland, displacing the previous inhabitants. Members of these groups, Ngaati Pou and Ngaati Uru, were with Marion du Fresne when he breached a tapu in Ngaa Puhi territory during 1772, and they were held responsible for his killing and the French retaliations.[25] Skirmishes followed, and in a series of decisive battles, Ngaati Pou and Ngaati Uru were driven out of the Bay to Whangaroa and Hokianga. While these battles were still raging, the *Daedalus* kidnapped Tuki-tahua and Huru-kokoti off the Cavalli Islands in 1793. This did not improve the Europeans' local reputation, and it was not until almost ten years later that other European ships ventured back into the Bay of Islands.

In 1802, the *Harriet*, commanded by Samuel Rodman Chace, visited the Bay, followed by the *Alexander* (Robert Rhodes) in 1803.[26] The *Alexander* had sailed from Port Jackson to North Cape,[27] where the *Venus*, *Greenwich* and *Albion* (Captain Eber Bunker) were cruising. When the *Alexander* called at the Bay, a young local man joined her crew as a sailor. Upon the ship's return to Port Jackson via Norfolk Island on 1 June 1803, the *Sydney Gazette* reported:

> A youth, about 16 years old, the son of a Chief at the North End of New Zealand went on board the Alexander soon after she arrived off the Coast, and is now landed from that ship: he is very intelligent, and of a good disposition; and, as he resides with the GOVERNOR during the Alexander's stay, it is to be hoped the attention he may receive from all descriptions of persons in the Colony will impress him and his countrymen with such favourable ideas of Europeans as may insure a continuance of the hospitable reception our whalers have met with on that Coast, of which Captain Rhodes speaks in the highest terms; he procures seven or eight tons of very fine Potatoes, and other refreshments; with much assistance from the Natives in wooding and watering, for the most trifling returns. [28]

The Governor at Port Jackson at this time was Philip Gidley King, who had befriended Tuki and Huru at Norfolk Island. The young Maori traveller, 'Teinah' or 'Tyeena' [29] (Teina), may well have been a kinsman of Huru-kokoti, and memories of King were still vivid in the north at the time of the *Alexander*'s arrival. The ship may also have visited Doubtless Bay during this voyage, because the *Sydney Gazette* added that while she was 'cruizing off New Zealand', Tuki came out to the ship. He could still speak some English, and reported that Huru had 'died some time ago' (which was not true, since Huru met the missionary Samuel Marsden many years later), and asked to be remembered to his friends at Norfolk Island.[30]

Teina stayed with King at Government House in Sydney from early June to mid-September 1803. When the *Alexander* left Port Jackson again, he went aboard, laden with gifts (including some pigs[31]), and was soon whaling again off the coast of New Zealand. The *Alexander* had a good voyage on this occasion. A number of whales were taken, and Teina was landed back at the Bay of Islands. It seems likely that Teina's pigs were the first to be introduced to the Bay of Islands. One young pair, a boar that came to be called 'Hani-kura' ('red taiaha', named for its impressive propagating parts) and a sow, 'Te Maro-o-te-kopu' ('the apron of the womb'), was sent to Maahurehure people at Waima in the Hokianga. Thinking that the pigs were atua, they allowed the animals to wander. When the pigs went into kuumara gardens and began to root up the tubers, the people didn't dare to chase them out. As they heard the pigs grunting, Maahurehure became even more convinced that these creatures were supernatural in origin. When the pigs began to breed, they gelded some of the young boars, just as dogs were gelded to prevent them from becoming a nuisance. Finally, at a meeting, Maahurehure decided to kill some of their pigs and cook them in an earth oven. After feasting on the pork, the chiefs agreed that 'This is good food . . . and if man is to be killed, let him die from this food,' so they let the pigs increase in number as part of the food supplies at Waima.[32]

Although people in the Bay of Islands remembered Captain Rhodes for his gift of pigs, there were also less positive aspects to his visit. When the *Alexander* returned to Sydney in mid-May 1804, after visiting Norfolk Island, there was a flurry of complaints against the ship's crew and captain. Governor King convened a court of enquiry to examine Rhodes on charges of malpractice and excessive violence, viz:

> Breaking the ship's articles and neglecting the object of the voyage, and thereby injuring the interests of the owners of the said ship to the evident disadvantage of the Memorialists; and firing on the Natives of New Zealand, and flogging them on board the ship; and diverse other complaints exhibited in the said memorial.[33]

Rhodes was evidently not convicted, for soon after he sailed from Port Jackson again, with the Danish sailor Jorgen Jorgensen as first mate. They went to Adventure Bay and then to the Derwent, where a large number of right whales were harpooned; returning to Sydney on 14 December, where Rhodes enjoyed a high-spending lifestyle.[34] On 27 February 1805, the *Alexander* left for the fishery en route to England with a cargo of 200 tons of oil, 14,000 sealskins, some kangaroo skins and 22 tons of elephant seal oil. After a brief stay at Norfolk Island, where Rhodes tried to carry off some convicts, they visited the Bay of Islands. There Teina 'solicited mostly earnestly' to be allowed to re-join the ship. He went cruising on the *Alexander* off the north end of the North Island, where the *Harriet*, *Ann*, *Elizabeth and Mary*, *John Sebastian*, *Adonis*, *Britannia*, *Hannah and Eliza* and *Scorpion* were also fishing.[35] Teina became convinced that the salted beef and pork on board was human flesh. One day while the cooper was making a cask, he told Teina that it was for his body, once he had been killed, butchered and salted. Teina was terrified and could neither eat nor sleep. When the ship called at Norfolk, the sailors took pity on him and showed him oxen and sheep, trying to convince him that they were not really cannibals, and that they did not in fact intend to eat him.

After several months on the fishery, the *Alexander* returned to the Bay of Islands, where Jorgensen reported that 'we almost lost our ship in a skirmish with

A whaler's-eye view of Maori in waka — scrimshaw with portraits of Maori.

the natives'.[36] In 1805, according to his account, the lands around the Bay were divided among three chiefs: Tookahoorooh (Tuukahuru?), Kovow (Ko Whao) and Tippohee (Te Pahi). Teina had warned them against Tuukahuru, who he said was violent and deceitful (although the chief's hostility towards Rhodes and his men was probably due to the shootings and floggings that had marred the *Alexander's* previous visit). One day Jorgensen sent a party ashore to get water and stayed with the ship's boat, guarding pieces of hoop iron that Rhodes had given him to pay the local men for carrying and loading the casks. Without warning, a group of warriors swooped down on the boat and took the iron. When a fleet of armed canoes began to converge on the beach, Jorgensen called his men back to the boat and they rowed frantically for the *Alexander*. As they came alongside, Captain Rhodes, who had 'a perfect contempt for the natives', leaped into another boat with five men and one cutlass and headed for the beach, where he confronted one of the warriors, wresting an English tomahawk from him and throwing it into the bushes. Jorgensen had followed in his boat, bringing more sailors armed with muskets. As Rhodes came under attack, they tried to assist him, but their guns would not fire because the gunpowder was wet, and they were forced to beat a hasty retreat back to the *Alexander*. In their absence (according to Jorgensen's account), two or three hundred warriors had boarded the ship and were fighting a pitched battle with the sailors. They swarmed up onto the deck, where Jorgensen seized a rangatira named Whao and bundled him into the ship's cabin as a hostage. The sailors now drove the attackers off the deck and manned the cannons, firing one gun into the retreating war party, which did 'terrible execution'. Shortly afterwards a young man, Maki (the son of Whao's brother the high priest 'Marquus' [Maakuu?]), came back on board to say that if his uncle were freed, his people would load water onto the ship without charge, an offer that Rhodes accepted with alacrity.

When the *Alexander* left the Bay, Teina and Maki were still on board. According to Jorgensen, 'We faithfully promised to return them to their native land in eighteen moons. Their parents seemed extremely anxious about them, not being wholly free from suspicion that we might be inclined to eat them!'[37] They sailed east across the Pacific to Cape Horn, where a tremendous storm drove the ship almost three thousand miles off course and forced them to turn back to Tahiti. Thus Teina and Maki became the second Maori pair to visit Tahiti, almost forty years after Te Weherua and Koa of Totara-nui had been left there by Captain Cook. Jorgensen described the 'stately and elegant' women of the island, and 'King' Pomare from Raiatea, with his 'Swiss Guard' of two hundred warriors recruited from other islands (part of the Polynesian diaspora of those early whaling years), and even as far away as Peru. As they left Tahiti, a chief from the island and his young friend also joined the vessel. From Tahiti they sailed to Brazil, where the *Alexander* spent three months in the dockyard and the crew almost mutinied, then to St Helena, where they waited a further three months for a convoy to protect them from French warships on their way to England.

The *Alexander* arrived at Portsmouth on 13 June 1806, and in London at the end of that month. Most of her oil had leaked out of the barrels on board, and the sealskins were also badly damaged. Most had to be dumped, and the owners of the vessel were declared bankrupt. Rhodes, who had run up large bills during the voyage, was thrown into a debtors' jail, and many of the crew were left destitute. Teina, Maki and the two Tahitians received no payment for their work and were left so short of food and clothing that Teina soon fell ill and died (although in one version of this story, Jorgensen claimed that Teina had joined Pomare's people at Tahiti). On 13 July, Jorgensen wrote to Sir Joseph Banks 'on Behalf of two Otaheitean Boys and one New Zealand Boy, who certainly all will be miserable as they are afforded neither the least Protection nor Assistance except you Sir should be good enough to take them under your Care'. Banks obligingly paid for new sets of clothing and lodgings (which he noted cost '22 shillings a week & the Landlady Compleins of their appetites'[38]), and placed them under the care and instruction of the Reverend Joseph Hardcastle, the treasurer of the London Missionary Society, while trying to arrange their return to New South Wales, where Governor King and the Reverend Samuel Marsden could look after them.[39] Jorgensen recorded in his memoirs that, after some months in London, both of the Tahitians also died. Only Maki remained, 'who being a tolerable carpenter, kept himself profitably employed'. Shortly after, however, Maki was kidnapped by a notorious crimp (an agent who supplied labour to the ships) and sold to work without pay for the captain of another British vessel.[40] Jorgensen had meanwhile gone home to Copenhagen, which was being bombarded by the English, and joined a vessel that went to war on English shipping.[41]

GOVERNOR KING AND TE PAHI

In 1804, the numbers of whaling ships in New Zealand waters rose sharply. American interest in the southern fishery was growing. When war broke out again in Europe in 1803 and attacks on British shipping off South America increased, Port Jackson became a safe haven for the whalers,[42] and more European ships visited northern New Zealand. In 1804, for instance, a government vessel, the *Lady Nelson* (Lieutenant James Symons), visited New Zealand when rough seas drove her off Norfolk Island. After brief stops at the Three Kings and North Cape, the ship anchored in June 1804 off Cape Brett in the Bay of Islands. Symons sent a boat ashore for wood and water, and two hundred people came out in canoes to barter potatoes, vegetables, and mats for scraps of paper, button tops and old nails. The next day the lieutenant was offered a pig for a new razor, but a chief asked for it back, saying the animal had been a gift from Captain Rhodes (of the *Alexander*, who had delivered Teina with his gift of pigs to the Bay earlier that year). Shortly after this, Symons decided to set sail because too many people were swarming over his vessel. He sailed the *Lady Nelson* to the Hauraki Gulf, then back up the east coast into a bay opposite the Cavalli Islands, where wood and water were collected. There a prisoner named James Cavanagh ran into the bush, becoming the first white man to live in this part of the country.[43]

During some of these visits, more young Maori joined the ships. In late 1804, for instance, the *Hannah and Eliza*, a New Bedford whaler commanded by Micajah Gardner, arrived off North Cape in Muriwhenua. A local man came on board for a cruise, during which a whale was harpooned and processed. Several weeks later another local man joined the ship, and two more whales were killed and 'tried down'. This man evidently stayed on the *Hannah and Eliza* during visits to Norfolk Island and Port Jackson, and at least until the ship returned nine months later to Muriwhenua. During her cruises off Northland in 1804–06, the *Hannah and Eliza* spoke fifteen other ships,[44] some of which also took on Maori crew members. The *Hannah and Eliza* met local people in canoes on a number of occasions, trading for potatoes, turnips and other goods. In January 1806 she visited the Bay of Islands, where the *Carleton*, *Ann*, *Aurora* and *Brothers* were at anchor, then sailed via North Cape and Norfolk Island around Cape Horn and back to New Bedford.[45] The *Atlantic*, one of the ships the *Hannah and Eliza* met off North Cape during 1805, also had 'New Zealanders' in her crew, and during a stay in Port Jackson in late 1806 one of these men was killed by a lightning strike in Sydney Harbour (the verdict at his inquest was 'Death by the Visitation of God').[46]

These visits by young Maori to Sydney reawakened Governor King's interest in New Zealand, and he decided to forge new links with northern Maori leaders. In April 1805, he wrote to Earl Camden in London:

> I beg to add that from the Information of the Masters of those Ships that have for the last Four Years frequented the North-East part of New Zealand, I found that the quantity of seeds and other articles I gave the two New Zealanders who visited

A view of Port Jackson from Point Dawes.

Norfolk Island in 1794, and remained there Nine Months, have turned to a very beneficial account, not only for their own advantage, but also in supplying the Whaling Ships very liberally with potatoes and other productions derived from what my Two Visitors, whom I conducted to their Homes in 1794, took with them. The frequent intercourse those vessels have had with that part of New Zealand has been very advantageous. The New Zealanders have gone on board their vessels, assisted them in procuring Oil, and are found a very tractable People.

The many vessels that have put into the Bay of Islands and other parts of that coast have never, as far as I have learn'd, had any altercation with the natives, but have received every kind office and assistance in procuring their Wood and Water, &c., at a very cheap Rate in Barter . . .[47]

At the same time, King sent instructions to Captain John Piper, the commandant on Norfolk Island, to send by any trustworthy whaler proceeding from Norfolk to the north-east coast of New Zealand, 'Ten to Twenty Sows and a sufficient number of Boars to be given to the most powerful Chief or person in the place they may touch at for the express purpose of Breeding, & at the same time putting on board a sufficient quantity of Maize and Bran for their support'.[48] A month later, he issued a 'Government and General Order' that was published on the front page of the *Sydney Gazette*:

Whereas a number of Otaheitans and Sandwich Islanders have been brought from Otaheite . . . and several New Zealanders being brought here and left by South Sea Whalers from the East Coast of that Island; and it being intended by the Persons who have hitherto been allowed to frequent the Islands in Bass's Straits to send some of these credulous people to that place where their Treatment and Return are very suspicious and doubtful; and it being of the utmost consequence to the interest and safety of Europeans frequenting those Seas, and more particularly the South Sea Whalers, that these people should suffer no ill Treatment, but, on the contrary, experience every kindness until they can return to their native country; It is, therefore, hereby strictly forbid sending any Otaheitan, Sandwich Islander, or New Zealander from this Settlement to any Island or other part of this Coast, on any Sealing or other Voyage, or to any place to the Eastward of Cape Horn . . .

. . . During their stay here, those whose service they are employed in are not to beat or ill use them; but if their Employers; or those who brought them to this Colony, are not able to maintain and employ them, they are to report it to the Governor, who will take measures for their employment and maintenance until they can be sent home. And it is to be clearly understood that all such Otaheteans, &c., are protected in their properties, claims for wages, and the same redress as any of His Majesty's Subjects.[49]

This proclamation is significant, for it extended to Maori (and other Pacific Islanders) some of the civil rights of British subjects, long before the signing of the Treaty of Waitangi.

Te Pahi, a leading Hikutuu rangatira, was one of the first chiefs in New Zealand to become involved in King's diplomatic initiatives. As Sir Joseph Banks noted on the basis of King's reports, 'the South Whalers have . . . been in the habit of

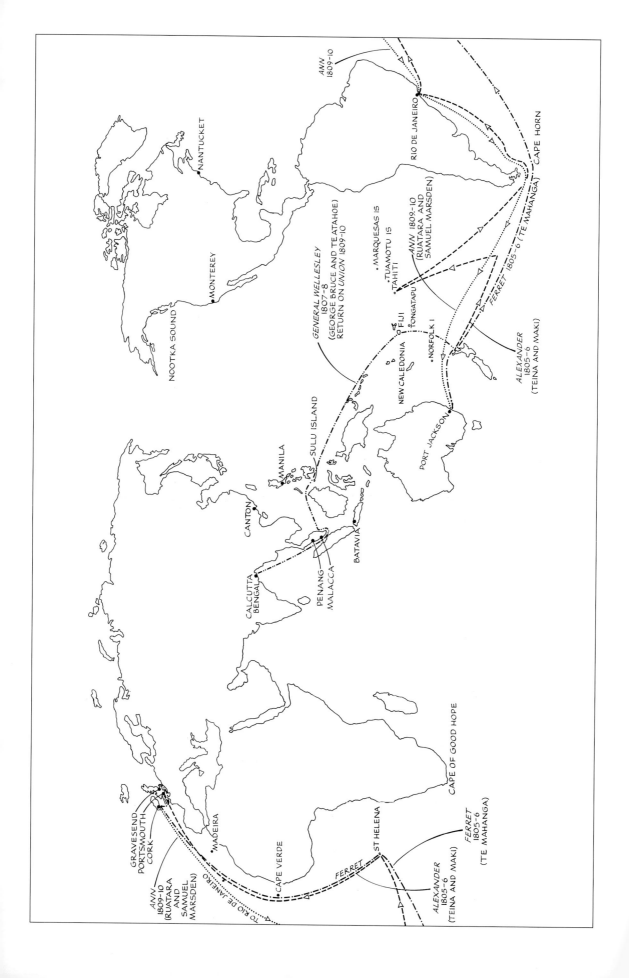

NANTUCKET

NOOTKA SOUND

MONTEREY

ANN
1809-10

RIO DE JANEIRO

CAPE HORN

GENERAL WELLESLEY
1807-8
(GEORGE BRUCE AND TE ATAHOE)
RETURN ON UNION 1809-10

MARQUESAS IS
TUAMOTU IS
TAHITI

ANN 1809-10
(RUATARA AND
SAMUEL MARSDEN)

FERRET 1805-6 (TE MAHANGA)

FIJI
TONGATAPU
NEW CALEDONIA
NORFOLK I

ALEXANDER
1805-6
(TEINA AND MAKI)

SULU ISLAND

MANILA

PORT JACKSON

CANTON

CALCUTTA
BENGAL

PENANG
MALACCA

BATAVIA

CAPE OF GOOD HOPE

MADEIRA

CAPE VERDE

ST HELENA

GRAVESEND
PORTSMOUTH
CORK

ANN
1809-10
(RUATARA
AND
SAMUEL
MARSDEN)

TO RIO DE JANEIRO

FERRET

FERRET
1805-6
(TE MAHANGA)

ALEXANDER
1805-6
(TEINA AND MAKI)

visiting the Bay of Islands for Refreshments & have Obtaind besides wood & water Potatoes both Sweet & the Common sort, said to have been Left behind by Capt Cook & fish in abundance They have always been well Receivd there by the Cheif [of] Ta-Poonah.'[50] Te Pahi had his headquarters at Te Puna on the Purerua Peninusula, where Ngaati Pou had formerly resided. One of his wives, Ngaaraa, was a woman of Ngaati Uru, a related group that had been driven from the Bay after the killing of Marion du Fresne, and Te Pahi often visited her people at Whangaroa.[51] He may also have been close to Tuki-tahua, for he had a son named Tuki, and certainly he knew a good deal about Governor King. In any case, Te Pahi decided to ally himself with the Europeans, and extended his protection to the whalers.

Soon after the *Alexander* first visited the Bay, Te Pahi sent one of his sons, 'Ma-Tara' (Maa-Tara), on a British whaler, Captain Skelton's *Ferret*, 'in order that he might see the English at their settlement'.[52] In December 1804, en route to Port Jackson off North Cape, the *Ferret* spoke the *Hannah and Eliza*. Micajah Gardner, who commanded that ship, wrote in his log: 'Ferret Capt Scilton Came Long Side in which was One of the New Zeland Princes that Capt. Skilton took On board at the Bay of Islands he appeard to be Vary happy & well contented on bord the ship.'[53]

Maa-Tara arrived at Port Jackson in June 1805, shortly after Governor King had issued his proclamation.[54] He was taken to Govenment House and introduced to King, who described his visit as follows: 'In consequence of the great intercourse of the South whalers with the natives of the Bay of Islands, on the N.E. part of New Zealand, some of the lower orders of them have been occasionally brought to Sydney, and among them a youth said to be the son of a powerful chief at the Bay of Islands who had always been extremely hospitable to the whalers.'[55] During Maa-Tara's visit, Governor King invited all the Pacific Islanders then living in Sydney (including Maa-Tara and other unnamed New Zealanders) to a meeting at Government House on 5 July 1805, where he questioned them about their situation and assured them of redress for any ill-treatment. King offered a passage home or training in European trades to any of them who wanted it. According to his report they left Government House well pleased with his concern for their well-being.[56]

King gave Maa-Tara tools and other gifts for his father and, towards the end of July 1805, sent him home on the *Venus*, a small Calcutta brig commanded by William Stewart. On 24 July, he wrote a note to Captain Piper: 'The Native Boy Myty, returns to New Zealand under Mr. Stewart's promise to deliver him to his Father, who I understand is Chief of a district in the Bay of Islands, where the Whalers frequent, I request you will give him two female and one male swine with two female and one male Goat from Government Stock, to be landed with him, for which the Master of the Venus will give receipts, as well as for Maize to feed them on the Voyage.'[57]

Opposite: *Voyages of Maori explorers, 1805–1810.*

'Myty' (or maitai, literally 'from the sea') was the term given by northern Maori to Europeans, and Maa-Tara had evidently adopted this name to commemorate his adventures on the *Ferret* and his stay in the European colony. The *Venus* sailed from Port Jackson to Norfolk Island, where Piper provided livestock and grain, according to King's instructions. From Norfolk they sailed to the Bay of Islands, where Stewart delivered Maa-Tara, and two sows and two goats as gifts from Governor King to his father.[58] Over the next few months Piper despatched more breeding stock from Norfolk to New Zealand. The *Adonis*, commanded by Robert Turnbull, sailed from Port Jackson in September, collecting eighteen sows and two boars at Norfolk as 'a present to Tip-pa-he'[59] and delivering them safely to the Bay of Islands at about the same time.[60] Te Pahi and four of his sons decided to thank Captain Piper and Governor King for these gifts in person, and boarded the *Venus* in mid-September 1805. By the time the *Argo* (John Bader) arrived at the Bay of Islands in October with six sows and two boars from Norfolk for Te Pahi, therefore, he found that he was gone; and when Bader called back at the Bay in March 1806, he found the settlement at Te Puna deserted.[61]

┌─────────────────────┐
│   │
│   *Fourteen*   │
│   │
└─────────────────────┘

JOHN SAVAGE AND TE MAHANGA

Shortly after Te Pahi and his sons had left on their trans-Tasman adventure, the *Ferret* under Captain Skelton returned to the Bay, arriving there on 20 September 1805. Te Puna was still occupied at that time, and John Savage, one of the passengers on board the ship, later wrote a vivid, detailed account of life around the settlement. A military surgeon with a royal commission, who had arrived at Sydney in 1803, Savage had settled at Parramatta, where he acquired several farms and became a justice of the peace in addition to his medical duties. He carried out a successful smallpox inoculation campaign in the colony, annoying the Principal Surgeon, who had him court-martialled for refusing to attend a woman in childbirth. Savage had appealed for his case to be heard in London, and when Governor King agreed, he left Port Jackson with his wife and another couple on the *Ferret*.[1] Despite this apparent disgrace, King had provided Savage with a letter of introduction to Sir Joseph Banks, which explained the circumstances of his case but commended him to Banks as 'much esteemed here by myself, particularly so by Paterson & indeed the greater part of all the Officers & Colony'.[2] The missionary Samuel Marsden, who was also a friend of Savage's, took care of his farms and stock during his absence from Port Jackson.

Savage's hundred-page description of the Bay of Islands, *Some Account of New Zealand*, was the first book to be devoted entirely to New Zealand. It began with a dedication to his patron, Earl Fitzwilliam, a portrait of the chief 'Tiarrah' (Te Aara), and an Arcadian poem:

> Remote in Southern Seas an Island lies,
> Of ample Space, and bless'd with genial Skies;
> Where shelter'd still by never-fading groves,
> The friendly Native dwells, and fearless roves;
> Where the tall Forest, and the Plains around,
> And Waters wide, with various Wealth abound.[3]

The *Account* is an important early account of northern Maori life, based on Savage's brief visit and his conversations with his shipmates, especially Te Mahanga, a young man who accompanied him to England. It found a ready audience, for

331

English interest in New Zealand was growing. By 1805, at least sixteen vessels, most of them from London, were whaling off North Cape, and many of these visited the Bay of Islands.[4] Savage's book received favourable reviews in Edinburgh, Paris and London. It is summarised here under the main categories that John Savage used to order his 'Description of the Religion and Government, Language, Arts, Manufactures, Manners and Customs of the Natives'.

SAVAGE'S ACCOUNT OF THE BAY OF ISLANDS
1805

First appearances
Savage began his *Account* with a description of the ship's arrival at North Cape and the Bay of Islands, complete with coastal profiles and suggestions for entering the Bay and anchoring safely. He commented that his first sight of local people upset all his preconceptions of Maori:

> In a country that has been described as being peopled by a race of cannibals, you are agreeably surprised by the appearance of the natives, who betray no symptom of savage ferocity, and by the patches of cultivated ground in the neighbourhood of the bay; on each of which is seen a well-thatched hut, and a shed at a little distance.
>
> These are the appearances observable from the ship; which, together with the abundant supply of fish and potatoes brought on board by the natives, tend forcibly to remove the prejudices you have imbibed from former accounts of this country and its inhabitants.[5]

Despite these fair appearances, however, he warned visiting captains to keep their firearms on hand and not to allow too many local people on board at any one time, for they were tempted by iron and might try to take over the vessel.

Around the anchorage at Te Puna, Savage described the country as almost bare of wood, although 'there are immense forests at fifteen or twenty miles distance', containing a fir tree 'which grows here to an amazing height, and of such dimensions, as to admit of being formed into a canoe capable of containing thirty persons, or in other words, five and six feet diameter'. Since the accounts from Marion du Fresne's expedition, this was the first significant description of the kauri, New Zealand's most valuable building timber. He also noted a hardwood tree more than a foot in diameter, from which weapons were made (probably the akeake). The woods were said to be full of birds, including many varieties of cockatoos and parrots, but around Te Puna there was little bird life, only large pigeons (kuukupa, as they were known in the north of New Zealand), which had beautiful plumage and were delicious to eat.

Around the Bay there were several villages and many scattered huts. Almost every small inlet where canoes could be hauled up had its little settlement of one or two families. Savage described the local flax, with its strong, silky fibres, four

Cape North, West 25 Miles.

Entrance to the
Bay of Islands.
Point Pocock, or N.W.Point, S. by W. 6 Miles.

Cape Brit, West by South, 7 Leagues.

Rock at the extremity of Cape Brit, S.E.by S. 2 Miles.
Cape Colville, South 20 Miles.

John Savage's coastal views of the Bay of Islands.

or five feet long, and fernroot, or 'haddawai' (aruhe), which before the introduction of potatoes had been 'almost their only esculent vegetable'. Interestingly, Savage did not mention kuumara, taro or yams growing at Te Puna, nor the presence of any pigs. He did, however, describe the Polynesian dog, or 'coraddee' (kurii), 'usually black and white, with sharp, pricked up ears, the hair rather long, and in figure a good deal resembling the animal we call a fox-dog'. The local fisheries were abundant, with 'uncommonly fine' snapper and bream, excellent crayfish and crabs, and tasty oysters, with cockles, mussels and other shellfish providing 'a great variety of rare and beautiful shells for the cabinets of the curious'.[6] He added that there was great scope for mineralogical investigations in the Bay, although the people there did not work metal. They used a hard, green, semi-transparent talc (pounamu) for most of their tools and ornaments, although this was already losing value as iron became increasingly available.

Settlement at Te Puna
Savage noted that the settlement at Te Puna extended from the coast to a small, steep island offshore, and consisted of about a hundred dwellings. These houses were about five feet high, with wattled walls lined with rushes, a single entrance,

and roofs thatched with 'strong bladed grass'. Each had a cooking shed nearby, with four posts about five feet high, covered by a flat roof thatched with rushes. Each coastal dwelling also had a small garden, but on the island there were no cultivations. This served as headquarters for Te Pahi and his close kinsfolk, and as a retreat in times of fighting. Te Pahi had a well-constructed house there, and an arsenal full of war mats, spears and other valuable items. Near his house stood a small storehouse elevated on a single post, which Savage likened to a dovecote. In this structure, he was told, Te Pahi had confined one of his daughters for several years, because 'she had fallen in love with a person of inferior condition'. During this confinement she could neither stand up nor stretch at full length, and her food was brought to her in a trough. Chastened by this punishment, this daughter eventually made a suitable marriage, but Savage commented that 'This barbarous cage, which is ornamented with much grotesque carving, still remains as a memento in terrorem to all the young ladies under Tippeehee's government'.[7]

The people
Savage was greatly impressed by the people at Te Puna. He considered them to be 'of very superior order, both in point of personal appearance and intellectual endowments'. The men were strong and well proportioned, and generally between five feet eight and six feet high. They had open faces, expressive of 'undaunted courage, and a resolution not easily shaken', although he thought that some of the older people were capable of dissimulation. They disliked alcohol and avoided intoxication. Accordingly, it seemed to Savage that many of them lived to a great age, although he cautioned that 'it is impossible to speak with certainty on the subject, there being no positive criterion for determining the age of man'. Their skin colour ranged from dark chestnut to brunette, and the women were attractive, according to their compatriots' ideas of beauty:

> Their features in general are regular and pleasing, with long black hair, and dark penetrating eyes. The tattooing of their lips, and the quantity of oil and red earth with which they anoint their persons and hair, would not be agreeable to the taste of a refined European; but I can conceive to a New Zealand lover, their well-formed figure, the interesting cast of their countenance, and the sweet tone of their voice, must render them extremely desirable companions, to soothe his cares, and strew his path through life with flowers; for savage life has its cares and perplexities as well as that of the polished native of the most enlightened country.[8]

Religion
Savage commented that the people in the Bay were divided into classes of priests, warriors and commoners, each distinguished by 'devices variously tattooed on their faces and persons'. The people paid homage to the sun, the stars and especially the moon, which they believed to be inhabited by a man who long ago had visited New Zealand (evidently a reference to Rona, the 'man (or woman) in the

An engraving of a hei tiki, from Savage's
Account.

A New Zealand Deity.

moon' of Maori legend). Savage believed that the greenstone tiki illustrated in his book was an image of this 'protecting deity', worn by both men and women around their necks, particularly in times of danger. When they greeted the rising sun in the morning, they spread their arms and bowed their heads 'with the appearance of much joy in their countenances, accompanied with a degree of elegant and reverential solemnity'. At this time they sang a cheerful, harmonious song, while at sunset the song was mournful, led by one person and with all the others joining in the chorus. Savage thought that the song sung to the moon was sad, blending anxiety and adoration.[9] Many early sources other than Savage, including Thomas Taylor, the runaway sailor at Hauraki, have claimed that Maori 'worshipped' the sun and moon. Maori seem to have greeted the sun at sunrise and farewelled it at sunset, but little is known of the beliefs involved in these ceremonies.

Savage also noted a number of practices related to tapu, although he had no knowledge of that term. For several days after cutting or combing their hair, people were fed by their relatives, and they would not allow their heads to be touched with food, nor food to be passed over their heads at any time. In the ship, where there were nets filled with potatoes slung between the beams, no-one would sit there. If anyone was led to that part of the ship, 'they always expressed their disgust in the strongest manner, and . . . nothing but force could induce them to remain in that situation'. (The head, as the resting place of the ancestor gods, was tapu; whereas food was noa, or common.) Savage discovered that a sacred island near Te Puna served as a burial ground. When one of Te Pahi's wives fell ill and was thought to be dying, she was sent to this island with two female attendants who nursed her there until she died. The graves on this island were marked with pieces of wood at the head and foot, and were never disturbed. Savage compared this with the Hindu custom of taking the dying to the Ganges.[10]

Government

Savage commented that 'this country is divided into small principalities, whose chieftains are almost constantly at war with each other'. He thought that 'the form of government of this part of New Zealand, and perhaps of the whole island [was] aristocratical, and hereditary', and that the chiefs on the coast were subservient to those who governed the interior. The people, when they spoke with Savage, described 'their ruler at this part [presumably Te Pahi] . . . as a personage of small note compared with other chiefs dwelling at a considerable distance in the country'. Chiefs in the Bay of Islands were said to walk barefoot, while those in the interior were carried in a kind of barrow on the shoulders of their attendants (so that their tapu feet – waewae tapu – did not touch the ground), and were accompanied by 'some hundreds, or even thousands of dauntless warriors, armed with spears and battle-axes, and decorated with war-mats, feathers &c.'[11]

The chiefs depended for their power upon martial prowess, but they always consulted their elders before going to war, and tried to 'find out how the destinies are disposed towards them'. According to Savage, fighting was prefaced by 'threatening gestures, shouts, grimaces, and other tokens of defiance, which, to an European tactitian, would appear extremely ridiculous, and, to an indifferent spectator, at least ungraceful and unbecoming, though they would strike both as exceedingly terrific'. The elders had great influence, deciding all but military matters independently of the chiefs, although the chiefs could veto the elders on a given matter if they felt disposed to assert their authority.

Civil power was exercised by the elders during the 'short intervals of peace', but Savage considered that justice was usually summary. He gave the example of a chief called 'Awkeeterree' (Au-ki-tere?) who had been absent from the Bay, and on his return discovered that his wife was having an affair. He went in search of her lover, armed with a European cutlass, and when he found him almost severed his head from his body. He did not hurt his wife, but left her and took another consort. Although this man was of 'noble blood', Savage was convinced that he would have been punished by her kinsfolk had he acted contrary to custom. As it was, however, his behaviour was considered laudable, and he was 'applauded for prompt administration of summary justice'.[12] Savage also believed that theft was punished by hanging, although he gave no evidence for this assertion.

According to Savage, in Te Pahi's absence Te Puna was being run by 'Tiarrah,

Drawn by J.Savage.

TIARRAH,
*a Chief of the Bay of Islands,
New Zealand.*

Engraved by d'Evôir.

John Savage's sketch of 'Tiarrah' (Te Aara).

his brother', whose sketch he affixed to the beginning of his narrative. This is of particular interest, for Te Aara was, in fact, Te Pahi's Ngaati Uru uncle by marriage from Whangaroa,[13] who was to play a signficant role in early contact history. Ngaati Uru still thus had influence, if only by marriage, in this part of the Bay. Savage described Te Aara as 'mild, and rather deficient in energy', unlike Te Pahi, who was said to have 'a good deal of the tyrant in his disposition'.[14]

On both religion and government, Savage admitted that he had great difficulty in getting reliable information from local people:

> [T]hey are subjects that, in my opinion, require to be handled with great caution, even by those who are well qualified to treat of them; the less, therefore, according to my judgement, that is said upon either the better; and probably, were we resident among them, we should find this line of conduct necessary to our personal safety.[15]

Character
Savage thought that 'in New Zealand, as in all uncivilized countries, the passions are the principal guide to the actions of its inhabitants', but that these were restrained by the authority of the chiefs, and 'a natural proneness to affection'. He

noted with some surprise that 'a great degree of subordination and affection is observable among them upon all occasions'. Although the people had been described as 'cannibals of the worst description', they ate human flesh only at times of great food scarcity, or when excited by a passion for revenge. He thought that the introduction of potatoes had saved many lives, for the people preferred potatoes to human flesh as food, and now only ate people as an act of vengeance. Even then, 'this . . . is not pursued without limitation. Thus, after a conquest, the victors do not devour the whole of their prisoners, but are content with shewing their power to do so, by dividing the chief of the vanquished tribe among them [so destroying his tapu and that of all his people]: he is eaten, it is true, but I do not believe that food is the inducement.' Savage considered that if a European acted angrily towards them, he might very well be eaten, but if cast defenceless on their shores, he would be unlikely to meet with such treatment.[16]

By and large, the people of the Bay seemed kind and affectionate. On one occasion, a canoe full of women and children had capsized when it was coming out to the ship. The local people on board wept and lamented, while each of the women in the water supported a child. A boat was lowered and soon gathered them up, and when the shivering survivors were brought on board the ship, 'the congratulations on their escape, and their kind and soothing attentions, were such as would by no means have disgraced the moral character of the most refined European; those who had remained on board immediately stripping themselves of their mats to cover their friends or relatives'.

The ordinary ceremony of greeting involved 'bringing the noses of the parties in contact' (hongi), but when people left on a journey they also embraced and wept for a long time, uttering 'a variety of plaintive sounds'. When they returned, the same ceremony was repeated, although if the absence had been long, the female relatives of the traveller also 'scratch and disfigure their faces with broken pieces of shell, so as to produce considerable suffering'. As Savage drily remarked, 'this custom must prove exceedingly distressing, if the male branches of a family were much in the habit of wandering'.[17]

Marriage and children
According to Savage, men commonly married several sisters at one time. Te Pahi, for instance, 'had four sisters [although 'tuahine' meant 'closely related woman of the same generation'] as his wives, besides several concubines: he was far advanced in years, and had become paralytic [one of his legs was lame]; a combination of these circumstances had probably induced him to try the effects of a change of air'. Children were regarded with great affection by their parents, and were robust, lively and with 'pleasing countenances'. They were carried about sitting astride their mothers' shoulders while she held one of the child's hands and with the other it played with the ornaments on her head — feathers, shells, buttons and sharks' teeth. Small children had their ears pierced, and the holes were gradually stretched with soft packing until they were quite large and could carry small tools as well as

ornaments. Tattooing, though, was not begun until they were eight or ten years old, because of the dangers of inflammation and fever. The patterns were marked out with red earth or a burnt stick, then punctured with a piece of sharp bone and some vegetable fluid was inserted to make the lines permanent. As well as the face, the 'pantaloons' were often highly decorated, to the great pride of the wearer. Those intended to be religious experts wore only a small square patch of tattooing over the right eye (an interesting comment), while women carried just a small spiral figure on either side of the chin, a semi-circular figure over each eyebrow, and two or three lines on each lip to make them seem thicker.[18]

Clothing and ornaments
Most people ordinarily wore a thickly woven, shaggy mat, which reached halfway down the thigh. Savage commented that, from a distance, a group of squatting people looked like a hamlet of thatched huts. Fine, glossy mats decorated with fringes were also worn and fastened at the neck; or war mats, woven very tightly and ornamented with a 'Vandyke' border (taaniko). When dress cloaks were worn, the hair was also dressed with red earth and fish oil, combed up and secured in a knot on the crown of the head with 'ligatures and bodkins', and decorated with feathers, sharks' teeth, pieces of bone, European buttons, beads and bugles. The same items were also made into necklaces, as were pieces of reed. The 'man in the moon' (or tiki) was always worn in full dress, or indeed on most occasions, and small versions of this ornament were worn by children. On formal occasions, the men carried a whalebone or hard black stone 'waddy' (patu), and men and women alike anointed their bodies with red earth and fish oil, especially if they wanted to look particularly splendid. The 'priests' wore little of this red earth, however, and very few ornaments. Children went naked until they were about eight years old, although from infancy they wore ear ornaments.[19]

Cultivation
Savage reported that, by 1805, the people around Te Puna were growing only potatoes (perhaps because these were preferred by the whalers). He did not know when these had been introduced, but noted that they were propagated from seed potatoes, which had been renewed on several occasions. He added, 'I never met with that root of a better quality.' The gardens 'are not planted with European regularity', but were highly productive, cropping twice a year, and the light soil was kept well cultivated with wooden spades. Most of the crop was kept for bar-ter with European ships. By 1805, people were desperate for iron – 'they would suffer almost any privation, or incovenience, for the possession of it'. Accordingly, they ate little of their own produce, but kept it on platforms erected each on a single post about ten feet high. Potatoes were brought out to the ships in flax baskets from eight to thirty pounds in weight, and bartered with considerable virtuosity. Although they had other European vegetables in seed, these were less valuable for barter and were not being grown, although cabbages grew wild everywhere.[20]

Fishing

Both men and women went fishing. Savage noted that 'the women here are as expert at all the useful arts as the men, sharing equally the fatigue and the danger with them upon all occasions, excepting war; in which, though they undergo considerable fatigue, they do not participate in the danger'. Large fish were speared, but most were caught with large nets or excellent fishing lines made of flax, with barbed hooks made from the outer rim of the ear-shell (paaua). These were baited with limpets or raw fish, and 'from the great dexterity of the fishermen, and the vast quantity of fish, with which this harbour abounds, the natives of this part are most abundantly supplied with this excellent article of food'.[21]

Cooking

Most food was roasted or broiled, but fish was cleaned, wrapped in cabbage leaves and tied up with tendrils, then laid on a heated stone and turned occasionally. In this way the fish was cooked in the steam of the leaves, and both the fish and the leaves were eaten together. Potatoes were cooked in a similar fashion. Dog meat was roasted. Since these dogs were not scavengers, Savage agreed that they could be regarded as 'good eating'. Salts and condiments were not used, and people did not overeat:

> Thus it will appear that the operations of a New Zealand kitchen are few, and exceedingly simple, but they accomplish the principal object of all cookery, the action of fire upon the food; and though they would not please the palate of an European, the natives here are perfectly well satisfied with them, and rise from their meals with as much chearfulness as an alderman, and with much more activity.[22]

Canoes

Savage gave an excellent account of local canoes. These were made from the trunk of a kauri tree, hollowed out by adze and usually raised with a plank a foot deep on each side. They were from thirty to sixty feet long, or longer; from two feet six inches to more than five feet wide; and three feet deep. The gunwhale plank was tied to the body of the canoe by ligatures, and the gap caulked with rush or flax. War canoes were ornamented with carving and painting, and held upwards of thirty warriors. Sometimes two such canoes were lashed together, and ten or fifteen of these double canoes made a powerful fleet. Ordinary canoes were rarely more than thirty feet long (a surprising comment – perhaps the war canoes, which were generally much longer, were elsewhere), and sometimes carried a couple of families out to the ship to trade. In this situation, the hull of the canoe was divided by a wattle partition, so that each family had its own section. Canoes carried nets, hooks, lines and paddles, and large anchor stones. 'From the great strength and activity of the natives,' added Savage, 'the canoe is impelled forward with uncommon velocity.'[23]

War and weapons

During his stay at the Bay of Islands, Savage remarked with barely concealed disappointment, 'it did not happen . . . that any warlike operations took place among the natives: this, I conceive, was not the case, from the neighbouring chiefs being at peace with each other, as I believe those "piping times" are rarely known here, but that there did not occur any convenient opportunity for meeting in the field'. Savage's expectation of perpetual hostilities is interesting, and so are his comments on Maori weaponry, largely based on discussions with a local man, 'Moyhanger' (Te Mohanga, according to an early Maori account of him collected by John White;[24] known to his modern descendants as Te Mahanga[25]).

The spear was made of hardwood, about thirty feet long and often pointed at both ends, and was thrown. The 'battle-axe' (tewhatewha), a weapon about five feet long, had a semi-circular head with a sharpened edge and was used as a pike and for deflecting spears. The 'waddy' (patu) was used at close quarters, like a tomahawk; and shields were not used, only war mats. Savage believed that, unlike European weapons, which were sometimes used just for show, Maori weapons 'are rarely formed without their subsequent performance of some death-doing deed, either in the service of the chief, or to execute the vengeance of its owner in cases in individual animosity'. Young men were drilled in warlike exercises, including the prefatory shouts and grimaces that were also used in naval fighting:

> [A]fter the preparatory shouting, grimace, &c. have been carried on in the adverse canoes for some time, the paddles impel the warriors to the contest, which instantly commences with unbounded fury.[26]

Ordinary mats were made of flax, left with a shaggy two-inch outer thatch to keep off the rain; while dress mats were made of untwisted flax, which looked like 'flos silk of a light yellow colour'. War mats were manufactured from tightly twisted flax, rolled on the knee and woven mainly by women, who held the weft in the hand in a ball and passed it alternately through the threads of the warp, pressing it closely together. Patterns were made by using different-coloured threads, or by sewing them in with a needle (if he was referring to taaniko here, the patterns were made by twining not sewing). The men made weapons, tools and musical instruments, carving these with great care. Adzes, chisels, small carving tools and needles were all manufactured from greenstone, although they preferred to use iron, despite the difficulty of keeping an edge on iron tools. At this stage local people were unfamiliar with any method for hardening or sharpening iron.

Language

Savage thought that the language was 'by no means wanting in harmony', possessing 'a considerable degree of softness'. During the voyage to England, with Te Mahanga's help, Savage acquired 'as much practical knowledge of their tongue as would enable me to make myself understood upon most subjects. It is true,' he added, 'he would sometimes laugh at my ignorance and want of comprehension;

but, on the whole, he was so complaisant as to pronounce me a tolerably apt scholar.' The vocabulary published in the *Account* included only a hundred items, plus a set of numerals. It included parts of the body; terms for close kin; commonplace actions including walking, crying, singing and speaking; some colours; terms for time; and counting from one to twenty. Most of these words can be readily identified with contemporary equivalents, but do not suggest that Savage acquired a complex speaking knowledge of Maori. He said that the people counted higher numbers in scores, or with pieces of stick, counting as high as twenty score or 'catteekow-catteekow' (ka tekau ka tekau), after which they simply repeated 'catteekow' a number of times to indicate great numbers:

> [T]hus, were you to enquire the population of their island, the answer would be catteekow, tungata-catteekow, catteekow, repeated ten or a dozen times, constantly clapping the hands, and accompanied with a tone of voice sufficiently expressive of their idea that the number is far beyond their power of ascertaining.[27]

Music and dancing

Savage described local music as melodious, with instruments 'such as afford a variety of pleasing simple notes'. 'Here every man is his own musician,' he remarked, 'he is never at loss for the means of entertainment.' Songs were variously pathetic, amorous and funny. The pathetic songs seemed sad, while amorous songs were accompanied by gestures and grimaces that he considered 'both extravagant and indecent'. The humorous songs were so hilarious 'as, in many instances, to occasion a total suspension of the performance, by the laughter of the audience'. Often, when they sang, people kept time with beating their breasts like 'a sort of natural drum'. A song was often begun by one person, who was then joined by others in chorus, beating their chests in a style of performance called 'aroroikee'.

Musical instruments included flutes, six or seven inches long, inlaid with paaua and carved in patterns, some of which Savage also found indecent. They had three holes on one side and one on the other, and were open at each end. These flutes were often played in the open by groups of performers, making music that was 'simple but pleasing'. There was also an instrument (puutorino) made of two pieces of wood bound together, with a bellied centre, where there was a small hole. The performer blew into one end, occasionally stopping and opening the other end 'to produce some variety in the modulation of the sound'.

Savage thought that local dances were intended to promote cheerfulness, but 'as their modes of expressing cheerfulness are unrefined by education, and unrestrained by the customs of the country, they frequently are such as to violate the laws of delicacy in point of gesture, grimace, and other accompaniments: they are, indeed, so faulty in this respect, that I shall not enter into a description of them'.[28]

General observations

Savage ended his description of life in the Bay of Islands in 1805 with some general observations. He noted that the whalers were already beginning to drive whales away from the coast. The climate in the Bay seemed mild and salubrious, 'for neither the appearance or accounts of the natives indicate the prevalence of disease'. Venereal disease was already established on shore. As a medical man, he thought that 'the captain of a ship might be required to ascertain that his sailors were incapable of communicating a disease which would entail misery upon the future population of a healthy and happy country'. Savage also expressed sympathy for local people in their dealings with European visitors:

> I am inclined to believe, in many instances where disagreement takes place between Europeans and savages, the former are the aggressors. The lowest profligate of Europe fancies himself a superior being, and treats the untaught native of a peaceful isle, as an animal almost unworthy his consideration; he communicates the diseases of civil life, and commits acts of treachery and outrage without the least remorse. Acts of this description are handed down to posterity, by tradition, among the natives, and they revenge the injuries done to their ancestors upon all Europeans that come within their power.[29]

Savage noted that there was a white man living in the Bay (perhaps James Cavanagh, who had run from the *Lady Nelson* in 1804 opposite the Cavallis), who 'shuns all communication with Europeans, and on the approach of a ship retires from the coast to the interior. His country, or the motives that induce him to remain here, are unknown: he is spoken well of by the natives, and has adopted their manners and customs.' Savage had seen this man's wife and one of his offspring, a bashful, flaxen-haired child, on several occasions.[30] He ended by recommending New Zealand as a place for future colonisation – 'the harbours are safe and capacious, the country beautiful, the soil favourable to cultivation; and the natives are in all respects a superior race of Indians'. He thought that the local people would work hard to help new colonists, for 'their intelligence is such as to render them capable of instruction, and I have no doubt but they would prove as essentially useful to a colony established in their country, as the natives of India prove to our Asiatic dominions'.[31]

TE MAHANGA'S VISIT TO LONDON
1806

While he was at the Bay of Islands, John Savage sketched a likeness of the chief Te Aara, and people came from miles around to admire it. Several of these visitors offered to accompany Savage to Europe, and he chose one, 'a healthy stout young man, of the military class, and connected with families of the first consideration in these parts' to travel with him on the *Ferret*. Savage described 'Moyhanger' (Te Mahanga, according to his descendants) as 'a most affectionate kind-hearted creature', and several days before they left the Bay, he came to live on board the ship, where he was visited by his relations. Some approved of his venture, and others disapproved, but Mahanga was unshaken in his resolve. Savage gave him a set of sailor's clothing when he came on board, which he wore with great pride and his relatives examined with obvious admiration. When it came time for the ship to leave, his family came out in a canoe, and his father, 'who is of the religious class', embraced his son and they wept together for about twenty minutes. Mahanga climbed down into the canoe and embraced his mother, weeping and making plaintive noises for about ten minutes more, and then his brother, and sisters, in 'a less ceremonious manner'. After this Mahanga went back on board cheerfully enough.

Savage was disconcerted by these displays of grief, and offered gifts of poultry to Mahanga's father, which were politely refused (although his family took them gladly), assuring the man that there was no need for his son to leave. He found, though, that such farewells were a usual way for kinsfolk to say goodbye, and that 'I should offend all parties by retracting my permission for Moyhanger to accompany me'. As the ship sailed, Mahanga's father and mother kept raising their arms and looking to the sky, 'as if supplicating the protection of a superior power in behalf of their son', until they were lost to sight.

As it happened, the winds were contrary and the ship could not sail out of the Bay that day. When she came back to anchor, Mahanga's family visited the *Ferret*, returning to the vessel on a number of occasions. When the ship finally sailed a few days later, he gazed at the land until darkness fell, and cried, but he 'was determined to be a man: he sung his evening song and retired to rest'. During the voyage to Cape Horn, Mahanga often looked to the west, each day singing his morning and evening song, but he was good-humoured and merry, frequently exercising his talent for mimicry at his shipmates' expense. At the Cape, he was sorry to see the land covered with snow, and 'concluded that he had done wrong in leaving a fine fertile country for one that appeared to be sterile in the extreme'. He enjoyed the passage to St Helena, marvelling at the flying fish and the new kinds of sea bird he saw. Mahanga often swam in the sea when the ship was becalmed, although on one occasion he was almost taken by a very large shark. After he had clambered back on board, the shark followed the ship for a time and he looked down at it, muttering, 'kiooda eka, matta matta, Moyhanger [kuare ika, mate mate Mahanga] – very bad fish to destroy Moyhanger.'[32]

Mahanga was delighted with St Helena, where they arrived in February 1806, admiring the buildings on shore and the many ships at anchor. He danced and sang with delight, repeatedly exclaiming, 'Piannah-miti' (Pai ana, maitai – Very good, very fine). When Savage told him that many potatoes were grown on the island, he was impressed, although when he looked at the soil later he commented, 'kiooda oota, very bad land' (kuare uta – useless land).

As the ship came to anchor, the battery on shore fired a salute. Mahanga clapped his hands over his ears and lay down on the deck, but as the salute continued he gained confidence and soon looked about. When he went ashore, he was astonished by the iron goods on display. He was fascinated by the soldiers, their uniforms and drill. When he first saw a yoke of oxen, he was amazed by their size, and when he noticed a man riding, he found this method of locomotion so ludicrous that he burst out laughing and ran after the rider as he cantered up the valley. Mahanga enjoyed European music, especially the regimental band and the sound of violins. He met Patten, the Governor of St Helena, who impressed him. He soon became bored with the island, however, and stayed on the ship in preference to going ashore. He liked the company of his fellow sailors, and enjoyed catching fish from the deck.

During the voyage to England, Mahanga's shipmates remarked on the acuity of his hearing and sight. He saw sails and could hear a distant gun when no other man on board could perceive them. When the ship finally arrived at Ireland, Mahanga was impressed with the abundant supplies of fish, meat and vegetables, and when they docked at London, in late April 1806, he was astonished by the quantity of shipping. Savage had left the ship at Cork to go straight to London with despatches, and Mahanga grieved at his absence. When the *Ferret* docked in the River Thames, Savage went to meet Mahanga, who was glad to see him again, although somewhat cast down by the size and grandeur of London. 'He told me that in New Zealand he was a man of some consequence, but he saw that in such a country as he was now in, his consideration must be entirely lost.' All the same, he went ashore cheerfully with Savage, and as they walked in the town he admired his surroundings:

> The shops with immense stores of ironmongery excited much of his attention; as we passed houses where those items were presented for sale, he always observed to me, Piannah Oota nue nue tokee [Pai ana uta nui nui toki – a kind of shipboard pidgin, as presented here] – very good country, plenty of iron. Commodities of real utility uniformly claimed his first consideration. The shops that exhibited articles of dress and ornamental finery excited his laughter; while those that displayed substantial cloathing appeared to give him real satisfaction.[33]

The sailors had taught Mahanga to shake hands and say, 'How do you do, my boy,' and when passers-by stood and stared at him, he offered to shake their hand, greeting them with this salutation. They found his appearance frightening, however, and withdrew from his handshake as quickly as possible.

Savage took Mahanga across London on a hackney coach. He was startled when the coach started off, but soon relaxed, and when Savage asked him how he liked this form of transport, he replied, 'Piannah wurrie nuenue yaieda [Pai ana whare, nui nui haere] – Very good house, it walks very fast.' As they crossed to Savage's lodgings on the west side of town:

> [N]othing escaped his observation. The church steeples – the shops – the passengers – the horses and carriages, all called forth some singular remark. Of the height of the steeples he observed, Piannah wurrie tauwittee tuwittee paucoora [Pai ana whare, tawhiti tawhiti ?] – Very good house, it goes up in the clouds. On noticing any singularities, decrepitude, lameness, or infirmity, in a passenger, he always remarked, Kiooda tungata, or Kiooda wyeena [Kuare tangata, kuare

wahine] – Good for nothing man or woman. His eye was constantly seeking articles of iron, cloathing, or food. Of some of the streets he observed, Nue nue tungata, nue nue wurrie, ittee ittee eka, ittee ittee potatoe [Nui nui tangata, nui nui whare, iti iti ika, iti iti potato] – Plenty of men, plenty of houses, but very little fish, and very few potatoes.[34]

As they went along, Mahanga again became despondent, commenting, 'Nue nue Europe, ittee ittee New Zealand' (Europe is large, New Zealand is very small). When they arrived at Savage's lodgings, however, and were greeted by Savage's servant boy, who had been his companion during the voyage, Mahanga soon regained his good humour.

Soon after their arrival in London, Savage took Mahanga to meet Earl Fitz-william, using the young Maori as a means of gaining access to his aristocratic patron. He told Mahanga that the Earl was a chief, and he entered the house with suitable respect. He was pleased by the furniture and paintings, and by the affability of the Earl and his countess, Lord Milton and others of the Earl's noble relatives. Mahanga also approved of Fitzwilliam's face, and when shown a marble bust of the Earl, took a chair and sat examining it attentively for some time, telling Savage that when he returned home he would try to carve a figure just like it. He was not much impressed by the mirrors and fine ornaments, however. Savage noted ruefully, 'While I thought he was admiring the more striking objects, I found he was counting the chairs. He had procured a small piece of stick, which he had broken into a number of pieces to assist his recollection [perhaps an old Polynesian way of counting, since Hitihiti had also used it]. He observed, "Nue nue tungata noho tippeehee – A great number of men sit with the chief."'

Mahanga spent only a few weeks in London before being sent home again on the *Ferret*. He had enjoyed his visit to the metropolis, visiting St Paul's Cathedral with Savage, where he particularly admired the dome and the monuments of great men. He was constantly amused by the people he saw in the streets, particularly a man with two wooden legs, and several very corpulent men, of whom he remarked, 'Tungata nue nue kikie [Tangata nui nui kai kai] – That man has plenty to eat.' He liked the markets, with their large quantities of food, and soon realised that the food was produced elsewhere and brought in carts to the city. He disliked the raucous cries of the vendors, and the noise of the streets, however, commenting, 'Kiooda tungata, or kiooda wyeena [Kuare tangata, kuare wahine] nue une mum mum mum – Bad man or woman to make such a noise.' Earl Fitzwilliam presented Mahanga with a good stock of tools and asked Savage to make sure the young man was instructed in 'the rudiments of the mechanical arts'. Savage showed him how to use the carpenter's and cooper's tools, and when Mahanga said goodbye, holding his hand for a long time and crying bitterly, Savage tried to console him:

> I reminded him of his riches, and the man of consequence he would become upon his return to his own country – of his power to entertain all his friends by a recital of the wonders he had seen, and the knowledge he had acquired: he admitted it all,

and the idea pleased him, but he left me shedding tears, and assuring me that I might expect him again when he had distributed his wealth, and made some family arrangements he considered of material consequence.[35]

Many years later, when Peter Dillon came to the Bay in the *Research* in 1827, he met Mahanga, who by then was known as 'King Charley', the brother of 'queen Terrooloo' and uncle of 'King George' (or Whareumu), the Ngaati Manu leader at Kororareka. Mahanga asked after 'Missi Savage', whom Dillon had recently met as a full surgeon in the East India Company's service at Calcutta. Mahanga told Dillon that, during his visit to London, a friend of Dr Savage, whom he identified as Earl Fitzwilliam, had taken him to see King George, dressed in his New Zealand garments. He had been very disappointed to find both the King and Queen Charlotte bent over with age. They were kind to him and asked him what he wanted most to take home. He told them 'tokees' (adzes) and nails, which he now deeply regretted, for he should have asked for muskets. Queen Charlotte had given him some 'red money' (guineas) from a purse and asked him to perform the New Zealand war dance. When he did so, she seemed frightened, but the King laughed. Mahanga had used some of the Queen's money to get himself a 'wife', named Nancy, who soon became pregnant (indeed it must have been quick, since he was only in London for several weeks). According to Mahanga, she asked him if the child should go to New Zealand when it was born, and whether it would have markings on its face like his own.[36]

Mahanga left London on the *Ferret* on 13 June 1806,[37] just a day after the *Alexander* arrived at Portsmouth with Jorgen Jorgensen, Teina and Maki on board. He is, therefore, the first Maori known to have visited England. The *Ferret* arrived back at Port Jackson in December 1806, and Mahanga made his way back to New Zealand.

Many years later, John White collected an account from a Ngaa Puhi source who spoke of Mahanga's odyssey:

> In the days when our fathers were alive, there were many vessells came down into the Bay of Islands, these came there to procure food for their crews . . . and some of our people were induced to go as sailors, who went out far on the sea, some of whome came back and some of whom were lost for ever, may be these were killed by the Europeans, or by disease, a slave man of the Nga-puhi called Mohanga (accident), and he said [on his return] he had been to the land on the other side of the sea, and that he had seen the King of England, and the many wonders of the land, and he brought back some European tools with him to build houses, Now Mohanga was a slave of the Nga-ti-uru, the tribe who occupied the islands at the Bay of Islands, and at Motu-arohia . . . and they also occupied the Whangamumu Harbour. When a vessell came into the Bay of Islands Mohanga stole an ax, and the master of Mohanga was blamed for the theft, and Mohanga in fear lest he be killed fled to Whangarei, to a tribe residing there called Te Para-whau, with whom he died under the name of King Charles.[38]

Mahanga was not a slave when he left the Bay of Islands, however, for Savage described his father as a priest of aristocratic descent and Mahanga himself as a warrior, while Dillon described him in 1827 as Whareumu's uncle and a significant chief with white sawyers under his protection. The taking of an axe, however, is supported by other contemporary accounts,[39] and for a time he was exiled from the Bay of Islands. By 1827, this punishment had been forgiven and he had returned to his former status. It was as a chief that Mahanga accompanied Dillon on a further adventure to Tonga, Rotuma and Vanikoro.

CONCLUSION

Savage's account of life in the Bay of Islands circa 1805 and Te Mahanga's visit to London was excellent. His account of material life in the Bay was accurate and systematic. When he commented on more abstract matters, Savage admitted that his understanding was limited. His descriptions of local practices, though, were enlivened with particular incidents – the imprisonment of Te Pahi's daughter in a storehouse, for instance, or Mahanga's farewell to his family. It included fascinating details – tohunga whose calling was marked by a small square tattooed over the right eye; inland chiefs being carried around on a kind of barrow. His narrative of Mahanga's visit to London is unforgettable. Although Savage's insight into Maori life was limited by a restricted knowledge of the language, he learned a good deal from Mahanga, despite the fact that they conversed in a kind of pidgin. Given the brevity of his stay in the Bay of Islands, his *Account* was a considerable achievement, a tribute to Mahanga's capacity for instruction and Savage's training as a surgeon.

Fifteen

TE PAHI, GOVERNOR KING, GEORGE BRUCE AND ATAHOE

While John Savage was visiting their home at Te Puna, Te Pahi and his four sons were on their way to Port Jackson. Having decided to visit Governor King to thank him for his gifts of pigs, Te Pahi asked the captain of the sealing brig *Venus*, William Stewart, to carry them to Norfolk Island. Stewart treated them harshly, however, threatening to kidnap Te Pahi's youngest son at the end of the journey to pay for their passage. It seems that Te Pahi did not understand that payment was expected and had offered no recompense for the voyage. Still, Stewart's conduct was in breach of the Government and General Order that Governor King had issued before the *Venus* had left Port Jackson, and when King heard about it, he was furious:

> I am sorry to say [that William Stewart] treated him so ill as to occasion the most bitter reproaches of Tip-a-he and his sons, who accompanied him. Fortunately the kind reception and attention he met with from Captain Piper, Commandant of Norfolk Island, and every person on that island, greatly removed the unfavourable ideas he was impressed with, and which he has often assured me would have been sufficient to have deterred him from the voyage to this place and returning to New Zealand but for the knowledge he had of my treatment of the two New Zealanders, Tookee and Woodoo, who visited Norfolk Island in 1794 [*sic*], and the kindness shown him by Captain Piper, whose absolute authority was requisite to rescue Tap-a-he's youngest and most beloved son from the master of the vessel, who, there is too much reason to apprehend, had destined the son for the payment of the father's passage, although he could not be ignorant that the kindness this family received at our hands would be abundantly repaid to the English whalers frequenting the Bay of Islands. Such wretches are who have no hesitation at committing these acts, and such was the master's conduct as to occasion the observation from Tip-a-he that he considered him as an *emoki* [mookai – war captive, servant] (i.e. of the lower class) as the only excuse for his conduct.[1]

As King noted, Captain Piper treated Te Pahi and his sons with respect and kindness upon their arrival at Norfolk. He looked after them during their brief stay on the island, and when HMS *Buffalo* arrived to collect supplies for Port

349

An engraving of Te Pahi, after an original sketch by G. P. Harris.

Dalrymple (on the north coast of Van Diemen's Land), Piper arranged for their passage on that ship to Port Jackson.[2]

The *Buffalo* sailed from Norfolk and spent a week at the Derwent River (by Hobart), where Te Pahi was entertained by the local officials, Colonel Collins and his officers. Soon after they left the Derwent for Port Dalrymple, the ship was caught in a storm and was forced to put in to Port Jackson instead. When the *Buffalo* arrived there in late November 1805, Lieutenant Houston took Te Pahi and his sons to Government House and presented them to the Governor. Te Pahi was dressed in his own clothes and carried cloaks and a stone patu, which he laid at King's feet, pressing noses with him in greeting. He told King that after Tuki and Huru's sojourn at Norfolk Island, he had promised his father that he would visit 'Kaawana Kingi'. This journey with his sons was in fulfilment of that vow. Te Pahi praised King for the introduction of potatoes to New Zealand, adding that

> leaving New Zealand was much against the wishes of his dependants, but that objection was much outweighed by the probable advantages they would derive from his visit, and concluded by saying that he considered himself under my protection. If I wished him to remain here, go to Europe, or return to his own country, he was resigned to either, and in the most manly confidence submitted himself and his sons to my directions. All this was said in such an imposing manner that no doubt could be entertained of his sincerity.[3]

Once again King found himself impressed and disarmed by Maori chiefly behaviour. He showed Te Pahi around Government House, which provoked 'many exclamations of surprise', and invited him to live there with his family during his visit to Sydney. This invitation included Te Pahi's sons, from the eldest, Tuki (no doubt named after King's companion on Norfolk Island), to the youngest, an eight-year-old boy who seemed to be Te Pahi's favourite.

Te Pahi's stay in Sydney with his sons was recorded by the *Sydney Gazette* and by Governor King in his private papers, official letters and despatches. He was described as a 'friendly chief', with considerable character and bearing. The *Sydney Gazette* described Te Pahi as 'about fifty years of age; 5 feet 11 and a half inches high, and of an athletic form: His countenance is expressive and commanding, though much disfigured by his face being completely *tattowed*.'[4] King's reports were even more admiring:

> Tip-a-he is 5 feet 11 inches high, stout, and extremely well made. His age appears about 46 or 48. His face is completely tattooed with the spiral marks shewn in 'Hawkesworth's and Cook's Second Voyage', which, with similar marks on his hips and other parts of his body, point him out as a considerable chief of Etangatida Etikitia [Rangatira tiketike?] of the first class. To say that he was nearly civilized falls far short of his character, as every action and observation shows an uncommon attention to the rules of decency and propriety in his every action, and has much of the airs and manners of a man conversant in the world he lives in. In conversation he is extremely facetious and jocose, and, as he never reflected on any person, so Tip-a-he was alive to the least appearance of slight or inattention in others.[5]

In a letter to Sir Joseph Banks about Te Pahi's visit, King added, 'His Manners are that of a well bred Gentleman allowing a little for the Country he comes from; he is about 50 Compleatly Tattowed, & possessed of much good natured facetiousness, In short his Company & manners has been highly interesting to us.'[6]

Te Pahi's visit to Port Jackson was no idle journey. He had come to see King, but also to investigate Governor King's society. He and his sons studied European carpentry, gardening (particularly the cultivation of potatoes), spinning and weaving techniques, and social institutions. Te Pahi collected seeds and young fruit trees fanatically. He visited John McArthur's farm at Parramatta for several days, and examined McArthur's 'cloth and woollen manufactory' with close attention. He also met the Reverend Samuel Marsden at Parramatta, whom he quizzed about the Christian God, and who later spoke of Te Pahi's 'Clear, Strong and Comprehensive mind'. It was after this meeting that Marsden first conceived the idea of taking a mission to New Zealand.

If Te Pahi impressed the Europeans, though, not everything he saw at Port Jackson impressed him. He was dismissive of the Aboriginals, expressing 'the utmost abhorrence at their going naked, and their want of ingenuity or inclination to procure food and make themselves comfortable'.[7] During his stay at Sydney, he and his sons were present at an Aboriginal mortuary ceremony, when the man who had killed the dead person stood amidst flights of spears hurled at him by the aggrieved mourners, defended only by a shield and his own agility. The *Sydney Gazette* described Te Pahi's reaction:

> Tip-pa-he regarded with contempt their warfare; he frequently discovered much impatience at the length of interval between the flights; and by signs exhorted them to dispatch; he considered the *heel-a-man*, or shield, an unnecessary appendage, as the hand was sufficient to put aside and alter the direction of any number of spears; he nevertheless, highly praised the *wommera*, or throwing stick, as, from its elasticity, he acknowledged the weapon to receive much additional velocity . . . The natives have formed some extravagant notions of this stranger; they dreaded to approach him, and as much as possible avoid him . . .
>
> It cannot be supposed that Tip-pa-he's high relish for civilization would find an agreeable object of contemplation in the manners of a naked race, who have for so many years disregarded its advantages; nor can it be imagined that the implacable ARRAIGNMENT of a fellow-creature for an offence which custom compelled him to commit, as was here the case, would in any wise accord with his sentiments of justice.[8]

The European idea of the Great Chain of Being was at work in this report, ranking one group of 'natives' above another. Te Pahi and his sons, however, also clearly considered that as people, they were superior to Aboriginals.

Te Pahi found some of the Europeans at Port Jackson to be ill-mannered and gauche. On one occasion, when someone mocked his tattoos, he retorted that the European custom of putting grease and powder in their hair seemed to him far more absurd.[9] On another occasion, when an officer's wife reproached him for presenting some earrings she had given him to a young woman, and took the jewellery back from the hapless recipient, Te Pahi was furious. Redistributing gifts was a rangatira practice, and to be scolded for it was galling. He packed up all the gifts she had given him, sent them back to her and refused to speak to her or see her again. As King commented:

> [He] constantly expressed his disgust at hearing of the presents he had received being in any way mentioned except by himself; and to do him justice, he always took every opportunity to speak of the donors with the most grateful respect.[10]

Above all, Te Pahi was appalled by European ideas of punishment, regarding these as excessive and barbaric. While he was at Port Jackson, two soldiers and a convict were brought from Port Dalrymple and tried for stealing pork from the King's store. One of them was sentenced to death. Te Pahi was horrified when he heard this, and went to visit them in jail, later taking a petition for clemency from them to Governor King and trying to arrange a passage for them to New Zealand on an American vessel. According to King:

> He came into the room where I was writing, and in a very earnest manner, and I believe from the full force of conviction, he endeavoured to reason with me on the injustice of slaying men for stealing pork, and at the same time shewing the severest sorrow and grief for their fate, which he concluded by taking the petition out of his pocket and giving it to me, at the same time shedding tears. He threw

Above: *The landing place at Parramatta.*

Below: *A view of Sydney, showing Aboriginals with their spears.*

himself prostrate on the ground, sobbing most bitterly. Observing that I did not give him any answer or hopes than by saying I should consider of it he left the room and did not make his reappearance until the hour of dinner, having taken off the dress he had made here, and appeared very violent, exclaiming in the most furious manner against the severity of our laws in sentencing a man to die for stealing a piece of pork, although he admitted that a man might very justly be put to death for stealing a piece of iron, as that was of a permanent use; but stealing a piece of pork, which to use his own expression, was eat and passed off, he considered as sanguine in the extreme.[11]

When the matter was subsequently discussed during a dinner party at Government House, Te Pahi was assured that justice had been done, since British law 'secured to each individual the safe possession of his property, and punished with death all those who would deprive him of it by theft or robbery'. He retorted, 'Then, why you not hang Captain ___ [pointing to this man, who was present]? He come to New Zealand, he come ashore, and tihi [taahae – steal] all my potatoes – you hang up Captain ___,' a response that discomfited the captain and greatly amused the rest of the company.[12]

Te Pahi reported his own authority in New Zealand to be very extensive. He said that to the south his main rival was 'Mowpah' (Te Haupa), and to the north,

Government House, Sydney, 1809.

the people of 'Moodee Whenua' (Muriwhenua). He claimed authority over the territory of 'Wai-po-poo' (Waipupuu) to the north of the Bay of Islands, and across the island, presumably to Hokianga. When King asked him about cannibalism, he said his people did not practise it, but that those about Thames did (according to King, however, he had been assured by a man named 'Ti-a-pe' from Muriwhenua that Te Pahi's people were also cannibals). Te Pahi often attended church at Port Jackson, and when the conversation turned to matters of religion, he told King that his people believed in a god who resides above and whose shadow often visited the earth. The priests were the only people who could see this shadow. They were able to invoke it with incantations to cure the sick or for help in times of crisis, when its presence became known by the sound of a gentle whistling. According to King, 'the dead are buried, and they believe that the spirit ascends; but if it enjoys a new state, or this "death is an eternal sleep", we could not ascertain'. Te Pahi also explained about chiefly polygamy, saying that he had several wives and fifty-two children, although he had killed one wife 'for having a troublesome tongue, nor could he help testifying his surprise that many of the women here did not suffer the same fate'.

Te Pahi often complained about the behaviour of the whalers, saying that on one occasion a Maori had been flogged by a whaling captain, and asked King to control them. King explained to him the difference between the English and American colours, suggesting that he should be kind to crews of both nationalities. Some Maori 'of the lower class' had made their way to Sydney on various ships, and King requested Te Pahi to send a number of his people to the colony to work as shepherds. It seems that war captives and other Maori without mana were escaping into European society, and Te Pahi was quick to insist that 'emoki' (mookai – slaves, war captives) should not participate in such a scheme, for they were 'too idle and vicious to send here and from whom no good could be got'.

King, who had long aspired to become the first Governor of New Zealand, began to plan a five-month expedition to the Bay of Islands under the command of Mr MacMillan, the surgeon of the *Buffalo*, 'for the purpose of making such observations on the inhabitants, their manners and customs, with the formation of the country, as the time and their situation might admit of'.[13] Te Pahi was enthusiastic about the project and promised to protect the travellers, but the plan was cancelled when King (who was suffering from ill health) heard that he was about to be relieved as Governor of New South Wales. Te Pahi stayed with King for three months in all, and when the time came for his departure in February 1806, King had a silver medal struck and engraved on one side: 'Presented by Governor King to Tip-a-he, a chief of New Zeland, during his visit at Port Jackson, in January 1806'; and on the other: 'In the reign of George The Third, by the Grace of God King of the United Kingdom of Great Britain and Ireland'. King hung this medallion round Te Pahi's neck on a silver chain, and he and his officers gave him iron utensils, tools, a box of fruit trees, and bricks and the framework for a prefabricated house to be erected on his arrival back at Te Puna. On the eve of his departure, the

Sydney Gazette noted, '[Te Pahi] appears sensibly affected at the necessary separation from those Friends, to whose unlimited hospitality he feels the warmest obligation; and as the children of nature are but little versed in the refined accomplishment of dissimulation, we cannot doubt the sincerity of his professions, or his friendly disposition towards our countrymen, which his treatment from our Government has very much improved.'[14] King added in a letter to Sir Joseph Banks, 'During his Stay here he has been treated with the utmost kindness & attended by every description of People who have heaped considerable useful presents on him & his Family with which & what he will receive from me he will return to his own Country the greatest Monarch that ever left it.'[15]

While Te Mahanga was leaving the Bay of Islands for his world tour on the *Ferret*, Te Pahi was returning to Te Puna from Sydney. Governor King ordered Lieutenant Symons of the *Lady Nelson*, an armed tender, to take Te Pahi and his sons home, so that there was no further risk of their ill-treatment.[16] Symons had already visited New Zealand on the *Lady Nelson* in 1804 before returning to Port Jackson, where the ship worked as a colonial transport until January 1806, when he was ordered to take Te Pahi and his four sons back to New Zealand.[17] Bricks and a house in frame for Te Pahi were loaded on board, and the ship sailed on 25 February. Te Pahi became ill during the month-long journey to New Zealand, and was nursed by a young man named George Bruce (or 'Joseph Druce', according to the ship's log). Bruce had been transported from England when he was twelve years old for stealing , and arrived in Port Jackson on the *Royal Admiral* in 1792.[18] At first he had been assigned as a water carrier for a party of tree-fellers, then as a servant for George Caley, the botanist who was collecting in Australia for Joseph Banks. After that he received a free pardon from Acting Governor Grose and served on various colonial vessels, including the *Cumberland*. Bruce then joined the New South Wales police force, but was caught up in a brawl between English and Irish convicts and sentenced to two hundred lashes. He ran into the bush to escape this punishment and lived as a bushranger for several years, praying constantly for deliverance. According to his autobiography, his prayers were answered when Philip Gidley King became Governor and had given him a pardon, sending him on board the *Lady Nelson*.[19]

As the vessel passed Motu-o-pao (an island off Cape Maria van Diemen) on 31 March 1806, five canoes came out to the ship to trade, and then two more; and the next day five canoes came alongside with friendly local people. Off North Cape there were three islands, one of which – 'Titteranee' (Titirangi?) – was thinly inhabited, and three chiefs came out to greet the ship. These chiefs, who were friends of Te Pahi's, bartered fish for bread and allowed the sailors to cut brooms and wood on the island. Tuki-tahua also came out from the cape to meet the ship, perhaps hoping that Governor King had sent him a message. After a week anchored off Titirangi, however, Te Pahi 'became very mutinous'. According to a Tahitian on board, he sent messages ashore inciting his friends to attack the ship, and then created a disturbance on board, threatening the sailors with his

An engraving of the Lady Nelson, *1803.*

weapons. He may have been impatient at the delay in returning to the Bay of Islands, or perhaps one of the sailors had insulted him. Symons was unmoved, and stayed at anchor for another week, collecting greens and water on shore, and sending the ship's boat to explore a deep bay to the south-west, with a lagoon and a river running into it. On 13 April, 'Joseph Druce' was flogged for 'theft, disobedience and embezzlement', and a week later he ran from the ship, just before the *Lady Nelson* sailed south to the Bay of Islands.

Upon their arrival at Te Puna, the ship's carpenter began to erect Te Pahi's house on his island, all his goods were landed ashore, and Te Pahi sent seven spars and a sample of flax cloth and fishing lines[20] on board the *Lady Nelson*. The ship sailed on 7 May for Norfolk Island. When Symons returned to Port Jackson in June, the *Sydney Gazette* reported that 'Tip pa hee was known and acknowledged as a great Chief, from the North Cape to his own residence'.[21] He had sent back many gifts to his friends, including weapons, flax and a quantity of fine seed potatoes, which were scarce in Sydney at that time. His house had been erected on the island described by John Savage, and Symons said that he thought it would be 'impregnable, and able to withstand the attacks of any force that the country at that time could bring against it'.[22]

After the departure of the *Lady Nelson*, George Bruce made his way south. Within a few months he was married to Te Pahi's youngest daughter, Atahoe (then about fifteen years old), and tattooed as a warrior. According to Bruce's memoirs, dictated in England in about 1818, Te Pahi was 'anxious to introduce the customs and arts of the English' to his people, and sent Bruce inland for six or eight months to become familiar with the local language and habits. The people were 'frank and hospitable', and made Bruce very welcome. He was made chief of 'Oongarua' (Uungarua), his wife's land, and Te Pahi put him to work as an interpreter and advisor in his dealings with European whalers. Te Pahi may also (as Bruce claimed) have gained useful information about European weaponry and fighting techniques from his new son-in-law.

Some of the things that Bruce learned from local people were later recorded in his autobiography. He noted, for instance, that if a New Zealander had no children, he felt abandoned by 'God', and it was for this reason that men took many wives[23] (although most men, in fact, remained monogamous). Eating, drinking and defecating in the gardens was strictly prohibited, and if this prohibition was broken, the crops would be blighted. No man could sleep with his wife while his crops were being planted. Anyone who ate food from a garden where any of these prohibitions had been broken would die (a reference to the tapu involved in agriculture). In childbirth, each man delivered his own wife, and for the next eleven days neither of them could touch food, but had to be fed by hand or eat off the ground. They could not go into any house that had been consecrated by a priest, but had to sleep outside in 'the open wilderness', where all children were delivered. After the birth, at an appointed time, a priest would take the child and lead the parents to a stream, where the baby was dipped three times under the water and named (a description of the tohi ritual, which dedicated children to particular ancestor gods). From this time onward the parents were freed from their restrictions.[24]

After death, according to Bruce, the souls of the dead climbed to the top of a mountain by the sea and, after 'moaning in A most dreadful Mamnar', turned their faces to the rising sun and descended through the mountain core under the sea. The mountain was an extinct volcano, whose fires had been extinguished by the sea rushing in through an underground tunnel. The only way for a living person to climb this mountain was to catch a particular type of fish, strip the flesh off its bones and touch it to his nose. At the top, one could look down into the crater, which was like a furnace on fire, where the souls could be seen torturing each other (this Maori 'hell' is not mentioned in other early accounts, and was probably a Bruce fabrication). Bruce was told that by both day and night, souls could be seen like shadows travelling on the road to this mountain. (This 'spirit's pathway' is recorded on Tuki-tahua's map of the North Island, and was often referred to in early Maori manuscripts and waiata.)

Human life, Bruce was told, began when a man and woman (presumably Rangi and Papa, the Sky Father and the Earth Mother) fell from heaven and had a great many children. When the children grew up, some of them ran away from their parents, each brother taking one of his sisters with him. They reached a very remote place, and met to discuss what they would do if their father caught them.

The eldest son wanted to kill him, but the youngest disagreed and suggested that they should all mark their faces instead, so their father would mistake them for devils. There were fourteen of these children, seven boys and seven girls, and the eldest marked the faces of all the others, and the youngest marked the face of the eldest (an account of the origin of moko, or tattoo). Thirty years later, their father found his runaway offspring, who by then had mated and had many children. They tried to deny that they were indeed his children, but despite the strange marks on their faces he recognised them from the patterns at the ends of their fingers. When he returned to his other children, he told them he had found their brothers and sisters, although they had disguised their faces with patterns that came from the 'devil'. He showed them the marks on their finger ends, told them their meaning and said that he would soon die, and at the end of the world he would take them to heaven with him. Their brothers and sisters would come to them soon, and they would fight, because of the ingratitude of the runaway siblings and their attempt to deceive their father. For this reason, Bruce commented, 'to this day, The new zealanders make war one with the other'. The father told his children at home that once he had gone, they should mark their faces with the patterns from their finger ends, and not be frightened of the marks on the faces of their brothers and sisters (a fascinating version of the story of Rangi and Papa's children).

Bruce added that at the death of a chief, his heart was taken out of his body and buried in a wood where no-one went, on pain of death. The body was trussed and taken to a large lagoon, where it was decorated and dressed in a cloak of flax and dogskin, with the outer side covered with feathers. The head of the chief was also decorated with feathers. For six or seven nights there were ceremonies while all his people gathered round him, cutting themselves with glass (obsidian) and wailing aloud (a description of the custom of haehae, or mourning by laceration). Then they lined themselves up in ranks, about two hundred yards from the body, holding their weapons, and advanced on the chief in unison, retreating three times, shouting and pronouncing vengeance 'in A most dreadful manner' (a description of the mourning haka). After these ceremonies the body was taken into the woods and put on a stake, where it was left until it rotted.

While his son-in-law was learning about Maori customs and views of the world, Te Pahi was engaged in a flurry of European-influenced activities. He began planting quantities of maize and potatoes – although his people went to the field when the maize was nearly ripe and ate all of the cobs he had intended for seed, ruining his enterprise. He also introduced whipping as a punishment for theft among his people, and moved into the prefabricated house that had been erected for him on the island.

In the middle of June 1806, the *Venus* (the colonial brig that had brought Maa-Tara home in 1805 with gifts of pigs and goats from Governor King, and took Te Pahi and his sons to Norfolk Island) was seized at Port Dalrymple and brought to the Bay of Islands. Owned by Robert Campbell and now commanded by Samuel Rodman Chace, the vessel had been carrying a cargo of grain, flour and salt pork to Port Dalrymple. Chace was on bad terms with his crew, having accused his American mate Benjamin Kelly of tapping a cask of spirits during the voyage. He had also argued with Kelly's lover, Catharine Hagerty, a strong-willed convict woman with 'light hair [and a] fresh complexion much inclined to smile', accusing her of tossing valuable papers overboard. When Chace went ashore at Port Dalrymple, the mutineers (Benjamin Kelly, his mate; the pilot David Evans; and Richard Thompson, a private of the New South Wales Corps) armed themselves and took control of the ship with the support of the convict women on board, sending ashore five sailors. The *Venus* was sailed to the Bay of Islands, with Richard Edwards, the second mate, who had been knocked down and confined; Joseph Redmonds, a mulatto seaman; Thomas Ford, cabin boy; William Evans, an Aboriginal cabin boy; Richard Evans, convict; a Malay cook; Catharine Hagerty; and John Lancashire, a convict, and his lover Charlotte Badger, a 'very corpulent, light-haired' ex-thief, with her child, all still on board the vessel.[25]

At the Bay, some of the passengers and crew shifted ashore, to join a scattering of other Europeans already living in the region (James Cavanagh, George Bruce and some sailors who had been left at the Bay by a whaler). About this time Te Pahi sent his son Maa-Tara off on another jouney, on the whaler *Richard and Mary* (Captain Lucas), to 'see the King and obtain from his Majesty and the English nation axes, Iron and musquets in order that they may be enabled to build houses and live as English men do'. When Maa-Tara arrived in London in April 1807, he met Sir Joseph Banks and told him that before the *Richard and Mary* left the Bay, the *Venus* had landed six people there: two men, two women and two children (evidently Kelly and Catharine Hagerty; Lancashire and Charlotte Badger, with her child; and perhaps Evans, the Aboriginal cabin boy). The women had been kept apart in their own quarters, which the chiefs declared 'toppi toppi' (taputapu – strongly tapu), and nobody had dared to approach them.[26]

As it happened, news of the *Venus*'s arrival at the Bay reached Sydney just a month before Banks heard of it in London. On 12 April 1807, the *Sydney Gazette* reported that the snow *Commerce* had arrived from the Antipodes and the Bay of Islands, where they found the *Inspector* and *Albion* at anchor. There Captain Birnie had met Te Pahi, who treated him kindly, supplying him with potatoes and lamenting the loss of his first crop of maize, eaten in one night by a marauding group of his subjects (although he reported that he had managed to raise a series of crops of potatoes from a single root brought back from New South Wales). During this visit Te Pahi also told Birnie that the *Venus* had been in the Bay, and that two of the pirates had been delivered up as prisoners to visiting ships: Kelly to the *Britannia* and Lancashire to the *Brothers*.[27] The same issue of the *Gazette* reported another account of a recent visit to the Bay, by Captain Eber Bunker of the *Elizabeth*. He reported that the *Venus* had been at the Bay of Islands but had recently left under the command of a 'black man [presumably the mulatto sailor Redmonds], who had avowed an inclination of returning to Port Jackson, but was incapable of piloting her to any determinate place whatever'. A hut built by Kelly and Lancashire had been taken over by eight or nine men from the *Inspector*, while five or six sailors left in the Bay by an earlier ship had left on the visiting whaler. The two white women brought to the Bay on the *Venus* had been living on shore, but one of them (Hagerty) had died soon after their arrival. Badger with her child stayed on in the Bay, refusing to return to Port Jackson with Bunker. It is said that she lived with a local rangatira for some years before running off with a New England whaling captain.[28]

It was quickly rumoured that the *Venus* mutineers had come to a grim end. Philip Gidley King, who had been relieved as Governor of New South Wales in August 1806 and was now back in England, reported to Banks in November 1807 as follows:

> A few days ago I saw the Master of a Whaler 6 Months from the Bay of Islands from whom I received very satisfactory Accounts of my Friend Tipahe since his return, the Prizes he carried and his unlimited authority caused him to be joyfully received by his Subjects – Some weeks previous to my being relieved – sent a Schooner to Port Dalrymple & the Derwent with some prisoners & convicts – on arriving at the former place she was seized by some Convicts & taken away with her Cargo – from the Account of the Master of the Whaler it appears that the Schooner put into the Bay of Islands the pirates having quarrelled with each [other] six of them left the Vessell & went on shore while others consisting of Twelve remained on board the Schooner. A whaler soon after came in – when the Six on shore – interest with those afloat to seize on the Inspector So. Whaler – It soon came to Tipahe's knowledge as some of his subjects were prevailed upon to join the pirates, which Tipahe encouraged, & with much address seized on the Schooner which had Four guns while the attack was making on the Ship, those belonging to the Ship were sufficiently prepared in consequence of being warned by Tipahe in short the attack failed – & the Pirates were dismissed under a promise of leaving the Bay the next day, but Tipahe did not chuse to give up the Six that had taken refuge on shore but claimed them – the Master of the Whaler readily agreed to give them up – as this piratical attempt was regarded by His Majesty in a very different point of view to the crime of stealing a piece of Pork, he *hung* the whole *Six*, and desired the Captain of the whaler to tell King George & Governor King what he had done – & was sure they would approve of it.[29]

This account was inaccurate, however, and may have been entirely fictional. Reports had been brought to Sydney that Kelly and Lancashire had been handed over to visiting ships (although the whaling captains might have handed them over to Te Pahi instead, and concealed this from the authorities). While Kelly's lover Catharine Hagerty died soon after their arrival in the Bay, her friend Charlotte Badger, Lancashire's lover, stayed on for some years after his capture. Apparently she and her daughter eventually made their way to Tonga – not bad for an ex-housebreaker.[30]

In this same letter, King told Banks that he had sent him the head of 'To Mau [Tuu Mau?] o Wegeoo a Young Chief of the District of Moodoo Whenua at the N. point of New Zealand' (along with a 'water mole' [platypus]), by care of the *Buffalo*'s surgeon. It is not clear how King had come by the head of a Muriwhenua chief, although he probably acquired it from one of the whalers.

Te Pahi must have wished later that he had hanged all of the *Venus* pirates. When its crew (apart from Kelly and Lancashire) took the ship out of the Bay, they kidnapped the sister and niece of Te Morenga, a great chief on the Taiamai plains, and a woman related to another great chief, Hongi Hika. Te Morenga's sister was later exchanged for mats with men of Ngaati Porou on the East Coast, who killed her. His niece was made a slave by a Thames chief, Huukori, and later killed and eaten by Te Waru, a chief at Tauranga. Hongi's female relative was killed near East Cape, and their deaths provoked separate war expeditions in 1818 against Thames, Tauranga and the East Coast, which caused widespread devastation.[31] The *Venus* was last seen in distress off the coast of New Zealand during May 1808, and shortly afterwards it vanished.[32]

The sealers and whalers were a lawless lot, and often indiscriminately violent. Many of the crew were ex-convicts, or sailors hardened by serving on convict transports. In March 1807, for example, the medical missionary Gregory Warner, who visited the Bay of Islands on the brig *Elizabeth* (with 'George', or Te Aara, on board), described their conduct with horror. In a letter to the Missionary Society in London, he complained of the 'extreme wickedness' of the sailors and the viciousness of their conduct toward local people.[33] In response to this and other complaints, the new Governor, William Bligh, issued another proclamation at Sydney in April 1807, intended to protect the South Sea Islanders. The masters of ships were prohibited from taking such people from the colony to Great Britain, and ordered to deposit a bond of £20 for each Islander brought to Port Jackson.[34] Many captains ignored these regulations, however. During 1806, for instance, Captain Wilkinson of the *Star* came into Whangaroa Harbour. The local people came out in a fleet of canoes with plentiful supplies to trade, and Wilkinson met Kaitoke, the chief who ruled the district, a man 'equally feared and beloved' by his people, who possessed great courage, bodily strength, an excellent understanding and a pacific disposition. Wilkinson's first visit to Whangaroa was peaceful, and when he left the harbour, a Maori described as 'George and Teara, New Zealander' [Te Aara], Kaitoke's kinsman and Te Pahi's brother-in-law, joined the ship as a sailor.[35] After a trip south to the Antipodes Islands, Wilkinson brought Te Aara back home to Whangaroa.

At this time, George Bruce was still in the Bay of Islands, advising his father-in-law Te Pahi. He later claimed that during his time there he had helped various whalers in their dealings with local people – *Inspector*, *Betsey*, *Venus*, *Governor Bligh*, *Ferret*, *Star* (a sealing vessel), *William*, *Three Brothers*, *Vulture* and *King George*, commanded by William Moody, to whom Bruce claimed to have introduced Te Pahi's kinsman Ruatara.

In October 1807, the *General Wellesley* came to the Bay of Islands. This vessel was commanded by Captain Dalrymple with James Ceroni as chief officer. The *General Wellesley* had left Port Jackson in late April with a number of passengers (including some children and at least seven women),[36] bound for Pulo Penang on a trading voyage via the South Pacific. In June, she had arrived at Tahiti, looking for supplies, where Edward Robarts, an English deserter who had formerly lived in the Marquesas, came on board as pilot, accompanied by his highborn Marquesan wife and their two daughters.[37] James Elder, a missionary who visited Hauraki in 1801 on the *Royal Admiral*, had just been expelled from the Tahitian mission for adultery, and Dalrymple recruited him as interpreter. The ship sailed from Tahiti to the Tuamotus, where some of the crew went ashore to look for pearl oysters on the reef. According to Robarts, about four or five hundred people tried to cut them off, although Elder later claimed the Tuamotuans had only gathered to gaze at these apparitions. Dalrymple, a drunkard given to casual violence, fired cannons loaded with grapeshot into the crowd, claiming that 'it was necessary to strike terror into the minds of these natives and to convince them what Power we Possessed'.[38]

From the Tuamotus, the *General Wellesley* sailed to the Bay of Islands, where they found the whaler *Santa Anna* already at anchor. According to Robarts, canoes full of men and women came around the ship, and the women retired below decks with the sailors. During these exchanges a man whom he later identified as Te Pahi grabbed hold of Robarts's wife, and 'behaved in a rude manner'. Robarts knocked him down and took away his stone hand club, then cleared the ship by firing a musket down the hatchway. He also reported that during their stay George Bruce arranged for Te Pahi's people to cut and haul spars in exchange for iron axes. He said that Bruce worked hard and behaved well, organising the work of cutting spars and having them dragged down to the river.

On one occasion during the visit, the ship's boat, which landed at the same spot where Marion du Fresne had set up his shore camp, was almost cut off by local warriors. Robarts saw this incident from the ship and wrote a vivid description:

> One day the carpenter was sent with the boat to a small Island close to the ship, a musket shot distance, to cutt a spar to make a mizen top mast for the ship. I was on the poop with the spy glass watching the boat and people. They got the spar cutt & cleard and was getting it towards the water edge, when I espied a great number of natives running Down a hill towards our people, and two large canoes came round a point of land padling as fas as they could. They sett up the war whoope. I calld out to Capt. D. that the boat & people would be cutt of. Mr. Randall and Capt D. run on the poop with two musket which was Kept fireing, while I loaded a six pounder with one double head and grape shot. Capt D. says: 'Don't hurt them.' 'No,' I answerd, 'but I will break their canoe.'
>
> The natives was very near our boat. I fired at the headmost canoe. The double head shot struck the canoe nearly the middle. The other canoe ran away, and the natives on the hill ran back. I loaded with grape and fired a second time to scour the hill. The grape made the dust fly among them. I could see them tumble, but they never acknowledged that any of them was Killd. This was evident: if the grape had not been fired, they would have murderd our people. A French Ship had been there some time before and had sent two boats to the very same spot, and the whole of the two boats crew was murderd and carried away by the natives [a reference to the killing of Marion du Fresne].[39]

363

According to Robarts, after this violent exchange they had no further trouble with local people.

While the *General Wellesley* was still at anchor, a whaler (perhaps the *Inspector*, Captain Poole, or a new colonial craft named *Venus*, Captain Birbeck, which also visited the Bay that October[40]) arrived with a warrant signed by Governor Bligh for Bruce's capture, dead or alive. The captain accused Robarts of being either Bruce himself or another escaped convict. As the visiting captain began to search the ship, Bruce begged Robart's Marquesan wife to hide him. She hid him under her bed and sat on it with her children while the ship was searched for the deserter. No doubt in gratitude for his escape, Bruce told Robarts about a gold mine at North Cape, and guided the *General Wellesley* north. En route they visited a 'land-locked' harbour (Whangaroa), where Robarts later heard the 'King's brig' (the *Boyd*) was cut off. There Bruce's wife Atahoe, a 'good-looking but dark young Lady', and three young Maori sailors came on board. Two days later they arrived at North Cape. The 'gold' proved to be fool's gold, however, and a storm blew up that drove the ship out to sea. According to Robarts, Bruce was offered a small boat to take back to land, with a musket and some axes, but he considered the passage too dangerous.[41] To their great distress, Bruce and Atahoe were forced to stay on board and were carried away across the Pacific.

At Fiji, where Dalrymple tried to obtain a cargo of sandalwood, Bruce offered to act as an intermediary with the local people. According to Robarts,

> [He] said that he understood them and began to speak some broken New Zealand words to them. 'O, Sir,' says he, 'I understand them perfectly.' 'Well,' says the Capt, 'you are the most proper person to go on shore and see if you can find any sandall wood. If you do, I will reward you handsomely when I reach India.[42]

Bruce dressed himself in a Maori cloak, buckled on a sword and went ashore with two young Maori companions. The next morning, when the boat was sent to pick him up, he was found stripped naked on the beach and one of the young Maori had been wounded with a spear. Despite his tattoos, the Pakeha Maori had not fooled the Fijians.

Bruce reported that he had met a white man on the island whose ship had been captured, so Dalrymple took two Fijians and put them in irons, ordering that this man should be brought out to the ship. A canoe was sent to the ship with a corpse and a roll of cloth instead, in exchange for the Fijian hostages. Dalrymple was horrified by this gesture, and immediately released his captives. According to Bruce, the captain blamed him for this episode and turned him out of his cabin (although Robarts said it was because of Bruce's own bad and abusive behaviour). He was separated from his wife, Atahoe, who was forced to work as a servant for a woman passenger from Sydney, and made to sleep on deck on the sandalwood logs. Dalrymple took all of their possessions and put them on the same rations as the Lascars. A young English man had joined the ship at New Zealand, and he was put ashore on another of the Fijian islands, where he went to live with the local people.

The *General Wellesley* sailed on to New Ireland, where local warriors twice tried to take the ship, but were foiled on each occasion. Edward Robarts complained bitterly of the cowardice of the crew, whom he described as 'China men manilla men & mongrel Portugues'. He shot down the New Ireland warriors without compunction, remarking, 'I cannot charge my mind of injustice or cruelty, harmless natives I would allways protect but treacherous tribes I would cutt them off.'[43] After they left New Ireland, the ship was becalmed and the food ran out. Bruce claimed that the white people on board, driven near to starvation, had made a plan to kill and eat the Lascar sailors, but a providential wind carried them to Sulu Island. The ship then sailed to Malacca, where, after nine months at sea, Captain Dalrymple sold one of the young Maori sailors as a slave for seventy-six dollars (according to contemporary accounts, young men and women were regularly offered for sale in the Malayan bazaars, at prices varying from thirteen to twenty shillings[44]). Bruce was landed in New Zealand costume, and while he was still ashore the *General Wellesley* sailed to Penang with his wife. There, Dalrymple sold Atahoe to a Captain Ross as a slave for his wife. Admiral Drury arranged for Bruce to be sent to Penang, and with the help of the Commandant he eventually found Atahoe. When he met her at Ross's house, she burst into tears, and Ross locked her away in a room, but the Commandant forced him to release her.

Bruce and Atahoe went to Bengal, seeking a passage back to New Zealand, and there their plight was reported in the local newspaper, the *Calcutta Gazette*. Atahoe was described as 'a daughter of the King of New Zealand', and Bruce as 'a man of consequence and authority there'. He gave an account of New Zealand to the *Gazette*'s reporter that emphasised its natural resources and discussed the introduction of new plants and animals:

> New Zealand abounds with a great variety of useful Timber; among which are the pine and the fir; the forests are of great extent, and may be considered as inexhaustible. Flax and hemp, which are both indigenous to that Country, grow in the utmost profusion . . . The tree producing the white Benjamin [kauri gum], is also found in many parts of the Island.
>
> Mines of different valuable metals, are known to exist in the interior. Specimens of their ores have been obtained; but from the total ignorance of the people in metallurgy, or in any other art of civilized Countries, their mines remain unwrought. Iron ores are found in great abundance; and with these the natives paint both themselves and their canoes.
>
> Cabbages, the common and the sweet potatoe, yams, parsnips, turnips, carrots, &c. rank among their garden vegetables. They have a plant somewhat resembling a fern, with a large farinaceous root, which when roasted, is a pleasant, wholesome food, and is a most excellent substitute for bread. They also have fruit trees, some of which are indigenous, others are exotic. The orange and the peach have both been introduced from the Cape of Good Hope, and are in a very thriving way.
>
> Breeds of swine and goats have been lately brought into New Zealand; and are increasing rapidly. Fish they possess in great variety and profusion, and during all the months of the year. In the summer season they are visited by shoals of

mackerel; and during the winter, their Coasts are frequented by immense quantities of herring. The Island is watered by many fine rivers, which abound with fish,
some of which are well known in Europe . . . the shores of the rivers and their
lakes are frequented by wild geese and wild ducks; but it is remarkable that they
have no tame web-footed Birds. The only quadruped on the Island is a kind of fox
[presumably the kurii, or Polynesian dog], and their only reptile a dull, sluggish
lizard [the tuatara].[45]

Lord Minto took pity on the couple and paid two thousand rupees for the
Union (Captain Luttrill) to take them to New Zealand. By now Atahoe was pregnant, and during the voyage she went into labour. There was no surgeon on board,
and a French prostitute who had offered to act as her midwife wept and wailed
instead. Eventually Bruce delivered his 'princess of New Zealand' of a fine
daughter. Instead of taking them to the Bay of Islands, Captain Luttrill delivered
them to the Derwent.[46] Upon their arrival at Port Jackson on 17 January 1810, a
man named Francis McKann offered them hospitality, and Bruce was hired by
Robert Williams and Simeon Lord to lead a flax expedition to New Zealand.
Atahoe (also known in Sydney as 'Mary Bruce') contracted dysentry, however,
and when she died two weeks later, the merchants cancelled their agreement.[47]
Bruce erected a gravestone to her in a Sydney church cemetery, with the following inscription:

> Sacred to the memory of Mary Bruce, Princess of New Zealand
> who Departed this Life Feb 27 1810, Aged 18 years
>
> Good Christian all that see this tomb
> What I am come to is your doom.
> These words is true that I do say
> The secret that is between this soul and me
> No mortal soul that in this life
> Will ever know the secret between me and my wife
> Altho she, is gone, and I am here,
> Never till our souls, before the Lord does appear,
> When we are there, both great and small
> God will discover our secrets all.[48]

Threatened with arrest for desertion, Bruce abandoned his daughter at the
Female Orphanage in Port Jackson and fled to England. Strangers on the streets
in London, seeing his tattoos, jeered at him and made his life a misery. For the rest of
his days, so far as we know, Bruce tried desperately to get back to New Zealand.[49]

CONCLUSION

Governor Philip Gidley King, Te Pahi, Maa-Tara, George Bruce and Te Atahoe
were boundary-crossers – cross-cultural travellers – each in their own fashion. They
investigated the knowledge and practices of a strange society, and negotiated

relationships across the edges. Once Governor King had decided that Maori were human, he made an unauthorised visit to New Zealand, risking his naval career. Once Te Pahi had decided that Europeans were human, he sent his son Maa-Tara to 'see the English at their settlement'. On the basis of Maa-Tara's reports, Te Pahi then set off with his sons to Norfolk Island and Port Jackson on an exploratory expedition. At Port Jackson, Te Pahi met with King, rangatira to rangatira, and carried out enquiries into European society. When Te Pahi liked what he saw, he tried to master it – especially European manufacturing and agricultural technology. When he disliked what he saw, he was outspoken, condemning the idea of hanging the men for stealing pork from the King's stores, or reacting with disgust to the manners of some colonials. Equally, King had become involved with New Zealand and its people. After his brief visit with Tuki and Huru to Muriwhenua some years earlier, he had become curious about the New Zealanders. He conducted his own enquiries, asking Te Pahi about his customs and mode of government. In the process, King found it difficult to maintain a view of Te Pahi and his former friends Tuki and Huru as 'savages'. Instead, he described Te Pahi to Sir Joseph Banks as 'a well bred Gentleman', who contradicted the idea of barbarians as vicious subhumans.

Both King and Te Pahi were acting strategically as leaders of their communities. King hoped to establish a colony in New Zealand; Te Pahi hoped to acquire useful European technologies and understandings. They conducted their enquiries in person, as well as using subordinates (minor officers on the one hand; junior relatives on the other) to carry out investigations.

George Bruce and Te Atahoe were caught up in their machinations. Bruce was recruited by Te Pahi as a useful source of skills and information. He ran from his ship on the gamble that life as a young rangatira in New Zealand would be better than life as a convicted pickpocket at Port Jackson. Te Atahoe, like her sister, had little choice about her marital arrangements. As a young puhi (chiefly woman), she was expected to marry in the interests of her kin group, to enhance their mana and status.

Once they had been carried off into the Pacific by Captain Dalrymple, both Bruce and Te Atahoe fell foul of European prejudices. Although he was a white man, Bruce had accepted the symbolic trappings of 'savagery' (including facial moko), something that other Europeans (and indeed Polynesians) mocked and resented. His aristocratic wife became fair game for the captain, a notorious drunkard, who sold her as a servant in colonial India. Te Atahoe died at Port Jackson, while George Bruce was taken off to England, where strangers mocked his tattoos and made his life a misery. Moko was a mark of mana in New Zealand but a stigma in Europe – especially on the face of a European. Boundary crossing was a dangerous game, and some people did not survive it.

Sixteen

THE BURNING OF THE *BOYD*

Back in England, ex-Governor King was not aware that relationships between Te Pahi and the whalers were deteriorating. In December 1807, he wrote to the Board of Revision suggesting that hemp and very fine masts and planks could be procured in New Zealand, 'which the good terms we are on with Tip-a-he, Chief of the Bay of Islands, would greatly facilitate the acquiring any quantity'.[1] In the Bay of Islands, however, there was increasing ill-will and violence. Early in 1808, shortly after Atahoe and Bruce had been kidnapped, the *Parramatta* put into the Bay in distress, and local people supplied Captain Glenn with pork, fish and potatoes. When they requested payment, they were thrown overboard and several were shot and wounded. The ship weighed anchor and sailed out of the Bay, but a gale blew up that drove the ship onto rocks between Cape Brett and 'Terra's' district, the Kororaareka region governed by the Ngaati Manu rangatira Tara and his younger brother Tupi. The crew were all killed and the vessel was plundered.[2]

In February or March 1808, when the whaler *Elizabeth* visited the Bay, there was another ugly incident, described by one of the whalers:

> One day while [the ship] laying at Anchor, Tippahee went on board to pay [Captain Bodie] a Visit and was very kindly received . . . In the mean time a Native came on board with whom Bodie made a Bargain to give him 20 Nails for 20 Baskets of Potatoes, the Man brought his Potatoes on board and Bodie having occasion to go below desired the Mate to receive the Potatoes and give him 20 Nails, which was done, – a Shower of Rain happening at the Instant the whole of the Natives then on board went on shore except Tippahee – when the Shower was over, Bodie came on Deck and counted his Baskets, and finding only 19 he fell into a violent Rage, seized Tippahee up to the Rigging and there kept him for 5 or 6 Hours 'till he was ransom'd with a Basket of Potatoes, tho' Tippahee offered to go on shore in his own Canoe . . . and bring him the Potatoes. Bodie . . . was sorry afterwards, as he found the Basket of Potatoes in the Forecastle of the Ship it having been stole by one of his own Sailors.[3]

This was a terrible assault upon the mana of a chief, and Te Pahi and his people must have been extremely angry.

368

In May, there were further conflicts. A ship called the *Harrington* was seized by pirates in New South Wales, and it was supposed that they had headed for the Bay of Islands in pursuit of the American brig *Eliza*, which was loaded with cargo and specie. The colonial authorities chartered another vessel, the *Pegasus*, putting Captain Symonds and Eber Bunker in charge with a military detachment of two sergeants, two corporals and twenty privates. The *Pegasus* sailed for the Bay, but neither the *Eliza* nor the pirates had been there, although the *Inspector*, *Grand Sachem*, *Seringapatam* and *Commerce* were all anchored at Te Puna. Several days later a brig hove in sight that they thought was the *Harrington*, but, seeing the ships in the Bay, she hauled her wind suddenly and sailed off to the east.[4]

James Elder, the former missionary who was on the *Seringapatam* at the time, reported numerous offences against local people. Potato plantations and store-houses were raided by the sailors, and people were lured below decks with the promise of food or gifts, and stripped of their cloaks and possessions. Elder later stated in a deposition sworn before Samuel Marsden:

> When they complained [the whalers] Beat them severly and sent them ashore Strip'd and weeping; at that time the Natives of the Bay of Islands, were very friendly, and very ready to supply every refreshments to the Ships in their power. I was often surprised from the ill treatment I saw them receive, they did not raise and murder us all. I have no doubt but that the Natives would be kind and atten- tive to the Crews of the Ships that put in there, if they were treated with any degree of common Justice honesty and civility.[5]

Towards the end of May, angry and frustrated by these repeated outrages, Te Pahi and his sons decided to return to Port Jackson to meet the new Governor, William Bligh, and report the kidnapping of his daughter and her husband by Captain Dalrymple. Te Pahi boarded the *Commerce*, which had previously visited the Bay of Islands several times, with three of his sons and several attendants. A number of logs for flooring boards and masts were loaded on the *Commerce*, perhaps as Te Pahi's payment for his passage.[6] Jacky Marmon, a cabin boy on the ship, well remembered Te Pahi in later years, saying that 'his countenance was expressive of much intelligence, his manners were affable, and in every way he seemed anxious to evince his regard and esteem for the pakeha . . . He was one of the finest natives it ever was my fortune to meet.'[7]

Supplies were scarce in the Bay at this time, because so many whalers had recently been there, and Te Pahi advised Captain Ceroni to put into Whangaroa (home of his wife's relatives) for provisions. Apparently Ceroni had a watch that he often showed to the local people, who thought it was an atua (or perhaps a waka atua – 'god receptacle'). To their horror, during one of these demonstrations Ceroni dropped the watch into Whangaroa Harbour. The *Commerce* sailed away that night without the usual farewells, and soon after she had sailed an epidemic broke out, killing many local people, including the chief Kaitoke.[8] The ship sailed to Norfolk, where the penal colony was being evacuated. There Alexander Berry, a former surgeon and a trader, met Te Pahi, whom he described as wearing 'robes of state' covered with tinsel given to him by Governor King, and looking like a 'merry Andrew'. He was lame in one leg and 'appeared a man of considerable gravity, displaying an easy consciousness of his own dignity. Upon the whole, he showed himself a man of some observation, and was by no means deficient in intellect, but the most prominent features of his character were a certain shrewdness, and low cunning.'[9] These comments of Berry's, however, were written after the loss of the *Boyd* and are based on hindsight.

During the voyage to Port Jackson, Te Pahi fell ill. He arrived on 10 July 1808 in a grave condition. Major Johnston, commander of the New South Wales Corps, ordered that he should be given every care, providing him with an apartment in Government House during his convalescence.[10] At this time, the authorities at Port Jackson were in an uproar. Governor William Bligh, notorious for the mutiny of his men on the *Bounty*, had exercised a brusque and arbitrary style of administration since his arrival in the colony, and he was soon deeply unpopular. He fell out with many of the colony's leading settlers, and threatened several of them with imprisonment. By the end of January 1808, the Governor had been deposed and put under house arrest by a group including Major Johnston, John Macarthur, John and Gregory Blaxland (friends of Sir Joseph Banks) and Simeon Lord. Alexander Berry, who was in Sydney at that time, recorded a memorable description of this mutiny:

> Johnston dispatched four officers of Government House to announce to Governor Bligh that he was coming to arrest him. In the meantime Governor Bligh had invited some of his partisans to dinner. One of the party told me afterwards that Atkins [the Judge Advocate, who was implicated in the judicial reprisals] was particularly uneasy, and that, as soon as he had dispatched his dinner, he left the table with a view to examining the state of affairs in Barrack-square. He returned thence in great trepidation and said, 'There is a great movement in Barrack-square, and the military are all under arms.' Bligh said, 'Surely they dare not attack my person?' To which Atkins replied, 'I have no doubt but that they will.' Bligh poured out a glass of wine, and rising with great trepidation, said, 'The Health of the King!' He then drank off the wine, and left the table.
>
> He went and dressed himself in his naval uniform, and fastened his dirk by his side, that he might impress his assailants with awe. When, however, he looked out at the warlike array coming towards him his heart failed him, and he hid himself under a feather bed. On his discovery, in that place of concealment, it was found that the uniform which Nelson and Duncan had worn with so much honour, was befouled with white feathers!
>
> I never saw Bligh after this event, except at a distance, when he was walking in his gardens, accompanied, I think, by a guard; but I heard many things of him in England, from an officer who had sailed under him, which were greatly to his disadvantage.[11]

This was the Governor whom Te Pahi had come to visit. Shortly after he landed at Sydney, however, Lieutenant-Colonel Joseph Foveaux, who was Johnston's senior officer, arrived from England, assumed the title of Acting Governor and decided to

The arrest of Governor William Bligh.

keep Bligh under arrest in Government House. Since Te Pahi was also living there, at least for a time, he must have witnessed Bligh's frustrated rage and the manoeuvrings of local settlers and officials.

By the time of this second visit to Sydney, Te Pahi's closest European friends, Philip Gidley King and Samuel Marsden, were both absent from the colony. King's term of office had ended, and Marsden was on leave in England. Once he had recovered from his illness, Te Pahi was asked to leave Government House, and he and his companions were sometimes forced to sleep under bridges, or in the open air.[12] Te Pahi was snubbed by some local residents, although others treated him kindly. Bligh's ally, the shipowner Robert Campbell, for instance, often invited Te Pahi to his home, but could not guarantee the good behaviour of other visitors. On 14 August, Te Pahi dined at Campbell's house with his son and two of his captains, James Gordon, and Captain Bodie of the *Elizabeth*.[13] At the dinner table Gordon noticed that Bodie seemed uneasy, and asked him what was the matter. In Te Pahi's presence, Bodie boasted of the incident earlier that year, when he had lashed Te Pahi to the rigging of his ship for five or six hours because one basket of potatoes of twenty he had traded for nails had gone missing. Angered by Bodie's 'exulting Manner' as he told this tale, Te Pahi flew into a rage, gnashing his teeth and contorting his face, so that Gordon had to walk him out into the garden to calm him. Afterwards Bodie told Gordon that when Te Pahi had gone back on shore, he had found the missing basket in the ship's forecastle, hidden by the sailor who had stolen it, and felt sorry for what he had done.

Despite Bodie's confession, it is unlikely that Te Pahi got much satisfaction from Acting Governor Foveaux. During his administration of Norfolk Island, Foveaux had been notorious as a flogging bully who sold female convicts to the free settlers. Te Pahi's faith in the mana of governors must have been shaken by Bligh's intemperate behaviour and by his own observations. With the collapse of legitimate authority in Sydney, European captains were no longer under the control of the colonial authorities (shipping returns lapsed until 1 January 1810, for instance[14]), and redress for their offences was unlikely to be forthcoming. On 26 September 1808, after a two-month stay at Sydney, Te Pahi and his sons returned to the Bay of Islands on the *Commerce* with Captain Ceroni.

A cartoon of Te Pahi in European uniform,
by the convict artist John Finucan, 1808.

Just three weeks later, Maa-Tara finally arrived back at the penal colony from England. In February of that year, King had reported from London that Sir Joseph Banks had equipped Maa-Tara and organised a passage 'for his return to his father Tipahe',[15] along with several officers from the *Buffalo* who had sailed with Te Pahi in 1805. On 15 November 1808, Maa-Tara was landed from the *Speke* (Captain Hingston) with ninety-seven female convicts and other passengers at Sydney.[16] Bligh reported his arrival to Viscount Castlereagh with the following brief comment: 'The New Zealand youth arrived safe, with his presents for his chief, Tippahee, to whom he had an early opportunity to return.'[17] While he was waiting for a passage to New Zealand, Maa-Tara lived at Government House with Bligh, who was still confined to his house and gardens.

Early in January 1809, Bligh asked Berry to take Maa-Tara back to the Bay of Islands on his Spanish prize ship *City of Edinburgh*,[18] which was sailing there for a cargo of timber. Simeon Lord (now back in favour and in partnership with Berry) also requested a passage for one of his sailors, a man from the Bay called Metatau. The *City of Edinburgh* left Port Jackson under the command of Captain Pattison on 27 January, and Ceroni, who had carried Te Pahi to Sydney and back on the *Commerce*, travelled with them as a passenger. According to Berry, Maa-Tara had been introduced to the royal family in England, and had acquired some European habits:

> He spoke English tolerably, dressed and behaved like a gentleman, and, of course, lived in the cabin; he spent, however, the greatest part of the day in company with a countryman of his own, who was employed as a sailor on board, and was indefatigable in his endeavours to regain a knowledge of his national songs and dances. His first appearance at New Zealand in the uniform of a naval officer, not only gratified his own vanity, but excited the greatest applause from his countrymen. In a few days, however, he resumed his national costume, and with it his national habits.[19]

In February, the *City of Edinburgh* arrived on the New Zealand coast, where Berry intended to visit Whangaroa, on Ceroni's recommendation. As the ship approached the harbour, however, it became obvious that Ceroni was reluctant to return there. They carried on to the Bay of Islands instead, where they arrived on 1 March. Te Pahi welcomed his son and informed the party that Kaitoke, the head chief of Whangaroa, had died and was lying in state waiting for his arrival. Te Pahi observed that 'an evil Etua had been busy amongst them', but offered no further comment. He urged Pattison and Berry to take their ship to Whangaroa to get spars and supplies, since the area belonged to him now that Kaitoke had died.

Pattison and Berry ignored this advice and turned their attention instead to the brothers Tupi and Tara, two Ngaati Manu chiefs related to Te Morenga of Taiamai, who were opposed to Te Pahi and his allies.[20] Tara, according to Berry, was a 'venerable old man, blind of one eye', about three score years, with a considerable air of dignity and authority. He could remember the *Endeavour*'s visit to the Bay of Islands in 1769, speaking highly of Tupaia, Cook's Tahitian high priest interpreter, although he was dismissive of Captain Cook, 'a surly old fellow [who] fired upon the natives'. Berry defended Cook, saying that he had been attacked by a crowd of warriors in the Bay, but Tara responded that his people had only wanted to see the Pakeha's weapons. Tupi, his brother, was much younger, about forty-five years old, tall, athletic and prepossessing; 'his face and manner equally bespoke a man of judgement and humanity'. Tupi spoke 'with great fluency, a mixed jargon of English and New Zealand', and dressed in European clothing – duck-trousers, a check shirt, waistcoat and an old slouched hat. He greeted Berry with a hand-shake, not a hongi, and seemed eager to assist him. The brothers controlled Kororareka and the Kawakawa district, where plenty of timber was available. Berry and Pattison were welcomed at their village by people waving their flag, a large scarlet banner (an innovation based on the custom of waving a red feather cloak in welcome – and maybe an echo of the Red Ensign), with an enthusiastic hongi from Tara.[21]

Tara, according to Berry, 'liked white men on account of the physical advantage which he saw they might render his country; but being of the order of the priesthood, was strongly attached to his own national customs. His general integrity might be depended on, and his word was sacred.'[22] Tupi, on the other hand, was more passionate and impulsive. He had only one wife and an infant daughter, 'the heiress of Cowa Cowa'. He was enthusiastic about new ways and was privately ridiculed by many of his countrymen for imitating European customs. In accompanying Berry and Pattison to the *City of Edinburgh*, which was anchored at about seven miles distance, Tupi fired off some of the muskets in their boat, to show that he knew how to use them, and kept up a stream of amusing chatter. He told the sailors in English to 'pull stronger', and asked Berry how many wives King George had. When Berry told him only one, he retorted, 'Your king, then, must be a poor fellow compared with Tippahee, the chief of Tippuna, who has four wives.' Berry asked him how many wives he had. 'Only one,' he replied. 'Well, Tupe,' said Berry, 'You must be as poor a fellow as King George.' 'Oh,' he responded wryly, 'when there are more wives than one, there is never any peace in the house.'[23]

The next day Tupi piloted the ship to Kororareka, showing an intimate knowledge of the harbour floor, its shoals and sunken rocks. The day after, he took Berry to the timber district, up a creek several miles beyond the Kawakawa Inlet. There were some old dry spars already cut lying on the forest floor, which Berry had made into a raft and floated down the river. The *City of Edinburgh* had been leaking badly during her passage from Sydney, so Berry decided to careen the ship by hoisting empty water casks to the head of each mast and filling them with water, tipping the ship on its side. The carpenters then replanked the entire bottom of the ship with new sheathing boards, which were fastened with iron spikes Berry had acquired in Sydney, and thousands of hardwood tree-nails. Not long after the work began, Tupi warned Berry that a fleet of canoes intended to attack his Kororareka camp and take the ship, a warning that Berry did not take seriously.

Tupi's people had built a snug dwelling for Berry, and the morning after the first night he had slept ashore, Tupi came and shook hands with him, saying that he

A portrait of Alexander Berry.

was going to spend several days at his house at Kawakawa. Soon afterwards, Berry's Bengal servant brought him hot water for shaving and told him that a fleet of canoes was coming around the point to attack them. Berry threw on his clothes and rushed outside, where his men were firing off their muskets. Two cannons stood on the beach that had not been loaded. The American officer in charge of the camp told Berry that there were no cartridges, so Berry took his stockings out of his hut and manufactured some cartridges on the spot. He loaded one of the cannons and fired at the approaching canoes. The first shot fell short, but the second flew over the heads of the paddlers. They panicked and several canoes capsized, tossing their crews in the water. Berry then launched two boats, filling them with men armed with muskets, who fired on the swimmers and killed many of them. One of these canoes was commanded by the sailor Metatau, whom Berry had brought back from Port Jackson. As his boats returned to the beach, an old warrior congratulated Berry, saying, 'You have conquered Waraki.'[24] Waraki was the chief of Waitangi, and an ally of Te Pahi's. His daughter Miki had married Te Pahi's kinsman, Ruatara.[25] It seems that Te Pahi and his allies regarded the *City of Edinburgh* as fair game, since it was anchored in Tara's territory.

The canoes were captured and hauled up on the beach, and several days later Maa-Tara came and asked Berry to return two of his father's canoes, which he said had been 'stolen by the bad people'. By now Maa-Tara was very ill with bronchitis. Berry, 'although I did not believe one word that he said', considered that 'I was an intruder on their country for my own personal advantage', and gave him the canoes for his father. Over the next few weeks Berry had difficulties with some of his crew, who demanded an increase in their rations. Tupi, who helped him to discipline them, was affronted when some days later, he and Tara were summoned to Berry's camp along with Te Pahi and Waraki because two sailors on sentry duty had deserted with their muskets. Berry told Te Pahi and Waraki that if the sentries were not returned, he would take them as prisoners to King George in England. Tupi then enquired whether he and Tara would also be taken, and when Berry said that they would, he replied angrily, 'That may be European custom, but it is not New Zealand custom. The New Zealanders never punish their friends because their enemies have injured them!'[26]

Tupi assured Berry that he would find the deserters and bring them back within three days, and if he failed, Berry could do what he liked with him. Tara added, 'I know Tupe will keep his word. Tarra will remain in the camp as security for Tupe; and if Tupe does not keep his promise, kill Tarra!' Waraki seemed ill at the time of this meeting, saying that a 'demon had entered into his body and was gnawing his entrails'. Berry dosed him with calomel, which eased him. Several days later, when Tupi returned with the two deserters, a Tahitian and an Irishman called McEwers, in hempen handcuffs, Berry sentenced the latter to twelve lashes, to be laid on by the Tahitian. That night there was a feast at the camp. The Europeans fought a mock 'English duel' with pistols, which Tupi considered barbarous. The local Maori then fought a sham fight in which one man was 'slain', the victors making torches out of old ship's canvas and singing a song of victory. During this song two little boys went to the 'corpse' and pretended to cut it up with shells, offering 'pieces' of the body to the people, and when the chiefs saw what they were doing, they were ashamed and slipped off into the dark. The local people had been trying to convince the Europeans that they were no longer cannibals.

As the *City of Edinburgh* prepared to leave the Bay, an old lady came to Berry with her son, a 'smart little fellow' called Taranui. She said that her husband had been a great chief but was now dead, and asked if he would take Taranui with him on the voyage. Berry agreed and asked the ship's tailor to make a suit of clothes for the boy, who learned to wait on table in the mess and soon became a general favourite. A few days later Berry took Taranui on a duck-shooting expedition near Waitangi. The place seemed deserted, without houses, trees or gardens, and the boy warned Berry to go back because it was too dangerous. Berry ignored him and carried on by himself. While he was wandering up the river, he stumbled upon an encampment of twenty or thirty men armed with spears, who began to chase him. He ran away as fast as he could and managed to get back to the place where Taranui was waiting. The boy fetched several sailors armed with muskets and some friendly Maori, who accompanied them back to the camp. There were some earth ovens cooking in a clearing, and when they opened them up they found a number of large fat dogs, which Berry's Maori companions soon slung on their backs, intending to carry them back to the ship. He made them put the dogs back and assured the few men left at the camp that he only wanted to buy some potatoes from them. They gave him several baskets and carried them from the camp to the boat, where Berry paid for them. He commented quizzically in his account, 'And thus I escaped being barbecued in a native oven.'[27]

After a three-month stay at Kororareka, the *City of Edinburgh* was fully refit-ted and in excellent condition. Berry took six or eight Maori on as crew, includ-ing Taranui, and in late May 1808 they set off for a voyage across the Pacific. Tupi and Tara came with them as far as the heads. As the ship sailed up the harbour, Captain Ceroni took out his watch to show it to some of his Maori companions. Shortly afterwards Tara let out a cry of horror, for Ceroni had dropped his watch in the sea, as he had done at Whangaroa. Tupi said with annoyance, 'Tara is an old fool. [He] thinks that the watch is a demon, or "Etua" [atua].' He told Berry that Tara believed that Ceroni had done it on purpose, intending to devastate the Bay with an epidemic, just as the people at Whangaroa had been decimated.

In his *Reminiscences*, Alexander Berry gave a lively account of the *City of Edin-burgh*'s Pacific odyssey and the adventures shared by his Maori sailors. They stopped first at Tongatapu, where they traded for fresh food and quantities of sinnet. Two men, 'very clean, fat and comely; [in] flowing robes', came out to the ship. They told Berry that there had been a civil war in Tonga, but it was now over and a new chief was in charge, who wanted the Europeans to come ashore. Berry decided not to land, however, and carried on to Nomuka. There, an elderly chief, Kino Kino Loa, and his son Taomaal came out to the ship and invited them to the place where 'Toote' (Captain Cook) had anchored. Taomaal presented Berry with a large pig and asked if he would become his ceremonial friend. Berry agreed and brought Taomaal on board for a meal, where he had his beard shaved off by the ship's barber. Taomaal offered them the use of the same boat-house that 'Toote' had used in his grandfather's time, and was thanked with a number of presents. Kino Kino Loa supervised the trade with the Europeans, threatening to strike down with his cutlass a man who had stolen a pistol from the captain. After exploring on shore, the visitors were given a festive meal followed by kava, and Berry was shown a pineapple plant that Cook had given to the Tongans. Taomaal asked to accompany them on the voyage, but Berry refused, saying it would be too dangerous. As they left the island, Taomaal presented Berry with his club as a keepsake, and in return Berry gave him one of his best razors.

Berry was looking for sandalwood, and at Fiji they anchored at the island of Opuna (Vuna, in Taviuni). They were welcomed by the local chief, a tall, corpu-lent old man who invited them to sleep ashore, and offered to supply them with sandalwood. A Fijian sailor called 'Jimmy' told Berry that the chief was trying to deceive them, and that there was no sandalwood on Vuna. They left the island but were forced back by contrary winds, so Berry decided to check out the truth of the old chief's story. He went ashore in a large decked boat and slept that night in the village. The next morning, however, when he went back to his boat, he found that yams had been piled up in front of it so that it couldn't be launched. As soon as he and his men began to shift the yams aside, each of them was seized by several warriors. Berry fought back but was pinioned and taken to a house where the local chiefs had gathered. Berry berated them for their treachery, but they steadfastly ignored him. They offered the Europeans food and began to drink 'angona' (kava), giving Berry a root so that he and his men could make their own kava. That night they all slept in the house, and in the morning Berry heard one of his sailors, a Tahitian, crying. This man had heard the local people saying they would all be killed, but Berry told him not to cry about that. Soon afterwards a Hawaiian man named Wainio came into the house and tried to persuade the chiefs not to kill the visitors. He had sailed on various ships and visited Sydney, and he scolded Berry, saying, 'How could you be such a *fool* as to risk your life among such a set of savages?' – an illuminating remark, exhibiting Polynesian cross-cultural prejudice.

The head chief allowed Berry to take a walk with Wainio. They visited the house of a Tongan woman, a 'kind, motherly' person, who fed them and asked Wainio to help a member of her family who was sick. When they returned to the chief's house, Berry told him that the captain was about to land with an armed party to rescue him and his men, and it would be wise to release them. Berry later learned that the chief hoped to recruit him as a fighting advisor and had not intended to harm him. The next morning the chiefs held another council, and Berry again asked to be set free. The head chief said that he would release him if he was given a tambua (whale's tooth). One of the sailors was sent out to the ship in a canoe to deliver this message to the captain. The captain sent Jimmy, the Fijian sailor, ashore with a tambua, and then McEwers, the Irishman, followed with another. The two men brought their gifts to the chiefs' house, and Berry told the chiefs that they now must keep their word and release him. Jimmy assured the chiefs that the men on the ship were getting their muskets and cutlasses ready to attack, and they all left the house except for the head chief, who ordered Berry to leave immediately. He walked with Wainio through a crowd of armed warriors, who let them pass. On the beach he found Ceroni with a boatload of armed men (no doubt including some of the Maori sailors) who were eager to attack the Fijians. Berry told them not to shoot, for no-one had been hurt, and so they left the island.[28]

From Opuna they went to Bau, where Ceroni left the ship and they found a number of runaway convicts and sailors living on shore, acting as the chiefs' military advisors. They obtained sandalwood at an island called 'Ilea' (Wailea, a district of Vanua Levu), where the sailors got into an argument with local people and were threatened with violence. For this or some other reason, some of the crew plotted with the runaways on shore and began to plan a mutiny. Berry and Pattison had decided to take the boats to Viti Levu, but Wainio (who had joined their expedition) told them about the talk of mutiny on board and warned them not to leave the vessel. Berry ordered the would-be mutineers off the ship, and left them behind at 'Ilea'.

During a brief visit to Viti Levu, where they were invited to join an attack on a visiting Tongan canoe with the offer that 'if we would assist them to kill them we could eat them together', they traded whale teeth for more sandalwood. The *City of Edinburgh* did not get a full cargo of timber, however, so Berry decided to return to New Zealand. At first he intended to enter Whangaroa, but the Maori sailors on board pleaded with him not to go there. They said that the local people had sworn to attack the next ship that entered the harbour, in revenge for the epidemic that Ceroni had caused by dropping his watch into the water. Berry thought they were speaking out of jealousy against the Whangaroa people, so he ignored their story. The Maori sailors wept as the ship sailed towards Whangaroa, but the winds were contrary and carried them to the Bay of Islands, where they arrived at the end of October. This voyage of the *City of Edinburgh* illustrates the Polynesian diaspora, and cross-Polynesian exchanges so characteristic of the Pacific whaling era.[29] Maori sailors had visited Tonga and Fiji during the voyage, and worked with Tahitian and Hawaiian (and no doubt other Polynesian) shipmates.

When the *City of Edinburgh* anchored at Kororaareka, Tupi and Tara were delighted to see the Europeans, offering every assistance in completing their cargo. Waraki also visited the ship to thank Berry for expelling the atua from his entrails during his previous visit. The local men cut down trees, barking and squaring the larger logs, and helped to load the spars into the vessel. Each Saturday night they were paid for their work. During this time, the news came that an important chief who had gone south had been treacherously killed. A series of meetings were held to discuss the matter, the orators pacing in front of seated crowds of people, and eventually it was decided to stay and load the ship, after which they would all go to seek revenge on their enemies.

Not long after this, Te Pahi came to visit Berry, saying that he wanted to get spars from Tupi for his own ship, and asking for 'a bottle of porter to drink in the bush'. He seemed quite changed and was in mourning for his son Maa-Tara, who had died during Berry's absence. Te Pahi may have had other reasons for resentment against the Europeans. According to depositions made later at Port Jackson, the *Speke*, which had brought Maa-Tara from England, had recently revisited the Bay of Islands. Hingston, its captain, later admitted to a colleague that he had flogged Te Pahi when an axe (which one of his men had probably traded for a mat) had gone missing.[30]

European interventions in relations among local people were often unhelpful and disruptive. At about this time, Berry mischievously teased Tupi's wife, 'a clever woman [who] used to act as his deputy, and share the cares of government' (an interesting reflection of the status of rangatira women), by saying that while he was on the ship, Tupi had been unfaithful to her with another woman. In fact, Tupi was a 'model of domestic felicity' and innocent of any adultery, but Berry's malicious joke caused marital difficulties. Tupi's wife went off in a fury to remonstrate with her husband, who had to give her all his greenstone ornaments to placate her.

About two weeks after the ship's return to the Bay, while the working party was on shore, Berry was on board the *City of Edinburgh* with the chief mate, his own Indian Portuguese servant, Taranui, the ship's cook, two blacksmiths (one of whom was Chinese), a Chinese carpenter and two other men. They saw a large war canoe approaching the ship, full of armed warriors. Berry ordered his men to load their muskets and man the large guns, one of which was loaded with ball and the other with pebbles. As the canoe approached the ship, Berry could see that Metatau was in charge, instructing his men on how to board the vessel. A random musket shot was fired, and Metatau fell back wounded as the canoe paddled off down the harbour.

According to later reports, a number of whalers were anchored in the Bay when the *City of Edinburgh* arrived on this occasion, including the *Mercury*, *Mary*, *Inspector* and the *New Zealander*. Te Pahi had supplied these ships with fish and wood, but his gardens had only just been planted and potatoes were in short supply. Several members of *Mercury*'s crew later testified that after Te Pahi had refused to sell him potatoes, Captain Theodore Walker, who was drunk at the time, led an armed raid on his garden one night, although the plants were immature and had not yet begun cropping. The sailors pulled up plants and trampled over them, and returned with just one bag of potatoes. Walker was still angry and ordered his crew to go the next day and plunder Te Pahi's storehouse, but they were forcibly driven off the island.[31] This was the second time that Metatau had tried to attack the *City of Edinburgh*. The crew of that ship were allied with Tupi and Tara, the chiefs of a rival alliance, and they may also have been involved in raids on Te Pahi's people. It is possible, too, that Berry and his men, having brought Te Pahi's son Maa-Tara home with a lung complaint, had been blamed for his death from this illness.

When the *City of Edinburgh* was fully loaded, they sailed to an anchorage off Kororareka. Tupi acted as the pilot on this occasion, and asked his wife to stay behind to look after the ship's boats, which had been left near the wooding encampment. Anxious about this arrangement, Berry said to him, 'You are very kind, Tupee but Mrs. Tupee is only a woman and unable to protect the boats.' Tupi drew himself up and retorted with some heat: 'True Mrs Tupee is only a woman but she is Tupee's wife. If anyone dares to injure anything under the care of Tupee's wife I will show you what kind of man Tupee is!'[32]

Soon after this, Tara met some strangers who told him disquieting news that he passed on to Berry. The Whangaroa people had captured a ship with twenty large guns and forty men, and killed and eaten all the crew, seizing their muskets and gunpowder. They were intending to come south to attack the *City of Edinburgh* as well. Tara told Berry to call his men back from the bush and to leave New Zealand as soon as possible. Until then he and Tupi and their men would stay on board to protect them. Berry thought that this report was fictitious, and when he asked Tupi about it several days later, Tupi denied it. Some time later young Taranui asked to leave the ship so that he could go and see his mother, and went away for a brief visit. He came back after several days, followed by his mother, who came on board to beg him to return on shore to live with his own relations. Taranui told her, 'I prefer living among the pakeha to living among the Maoris. The Maoris have so many *loutrou* [kutu – lice] about them.' His mother told him he ought to be ashamed for talking in such a way about his relations, and opened her cloak to show him her breasts, upon which he had suckled. Taranui stayed on the ship for a while, and then left without saying goodbye to his companions.[33]

Rumours continued to fly about the attack on a European ship at Whangaroa, and some of these seemed plausible. Finally, Berry decided to take three armed boats to the harbour to check on the truth of these reports, and called for volunteers to man them. None of the local Maori would go. 'They, to a man, inveighed against the danger and folly of such an attempt, and made use of every argument to dissuade me from undertaking it . . . They observed, that, after the fidelity with which they had so long served us, it was ungenerous to ask them, as such a thing would inevitably embroil them with the natives of Wangeroa.' Berry eventually mustered a party of twenty-two sailors and persuaded one young man, 'Towaaki' (Tuuhawaiki?), who had sailed with them to Fiji and intended to carry on to Europe, to accompany them. Berry asked Tupi and Tara for all their spare fire-arms to defend the ship in his absence, but these had not arrived before he left. The party guarding the vessel had just two six-pounders and a few defective muskets. The men left the ship in three boats after dark, so that news of their absence would not become generally known, but a gale blew up, and first one boat turned back to the Bay, and then another, and Berry was forced to follow them.

Several days earlier, a young Tahitian sailor called 'Tom' or 'Jemmy', their interpreter (who spoke English and Maori as well as Tahitian), had deserted the ship to live with a local woman. When Berry returned to the ship at about mid-night after this fruitless excursion, he was told that Tom had been persuaded to run away by a chief called 'Matingaro' (Matengaro?). Matengaro was on board the vessel that night, and Berry reproached him for luring Tom away, saying 'that it was a pity to see a man of his rank disgrace himself by decoying away our sailors, after all the attentions we had shown him', then turned his back contemptuously. The chief was infuriated by this public rebuke, insisting that he had nothing to do with the matter. He said that he had befriended the Europeans from the beginning and had always helped them, and could not bear to be treated so badly. He was about to leave the ship in a rage when Berry offered his hand, saying that if he would accompany them to Whangaroa, nothing more would be said on the subject. Matengaro shook Berry's hand and told him that he would go with them, adding: 'My presence will insure you every thing you require at that place. You shall see what a great man I am. The men of Wangeroa are a small people, and must do what I order.'[34]

The next day was fine, so Berry took a new party of volunteers and set off again for Whangaroa. This is a deep, sheltered harbour on the east coast north of the Bay of Islands, encircled by steep, bush-covered hills. Whangaroa was occupied by two main hapuu at this time, Ngaati Pou and Ngaati Uru, who had been driven out of the Bay after the killing of Marion du Fresne in 1772. They had accompanied the Frenchman on the fatal day when he ignored a death tapu, and had been forced to take utu by killing him. After that they were eventually exiled to Whangaroa, where they lived in uneasy proximity. Ngaati Pou now occupied

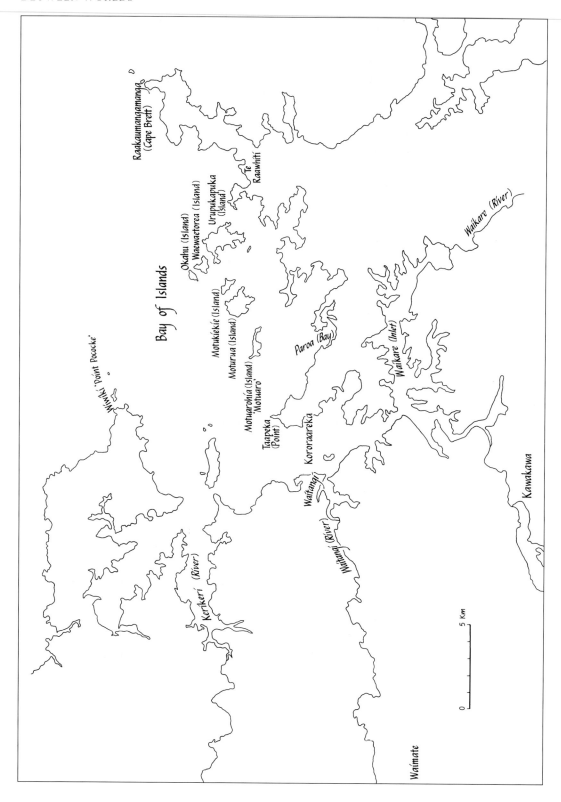

Raakaumangamanga
(Cape Brett)

Te Raawhiti

Okahu (Island)
Waewaetorea (Island)
Urupukapuka (Island)

Waikare (River)

Bay of Islands

Paroa (Bay)

Waikare (Inlet)

Wiwiki 'Point Pocock'

Motukiekie (Island)

Moturua (Island)

Motuarohia (Island) 'Motuaro'

Taapeka (Point)

Kororaareka

Kerikeri (River)

Waitangi

Waitangi (River)

Kawakawa

5 Km

Waimate

the heads and the large island at the mouth of the harbour, and were led by Te Pere; while Ngaati Uru lived on the inner shores, and were led by Pipikoitareke, the father of Te Aara and his elder brother Te Puhi, the father-in-law of Te Pahi.[35]

The boats anchored inside the Whangaroa Heads, and in the morning Matengaro took a boat ashore. There he talked with two Ngaati Uru chiefs, who were wearing garments made from the captured ship's canvas, and soon brought them to meet Berry and his party. The chiefs (very likely Te Puhi and Te Aara, who were key players in what had happened) freely admitted the sack of the ship, talking of it as a heroic achievement. The vessel they had attacked and plundered was the *Boyd*, a transport commanded by John Thompson, which had visited Whangaroa for timber, en route from Port Jackson to London with a cargo of coals, cedar and other timber, salted skins, passengers, and various supplies and papers.[36] The chiefs complained that the captain of the *Boyd* had been a bad man, who had taken one of their chiefs (later identified as 'George', or Te Aara) as he was leaving the vessel with a carpenter's axe under his cloak. He had been tied to the capstan for several hours while the captain threatened to flog him. Berry suggested that perhaps the chief had deserved to be punished, but they retorted 'that any indignity offered to a chief was never forgiven'. They told Berry there were several survivors from the ship, including a woman, her infant and a young boy, speaking of them with kindness and even sympathy. Berry told them that they had two choices: either they could accept a pile of axes he had brought and deliver up the survivors, or he and his men would attack and shoot them.

The principal chief (Te Puhi) thought for a moment, then remarked that 'trading was better than fighting'. He and his companions decided to take the axes, and invited Berry and his men to visit their settlement. Berry told the chiefs to get into his boat, and as they rowed up a narrow and winding tidal river (the Kaeo, where Pipikoitareke had his main paa Te Pohue[37]), warriors hidden among mangroves along the shore saluted them by firing off muskets. When they arrived at the village, a great crowd was waiting, some of the women wearing European clothing. The chiefs pressed Berry to sleep that night in the village, where they would feed them with fish and potatoes. Berry refused his invitation, and instead the Europeans slept on a small, rugged island (Motu-wai, now known as Red Island). The *Boyd* lay wrecked and burnt to the waterline in shoal water nearby, with 'the mangled fragments and fresh bones of our countrymen, with the marks even of the teeth remaining upon them'.[38]

The next morning the one surviving woman passenger, her baby and a young boy called Davis were brought to the island. The woman, Mrs Morley, a publican's wife from Sydney, had been held by local women in bushes just beyond the village the previous day and had overheard the discussions. After the chiefs had been given the axes, Mrs Morley told Berry that she knew of two other survivors, the second mate and Betsey Broughton, the illegitimate youngest daughter of the

Opposite: *A map of the Bay of Islands.*

Deputy Commissary at Sydney, William Broughton, who had accompanied her mother on the *Boyd*. The principal chief now informed Berry that the second mate had been taken by a chief who kept him alive for a while to manufacture fish-hooks out of iron hoops. Because he was no good at this work, however, he had since been killed and eaten. The girl was in the possession of a chief who lived on the island at the entrance of the harbour, and he would send one of his men to go and get her. Berry told him that the child was his 'brother's daughter', and held a pistol to the chief's head, saying that he would have to go himself to fetch her. The two chiefs with their attendants were forced onto a boat at gunpoint and rowed to the offshore island. This was the stronghold of Te Pere, the leader of Ngaati Pou (which accounts for the reluctance of the Ngaati Uru chiefs to go there), later identified as Betsey Broughton's protector.[39]

At the island, one of the chiefs' attendants was sent ashore with a message to deliver up the child, while Berry held them hostage. Fearing that the child might be killed, Berry waited for a while and then ordered the principal chief to send another of his companions ashore with a message. If the child was not brought to him at once, the two chiefs would be shot and then he would go ashore and kill everyone on the island. According to Berry, at this 'he gave me a most ferocious look, his eyes became blood-shot and resembled the eyes of a Tiger springing on its prey'.[40] Berry drew his sword and pointed it at his chest, and the chief began to cry. Shortly after this, the second man went ashore and came back with the little girl, clean and with white feathers in her hair, but thin and with sores all over her body, and dressed in a linen shirt that had belonged to the *Boyd*'s captain. When she was brought to the boat, Berry reported that the child 'cried out in a feeble and complaining tone, "Mamma, my mamma!"' Later, when she was asked what had happened to her mother, she drew her hands across her throat, saying that she had been cut up, cooked and eaten.[41]

Berry's men wanted to land on the island and kill all the people, but Berry refused, saying (according to his own account) that such an act would be wanton and cowardly. Instead, he decided to take the two chiefs to the Bay of Islands and hold them there as prisoners until the ship's papers had been delivered. Matengaro reproached him for breaking his word, telling him that he was a great man and trying to appeal to his sense of honour. Berry replied, 'We have long been friends and as a proof of lasting friendship, let us exchange names.' Matengaro agreed, and from this time on he was called 'Berry' while Berry was addressed as 'Matengaro'. The chiefs' companions were released with instructions to get the ship's papers and bring them to the Bay of Islands. If they were not brought within three days, Berry said that he would take the chiefs to England and deliver them up to King George for punishment.

The boats returned to the Bay, where the chiefs were put in irons on board the *City of Edinburgh* and guarded. Mrs Morley told Berry at this time that the boy Davis had been saved because he had hid in the hold for several days, and that her life had been spared by an old 'savage' moved to pity by her tears and embraces.

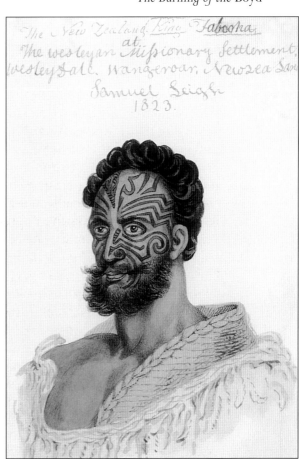

Two portraits sketched by Samuel Leigh in 1823: 'George' (Te Aara) and 'Tabooha'(Te Puhi).

Tuuhawaiki, the young Maori who had accompanied Matengaro, now travelled overland to Whangaroa and came back three days later in one of the *Boyd*'s boats with a box of letters, the ship's log book and a bundle of loose papers. Among these Berry found some valuable Bills of Exchange that he had left in Sydney to send on to his agents in London. As he commented later, 'When I undertook the expedition to Wangaroa . . . I thought I did it from a pure love of humanity for the purpose of saving the survivors from the hands of the Cannibals but it appears I was unconsciously acting for my own benefit, and that one of the results of the expedition was the recovery of my own documents.'[42]

Berry was still not content with the punishment the chiefs had received, although Matengaro often urged him to release them. Finally, he summoned all hands to the poop and announced that because of the atrocities the chiefs had committed, he was going to kill them:

If an Englishman committed a *single* murder, he was hanged, [but] they had massacred a whole Ships Crew and therefore could expect no mercy but as they were Chiefs I would not degrade them by hanging but would shoot them.[43]

Tara was present at these proceedings, smiling and nodding his approval. His only son had been killed a few years earlier on a visit to Whangaroa, leaving him childless. Two muskets were brought, and Berry loaded them himself, then handed them to a couple of Pacific Islanders, who seemed honoured to act as executioners. They took careful aim, while the chiefs covered their faces with their cloaks. The Islanders fired, and the chiefs stood motionless. Everyone thought they had been shot, but Berry had only loaded the muskets with powder. Once they had recovered their self-possession, Berry told the chiefs that he would spare their lives on one condition: that they would become Matengaro's slaves, serving him food and bringing him wood and water as long as they lived, and they agreed. This, he felt, was a fitting punishment. The Maori on board congratulated Berry on his judgement, and Tara, after weeping for a while with emotion, declared that 'they would all in future be warm friends of the Pakeha or Whiteman' (an early northern example of the use of the term 'Pakeha').[44] In return, Berry presented him with the *Boyd*'s boat, and a certificate of good character and behaviour.

While they were still at the Bay of Islands, Berry, Pattison and James Russel, the ship's mate, wrote a Notice warning shipping masters about the 'Massacre of the crew of the Boyd', which squarely blamed Te Pahi for the killings. They claimed that three days after the *Boyd* entered Whangaroa, Te Pahi – 'that old rascal . . . who has been so much, and so undeservedly caressed at Port Jackson' – had arrived from Te Puna. According to their account, he went on board the *Boyd* briefly, then waited alongside the ship in his canoe. As soon as the master went ashore to look for spars, Te Pahi gave a signal and all the people who had been sitting peaceably on the deck pulled out their weapons and killed most of the crew. Five or six sailors escaped into the rigging, but Te Pahi hailed them with a speaking trumpet, ordering them to unbend the sails and cut down the rigging. He told them them that if they came down, they would not be hurt. When they complied, Te Pahi took them to a canoe and killed them all. The shore party was not armed, and they were soon all killed. The survivors were Mrs Morley and her child, Betsey Broughton, and a boy, Thomas Davis.[45]

The source of this information may have been Matengaro, who accompanied Berry to Whangaroa. He was associated with Tara and was probably an enemy of Te Pahi's. Nor was Berry a neutral party, for he had twice been attacked by Te Pahi's allies. Despite this, the effect of his report was unequivocal. For the next few months Te Pahi was universally blamed by Europeans for the *Boyd* killings.

When the *City of Edinburgh* left the Bay in early January 1810, Berry gave copies of this Notice to Tara, telling him to show it to all visiting ships' captains. He also drafted a brief letter to the new Governor of New South Wales, Lachlan Macquarie, dated 6 January 1810, which again blamed Te Pahi for the 'Massacre', adding that 'Tippahee has betaken to the Bush and has eluded my researches'.[46]

When the *City of Edinburgh* prepared to leave the Bay, Tara and Tupi came on board as pilots. As the ship sailed past Te Puna, according to Berry, Tara asked him to fire one of his cannons at Te Pahi's residence to punish him for the part he had played in the destruction of the *Boyd*, and Berry did so. The ship left the Bay and sailed across the Pacific to Valparaiso and Lima, where Thomas Davis went on board a ship that was en route to London. Mrs Morley died, leaving her baby in the care of a Spanish family, and Betsey Broughton was looked after in Lima by another Spanish family who restored her to health, later sending her home to her father at Sydney.

News of the burning of the *Boyd* and the killing of her crew came to Port Jackson on 9 March 1810, just days after the death of Te Pahi's daughter Atahoe was announced in the *Sydney Gazette*.[47] Captain Samuel Rodman Chace of the *King George* had spoken the *Ann* and *Albion* immediately after those ships had left the Bay of Islands, and he brought the report to Port Jackson. Captain Gwynn of the *Ann* had been told by local people that the *Boyd* had been cut off at Whangaroa. Most of the crew had been ashore, where they had taken two boats to collect spars in the forest. The rest of the crew had been repairing the ship's rigging. The local people on board seemed friendly, but at a signal, they took weapons from under their cloaks and killed all the Europeans except for two women and a child. After this their arms and legs were cut off and their bodies were roasted. Chace blamed 'Prince Mattarra, who had lately arrived from England' for leading the attack, but he was mistaken, for Maa-Tara had died of a bronchial complaint several months earlier. He added that 'Tippo-hee' was in his canoe at some distance when the attack occurred, but had joined in plundering and sinking the *Boyd*.[48] Te Puhi was a Ngaati Uru chief and Te Aara's brother, and was indeed involved in the *Boyd* killings.

When a version of this report was published in the *Sydney Gazette*, however, his name was given as 'Tip-pa-hee'. The *Gazette* added that he was helped by his son, known in Sydney as 'Mytye'. Chace had already taken this news to East Cape, where he sent a Maori sailor who had crewed with him for the past three years ashore with a letter warning all ships' captains of the disaster. There he also learned that the *Mary* had foundered off East Cape, but that the crew had been rescued by other whalers.[49]

These reports of the loss of the *Boyd* were a disaster for Te Pahi, who had now been fixed with responsibility for the killings. This 'friendly chief', who had lived with Governor King at Sydney and whose son had met Sir Joseph Banks and the royal family in England, was castigated as a treacherous cannibal. Berry, Pattison and Russel ended their account: 'let no man (after this) trust a New Zealander'. Governor Macquarie had just arrived from England to replace Bligh, and when he reported the loss of the *Boyd* to Viscount Castlereagh in London and Lord Minto at Calcutta shortly afterwards, he also blamed Te Pahi, asking them to warn all South Sea whalers and East India Company vessels 'to be very vigilant and guarded in their intercourse with the New Zealanders, as well as with all the Natives of the South Sea Islands, who are in general a very treacherous race of People, and not to be trusted'.[50] A broadsheet was printed in London, describing the 'Atrocious and Horrible Massacree Of the Crew of the Ship Boyd', and circulated to the sailors. It was illustrated with a woodcut and ended with a ballad:[51]

Ye British seamen hearts of gold,
Who plough the raging sea,
Attend, while I to you unfold,
A horrid Massacree,
Which did of very late take place,
Upon a British crew,
So dismal and so foul a case,
Before you never knew.

Returning home from Botany Bay,
The Captain and his crew,
At anchor in New Zealand lay,
Some timber for to view.
And while the Captain went on shore,
The timber for to see,
Chief Tippohee came on board,
With all his company.

Some time he view'd the vessel o'er,
Then gave a dreadful yell,
Which was the signal to begin,
Upon the crew they fell.

Thirty of whom the monsters tore,
Limb from limb with speed,
And while their teeth did reek with gore,
They eat it as 'twere bread.

Two women and a lad they took,
On shore, and both were saved,
The Captain murder'd was on shore,
All by these blood-hound knaves.
The ship they robb'd of all her store,
Then burnt her up with speed,
The Monsters hasten'd to the shore,
When they had done the deed.

Be warn'd, ye Captains, by the fate,
Of Thomson, and his crew,
Touch not that cursed shore lest you
These Cannibals pursue.
Those murd'rous fiends who live by blood,
Like Tigers watch their prey,
For while they smile they're bent the while,
To take your lives away.

Stories of the *Boyd* 'Massacree' were told and retold, in Port Jackson, Calcutta, Paris and London. The tale played its part in an ongoing European debate about the essential nature of 'savages'. On one side of the argument, savages were said to be human and entitled to be treated as such. Although they were not yet civilised, they were thought to be capable of instruction. Like women and children, they might be immature, and thus in need of guidance and protection, but yet they had rights as human beings, which must be respected. According to the contrary view, however, savages could never be trusted. No matter how intelligent and attractive they might seem, they were wild animals at heart, vicious, bloodthirsty and violent. In this debate, Te Pahi was cited as an archetypal 'Ignoble Savage' whose impressive demeanour had hoodwinked Samuel Marsden, Governor King and the Port Jackson settlers into treating him as a reasonable being. The *Boyd*'s crew had paid for this mistake with their lives. 'Monsters' like Te Pahi and his people were bestial and beyond human rights, to be handled by avoidance, caution and violence. In response, Marsden and others of the missionaries depicted Te Pahi as innocent and noble, a victim of brutal degraded Europeans.

By and large, the whalers were illiberal in their views, and the violence was not long in coming. News of Te Pahi's involvement in the *Boyd* killings spread rapidly by word of mouth among the whaling vessels. In his letter to Castlereagh, Macquarie reported that an expedition proposed by Simeon Lord and other local merchants to establish a flax-collecting colony in New Zealand was still going

Opposite: *A broadsheet about the* Boyd.

Atrocious and Horrible MASSACREE,

Of the Crew of the Ship Boyd, Capt. Thomson, Newcastle, who were Murdered & Devoured by the Cannibals of New Zealand, where the Ship had touched on her passage home from Botany Bay.

IT appears that whilst the Boyd was at Botany Bay the Captain went with one of the two Chiefs who govern the Island of New Zealand, named Tippohee & agreed with him to purchase some timber to take to England. As soon as the voyage would permit, the ship arrived at the Island, and the Captain was promised the timber in two days. In the mean time, he was invited on shore, and attended the Chief with part of the ship's company in the boat. Nothing particular transpired on this occasion; but the Chief returned on board, the ship attended by a number of canoes full of men. They were permitted to examine the ship, as a matter of curiosity. Tippohee was treated with great respect; and having continued on board some time, he got into his boat, for the purpose as was supposed. of meeting the Captain who had gone to see the timber. Instead however, he gave a dreadful yell, which was the signal for the massacre of the whole ship's company.—There were about 40 in all, 30 of whom the horrid monsters tore limb from limb, and regaled themselves on the flesh of the unfortunate victims. Ten of the men, 2 women passengers, and a lad, ran below; the Chief hailed the men, and told them they had got all they wanted, having plundered the ship, and if they would come down their lives should be spared. The deluded men obeyed, and fell like their comrades, a sacrifice to the inordinate and brutal appetites of the cannibals. The 2 women and the boy were taken on shore, and their lives spared but the ship was burnt. The rival Chief, Pari, situated at a different part of the Island, heard of the affair, and expressed his sorrow on the occasion to the Captain of the City of Edinburgh, who was at the Island for timber, and prepared to accompany him with an armed force to release the women & boy, in which they perfectly succeeded.

The following address has been circulated on the subject of the late massacre by the cannibals natives of that quarter;—" All Masters of ships frequenting New Zealand, are directed to be careful in not admitting many natives on board, as they may be cut off in an instant by surprise. These are to certify, that during our stay in this harbour, we had frequent reports of a ship being taken by the natives of the neighbouring harbour of Wanganoa, and that the crew were killed and eaten. In order to ascertain the truth of this report, as well as to rescue a few people who were said to be spared in the general massacre, Mr. Berty accompanied by Mr. Russel, and Metangangoa, a principal Chief of the Bay Islands, who volunteered his services, set out for Wangangoa in three armed boats, on Saturday the 4th of May and upon their arrival they found the miserable remains of the ship Boyd, which the natives after stripping of every thing of value, had burnt down to the water's edge. From the handsome conduct of Metangangoa, they were able to rescue a boy, a woman. and two children, the only survivors of this shocking event; which, according to the most satisfactory information, was perpetrated entirely under the direction of that old rascal Tippohee who had been so undeservedly caressed at Port Jackson. This unfortunate vessel intended to load with masts, &c. She had been there 3 days; after her arrival, the natives informed the master, that in two days they would shew the spars. Next day, in the morning, Tippohee came from Tippusia, and went on board; he staid only a few minutes. He then went into his canoe, and remained along-side the vessel, which was surrounded with a considerable number of canoes that had collected for the purpose of trading; and a great number of the natives gradually intruded into the ship, and sat down upon the deck. After breakfast, the master left the ship to look out for spars with two boats. Tippohee, after waiting a convenientt ime now gave signal for Massacre—in an instant the savages, who appeared peaceable on deck, rushed upon the unarmed crew who were variously employed about the ship: the greater part were massacred in an instant, and were no sooner knocked down than they were cut to pieces still alive. Five or 6 men escaped by the rigging. Tippohee now having possession of the ship, hailed them with a speaking-trumpet, and ordered them to unbend the sails and cut away the rigging and they should not be hurt they complied with his commands, and afterwards came down upon the deck he then took him on shore in a çanoe, and immediately killed them The master went ashore without arms, and of course, was easily dispatched. The natives of the Spar district in this harbour have behaved well, even beyond expectation, and seem much concerned on account of the event! and dreading the displeasure of King George, have requested a certificate of their good conduct, in order to exempt them from his vengeance; but let no man after his trust a New Zealander.

(Signed)   Simon Pattinson, Alex. Berry, Supercargo, James Russel.

" Given on board the City of Edinburgh, Captain S. Pattison, at the Bay Islands.

The boy Davinson, mentioned above, owed the preservation his life to his being club footed, the natives taking him for a so n of the devil.

Printed by J. Catnach, 2, Monmouth-court, 7 Dials

YE British seamen hearts of gold,
  Who plough the raging sea,
Attend, while I to you unfold,
  A horrid Massacree.
Which did of very late take place,
  Upon a British crew,
So dismal and so foul a case,
  Before you never knew.

Returning home from Botany Bay,
  The Captain and his crew,
At anchor at New Zealand lay,
  Some timber for to view.
And while the Captain went on shore,
  The timber for to see

Chief Tippohee came on board,
  With all his company.
Some time he view'd the vessel o'er,
  Then gave a dreadful yell,
Which was the signal to begin,
  Upon the crew they fell.
Thirty of whom the monsters tore,
  Limb from limb with speed,
And while their flesh did reek with gore,
  They eat it as 'twere bread.

Two women and a lad they took,
  On shore, and both were sav'd,
The Captain murder'd was on shore.
  All by these blood-hound knaves.

The ship they robb'd of all her store,
  Then burnt her up with speed,
The Monsters hasten'd to the shore,
  When they had done the deed.

Be warn'd ye Captains, by the fate,
  Of Thomson, and his crew,
Touch not that cursed shore left you
  These Cannibals pursue.
Those murd'rous fiends who live by blood,
  Like Tigers watch their prey,
For while they smile they're bent the while.
  To take your lives away.

ahead, although several of the partners had pulled out because of the 'recent melancholy occurrence.'[52] This was the expedition that George Bruce and his wife had been supposed to lead, but by now Atahoe had died and Bruce's contract with Lord was cancelled. The expedition left Sydney on the *Experiment* on 17 March 1810 with William Leith (who had lived in Tamatea with the *Britannia*'s sealing gang) on board, and sailed to North Cape, anchoring at the entrance of the Bay of Islands on 5 April.[53] There they were told that, ten days earlier, Te Pahi's island had been raided by a vengeful party of whalers, who learned of the *Boyd* killings from a young woman. She told them that four white men, named Brown, Cook, Anthony and Harry, were being held prisoners inland. It was also suggested that Te Pahi had murdered his son Maa-Tara in a rage. According to Leith, sixty of Te Pahi's people had been killed in the raid, and the chief had escaped to Whangaroa.[54]

A report on this raid was forwarded to Governor Macquarie[55] by the captains of the vessels involved – the *Speke* (John Hingston, later identified as 'the ringleader in this horrid affair'[56]), *Inspector* (John Walker), *Diana* (William Parker), *Atalanta* (Josh Morris), which had sailed to the fishery about the same time as the *Boyd*,[57] and the *Perseverance* (Frederick Hasselberg), a sealing vessel that collected a cargo of spars at the Bay. According to their report, the captains each took an armed boat to the island to look for arms, ammunition and *Boyd* survivors. When they landed, they found the 'natives in a hostile disposition'. The local people had 'set up a General Cry' and threw spears and fired muskets at the sailors. The whalers took the island 'by force of arms', while 'the natives with Tippahee escaped to the Main', taking their muskets with them or throwing them into the water.[58]

When the Lords' Committee of the Privy Council held an inquiry into this incident in 1812, however, the Thames Police took depositions from Henry Bryers, a Prussian sailor from the *Inspector*, who had been present during the attack, and William Smith of Salem, chief mate of the *Inspector*, who had stayed on board the vessel. The police referred to this attack as an 'outrage', but were unable to locate any more eyewitnesses.

According to these depositions, at about four o'clock in the morning, a party of five armed boats had been sent to row the twenty miles from their anchorage to Te Pahi's island in an effort to recover the *Boyd*'s longboat and stores. Te Pahi, thinking they came for wood, had welcomed them in broken English. When the mate of the *Perseverance* found the *Boyd*'s boat, they landed on the island, where local people armed with spears and muskets confronted them. Captain Walker ordered the sailors to fire, and four of the local people fell, while the rest fled to a larger island. (A later account from Philip Tapsell, who arrived in the whaler *New Zealander* just after the raid, added that Te Pahi was shot by Captain Parker in the chest or neck, but managed to escape to the mainland, swimming with the assistance of two women[59]). The boats of the *Inspector* and *Speke* followed them and many men and women were shot in the water. At least fifteen people were killed in the attack, only one of them being a European, who was shot when a Portugese sailor accidentally fired his musket. The sailors burnt all the houses at Te Puna and some on the larger island. Bryers said that the people of Whangaroa were 'at enmity' with the people of Te Puna.

The Solicitor-General wrote to the Lords' Committee that in his view Captain Walker and those who had participated in the attack were guilty of murder. By then Bryers and Smith had left the country. The Lords asked the Thames Police to keep watch for the return to England of any of the ships or sailors involved, and there the matter seems to have rested.[60]

After the *Experiment* joined the whalers responsible for the attack at the upper end of the harbour soon after this affray, Te Mahanga came on board and managed their dealings with local people. There was almost no food to be had, because 'all the natives of this bay [are] at war with one another'. A war party of nine hundred men had recently left on an attack to the eastward (presumably to Raawhiti, or thereabouts). On 9 April, the Europeans travelled to a river (probably the Mangoonui Inlet) to the north of the Bay, where the four white men were rumoured to be held captive. They walked ten miles inland, and then returned to the ship before dark, having seen no white men, very few trees and almost no flax. Leith wrote to Messrs Lord, Williams and Thompson that Bruce had grossly deceived them with his stories about flax and timber in the Bay, adding 'that the masters of the different ships have to thank themselves for all the evils they have brought on by their injustice and ill-treatment of the natives'. Colonel Foveaux, who was a passenger on the *Experiment*, transferred to the *Speke* at the Bay for the voyage back to England.[61] Leith decided to collect a cargo of spars and go to Whangaroa if Captain Dodd was willing. From there they could sail to North Cape to join the schooner *Governor Bligh*, and then proceed to East Cape, where good flax and mats could be procured, and from there to Queen Charlotte Sound, where the whalers reported plenty of flax and very few inhabitants. After visiting almost every town in the Bay of Islands, however, Leith had to report that he had procured only four pounds of flax, no mats, and very little timber. Some locals had told him that the *Parramatta* had been cut off earlier in the Bay, an attack for which they also blamed Te Pahi (although it seems more likely that Tara's people were responsible).[62]

The *Experiment* failed to meet up with the *Governor Bligh*. Leith's men, abandoning all hope of finding a suitable site for a flax-collecting settlement, transferred to the *New Zealander* and went back to Sydney.

When Captain Chace returned in the *Governor Bligh* to the north-east coast of New Zealand on 28 April 1810, eight fishing canoes came out to meet him. A man who had served with him on the *King George* told Chace that a brig, which he assumed to be the *Experiment*, had left the Bay ten days earlier. He also told Chace about the attack on Te Pahi's stronghold, and that the chief had subsequently been killed by a spear thrust in a fight with a Whangaroa rival. Te Pahi's son had also died, along with his fighting chief 'Whaetary', both victims to 'the arts and connivances of Tettua, or god' (presumably referring to their deaths by illnesses picked up from the Europeans), and the head chief of Whangaroa . The people had told him that 'they had no kings remaining on the coast, but that every man was the ruler of his own family'.

When they arrived at the Bay of Islands, Chace found Te Pahi's settlement in ruins and many of the people in the vicinity walking about dressed in the clothes of the *Boyd* sailors. He talked to them, trying to dissuade them from any more such attacks, but their minds were preoccupied with fighting and food shortages, and they paid him little attention.[63] Te Mahanga came out to the *Governor Bligh*, bringing letters from Captain Clark of the *Ann* and a letter from Leith, advising him of the likely course of the *Experiment*. Chace was able to frustrate an attack on his ship, and talked with a Tahitian settled in the Bay, who gave him a detailed account of the *Boyd* killings, which was quite different from Tara, Berry and Pattison's original version.

When Chace returned to Port Jackson, the *Sydney Gazette* published this account of the 'Massacre', which exonerated Te Pahi and Matara from responsibility for the killings. The Tahitian (probably 'Tom', or 'Jemmy', who had arrived on the *City of Edinburgh*) claimed that when the *Boyd* left Port Jackson, there were four or five Maori on board, who had been mistreated during their passage. As soon as they arrived at Whangaroa, they told their friends and relations what had happened, and it was decided to take the ship as utu. Captain Thompson was invited ashore and went, taking three armed boats. He and his men were led into the bush, where they were confronted by their Maori shipmates, who upbraided them for their mistreatment. When Thompson turned to go back to the ship, he and his men were attacked with clubs and axes, and killed and later eaten. The warriors returned to the ship in darkness, dressed in their victims' clothes, and told the second officer that Thompson had decided to sleep on shore but told them to begin loading the spars on board. They came over the side and attacked the rest of the crew, who were soon all killed, except for a few who ran up the rigging and stayed there all night. One man was sent to call the passengers up on deck to look at the spars being loaded, and they were also killed. Only a woman and her two children, who had hidden below, and the boy Davis were saved.[64] The next morning, when Te Pahi arrived at the ship, he was angry about what happened. He tried to save the men in the rigging, telling them that if they could get to his canoe, he would rescue them. They made the attempt but were intercepted and killed while Te Pahi was held back forcibly. The woman and the two children were then taken ashore and the ship was plundered. Te Pahi was allowed to take away three boatloads of goods from the ship, except the guns, which the local people kept for themselves. One man (later identified as Te Aara's father, Pipi), who was anxious to test a musket he had taken, snapped it over a cask of powder, which blew up, killing five local women and eight or nine men, and setting fire to the *Boyd*.[65]

Several years later, the missionary Thomas Kendall heard a similar story at the Bay about the *Boyd* killings, which added a few extra details. He was told that during the voyage to New Zealand, Te Aara had been ill for five days and had heard Captain Thompson say that he would throw him overboard. Thompson flogged him from his sickbed and forced him back to work. At Whangaroa, when Te Aara's people attacked the *Boyd* in retribution, the boy Thomas Davis was found hiding in the hold. He appealed to Te Aara, saying, 'George, you will not kill me?' and George replied, 'No, you are a good boy; we will not kill you.' Like the Tahitian, Kendall's sources were adamant that Te Pahi had played no part in the killings.[66]

The most direct account of the taking of the *Boyd* was given by 'George' (Te Aara, Te Pahi's brother-in-law) in a letter to Governor Brisbane in November 1823, quoted here in the original translation. According to this account, people from Te Puna were involved in the affray:

> My Friend,
>
> Let our anger cease for the killing of Capn. Thompson, and all his men. I came from Port Jackson on board his Ship and he flogged me thrice. As soon as his Ship was at anchor, I went on Shore and told my tribe the Tribe at Whangaroa, the Kiddi Kiddi (Kerikeri), Tippoonah (Te Puna), and the tribe at Shukianga (Hokianga), and they all came to this Place and killed Capt. Thomson and his crew. A little time after A Ship came from England to revenge the loss of the Boyd where Tippehee, his son, and Ruatara were killed. That is enough, let our anger cease, and as a token of this I have given A New Zealand Matt to Mr. White for you. You give me a Fowling piece to shoot Birds for food. That will do. No more from your
>
> Friend George.[67]

The truth of the matter can never be finally known, but it seems that Te Pahi was not personally involved in the *Boyd* killings. Nevertheless, he certainly shared in her plunder. In the end, he himself was killed by a lethal combination of inter-tribal animosity and European antagonism. Berry had a score to settle, Tara had seized the opportunity to blackguard a rival, and the whalers were only too happy to believe them. Te Pahi's friendship with Governor King, which aroused the jealousy of local chiefs and European settlers alike, eventually proved fatal.[68]

Te Pahi's death, and the loss of the *Boyd*, also had long-term reverberations in Port Jackson. Simeon Lord, who during Bligh's time as Governor had been margin-alised, hoped to use the *Boyd*'s voyage to regain his pre-eminence as a trader. He had loaded a cargo of sealskins, coal and timber on board the ship and sent her to New Zealand for spars, asking Acting Governor Paterson (who had taken over from Foveaux) to recommend Captain Thompson to the Governor of the Cape of Good Hope as a supplier of timber, coal and spars in exchange for South African wine.[69] The burning of the *Boyd* ruined this scheme, and over the next few years Lord and his fellow entrepreneurs in Sydney went through difficult times.[70] An oversupply of goods from India and a period of severe drought led to an economic depression in the penal colony, and a sharp decline in the numbers of European vessels to visit New Zealand. The idea of establishing a settlement there had been canvassed in Port Jackson just before the *Boyd*'s voyage, on the grounds of economic and social advantage:

> The natives of New Zealand are a very different race to those of New South Wales;

they are of a different colour, athletic, muscular men, arising no doubt from the superior nature of the soil and its production. The sea also furnishes great quantities of superior fish of every description, and the forest timber is reported excellent. The spars for masts and yards are cut down upon these islands and carried to China where they fetch a very high price. Hemp and flax can be produced in any quanitity, and in the southern parts of the South Island the wool might be improved equal to the best in Europe.[71]

This, indeed, had been the motivation behind the 1810 voyage of the *Experiment*. The attack on the *Boyd*, though, reminded the merchants and officials in Port Jackson that Maori were cannibals, as well as formidable warriors. Colonial ambitions were set aside once again, at least in the meantime.

Conclusion

Utu, Law and Commerce

In Maori ways of being, utu was a pivotal dynamic. Hau, or vitality, was needed to master the art of successful exchanges. A person of mana engaged in oratory, song, fighting, gift exchange or in spiritual contests (commonly translated as 'magic' or 'witchcraft'). These were competitive arts, in which mana might be lost or diminished. As the lives of Maori and Europeans tangled more closely together, the danger of their encounters intensified. For Maori, this pattern was far from surprising. The word hoa in Maori, for instance, means 'companion, friend', while hoariri (literally 'angry friend') means 'enemy', or 'antagonist'.

In Maori, intimacy was a risky business. Aapiti, used in many incantations, means 'to bring together, place side by side', and 'lay a spell on, curse' or 'to begin hostilities'. Awhi means at once 'embrace' and 'beseige'. The most powerful metaphors in the language relate to the crossing of boundaries. Pae refers to a place between worlds – earth and sky, light and darkness, local people and strangers. It means the horizon, over which enemies or friends might appear; or the edge between people (taangata Maori) and supernatural beings (taangata atua). Pae o te riri is the resting place of a war party on the march; kai paepae refers to offerings of food between one kin group and another; pae arahi is a person who leads strangers onto a kin group's ceremonial ground, while paepae hamuti is the latrine beam, a ritual edge between the everyday world of light and the dark realm of ancestor spirits. Whakapae means to cross such a boundary; to beseige a fortification; or to make peace with an offering. In Maori, at least, it was taken for granted that boundary crossing was spiritually and physically dangerous. Power lived in liminal places.

Success in such exchanges required ancestral power, to survive the encounter. The word hau, the vitality of person or land, also referred to gestures of assertion – the food offered to atua in rituals of propitiation; a return gift for one received from an exchange partner; to strike, or to smite. The worst thing, always, was to be unable to act. Captivity and imprisonment were the stuff of a nightmare. Harm to the hau demanded utu, a response, otherwise the life force would perish. Verbal insults, or rhetorical attack, provoked retaliation. If women were raped, the hau of the descent group was hurt and the offenders were punished. If a rangatira was tied up and flogged, the hau of his people was damaged. The destruction of the *Boyd*, the *Parramatta*, and other European ships were utu for such inflammatory gestures. Encounters with Europeans were also characterised by forbearance, however, and attempts at negotiated peace-making. Te Pahi's restraint in the face of repeated abuses, and his attempts to ally himself with the Kaawana (Governors) at Port Jackson foreshadowed the signing of the Treaty of Waitangi in New Zealand.

Although cross-cultural journeys were dangerous, they were also thrilling. The young men who boarded European vessels and sailed to Norfolk Island, Port Jackson, Tahiti, Tonga, Fiji, South America, Britain, North America and India sought new knowledge, experience, wealth and excitement. Exploration and discovery in these adventures were two-way processes. Maori, as well as other Polynesians on the ships, were experimenting with new ways of living. Risk-taking had its own heady rewards, even if one might die in the process. One can recognise in these sailors (and the women who sometimes went with them) the voyagers who first peopled the Pacific.

Both Europeans and Maori gained much from their repeated encounters. For Maori, this included iron tools, textiles, European plants and animals, building techniques, firearms, and adventure. They risked exposure to European infectious and epidemic diseases (formerly unknown in New Zealand), physical danger on board the ships and the possibility of degrading treatment. Europeans, on the other hand, gained access to the resources of a new archipelago and its surrounding seas – flax, timber, seals and whales in particular. They recruited local men to help them with the harvest, and sought local women for sexual satisfaction. Wood, fresh water, green stuff for scurvy, root crops (including introduced species such as turnips and potatoes) and fresh meat (especially pork) were acquired as provisions for their sea journeys. They risked the dangers of surprise attack, shipwreck and marooning. Many of them preferred perils such as these to convict life or a menial metropolitan existence.

Although most Europeans in this period assumed themselves to be superior to barbarians and savages, the nearest colonial outposts to New Zealand were the 'thief colonies' at Norfolk Island and Port Jackson, peopled by outcasts from Britain. The convicts had been 'projected, and as it should seem purposely – as far out of sight as possible' for breaking the laws of their own society. In the new world, it was hoped they would redeem themselves through good behaviour and hard labour. In such a situation it seemed important to consider themselves a higher form of life than tattooed heathens and cannibals.

The colonial representatives of British law – the governors and colonial officers – on the other hand, often saw (and treated) the convicts as savages. They sometimes suspected that the 'children of nature' might be preferable to such 'unnatural' villains. Philip Gidley King, for instance, regarded Tuki-tahua and Huru-kokoti, and Te Pahi and his sons, as 'sensible men', even 'Gentlemen'. They slept in his house and dined at his table – a liberty never extended to the convicts. The extension of civil rights to Pacific Islanders, including Maori, through various proclamations was intended to protect them against lawless Europeans. In establishing such constraints, successive governors treated Maori chiefs (at least rhetorically) as diplomatic partners, and important leaders.

Both commerce and law were global forces, which flung people across geographic expanses. Wars in Europe created a demand for timber and flax; while European cities and machines required sea-mammal oil for lubrication and lighting. Treaties were signed that handed over Pacific continents and islands; while disputes among European powers led to ships being sunk or taken as prizes. Maori men and women were drawn into this vortex of events, by foul play, accident or free decision. They found themselves far from home, speaking new languages, eating new foods and undergoing cultural mutation. Equally, European men and women came to New Zealand and underwent cultural transformations. Important cross-cultural alliances were forged – Honekai and James Cadell in the south; Thomas Taylor and Te Haupa in Hauraki; and Governor King, Tuki and Huru, and Te Pahi in the north are just the more obvious examples. The relationship between King and Te Pahi affected many other lives – those of George Bruce, Atahoe, Maa-Tara, Sir Joseph Banks, Charlotte Badger and her unnamed rangatira. Tattooed Europeans dressed in cloaks and Maori dressed in European suits were the more exotic products of these existential migrations. Not only people, but plants, animals and diseases were moved about. Whole worlds were being re-created.

TAPU
AND
RELIGION

THE EVANGELICAL VOYAGES

REFLECTIONS ON TAPU AND RELIGION

In 1865, fifty years after the introduction of Christianity to New Zealand, a tohunga (priestly expert) named Te Maatorohanga spoke to the students in his tribal waananga (school of learning). He said:

> The tapu (pl.) have ended, the ancient teachings are gone, the karakia (incantations) are lost and they are no longer known. Because tapu is the first thing, if there is no tapu all the works of the gods have no mana, and if the gods are lost, everything is useless – people, their actions and their thoughts are in a whirl, and the land itself becomes confused.[1]

In this lament, Te Maatorohanga claimed that tapu was at the beginnings of creation. Since tapu was the first thing, without it the works of the gods were devoid of mana. If the gods were lost, the world itself became confused. Gods, people and land were left in a state of whirling chaos.

According to the waananga chants, we have noted, the cosmos began with a surge of primal power. From this, thought emerged, followed by memory, the mind-heart, knowledge, darkness and the kore (nothingness, potential forms of existence). Tapu, or cosmic power, was the source of all creation. It brought complementary forms of life together, generating new beings.[2]

When Earth Mother and Sky Father came forth, they were locked together in a tapu state of union. Their children were born, cramped between their parents, until Taane pushed earth and sky apart, letting light into the cosmos. Now life began for plants, fish, birds and people. It blew through the cosmos like a wind, bringing freedom and renewal. Once present in the world of light, this power could be called upon by humans, and channelled through ritual pathways of flax, rods or hair into stones, receptacles or people.

One can see these ideas at work in the patterns of the language. An aho was a string or line, the cross threads woven into a cloak, a line of descent, and the medium for an ancestor god, or atua. An ahorangi was a man like Te Maatorohanga, a teacher in the whare waananga. Kaha was a boundary line, a rope, strength, a line of ancestry, and the line of niu rods used in divination. A kaupapa was a trail or track, the groundwork of a cloak, the medium for communicating with an atua, the navel string, or rods used in rituals of divination. Power travelled through all these pathways. If karakia and rituals were neglected, though, the gods abandoned their people. Sickness came, and defeat and failure. The wind of life ceased to blow. The world had lost its bearings.

The evangelical voyages that brought the first missionaries to New Zealand were inspired by a different cosmological theory. This was expressed in Genesis, in the Bible:

> In the beginning God created the heaven and the earth.
> And the earth was without form, and void; and darkness was upon the face of the deep. And the Spirit of God moved upon the face of the waters.
> And God said, let there be light: and there was light.
> And God saw the light, that it was good: and God divided the light from the darkness.
> And God called the light Day, and the darkness he called Night. And the evening and the morning were the first day.
> And God said, Let there be a firmament in the midst of the waters, and let it divide the waters from the waters.
> And God made the firmament, and divided the waters which were under the firmanent from the waters which were above the firmament: and it was so.
> And God called the firmament Heaven. And the evening and the morning were the second day.
> And God said, Let the waters under the heaven be gathered together unto one place, and let the dry land appear: and it was so.
> And God called the dry land Earth; and the gathering together of the waters called he Seas: and God saw that it was good.
> And God said, Let the earth bring forth grass, the herb yielding seed, and the fruit tree yielding fruit after his kind, whose seed is in itself, upon the earth: and it was so.
> And the earth brought forth grass, and herb yielding seed after his kind, and the tree yielding fruit, whose seed was in itself, after his kind: and God saw that it was good.
> And the evening and the morning were the third day . . .

On the fourth day, God made the sun and moon; on the fifth day He created fish and birds; and on the sixth day He created animals, and man and woman in his own image. He blessed them and said, 'Be fruitful, and multiply and replenish the earth, and subdue it: and have dominion over the fish of the sea, and over the fowl of the air, and over every living thing that moveth upon the earth.' On the seventh day he ended his work, and rested, and sanctified that day, 'because that in it he had rested from all his worke, which God created and made'.

Whereas in the Maori account the cosmos began with a burst of primal energy, in the Christian account the spirit of God moved in the void, calling up the elements of creation. God summoned up the light and divided it from darkness, naming them 'day' and 'night', and called up the firmament, dividing the waters above and below Heaven. He divided land from sea, naming them Earth and Seas; and made the earth productive. He set lights in the heaven, to divide and rule over day and night; and made fish, birds and animals, and then man and woman. Man and woman were commanded to be fruitful and subdue the earth, and God gave them dominion over all living creatures. While in the Maori account each form of life came together with another to make something new in a network of genealogical connection, in the Christian account God created the world by splitting its parts into binary sets. The Deity was depicted as an analytic logician.

God dividing up the Universe, by William Blake.

The first missionaries to New Zealand took the biblical account of the cosmos for granted. It is fascinating to see how it resonated with other contemporary ideas that influenced them. The European idea of the Great Chain of Being, for instance, so often echoed in their writings, took the notion of dominion from the creation story and turned it into a cosmic hierarchy.[3] All forms of life were ranked, from an omiscient and omnipotent God to the angels, to cherubim and seraphim, kings and queens, princes of the church and aristocrats, down to ignorant commoners, barbarians and savages. From savages the Chain descended to apes and other intelligent animals, through insects and plants and finally stones and earth, which had no sentience whatever. The upper end of the Great Chain of Being was lit with the light of knowledge and understanding; the lower end was sunk in ignorance and darkness. The missionary enterprise was understood as taking the Gospel of God to savages lost in epistemic murk, and raising them up to Enlightenment.

Seventeen

'THE SWEETS OF CIVILIZATION'
RUATARA AND SAMUEL MARSDEN

Enlightenment, however, had to wait its turn to come to Aotearoa. One immediate consequence of the burning of the *Boyd* was to delay the arrival of missionaries at the Bay of Islands. For years, the principal chaplain at New South Wales, Samuel Marsden, had been contemplating a mission to New Zealand. According to his own account, the notion first occurred to him when he heard about Tuki and Huru during a visit to Norfolk Island.[1] Some years later, when he met Te Pahi and his young relative Ruatara at Port Jackson, he decided to send a mission among the New Zealanders.[2] Marsden saw his meetings with these men as part of a divine plan that controlled the great events of world history:

> When the fulness of time drew near for these poor heathen nations to be favoured with the knowledge of Divine revelation, the Supreme Governor of the World overruled the political affairs of America and England to further this object, and made the wrath of man to praise him. One great step was accomplished when America, in July 1776, was declared a free and independent nation. A short time before this important event took place, Captn. Cook, accompanied by the late Sir Joseph Banks, had been sent by the British Government to visit the South Sea Islands; and during this voyage the great navigator visited New South Wales and anchored in Botany Bay.
>
> After peace had been established between England and America; in the year 1783, the British Government found that it had now no place to which the national convicts might be transported . . . The above single fact . . . clearly shows that the whole was under the superintending providence of an all wise and merciful God . . . He did not establish a colony in New South Wales . . . by selecting men of character and principle:– on the contrary, He took men from the dregs of society – the scrapings of Jails, Hulks and Prisons – men who had forfeited their lives or liberties to the Laws of their country:– but He mercifully gave them their lives for a prey, and sent them forth to make a way for His missionary servants – for them that should bring glad tidings – that should publish peace to the Heathen world, that should say unto them in the name of the Lord 'Look unto Me and be ye saved, all the ends of the Earth, – "For I am God, and there is none else."' Well may we

The Reverend Samuel Marsden, portrayed by Richard Read in 1833.

exclaim with the apostle: 'How unsearchable are His judgements, and His ways past finding out.'[3]

Marsden was impressed by the intellectual capacity of the Maori he had met: 'Their minds appeared like a rich soil that had never been cultivated, and only wanted the proper means of improvement to render them fit to rank with civilized nations.' The fact that Maori ate people only convinced him that they were in urgent need of salvation. 'I knew that they were Cannibals – that they were a savage race – full of superstition, and wholly under the power and influence of the Prince of darkness; and that there was only one remedy which could effectually free them from their cruel spiritual bondage, and misery; and that was the Gospel of a cruci-fied Saviour.'[4] He added in a letter to the Church Missionary Society (CMS):

> Having an ardent wish, that the New Zealanders may enjoy the Sweets of Civiliza-tion, and the more inestimable Blessings of divine Revelation; I shall feel a pecu-liar Pleasure in seconding any Attempt the Society might be inclined to make for their general Improvement, and Advantage.[5]

Samuel Marsden was an energetic, strong-minded Yorkshireman who had come to minister to the convicts at Port Jackson. In the 1780s, while working as a blacksmith's apprentice, he had been chosen as a potential cleric by the Elland Society. He was tutored, and sent for training to Hull Grammar School and Magdalene College in Cambridge. After securing the post of assistant chaplain at Port Jackson, he settled in the colony where he became a magistrate, Principal Chaplain to successive governors, and a wealthy farmer.[6] As a magistrate, Marsden became notorious when he meted out brutal floggings to Irish suspects during the 1800 convict uprising. He disliked Catholicism and regarded the Irish as 'the most wild, ignorant and savage Race that were ever favoured with the Light of Civilization . . . extremely superstitious artful and treacherous'.[7] In his role as Principal Chaplain, he acted as agent for the London Missionary Society's Tahitian mission, and was co-founder of the Female Orphanage with Governor King, and an ardent campaigner against drunkenness and 'immorality'.[8] On his estates at Parramatta, where he experimented with artificial grasses and cross-bred sheep (mainly merinos), he prepared the first commercial shipment of wool to England. By the time he met Te Pahi in 1805 and Ruatara during the following year, Samuel Marsden had become a substantial citizen. He owned 2,974 acres at Parramatta, on which there were 1,416 sheep, twelve horses, sixty-three cattle, twenty goats and twelve hogs.[9] Having conceived of a mission to Maori, he acted with characteristic purpose and decision. He opened his home to Maori visitors, and in February 1807 sailed to England to recruit evangelists for New Zealand.[10]

Thus Marsden was absent from the colony during Te Pahi's second, ill-fated visit to Sydney. He missed the mutiny against Bligh led by John Macarthur and his business colleagues, a circumstance that he later considered fortunate. Macarthur and Marsden were rivals, and Marsden might have suffered at the hands of the mutineers. In England, he persuaded the leaders of the CMS that it would be best to begin by establishing a self-supporting mission, under the protection of the Principal Chaplain and the Governor of New South Wales. In such a mission, the arts of civilisation should be taught to 'the Heathen' Maori by artisan missionaries. Marsden ardently believed that 'Commerce promotes Industry – Industry Civilization and Civilization offers a way for the Gospel'.[11] After commerce and trade, the 'mechanic arts' could open the way for religion:

> The attention of the Heathens can only be gained and their vagrant Habits corrected, by the Arts. Till their attention is gained, and moral and industrious Habits are induced, little or no progress can be made in teaching them the Gospel. I do

Marsden's parsonage at Parramatta.

not mean that a native should learn to build a Hut or make an Axe before he should be told any thing of Man's Fall and Redemption, but that these grand Subjects should be introduced at every favorable opportunity while the Natives are learning any of the simple Arts. To preach the Gospel without the aid of the Arts will never succeed amongst the Heathens for any time.[12]

As his friend John Nicholas later explained, Marsden resolved to pave the way 'by creating artificial wants to which they had never before been accustomed, and which he knew must act as the strongest excitement to the exercise of their ingenuity'.[13]

Accordingly, Marsden recommended that pious carpenters should be sought to demonstrate the construction of houses, boats and wheeled carts; devout smiths to forge edge tools and nails; and godly twine-spinners to make clothing, fishing lines and nets from local flax.[14] It proved difficult, though, to find young clerics to send out to the New Zealand mission, for 'few would venture out to a country where they could anticipate nothing less than to be killed and eaten by the natives'.[15] Finally, two lay men were found who seemed suitable for the mission. William Hall, a carpenter from Carlisle, was given intensive training in navigation and the design and building of small ships, while John King was already trained as a ropemaker, flax-dresser and shoemaker. Once they had been recruited, Marsden was anxious to get the mission started. On 28 August 1809, he, his wife Elizabeth and Hall and King boarded the *Ann*, a convict transport bound for New South Wales. There, by a coincidence that seemed providential, Marsden found Ruatara, a Maori sailor whom he had previously met in Port Jackson.

Ruatara was a young rangatira from the Bay of Islands, a close relative of Te Pahi and the fighting chief Hongi Hika. Almost as soon as whaling and sealing ships arrived at the Bay, he had embarked on a series of European vessels.[16] His first voyage was on the British whaler *Argo* (Captain John Bader), which in September 1805 carried gifts of livestock to Te Pahi at Te Puna. Te Pahi had already left on his voyage to Port Jackson, but Ruatara and two other Maori joined the *Argo* and cruised off the coast for six months, returning to the Bay in March 1806. After this the *Argo* briefly visited Port Jackson, then cruised off the Australian coast, and in September 1806 Bader discharged Ruatara without pay at Port Jackson.[17] There the young Maori sailor met Samuel Marsden for the first time. A month later he joined the whaler *Albion*, which sailed in New Zealand waters for about six months before landing him at the Bay of Islands.[18] Captain Richardson of the *Albion* treated Ruatara kindly, paying him for his services with an array of European items. After this he joined a whaler/sealer, the *Santa Anna* (Captain Moody), which left Port Jackson in July 1807 and sailed to the Bounty Islands and then to the Bay of Islands. Ruatara and the rest of his sealing gang, another New Zealander, two Tahitians ('Toomah' and 'Toobutta') and ten Europeans, were dropped off on one of the Bounty group in November 1807 with little water and very few provisions.[19] For almost a year they were forced to survive by eating seals and sea birds and drinking rainwater. Two Europeans and one Tahitian died of thirst and hunger before another ship, the *King George*, arrived at the island.

Several weeks later, in October 1808, the *Santa Anna* collected the survivors, with their harvest of 8,000 skins, and in June brought them back to Port Jackson.[20]

Despite his sufferings on the Bounty Islands, Ruatara decided to stay with the *Santa Anna* for her voyage back to England, because he was determined to see King George III in London. There is no account of Ruatara's experiences on this journey, but a sailor called George Miller, who sailed on the *Santa Anna*'s next voyage with Captain Dagg, later wrote a vivid memoir of his adventures. At Port Jackson, according to Miller, everything was very dear. Cape wine was ten shillings a bottle, and kangaroo hindquarters cost one shilling and sixpence a pound. The sailors lived on board most of the time, working on the ship, but every now and then visited a tavern. From his account, one of their favourite recreations was drinking gin and other spirits. Miller also made an excursion by horseback to Parramatta, which Ruatara had already visited. In his memoir, he described whaling off New Zealand, after leaving Port Jackson:

> We got ready for sea, and set sail . . . for New Zealand, on the look-out for sperm-whales. Three boats with stores were always kept ready, and every one in the watch, at daylight, took his turn at the mast-head, to look out for them. Sperm-whales breathe out of their nostrils, and blow the water up into a form similar to a thick thorn bush. When they do this, they are said to 'spout'. They make a 'breach' when they leap with their immense carcases clear out of the water, for they can spring up, like a dog over a gate, though their weight is from 20 to 50, and sometimes 60, tons each; and these weights are not improbable, as some produce 9 or 10 tons of oil. The males are called 'bulls' and the females 'cows'. The latter have two tits, and I have milked them. They give birth to their young, and the females have been known to give birth to 'calves' fourteen feet in length.
>
> The right whale, finner, sword fish and killer, all breathe out of their nostril, and spout the water straight up into the air like a poplar tree.
>
> During our watch upon deck, at 4 a.m., the man at the mast-head sang out, 'Yonder she breeches'. The second mate immediately ran aloft, knocked all hands up, and manned the three boats. It is a beautiful and exciting scene to chase these huge monsters, as they tear along and spout the water up; and it takes great coolness and dexterity to escape from destruction when too near them.[21]

Ruatara had shared such experiences. He also must have participated in the 'Crossing the Line' ceremonies on the way to England, when the *Santa Anna* crossed the Equator.

> On crossing the line, the frolic begins at noon, at which time the hatchways are ordered to be fastened down, as Neptune is coming on board to make all those who have not passed before free of the sea.
>
> A quantity of tar and grease was mixed together in a tar-pot, whilst a large tub filled with water was put upon deck just before the main rigging. All those who had crossed the line went upon deck, where the guns were drawn backwards and forwards, and during the din, the best speaker, as Neptune, dressed for the occasion, in a hoarse voice, hails the officer upon deck, who answers, and receives him on board. All the buckets and tin pots of every kind are filled with water, and the

boatswain and another man then go below, where they blindfold the first they get hold of, lead him upon deck, and cause him to be seated on the edge of the water-tub. Another man lathers his face well with tar and grease, and afterwards, with a piece of iron hooping, scrapes it well over his face. The two men who brought him upon deck, one hold of each arm, and two others, one hold of each leg, then pop him backwards into the tub of water [on some ships, neophytes were ducked overboard, or even keel-hauled]. Neptune was all this time stating, that he was come on board to do his duty, and make all strangers free of the sea. After three ducks, off comes the bluff, and then every one takes up either a bucket or a pot of water, and pitches it at the poor fellow, who runs fore or aft, which way he can, but whichever way he runs he is doused with water.[22]

One may wonder what Ruatara made of these antics. They must have seemed an exotic way of celebrating the relationship between sailors and the god of the ocean.

When the *Santa Anna* finally arrived in London in late July 1809, Ruatara was scarcely allowed to go on shore. The sailors told him that they did not know where King George lived, and in any case no one was allowed to see him. He was forced to work without pay and was beaten and abused by the captain. When the ship was discharged, he was transferred to the *Ann*, which sailed almost immediately to Portsmouth. Captain Clarke refused to take Ruatara on board unless the master of the *Santa Anna* supplied him with clothes, otherwise he would have been sent on the *Ann* naked. There Samuel Marsden found him, wrapped in his greatcoat and spitting up blood, just fifteen days after his arrival in England. Ruatara was dismayed by his failure to see the King and to receive proper payment for his labours. He told Marsden disconsolately that 'his countrymen [would] find great fault with him for coming back without attaining the object of his voyage'.[23]

Ruatara was depressed and homesick for his friends and country. Marsden took him into his own cabin and, over the next few weeks, nursed him back to health. To the patrons of the New Zealand mission, this encounter seemed providential.[24] When Marsden wrote to Dr John Mason Good, a friend of Sir Joseph Banks and a distinguished medical practitioner in London, telling him about Ruatara, Good replied:

> Poor Duaterra! How sincerely do I pity him that he should have fallen into the hands of a wretch so unworthy of the British name, and so careless about its reputation: but [there are] yet savages among Englishmen, and philosophers among savages. I rejoice most ardently . . . that he at length fell so marvellously into your care; whose kindness, and moral and religious instruction have already, I doubt not . . . atoned for all the brutal treatment of his first master. [If he is not yet] too much discouraged to repeat his voyage, we will take care that he shall not again quit England without feasting his eyes upon King George, and obtaining a full insight into the chief productions and curiosities that King George's country has to boast of.[25]

From a Maori point of view, this meeting between Ruatara and the missionaries was consequential. By caring for Ruatara during his illness, their hau and

Ruatara's had been brought together. As Marcel Mauss said of such exchanges of hau: 'In short, this represents an intermingling. Lives are mingled together, and this is how, among persons and things so intermingled, each emerges from their own sphere and mixes together.'[26]

During his convalescence on board the *Ann*, Ruatara was befriended by John King, to whom he soon became devoted.[27] William Hall's wife had a miscarriage during their passage and lost twin babies, so he was distracted and spent little time with Ruatara during the voyage.[28] Marsden often conversed with Ruatara in English, and in a letter to the Church Missionary Society committee, remarked:

> Duaterra is a very fine young man, about two-and-twenty years of age, five feet
> ten inches high. He possesses a most amiable disposition; is kind, grateful, and
> affectionate: his understanding strong and clear. He is married to one of the daugh-
> ters of a chief called Wanakee [Waraki, a leading Ngaati Rahiri rangatira at
> Waitangi[29]]. His wife's name is Mike [Miki, a name taken from the name of Marion
> du Fresne's 'wife', according to local tradition]. Having learnt the English alpha-
> bet, and the various sounds of the letters, [he] makes progress in the pronuncia-
> tion of the English Tongue. We are able now to converse on most subjects so as to
> understand each other.[30]

Marsden began compiling a Maori vocabulary during the voyage, and made notes on Maori customs and political structures. He sent copies of this material to various correspondents, including Dr Good in London. Of Maori traditions, he wrote that since time immemorial the New Zealanders had been taught that three gods – Mowheerangaranga (Maaui-Rangaranga), also known as 'Tupuna' (Ances-tor), Mowheemooha (Maaui-Mua) and Mowheebotakee (Maaui-Pootiki) – made the first man, and that the first woman was made from a bone (or 'Eve' – iwi [bone]) taken from the first man's side. This refers to the great cycle of traditions concerning the ancestor Maaui.[31] The notion that Maaui made the first man is not supported by later Maori accounts, however, which attribute this feat to Rangi and Papa, the Sky Father and the Earth Mother. Nor do these accounts mention a woman being made from the first man's side, a notion apparently borrowed from the Bible.

Ruatara told Marsden the story of Rona, the man (or, in some tribal accounts, woman) in the moon, who one night went out to fetch water. At that time there was no light from the moon or the stars, and in the darkness he hurt his foot. In this weakened condition he was seized by the moon, and although he clung to a tree, the moon pulled so hard that he uprooted the tree and carried both tree and Rona up into the heavens.[32] Ruatara also told a tale about sharks and the serpent (or rather, the lizard, since there are no snakes in New Zealand). The sharks wanted to come ashore to live, but the serpent would not allow it, saying that if sharks came on land, men would eat them. The sharks retorted that they would be as safe as the serpent on land, to which the serpent replied that it lived in a hole in the ground, where it could hide itself away from people. (This account is similar to a fable of the tuatara and the shark reported later by the missionary William Colenso.[33])

Marsden said of this tradition that if the New Zealanders believed that snakes could speak, it should not be too difficult to persuade them to accept 'the account of Man's Fall [in the Garden of Eden], as recorded by Moses'.

As Marsden understood him, Ruatara said that the New Zealanders had six gods; the three Maaui ancestors, and Teepocko (Te Upoko – the head), Towackhee (Tuuhawaiki?) and Heckotoro (Hekotoro?). When all the world was still under water, Maaui-mua had been sent from the sky by Maaui-rangaranga. He made the land, then fastened fish-hooks to rocks under the sea so that Maaui-pootiki, who came down from the sky in a canoe, could haul up the islands (a reference to the tale of the demi-god Maaui hauling up land from under the sea). Maaui-pootiki was also the god who created birds and dogs, and afflicted people with diseases, although he had no power to kill them. This was left to Te Upoko, the 'God of Anger and Death' (a god more commonly named in Maori tradition as Whiro). Tuuhawaiki was the 'God of Rain, the Wind, Sea, Lightening, Thunder &c.', roles that Maori traditions commonly ascribe to the gods Tangaroa, Taawhiri and Whaitiri. Heketoro was the 'God of Reptiles, and also of Human Tears and Sorrow', so named because he had lost his wife, who had gone down to earth. When he finally found her, they boarded a canoe that was hauled up to the sky by ropes fastened to its stem and stern. Maori called the sky 'Ranghee' (Rangi), while 'Trayhinga Attua' (Te Reinga Atua) was the home of the gods, who could see everything that was done on earth, both in daylight or darkness.[34]

According to Marsden, Maori religious beliefs prevented 'those crimes which affect the general happiness and welfare of society'. Adultery was uncommon among married women, and the gods punished those who were guilty of this wrong, although they did not concern themselves with mere fornication. Theft was punished by the gods with disease. If a man was robbed, he immediately went to his tohunga, or priest, who consulted the gods, or atua. The atua then cast the shadow of the thief up on a wall (his ata-a-rangi, shadow or spirit[35]) so that he could be identified and punished. Although this effectively prevented theft among Maori, they often stole from Europeans, such was the temptation to acquire iron and axes. (In such a situation, one might speculate that they would not have been surprised when they fell ill with European diseases.) If a man behaved well, the gods were kind, but if he was wicked, he suffered their anger. His potatoes would not grow, he caught no fish, and 'his wife and children would also be evil'. Cannibalism was practised, but on enemies after fighting as a form of 'mental gratification'. Religious ceremonies were held after the potato harvest, and at the death of a chief, when for two or three days all work stopped, and thousands of people assembled.

Ruatara was troubled that 'New Zealand Man did not know how to make a Sunday'. He liked the idea that one day each week should be kept sacred, and decided to acquire a flag at Port Jackson and hoist it each Sunday at Te Puna, signalling that this was the Sabbath. It is intriguing that Maori associated flags with Christianity, presumably regarding them as a way of communicating with the European atua.[36] He told Marsden he would call that day 'Rattapoo Jheena

Attua' (Raa Tapu ki ngaa Atua – Day Sacred to the Gods), and invented names for each of the other days of the week – the first step towards a European calendar. His people relied on the phases of the moon and the flowering of plants to calculate time. Potatoes were planted when trees first burst into bud, and new potatoes could be eaten two moons later. After four moons all the potatoes were ripe, and that was the time for the harvest. During his travels Ruatara had collected some European seeds to take home and plant in his gardens. When Marsden inspected them, however, he found that Ruatara had been given unground peppercorns. When he was told that these would not grow, Ruatara was upset, but Marsden consoled him by promising to give him seeds and grain at Port Jackson for his people.

Marsden also learned a good deal about Maori political structures from Ruatara:

> New Zealand is governed by a number of Chiefs, each of whom appears independent within the limits of his own district. Some of them possess a much larger extent of country and a greater number of subjects, than others. Their families intermarry very much with one another. These marriages tend to unite them together, and promote their general peace and welfare.[37]

This was not a bad snapshot of Maori kin-group geopolitics. Ruatara gave Marsden the names of the principal chiefs in the Bay of Islands, in four genealogical groupings. First, he named five 'brothers', his 'uncles' (his mother being their 'sister'), the leaders of an alliance of descent groups on the north-west side of the Bay – 'Moca' (Moka), 'Kaingroha' (Kaingaroa), 'Shunghee' (Hongi), 'Howhowkee' (Hauraki) and 'Repuro' (Ripiro). Ruatara added that Moka (Kaingaroa's predecessor) was the greatest of these chiefs, occupying large estates in the interior. He had more than ten thousand men under his command (although it is not clear what expression Ruatara used in Maori for 'ten thousand'[38]), who were clearing new lands for sweet and common potatoes. Most of these men were not 'brothers' in the European sense, although Kaingaroa and Hongi Hika, the elder and younger sons of Te Hootete, did fit that description. Rather, they were all 'brothers' (tuakana or teina, senior or junior kinsmen), men of the same generation descended from a common ancestor, Raahiri, allied with Ruatara's own family.[39]

Second, Ruatara named a group of four brothers, the leading chiefs at Te Puna on the north-east side of the Bay of Islands – 'Tippahee' (Te Pahi – Governor King's friend), 'Caparoo' (Kaparu, Ruatara's father), 'Tippepiphee' (Te Pepipi?) and 'Tittuerra' (Te Tuara). He also mentioned his brother 'Ogateeree' (Hoka-tiri) as Te Pahi's successor. He said that Te Pahi's sons were too young to know how to govern, and that Hoka-tiri would take Te Pahi's name if he succeeded him. Marsden noted, 'It appears to be the custom, for the person who succeeds to the command of a district, to take the name of his predecessor: he then becomes heir of all his lands and vassals, and of whatever the former Chief was possessed at the time of his death.'[40] (It is true that sometimes at least, a rangatira who took over the lands of another, whether by inheritance or conquest, assumed his predecessor's name.[41]) Hoka-tiri makes no further appearance in the historical record, and he may have been one of those shot by the whalers during their attack on Te Pahi's island.

Third, Ruatara named two brothers, the leading men at Waitangi, on the central west coast of the Bay of Islands – 'Warrakee' (Waraki) and 'Houkee Cappee' (Hoki-kape). Waraki was the leading Ngaati Raahiri rangatira at Waitangi and the father of Ruatara's wife 'Mike' (Miki).[42]

Fourth, Ruatara named two more brothers, the leading chiefs of an alliance of descent groups in the southern Bay of Islands – 'Terra' (Tara) and 'Tuphoo' (Tupi). Tara was an old man and blind in one eye, who controlled a district that 'abounds with fine timber and is situated on the banks of a fresh water river, which makes it very convenient for him to supply ships with timber'. He and his brother Tupi were Ngaati Manu chiefs with territory that extended from Kororaareka to south of the Waikare Inlet. They had been rivals with Te Pahi for access to European trade and were partly responsible for his death, since they had fixed him with blame for the *Boyd* killings. Ruatara knew nothing about these events, however, which had occurred during his absence in England. If he had been better informed, it is unlikely that his comments about Tara and Tupi would have been so non-commital.

Some of Marsden's notes on status and leadership in the Bay are worth quoting verbatim:

> There is no middle class of inhabitants. They are all either *Rangateeda* (rangatira – aristocrats) or *Tungata* (taangata – ordinary people). The *Tungata* are employed in all kinds of servile labour, while the *Rangateeda* are considered as gentlemen. A *Rangateeda* never strikes a *Tungata*. A *Tungata* will immediately do anything which a *Rangateeda* commands him: he never presumes to dictate, or to resist the authority of his Chief. One Chief will have many *Rangateedas* under his command. These are all considered as gentlemen; they superintend the cultivation of the lands and attend to all the inferior offices of government: they do not labour, but are maintained by the produce of the labour of the *Tungatas*. The strictest subordination exists; and few capital crimes seem to be committed, or punishments inflicted.
>
> The Chiefs muster all their men at particular times of the year. The Great Muster is made after the Potatoe Harvest. The ground from which the potatoes have been lately dug is cleared of the stems and weeds and then levelled. On this ground they all assemble – men, women and children. The men are all drawn up like a regiment, and stand in ranks, five, six, or seven deep, according to the will of the Chief. One of the head officers, or *Rangateedas*, begins to muster them, not by calling over their names, but by passing in front of their ranks and telling their numbers. At the head of every hundred men he places a *Rangateeda*, and continues in this manner to muster the whole, leaving a *Rangateeda* with every hundred men. Thus ten *Rangateedas* answer for a thousand men. The women and children are never mustered. This custom is something similar to that of the kings and rulers of the Israelites – mustering the men of the different tribes among them, while they took no account of the women and children.
>
> After the Muster is taken, their Holidays begin. They now spend several days and nights, in feasting, dancing and performing their religious ceremonies. Many

hundreds join in these amusements. The Chiefs do not dance themselves: they only look on, and give directions to their men. The Chiefs appear, on all occasions, to keep up great state and dignity among their subjects, and to treat them at the same time with kindness and humanity.[43]

Ruatara's description of the annual musters of men in their kin groups is fascinating, and well supported by other early sources,[44] for instance, the missionary William Williams.[45]

Others of his political observations appear to reflect local ideals rather than actual practice. According to most eyewitness accounts, rangatira in the north were quite often ignored, and relationships between commoners and their aristocratic leaders were regulated by checks and balances.[46] Furthermore, some rangatira at least – those dedicated to the ancestor god Rongo – worked in the cultivations. Laziness was not appreciated in Maori communities, as attested by many sardonic proverbs on the subject.[47] It is also interesting to note that in these remarks Marsden made his first comparison (although by no means his last) between Maori and the Children of Israel.

In conclusion, Marsden commented that 'a finer race of men has seldom, if ever, been found in any country, than the New Zealanders; which is strong evidence that they are well fed, and their habits and employments are congenial to the health and vigour of the human constitution'. Not only were the New Zealanders healthy and robust; they were also intelligent and enterprising. Although they were in 'a state of nature', the chiefs he had met seemed anxious to adopt 'the Arts of Civilization'. Marsden recalled that when he took Te Pahi to a small rope walk during his first visit to Parramatta in 1805, and showed him how Europeans spun their rope, Te Pahi had wept and said, 'New Zealand was no good.' Ruatara was more interested in agriculture, but had learned to sole and mend shoes, and had collected some shoemaker's tools. Marsden commented how interested these men were in European technologies, and concluded: 'I am fully convinced that they would soon become a great nation, if the Arts could be introduced among them, without the ruinous vices and prevalent diseases of Civilized Society.'[48]

When the learned Dr Good received Marsden's reports on Maori customs and language in London, he was ecstatic:

> You who never suffer a single opportunity of improvement to fleet away without availing yourself of it, have used it to the best of all possible purposes. I feel confident that by this time you have become a proficient in the New Zealand tongue, and ought to have a patent from his Majesty to assume the professorial chair in this new department of *literature*.
>
> Are you aware of the full extent and usefulness of the learning you are thus acquiring? Do you know that the language of New Zealand is precisely that of Otaheite; and probably of the Society Islands in general? It is not improbable . . . that the greater number of those clusters of islands that lie scattered over the Pacific Ocean from the Ladrones to the Marquesas only use different dialects of the same mother tongue, and this the tongue which you are now studying and analysing.[49]

Good noted in this letter that although it was often argued in Europe that the 'black-coloured, bush-haired and less intelligent tribes' of New South Wales and New Guinea were African in origin, and the 'fairer-complexioned, long-haired and more enterprising people' of New Zealand, Tonga and the Society Islands were Asiatic, the vocabularies he had seen from New Zealand and Tahiti suggested an ancient Sanskritic origin for those last groups, 'softened by passing through a Malay dialect'.[50] He thought that the people of New South Wales might have first colonised New Guinea, New Britain, New Ireland and the Solomons, then 'intermixed with successive influxes of restless Malays' in those places. The boundary tribes of Asia, he remarked, had 'from time immemorial, exhibited a most restless and roving disposition', overrunning most of Europe, as well as much of the Pacific. Attila the Hun, Genghis Khan and the Saracens had all migrated out of Asia, like the Malayans, 'who were equally restless and intrepid, [and] by their peninsular site accustomed to navigation'.

He then outlined an early version of the modern theory of Pacific migration:

> [They] bade defiance even to the ocean itself. We find them . . . migrating from shore to shore, from island to island; a few of them perhaps remaining behind as the rest advanced, and producing a cross breed in the countries they traversed, but the greater number . . . still passing forward and only settling in the remotest regions and in the farthest shores they could explore; viz in New Zealand, the Friendly and Society Islands and the Marquesas.

Good posed a flurry of consequent questions. How far back could the New Zealanders trace their political history? What were the names and histories of their most celebrated princes, legislators, warriors, priests and poets? What was the nature of their oral traditions – did they have ballads, like the Greeks and the Highland minstrels? Did they have traditions of the Garden of Eden, the Great Deluge, and what were their calendrical systems? He told Marsden that his last letter had been discussed with Sir Joseph Banks and among many of their friends, and they thought that Tahiti and New Zealand may once have been 'in a state of much greater civilization', but may have degenerated in both knowledge and moral virtue. In that case, they might be ready for regeneration. Although Europe was undoubtedly in a state of decline, in the Pacific, the opportunities were exciting. 'You, with small resources, are recovering a world; while we, with every resource around us, are, I am afraid, daily sinking beyond all hope of recovery.'[51]

In his letter to Marsden, Good was referring to ideas that were in common circulation among European intellectuals.[52] In a counterpoint to contemporary ideas of 'progress', some European thinkers had decided that while civilisations might rise, they could also fall; and that Europe was in the process of falling.[53] High taxes, corrupt élites, restless commoners, the betrayal of the hopes of the French Revolution and incessant fighting culminating in the Napoleonic Wars all indicated a state of decay and decline. The Pacific, however, might rise again and offer new hope to humanity. Indeed, they toyed with the notion that as Europeans now visited Roman ruins, to marvel at the decline and fall of the Roman Empire, some day New Zealanders (or other Pacific Islanders) might come and visit European ruins, to marvel at the decline and fall of Europe.[54] Finally, Good suggested in his letter that while building a wealthy new Pacific world, Marsden should look upon New Zealand flax as one of its finest resources. It produced a fibre that seemed more silky than silk itself, and they could ask Te Pahi to help them cultivate and work it.

Marsden had intended to send Ruatara, King and Hall directly to the Bay of Islands on the *Ann*, but almost as soon as the ship arrived back at Port Jackson in late February 1810, news arrived of the fate of the *Boyd*. These reports blamed Te Pahi and his son Maa-tara for the killings. Marsden was devastated. His hopes of establishing the mission under Te Pahi's patronage were dashed, and it seemed that he had utterly misjudged Te Pahi. Hall and King were also horrified by the news, and reluctant to proceed with the mission. John King wrote to the secretary of the Church Missionary Society:

> We have receiv'd an awful account of the New Zealanders destroying a whole Ships Crewe Excepting one Woman and three Children in the most Cruel manner immagnable which must fill every feeling soul with remorse and sorrow for the destroyed & for those that sit in darkness & in the region of the shade of Death if God has a work for us to do there he will open a way for our entrance in among them in his own good time and Bless our labours of love toward them & make crucked things strait & ruff pleaces plain. In stead of the thorn shall come up the fir tree . . .
>
> I ham greatly disapointed that the Chief of the Bay of Island who was to protect us and we was to put our selves under him as our temperal Refuge but alass he is the Chief of the Murderers he hath no pity he him self was at the head of this shocking scene . . . so we must leave it in the hands of God who knoweth what is best for them and us for the present and has soon as it is thought wisdom to go & there is any probability of doing them good I shall (if it please God) go with pleasure and with a witting mind, so wether we live or die may we be the Lords.[55]

William Hall added, 'It has proved very providential to us that we were not left upon New Zealand before we were aware of the danger of it, the New Zealanders are all at war at present and appear to be a very hostile savage kind of people, it being proved by the fate of the unfortunate ship *Boyd*.'[56]

When news of the burning of the *Boyd* was published in the *Sydney Gazette*, just days after Marsden's arrival, feelings against the New Zealanders ran high in Sydney. Soon after the *Ann* arrived at Port Jackson, therefore, Ruatara travelled with Marsden to his estates at Parramatta. He was apparently in no hurry to return home, for he stayed with Marsden for eighteen months, working as a labourer and learning to cultivate cereals, as an alternative to the root crops (sweet potato, taro, yam and fernroot) that were raised in New Zealand. During this time John King and William Hall, the artisans recruited for the New Zealand mission, were supposed to be teaching him practical skills, and to be learning Maori. They

A view of part of Parramatta, in about 1809.

complained to the Church Missionary Society that although they had built a small house out at Parramatta, where they hoped to teach Ruatara and another young New Zealander (another of Te Pahi's sons) to make rope and spin twine, Marsden kept them and the two Maori so busy working on his estates that there was no time left for this mutual instruction:

> But for a work consisting of no less than the conversion of the Heathen, to be so neglected and laid aside has been a daily and nightly reflection, and grief upon our minds; and especially we have to lament the favourable opportunity that has elapsed for learning the language, which we never had it in our power to embrace – and if it had not been that were put so much under the direction and influence of Mr. Marsden, that we would have taken a Native or two home to our own house, and then we might have both learnt the language and taught the Natives many a useful lesson, and yet spent a part of our time in the cultivation of garden ground or other such work as would contribute greatly to our support and theirs.[57]

Marsden, on the other hand, complained that Hall was obstinate and self-willed, and that neither he nor King showed much interest in spending time with the New Zealanders. Hall had found he could make a better living as a carpenter in Sydney than as a missionary, and showed 'a want of love for the heathen'.[58] Nevertheless, Marsden was determined to pursue the New Zealand mission, and to 'make some little establishment for the accommodation of our own natives, and those of the islands who may visit us, and who have no place of protection', where visiting New Zealanders, whom he described as 'very attentive, sober, and willing to learn', could be taught 'the simple Mechanics, Agriculture, and the knowledge of the Scriptures'.[59] Marsden was evidently hoping that his artisan missionaries would replicate themselves by training a cohort of devout Maori tradesmen.

During 1810 and 1811, while Ruatara was living at Parramatta, the numbers of ships visiting New Zealand plummeted. In 1810, a five-year economic depression began in New South Wales, caused by successive droughts, falling prices for grain and meat, a glut of goods from India and a diminishing flow of convicts, who were being diverted to the English dockyards in the last phases of the struggle with Napoleon. Contact with the penal colony was costly, and a low priority for the British Government.[60] A number of local businesses collapsed, leading to a reduction in local shipping.[61] The burning of the *Boyd* also acted as a deterrent. Some whaling ships still visited the fishing grounds north-east of New Zealand, but were reluctant to enter northern harbours. In November 1810, for example, the *Atalanta* sprang a serious leak while crossing the Tasman on its way to London. Her captain, William Wilson, instead of sailing north to the Bay of Islands (where the ship had joined in the raid on Te Pahi's island earlier that year), headed south for Totara-nui. Ensign Huey of the 73rd Regiment of Foot was on board the *Atalanta*. On 15 November, as the ship entered the Sound and sailed past 'Canibal's Cove', he noted in his journal:

> We saw about a dozen old huts close to the beach on the very spot where Captain Furneaux's people were eaten [in fact this happened at Grass Cove, on the opposite side of the Sound]. Some of the men on board imagined they saw natives in the huts but for my part I could see none. We did not wish to see the gentlemen at all, knowing they were cannibals and would serve us in the same way as they did the 'Boyd' if it lay in their power.[62]

The people of Totara-nui, however, were just as anxious to avoid the Europeans, and abandoned their hamlets immediately upon the ship's arrival. During their four-day stay the *Atalanta*'s men collected shellfish, fish, birds, eggs, fresh water and firewood, and Huey saw a wild dog (perhaps a kurii) in the bush, and celery, parsley and turnips sown by Captain Cook's men, but not a single local inhabitant.

After the attack on Te Pahi's island, during 1810 only five ships – the *Atalanta*, *New Zealander*, *Spring Grove*, *Experiment* and the *Governor Bligh* – are known to have visited New Zealand. As time went on, successive reports arrived at Port Jackson that the attack on the *Boyd* had been provoked, and that most Maori were not hostile. In May 1810, for example, a Maori woman who had arrived on the *Perseverance* (which delivered a load of spars from the Bay of Islands) reported that the attack on the *Boyd* had followed serious provocations. During Maa-Tara's return voyage from England, most of the gifts that had been given to him were stolen; and he had died of disease just days before the attack on the *Boyd*. Te Pahi had been neglected and ill-treated during his last visit to Sydney, and the whalers had taken to stealing crops of potatoes from gardens in the Bay and carrying off cargoes of spars without payment. In July 1810, moreover, a sailor from the *Brothers* informed Marsden that the people there had treated them very kindly. They had continued to supply the ship with potatoes, even though a local man had been murdered during a raid on a plantation.[63] In October, Marsden was told definitively that Te Pahi was not responsible for the attack on the *Boyd*. A young Maori sailor who came to stay with him at Parramatta reported that after Captain Thompson had flogged Te Aara and his three companions on the *Boyd*, Te Aara had informed his father and his brother Te Puhi. They attacked the ship, and Te Pahi, who happened to be visiting Whangaroa at the time with gifts of fish for his in-laws, had tried to rescue some of the sailors. He had then been attacked by the whalers, who shot him through the neck, and his house and settlement had been burned and plundered.

In 1811, reassured by such reports, a few more ships visited New Zealand. During that year the *Spring Grove, New Zealander*, *Indispensible*, *Industry*, *Santa Anna*, *Hawich* and *Frederick* went whaling in New Zealand waters. Like the *Atalanta*, the *Hawich* was caught in a storm and forced to run for shelter. The ship briefly called at the Bay of Islands, where Captain Brodie said that the people were quiet and friendly.

Later in that year, two more Maori came to visit Marsden at Parramatta — another of Te Pahi's sons and 'Cawheetee [Kawiti], the Son of one of their great Priests'[64] (whom he described as the 'son of Terra', and who later became a tohunga and a great northern leader).[65] They refused to take any alcohol when Marsden offered them a drink, and Kawiti sang a song for Ruatara, which Marsden referred to as 'Mike's [Miki's] Song', composed by Ruatara's wife for her absent husband. Kawiti told Marsden that his 'father' (matua — senior relative) Tara had sent him to Port Jackson on a sealing ship to acquire useful goods and knowledge for their people. He had been taken with a gang to Macquarie Island instead, where they were left without adequate food and clothing. It was miserably cold, and they had been forced to eat sea birds' eggs and elephant seal tongues to survive. The owners at Port Jackson paid him one shirt, a handkerchief and a pair of trousers, and three shillings for ten months' work on the island. Kawiti also reported that another ship from Port Jackson had recently visited the Bay en route to India, and had agreed with Tara to supply a cargo of spars. Once the ship was loaded, however, it sailed without Tara receiving the agreed payment. Kawiti commented to Marsden that 'the English treated the New Zealanders very bad':

> I was a King in New Zealand, but now I am a Cook at Port Jackson – I make Fires on Board of the Ship and on Shore, and cook in both Places. When I return (he added) my Father will say, Coweetee Tee tooa [Kawiti Tiitua] what have you brought me? I tell him I brought nothing, I learn nothing white man at Port Jackson make me a Cook. My Father will be very angry with me. I a King at Home, I a Cook at Port Jackson.[66]

Cooked food, we have noted earlier, was inimical to tapu. Rangatira, if they were forced to act as cooks, understood that their ancestral powers were being destroyed in the process. Kawiti was also aghast at the sailors' habit of swearing. He remarked that 'he had never worn an oath in his Life – if he shod Swear at a Tree, or a man, or woman or at any thing, his Father would punish him very much'.[67] Kanga, or cursing in Maori, was a form of spiritual attack, and not to be casually practised. Marsden was impressed by Kawiti, whose conduct contrasted favourably with most of the convicts, sailors and soldiers who made up Port Jackson society:

> The more I see of these People, the more I am pleased with, and astonished at their moral Ideas, and Characters. They appear like a Superior Race of Men. Was Christianity once received amongst them, New Zealand would be one of the finest Parts of the Globe.[68]

During their brief visit to Parramatta, Kawiti and his companions visited Ruatara's farm, where he had planted wheat, peas and beans. They marked a line across Marsden's land, cutting notches in the stumps of trees with a knife. When he asked them what they were doing, they answered that they were marking out a farm for Kawiti, who would return as soon as possible with one hundred men to work it. Marsden replied, 'I would give him as much Land as he liked, and he might begin to morrow' – a response worthy of a rangatira. He was hoping that

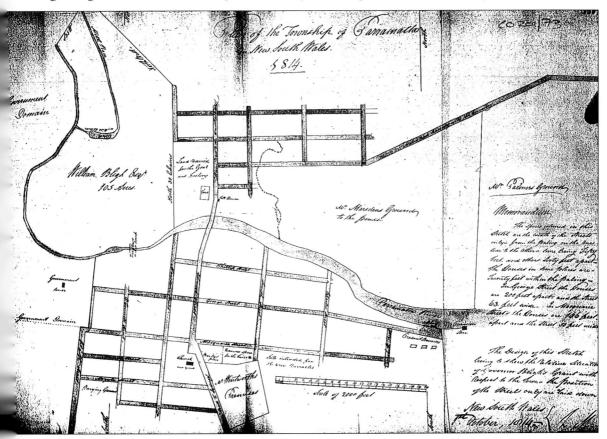

A plan of Marsden's land at Parramatta.

by introducing a wider variety of crops to these men, a more settled and peaceful style of life might be established in New Zealand. Marsden was concerned that if Maori continued to plant potatoes without manuring their lands, the soils would soon become exhausted. He had been told that a great chief named Moka had already attacked a neighbouring district in the Bay of Islands to get good land for planting his potatoes. Unless new agricultural techniques and an alternative food supply such as cereal crops were introduced, it seemed likely that inter-group fighting there would intensify.

This perception was accurate, but it was worse than Marsden thought. Although potatoes had been received as a great gift by Maori and redistributed throughout the North and South Islands, they were a mixed blessing. Unlike kuumara, which cropped once a year, potatoes cropped at least twice, providing more food but also requiring a larger labour force to keep the gardens weeded and fenced from pigs.[69] Potatoes soon caused groups to raid each other, not only for fallow land, but for mookai (war captives, without mana) to work the plantations. The health of these people was harmed by continuous hard labour, their families were often killed in the fighting, and their wairua was damaged when their connection with ancestral lands and powers was broken. This made them more prone to introduced diseases (including venereal infections). While mortality rates in many parts of New Zealand soared at this time, fertility rates were dropping.[70]

Moved by his wife's waiata, and now anxious to return home, Ruatara asked Marsden to arrange a passage for him and his friends back to the Bay of Islands. Marsden realised that this could also be a useful step towards establishing the mission, so he talked with Alexander Bodie, master of the *Frederick*, who agreed to deliver the four men to the Bay, provided that they worked their passage. In late November, Hall and King reported to the CMS:

> [The New Zealanders] sailed in a small vessel for the fishery, in the beginning of October 1811 – Mr Marsden have given them two large Saws belonging to the Society that we had in our possession, and several other articles . . . and we gave them some small articles such as hooks, axe blades, pocket knives, Writing paper &c. [Ruatara also carried with him a 'colour' or flag which Marsden had given him to fly each Sunday, a large piece of Muslin[71] .] We parted with them in great friendship, and D — [Duaterra] promised that he would sent a man-or-two by the first vessel to Port Jackson, to let us know the minds of the people, and the state of the Island, and likewise he has promised that he will do all that lays in his power to make peace and serve our interests among the people, so far as his power and influence extends – and may the Lord exert all powers for the advancement of his own Glory – and our daily prayers are, that he may support and qualify us for the work he has given us to do, and be pleased to make the way plain before us.[72]

The *Frederick* went directly to North Cape, where Ruatara asked his Muri-whenua friends to provision the ship with pork and potatoes. After that the vessel went whaling for six months off the New Zealand coast, then Captain Bodie called at the Bay of Islands for provisions. He refused to allow Ruatara and his friends to go ashore, despite their entreaties. According to Ruatara's own account, given later to Samuel Marsden:

> Duaterra felt great distress on this occasion, as he had been from home about three years and was most anxious to see his wife and friends. He earnestly solicited the captain to land him on any part of the coast – he cared not on what place – as all he wished was to get put on shore and he would find his way home. The master was deaf to all his entreaties, and told them they would proceed to Norfolk Island and from thence direct for Britain, and that he would be landed as they passed New Zealand on their way to England.[73]

At Norfolk Island, Bodie sent Ruatara and his friends ashore to fetch water for the ship. They almost drowned in the surf as they tried to get ashore. Once the *Frederick* had been supplied, Captain Bodie told Ruatara that he had no intention of returning to New Zealand. He sailed for England without paying Ruatara for his work, and forcibly took Te Pahi's son with him, ignoring his protests and entreaties. Alexander Bodie was the captain who had tied Te Pahi to the rigging of his vessel during a visit to the Bay of Islands in 1807, and subsequently taunted him at a dinner party during his 1808 visit to Port Jackson. He may well have taken the burning of the *Boyd* as an excuse for further ill-treatment of New Zealanders. Interestingly, though, it was another whaler, Captain Gwynn of the New Bedford ship *Ann*, who eventually rescued Ruatara (and perhaps also Kawiti) from Norfolk and, in August 1812, brought them back to Port Jackson. Gwynn was indignant that Ruatara and his companions had been cheated of their 'lays' for the voyage (which he estimated at about £100 each), as well as the tools and seed wheat that Marsden had given him, and he supplied Ruatara with clothing and other necessities. Again, Ruatara lived with Marsden at Parramatta for a time, 'labour[ing] early and late to obtain knowledge, and particularly, to make himself acquainted with practical agriculture'. In late 1812, the captain of the British whaler *Ann* agreed to take him home, provided that he worked his passage. Before he left Parramatta, however, Ruatara asked Marsden to send him someone as soon as possible to the Bay of Islands to 'teach his Boys and Girls to read & write'.[74]

During 1812, war broke out again between the United States and Britain, and American ships were forced to avoid Port Jackson. Nevertheless, at least ten ships went whaling or collected spars at New Zealand. Several of these vessels (including the *Active*, a trading vessel owned by a Salem firm) visited the Bay of Islands. Another was the colonial vessel *King George*. Her captain, Lasco Jones, was later accused of ill-treating one of the two New Zealanders, 'Bevan' and 'Jack', who had sailed with him from Port Jackson. According to these reports, he beat the man, stripped him naked and took away all of his property.[75] An American sailor on the *King George*, John Besent, afraid that the vessel would be destroyed and all the crew killed in revenge, ran from the ship and lived for twelve months in the Bay on excellent terms with local people. During this time he met Te Aara (or 'George'), who spoke fluent English. Te Aara gave him a detailed account of the loss of the *Boyd,* saying that it had happened because Captain Thompson flogged him and took all his things while they were at anchor in Whangaroa, and that Te Pahi was not responsible for the killings.[76] Te Aara's people had helped to cut a cargo of spars but, after the flogging, they refused to load it. Thompson took all but two of his crew ashore to haul the logs, where Te Aara's father confronted and killed him. Like Besent, many of the sailors who visited New Zealand after the *Boyd* described the New Zealanders as friendly and co-operative. According to Marsden, they believed that in the attacks on various ships, Europeans had been the aggressors.[77]

In early 1813, after five months at sea on the *Ann*, Ruatara finally returned to Rangihoua. He was received by his people with joy, and Marsden reported that they had made him their 'King'.[78] Both Te Pahi and his elder brother had died, and Ruatara had inherited Te Pahi's lands at Te Puna. It is likely that he was chosen as their new leader because of his capacity to deal knowledgeably with Europeans. He took the seed wheat that Marsden had given him at Parramatta and distributed it to a number of his relatives, including his uncle Hongi Hika. Ruatara told them that wheat was the plant from which the Europeans made their biscuits and bread, but when the seeds sprouted and the plants grew tall, his people pulled them up, expecting to find wheat at the roots. Finding nothing, they reproached Ruatara for telling them such ludicrous stories, and burnt all their wheat crops, along with some peas they had planted.[79]

Ruatara had his own wheat crop, however, and when it ripened, he harvested and threshed it. He showed the grain to his relatives, but they still refused to believe that this could be made into bread. He sent a message to Marsden asking for more grain; with gifts of a fishing net and a spear or club (probably a taiaha), which Marsden sent on to the CMS. The net arrived safely, but the club was lost in passage. When he received the net, the secretary of the CMS asked the missionaries to send other 'curiosities of nature or of art' – particularly objects that illustrated the 'superstition and moral state of the Heathen . . . as such things – images of Deities &c. &c. speak in forcible language to the pity and the conscience of those to who they are shewn' – for a museum the Society was establishing[80] – an interesting way of raising funds for the mission.

In return for these gifts, Marsden sent Ruatara more tools and seed wheat (probably by the *James Hay*). When the *Jefferson* arrived in the Bay soon after these gifts had arrived, Ruatara borrowed a pepper mill from Captain Barnes to grind his grain into flour, in an effort to prove his assertions. The pepper mill was too small for the task, so he asked Barnes to deliver another urgent message to Marsden. He requested a hand mill to be sent so that he could grind his grain, and some tools for working his gardens. Marsden gathered a selection of hoes and other agricultural tools, and sent them with several bags of seed wheat by the *Queen Charlotte*, which had planned to visit the Bay of Islands. This ship sailed past New Zealand without landing, however, so the gifts were never delivered.

In April 1813, Marsden suffered one last setback in his plans for the mission. The sealing ship *Perseverance*, owned by Robert Campbell and commanded by Robert Murry (who had visited southern New Zealand on the *Britannia* in 1792, the *Endeavour* in 1795–96 and the *Fox* in 1809, where he lived with a sealing gang in Foveaux Strait for nine months), sailed to New Zealand to find a place where flax could be harvested and manufactured. The voyage was sponsored by the Sydney entrepreneur James Birnie, represented on board the ship by James Gordon, a sea captain who had sailed with Maori on a number of occasions. According to Gordon, Maori sailors (including the two on board the *Perseverance*, 'Jacky Mytye' and 'Dick') were 'obedient, quiet and industrious men' who made excellent shipmates.[81] An emancipist rope-worker, Robert Williams, was also on board. Williams had a rope walk in Macquarie Street in Sydney, and claimed to have invented a machine for dressing New Zealand flax that would allow a thriving and lucrative industry to develop.[82] Marsden asked William Hall to sail on the *Perseverance*, and arranged a passage for him so that he could 'see the natives, and the Country and form his own Opinion of the Propriety of establishing the mission',[83] but Hall refused to leave Port Jackson.

Although Marsden was annoyed by Hall's refusal, it seems unlikely that Hall would have learned much of value to the mission on this voyage. Murry took the ship directly to Port Williams, an abandoned sealing station in Foveaux Strait, where Williams took a party ashore. Gordon cut his leg with an axe and immediately returned to the ship, retiring to his cabin. A group including Williams, and Birnie's clerk, Mr R. Jones, crossed the strait in two armed boats and visited Bluff Harbour. Williams drafted a chart of the bay (which he called Port Macquarie), where he met a local man who seemed friendly. He found he could not communicate with him, however, since the man could only speak in Maori. They landed and walked along the coast through swamps to Mokomoko Inlet, which they waded, then climbed over a ridge to a village by a high, sandy hill, inhabited by a few old men, and women and children. The men of this village were away on an expedition, but the remaining residents were kind to the Europeans, offering them food and shelter. They seemed poor, living mainly off fish and potatoes, which they grew in 'remarkably clean' gardens. These gardens were laid out in about a hundred acres of well-tilled ground, filled with plants at various stages of maturity.[84] The Europeans posted sentries that night and slept in a hut together.

The next morning when they returned to Mokomoko Inlet, women from the village loaded themselves with potatoes, carrying these as provisions for their visitors. Williams and his companions, finding the inlet dry and flocked with paradise ducks, named it 'Duck Bay'. At the back of this bay Williams discovered a large valley full of 'the best hemp we had seen, and as regularly set out as if planted by the hands of man'.[85] On the western shore, flax was growing abundantly. That afternoon one of the boats arrived with two local men, and they camped overnight in Duck Bay, where Williams thought the flax settlement might be established. He was anxious to stay longer and to explore the coastline around Bluff, but Jones was determined to return to Sydney. He ordered them to go back to the ship, which they did, to the distress of their Maori companions, and commanded Murry to hoist up the anchor.

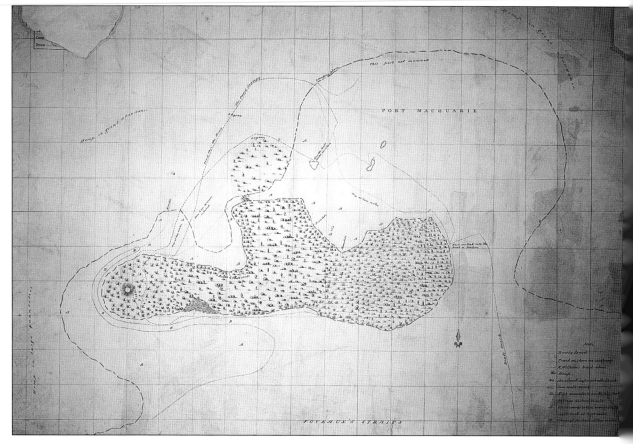

Robert Williams's 1813 chart of 'Port Macquarie'.

From the strait they cruised up the east coast, passing 'a fine harbour' with a large village (probably Otakou), and some days later a very large bay, which proved to be Te Matau-a-Maaui (Hawke's Bay). There they saw fires lit on the shore, and numbers of local people. When 'large tribes of natives' launched their canoes, Jones ordered Murry to take the *Perseverance* around Table Cape, but Murry hove to instead. The local people brought out potatoes and mats to trade, bartering a hundredweight of potatoes for one spike nail, and one woman offered to exchange her small son for a tomahawk, but the boy was crying so bitterly that they refused to take him. Jones then insisted that they sail out to sea and return to Port Jackson as quickly as possible. Williams was frustrated by Jones's cowardice and his reluctance to spend much time ashore. He commented in his report on the expedition:

> We made Port Jackson after a voyage of twelve weeks as wise as we went had not Port Macquarie fortunately formed by nature to answer all the purpose for a large establishment, and I [was] . . . greatly disappointed in not having numerous choices of situations which most likely would have been the case had our means been made good use of.[86]

By the end of 1813, the tides of world history were turning. From London came jubilant reports of Napoleon's retreat from Moscow and new hopes of peace in Europe.[87] A succession of ships also brought good news from the Bay of Islands, and the establishment of a mission there seemed to be imminent.[88] Captain Parker of the *Phoenix* reported that upon the ship's arrival at the Bay, Ruatara had welcomed him warmly and supplied spars, firewood and potatoes. The *Phoenix* brought John Besent (the young American sailor who had deserted the *King George* in 1812 and lived there for more than a year) from the Bay back to Port Jackson. He assured Marsden that the local people were friendly and his missionaries would be in no danger. If the mission was to be established in the Bay, he would gladly go with them to New Zealand.[89] Another ship (probably the *James Hay*) also visited the Bay of Islands at this time, bringing two young men to Port Jackson. They were the sons of chiefs, and one of them, 'Tohi' (Tui, of Ngare Raumati, the tribe which occupied the eastern islands and coastline in the Bay), a young man about seventeen years old, went to stay with Marsden at Parramatta, where Besent was working as an apprentice brickmaker. They were soon joined by Maaui (also known as 'Tommy Drummond'), whom Marsden described as 'a good young man very moral, and well behaved', a relative of Tara's.[90] When Maaui was about eight

A sketch by James Barry of Tui made during his 1818 visit to London.

427

years old, inspired by stories of Tuki and Huru's adventures, he had embarked on a whaler bound for Norfolk Island. There the local harbourmaster, John Drummond, had taken him into his family and enrolled him in a day school, where he learned to read and write and to speak good English.[91] When the Drummonds moved to Liverpool, about seven miles south of Parramatta, Maaui worked on the family farm as a shepherd. He was now about seventeen years old and anxious to 'learn more of civil life', so Marsden invited him to live at Parramatta.

In October 1813, Thomas Kendall, who had been recruited as the mission's school master, arrived with his wife and five children. He was a linen draper and former tutor from Lincolnshire, who had become inspired with the desire to carry the Gospel to the heathen. Marsden asked him to begin teaching the two young New Zealanders, Tui and Maaui. Hall was reluctant to do so, and King was not fit for the task, since he was suffering an attack of 'family insanity' (apparently, a kind of melancholia). In the meantime, Marsden himself instructed them in agriculture and iron-working.[92] Tui had apparently also investigated the more intimate aspects of European life, for he later boasted that he had 'enjoyed the favours' of one of the young Miss Marsdens (if this was true, her father apparently knew nothing about it).[93]

Thomas Kendall was eager to begin his mission to New Zealand. He had read John Savage's *Account*, which had whetted his appetite for evangelical endeavours among the Maori.[94] The secretary of the Church Missionary Society asked him to act as a peace-maker in the disputes between Marsden and his fellow missionaries, and to deliver letters to Hall and King, urging them to rededicate themselves to the great task of 'saving the souls of the poor perishing heathens'.[95] He did this, and about a month after Kendall's arrival Marsden wrote a strongly worded letter to Hall, telling him that he must either go to New Zealand or resign from the CMS, in which case he must return all tools and other goods the Society had given him.[96] Hall was duly chastened and told Marsden that he was now ready to travel to New Zealand.

Throughout 1813, Marsden had been having long discussions with Governor Macquarie about the New Zealand mission. He had collected a sheaf of sworn affidavits about European aggressions in the Pacific, which he placed before the Governor. These affidavits described injustices against South Sea Islanders (particularly New Zealanders) by captains of British ships – Wilson of the *Royal Admiral* and Reid of *El Plumier* in 1801; Dalrymple of the *General Wellesley* in 1807; Clarke of the *Seringapatam* in 1808; Glyn of the *Parramatta*, Theodore Walker of the *Mercury*, Thompson of the *Boyd* in 1809; and Jones of the *King George*, Theodore Walker of the *Endeavour* and Fodger of the *Daphne* in 1812.[97] Jones had frequently recruited New Zealanders as sailors but ill-treated them during his voyages, and Marsden laid official complaints against him and Walker, and the latter was subsequently brought to trial and convicted for abusing New Zealanders, and tried for hanging a Lascar on his vessel in Tahiti.[98] On 1 December 1813, as a result of Marsden's complaints, Macquarie issued a proclamation:

Governor Lachlan Macquarie.

Whereas many, and it is to be feared just, complaints have been lately made of the conduct of divers masters of colonial and British ships, and of their crews, towards the natives of New Zealand, of Otaheite, and of the other islands in the South Pacific Ocean: And whereas several ships, their masters and crews, have lately fallen sacrifice to the indiscriminate revenge of the natives of the said islands, exasperated by such conduct: And whereas the lives and properties not only of His Majesty's subjects, but of the subjects of other Powers, touching at such islands, are likely to be put in continual jeopardy, and the farther trade and intercourse with the said islands greatly endangered, if not wholly prevented, unless some effectual measures are taken to prevent the continuance of a conduct and behaviour, at once repulsive to humanity and interest.[99]

This proclamation ordered all ships (from Britain, India or the plantations), before clearing Port Jackson, to enter into a bond that the master, officers and crew would behave peaceably and well in New Zealand and the South Sea Islands:

They shall not commit any act of trespass upon the plantations, gardens, lands, habitations, burial-grounds, tombs, or properties of the natives . . . they shall not make war or cause war to be made upon them, or in any way interfere, stir up, excite or foment any animosities among them; and they shall leave the natives of the said islands to the free, uninterrupted, and undisturbed enjoyment of their religious ceremonies, rites, or observances; and [they] shall not ship any of the male natives, or take away any such natives without their free will and consent and the free will and consent of their chiefs, parents, or others to whom they are subject; and [they] shall not ship or take away any of the female natives of the said islands without such free will and consent; and also without having first obtained

Natives of South Sea Islands;

No Ship or Vessel shall clear out from any oth[er] within the Territory for New Zealand, or any other Island in the South pacific, unless the master, if of British or Indian, or the master and owners if of plantation registry, shall enter into bonds with the Naval officer under £600 penalty that themselves crew shall properly demean themselves towards the natives, and not commit acts of trespass on their Gardens, lands, habitations, burial grounds, tombs, or properties, and not make war or at all interfere in their quarrels, or excite any animosities among them, but leave them to the free enjoyment of their rites and ceremonies; and not take from the Island any male Native without his own and his Chiefs and parents consent, and shall not ship or take from thence any female Native, without the like consent and without having first obtained the consent of His Excellency the Governor or his Secretary in writing, or in case of Shipping any male natives as Marinars divers &c. then at their own request at any time to discharge them, first paying them all wages &c due to them and the natives of all the said Islands being under His Majestys protection all acts of rapine, plunder, piracy, murders, or other outrages against their persons or property will upon conviction be severely punished ———

December 1 1813

The above was written by a native of New Zealand who [re]turns with the Vessel to his own country — he is a young the consent and approbation in writing of His Excellency the Governor; [and on receiving this consent and discharging such a person at the end of a voyage] shall first pay him or them such wages or price as may be lawfully or reasonably due . . . And whereas the natives of all the said islands are under the protection of His Majesty, and entitled to the good offices of his subjects; all persons whatsoever charged by the oath of credible witnesses with any acts of rapine, plunder, robbery, piracy, murder or other offences against the law of nature and of nations, against the persons and properties of the natives of any of the said islands, will, upon due conviction, be further punished with the utmost rigour of the law.

LACHLAN MACQUARIE.

Macquarie also assured Marsden that he would write to the Governor-General of India, and British Government ministers, asking them to issue similar orders at ports in India and Britain. Following earlier proclamations by Governors King and Bligh, this document placed Maori under the protection of the King, and declared that British subjects were bound by international and British law in their dealings with Maori and other Pacific Islanders. Furthermore, on 20 December 1813 Marsden established a 'New South Wales Society, for affording Protection to the Natives of the South Sea Islands, and Promoting their Civilization' (better known as the 'Philanthropic Society'), with Macquarie as its patron. In the minutes of its first meeting, attended by settlers as well as missionaries, the purpose of the Society was stated:

> To afford Protection and Relief to the Natives of the South Sea Islands who may be brought to PORT JACKSON, and to defend their just Claims on the Masters and Owners of the Vessels who bring them, and to see justice done to their Persons and Property; and also, to instruct them in the Principles of Christianity, and in the different Branches of Agriculture; and in such other simple Arts as may best lead to their Civilization and general Improvement.[100]

At this meeting an elected committee of three members was set up to hear any complaints from South Sea Islanders against the owners, masters or crews of vessels, and to bring such people before the courts, if it was necessary to do so.

Marsden was thrilled. In a letter to the CMS he exulted, 'In this I [have] obtained the utmost of my wishes. The Society will see from all these Circumstances that divine Goodness is preparing a way for these poor Heathens to receive the glad tidings of the Gospel.'[101] Since 1805, he had been asking the CMS to buy a vessel to support missionary work in the Pacific, but although his patron William Wilberforce (the anti-slavery campaigner and a member of the society) had given strong support to the idea, no funds had been forthcoming. Marsden now took decisive action. When he found that it would cost at least £600 to hire a ship to carry the missionaries to New Zealand, he purchased the *Active*, a 120-ton

Opposite: *A draft of Governor Macquarie's proclamation, copied by Maaui at Parramatta on 1 December 1813.*

Indian brig, from a Sydney merchant for £1,400,[102] and engaged Peter Dillon as captain. Dillon was an Irishman and an old Pacific hand who had been honoured by the French Government for discovering the fate of La Pérouse. He was familiar with New Zealand, having visited the Bay of Islands in the *Mercury* in 1809, and Marsden intended to benefit from his experience.

Marsden's rejoicings were premature. He wanted to go on the *Active* to New Zealand, but could not leave Port Jackson without the Governor's permission. Early in February, however, he fell out with Macquarie. He refused to read a Government Order from his pulpit instructing the settlers to supply the government stores with grain. This order applied to Marsden himself, and Macquarie was infuriated by his refusal.[103] Marsden also resisted Macquarie's attempts to appoint prominent ex-convicts to the magistrates' bench, which further alienated the Governor. Macquarie began to turn a sympathetic ear to some of those men, who disliked Marsden for his moralising and mistrusted his 'Philanthropic Society's' efforts to restrain the conduct of their ships' captains and crews in the Pacific. Caustic comments in Macquarie's despatches about Marsden's preference for the 'cannibalistic and treacherous natives of New Zealand and Tahiti' over the Australian Aboriginals, his low rank and 'Methodistical Principles' suggest that the Governor's support for his Principal Chaplain was waning.[104] To Marsden's chagrin, after some initial encouragement Macquarie refused him permission to join the first evangelical voyage to New Zealand, saying that the venture was too dangerous.

Kendall and Hall, however, were allowed to take the *Active* on an exploratory expedition to the Bay of Islands. Kendall was ecstatic, seeing their venture as a fulfillment of Biblical prophecy: 'That sendeth ambassadors by Sea; even in *Vessels of Bulrushes* upon the Waters. Who are these that fly as a cloud, and as the dove to the window? Surely the *Isles* shall wait for me, and the *Ships of Tarshish* first to bring thy Sons from far, their silver and their gold with them, unto the name of the Lord thy God, and to the Holy one of Israel, because he hath glorified thee.'[105] Early in March 1814, Kendall, Hall and Tui boarded the brig, with a crew that included two Tahitians, one Hawaiian, one Australian Aboriginal, one American, a Swede, a Norwegian and one man each from Prussia and England, and two Irishmen.[106] Marsden was convinced that ownership of the vessel was the only way to ensure that 'native' crew members were fairly treated during the voyage. 'Few Masters of Vessels can be trusted, when once they lose Sight of Land. Their Tyranny and Avarice is incredible. I pledged myself to Duaterra, that I would send a Vessel to the Bay of Islands, and that the Master and Crew should be instructed to treat them with more Justice and Humanity.'[107]

His instructions to Dillon honoured that pledge. Polynesian crew members were to be paid at European rates, and the *Active* was to proceed directly to the River Derwent, where her cargo should be discharged, and from thence to the Bay of Islands, where 'a friendly intercourse [should be opened] with the natives of New Zealand'. Dillon was asked to deal particularly with Ruatara, Tara, Kawiti and Korokoro (Tui's brother), and to prevent all quarrels between his sailors and the local people. If any of them, especially Ruatara or any of the chiefs' children, wished to come to Port Jackson, he should give them a free passage on the *Active*, and promise to bring them home again. He should announce that Marsden wanted a chief to come to Sydney to make some arrangements for their benefit, and that Marsden himself would then come to visit them. No private trade was to be allowed, nor were any local women to live on board, and the Sabbath should be strictly observed during the voyage and upon their arrival in the Bay of Islands. In New Zealand, quantities of flax, spars, pork, salt fish, rosin (kauri gum) and potatoes were to be obtained, to help defray the ship's expenses. Marsden also gave Kendall a steel mill, a frying pan, and the following letter for Ruatara:

> Duaterra King,
> I have sent the Brig Active to the Bay of Islands to see what you are doing; and Mr Hall and Mr Kendall from England. Mr Kendall will teach the Boys and Girls to read and write. I told you when you was at Parramatta I would send you a gentleman to teach your Tamoneeke's [tamariki] and Cocteedo'es [kootiro] to read. You will be very good to Mr. Hall and Mr Kendall. They will come to live in New Zealand if you will not hurt them; and teach you how to grow corn Wheat and make Houses. Charles has sent you a cock and Mrs Marsden has sent you a shirt and jacket. I have sent you some wheat for seeds, and you must put it into the ground as soon as you can. I have sent you a mill to grind your corn. If you will come in the Active to Parramatta, I will send you back again. Send me a man or two to learn how to make an axe and everything. You will send the Active full of moca [muka – dressed flax], potatoes, lines, mats, fish and nets. I have sent a jacket for Kowheetee [Kawiti]. Tell him to assist you and Terra [Tara] to lade the ship. You will be very good to all my men and not hurt them, and I will be good to you. Anne, Elizabeth, Mary, Jane, Charles, Martha, Nanny and Mrs. Bishop, Mrs. Marsden are all well, and wish to know how you are. If you do not come to see me send me word by Mr. Kendall and Mr. Hall what you want, and I will send it to you. – I am,
> Your friend,
> Samuel Marsden.[108]

On 11 March, Kendall wrote to the secretary of the Church Missionary Society from the ship, announcing their imminent departure:[109]

> We expect to sail as soon as we have a fair wind . . . A young man, a native of New Zealand, whose name is Tohi has been with me about a month. He can speak English a little, and we can now begin to understand each other tolerably well. I am trying to learn the language, and Tohi who knows what I want, makes himself to be as clearly understood as possible. He says he will return with me in the Active and dwell with me. The New Zealanders are certainly a fine race of men, and much superior in point of mental capacity to any savages which I have hitherto seen. Tohi is strongly attached to my servant Richard Stockwell (a young man who was recommended to my care by some clergymen at Bristol); he calls himself his Brother [although if Stockwell's affair with Jane Kendall had already begun by that time, he and Tui were a sad pair of libertines].

One object in going at this time to New Zealand is to see whether it would be prudent for us to take our families from New South Wales and reside there. In case the prospect is fair, Governor Macquarie has promised to give us all the support in his power.[110]

On 14 March, the *Active* finally sailed from Port Jackson. Although he was disappointed to be left behind, Marsden had great faith in Thomas Kendall. He wrote in a letter to the CMS: 'His heart is engaged in the Cause – he is very mild in his manners – kind, tender and affectionate; and well qualified to treat with an ignorant Heathen.'[111]

Kendall was ardent in his beliefs and liberal in his sentiments. When they visited the east coast of Australia en route to New Zealand, for example, he befriended the local Aboriginals, and at Hobart (where they arrived on 12 April) he wrote of the Tasmanians, 'The Natives of Van Diemens Land have been very ill treated indeed, and banished entirely from those parts which are colonised by Englishmen. Great numbers of them have been shot like Beasts of Prey by our people, and the Bush-rangers . . . have killed them without mercy'[112] (although at the same time referring to them in prayer as 'benighted idolaters' and the 'perishing Heathen').[113] During the voyage, Kendall spent a good deal of his time with Tui, trying to learn Maori. He heard Tui's version of the *Boyd* killings, and Tui assured him of Tara's good will, despite his enmity towards Ruatara's people. Kendall also looked forward to meeting Kawiti, a Ngaati Hine chief who had spent some time with Hall at Parramatta, and Korokoro, Tui's brother, a chief of Ngare Raumati who controlled the east side of the Bay of Islands.[114]

At Hobart, Waraki, a young Ngaati Raahiri chief from Waitangi in the Bay of Islands (named after Ruatara's wife's father), came on board and asked for a passage. He was homesick for his mother, his brothers and sisters, but had signed articles to serve on the *Spring*, and neither the owner, Simeon Lord, nor the master would release him. On 11 May, while the ship was still anchored in the Derwent, 'Moroo' (Maru), another Bay of Islander, arrived from his ship at Port Dalrymple. Maru had previously lived with Hall at Parramatta, and had walked overland through the woods for five days to Hobart to see him. Maru had been serving with a Captain 'Stuart' (probably William Stewart, who often visited New Zealand), but complained that he had been given little to eat and was abused on board his vessel. Kendall secured his release by arguing that Maru had been mistreated and did not understand the binding nature of the articles he had signed.[115] Finally, Maru was allowed to travel with them to New Zealand. Before they left Hobart, Kendall received a loving letter from his wife, revealing some of the anxieties that plagued the missionaries' families:

My dear love, I did not think I could bear your absence from me so long as we have lived ten years together so very happy. God grant we may meet again and spend many more years together as happy. I do not care where I am if we are together; I cannot bear the thoughts of being parted. I think the time very long. I always pray for you every night and morning that God may bless you in your undertaking and protect you from the cruelty of the Heathen, and conduct you in safety to your family so that we may unite again in praying to and praising Him. Our Dear Children join with me in love to you. Joseph says his father is gone to New Zealand; he will kiss him when he returns home. They all want to see you very much.

I am, my dearest,
Your
Jane Kendall.[116]

On 23 May 1814, the *Active* sailed from Hobart for the Bay of Islands, and on 10 June the ship anchored near the paa at Rangihoua. Ruatara was at his farms in the interior (to the west, at Te Puna, for there was little good agricultural land around Rangihoua[117]). News of their arrival brought him hurrying back, and he soon arrived to welcome Hall and Kendall.[118] When the missionaries landed, they were surrounded by the inhabitants of Rangihoua, who greeted them warmly. The local tohunga 'kaioos' (tohunga whakairo?, or carvers) paid Hall, the carpenter and ship-builder, particular attention. As soon as Kendall had managed to over-come their fear, the children followed him everywhere and held onto his hand (Kendall was particularly fond of children[119]). He described Rangihoua as a cluster of small houses, mostly five feet high, eight feet wide and ten or twelve feet long. Ruatara had storehouses in the paa filled with rum, tea, sugar, flour, cheese, and two chests of European clothing. Although one of these was unlocked, and Ruatara's main residence was sixteen miles away, nothing was ever taken. There were many small fenced gardens on the hillsides, where potatoes, cabbages, turnips, carrots and onions were growing, and outside the garden fences a number of pigs were grazing. Pork was freely available for barter, with an axe or adze buying

Rangihoua, sketched by Augustus Earle.

one or two pigs. Where the hilly ground was not cultivated, it was generally covered in bracken.

On the Sunday after their arrival at Te Puna, Hall read a service on the deck of the *Active*. It was raining, so only the two or three local people who had slept on board attended the service. When Kendall and Hall went to the paa that afternoon, the people wanted to trade with them, but the missionaries told them that it was a sacred day and there could be no barter. Men might work for six days, but on the seventh they must rest and 'krarkia atua' (karakia ki ngaa atua – pray to the gods). According to Hall, he and Kendall 'told them that we loved them very much and that we would come and live with them and bring our wives and families if they would not injure them, and I told them that I was a Carpenter and that I would build them large houses and fine Canoes, and they seemed very much pleased with the Idea and expressed their joy by saying, "Nuee nuee rungateeda pakehaa" – a very great Gentleman white man' (another early northern use of the term Pakeha).[120] Kendall also invited some of the children to travel to Port Jackson in order to learn to read books and to see Mr Marsden, who was well known in the Bay. The people mentioned his name in their songs and often spoke about him. In a corner of the paa, Kendall noticed an old man fenced around with some sticks, who had been isolated because he was tapu. He was not allowed to eat with other people, or to feed himself with his own hands for the next five months – showing the rigorous nature of some tapu restrictions (in this case, probably the death tapu).

On 13 June, three days after their arrival, Kendall, Hall and Tui walked with Ruatara into the interior to see his cultivations. They passed by a paa called 'Teepookay' (Te Puke), on the inland plains, where the people took them by the hand and invited them to dinner. After some conversation they carried on, crossing swamps and high hills, where the soil seemed very fertile. Little bush was visible in this part of the Bay. When they reached Ruatara's cultivations, at a place called 'Motoo Terra' (Motu-tara), they found wheat about six inches high growing in an enclosure. Fifteen of his people (including Te Pahi's son 'Towwha' [Taua]) were clearing more land for potatoes and the two bushels of wheat that Marsden had sent as a present to Ruatara. Hall also had brought two boxes of young fruit trees, including peaches, apples and quinces, and a hundredweight of potatoes as gifts, while Charles Marsden had sent two cocks and two hens. In addition, Marsden sent a steel mill for Ruatara by the *Active*. As soon as he received this, Ruatara ground some wheat into flour and made a cake, which he cooked in a frying pan then gave to his relations. When they tasted the cake, they 'shouted for joy', at last believing that bread was made from the wheat plant.[121]

On 15 June, the brig *James Hay* returned to the Bay, and Kendall and Hall dined with Captain Folger. Shortly afterwards, Tara, the old high chief of Kororaareka, and his wife came out to the ship with an attendant, and Kendall gave them a letter almost identical to the one that Marsden had sent to Ruatara, addressed to 'King Terra'. This included an invitation for Tara to come to Port

Jackson, where he would meet 'King Macquarie'.[122] In response to these regal greetings, Tara said that he would be glad to visit Marsden, and invited Folger to bring the missionaries across the Bay to Kororaareka. Upon their arrival there, Tara presented the crew of the *James Hay* with five baskets of potatoes. Tara was about seventy years old and the leader of 'seventeen places' (presumably dwelling places, or kaainga). He and his southern allies were inveterate enemies of the people to the north of the Bay, and this friendly gesture made the northern allies nervous. The very next day Ruatara brought his uncle Hongi Hika to meet Hall and Kendall.[123] He told them that Hongi was the commander of six hundred fighting men, while he himself had four hundred, his friend Wai had two hundred, and Hongi's brother Kaingaroa another three hundred. Kendall was impressed by his meeting with Hongi Hika:

Thomas Kendall, with Hongi Hika and Waikato.

> Shunghee . . . is a warrior, but apparently a man of a very mild disposition, and altho', this is the first time he has had any intercourse with Europeans he is remarkably steady and decent in his outward behaviour, and has little appearance of the Savage about him. He is a chief over the People of seventeen places[124] is a man of a very ingenious turn, and is very desirous to learn the European Arts. He showed us a Musket which had been stocked and mounted by his own hands, and the performance does him much credit, since he had no man to instruct him. He has several [Kendall's journal says ten] Muskets in his Possession.[125]

This is a very early mention of muskets in Maori hands, which according to Kendall were acquired from visiting ships in exchange for fresh water, provisions and spars, or for the services of Maori sailors.[126] Hongi was perhaps the first local commander to grasp the power of these weapons to kill and wound at a distance, and to exploit this in campaigns against other kin groups. He was later to do this to devastating effect throughout much of the northern North Island.

Friendly relations with Europeans gave significant strategic advantages, in acquiring iron tools, European plants and animals, and knowledge, as well as weapons. The next day Pomare, the leader of Ngaati Manu at Matauwhi, also made contact, inviting the missionaries to visit his paa and offering to take them to a place where the ship could get timber. Pomare, formerly known as Whetoi, had recently renamed himself after the high chief of Tahiti, who allied himself with the LMS missionaries, and became famous in the Pacific as the 'king' of his people. Whetoi had also renamed his kaainga (settlement) 'Matauwhi', after Matavai in Tahiti, Pomare's main settlement.[127] It was a lovely afternoon, and Kendall and Hall set out in a canoe manned by Pomare's people. After they had paddled for several miles, it began to get dark, so they headed to shore and landed. Kendall wrote in his journal:

> We made a good fire and I slept by the side of Pomarre having for my bed some dried fern, and Pomarre's Cakkahow [kakahu – cloak] for my covering. I mention this event with great pleasure and satisfaction, because the natives of New Zealand have been called a dangerous set of men, & that there is no trusting to them. But here was a strong temptation. I had two muskets and a pair of pocket pistols with me. Pomarre knew they were unloaded for he had several times discharged them, and the natives are very fond of articles of this kind. They will almost give anything for them. However I slept secure, and felt happy that God had been pleased (for some good purpose, as I trusted) to send me amongst them.[128]

Kendall was overjoyed with the welcome that they had received, and content to be in Maori company. The next morning Hauraki, a rangatira of Ngaati Hineira, a kin group allied to Tara, took them to some woods by a river. Two spars that had already been cut were hauled to the river's edge, and after payment was received of one 'tokee' (toki – adze) each, these were floated fourteen miles or more out to the *Active*.

The next day, 19 June, was a Sunday. Two or three chiefs were on board, several canoes came alongside, and Kendall read prayers on the deck of the vessel.

The local people were entranced with the idea of a day of rest, and in honour of the Sabbath the *Active* flew the Union Flag while Tara flew his own flag at Koro-raareka. (Flags were like raahui poles, which staked out mana, and often had a local rangatira's garment tied to them.) That afternoon Kendall and Hall paid a visit to Pomare at Matauwhi. Again, the men, women and children clustered around the missionaries, and Kendall distributed religious tracts among them. He re-flected in his journal: 'To have noticed the eagerness and delight with which they all received them would have caused a tear, and excited a pious desire in the true Believer, in behalf of a people whom Satan has so long held in captivity.'[129]

Over the next three weeks a cargo of spars and flax leaves ('koraddee' – korari) was loaded, and various chiefs attended Sunday service on board the *Active*. During this time Kendall attended the tangi for a kinsman of Tara's. He noted that the dead man was neatly wrapped up in his cloak, with his feet pulled up under the body. A group of about six women lamented bitterly and cut their faces, breasts and arms with sharp shells (the haehae ceremony) while the men sang songs of mourning. During the tangi there was a mock fight, an interesting feature of this funerary ritual for a rangatira; then two or three hundred people sat down to feast on sweet potatoes, which concluded the ceremony. During the feast Kendall was presented with six baskets of kuumara, gifts for an honoured visitor.

Just before the *Active* prepared to sail from the Bay, Kendall took the brig back to Kororaareka. He invited Tara and Hauraki, chiefs of the southern alliance, to go with him to Port Jackson, but they declined the invitation. The next day Tara, Tupi, Pomare and Hauraki came to say goodbye. As the two missionaries prayed, the chiefs knelt down beside them. Afterwards the vessel was sailed to the Mangoo-nui Inlet on the north side of the Bay, where the chiefs of the northern alliance, including Hongi and Ruatara, came on board. Unlike Tara and his chiefs, Hongi decided to go to Port Jackson, and came on board with his wife Turikatuku and five of his children, including his two small sons, Ripiro and Ruinga. The two boys stayed with their father on the ship while Turikatuku and the other children camped nearby on the shore. Hongi now insisted that Ruatara should travel with them, to act as their interpreter. Ruatara's three wives and his tohunga begged him to stay, the priest warning him that his head wife would die if he left her. Hongi's mana was greater, however, and Ruatara agreed to accompany his uncle.

On 22 July, after six weeks in the Bay, the *Active* was ready for departure. People crowded on board to farewell the voyagers – Hongi, Ruatara, Tui, Tinana and Pounaho. Their womenfolk, especially Hongi's wife Turikatuku and one of Ruatara's wives, Tehu, wept bitterly. That evening Tui's brothers Korokoro and Te Rangi, who had arrived back in the Bay from a trading voyage to 'a distant part of New Zealand', embraced Tui and wept over him. The ship set sail that after-noon, but adverse winds forced it back to Te Puna. On 25 July, the *Active* finally left the Bay for Port Jackson. Hongi had allowed his eldest son, Ripiro, a boy about eight years old, to go with him on the voyage; Ruatara took his half-brother, a boy of about ten; and Tui's brother Korokoro, the chief of Paaroa, also decided to join them. As they sailed out of the Bay, the main boom swung from one side to the other of the ship and Kendall (who could not swim) was knocked overboard. A canoe that was following the *Active* soon picked him up and rescued him from drowning.

It is obvious from Kendall's account that he had conceived an affection for the Bay of Islanders. He protested the way that they had been depicted in British newspapers and by 'authors on geography' as uncouth and aggressive. On the contrary, he argued, they had been provoked by the tyranny and wanton abuse of visiting sailors:

> For, in my opinion, the true character of the New Zealanders is not so despicable as Europeans are apt to imagine, and it has by some writers been very unfairly portrayed. Because there are practices amongst them which are in their nature abhorrent to the tender feelings of humanity they have been condemned as the most dangerous and degraded of the human race. I cannot from a few days observation form a true estimate of their general character, but I am told that there are usages and customs amongst them which are not approved by them all, and these followed by some to which others more enlightened are averse and which they hold in detestation . . . In giving a fair account of the general character of a savage nation, great allowances must be made for ancient usages . . . Their raiment it is true is the most uncouth in appearance of any that I have ever yet seen. But then, neither the men nor the women expose their persons, like the natives of New Holland. The men are also intelligent, industrious and full of ingenuity; fit for husbandmen and mechanics as soon as they shall be favored with the means of instruction. The women employ part of their time in making Cakkahows [kaakahu – cloaks], Pargattis, Mats, Moka [muka – dressed flax] &c., and in all probability would gladly learn to spin, and knit stockings and the use of the needle; and the children are lively, active and witty. They made no stranger of me. As soon as they saw me they usually said, 'How do you do, Mr. Kendarro?' They then offered me their little parcels of thread which they had made with their own hands, and asked me for Fish Hooks, Nails, and Buttons in return. It has been truly said of these People, that they are a Noble Race. They stand in need of our friendship, and if proper attention was paid to their wants, and they were dealt with upon just and good principles, they would by the Divine blessing soon be brought over to a state of civilization.[130]

During the voyage Kendall took great pleasure in teaching Hongi, Korokoro, Ripiro and Pounaho to sound and write the letters of the English alphabet. He had some cards on which letters and monosyllables were written, from 'Dr Bell's System of Education'. He offered them a prize of one fish-hook for every page they could memorise. They were delighted, and in particular his 'little pupil Depero [Ripiro] seemed transported with the idea of possessing some riches which he should have to show his mother and his uncle Kangroha [Kaingaroa] upon his return to his native land'. Within five or six days, Hongi, his son and Pounaho had learned the alphabet by heart, and Hongi copied out several letters that Kendall sent on to the Church Missionary Society. On 5 August, the brig *Campbell Macquarie* was sighted, and Kendall and Hall went on board her with Captain Dillon. Kendall got very drunk and swore at Dillon, who hit him. Kendall was ashamed of himself and afterwards remarked that the New Zealanders mistrusted and disliked alcohol, and were dismayed by abusive language. While they were still in the Bay, Pomare had remarked to him that 'Europe Tungata [European people] said D—n your Blood, D—n your Eyes and G—d D—n you you Buggar, these Expressions were no good'.[131]

According to Kendall, Maori were very fond of bread and were now keen for wheat to be established. They had many gods but did not seem to worship them.

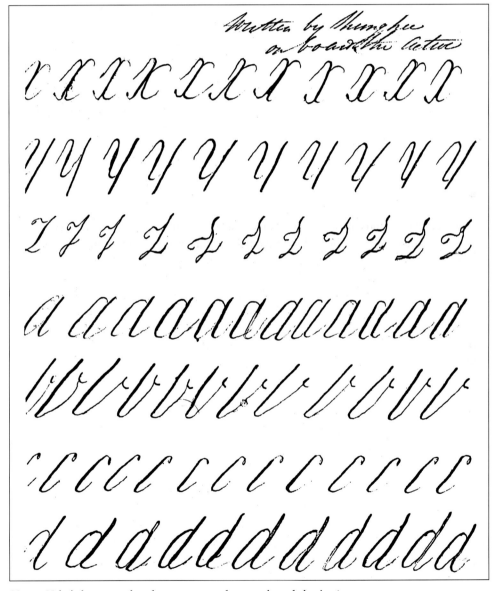

Hongi Hika's lessons in handwriting, copied out on board the Active.

A marriage was contracted when a young man, having been attracted to a young woman, sought her family's permission. If they agreed and when this was announced to her, she did not cry, the marriage was consummated. If she cried each time he visited her for two or three nights, he must cease to press the matter. Kendall added, of moral issues that were later to cause him great personal tribulation, 'Simple fornication is not considered a crime, but if a woman is unfaithful to her husband he spears her.' During the voyage Kendall forged excellent relationships with the chiefs, and his affection for them was reciprocated. Marsden later reported:

> Mr. Kendall is a most valuable man. His Heart is wholly engaged in the work – he is making very considerable Progress in the Language, and some of the natives are always with him. His manners are mild – he is naturally kind, tender and affectionate; and will most assuredly attach the natives of New Zealand to him. He loves to be constantly with them, and can with ease meet their wishes – They all pay him the greatest Respect, and speak of him with the warmest Affection – If I inquire of the Chiefs how Mr. Kendall treats them, their answer always is, 'Mr. Kendall is too good.'[132]

On 22 August, when the *Active* arrived back in Port Jackson, Kendall's family were all well and his Maori companions were taken to Parramatta. Kendall and Hall gave rhapsodic accounts of the Bay of Islands, describing the area as

> beautifully picturesque in point of scenery, with a soil that only required the hand of cultivation to produce every thing in the greatest abundance. The climate was . . . salubrious and inviting, [and winter was marked by] a few refreshing showers, which gave a mellow and vernal softness to the fields, while no sudden or violent transitions ever disturbed the serenity of the mild atmosphere.[133]

There were twelve Maori from this Arcadia now living at Marsden's establishment – the chief Ruatara and his young half-brother, Hongi Hika and his son Ripiro ('a fine boy'), Korokoro ('A warlike Chief on the opposite Shore in the Bay'), Tui (his brother) and 'Horow' (Horo) ('Related to old Tippahee'); and the commoners Maaui ('reads and writes the English language'), Waraki ('A common man'), Waihi ('Servant to Duaterra'), Tinana ('a fine young man, learning to make nails') and Waikato, another commoner.[134] According to Marsden, they enjoyed their time at Port Jackson:

> Their minds [are] enlarging very fast. Beholding the various works that are going on in the Smiths & Carpenters Shops, the spinning and weaving, Brickmaking and Building Houses, together with all the operations of Agriculture and Gardening, has a wonderful Effect upon their minds; and will excite all their natural Powers to improve their own Country. The Idea of my visiting them is very gratifying to their minds. At present I spend all the time I can spare with them, in conversing with them upon . . . the Subjects of Religion, civil Government, and Agriculture.
> With respect to Religion, I talk to them of the Institution of the Sabbath Day by God himself – and they see it observed by us with particular attention. They see the Prisoners mustered on Sunday morning, their names called over, and then

marched to Church. They also see the Soldiers and Officers march to Church likewise; and most of the People in the Town of Parramatta.

As I have many Complaints to settle as a magistrate – they frequently attend – when I explain to them afterwards the different Crimes, and Punishments that each have committed and what sentence is past upon them – Some men confined for one moon, and some for more in Prison, according to their Crimes.

With respect to Agriculture, they visit different Farms, observe the Plough at work, some men with the Hoe, some thrashing &c. &c. They tell me when they return, they shall sit up whole nights, telling their People what they have seen, and that their men will stop their Ears with their Fingers – We have heard enough, they will say, of your incredible Accounts, and we will hear no more – they are impossible to be true.[135]

Soon after their arrival, the chiefs were taken to meet Lachlan Macquarie. Ruatara asked the Governor to give him a flag, or a bell or drum so that he could signal the Sabbath to his countrymen each Sunday. Macquarie promised to give them a bull and three cows when they returned home; and ordered a new suit for each of them, with scarlet coats, and a supply of provisions from the government stores throughout their visit. They toured buildings and other facilities around Sydney, practised reading and writing, and Tinana learned to make nails. Hongi studied the mechanical arts, while Ruatara studied agriculture. When they were taken to see stockings being woven on a loom, Ruatara remarked, 'Hoes they wanted, and not Stockings – They could do without Stockings at present, if they could only get Bread.'[136] Wheat was very scarce at Port Jackson during their visit, and Ruatara decided that when he returned home his people could cultivate surplus crops of wheat for sale at the penal colony – the first Maori scheme for an export venture.

At the same time Marsden, who was eager to escape his troubles in Port Jackson, threw himself into planning the establishment of the missionary settlement at the Bay of Islands. He wrote to the CMS requesting a long list of tools, blue and red cloth, and other items for the mission, and sending gifts of mats and a carved self-portrait by Hongi. He had told Hongi that 'I wanted his Head to send to England, and he must either give me his Head, or make one like it of wood'. Marsden's joke about taking Hongi's head was dangerous, since the head of a chief was intensely tapu, but Hongi chose not to be offended. Instead, he made an iron tool about five inches long out of hoop iron, tied a handle to it and fashioned the bust from the end of an old post, carving it with a likeness of his own moko. Like Kendall, Marsden was impressed by Hongi, considering him to be 'a very fine Character; appears uncommonly mild in his manners, and very polite, and well behaved at all times'. Korokoro, the Ngaati Manu chief, he described as war-like, an avid voyager and trader. Korokoro had told him that he sometimes went on trading voyages four months long, from the North to the South Cape of New Zealand, where wild weather, snow and hail were common. Tui, Korokoro's brother, had learned the Lord's Prayer off by heart, and understood much of its meaning.

Hongi's self-portrait, carved for Samuel Marsden at Parramatta.

Marsden had told him, 'Since [your] Father [was] a New Zealand Priest, [you will] be an English one' – anticipating a role for Maori evangelists in New Zealand. He was fascinated by these men, and by the prospect of evangelising their home-land.[137] In another of his letters to the CMS, he wrote:

> I consider New Zealand as the Great Emporium of the South Sea Islands, inhab-ited by a numerous race of very intelligent men. I hope to erect the Standard of Christ's Kingdom there, and to hear the sacred Trumpet sound the Glad Tidings of Salvation . . . Faith and prayer will again build the walls of Jerusalem, even if we are obliged to hold the Trowel in one Hand, and the Sword in another.[138]

Kendall and Hall also wrote to the Society, reporting on their New Zealand adventure. Hall asked for a shotgun 'as a kind of defence' to take with him when they set up the mission, commenting briefly but enthusiastically on their visit to New Zealand. Kendall sent a journal of their expedition and a sample of Hongi's writing, along with a collection of 'curiosities' as gifts for various clerical colleagues. These included a 'Curious Box' (probably a waka huia, or carved feather box), cloaks of various kinds, upper garments, woven belts, flutes, a greenstone hei tiki, a war club, parcels of flax thread, fishing lines and the 'Head Tattowed in the New Zea-land Stile' carved by Hongi.[139] Both men were eager to return to the Bay, and their wives and children, once they had got to know the New Zealanders at Parramatta, had lost much of their fear of living amongst 'the heathen'. According to Marsden, Mrs Kendall was 'very attentive to the Heathens, and they are very much attached to her', while Mrs Hall was a 'mild, obliging and attentive' woman who also had good relationships with their Maori visitors.[140]

In October 1814, Simeon Lord approached Governor Macquarie with a pro-posal to establish a commercial settlement and factories in New Zealand. Although his 1810 venture with Francis Williams and Andrew Thompson had failed, incur-ring considerable losses, Lord now proposed with Garnham Blaxcell and several other merchants to set up a 'New South Wales New Zealand Company' to bring flax and timber from New Zealand. They intended to sell shares in the company, which would operate under charter, and with the capital thus subscribed to purchase two small vessels and establish a settlement at Port William in Foveaux Strait. Lord and his partners declared that they had the best of intentions in negotiating with Maori:

> Endeavouring to form, and preserve by every mode of conciliation and kindness, a friendly intercourse with the natives, by bartering with and encouraging them to procure and prepare the hemp and flax, by shewing them the best way of dress-ing those articles by hand . . . making them first usefull, and then leading them on to progressive civilization, by allowing and inviting such of them as may be so disposed to proceed to the establishment, where they may learn our tongue, and be taught to assist in the various processes attached to the arts before them, to facilitate which there will be a kind of dock yard, where black-smiths, ship-wrights, carpenters, and sawyers will be employed.[141]

The Sydney ship-owners, however, had a poor record in their dealings with South Sea Islanders. Marsden had already presented affidavits to Macquarie concerning the brutality and greed of some of their ships' captains, and in late October further evidence came to light of bloody affrays in Rarotonga caused by the *Cumberland*, one of Blaxcell's ships, and the consequent death of one of Ruatara's relatives. When Marsden tried to have the matter discussed at a meeting of the Philanthropic Society, however, he was blocked by members from the ship-owning families whose relatives and employees were involved in the violence. Macquarie was well aware of the debate, and its implications for government policy on the rights of Pacific Islanders.

In early November, the Governor gave Marsden permission to travel to New Zealand, on condition that he report on the suitability of the country for a settlement under the control of 'His Majesty's Government'. It seems that he had decided to further extend the rule of law over New Zealand. Kendall was sworn in as a resident magistrate,[142] and Macquarie published a proclamation intended to protect the 'just rights and privileges' of the New Zealanders, forbidding captains of visiting ships to land or recruit sailors in the Bay of Islands, without the written permission of Kendall and the agreement of the chiefs Ruatara, Hongi or Koro-koro:[143]

> It having been represented to His Excellency the Governor, that the Commanders and Seamen of Vessels touching at or trading with the Islands of New Zealand, and more especially that part of them commonly called 'The Bay of Islands', have been in the Habit of offering gross Insult and Injury to the Natives of those Places, by violently seizing on, and carrying off several of them, both Males and Females, and treating them in other respects with injudicious and unwarrantable Severity, to the great Prejudice of the fair Intercourses of Trade, which might be otherwise productive of mutual Advantages; and his Excellency being equally solicitous to protect the Natives of New Zealand and the Bay of Islands; in all their just Rights and Privileges, as those of every other Dependency of the Territory of New South Wales, hereby orders and directs, that no Master, or Seaman of any Ship or Vessel belonging to any British Port, or to any of the Colonies of Great Britain resorting to the said Islands of New Zealand, shall in future remove or carry therefrom any of the Natives without first obtaining the Permission of the Chief or Chiefs of the Districts within which the Natives so to be embarked may happen to reside; which Permission is to be certified in Writing under the Hand of Mr Thomas Kendall, the resident Magistrate in the Bay of Islands, or of the Magistrate for the time being in said Districts.[144]

These were fine sentiments, but after one or two initial gestures, Macquarie had done little to enforce his earlier declaration of Maori rights. The whalers who devastated Te Pahi's island, for instance, had escaped without any kind of punishment. It seems likely that this proclamation was intended to placate the missionaries and their influential friends at home, rather than as a serious political commitment.

In recognition of their new status, he gave the chiefs officer's uniforms. They also received one cow each, and Ruatara was given a 'fine mare' by one of the local gentlemen. A new crew came on board the *Active*, including Thomas Hansen (Mrs King's father) as captain, Alexander Ross as mate, Thomas Hamilton, cook, and one European, two Tahitians and five Maori 'common men' (Waraki, Maaui or 'Tommy', Tinana, Paihi and Mutu, also known as 'Jacky Miti' [Maitai]) as sailors. They were joined by the missionary party on 19 November – the Reverend Samuel Marsden; Mrs Hansen, the captain's wife, with their son Thomas junior; Thomas and Mrs Kendall with their three sons Thomas, Basil and Joseph[145] (their two daughters, Susanna and Elizabeth, stayed behind with the couple who ran the Female Orphan School in Sydney, for fear of the 'filthiness' of the heathen), and their convict servant Richard Stockwell; John and Mrs King (who was heavily pregnant), with their fifteen-month-old son Phillip; and William and Mrs Hall with their three-year-old son. Two other convict servants; two emancipist tradesmen, John Hunter, a carpenter, Walter Hall, a blacksmith, William Campbell, a weaver and flax dresser; and John Liddiard Nicholas, a free settler whom Kendall had met on the *Earl Spencer* during their voyage from England, and who was travelling as Marsden's companion, also joined the ship.[146] Nicholas had planned to set up a business in Sydney, but this had fallen through, so he was 'at liberty to indulge the ardent desire I felt from my earliest days, of learning the manners and customs of different nations'.[147] When the chiefs Ruatara, Korokoro, Tui and Hongi (with his son) came on board, the ship's complement was complete, for Ruatara's young half-brother had stayed behind at Parramatta to study English, reading, carpentry and agriculture. The *Active* was detained for nine days in Watson's Bay by contrary winds. On 28 November 1814, the ship, with its entourage of missionaries and rangatira, sailed for the Bay of Islands.

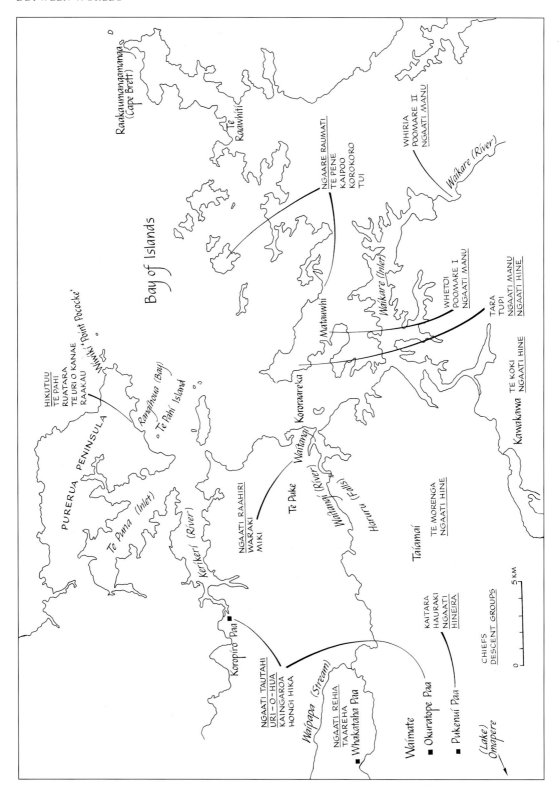

Raakaumangamanga
(Cape Brett)

Te
Raawhiti

WHIRIA
POOMARE II
NGAATI MANU

Waikare (River)

NGAARE RAUMATI
TE PENE
KAIPOO
KOROKORO
TUI

Bay of Islands

Waikare (Inlet)

WHETOI
POOMARE I
NGAATI MANU

TARA
TUPI
NGAATI MANU
NGAATI HINE

Matauwhi

KAWAKAWA   TE KOKI
NGAATI HINE

HIKUTUU
TE PAHI
RUATARA
TE URI O KANAE
RAAKAU 'Point Pococke'

Rangihoua (Bay)

Te Pahi Island

PURERUA PENINSULA

Te Puna (Inlet)

Kerikeri (River)

NGAATI RAAHIRI
WARAKI
MIKI

Te Puke

Waitangi

Kororaareka

Waitangi (River)

Haruru (Falls)

Taiamai

TE MORENGA
NGAATI HINE

Koropiro Paa

NGAATI TAUTAHI
URI-O-HUA
KAINGAROA
HONGI HIKA

Waipapa (Stream)

NGAATI REHIA
TAAREHA
Whakataha Paa

KAITARA
HAURAKI
NGAATI
HINEIRA

Okuratope Paa

Pukenui Paa

Waimate

Okuratope Paa

Pukenui Paa

CHIEFS
DESCENT GROUPS

0   5 KM

(Lake)
Omapere

Eighteen

THE MISSION AT RANGIHOUA

According to John Liddiard Nicholas, Samuel Marsden's New Zealand venture was regarded with intense scepticism in Sydney:

> His plan was by most persons deemed wild and chimerical, and a sacrifice of the life of every one was foreboded, who should venture to carry it into execution. The New Zealanders . . . were represented at the Colony in the blackest colours; and any attempt to impress their minds with a sense of religion and morality, was judged not only hopeless and impracticable, but rash, absurd, and extravagant . . . Dreaded by the good, and assailed by the worthless, their real dispositions were not ascertained; the former dared not venture to civilize them, the latter only added to their ferocity . . . The fatal attack upon the Boyd was still fresh in the recollection of every one, and left an impression of horror and detestation which nothing could efface. This ill-fated ship having touched at New Zealand in 1809, while on her return to Europe, was actually seized by the natives in spite of the resistance of the crew, who were all of them murdered, and many of them in like manner eaten.[1]

Marsden understood his mission as an act of generosity and faith, in the face of such dire forbodings. He was distraught to find that while they were still at anchor in Watson's Bay, Ruatara had been warned against the missionaries:

> He was informed by a gentleman at Sydney, that the Missionaries then going, would shortly introduce a much greater number; and thus, in some time become so powerful, as to possess themselves of the whole island, and either destroy the natives, or reduce them to slavery. The gentleman . . . bid him to look at the conduct of our countrymen in New South Wales, where, on their first arrival, they despoiled the inhabitants of all their possessions, and shot the greater number of them with a merciless cruelty; while, in some few years, the whole race of that once happy people would be entirely extinct. This diabolical reasoning succeeded by too well in awakening all the fears and suspicions of Duaterra . . . Dismayed by this infamous calumny, we knew not how to act.[2]

Opposite: *Map of the Bay of Islands, showing the leading rangatira in 1814–15.*

Marsden tried to reassure Ruatara but found that he could not undo the damage. He offered to take the ship back to Sydney Cove and put the missionaries ashore, if that was what Ruatara wanted. Ruatara demurred but was obviously still full of doubt. Marsden remarked disconsolately, 'The poison infused into his mind was too subtle and infectious ever to be removed.' It was not until Marsden promised that the missionaries would settle amongst his people at Rangihoua, and nowhere else, that Ruatara 'resumed all his usual good humour'[3] — a commitment that shaped the future of the mission.

THE VOYAGE

As soon as they left Port Jackson, the *Active* sailed into a gale that tossed the ship about unmercifully. Marsden, the other missionaries, the Maori passengers and the animals on board (one stallion and two mares, one bull and two cows, sheep, pigs, dogs, chickens, goats, cats and dogs) were all prostrated with sea-sickness. The Maori chiefs lay down in their cots and stayed there until the storm subsided. Kendall vomited over the side, his wig fell into the Tasman and he tied a red handkerchief around his head. With his white, anguished face he looked like 'Banquo's ghost — a complete spectre'. The next day when the wind died down, two convicts who had stowed away came on deck and walked about nonchalantly. Nicholas played draughts with Ruatara, while Hongi worked on a cartridge box he was making. Korokoro, who had been greatly struck with Governor Macquarie (whom he considered a 'nuee nuee arekee' [nui nui ariki – a very great chief]), now assumed his name and insisted in being treated with the same formality as the Governor, inclining his head in an elegant manner. 'Thus even are the rudest barbarians dazzled with the distinctions of office and the pageantry of power,' Nicholas commented sardonically.[4]

Several days later, the Maori on board put on a musical performance. They entertained their companions with a song composed by Te Pahi's daughter, describing his visit to Port Jackson. According to Nicholas, 'it forcibly reminded me of the chanting in our cathedrals, it being deep, slow and extended; [and] . . . divided into parts, which the chiefs sung separately, and were joined in chorus, at certain intervals by the other New Zealanders; while they all concluded it together'[5] — a vivid description of waiata chanting. They often sang together during this voyage, and Nicholas eventually recorded the words of three more waiata.

One of these told of the destruction of a potato crop by the east wind, followed by a successful harvest, and was accompanied by actions that portrayed the work of planting and digging up potatoes. During this song they stood and danced in a line, '[throwing] themselves into a variety of easy attitudes'. Another, which was sung without actions, was about a man who was ambushed while carving a canoe, and captured and then killed by his enemies.[6] According to

Nicholas, most of their songs were composed by people at the East Cape, whom they described as 'the bards of their country'.

Nicholas spent much of his time during the voyage talking with Ruatara. He described him as being 'in the full bloom of youth . . . a man of tall and commanding stature, great muscular strength, and marked expression of countenance: his deportment, which I will not hesitate to call dignified and noble, appeared well calculated to give sanction to this authority, while the fire and animation of his eye might betray even to the ordinary beholder, the elevated rank he held among his countrymen [although, unlike Hongi and Korokoro, he had no moko].'[7] Ruatara told Nicholas that his people were fond of observing the stars and constellations, which were named and associated with 'curious traditions'. During the summer the priests often stayed awake all night, watching the sky and waiting for particular stars to make their appearance. If a star was not seen at the appropriate time, they became worried and tried to deduce the reason.[8] They called Orion's Belt the 'Waka', or Canoe, and a nearby star (which set at night and rose in the morning) the 'Anchor'; while the Pleiades were the glowing eyes of seven deceased ancestors.[9] He said that no thief went undetected in New Zealand. If a man stole, the atua (god) 'rises upon him like a full moon, rushes upon him with the velocity of a falling star, and passes him by like a shot from the cannon's mouth', afflicting him with illness in its passage.[10]

Because Nicholas's command of Maori was limited, he could not grasp all of Ruatara's explanations. Nevertheless, he took it for granted that Maori were ruled by unreason and mistaken in their cosmological understandings:

> Though the savage does possess all the passions of Nature, pure and unadulterated, and though he may in many instances feel stronger and more acutely than the man of civilized habits; still is he inferior to him in every other respect: the former is a slave to the impulse of his will, the latter has learned to restrain his desires; the former stands enveloped in the dark clouds of ignorance, the latter goes forth in the bright sunshine of knowledge; the former views the works of his Creator through the medium of a blind superstition, the latter through the light of reason and of truth; the one beholds Nature and is bewildered, the other clearly 'Looks through Nature up to Nature's God'.[11]

Like most of his contemporaries, Nicholas echoed the claims of European 'common sense', which linked reason and truth with Christianity and civilised life, and savagery with ignorance and superstition. He assumed that Western science offered decisive proof of the superiority of rational, restrained Europeans over passionate, ignorant savages.

Despite some unflattering judgements and mutual doubts, relationships on board the *Active* were friendly. When Nicholas came on deck wearing his spectacles one day, Tui teased him by asking whether he could see Brush Farm, his residence in New South Wales, more than four hundred miles distant. There was much joking back and forth, and exchanges of information and experience. Korokoro, for instance, drew Nicholas a sketch of the North Island indicating a high island (White Island) between East Cape and Totaranui, which periodically erupted.[12] He also told the missionaries about being ill-treated by Captain 'Seddons' (Richard Siddons of the sealer *Elizabeth and Mary*, which had visited the Bay of Islands in 1812). Siddons had accused Korokoro of having stolen an auger, and tied him up in his cabin. In a fury, Korokoro had burst his bonds, knocked Siddons down and jumped out the cabin window. He swam to his canoe and took up a spear, which he hurled at the ship, wounding a sailor. Siddons fired a musket at him but missed, and was relieved about this when he later discovered that some-one else had taken the auger. Galvanised by this memory, Korokoro broke into a haka, gesturing violently, stamping his feet, thrusting out his tongue, distorting his face and glaring 'with wild frenzy' (the puukana, in which the eyes are rolled downwards), and gesticulated to show how enemies should be treated.

Nicholas found Korokoro paradoxical: 'Furious to a degree when provoked, his rage knew no bounds; but when well treated, he was both gentle and affec-tionate; and such too was his fidelity, that when once conciliated by friendship, it might for ever after be confidently relied upon.'[13] By contrast, Hongi Hika seemed calm and mild-mannered. Although Hongi had 'the reputation of being one of the greatest warriors in his country', yet he found him likeable and inoffensive.[14]

As the *Active* approached the New Zealand coastline, flocks of birds flew around the ship, and the chiefs began to prepare for landing. They stayed below in seclu-sion, fearing that the sailors would steal their possessions. Ruatara seemed par-ticularly uneasy. He was anxious that his tohunga's warnings might prove correct and something dreadful had occurred in his absence. He took off his European clothing and donned cloaks, and spoke often of his head wife, who had been about to give birth when he left her. If the Whangaroa people had attacked Te Puna while he was away, he vowed to take a fleet of war canoes and destroy them.

On 16 December, they passed the Three Kings, where Nicholas was told that pigs and goats were now established. Early the next morning the ship anchored off North Cape. The chiefs, dressed in their uniforms and armed with swords, pistols and muskets, went ashore accompanied by three of their attendants and an armed party of sailors carrying sickles to cut grass for the ship's animals. In Sydney, the missionaries had been warned that two boats belonging to the *Jefferson* had been attacked by the North Cape people. When a canoe paddled by fourteen men came out to the *Active* at high speed, therefore, the remaining crew prepared for action. Their fears were groundless, however. Six of these men, including a chief and his son, swarmed up the side of the ship and approached them without hesitation. Using one of the English-speaking Maori sailors as an interpreter (almost certainly Maaui), Marsden told them about his plans to establish a mis-sion in the Bay of Islands. He assured them that his missionaries would befriend the North Cape people, and that if they brought flax and pigs to the mission in the Bay, they would be paid with iron axes or adzes. They seemed delighted with the news, and the chief told Marsden that he knew Ruatara, who had once given him a pocket knife, which he kept tied by a string around his waist and highly valued.

When he heard Marsden's name, he enquired after a young North Cape man who had lived with Marsden at Parramatta. This man's brother was in the canoe, and asked Marsden many more questions about him. They were soon on friendly terms, and Marsden gave the chief a piece of India cloth, which he threw around his shoulders with joy; and a printed copy of Governor Macquarie's proclamation.

More canoes came out, with an abundance of fish to trade. A 'tenpenny' nail[15] was exchanged for a ten- to twenty-pound snapper. The chief sent his canoe ashore with one of the Maori sailors to fetch pigs and potatoes for the ship's provisions. While he was waiting for them to return, he and his companions explored the *Active*. They were intrigued by Nicholas's spectacles, entranced at the sight of Marsden shaving his face, and astomished at the array of European animals on board the *Active*. They hugged the Europeans affectionately, who recoiled from the kutu (lice) in their hair and clothing. Nicholas noted, with some surprise, a woman lying face down in one of the canoes, who never once raised her head or looked at them. He thought that she might have been in mourning, though more likely she was avoiding their gaze for fear of some spiritual affliction.

Before long, two large war canoes came sailing out to the ship, riding smoothly over the rough water. One carried twenty-four and the other thirty-three 'stout fine-looking men'. They were led by a high chief 'Tarapeedo' (Te Arapiro?) with his brother 'Tishopango' (Te Hiipango). The chiefs were accompanied by a young Tahitian known as 'Jem', their brother-in-law, and their sister, his wife. Marsden knew this young man, who had lived for many years with the Macarthurs at Parramatta. John Macarthur had sent him to school, where he had learned to read and write and to speak fluent English. Jem was now about twenty-three years old and dressed in chiefly style, wearing a fine feather cloak with feather head and ear ornaments, and carrying a musket. He was well mannered and very good-humoured, and appeared to be highly regarded by his in-laws. His brother-in-law, the high chief, presented Marsden with a pig, and in return received an axe and a printed copy of Macquarie's proclamation. Marsden explained about Macquarie's orders to the captains of visiting ships, and announced that a mission was going to be established at the Bay of Islands. When he reproached them with 'great cruel-ties towards the Europeans, particularly in the case of the Boyd', however, they retorted that the Europeans had been the aggressors. Marsden added that Captain Barnes of the *Jefferson* had reported that during a recent visit to North Cape in company with the *King George*, two of his boats had been attacked by local people; and that if they continued to behave in this way, no European vessels would visit them. This provoked a storm of protest. Jem indignantly informed Marsden that the masters of these two ships had agreed to trade a musket for eight pigs and 150 baskets of potatoes. The potatoes and pigs had been delivered, but when he and the head chief's brother (Te Hiipango) went out to collect the musket, the cap-tain of the *King George* had detained Hiipango and sent Jem to fetch more pigs and potatoes. The high chief refused this demand, and when Jem delivered this message to the *King George*, he was also imprisoned. Several days later the captives were moved to the *Jefferson*, where they were kept for three more days until a ransom of five pigs and 170 baskets of potatoes was delivered. As soon as two armed boats dropped them on shore, Te Hiipango's people had fired on the sailors. Marsden promised that these offences would be reported to Governor Macquarie, who would surely punish the offenders. In the meantime, they must not attack European ships but, instead, refer their complaints to the Governor at Port Jackson.

Soon after this exchange, Ruatara returned to the ship, where he greeted the high chief and his brother with gifts and a hongi. He ignored the first chief who had come aboard, telling Nicholas that he was an 'ittee ittee rungateeda' (itiiti rangatira – a small, small chief). He reported that on shore he, Hongi and Korokoro had been received with friendship. During their absence in Port Jackson all wars had ceased and the tribes were now living in peace with one another.

A brisk trade in various goods soon began on the decks of the *Active*. Turnips and other greenstuff were brought aboard, and mats, spears, hooks and fishing lines, thread and hand clubs were exchanged for plane irons, hoop iron, nails and hatchets. Only three local people were allowed on deck at any one time, to guard against any ambush. Both Marsden and Nicholas were impressed by the Muri-whenua people, although Ruatara warned them to be on their guard against them. Nicholas remarked:

> I never thought it likely they could be so fine a race of people as I now found them. In their persons they generally rose above the middle stature, some were even six feet and upwards, and all their limbs were remarkable for perfect symmetry and great muscular strength. Their countenances, with few exceptions, were pleasing and intelligent, and had none of those indications of ferocity which the imagina-tion naturally attributes to cannibals. They displayed, on the contrary, strong tokens of good nature and tender feeling, and I thought I could trace in them, some of the finest evidences of human sympathy. Though too often ill-treated by Europeans, they shewed not the least distrust of coming among us.[16]

As the *Active* left the North Cape that night, the local chiefs promised to pre-pare flax for the ship's next visit, and their parting was 'warm and affectionate'. Later that evening Hongi took a fine war mat he had been presented with at the Cape and gave it to John Nicholas.

The next day, 18 December, they sailed into Doubtless Bay, which reminded Captain Hansen of the coast of Norway. The local people had renamed an island in the harbour 'Norfolk Island', to commemorate Tuki's visit to that place. Accord-ing to Ruatara, two large rivers ran into this bay. At the foot of a high hill inland, a stream ran from a 'remote part of the island'. This stream was navigable for a distance, with beautiful, tree-lined banks. At a certain point it divided and became the two rivers that ran into Doubtless Bay, at Oruru and Mangoonui. He described the hinterland as fertile, with excellent soil. It was inhabited by people who came down the rivers in summer to fish along the coastline. Marsden and Nicholas thought of walking overland from Oruru to the Bay of Islands, but Captain Hansen dissuaded them, saying that it was too risky a venture.

That evening they were becalmed in Doubtless Bay. The coastline south of Mangoonui sent Nicholas into rhapsodies about the glories of nature. At the same time he reflected upon the inglorious nature of humanity, for Korokoro and his brother Tui had been grumbling about the gifts they had received from Marsden. The Ngaati Manu chiefs were no doubt disgruntled that he had promised to establish the mission amongst their Hikutuu rivals at Te Puna, and their complaints hinted at a more general dissatisfaction. Marsden soon restored their good humour, however, with a distribution of adzes and hoes, and extra gifts of spades, axes and red India print cloth for the rangatira.

On 19 December, the *Active* sailed past Whangaroa, the scene of the *Boyd* 'massacre'. When the ship was detained again by contrary winds, Marsden decided to visit the nearby Cavalli Islands. At 10 a.m. they anchored close to Panaaki, where Marsden went ashore with Nicholas, Kendall, and Korokoro and Tui. They crossed a stony beach, passed a small fenced garden and climbed a hill, which the chiefs 'skipp[ed] up like so many goats, leaving us below to wonder at their agility'. At the top of the hill they found a small village of about fourteen houses, each about eight feet wide, four feet high and fourteen feet long, with walls of interwoven 'sticks and reeds' and a door so low that it had to be crawled through. There were neat little gardens of turnips, potatoes and kuumara beside each dwelling. The inhabitants had run away when the Europeans landed, and hid themselves in the bushes. Only an old lame man was left behind. He had relaxed as soon as he recognised Korokoro as a kinsman, however, and greeted the Europeans courteously. Soon after this, Korokoro left the village to try to find the rest of his relations.

Kendall, who was exhausted by the climb, stayed in the village with this old man, while Marsden and Nicholas followed Korokoro. As they walked, they passed groves of flax on the hillsides, and tutu plants growing wild, the berries of which could be expressed and made into a delicious juice.[17] Marsden and Nicholas climbed up to the summit of the highest hill on the island, where the view was breathtaking. Nicholas wrote in his journal:

> How should I venture to describe the countless interesting combinations which were here grouped together . . . to give a more powerful effect to their varied beauties! The swelling rocks which seemed to frown on the convulsions of the elements; the scattered islands; the broad expanse of ocean; the sublime diversities of the country itself; the singular prospect of an Indian village, and of the natives paddling to the ship in their canoes; formed altogether such an extraordinary assemblage of views, as it would be impossible for the most vivid imagination to conceive, or the most animated pencil to depict.[18]

Marsden remarked more succinctly, 'the view of the Main, together with the Ocean and the numerous small Islands scattered upon it, is the most delightful I ever saw (at least I thought so)'.[19] On the summit they found Korokoro chatting with a commoner, or 'cookee' (literally 'cook' – male captives handled cooked food, which was noa, the antithesis of tapu). He was a man of about forty who stood there naked, carrying a spear. When he caught sight of some women and children below, he called out to them to come and greet the visitors. At first they were reluctant, but when Tui reassured them of their safety, the women climbed the hill and approached them in a group, faces turned to the ground with an air of melancholy sadness (the usual manner of approach on ceremonial occasions). The old woman who led them (an aunt of Tui and Korokoro's) leaned on her staff and chanted 'in a low plaintive voice a number of words' – a karakia of greeting. She was wearing a green wreath around her head, greenery around her waist (signs of mourning and respect), and carried a small child on her back. According to Marsden:

> She advanced to Koro-Koro with a slow pace. Koro-Koro appeared much agitated, he stood in deep silence, like a Statue, leaning upon the top of his Musket, as his Aunt advanced she prayed aloud and wept exceedingly [the tangi, or weeping for the dead, a ritual element in all such meetings]; Tooi, Koro-Koro's Brother [who had joined them], seemed much affected, and as if ashamed of his Aunt's conduct, he told us he would not cry; I will act like an English Man, I will not cry. Koro-Koro remained motionless till his Aunt came up to him, when they laid their heads together, and in this situation they wept aloud for a long time, and repeated short sentences alternately, which we understood were prayers, and continued weeping the tears rolling down their sable countenances in torrents. It was impossible to see them without being deeply affected; at this time also the Daughter of Koro-Koro's Aunt sat at her Mothers feet weeping, and all the Weomen joined their lamentations, we thought this an extraordinary custom amongst them of manifesting their joy but we afterwards found that this custom [the tangi of greeting, in which dead kinsfolk are recalled; and the haehae, or ritual laceration] was general in the Island of New Zealand. Many of these poor Weomen cut themselves in their Faces, Arms, and Breasts with sharp Shells or Flints till the Blood streamed down.[20]

Nicholas was moved by these exchanges, and had tears in his eyes. As he remarked, 'indeed it were no praise to the heart, that could on this occasion repel the gentle emotions of tender sympathy'.[21] It is interesting, though, that one effect of contact with Europeans was to discourage Maori men from crying, at least in front of Europeans.

Marsden's party spent an enjoyable morning on Panaaki, chatting with the local inhabitants. A young chief, one of Tui's friends, 'a fine handsome fellow of an open and ingenuous countenance, and not tattooed', soon came over from the mainland to join them. He had paddled across from Matauri Bay with seven or eight of his people, and when he saw Tui, they embraced and wept together. At North Cape, both Ruatara and Korokoro had learned that during their absence one of Korokoro's relatives had seduced Ruatara's youngest wife. This man, a sailor called 'Waree' (Waari), had escaped to Panaaki, and the local people now handed him over to Korokoro.

In the afternoon, when they went to the beach, the young chief gave them a 'manly and intrepid' demonstration of spear-handling. They returned to the *Active*, where Korokoro's errant kinsman was locked up. It had been an eventful morning. While Marsden visited Panaaki, Ruatara and Hongi had gone to Matauri Bay, which was controlled by Hongi's brother Kaingaroa. There they learned that the Ngaati Uru chiefs 'George' (or Te Aara) and his brother Te Puhi, central figures in the *Boyd* killings, were camped with some of their warriors nearby, on their way home from a chief's funeral. Ruatara decided to go and see them. As he approached their encampment, Te Aara had run away, until Ruatara threatened him with his pistol. Ruatara told him that it was time they made peace, and informed him of the mission that was to be established at Rangihoua. After some talk, he had invited Te Aara to the *Active* to meet Samuel Marsden and his missionaries.

When Ruatara returned on board with this news, he found that one of the Maori crew members had died of dysentery in his absence. It is not certain whether this diagnosis was accurate, but if it was, dysentery was highly infectious. Ruatara carried this man's body up on deck, pressed the knees up close to the head and wrapped the corpse in his kaakahu (cloak). The dead man was taken ashore, where they dug a hole in the sand and buried him. After this, Hongi, Ruatara, Marsden and others of the missionary party went ashore to see Te Puhi and Te Aara. This was to be a momentous encounter. Since the attack on the *Boyd* and the whalers' raid on Te Pahi's island, the people of Whangaroa and Te Puna had been at war, locked in a cycle of mutual retaliation. This was a threat to the security of the mission, and Marsden was anxious to reach a settlement between them. He also hoped to meet the Whangaroa chiefs, to get a first-hand account of the *Boyd* disaster.

They landed at Matauri Bay, near a large village under the mana of Hongi's sister. Ngaati Uru were camped on a high hill by the sea about half a mile away, with their colours flying. As Hongi and Marsden walked towards the encampment with a crowd of Hongi's people, some of its occupants fled. As they came closer, however, the people formed into lines on either side of them, and an old woman waved a red cloak in the air, calling out loudly, 'haromai, haromai, haromai' (haere mai – welcome) – the karanga. The Ngaati Uru chiefs were standing together, armed with pistols and surrounded by about a hundred and fifty warriors who sat on the ground, their long spears stuck in the earth beside them. Ruatara and Hongi went ahead of the Europeans to press noses with the chiefs, Te Aara, Te Puhi and another rangatira. They exchanged a few words, and then beckoned Marsden, Kendall, Nicholas, Hall and Captain Hansen forward. The Europeans shook hands with the rangatira while the old woman waved the red mat and chanted. Te Aara greeted Nicholas by saying, 'How do you do, my boy?' while the warriors watched gravely. When these greetings were over, Ruatara, Hongi, Te Aara and Te Puhi each fired their pistols into the air, and Nicholas fired his fowling-piece in a gesture of reconciliation. Six or seven warriors now discharged their muskets and, grabbing their spears or firearms, all the warriors jumped to their feet and performed a resounding haka.

The chiefs were tall, robust men, tattooed and wearing 'cloaks of different coloured furs' (dogskin cloaks) or mats with variegated borders (taaniko) around their shoulders and waists, the waist mats tied with woven belts in which were stuck their 'pattoo pattoo' (patupatu – hand clubs). Fine mats shone white in the sunshine, or glowed red with kokowai dye. The warriors had their hair combed up and tied into topknots ornamented with white gannet feathers. Some had the teeth of deceased enemies hanging from their ears, while others wore greenstone tiki or dollars from the *Boyd*'s cargo as neck ornaments. They carried short throwing spears or long lances tipped with whalebone points, battle-axes (tewhatewha), 'sergeant's halberts' (hani) ornamented with bunches of parrot's feathers, or long whalebone clubs (hoeroa), and each carried a greenstone or whalebone patu (hand club). Te Puhi carried a patu beaten out of bar iron and brought to a high polish, which he brandished about. In the midst of the haka, the warriors looked splendid.

As soon as the din died down, Marsden began to converse with the chiefs. After some polite exchanges, he asked them about the *Boyd* killings. Te Aara and the other chief (not Te Puhi) told Marsden that years before, they had travelled together to Port Jackson. When Simeon Lord had sent them home on the *Boyd*, Te Aara became sick during the voyage and was unable to work his passage. Captain Thompson had refused him food and threatened to throw him overboard, calling him a 'cookee cookee' (slave) and other insulting expressions. When they reached Whangaroa, Te Aara had been tied up and flogged at the gangway, and tormented by the other sailors. The captain had stripped him and sent him ashore almost naked. At the sight of his lacerated back, his people were so enraged that they had attacked the *Boyd* as utu.

It was obvious from their account that Te Puhi had led the attack, and that Te Pahi had nothing to do with the killings. He had arrived the next day at Whangaroa and tried unsuccessfully to save some of the survivors. Te Aara offered to take Marsden to the wreck of the *Boyd* so that his men could salvage its guns and some remaining cedar. He apologised that he could not give them the dollars that had been on board, for they had long ago been redistributed. Even so, Nicholas did not trust him. He thought that Te Aara's friendly demeanour masked 'a dark and subtle malignity of intention'.[22]

While they were at the encampment, Hongi's people had prepared a meal for the Europeans back at his village. Marsden and Nicholas now took their leave, promising to return after supper and spend the night with Te Aara and Te Puhi. Ruatara had told them that the ritual welcome with a red mat was never betrayed, and that they could stay with these people in safety. Ngaati Uru performed a sham fight, a haka and a song of victory as they left the encampment. They returned to the village, where Ruatara, Kendall and King went back to the *Active*, leaving Marsden and Nicholas with Hongi. The food was laid out in a wide open space, and as they ate, people crowded around to watch them. Marsden drew a circle on the ground and ordered them not to pass it. The local people exclaimed in wonder or burst out laughing as they watched the strangers, and tasted biscuits and sugar candies that were handed to them. Some sober old men stayed silent, however, and gazed at the Europeans intently. According to Nicholas, these 'mute sages [whom he likened to Roman senators] seemed occupied in forming conjectures as to the motives that induced us to visit their country'.[23] There were about fifty well-built houses in this village, each with a rounded or gabled roof, and its own eating shelter in a fenced enclosure. Two carved war canoes were hauled up on the beach, gaily embellished with feathers. The settlement was inhabited by about a hundred and fifty people, led by a chief called Kira, a subordinate of Hongi's elder brother, Kaingaroa.

That evening Marsden and Nicholas returned with Hongi and Maaui (who acted as their interpreter) to spend the evening with Te Aara and Te Puhi, who had shifted their camp to a large flat area. Te Aara gave them cooked potatoes for supper, and they continued their discussions. Marsden told them he hoped that they would make peace with the Bay of Islands people, so that the mission there could be safely established. In talking about the attack on the *Boyd,* Te Aara informed the Europeans that his father had been killed when the ship was plundered. He had taken some kegs of powder on deck and was trying out a flintlock musket. A spark from the musket had ignited the powder, which exploded, killing him and four other people. Marsden urged Te Aara to tell his people to give up war, which caused such terrible disasters: 'If they would only attend to the cultivation of their Lands and lay aside all Wars and Murders they would soon become a Great and Happy people.'[24] Te Aara replied, '[We do] not want to fight any more and [are] ready to make peace', an answer that pleased Marsden immensely.

At eleven o'clock they lay down to sleep. Marsden and Nicholas, wrapped in their greatcoats, lay on either side of Te Aara and his wife and child. Marsden later recorded in his journal:

> The Stars shone bright and the Sea in our front was smooth, around us were numerous Spears stuck upright in the Ground and Groups of Natives lying in all directions, like a flock of Sheep upon the Grass, as there were neither Tents nor Huts to cover them . . . Surrounded by Cannibals, who had Massacred and devoured our Countrymen, I wondered much at the mysteries of Providence, and how these things could be. Never did I behold the blessed advantages of civilization in a more grateful light as now. I did not sleep much during the night, my mind was too seriously occupied by the present Scene, and the new and strange ideas it naturally excited.[25]

The next morning he invited the Ngaati Uru chiefs to the *Active* for breakfast. They were rowed to the ship, accompanied by several canoes full of people. As they climbed over the side, they were saluted with 'three hearty cheers', orchestrated by Ruatara as master of ceremonies (a practice introduced to local people by Tuki). After the meal they were taken to the ship's cabin, where he introduced the chiefs to each of the Europeans. The role that each man was to play in the mission was explained (Thomas Kendall to instruct their children; William Hall to build houses and boats; John King to make fishing lines, and Captain Hansen to command the *Active*), and gifts including axes, billhooks, red India print, plane irons, scissors, nails and fish-hooks were distributed. Ruatara arranged Te Puhi and Te Aara on one side of the cabin table, and Marsden on the other. Everyone else stood around the cabin while each gift was presented individually, to the senior chief first and then to the other rangatira, each receiving items appropriate to his rank. This kind of ceremonious gift-giving acknowledged mana between people of similar status, opening up a relationship and requiring the recipient to reciprocate with a better gift at some time in the future.[26]

After the gifts had been distributed, Ruatara made a speech, saying that Te Aara was now forgiven for the *Boyd* killings. If he ever attacked Te Puna or cut off another ship, however, the revenge would be swift and terrible. At the end of this oration, Te Aara declared that he would never again injure any Europeans. Ruatara and Hongi and the Ngaati Uru chiefs shook hands (another new convention) and pressed noses, saying that they were no longer enemies. That afternoon Te Aara and Te Puhi left the ship and the missionaries sailed for the Bay of Islands.

ARRIVAL AT RANGIHOUA

Early in the morning of 22 December, the *Active* passed Cape Wiwiki (Point Pocock) at the head of the Bay of Islands. Two war canoes came out from the southern side, one with a large blue flag hoisted at its stern, and carrying a man in a seaman's jacket who was waving a handkerchief. This canoe brought out Kokokoro's brother and his ten-year-old son, who wore a cotton garment that the missionaries had given him during their previous visit. Korokoro embraced them both, weeping and talking in a low monotone. Taking his sea chest and all his possessions, he said goodbye to the missionaries and climbed into the canoe, promising to visit them soon at Rangihoua. As he paddled off, they saluted him with three cheers, which he and his people returned 'with double interest'.

As the *Active* sailed up the Bay, Ruatara acted as the ship's pilot. At three o'clock that afternoon the *Active* dropped anchor opposite Rangihoua, firing a salute in honour of the occasion. Marsden, Nicholas and the missionary party rowed to the beach east of Rangihoua, where a small stream entered the ocean. There the live-stock were landed. According to Nicholas, the local people were astonished:

> Cows or horses they had never seen before, and diverted now from every thing else, they regarded them as stupendous prodigies. However, their astonishment was soon turned into alarm and confusion; for one of the cows that was wild and unmanageable, being impatient of restraint, rushed in among them, and caused such violent terror through the whole assemblage, that imagining some preter-natural monster had been let loose to destroy them, they all immediately betook themselves to flight.[27]

Fear turned to awe when Marsden mounted his horse and rode along the beach. They had never seen a man ride an animal before, although, after his first visit to Port Jackson, Ruatara had tried to explain about horses and horse-drawn carriages. When he had told his people that Europeans rode about on the backs of large animals ('corraddee', or kararahe), they tried to ride their pigs, which immediately tossed them. When he had described the Europeans sitting in land canoes hauled by these creatures, they stopped their ears and told him indignantly not to tell so many lies. Now the Europeans and their animals were there in the flesh before them.

Later on that day, Ruatara took the missionaries up to Rangihoua for a formal reception. This settlement had about a hundred and fifty inhabitants and was built on a high hill, with fenced terraced gardens on the slopes, kept in perfect condition. The village was surrounded by a wide, deep trench, with a stout palisade along its inner margin. Inside the palisade, narrow lanes wound past fenced enclosures, each entered by a carved stile and containing a house, a small courtyard and a shelter. Ruatara's own enclosure was on the summit, and his dwelling was larger than any of the others. It was about twenty feet long, fifteen feet wide and eight feet high, with a ridged roof and a low doorway, and containing a stone-edged fireplace. Although the house was dark and smoky, the eating shelter, where his family took their meals, was light and pleasant. There was an enclosure beside it where kuumara and potatoes were stored in another shelter, with a flagstaff flying Ruatara's flag.

When Ruatara entered the compound with Hongi and the Europeans, his people wept for joy and the women cut themselves with flints and shells. Ruatara had three wives, his head wife, Miki, being a 'very fat' woman with 'fine black eyes sparkling with animation; teeth of an ivory whiteness; a blooming complexion; and all her features peculiarly expressive of cheerful complacency'. This woman was 'considered no less a personage than a queen by all the people within his territory'.[28] Contrary to Ruatara's fears, Miki was happy and well, and had a fine baby son born while he was at Port Jackson. Ruatara had brought her a red cotton gown and petticoat, and now helped to dress her in them.

Some grave old men were present, and Te Pahi's elderly widow, a 'poor decrepid old woman', was there with her daughter, a lively young woman who wore a silver chain that Governor King had given to her father at Port Jackson. Miki's father was also present, with two of her sisters and a number of their people. One of these sisters was a beautiful girl about seventeen years old, while the other was about forty, full of mirth and witticisms. Nicholas remarked wryly, 'We could easily perceive, from the effect her sallies had on her companions . . . that the *packaha*, or white man, was the subject of some extraordinary remarks, and called forth the rarest specimens of her witty effusions. I doubt not but her jokes upon us were indulged with a great deal of freedom, as all our movements excited the loudest bursts of laughter.'[29] Ruatara's second wife (presumably Rahu, the tohunga Raakau's daughter) sat with Miki, nursing her baby with evident affection. His third wife, however, having committed adultery with one of Korokoro's men in Ruatara's absence, was excluded from this gathering. Three young women danced for the Europeans, and afterwards they returned to the *Active*, followed by a good-humoured crowd who farewelled them from the beach, crying out, 'Ire atudo, eckeneedo' (Haere atu ra, ka kite anoo – Farewell, until we see you again).

The next morning the missionaries stayed on board the *Active* while Ruatara punished his junior wife and her seducer, Waari. At the Cavalli Islands, Korokoro urged Ruatara to kill the man, the usual punishment for adultery, but Marsden had suggested that a flogging of twenty lashes would be sufficient. During the passage to the Bay, Ruatara had fashioned a cat-o'-nine-tails and pondered on how many lashes should be inflicted. The prisoner was now sent ashore in chains, where he received thirty lashes, administered by one of Ruatara's people. Afterwards he was brought back on board and confined, and ordered to serve the next three years on the *Active* as a sailor. If he ever came back to the Bay, Ruatara promised that he would kill him. Nicholas was told that in cases of adultery, if the man was discovered in a woman's house, he was supposed to be the guilty party and killed, while the woman escaped with a beating. If the woman was discovered in a man's house, on the other hand, she was killed while he escaped with impunity.

That afternoon the Europeans went ashore, and Te Uri o Kanae (Kanae or 'Gunnah' for short), nephew to the late Te Pahi, took Nicholas along the beach to shoot sea birds. On their way Nicholas noticed a piece of wood, carved and painted with red ochre, stuck into the ground under a large tree. When he wandered over to look at it, Kanae cried out, 'Taboo, taboo' (Tapu, tapu), and told him to get away from it. He explained that the carving marked the place where a man was buried. Further along the shore they found a number of people sitting around in groups, eating a meal of fernroot. Nicholas understood that this was their staple food, kuumara and potatoes being luxuries. The cooks were roasting the roots on a fire, then beating them with mallets until they were soft, and throwing them in handfuls to the diners. Nicholas sampled some, chewing each root and spitting out the fibres. He found the starchy flesh sweet and pleasant.

After this, Nicholas and Marsden visited Miki at Rangihoua. She was sitting in her compound, weaving a cloak. Two wooden pegs were fixed in the ground, with the threads of the woof tied between them. She was knotting groups of six woof threads to the two threads of each warp (the warps being spaced about an inch apart), to make a silky open-weave textile. While they were there the wives of the missionaries came to be introduced to Miki, curtseying and nodding at her while she gazed at them in 'ineffable astonishment'.

December the 24th was marked by a spectacular sham fight, arranged between Korokoro and Ruatara. About eight o'clock that morning, a fleet of ten war canoes, flags flying and packed with men, women and children, came speeding out to the *Active*. Korokoro ('Kaawana Makoare') and Tui, painted with red ochre and with feathers in their hair, stood in their canoes, brandishing their spears and chanting a haka. The canoes were arranged in a line, their crews paddling in unison, following the signals of their leaders. Nicholas was struck by the 'wild grandeur' of the scene:

> The different chiefs were all standing up with their war mats thrown gracefully
> over their shoulders, their hair neatly tied in a bunch upon the crown of the head,
> and ornamented according to the general fashion of their country with the white

Te Pahi's nephew, Te Uri o Kanae.

feathers of the gannet. Their attitudes and gestures, violently impetuous, as if intent on making an immediate attack upon the vessel, might strike the most resolute beholder with terror; and their fierce countenances, furrowed over with hideous punctures all deeply painted with a blue pigment, or quite black, gave a horrible identity to the savage display.[30]

As it came alongside, the fleet was saluted with gunfire. Korokoro and Tui had brought out a number of important chiefs, who now boarded the vessel. Korokoro introduced his companions to each of the Europeans in turn, acknowledging the kindnesses that each individual had extended to him at Port Jackson, and explaining the role that each would play in the new mission. He then presented Nicholas and Marsden with two fine cloaks each, and a weapon called a 'hennee' (hani), shaped like a sergeant's halbert but carved and decorated with feathers.

After these ceremonies Ruatara went back on shore. Soon afterwards,

Korokoro invited Nicholas and Marsden to join him in his canoe, which led the fleet as it raced towards Rangihoua. As they landed on the beach, about a hundred and fifty of Korokoro's warriors stood up in their canoes, brandishing their paddles and 'making furious gesticulations'. One of Ruatara's men, stripped naked, ran up and down on the beach, 'making a . . . horrid noise' and shaking a long whalebone weapon in defiance. As soon as they ended their haka, Korokoro's men jumped out of the canoes and chased the challenger. He sprinted back to the rest of his party, who were hidden in a nearby valley. As Korokoro's warriors rushed towards their hiding place, Ruatara's men (about two hundred altogether) charged out to meet them. There were violent but bloodless duels in every direction. First, the combatants fought with spears and lances, then they took 'battle axes' and patu and engaged at close quarters. Ruatara's men retreated, then rallied, and the sham battle raged back and forwards. Finally, at a signal, they all joined in a haka. Ruatara's head wife was in the thick of the fray, wearing her red gown and petticoat and brandishing a whalebone hoeroa about seven feet long, and a large horse pistol. She was one of the leaders in the war dance, which left her panting and perspiring. Te Pahi's old widow also joined in the mock battle, with some of the younger women. Nicholas wrote:

> I observed likewise some other female warriors, who joined in the combat with much resolution, and following the example of their queen, exposed themselves in the thickest of the fight, to mimic dangers. From what I discovered, however . . . it was not a general practice for women in this island to take the field; and that the passion for war-like prowess was only to be found among certain ladies of a more intrepid character than the rest.[31]

After this entertainment the missionaries went back to the ship for breakfast. Later that day they returned to Rangihoua. Marsden took one of the boats, but forgot to tell Nicholas that he was leaving. Nicholas had to ask a woman in a small canoe alongside to paddle him to Rangihoua. This woman, 'Mary', was notorious for selling her favours to the sailors, and she was aggrieved because Marsden had forbidden her to board the *Active*. She paddled Nicholas to within six hundred yards of the beach, then told him that he could swim the rest of the distance. He pointed to his clothes, thinking she was joking, but 'Mary' was deadly serious. It was only when he gave her some fish-hooks that she agreed to paddle the extra distance.

That afternoon Ruatara's men worked to enclose a flat area of about half an acre as a stockyard for the European animals. It was Saturday, and as dusk approached, Ruatara set up a pulpit, covered with a black mat, and a reading desk made from an old canoe and a few planks. He also lined up old canoe hulls as seats ready for a service the next day, which was both Christmas Day and the Sabbath.

When Marsden woke the next morning, 25 December, he saw the British flag flying on the pole at Rangihoua (most likely the flag presented to Ruatara by Governor Macquarie). He wrote in his journal that night: 'I considered it the signal for the dawn of Civilization, liberty and Religion in that dark and benighted land. I never viewed the British Colors with more gratification, and flattered my-self they would never be removed till the Natives of that Island enjoyed all the happiness of British Subjects.'[32]

About ten o' clock everyone from the *Active* went ashore, except for one man and the ship's master. Marsden was wearing his surplice, ready to take the service. Korokoro, Ruatara and Hongi had put on the uniforms that Governor Macquarie had given them, swords at their sides and carrying switches. They had lined up their men, probably echoing the Sunday rituals at Port Jackson, when the Gover-nor and his officers reviewed the convicts in military style before they attended church together. After ushering the Europeans to the seats before the pulpit, Korokoro marched in his men and sat them to the right behind the Europeans, while Ruatara placed his men to the left (the appropriate positions in a meeting house for visitors [on the right] and local people [on the left]). The women, children and other local people sat in a circle around them. There was a solemn pause before Marsden stood to sing the 'Old Hundredth Psalm'. As he read the service, Korokoro followed the movements of the Europeans with his switch, signalling the people to sit or stand, and tapping them on the head or the shoul-ders if they chatted or were tardy.

Marsden preached from the second chapter of Luke: 'Behold I bring you glad tidings of great joy.' Some people protested to Ruatara that they could not under-stand what Marsden was saying. Ruatara said that they should wait until the end of the sermon, when he would translate it for them. When they asked him to explain some of the finer points, he replied that these would be made clear later. As they left the enclosure, three or four hundred people surrounded the Europeans, per-forming a rousing haka. That evening Marsden administered the Holy Sacrament on board the *Active*, rejoicing that 'the time was at hand when the Glory of the Lord would be revealed to these poor benighted Heathens'.[33]

The next day was devoted to more practical matters. Most of the iron tools on board had already been given away to various rangatira. Marsden realised that without such items to trade, his missionaries would be in a difficult situation. He instructed the blacksmith to begin burning charcoal and to build a smithy, then landed all the iron from the ship, placing it in Ruatara's keeping. Hall marked out a site for a temporary shed for the missionaries, and the sawyers and young Hansen were left in charge of its construction. Unfortunately, the land around Te Puna had long since been cleared and no timber was available for permanent mission buildings. Marsden decided to shift the *Active* to the timber district in the south of the Bay, where he could procure enough wood to build the mission and obtain a cargo of logs to help defray the *Active*'s expenses.

VISIT TO THE SOUTHERN DISTRICTS

On the morning of 26 December, the *Active* sailed south and anchored off Kororaareka. Like Rangihoua, this settlement was sited for access to the sea (and to visiting ships), for the surrounding lands were infertile.[34] There, Marsden, Kendall, King, Nicholas and Maaui went ashore to visit Tara, the old ariki who led the southern alliance. Tara had been a central figure in the *Boyd* saga, fixing Te Pahi with responsibility for the killings. He was now over seventy years old, and sat on the beach 'like some venerable patriarch in the midst of his people' to greet his visitors. Marsden saluted him, presenting him with an axe, an adze and two plane irons, and asked his permission to cut timber for the mission at Rangihoua. Tara urged him to set up the mission at Kororaareka instead, but Marsden told him that the decision to settle among Ruatara's people was final. The old chief was unhappy at this turn of events, but was mollified when Marsden promised that some Europeans would come to live with him later. In the end, he gave them permission to cut timber in his territories across the Bay at Kawakawa, and commanded his people to cook his guests a meal of kuumara. Nicholas found Tara impressive, remarking that although he 'had lost the use of one of his eyes . . . this had no effect on his temper, which was always cheerful; and there was a dignified serenity in his manner that was extremely prepossessing'.[35] When the food was cooked, Tara gave it to his visitors with his own hands as a particular honour.

After the meal Tara showed Marsden and Nicholas a flourishing crop of wheat he had raised from seed given to him by Kendall and Hall during their previous visit. He also introduced them to two of his wives, his elderly head wife and a young wife, 'Mrs. Go-shore', who had previously lived for some weeks with a Captain Jones on his ship (probably Lasco Jones, of the *King George*), where she had picked up a number of English expressions. 'Mrs Go-shore' took them to an enclosure where some peas and peach stones given to Tara by the missionaries had been planted. The peas were now flowering, and a fine young peach tree was springing up. She explained that a cock and hen the missionaries had brought had been banished from the village, the hen for abandoning her eggs, and the cock for persistently roosting on the roof of a tapu building. When they returned to Tara's house, they found him weeping over Maaui with two women, his distant relations.

During the next day two runaway convicts came on board the *Active*. They were in an emaciated and filthy condition. These men, a former shoemaker and a tailor, had stowed away on the *James Hay*, whose captain had handed them over to the *Active* during her previous visit to the Bay of Islands. They escaped from the *Active*, and had been living ashore for the last six months, where the local people treated them as taurekareka (war captives, slaves). After their escape Kendall had offered a reward for their capture, informing the local people that they had been transported for stealing. After this they were treated with contempt, for 'tungata tihi' (taangata taahae, or thief) was a term of opprobrium. Worse, they had refused to do any work, expecting to be treated as superior beings. The chiefs told them unsympathetically, 'Ittee ittee workee workee, ittee ittee kiki' (Iti iti workee workee, iti iti kaikai – Work little, eat little). Fearing that they would be killed and eaten, they had fled inland and lived in a cave in seclusion.

Finally they threw themselves on the mercy of Tupi, Tara's brother, who took them under his protection. He made them work for their living, the shoemaker in the gardens, and the tailor (who had smuggled his scissors ashore) as hair-cutter for his people. While Tupi was around, they were adequately fed, but in his absence the local cooks starved them. In the end, they decided to give themselves up, finding life as convicts at Port Jackson preferable to life as white slaves in the Bay of Islands. Nicholas knew one of these men, who had been transported on the *Earl Spencer*, the ship that brought him and Kendall to Port Jackson. He recalled his father, 'a respectable and wealthy tradesman in London', farewelling his son on the eve of their departure, and thought how anguished he would be to witness his son's degradation.

On 28 December, Marsden, Kendall, Nicholas and Hall were rowed up the Kawakawa Inlet to a densely inhabited part of the Bay that still had extensive forests.[36] They travelled for about ten miles upstream, although the river was navigable much further into the interior. The principal chief at this place was 'Te Kokee' (Te Koki), another rangatira of the southern alliance who was in some degree subordinate to Tara. This name, which does not appear on local whaka-papa,[37] was probably just one of his names, maybe honouring Captain Cook, whose visit to the Bay was vividly remembered.

The missionary party landed at a small village, where two young men took them about a mile inland to meet Te Koki. They walked past swamps and flatlands where large gardens planted with kuumara and potatoes were growing, then climbed a hill to find the chief seated on its summit (or tihi) with several attendants. Nicholas was greatly impressed by Te Koki:

> His demeanour was firm and convincing, and [on] his ingenuous countenance, the . . . qualities of honesty and candour were plainly legible to every beholder. In his person he was more robust than any man I had yet seen, and all his limbs displayed a perfect correctness of symmetry, evincing at the same time the greatest capability of laborious exertion. His broad shoulders were covered with a large skin of different coloured furs, and his tall figure, bold as it was stately, and perfect as it was commanding, might have supplied even to Phidias, had it existed in the days of that celebrated artist, a model not unworthy his inimitable powers.[38]

Te Koki greeted them courteously and offered to guide them to a place where they could find suitable timber. He took them back to their boat and they were rowed about two miles further up the river, where it divided into two branches. There they entered a forest of kauri trees about eighty to a hundred feet high, with trunks about six or seven feet in circumference. Marsden offered Te Koki a large English axe in exchange for his men felling some of these trees when the missionaries had returned to the *Active*.

On their way back down the river they were amused by the antics of Kanae,

Te Pahi's young nephew. He helped to row the boat for a while, then shaking his head, cried that 'workee workee was no good for rungateeda, only for cookee cookee' (work was no good for chiefs, only for slaves) – a sentiment he had probably picked up at Port Jackson, since it contradicted local ideas about rangatira. He put down his oar but soon picked it up again and resumed rowing. Further down the river they saw a large cross on a high hill, where Kanae said the bodies of thieves were hung (an odd echo of Christian history). After a thief was put to death, he was wrapped up in his cloak and buried for a time, then exhumed and hung up as a warning to others. This cross was probably a recent innovation, borrowed from the European practice of hanging thieves on a gibbet. Te Pahi, among others, had observed this practice during his visits to Port Jackson (although at the time he decried it), and it was later reported that he had adopted it to hang some European pirates. As they were rowed back to their ship, Nicholas admired the scenery, glad that civilisation was about to be introduced to so beautiful a setting:

> How anxiously did I wish, while contemplating these enchanting views, for the moment to arrive when civilization and well-regulated industry would take place of barbarism, and rational ideas supplant the gross delusions of superstition! To this happy period I looked . . . with impatient solicitude, feeling that so many of my fellow-creatures, who are now immersed in darkness, would then enjoy, as enlightened beings, those profuse bounties with which nature has supplied them.[39]

On 29 December, Nicholas, Marsden and the other missionaries travelled to Waitangi, a fertile district controlled by Waraki, the father of Miki (Ruatara's head wife) and an ally of Hongi Hika. They found some of Waraki's people hauling in an enormous seine net full of snapper. In nearby coves, lines of stakes driven into the seabed indicated the boundaries between fishing grounds belonging to different kin groups. Nicholas commented that the local fisheries seemed highly productive, and that the seine nets made by the local people were much larger than the nets used in Europe. The fish caught were cut open and their backbones removed before they were hung in the sun for drying.

Although Waraki was away on a visit into the interior, his people welcomed the missionaries warmly and gave them a meal of fish roasted over a fire on a stick. One of the *Active*'s Maori sailors, a namesake of Waraki's (whom they had rescued at Port Dalrymple), was already there, visiting his relations.

After the meal the missionaries walked along the coast to a large area of level ground, opposite the entrance of the harbour.[40] Hall and Kendall thought that this would be a better site for the mission than Rangihoua, where good agricultural land was limited. Marsden had committed himself to Ruatara, however, and replied that for their own safety the mission should be established among people who were friendly, with a chief whose intentions could be trusted. Kendall and Hall disagreed with him still, but they were overridden. Kendall afterwards disconsolately remarked, 'Mr. Marsden will have his way in every thing.'[41] On their return to the village they were met by Waraki's son Te Tuhi and his wife Rangi, a very affectionate couple. After this they rowed to the head of the Waitangi Inlet to a large waterfall (the Haruru), an excellent site for mills to grind corn or saw timber.

The missionaries returned to the ship without meeting Waraki. In their absence, Pomare, the Ngaati Manu chief from Matauwhi whom Kendall and Hall had met during their previous voyage, had arrived on board the vessel. This rangatira had the reputation of being 'artful and covetous', but was eager to do business with the Europeans. He wanted to supply Marsden's party with timber, and tried to negotiate an exclusive deal. Marsden was cautious, however, for he wanted to leave the missionaries on good terms with a range of local leaders.

On the following day, 30 December, Marsden and his companions rowed up the Waikare Inlet, another densely inhabited area with extensive forests. Although Nicholas called this inlet 'Waitangi', this was evidently a confusion. The journey he described, eight miles up the inlet and then two miles up the river through marshlands to a village called Waikare, was to the south-east side of the Bay of Islands. At this time Waikare was controlled by 'Wiveeah' (Whiria, also known as Pomare II). He was another Ngaati Manu rangatira, subordinate to Tara, and a namesake and nephew of Pomare's. On their way they saw some children launching a model of the *Active* they had made, fitted with two masts, a bowsprit and rigging, and playing with it in the water. When they arrived at Waikare, Whiria was not at home, but his people offered to take the Europeans inland to a place where good timber trees grew. They walked through neat cultivations of kuumara and potatoes, fenced (presumably against pigs) with stiles at convenient distances. The local men carried the Europeans across the Waikare River on their backs, laughing and occasionally pretending to drop them in the swampy water. They soon came to a small settlement, where most of the inhabitants had never before seen a European. There were large stands of kauri nearby, 'of an amazing height', that could easily be felled and floated down the river.

When they walked back to Waikare, Whiria was waiting for them. He was seated on the roof of his house, to signal his 'elevated dignity above the rest of [his] people'.[42] The chief had been talking with one of his subordinates, who had taken a pig to the *Active* that morning without receiving an axe in payment. After being introduced to Marsden, Whiria reproached him for favouring Tara and Tupi, who had each been given axes, while he and his people had received nothing. To pacify him, Marsden presented him with a large axe belonging to the ship, despite the inconvenience of being without it. Whiria became pleasant and good-humoured, but like Tara before him, tried to insist that the missionaries should settle in his district.

Nicholas described Waikare as a beautiful village, occupied by a hundred and fifty people. It was built on a bank fifteen or twenty feet above the river, which was about forty feet wide with crystal-clear water running over pebbles, and banks lined by shrubs where flocks of birds were feeding. Whiria's house was the largest they had yet seen — twenty-seven feet long, eighteen wide and nine high — an indication of his wealth and status. It had a carved doorway, and neat gardens

469

nearby, with kuumara and potatoes regularly planted. Outside another rangatira's house in the village, Nicholas saw a woman who had given birth to a baby two days earlier. Both mother and child seemed well and happy. He also noticed a boy in this village about twelve years old who seemed to be suffering from leprosy (the only person with this disease that they met). His skin was scaly and white, his eyes were half closed and his whole appearance was 'disgusting'. In later years Colenso commented that this disease was restricted to the north of New Zealand, and that in its later stages, fingers, toes and even hands and feet could drop off at the joints.[43]

During his visit Nicholas shot a bird that had landed in a nearby tree, throwing the whole village into confusion. People panicked and shouted aloud, gazing at the dead bird in consternation. While they were trying to work out what had happened, Nicholas shot another bird, provoking an even greater uproar. He showed his shot-bag to one of the old men, who scarcely dared to look at it (although by then quite a few rangatira in the Bay had muskets). At the same time they enjoyed the sight of his watch. Everyone in the village was keen to see this marvel and to listen to its ticking, which they described as the language of the atua. After these exotic entertainments, Nicholas and Marsden returned to the *Active*.

On 31 December, Maaui's mother came out to the ship, where she threw herself at her son's feet, weeping bitterly. She had not seen him for many years, and thought that he had perished. On an excursion inland that afternoon, Nicholas and Marsden met a family comprising a man, his head wife and two junior wives, with three or four fine children, living away from any settlement. Nicholas wrote:

> The harmony and happiness in which they appeared to live together, their content and cheerfulness, and the social cordiality that prevailed among them, were gratifying to behold; and our imaginations were carried back to those days of primeval simplicity, when every man lived quietly under his own vine, and enjoyed as his best riches, the innocence of his heart and the fruits of his industry.[44]

This Arcadian family prepared a meal of fernroot for the boat's crew while Marsden and Nicholas took a brief stroll into the interior.

The beginning of 1815 was marked by a violent easterly gale. Although the *Active*'s anchorage was sheltered, Marsden moved his people ashore for safety. On 2 January, the weather cleared again and another senior chief came to visit the missionaries. Korokoro and Tui had brought their uncle 'Bennee' (Te Pene, also known as Kaipoo[45]), the leader of Ngaare Raumati at Paaroa Bay and Moturua Island, who invited them to his village. Te Pene was Tara's second cousin, 'a formal old chief . . . fully impressed with a sense of his own importance'. Nicholas and Marsden accepted his invitation and boarded the war canoe that he had brought for the journey. They paddled about five miles to a cove, where they landed. From the beach they climbed across a narrow ridge, through marshy ground and into a forest, where Te Pene told them that Captain Cook's men (or maybe Marion's) had cut wood during their earlier visit. Te Pene had been a boy at the time and had visited the European ship on several occasions. From the ridgetop he pointed out the places where the sailors had pitched their tents, washed linen and collected water. Beyond the forest they came to some empty houses by a cultivation where wheat was growing. Marsden wanted to look at the crop, and climbed a stile into the garden, although Tui told him that it was tapu. The wind had risen again, and Te Pene invited them to sleep that night at his paa at Paaroa rather than risking a journey to the ship by water.

At Paaroa Bay, Te Pene hailed a boy in a small canoe, which he commandeered to take Marsden and Nicholas to his village. Although the sea was rough, he paddled them safely across the bay. As they landed, an old woman stood by a group of houses at the foot of the hilltop paa, calling out in a karanga of welcome. Paaroa was another densely inhabited area, with fertile garden lands and good fisheries.[46] Outside the paa very large nets were spread out on stakes, and three stages about twelve feet high stood by the landing, where large quantities of stingray and dog-fish were drying. Nicholas also noticed a pigsty, where a sow and ten piglets were sleeping. As they climbed the hill to the paa, they passed terraced gardens on its slopes, neatly weeded and planted with kuumara. The summit was fortified by a deep ditch and bank, and a palisade that surrounded the houses. The other side of the hill had been cut away, making it inaccessible.

Te Pene and his companions gave their guests a meal of cooked potatoes outside, although it was raining. Nicholas and Marsden had already learned that in the Bay people did not eat inside their houses[47] (for houses were tapu, and cooked food was noa, or profane). Women in labour were taken outside to the eating shed (or whata), and so were the sick, for fear of offending the atua. If a man was building a house, he was 'under the taboo taboo' (tapu tapu), 'a kind of quaran-tine'. A chief in this state was fed by hand, but if he was a commoner, his food was left on the ground for him to pick up with his teeth. If he used his hands, the atua would punish him with a slow and lingering disease. Nicholas and Marsden found these restrictions absurd, and sheltered under the eaves of Te Pene's house for their meal, although this was a breach of tapu. As the rain dripped down his neck, Nicholas grumbled to Tui that 'the taboo taboo was all *gammon*':

> Turning sharply round to me, he replied, that 'it was no gammon at all; New Zealand man,' said he, 'say that Mr. Marsden's *crackee crackee* [karakia – prayers] of a Sunday, is all *gammon.*' 'No, no,' I rejoined, 'that is not *gammon*, that is *miti* [maitai – good].' 'Well then,' retorted the tenacious reasoner, 'if your *crackee crackee* is no gammon, our taboo taboo is no gammon;' and thus he brought the matter to a conclusion; allowing us to prize our own system, and himself and his countrymen to venerate theirs.[48]

That night Nicholas and Marsden decided to stay under the eaves of Te Pene's dwelling. Marsden slept soundly, but Nicholas was kept awake by the wind and rain. Eventually he crept inside the house, where their companions were loudly snoring. He commented with chagrin, 'The packaha was the only one among them that was doomed to remain with his eyes open, and was plagued on till morning with these noisy slumbers, in which he could not participate.'[49]

The next morning, after a breakfast of potatoes, they crossed the cove again, passing some hidden gardens of kuumara and potatoes. According to Nicholas, these gardens indicated 'that state of disunited barbarism and feudal enmity, in which the different tribes reside among each other . . . resorting on all occasions to physical strength' – a remark that momentarily ignored Europe's war-torn state and the devastation caused by rampaging armies.

On their way back to the ship they stopped for a meal of eels and potatoes. Soon afterwards they came to a village of about twenty houses divided by a wicker-work partition, where they were welcomed and fed with fernroot. In this village forked poles were stuck in the ground, carrying baskets of dried fish and cockles, cooked potatoes, fernroot and calabashes of water. Mothers held out their children to the Europeans, saying, 'Homi pickeninnee wow' (Hoomai pickaninny whao – Give the child a nail), a mixture of Maori and pidgin. The rangatira of this settlement was an old man who proved to be Pomare's father. Unlike his son, he paid little attention to the Europeans, largely ignoring their presence.

After this, Nicholas and Marsden returned to the *Active*, where they found the ship surrounded with floating spars and canoes whose crews had come out to barter. Among the goods that were offered to the Europeans were tuuii birds in small wickerwork cages (some tuuii were taught to talk, after the bristles on their tongues had been shaved[50]). Although the local people struck hard bargains, the Europeans still did well, giving an axe worth ten shillings for three spars that would fetch £8 in Port Jackson.

On the morning of 4 January, Tara and Pomare came to eat breakfast on board. While Pomare ate with a knife and fork, Tara observed strict tapu restrictions. He took rice from his plate with a spoon and emptied the spoon into his hand, from which he ate the rice; and poured tea into his palm, drinking without touching his lips to the vessel. Since Tara was an 'areekee' (ariki – high chief), his head was intensely tapu, and if any of the vessels had touched it, they would also have become tapu. He was sarcastic about Pomare's efforts with the knife and fork, saying that only 'cookee' (slaves) would eat in this manner.

The next morning some other visitors arrived: 'Homarree' and 'Puttuti' (a friend of Hongi's) from Taiamai, about twenty miles inland, and Tahika from Bream Bay on the southern coastline. They had a canoe thirty feet long and four feet six inches wide, with carved head- and sternposts decorated with feathers. Nicholas showed them illustrations in a book of Cook's voyages (probably Hawkesworth), including an engraving of a war canoe. They were delighted with this image, and asked if the 'nuee nuee areekee' (nui nui ariki – the great high chief) King George had seen it. One of these chiefs was offered rum, which he tasted and spat out with tears in his eyes, saying that it was impossible to drink it. Another carried a sword he had beaten out of a piece of iron, which he carried wrapped in a cloth and treated as 'an inestimable treasure'. They danced and sang for their hosts, and Tahika invited them to visit his superior chief Te Haupa, the ariki of the Thames district.

On 6 January, large numbers of canoes came from the Waimate and Kawa-kawa districts, whose crews traded eagerly with the missionaries. Nicholas and

Marsden went to a nearby cove, where they visited a tiny hamlet of two houses. Its inhabitants (including several children) ran away, panic-stricken at the sight of Europeans. Only one young man, whose brother had gone as a sailor the previous year to Port Jackson, stayed behind to greet them. He called his mother back to meet their guests, and when she discovered that her sailor son had visited Marsden's house at Parramatta, she burst into tears. On their way back to the ship they noticed a canoe full of fernroot being paddled towards Waikare, a glimpse of the transfer of foodstuffs from one place to another.

During his explorations in the southern part of the Bay of Islands, Nicholas had been thinking about local leadership and power. He now produced a summary, based on his observations. It seemed to him that in New Zealand, some kind of feudal system was operating, not unlike the clan system in Scotland. From the Cavalli Islands to Hauraki, there were three main ariki – Kaingaroa, from the Cavallis to the north-west side of the Bay; Tara on the south-east side, as far as Bream Bay; and 'Shoupah' (Te Haupa) in the southernmost district to Hauraki. Although these ariki could command the inferior chiefs in times of war, for the most part their power seemed to be nominal. The ariki did not go to war themselves, but each had his own 'general, or fighting man', who was one of his close relatives. This man trained and controlled the warriors of the clan, and directed them in battle. Hongi was war leader for his elder brother Kaingaroa, while Tupi played this role for his elder brother Tara. The ariki of the interior were reputed to be very powerful, and attended with great 'state and ceremonious distinction'. They were so tapu that when they travelled in state, they were carried in litters on the shoulders of their attendants (so that the places where their feet had stepped did not become tapu, an observation also noted by John Savage).

Even in war, though, the lesser chieftains often acted without consulting their ariki. Many had large retinues of devoted followers over whom they exercised considerable authority. In some cases this power seemed absolute, while in others it was restrained by public opinion. The males of these families were styled 'rangatira', and seemed to be haughty and proud, but were neither cruel nor arbitrary in their behaviour. Although these rangatira insisted upon their consequence and were dignified in demeanour and dress, the commoners did not seem in awe of them. They spoke and acted with great freedom in front of their chiefs, and did not seem constrained by their presence. On the contrary, they were cheerful and good-humoured, and chiefs and commoners lived together in evident harmony. At Rangihoua, furthermore, the commoners held their land independently of the chief, who had no power to oust them. Their canoes were also their own property, and the chief could not control these for his own purposes.[51] All the same, rangatira and commoners could not intermarry, although most rangatira had several wives, all being involved in manual labour. It seemed to Nicholas that most wives were married as 'hard-working servants' rather than 'for the charms of their persons or the endearments of their society'.[52] By and large, his observations seem accurate and compelling.

Nicholas found the chiefs mistrustful in their mutual relationships. Ruatara, for instance, warned them against Te Aara, saying that he was determined to cut off the next European ship that came to Whangaroa, despite his protestations to the contrary. He also accused Pomare of being an inveterate thief and quarrelsome, having recently killed and eaten six of his people; and Te Morenga of being violent and untrustworthy. He added that he had recently been ambushed by another local chief and ten of his warriors, and had only escaped by threatening them with his pistols. Tara, too, assured them that Te Pahi had been a principal actor in the fate of the *Boyd*, although the Whangaroa leaders and the other chiefs emphatically denied it. Tupi, his brother, described Korokoro as a treacherous man who had killed and eaten two of his people, and spoke bitterly about Ruatara, Hongi and Pomare. Nicholas concluded that 'many of the chiefs entertain towards each other, not only a spirit of envy, but even of rancorous malignity'.[53] He described Pomare as the epitome of this attitude, speaking contemptuously of all his rivals.

Of the chiefs that he met (apart from Te Aara at Whangaroa), Pomare was the one whom Nicholas liked least, describing him as 'artful', 'avaricious' and 'obnoxious'. He was an expert in preserving the heads of enemies taken in battle, a practice that Nicholas found abhorrent. When Marsden asked Pomare if he could supply him with one of these heads, which were much in demand among scientists in England,[54] Pomare replied that for gunpowder and an axe, he could procure several. He would shoot some people who had killed his son and bring their heads back, and show Marsden how to preserve them. Taken aback, Marsden withdrew his request, unwilling to be party to such proceedings.

A VISIT INLAND WITH HONGI HIKA

On 7 January 1814, after Marsden had procured a quantity of timber, the *Active* sailed back to Te Puna. Ruatara flew his colours on the flagstaff at Rangihoua to greet them. A temporary building sixty feet long and fourteen feet wide had almost been completed by the beach, with walls made of posts interwoven with flags and rushes and a thatched ridged roof. The interior was divided into four compartments, one for each of the European families. The smithy was also nearly finished, and some charcoal had been prepared. The sailors pitched into the task of finishing the buildings while Nicholas wandered around Rangihoua. He watched men and women digging potatoes in the gardens near the village, using wooden sticks about seven feet long, sharpened at one end and provided with a footrest about three feet from the pointed end (the koo, or digging stick). When they were dug, the potatoes were stacked on stages eight or nine feet high and covered up with fern fronds. In the village no one seemed to be idle. Most of the women were weaving garments or mats, although two young women amused themselves by painting each other with shark oil and red ochre. People offered to trade fishing lines and carvings (some representing human heads, with paaua eyes; or copulating figures) in exchange for nails, which they eagerly accepted. When he and Marsden visited Miki later that afternoon, three young female attendants entertained them with singing and dancing. They gave Marsden a gift of a poi, a ball made of finely woven fabric, stuffed with bullrush down and hung on a long string, which was swung backwards and forwards over the forefinger.

The next day Kaingaroa and Hongi Hika came to visit the missionaries. The former, Hongi's older brother and ariki of the central Bay, was 'a middle-aged man, very well proportioned, but inclined to corpulency; mild in his manners, and easy in his deportment'.[55] Hongi had brought his daughter, a lovely girl about eleven years old, whom he presented to Marsden, suggesting in jest (or maybe not) that Charles, Marsden's son, should marry her. Marsden replied that 'he had no objection to the alliance, but only on condition that Miss Shunghi should reside at Port Jackson, at which her father shook his head, and would fain have the converse of the proposition, viz. that Charles should come and fix his abode with him in New Zealand'.[56] In fact, Marsden's evasion of Hongi's request reflected a personal aversion. In 1810, he had declared in a letter to Joseph Hardcastle in London, 'I do not hesitate to say . . . to have a daughter or a Son from necessity, united to an heathen would be to me the most dreadful of all human afflictions' (although if Tui's boast about sleeping with one of Marsden's daughters was accurate, this was an ironic comment).[57]

Since it was a Sunday, Kaingaroa and Hongi joined the missionaries in a service in the new mission building. Ruatara's flag had been hoisted to signal the Sabbath, and none of the local people was working. When Ruatara arrived at the mission, however, he was angry, complaining that his head wife Miki had refused to put on the English clothes he had given her to wear at the service. When he tried to insist, she had been adamant, saying that every time she wore them the women laughed at her. Ruatara must have been even more aggrieved when he found the next morning that Waari, the man who had seduced his youngest wife, had escaped overnight from the *Active*.

On 9 January, Hongi came out to the ship to take Marsden and Nicholas on an inland excursion. He had invited them to visit one of his villages, about thirty-five miles in the interior. He arrived in a war canoe, the largest they had yet seen, sixty feet long and four feet six inches wide, elaborately carved and with a wickerwork deck about a foot from the bottom of the hull. There were fourteen young men to paddle this canoe, helped by the rangatira. Their party included Hongi, Tinana, Wairua (one of Kaingaroa's sons) and Ruatara, with Miki and her child, as well as Nicholas and Marsden. When they began moving, Miki put her baby down on the wickerwork floor and joined in, paddling vigorously.

They chatted and laughed as the canoe raced along, accompanied by a smaller canoe carrying supplies for their journey. As they passed Te Pahi's island, Ruatara told Marsden and Nicholas about the 1810 attack by the whalers. When the whalers had arrived, Te Pahi's people were caught by surprise and were indiscriminately slaughtered. Te Pahi and Te Uri o Kanae had been wounded in the affray, but had managed to escape by swimming to the mainland. Nicholas commented:

> It will be regretted by every feeling heart, that these inoffensive creatures, who had uniformly conducted themselves towards our shipping with the greatest good faith and the most friendly treatment, were nearly all annihilated; while the guilty savages at Wangeroa have to this moment gone unpunished.[58]

At Te Puna Inlet, a favorite anchorage for the whalers, Nicholas saw fortified paa along the hilltops. After three hours' hard paddling they landed at the head of the Kerikeri Inlet, near a small garden belonging to Kaingaroa. This district, which was wealthy and well inhabited, was controlled by Hongi and his brother.[59] Ruatara and Miki went off to their cultivations while Hongi picked up a small stick, a piece of rotten wood and some dry grass and made a fire, twirling the stick between his hands till the touchwood ignited. The servants peeled potatoes and dug a circular hole in the ground, in which they put stones and then built a fire on top, covering this with another layer of stones. When the stones were hot, they were taken out of the hole and the embers swept out. The hot stones were replaced and covered with wet grass, a layer of cleaned potatoes, then more wet grass and hot stones, and a layer of soil. About ten minutes later the potatoes were ready to eat, beautifully steamed in the earth oven.

While the meal was being cooked, Marsden wandered off to look at the Wharepoke Falls, at the head of the inlet. He estimated these to be nine feet high, tumbling over a ledge of rock stretching from one side of the river to the other. This was another fine site for a mill and a European settlement.

After the meal, they set off for Waimate. Hongi wore a pistol stuck in his belt and carried Nicholas's gun. Two of his men were armed with loaded muskets, while the rest carried spears. They passed two small hills with a plantation of kuumara between them, then came out onto a beautiful fern-covered plain that extended for several miles. The surrounding low hills were covered with fern or trees, and the soil varied from dry and gravelly to wet and swampy. Most of the plain was covered with rich black earth, watered by streams in all directions. Marsden thought that this plain could be easily ploughed, and that it would make 'good strong wheat land'.

After walking across the plain for about six miles, stopping twice to eat, they entered a forest of tawa and totara. The trees were as much as thirty feet round and a hundred feet tall. As they rested in a clearing, six of the company danced and sang a song that they had composed for Marsden. The undergrowth was tangled and difficult to walk through, and they had to cross a stream in the middle of the forest. Shortly after this they met an old woman, loaded with flax, who gazed at them in astonishment. On leaving this forest they came to a village on the banks of the Waitangi River with a hilltop paa nearby (Whakataha[60]), where the inhabitants retired in times of danger. The leader of this settlement was Taareha of Ngaati Reehia, Hongi Hika's second cousin and a 'petty chief' at this time. He had visited the *Active* several days earlier, impressing Marsden as 'a very fine hand-some looking man'. He had told Marsden that when the whaler *New Zealander* visited the Bay (probably in 1810), her sailors plundered his cultivations. His father and some of their people went to keep watch, and were shot by the sailors. His father, another man and a woman were killed. The next night Taareha and his warriors kept watch, and they had killed three Europeans.

As they entered Taareha's village, Hongi fired off his pistol, and the women replied with shouts of 'Haere mai' (Welcome). Hongi pressed noses with an old woman, and they wept affectionately together. Taareha and most of his people were absent, but one of his ten wives greeted them warmly. Hongi had shot a duck by the river, which he presented to his guests for dinner. Taareha's people gave them cooked potatoes, and Marsden ordered tea to be made in an iron pot, with tea and sugar brought from the *Active*. Some visitors arrived from a neighbour-ing settlement, and after some singing and dancing, Hongi and Marsden decided to carry on to Kaingaroa's stronghold at Waimate. Taareha's people carried the Euro-peans across the Waitangi River on their backs, then they walked to another wood-land. There was a large garden of kuumara, potatoes and turnips at the edge of these trees, extending over thirty or forty acres, which belonged to Kaingaroa. This garden was fenced against pigs and was in a state of high cultivation. About half a mile into the bush the slope became steeper and they climbed through the trees to the foot of Okuratope Paa (or Waimate, as Nicholas called it), Kaingaroa's principal fortification. From this hilltop town he controlled the rich agricultural lands of the district.[61] As they entered the paa, they were greeted with 'the loud-est acclamations'. Darkness had fallen, so after supper they went to sleep in Hongi's house, lying on clean mats and wrapped in their greatcoats.

The next morning, 10 January, they woke to a marvellous chorus of birdsong. Nicholas said, 'we fancied ourselves for the moment in some enchanted ground, while the forest seemed to ring with the mellow warblings of nature, and a thou-sand feathered songsters poured their soft throats in responsive melody'.[62] As the sun rose, the people of the paa called out to greet it. The two Europeans went out in the early-morning light and inspected the fortifications. A strong palisade, twenty feet high, enclosed the settlement, with a postern gate five feet high and only two feet wide, carved with human heads to defy invaders. This palisade was backed by wickerwork to deflect spear thrusts, and loop holes were cut through at regular intervals, where muskets could be fired (a pioneering adaptation). Near the postern was a secret place where a defender could keep up a fire on attacking warriors. Behind this palisade was a space of about thirty feet, where a deep ditch had been dug at least nine feet wide, with a high bank beyond it. This bank was topped by another high palisade, with a postern gate set in it. Behind the palisade was a flat area about eighty feet wide, where the hill had been terraced. The sheer face of this terrace was about fifteen feet high, and surmounted by another palisade that encircled the summit. The summit held about two hundred houses and stores for kuumara, potatoes and weapons, each compound protected by its own palisaded enclosure. According to Hongi, this paa had been attacked the previous summer by a strong force from Whangaroa, but he and his warriors had repelled them. Two to three hundred people usually lived at Okuratope, but they were presently down at the coast catching and drying fish for their winter provisions.

In the centre of the paa was Kaingaroa's 'throne', a long seat about twenty feet long and three feet wide, set on a carved post about six feet high, with a step leading up to it. This elevated seat had a spectacular view of the surrounding plains, and the Europeans were told that Kaingaroa sat on it when he gave his commands to his people. There was another seat nearby, reserved for the use of his mother, and a small storage box raised about four feet off the ground, three feet long and two feet wide, with a carving by the door, where she kept her provisions. At this time in the north the Polynesian custom of elevating chiefs above their people was obviously practised. It has already been noted that high chiefs were carried around on litters, and that lesser chiefs sat on the roofs of their houses.

Nicholas was impressed by the storehouses in this settlement, which were up to thirty feet long and twenty wide, and built more solidly than the houses. One of these structures had a high door, a roof that projected about three feet from the walls on all sides, and two large openings to allow air into the interior. The door frame was mortised to the sides of the wall, with uprights projecting to take the bolt that fastened the door. Inside, the space was divided by a partition. The storehouse was surrounded by a strong fence about ten feet from the building, for extra security. Near one of the houses in the settlement Nicholas noticed a large wooden trough in which hinau bark was steeping. This trough was six feet long and eighteen inches wide. Hongi also showed him some hardwood spears, twenty-three feet long and tipped with bone points about nine inches long.

After breakfast outside Hongi's house they went to see Lake Omaapere. Having descended the hill and walked through the bush for about an hour, they came to a wide plain about four miles square. On the far side of this they arrived at a village surrounded by fertile gardens where kuumara, potatoes, gourds, cabbages, turnips and a little Indian corn were growing. The soil was very rich and dry, and the potatoes were excellent. The chief of this village was a genial young man who offered to take them to the lake, about two miles away. They walked through the bush, some of which was being cut down and burnt off for gardens. Stones had been collected from the ground and piled in heaps for removal. The landscape around the lake was beautiful, reminding Nicholas of the 'pleasure grounds' of England. The people told him that the lake was full of fish (presumably eels, as well as freshwater fish), which they caught in circular traps made out of mangimangi, which they showed him. The lake led to a river (the Utakura), which ran to the western coast, with 'canoes . . . constantly plying upon it' (no doubt carrying root crops and dried fish as well as people to and from the interior). It is interesting to note that in 1815 this river was navigable for canoes all the way to Lake Omaapere. Hongi reported that it came out in a 'very fine and extensive harbour' with a narrow entrance and high seas in a southerly wind – the Hokianga.

Nicholas took a small canoe out onto the lake to shoot ducks. From this unsteady vantage point he surveyed the lake and imagined on its shores the capital of a new British colony:

> Should an extensive settlement be ever formed in New Zealand by our people, and the Bay of Islands fixed upon as the principal harbour; the neighbourhood of this lake would form an admirable situation for the seat of government, and chief town of the colony. The extensive forests that line one side of it, would afford an immense quantity of timber, that might at a trifling expense be floated to the opposite bank, where, the ground being cleared to a considerable extent, the town might be built, and lands inclosed both for pasturage and husbandry.[63]

Nicholas believed that such a colony would be beneficial for Maori:

> A spirit of civilized industry would be diffused all over the country, and they would be gradually initiated into all our pursuits; while being protected in their persons and property by the wholesome laws of our inestimable constitution, they would have nothing to apprehend; and providing for their wants in conscious security, their physical comforts would always keep pace with their moral improvement.[64]

He did not believe, however, that New Zealand should be settled by convicts, who would only introduce 'a factitious contamination of morals among the natives . . . instructing them in the most depraved practices by their own example'. Nicholas's vision was of a colony of honest artisans and labourers, bent on self-improvement. It later inspired him to write his two-volume description of his journey, *Narrative of a Voyage to New Zealand*.

On returning from the lake, Marsden, Nicholas, Hongi and their companions walked back to the small village they had just visited. A duck that Hongi had shot at the lake was stewing in the pot, and the chief speared a pig for their provisions. Tinana mused aloud that in New Zealand people always fed their visitors, whereas at Parramatta you could walk about all day without anyone offering to feed you. As they left this village on their way back to Waimate, Nicholas noticed some fine taro plants growing in its gardens. They were planted in rows about eighteen inches apart, with earth carefully mounded up around the tubers (although taro was usually grown in scooped-out depressions). Hongi shot a kuukupa (pigeon) in the woods, and when they arrived at Okuratope, this was stewed in their iron pot while two pigs were baked on hot stones for their dinner. The servants butchered the pork with sharp shells and distributed it carefully, giving a large portion of the meat to the visitors. After the meal a local man took Nicholas to visit the latrine at the outer fortifications. The hill was cut down into a cliff, and a horizontal board had been fixed to an opening in the palisade, projecting about two feet out over the precipice. The man showed Nicholas how it was used, climbing on the board and perching there in an unmistakeable attitude. Nicholas was impressed by the cleanliness of this sanitary arrangement, but refused to use it.

That night Kaingaroa's son Wairua gave Marsden and Nicholas a fine mat each, and a man presented Marsden with a fragment of a letter from the *Boyd*, 'addressed to the unfortunate Captain Thompson'. Writing seemed to have magical powers, and even fragments of texts were treasured. They slept in Hongi's shelter, which was cold and damp, and early the next morning returned to Taareha's village with Hongi, Tinana, Wairua and twenty of their people. Food was soon prepared, and Marsden had tea made, which he offered to four of Taareha's wives. They refused, saying that they were 'tapu tapu', and only allowed to drink water. He then offered tea to one of Hongi's wives, a woman with a one-month-old baby, but Hongi refused to let her taste it. He told Marsden that if she did, her baby would die (from a breach of tapu). All the chiefs drank the tea, however, and everyone tasted his bread and sugar. Taareha's house was also sacred, as Nicholas discovered when he put a bundle of his things onto its roof. Amidst cries of 'Taboo Taboo!' they ordered him to remove it.

After leaving Waimate, they walked to the head of the Kerikeri Inlet. The tide was out and their canoes could not be launched immediately. While they waited for the tide to turn, Wairua painted the gunwhales of his canoe with red ochre mixed with oil. He used a tuft of feathers as a brush, painting the patterns with great dexterity. Another man in their party showed the Europeans a tattooing kit, comprising small pieces of bone worked to a very sharp point and fastened to short pieces of wood at right angles. He told Nicholas that although people were eager to be tattooed, they could only bear to have a small part done at a time, which took at least two months to heal. On their way back to the ship they dropped some of their party off at a paa, then carried on with twelve people in the canoe, three of whom were women. As they approached the *Active*, Ruatara came out with twelve men in his canoe, which was loaded with provisions, and fired a salute with his musket. Hongi returned the salute, signalling a race between their canoes to the vessel. Two women in Ruatara's canoe, who had their babies on board, laid them on mats on the wickerwork lattice and picked up their paddles. The crews of each canoe kept perfect time, changing the pace every few minutes from long and slow to quick and short strokes, at signals from their leaders, but Ruatara's canoe soon pulled ahead. As they reached the side of the ship, the two crews stood in their canoes, brandishing their paddles and singing a war song.

That afternoon Nicholas and Marsden went ashore, to find Thomas Kendall and William Hall installed in their new dwellings. After watching Mrs Hall teaching Te Uri o Kanae's wife to wash linen with soap and water, Nicholas commented, 'Though the wife of a *rungateeda* [rangatira], she felt herself highly honoured by this employment; and imagined it, very probably, the most suitable of any that the *packaha* could assign to her.'[65] He reflected once again on the glories of civilisation:

> Many interesting ideas occurred to me while I beheld the missionaries thus seated in their new residence, and preparing for the work of civilization in a land where never before was the least gleam of knowledge, except what nature instinctively supplied; and where man, roving about as a lawless denizen, acknowledged no

authority except that of an individual barbarous as himself, who constantly led him on to deeds of carnage against his fellows, and taught him not only to satisfy his revenge with their destruction, but to crown it with a bloody banquet. In such a land it was that a few civilized beings were now going to reclaim a whole race to subdued and regular habits; and afford, at the same time, another proof of the immense superiority of mind over matter.[66]

His comment reveals how readily Europeans translated the rule of mind over matter into the rule of 'civilized beings' (with their knowledge and laws) over ignorant, anarchic, 'savages'.

Soon after they arrived at the mission, Marsden received a complaint that Hansen's son had seduced one of Te Uri o Kanae's wives. Marsden had prohibited the sailors from having any dealings with local women, so he immediately set up an inquiry into the matter. The young man vehemently denied the accusation, and the next morning an impromptu trial 'for *crim. con*' was held on the beach. The woman concerned, the wife of Kanae's brother Waari, acknowledged that a sailor had given her a nail, and offered her another if she would sleep with him. She had refused, saying that she was tapu, but kept the first nail. When her husband found the nail, he was furious and accused her of adultery. He said, 'the *packaha* never gave nails away for nothing', and gave her a severe beating. The woman denied that Hansen's son was the sailor concerned, and that she had slept with any of the Europeans. The case lapsed because no offence could be proved, and Marsden dropped the matter.

After this inquiry was completed, the Halls came ashore with the rest of the stores, and the next morning the Kings were landed with all their possessions. Timber was also unloaded from the *Active* for the mission buildings. Marsden had decided to take the ship on a short voyage while these were being built. Visiting chiefs had invited him to Whangaroa and Hauraki, and he decided to follow up at least one of these invitations. At Whangaroa he could salvage the *Boyd*'s great guns, which might be a profitable venture. In the end, however, the itinerary of his journey would depend on which way the winds at sea were blowing.

AN EXPEDITION TO HAURAKI

On 12 January 1815, the *Active* sailed from Rangihoua. She was becalmed off Cape Brett, but the next morning the winds were fair for Whangaroa and the ship set sail for the north. There were thirty-five people on board, described by John Liddiard Nicholas as seven 'civilized people' and twenty-eight 'savages'. Kendall, Hall and King had stayed behind to get the mission station ready for occupation. Marsden's European companions were Nicholas; John Hunter, the carpenter; Hansen, the ship's captain; the Scottish mate Ross; the ship's cook; and one European sailor. All the rest of the party were Polynesian. They included two Tahitians and twenty-six Maori – three sailors, Ruatara and six of his warriors, Te Uri o

Kanae (Te Pahi's nephew) and Toa (Te Pahi's fifteen-year-old son, by a captive wife from Hauraki), all from the north of the Bay at Te Puna; Parore (Hongi's nephew) with Wairua (Kaingaroa's son) and Arawa (son of a Waimate priest), from inland at Waimate; Korokoro, his brothers Tui and Te Rangi, his ten-year-old son and three of their men, from the east of the Bay at Paroa; Te Morenga, a chief from 'Hekorangha' (Te Ruahoanga paa[67]) on the Taiamai plains, who was one of Hongi Hika's great rivals; Tohu (son of Moka, described as a chief from the west side of New Zealand); Hiinaki (grandson of Waraki) from Waitangi on the central coast of the Bay, and Kahi (son of Maru) from the Kawakawa district.

The *Active* headed north for Whangaroa, despite Korokoro's protestations. He had hoped to go south to Hauraki, and was anxious about the Whangaroa people's intentions. When they reached the Cavallis that afternoon, however, the wind turned round and they were forced to anchor inside the islands. Three canoes came out, and as soon as he saw them, Ruatara assumed command over the Maori on board the *Active*. He distributed muskets, pistols, cutlasses and spears, and ordered the men to lie on the deck behind the gunwhales. As the canoes came alongside, at a given signal Ruatara's party leaped up and rushed to the sides of the ship, performing a deafening haka. The people in the canoes were terrified and at first refused to board the *Active*. After a promise that they would not be attacked, however, they regained their confidence and climbed up the sides with alacrity. Another canoe approached soon afterwards, which was given the same startling reception. Ruatara told Marsden that he wanted these visitors to tell the local people that the ship was well armed and on the alert, so that no one would venture to attack them.

When these canoes had left the ship, the carpenter discovered that one of his chisels had been taken. Ruatara offered to get it back, and was permitted to take the ship's boat with twelve warriors, all heavily armed with muskets and pistols (although the firearms were unloaded), across to the island. Nicholas decided to go with them, but Ruatara made him stay in the boat with Inga (son of Tuu – a chief at Paaroa – and an inexperienced sailor) and Kanae, while he and the rest of his men landed. Nicholas ordered his two companions to row him along the coast, following Ruatara's party. At nightfall they landed at a small village, where Ruatara and his warriors were in the midst of an angry confrontation. Six or seven of the villagers were protesting that the man who had taken the chisel came from another island, and when Nicholas arrived they involved him in the discussion. He accepted their assurances that they were not responsible for the theft, and decided that further pursuit was useless. On their way back to the ship, Kanae amused the party by describing Nicholas's frustration with Inga's clumsy efforts to row the boat. He referred to Nicholas as 'New Zealand', a name that he had been given when he first arrived at Te Puna.

On 14 January, a stiff nor-westerly blew up and Marsden decided to take the *Active* south towards Hauraki. Ruatara and Korokoro were elated, and they and their companions began exuberant joking and singing. They engaged in mock duels and, stripping off their clothing, performed action songs during the voyage, including some the Europeans found extremely indecent. Korokoro's people also sang a dirge about one of their relatives who had been killed and eaten by the Hauraki people. As they sailed down the coast, Korokoro told Marsden that while the *Active* had been anchored in the south of the Bay of Islands, a chief at Kawakawa named Maru (whose son was on board) had plotted to ambush the vessel. He was angry because no payment had been received for timber his people had cut, and wanted to kill the Europeans. Pomare had urged them on, but in the end Tara was able to prevent the ambush. When Marsden asked Tui if this story were true, Tui assured him that it was all 'henereka', or lies. Since Tui was Korokoro's brother, Marsden was inclined to believe him.

On 15 January in the morning, a canoe came from Bream Bay, bringing out an old man with three male attendants and a woman. As they climbed up the gangway over the side, Ruatara's warriors leaped up and presented pistols, muskets and spears at the old man's chest. He fell back into his canoe, trembling with terror. Korokoro, who knew the man, called out to reassure him and invited him on board, but he was still shaking and was reluctant to go to see Marsden in the cabin. This old man was the chief of Ruakaakaa, a district with plenty of good timber. When he got over his fright, according to Marsden, he laughed at the trick that had been played on him.

Later that morning Marsden conducted a service on deck, attended by the chiefs and their warriors. Soon afterwards another canoe came alongside and 'received the same electric salute as the others'. When two more canoes came out during the afternoon, laden with fish, they flew from a spear printed cotton that Marsden had given their chief at Kawakawa. During the haka they rested quietly on their paddles, then came on board, bearing the fish as a present. They told Marsden that if the *Active* fired off its cannon as it rounded Bream Head, their chief had promised to come out and visit him. Some of these men joined the ship, and as the *Active* sailed south the cannon was fired, but no canoe came out to the vessel.

That night the ship entered the Hauraki Gulf, passing the Barrier Islands. Nicholas learned that the westernmost island was called 'Shouthuroo' (Hauturu), and the larger island was called 'Outhahah' (Aotea), where a chief named 'Coreo' (Ko Reo?) was living.

Early on 16 January, the brig sailed towards the mouth of the Waihou River. Two canoes came out to the ship, bringing Te Haupa, the ariki of Hauraki. Te Haupa stayed at a distance while Te Morenga called out to him, telling him about the Europeans and their mission at Rangihoua. Ruatara and his warriors then repeated their challenge, but less violently than on previous occasions. After Te Haupa and Te Morenga had spoken again, Te Haupa came on board with his son and presented Marsden with two fine mats, inviting him to visit their village. Nicholas found Te Haupa impressive:

> This chief, who appeared about the same age with Tarra, was in his person the
> finest and most venerable looking old man I ever beheld; in stature he rose above

the tallest of his countrymen; and his strength, though impaired with age, was yet extraordinary. In his countenance there was a thoughtful seriousness that bespoke him of a meditative cast of mind; and in his deportment a solemn gravity, which, even more than his high rank, served to distinguish him from all the others . . . Shoupah . . . was by far the most considerable chief we had yet met with; his authority reaching from this place as far as Bream Bay, a great extent in such a country to be under the power of one individual. Contrary to the usual practice of the areekees [ariki], he always commanded his warriors in person, and was accounted, notwithstanding his advanced age, one of the bravest men in New Zealand.[68]

Te Haupa gave them instructions on how to cross the gulf safely, then returned to the mainland. He was about to leave Hauraki the next day on a raid to East Cape, with a large contingent of people 'from the western side' (probably either from Tainui, or Taamaki-makau-rau – Auckland). These people, whose canoes were drawn up along the coastline, had formerly been his enemies. They had often attacked his territories until he married his daughter to their chief, securing them as allies. They had travelled fifty miles across rugged terrain to Hauraki to join the war party, hauling their canoes, loaded with provisions, with ropes over rollers. Nicholas likened their efforts to contemporary campaigns in Europe:

> [This] shews to what lengths ambition is carried, even among savages, and what difficulties are cheerfully encountered from the desire of plunder and devastation. This truth has been exemplified in New Zealand at various intervals, no less than in Europe, which has been deluged in blood for the last five-and-twenty years; and the only difference between the memorable expedition that passed the Dnieper never to return, and the noteless horde that proceeded to the East Cape, is the number and attributes of the respective forces, the principle and motives being exactly the same.[69]

Here he was comparing Te Haupa's East Cape campaign with Napoleon's disastrous march on Moscow, just two and a half years earlier.

Early on 17 January, Hansen tried to take the *Active* to the western side of the Hauraki Gulf, but a gale blew up that tossed the ship about, making the crossing impossible. The chiefs said that Te Haupa's atua had raised the storm in a fit of furious anger. When Nicholas asked Korokoro whether the god was angry with them or with Te Haupa, he was assured that Te Haupa was the culprit and that the god of Te Puna was not angry. All the same, the wind favoured Te Haupa's fleet, which had sailed in the night to the eastward. In the evening the *Active* finally anchored opposite a large village on the western side of the gulf, at Whakatiiwai. The boat was lowered and ten of their Maori companions went ashore to meet the local people. The people on the ship heard a loud outcry when they landed, but it was just the sounds of the welcome.

Early the next morning a canoe with five men on board brought Te Haupa's nephew, a man called 'Phiti' (Whiti) out to the *Active*. Marsden gave him some biscuit and offered wheat as a gift, telling him how to grow it. Accompanied by Whiti, Nicholas and Marsden went ashore with Ruatara, splendidly dressed in uniform with a sword at his side, and Kanae with a dozen armed warriors. They landed at a small village where the women greeted them with the karanga. Almost all of their men had gone with Te Haupa on his East Cape expedition, and only women, children and a few old male slaves (who Marsden discovered were bought and sold) were left behind in the village. One woman offered Marsden a fine cloak in exchange for some India print cloth. Kanae and his companions had brought fish-hooks, pieces of iron hoop, and white gannet feathers (a characteristic Bay of Islands product) with them, which they now offered to the local people:

> The Village was all in motion, they crowded together, like a fair, from every quarter, some of the inhabitants brought their Matts to sell and various other Articles, so that the whole day appeared a busy scene, and many things were bought and sold in their way. When the fair was over, the Ladies entertained us with several Dances and Songs. One of them had on a very fine upper garment which a Chief from Ranghee-Hoo [Te Uri o Kanae] . . . wanted to procure for his Wife. He had brought a box of feathers neatly dressed, the pithy part of the quill having been all cut off, and only the external part remaining, to which the feather was attached made the feather wave gracefully with the smallest breeze, when placed in the air. He opened it in presence of the Ladies, many of them wanted these feathers, he on the other hand wanted the fine garment. After placing them very tastefully two or three feathers in several of the Ladies hair, she that had got this fine garment, when she beheld how elegantly they appeared in the Heads of those, who had them, became seemingly impatient for some. He asked her to sell her garment, she stood hesitating for some time; at length he laid a certain number down at her feet, this proved a temptation she could not resist, and instantly threw off the fine garment and delivered it to him for his feathers.[70]

When these exchanges were over, the party walked about a mile along the beach to Te Haupa's village at Whakatiiwai. Its male inhabitants had also gone to the East Cape, leaving just a few women and children behind in residence. They were greeted by Te Haupa's daughter-in-law, a 'fine, tall woman' in mourning for her child, her body scarred with unhealed wounds from the haehae. Marsden offered her a pair of scissors in exchange for pork and potatoes, but she told him that she had no potatoes and that the only pigs in the village belonged to a man who lived elsewhere, and she had no right to dispose of them. Te Haupa's settlement straggled for about two miles below a high hill, fortified on its summit. One of its slopes was cultivated, with two comfortable houses in the gardens and a circular storehouse with projecting eaves. The palisades leading into the fortification were decorated with carved figures about fourteen feet high, some with round tops on their heads, which reminded Marsden of Kaingaroa's fortified village at Waimate.

About three miles further along the beach, they came to a large settlement built on an extensive plain. They were greeted by women waving cloaks in the air, and Whiti, the chief who had come out to the *Active* the day before, with his brothers Kawau and Te Kapuhoka received them. Whiti's father, a very old man with snow-white hair and a beard, sat on a high stage in the middle of the houses.

The inhabitants of this village were 'some of the finest men and women' whom Marsden had seen in New Zealand, and they danced and sang for their visitors. The women wore long, finely ornamented cloaks, but would only exchange them for axes, and Marsden had none left to offer. Ruatara tried to barter for a war captive, or mookai, but there was only one available, a boy about twelve years old. Some of the children wore dollars from the *Boyd* around their necks, and there was a large piece of iron from the plundered vessel in this village. On their way back to the *Active*, Nicholas noted a huge, empty pigsty about a hundred feet long, divided by a partition down the middle.

Soon afterwards the wives of two chiefs, very fine-looking women, came out to the vessel. Their husbands, three other rangatira and nine of their people soon followed with a load of goods to barter. Nicholas acquired an elegant cloak in exchange for a large toki (adze). Cloaks were particularly valuable items, for they took at least two or three years to manufacture. One of these chiefs promised to visit Ruatara at Rangihoua, and to visit Marsden at Port Jackson. He and his people sang and danced for their hosts, and when they finally returned to shore, Ruatara's group replied with a haka. The visitors responded from their canoes, standing up and chanting until they were out of sight of the ship. Ruatara assured Marsden that Te Haupa and his people were now their friends, but Te Morenga said that they could not be trusted. They were capable, he said, of showing the most ardent friendship to the Europeans while at the same time planning to kill them.

That night the *Active* sailed up the north-eastern coast past Cape Rodney, and next evening anchored at the mouth of the Whangarei Harbour, where Marsden hoped to meet a local chief who had visited him at Kawakawa.[71] The Europeans were told that a freshwater river with kauri forests along its banks ran into the harbour from the interior. When Marsden asked whether any European vessel had ever stopped at Whangarei, he was informed that the *Venus* from Port Jackson had been there. It had stopped first at North Cape, where the pirates on board had kidnapped two local women, and then sailed south. One woman (Hongi's relation) had been taken from the Bay of Islands, one from a small island opposite Bream Cove (probably one of the Hen and Chickens) and one from the cove itself. At Hauraki, the sailors had tried to kidnap Te Haupa and one of his daughters, but the chief had managed to jump overboard and was picked up by a canoe that had been trailing the *Venus*.

During the following day (19 January), Nicholas got bored and decided to test Korokoro's patience. First, he tossed some chips of wood at him, which Korokoro ignored. He then picked up a stick and hit him on one leg. Korokoro grabbed a piece of wood and hurled it at Nicholas, hitting him on the cheek in retaliation. Nicholas retired in a huff to his cabin, went to his sea chest and took out his pistols, threatening to shoot Korokoro for hitting him. Korokoro coolly replied that it was all his own fault, to which Nicholas retorted that 'nothing less than [your] life [can] satisfy my resentment'. Korokoro grabbed the pistols from Nicholas, who cried that he had only been joking. The chief gave him back the pistols, then went back on deck, where he picked up a spear and challenged Nicholas to fight him. After taking the balls and half of the powder out of his pistols, Nicholas followed Korokoro and threatened again to shoot him. Korokoro seized one of the weapons, which went off in the struggle, singeing his waistcoat. He was now in a fury, exclaiming, 'Mr. Nicholas no good, no good, shoot Mr. Korra-korra.' Nicholas quickly took the bullet out of his pocket to show him that he had only been teasing. As soon as Korokoro realised it had all been a joke, he burst into tears then took a piece of linen tied around his head and bandaged one of Nicholas's fingers that had been hurt in the struggle. Ruatara and Tui had watched this altercation calmly, unmoved by the threat of violence. When it was all over, Nicholas realised how stupid he had been, for Korokoro could easily have hurt or killed him.

During the morning of 20 January, they sailed past Bream Head, where a canoe came out with a local chief whom Marsden had met at Kawakawa. He had 'Moyhanger' (Te Mahanga) with him, the Bay of Islands man who had travelled with John Savage to England. The chief said that they missed them the night before because he and his men had been working in their potato gardens. Nicholas thought Mahanga 'a handsome intelligent fellow', although he showed no nostalgia for civilisation: 'perfectly content with his original condition, he shewed no disposition to resign it, nor had the roast beef of Old England produced in Moyhanger any distaste for the fern-root of New Zealand'.[72] When he came on board, Mahanga was given some nails, but instead he asked for a cat that he fancied, and Marsden presented it to him. Nicholas asked him whether he had met King George in London, and he replied, 'Yes, that King George was a great king; but that the Governor at Port Jackson was no king at all.' He invited them ashore to meet his high chief, who would give them plenty of pigs and potatoes. Nicholas described Mahanga as a 'cookee', or commoner. He was told that after the *Ferret* had brought him home to the Bay, Mahanga had stolen an axe. Tupi had ordered him to be flogged, and Tara had exiled him from the district.

That afternoon the wind turned in a contrary direction. Marsden decided to visit Mahanga's high chief to get pork and potatoes for their provisions, and at about six o'clock he took the boat ashore with Nicholas and Korokoro. When a high surf on the bar of the harbour threatened to capsize them, two canoes dashed from the beach through the waves and they were directed to a good landing place on the western shore. As they came in, people rushed out through the surf and brought the boat safely to land. The chief lived on the eastern side of the harbour, so they crossed over by canoe, marvelling at the coastal scenery:

> The whole place was surrounded with broken Rocks, which resembled more the ruins of old Abbies, than anything else. Some formed very large arches, others deep Caverns, some were like old Steeples and others like broken, massy, columns. In short, they represented the most curious group of ruins, which time, storms and Seas have made.[73]

Mahanga, who was waiting for them on the beach with crowds of curious people, greeted Nicholas and Marsden, linking arms with them with in 'Europee fashion'. Other people then joined in, laughing and joking, before the party walked about a mile to the village. There the women waved cloaks and saluted them with the karanga as they entered the settlement. The high chief of this harbour, 'Kiwacha' (Kiiwaka?), was 'a very old man, with a long grey beard and little hair on his head'. He was sitting on the ground with his war leader, Kukupa, the chief who had visited the *Active* the previous day, standing beside him. As his visitors approached, he ordered a clean mat to be spread on the ground and invited them to sit beside him. Marsden gave him three toki (adzes), explaining that he wanted potatoes and hogs in exchange. They chatted for a while, with Mahanga acting as interpreter. When Korokoro told the ariki about his visit to Port Jackson, he laughed and asked numerous questions. When Korokoro explained why Marsden had brought the missionaries to New Zealand, Mahanga interrupted often, trying to talk to the Europeans in English (which he had largely forgotten). He said that he would like to go back to England, and asked after Governor Bligh, Lieutenant-Colonel Foveaux, the Duke of York and Lord Fitzwilliam.

After they had been on shore about an hour, they heard musket-fire from the ship, a signal that the wind had turned in a favourable direction. The tide was out, so they had to wait until nightfall to row back to the vessel. While they were waiting, fires were lit and people sat around these in small groups, chatting and eating their supper. Nicholas wandered from one group to another while people gathered round, scrutinising every article of his clothing. They offered him food, and one old man brought him a young girl about twelve years old, 'presenting her to me with many commendations, and urging the alliance in a copious strain of native oratory'. Nicholas refused to accept her, however, saying that he was tapu. As they returned to the ship, Korokoro guided the boat through a rocky channel. Ruatara greeted them with a hearty handshake, saying that he feared his country-men had 'killed every one of us and made a meal of our bodies'. They immediately set sail, and the next afternoon arrived back at the Bay of Islands.

BACK AT THE BAY

At dawn on Sunday, 22 January, the *Active* anchored off Rangihoua. Marsden saw Ruatara's colours flying from the summit of the hill and remarked that the mission buildings on the flat were almost finished. He had now completed his explorations, and wrote in his journal:

> [I had] now completed every thing relative to the Establishment of the Mission, that appeared to me necessary . . . and opened a communication nearly 200 miles along the Coast, and made the Chiefs in all the different districts acquainted with the object in view; and they seemed all sensible of the benefits which they were

likely to derive from the Europeans residing amongst them. A more promising prospect never could be than the present, for civilizing this Part of the Globe.[74]

After they had greeted their friends, Marsden conducted a service on shore at Rangihoua. Hongi and Korokoro attended, but Ruatara and most of his people were absent. The reason was soon apparent. As the missionaries sat down to dinner at William Hall's place, a number of people rushed in, saying with great agitation that a 'nuee nee [big, big] fight' was imminent. Rangihoua was about to be attacked by a party from North Cape, and Ruatara was gathering his warriors. Marsden ordered his people to withdraw to the ship, where they sat and watched the ensuing action. Three large canoes soon paddled into the bay, loaded with men and women, cats and dogs, and quantities of fish and fernroot. When Tui, who had accompanied them out to the *Active*, saw these people, he told Marsden that these were not enemies after all, but his relatives from the Cavalli Islands.

As the canoes approached the shore, Ruatara's people rushed forward, chanting and brandishing their spears and muskets. Ruatara had a spear in his left hand and a large billhook in his right, while his head wife Miki carried a horse pistol and wore his sword belt over her shoulders. After a deafening haka, they sat down on the beach, where for quarter of an hour or more the two groups stared at each other in silence. Finally an old chief stood up in one of the canoes and spoke to his people, then turned to Ruatara. He said that hostile tribes from the North Cape had cut off thirty of Ruatara's kinsfolk near Doubtless Bay, and asked for his help to avenge the killings. After this speech Ruatara invited the visitors ashore for a meal. They hauled their canoes onto the beach, and the cooks began to light fires and prepare dinner. Realising that there was not going to be a fight, Marsden and Nicholas decided to go about their business. Korokoro came out to the ship in a canoe and accompanied them to Paroa, where they planned to get fish for the *Active*'s cargo.

At Paroa, Korokoro's head wife and her sister welcomed them, and for the next two days they stayed at the chief's village, a straggling settlement below a hilltop fortification. Korokoro set his people to work catching large quantities of fish in seines and by hook and line. In one small cove, four men and two boys used two canoes and a very long seine net to catch herrings. One man stood on a rock holding one end of the seine, watching for signs of a shoal. When he spotted ripples on the surface of the sea about a quarter mile off, he signalled to his companions. Another man, holding the other end of the net, paddled his canoe and drove the fish into the seine, surrounding them with a semicircle of netting. Although most of the shoal escaped on this occasion, three to four hundred fish were still caught in the net. Tui said that if they had used one of their larger seines, all of the shoal would have been taken. Other people caught bream and snapper with hooks and line, while Marsden and Nicholas worked to salt and cure the fish, which Marsden intended to sell at Port Jackson. Te Pene, the old chief of Paroa, watched them contemptuously, remarking, 'Mr. Marsden and Mr. Nicholas cookee cookee, Mr. Bennee, nuee nuee rungateeda' (Mr Marsden and Mr Nicholas are slaves, while Mr Pene is a great rangatira).

On 25 January, they returned to Rangihoua. Kendall celebrated by playing his barrel organ to an audience of astonished local people. They had arrived just in time to say goodbye to Ruatara, who was taking a party of his people to Doubtless Bay in response to his kinsfolk's summons. Miki and her older sister went with him, and his canoe, which was elegantly decorated, was paddled by 'a group of the most beautiful young women in the island'.[75] As he farewelled the missionaries, he asked if he could borrow a brace of pistols, which they willingly lent him. Marsden was now intent on completing the *Active*'s cargo. He decided to take the brig back to the southern side of the Bay to collect more timber.

On the evening of 28 January, the ship anchored at the mouth of the Kawakawa River. Early the next morning Pomare welcomed them and delivered five spars out to the vessel. He also invited Marsden to visit his people, who were cutting timber upriver. Shortly after they all sat down to breakfast, there was a commotion on board. Kanae had caught a local man stealing a marlin spike, which he was hiding under his cloak, and brought him to Marsden. Marsden decided not to punish this man himself but confined the thief on board to hand him over to Tara. The people were surprised that Marsden did not have the man flogged, remarking that a British captain had recently shot a thief who took a small axe from his vessel. Pomare told Marsden to hang the man, and when Tara came on board he hurled a block of wood at the thief so hard that he knocked him flat on the deck, where he kicked and beat him. When Marsden intervened, Tara spared the man's life but ordered him out of the district, saying if he ever returned he would be immediately killed (if they were not killed on the spot, thieves and adulterers in Maori communities were often exiled).

On 30 January, Marsden and Nicholas went upriver with Pomare to see the timber workers. They paddled up the Kawakawa as far as Te Koki's village, which they had visited during their earlier stay in the timber district. At this village, Pomare invited Marsden to walk with him through the woods while Nicholas followed with a canoe-load of trade goods that they had brought for the workers. Marsden went off with the chief, leaving Nicholas feeling uneasy. He mistrusted Pomare and was afraid that he had taken Marsden into the woods to kill him. Nicholas was paddled about a mile further up the river to a clearing where many people were gathered. He could not see Pomare or Marsden among them, and when several warriors daubed with blue paint appeared at the river's edge, he thought that his worst fears had been realised:

> The report that we had heard concerning [Pomare's] intention to cut off the ship now recurred to me with alarming certainty, while I could not help apprehending that he had brought us hither for the sole purpose of realizing his atrocious project, and thus securing to himself and his tribe all the property we possessed. Such were the dreadful suspicions that alarmed my mind, on finding myself separated from my friend, and surrounded by the dependents of a ruthless savage; who, according to all the accounts I had heard of him, had given repeated proofs of his

excessive cruelty; yet I thought it most prudent to dissemble my fears, and assume an air of implicit confidence in their sincerity.[76]

All was well, however, and soon after Nicholas was landed he and Marsden were reunited. They presented their trade goods to Pomare's people, who laughed and danced with pleasure. Nicholas noticed that one of the men wore a carved flute around his neck, and asked him if it was made of 'evee tungata' (iwi tangata – human bone). When he answered that it was, Nicholas began to reflect upon the use of human bone and the practice of cannibalism. He recalled that in Hawkeworth's edition of Captain Cook's first voyage, Cook had explained the local custom of eating people as due to a shortage of food. Nicholas thought that this explanation was highly unlikely. Fernroot seemed to be available in profusion, and the fisheries were productive. The people were industrious in storing food, and a shortage of provisions seemed unlikely. At the same time, Johann Forster had explained the custom by appealing to education. He claimed that New Zealanders were trained to enjoy the taste of human flesh, that male children were taught to be licentious and violent, and their mothers were forbidden to discipline them. In adulthood if they were insulted, men went into a frenzy, attacking their enemies without mercy and eating their bodies.

Nicholas found this explanation equally unconvincing. He had discovered no epicurean taste for human flesh among the Maori he met, nor were the children petulant and unruly. On the contrary, they were obedient, docile and cheerful. For himself, he attributed the practice of cannibalism to superstition, which 'teaches them to believe that their revenge can reach beyond the grave, and that the future existence of their wretched victims must be totally annihilated, by this unnatural destruction of their mortal remains'.[77] This was, in fact, quite a perceptive account of the belief that one could destroy an enemy's hau by ritually eating the flesh of their body.

After the distribution of goods to Pomare's people, Marsden presented the chief with five axes and three hoes. He was delighted and agreed to deliver sixteen more spars to the *Active*. As Nicholas and Marsden returned to the ship that evening, they passed a fleet of canoes with spars lashed to their sides, and a raft of spars being paddled out to the ship. There they found Tara, Tupi and Te Koki already on board with a chief called 'Tenanga'. In the cabin, this man gave Marsden a copy of Captain Pattison's 1810 letter warning ships' captains about the *Boyd* and blaming Te Pahi for the killings. Shortly afterwards Korokoro came alongside in his war canoe, with four others packed with warriors. They announced that they were on their way to make war on Whiria, Pomare's nephew, who had seduced the wife of one of Korokoro's allies.

On the morning of 31 January, a vast number of canoes came out to visit the Europeans. A slightly built Indian man who came on board told Nicholas that he had deserted from the *City of Edinburgh* (presumably during her visit in 1809) and had been living ever since among the local people. He was happy in the Bay and had married a local woman. He had 'experienced the kindest treatment from the natives', and when Nicholas offered him rice, replied that he now preferred fernroot. That same day Te Koki asked Marsden to take his son (who was about fourteen) with them to Port Jackson. Since he had a high regard for this kind, mild-mannered chief, Marsden agreed to his proposition.

The next day Thomas Kendall came out to the *Active* with Te Morenga. Some other chiefs had told Nicholas that this rangatira and his Taiamai people were plotting to kill the Europeans. He seemed perfectly friendly, however, and stayed on board for several days. When Kendall took the boat to Rangihoua, Marsden and Nicholas went with him, leaving Te Morenga on the *Active*. On the way they stopped at Moturoa, where the owner of the island offered to give it to the Europeans in exchange for two muskets, and to remove the tapu from those parts of the island that were under this restriction.

After examining the island, but making no commitment, they crossed the Bay to the mission at Rangihoua.[78] There they met Ruatara, who had just returned from his visit to Doubtless. He seemed troubled and anxious, telling them not to trust Te Morenga, for Waraki, the chief at Waitangi, had heard him boasting that he would cut off the *Active* and kill all the Europeans. Nicholas had become accustomed to hearing one chief accuse another in this way, and virtually ignored the warning. As he left the mission to check on one of his cows that had just calved, Ruatara armed himself with a pistol and a billhook. When Nicholas expressed surprise at these precautions, Ruatara replied that 'He was not sure of his life upon any occasion, since he became possessed of so much wealth, and he made it a rule . . . never to go any where without proper means of defence.'[79] These taonga (treasures) provoked jealousy and aggravated local political instabilities. It is clear that inter-hapuu (kin group) jealousies, with the presence of Europeans, were creating a particularly volatile environment.

The next day Hongi and Kaingaroa arrived to dine with Marsden at Rangihoua. Several days later, on 4 February, Nicholas decided to go by canoe to the *Active* to deliver a pile of axes that the smith had crafted. He asked Ruatara to arrange him a passage but was told that all of his canoes were busy and he could not order any of his people to take him. Nicholas finally prevailed on some men to paddle him to the ship. When they reached the *Active*, Tara and Pomare were on board, and as soon as he saw the axes Tara 'tabooed' the largest one for himself. Pomare was also keen to acquire his share, and told Nicholas that he was about to deliver more spars, although some of his people were angry that they had not yet received any presents.

On 5 February, the missionaries heard that the great battle between Whiria and Hinau, the chief whose wife he had seduced, was about to be fought . Te Morenga, who was still on board the *Active*, told Nicholas that he intended to attend the fight as a 'neutral' spectator. It was the Sabbath, so Marsden could not go, but Nicholas decided to go with Te Morenga. Accompanied by thirteen other Maori, they paddled across to the Waikare Inlet. When they arrived at the landing place, about half a mile from the village, two warriors, running up and down the beach with long whalebone clubs in their hands, brandished them defiantly in challenge. Nicholas's companions were all armed and leaped out of the canoe to pursue the challengers, but Te Morenga stayed behind with Nicholas and walked sedately with him to the village. It was a scene of chaos and confusion, with warriors rushing in all directions. As they came into the settlement, Nicholas caught sight of Tupi and two other chiefs, 'Guy' (Kae?) and 'Show' (Hau), sitting on a rooftop. They invited him to join them, so he climbed up onto the roof, which had a grandstand view of the proceedings. On the opposite bank of the Waikare River, Hinau was encamped in a large enclosure with about two hundred of his people. They were seated in groups according to their tribes, headed by their chiefs. Before them on the riverbank an old warrior was delivering an impassioned oration.

The old man was running up and down behind the paling on the opposite bank, shaking his head, brandishing his spear and speaking 'in a tone of violent resentment'. As soon as his speech was over, two speakers arose from Whiria's side of the river and answered in a conciliatory manner. First, Tupi (Tara's younger brother and his fighting leader) spoke briefly, followed by a quiet, measured speech from Te Morenga (the Taiamai chief, and Nicholas's companion on this occasion). After this another man stood on Hinau's side, who spoke 'in a masterly style of native eloquence'. He was a tall, impressive figure, wearing a long plain cloak and pacing up and down the riverbank with marked dignity. Tupi and Te Morenga each replied to this speech, then two more orators spoke from Whiria's side, followed by a third orator who spoke for Hinau. (This pattern of speech-making, where one visitor spoke, then two locals, followed by one visitor, two locals, two visitors, and one local, is different from contemporary rituals, where either all local orators speak first, then all visitors, with one local to conclude the ritual [known as paaeke]; or locals and visitors speak alternately [a pattern called utuutu].)

This final speech by Hinau's orator evidently concluded the matter. There had been various ceremonial exchanges before Nicholas arrived, and the groups had now decided against fighting. Tupi explained all this to Nicholas, saying that both Whiria and Hinau's people belonged to him, presumably because they both paid allegiance to Tara. According to his account, this was a domestic dispute amongst the rangatira of the southern alliance.

After the speeches were ended, Whiria, 'the gallant gay Lothario of this quarter', came to greet Nicholas and his companions. According to Nicholas:

> He appeared about five-and-thirty, of the middle size, but of a graceful figure, and remarkably well proportioned. He had a handsome mat, adorned with feathers, tied round his waist, leaving bare the upper part of his body, which was deeply besmeared with oil and red ochre; his hair was nicely tied up on the crown of his head, and a large comb, as white as ivory, made of the bone of some cetaceous animal, and curiously cut in filigree work, stuck in it. His cheeks were painted red, which giving fire and vivacity to his eyes, formed a curious and not unbecoming contrast to his black and bushy beard. His appearance altogether was such as

might attract the attention of the ladies of his country, who looked upon him as the very *acme* of elegant manliness.[80]

After this meeting Tupi took Nicholas across the river to meet Hinau, the aggrieved husband. Nicholas was carried across on a man's back (a courtesy frequently extended to Europeans), followed by others carrying quantities of potatoes, a gift from Whiria to Hinau. He greeted Hinau and his son 'Temoutee' (Timoti), who invited him to sit with them. Hinau, an old man of about seventy with a long snow-white beard, gazed fixedly at Nicholas but said nothing. Disconcerted, Nicholas soon left him and went to meet others of his party. The warriors gathered around, examining his boots and clothes and unbuttoning his waistcoat to look at his chest, to see whether he was a man or woman. When he showed them his watch, they were amazed, but the chiefs admonished Nicholas not to waste his time on such 'itee itee tungata' (unimportant people). Among the crowd he noticed a dwarfed hunchback with crippled legs, the only deformed person he saw in New Zealand.[81]

Whiria's gift of potatoes was carried into the centre of the enclosure. After various rituals, a rangatira from Whiria's side distributed the food and the cooks began to light the fires for dinner. While this was happening, Waari, the man who had seduced Ruatara's wife, came up to Nicholas, dressed in sailor's clothes, wearing a cartridge box and carrying a musket. He shook his hand and they talked for a while, until Te Morenga came up and gave Waari a loud and public scolding. During this altercation, a man called 'Hereco' took Nicholas aside and introduced himself, saying that he had been at Norfolk Island and Port Jackson and asking after Governor King and Captains Piper and Brabyn.

After this conversation, Nicholas returned across the river to Whiria's side for dinner. He joined the chief's group, but when he offered him some biscuit, Whiria refused, saying that he was in a state of tapu. As he ate his meal, Nicholas noted that the rangatira looked splendid in their dress costumes. Most wore dogskin cloaks, with the fur cut in white squares or long mottled stripes, while others wore feather cloaks, with long white feathers on their heads as decorations. One of Whiria's warriors was particularly impressive, a tall man wearing a feather kilt and a cloak around his shoulders covered by a piece of red India print, with a strip of the same fabric tied around his forehead. This man had painted his cheeks red and stuck long white feathers on his head. He carried a large iron pike, with a long patu stuck in his waistband, and 'paced about with an air of stately importance, holding up his head in as good style as the best disciplined grenadier, and regulating all his movements by a sort of military cadence'. When Nicholas shook this man's hand and congratulated him on his appearance, saying, 'Nuee nuee miti' (Nui nui maitai – Very fine), the warrior responded with amusement that Nicholas was 'nuee nuee miti Europee' (a very fine European – note that the word 'Pakeha' was not used here).[82]

After the feast Hinau divided his warriors into two groups for a performance of the haka. The first group, armed with long spears, charged down to the palisade shouting, followed by the second division. Then they all joined together, each section headed by their chief, and performed the haka, the chiefs prominent among them. After a second charge, three women appeared, who danced before the warriors. Whiria's men responded with a haka on their side of the river, followed by more speech-making. The old man who had opened the proceedings earlier stood on Hinau's side and gave another harangue, leaping and gesticulating violently. Whiria responded at some length, followed by two orators from among his people. Finally the injured party, Hinau, stood up and delivered a speech 'with much gentleness of manner'. After Whiria had replied in equally mild tones, his three wives concluded the orations. They spoke one by one with great animation, all of the warriors listening attentively. It is interesting to note the conventions in this part of the meeting. Chiefly women involved in the matter were free to speak, without fear of rebuke or retribution.

As soon as these ceremonies were over, Hinau's people began to disperse. Nicholas had admired the comb that Whiria was wearing on this occasion, and now offered him a billhook for it. Whiria hesitated because he was a tohunga as well as a chief, and his comb was intensely tapu. It sat on his head, the place where his ancestors alighted, and could not casually be handed over. At the same time, such a request could not easily be refused. It presented Whiria with a dilemma.

The next day the *Active* was crowded with visitors. Te Morenga's people brought twenty-four baskets of potatoes out to the ship, because he had decided to sail on the *Active* to Port Jackson. The day after, Nicholas met Whiria and gave him the bill hook, and on 7 February, Whiria came out to the ship, with three other chiefs as his attendants, to present the comb to Nicholas. He asked Nicholas to come into the cabin, where he told him to hold up the palms of his hands. Putting Nicholas's palms together and taking hold of one of his fingers with one hand, he dipped the other hand in a basin of water and sprinkled water over Nicholas's right hand, chanting a karakia. Next he spat on his fingers and ran them across Nicholas's palms, continuing his chanting. Finally he took a piece of dried fish, which he touched lightly to Nicholas's hands. He held this up to the mouths of each of the three chiefs in turn, and each bit a small piece from it. This part of the ritual was repeated three times in succession. Finally one of the chiefs gravely stepped to-wards Whiria and, taking the comb from his head, handed it silently to Nicholas. Nicholas received the comb and was about to put it in his sea chest when Whiria told him not to. He made him wrap it in a piece of paper and put it in a locker over his bed, telling him that it must stay there.

The ritual of giving the comb to Nicholas was dangerous for Whiria, for his hau might have been damaged in the process. By sprinkling Nicholas with blessed water, he was placing him under ancestral protection. By touching Nicholas's hands with his own spittle, he was preparing him to handle a taonga (treasure) imbued with ancestral presence. Tapu things were kept in high places, away from food and women. If the comb had been kept in Nicholas's sea chest, it might have been walked over by a commoner or a woman, or have cooked food passed across it. The presence of these noa (profane) entities could harm the tapu of the comb, damaging Whiria's mana.

That evening Nicholas had another brush with tapu. He and Marsden took Te Uri o Kanae ashore to cut down some small spars near the vessel. Kanae took an axe and, after making a platform against a tree, began to fell it. There was a burrow at the foot of one of these trees, which Kanae said was the home of some sort of lizard. Marsden asked him to poke with a stick in the hole, which he did with great reluctance. Lizards (probably a tuatara, in this case) were treated with caution, for they were held to have supernatural powers. Nicholas knew that there were no dangerous animals in New Zealand, although Ruatara had told him about a dangerous creature that lived in the interior, which carried off children and ate them. It sounded like an alligator from his description – no doubt a taniwha (supernatural monster).[83]

That same day, Marsden learned that the smith had no more iron to make tools at Rangihoua. Ruatara was refusing to hand over the iron in his keeping, saying that this was his own property. He also insisted that the site of the mission station at Rangihoua should be paid for, so that its owners would be satisfied. Ever since he had learned that Te Morenga was planning to accompany Marsden and Nicholas to Port Jackson on the *Active*, Ruatara had been showing signs of resentment and anxiety. He had hoped that by settling the missionaries at Rangihoua among his own people, he and his kinsmen could control European commerce in the Bay of Islands. They were clearing large areas to plant wheat on their lands, and he had exulted to Marsden, 'I have now introduced the cultivation of wheat in New Zealand. It will become a great country; for, in two years more, I shall be able to export wheat to Port Jackson, in exchange for hoes, axes, spades, and tea and sugar.' Ruatara had also begun laying out a town on a site with a spectacular view of the Bay, for his own people and to attract further European settlers. It was to have a church and European-style houses and streets. He must have been concerned that if Te Morenga was going to visit Port Jackson, he might forge a close relationship with Marsden and perhaps with the Governor, and gain equal access to the Europeans.

On 8 February, Nicholas went ashore to see if he could settle matters with Ruatara. Ruatara and Miki, however, had gone off inland to their cultivations. Kendall invited him to stay in his house while he was visiting Rangihoua. The next morning Nicholas wandered into the village, where the people crowded round him. An old man offered to exchange a large mat for his coat, and Nicholas agreed. He donned the cloak and the old man put on the coat, walking around with an air of 'pompous consequence'. As Nicholas walked about the village, he noticed a woman with terrible ulcers all over her skin, suffering from a venereal infection. Another woman approached him, saying that one of Kanae's close relations was dying. He asked if he could see the sick man, but was ordered to keep away, for '[the man] was under the taboo, and not to be approached till the Etua was pleased to deliver him from his sufferings, by putting an end to his existence'.

That afternoon Tui came to the mission to request more salt to cure fish for the *Active*'s cargo. Kawiti, a chief from the eastern side of the Bay who had previously visited Marsden at Parramatta, also arrived at the mission. Hall had given him an axe in exchange for a canoe, but Kawiti had failed to find one, so he brought a pig instead to honour the bargain. When Nicholas took him to shoot seagulls along the beach that afternoon, he proved to be an excellent marksman.

On 10 February, Nicholas heard that Kanae's relative had died and the tangi was to be held away at Te Puna. He went to the place, about a mile from Rangihoua, where crowds of people had gathered. The body was bundled up in its cloak with its knees drawn up and tied with a belt, and hung between two poles that had been used to bring it to the beach for the funeral. Te Pahi's widow and another woman stood beside the corpse, weeping bitterly. They told Nicholas not to come too close, because the body was 'taboo taboo'. One young man had lacerated his face in the haehae, and was also crying, but when Nicholas approached, he shook him by the hand and laughed in a hearty manner. Many of the mourners were talking and laughing, which Nicholas found disconcerting. The atmosphere was quite unlike the sombre constraint of an English funeral. After a feast the body was carried away between the two poles, with three or four people behind it, who forbade Nicholas to accompany them to the burial ground because of the tapu.

That afternoon Ruatara came back from his farm. He agreed to hand over the iron, providing that Kanae and Waari, the owners of the mission site, were properly paid for their land. He also told Nicholas that if he wished to use his people's canoes, payment would have to be made for each journey.[84]

Back at the *Active*, the work of loading the cargo was progressing well, as spars were brought out to the vessel. The ship was crowded with members of the southern hapuu, some of whom were living on board the vessel. There were very few thefts, although one day when Whiria's people were on board, two of Marsden's razors were taken. The chiefs were chagrined, saying that he had allowed too many commoners on board the ship, and that no chief would ever steal from him. They gave him a fine mat in compensation for the theft, and Whiria sat for the next two days and nights on the deck, refusing to eat in the cabin out of shame for his people's behaviour (whakamaa, a state of humiliation). When the chiefs told Marsden that they usually put thieves to death, he gave them a discourse on the British legal system:

> I explained to them the nature of a British Jury, told them that no man could be put to death in England unless twelve Gentlemen, examined into the case of a prisoner accused of any crime and if these twelve Gentlemen said he was not guilty King George had no power to put him to death; but if these twelve Gentlemen pronounced him guilty King George had the authority to pardon him if he wished to do so. They replied this law was very good, and one of them asked, what Governor we should send them, I replied that we had no intention of sending them any, but wished them to govern themselves. I mentioned some crimes, which we

punished with death and others, which we punished with banishment; and that punishment should be regulated at all times by the nature of the offence. I told them, if a man had two wives in England, tho he was a Gentleman, yet he would be banished from his Country.[85]

Most of the chiefs practised polygamy, and they found this last piece of information intriguing. A lively debate ensued, in which one rangatira argued that it was best to have only one wife, for if there were more they always quarrelled. Others protested that their wives made the best overseers, and that if they had no wives, they would have no gardens. When Marsden suggested that women should not be condemned to 'perpetual toil', according to him they responded that 'they [were] only claiming the right they are entitled to as superior beings, in making them, as an inferior species, work instead of themselves'.[86] When some women joined in the discussion, however, they had little sympathy for this point of view, declaring that a man should have only one wife. The chiefs were also interested to learn that there was only one king in England. Some thought that if there were fewer kings in New Zealand, they would 'have fewer wars and be more happy'. Marsden reported that in these discussions Maaui always acted as his interpreter. Through Maaui, he talked with the chiefs about religion, civil government, agriculture and commerce, and 'They always shewed an anxiety for information respecting the habits or customs of the people in other parts of the Globe'.[87]

When Marsden reproached the chiefs about cannibalism, saying that the practice was abhorred in other countries, they replied that 'it had always been customary to eat their enemies', and had no idea that it might be seen as improper behaviour. He reflected that 'these people consider the eating of their enemies in the same light as we do the hanging of a criminal (condemned by the laws of his country), and . . . the disgrace reflected on the surviving relations of the victim is nearly the same as that reflected on a family in Europe by the public execution of one of its members'.[88]

From these discussions, as well as his own observations, Marsden learned a good deal about authority and power in the Bay of Islands:

> From [what] I could learn there is no middle class of people in New Zealand, but they are all either Chiefs or, in a certain degree Slaves; at the same time the Chiefs neither give their commands indiscriminately to their people, like masters do to their servants in civil society, nor do their dependents feel themselves bound to obey them It is true they have the power over any of their people to put them to death for theft, but as the Chiefs have no means of remunerating the services of their dependants, there being no reciprocal contracts between them as Master and Servant, they cannot command them as a body to labour on their grounds &c. In time of War, and common danger they can then command them to put themselves under their authority, which they are compelled to do, and the inferior Chiefs are also obliged to attend with their people in the field of Battle. The Chiefs have their domestic Servants to dress their provisions and attend them in

their Canoes, cultivate their Lands, or any menial services, and these are wholly under their authority.[89]

When the *Active* returned to the timber district, Whiria had invited Marsden to go back to Waikare (a village he had previously visited when the ship was anchored off Kororaareka). Now that the ship was almost loaded, Marsden accepted his invitation. Whiria collected Marsden in his canoe and they set off, accompanied by another canoe-load of people. It was pouring with rain, and after paddling for about four miles, they came to a coastal village, where a chief waded out into the sea to invite them in for a meal. Marsden was wet and cold, and did not want to break the journey, so Whiria told him to give the chief a nail instead, and they carried on to the Waikare River. Once they entered the Waikare, they were paddling against the current, and the higher upriver they went, the faster the current ran, so that at length the men could no longer paddle against it. After dark they stopped and decided to walk the remaining mile or so to Whiria's place. They disembarked and Marsden followed his guide along a marshy trail, stumbling into holes full of water and mud, unable to see where they were going. Eventually a light appeared twinkling in the trees ahead, at the outskirts of Waikare village. The warrior went ahead to announce their arrival while Marsden followed the light to a house. He crept through its low door, looking for shelter, and women and children and several of Whiria's servants gathered around him. A small fire was flickering and smoking in the room, and the children (who were all naked) ran to get more firewood. When Whiria arrived shortly afterwards with two clean cloaks, Marsden stripped off his sodden clothes and dressed in local garments. Whiria asked him to accompany him to another house, but Marsden did not want to go out into the weather. Whiria left, saying that he could not bear the smoke, and left the women and children to entertain Marsden. A log, which ran about thirty feet along the length of the house, served as a communal pillow. People lay on either side of the log, with their heads resting on it. At about midnight Whiria returned, telling Marsden that one of his wives, who had just had a baby, was very ill, and asking him to pray over them in the morning.

Early the next morning Marsden got up to see the sick woman. He was horrified to find the invalid and her baby outside in the cold, miserable weather. A few reeds had been put up to shelter them from the rain, but the mother looked as though she was dying. Marsden prayed over her in English, and she smiled weakly, perhaps hoping that the Pakeha's atua could help her. She seemed hungry and feeble, but when Marsden gave her a biscuit, she refused, saying that she could only eat potatoes. Whiria took the biscuit away, telling Marsden if she ate it their god would be angry. He chanted over the biscuit, then placed it under her head, to heal the breach of tapu.

Marsden felt sorry for this woman, lamenting that babies, women after childbirth and sick people had to suffer because of tapu restrictions. They were left out in the open air and refused food and drink, when they needed all their strength to recover. Many of the young women seemed prematurely aged, which he thought was because of such exigencies. After Marsden left this pair and went into the village, he saw another infant lying naked on the ground with people gathered around it, gazing with concern. A rangatira told him that this was his child, and pointed to his wife, who was walking about. This baby, who was only two days old, seemed to be ill and suffering from exposure. Yet, as Marsden reflected, there was no want of feeling involved in these childbirth practices. Men treated their women and children with marked affection, and domestic life was harmonious: 'I saw no quarelling nor domestic broils while I was on the island. I never observed a mark of violence on any of them, nor did I see a woman struck.'[90]

Later that morning Whiria took Marsden to a small hut near his house, with a stage erected in it, carrying a round bundle. He said that this was the body of his father, who had been killed in battle. His corpse had been wrapped tightly and placed on the stage, where it would stay until 'the bones moulded away'. Marsden was surprised, because when a chief died, his body was usually hidden. It was put on a stage in a secluded place, guarded by a terrifying carving. It seemed odd that Whiria's father was kept so close to his son's house, in the middle of his village (although according to a later authority, dead bodies might sometimes be walled up in the verandah of the houses where they had lived[91]).

Like other chiefs whom the missionaries had met, Whiria was eager for them to settle in his territory. He asked Marsden to arrange a passage for him to Port Jackson, hoping to establish a closer contact with the Europeans. Marsden agreed to do this at a later date, but said that he must now return to the *Active*, which was about to leave Kawakawa. Before they left, though, Whiria insisted on fetching some pigs as a gift. He threw off his clothes and, taking a boy and a dog, swam supporting them across the river. He returned with three large pigs, which were loaded into Marsden's canoe. Whiria also put one of his sons on board, a boy about nine years old, asking Marsden to take him to Mr Kendall for instruction. Marsden replied that Kendall's house was not yet ready for pupils, but that he would send for the boy as soon as it was finished. In fact, Kendall had already begun to teach two boys, the sons of a commoner at Rangihoua, to read and write. The Rangihoua chiefs had reproached Marsden about this, saying that 'it was of no use to teach the children of the common people – that they had no lands or servants, and could never rise higher in rank than their parents, but that it would be very good to instruct the sons of chiefs'. Such people lacked mana, and valuable knowledge was wasted on them. It was plain that, like the Rangihoua rangatira, Whiria wanted his son to have every advantage. During his visits to the Europeans, Whiria had often brought the boy with him, carrying him on his back and looking after him with 'the gentlest attention'. As Nicholas had remarked, 'the tenderest parental affection . . . is remarkable among all classes, high and low in this country . . . [yet] I have never seen any father fonder of his child than the chief Wiveeah'.[92]

When Marsden returned to the ship, he learned that the *Jefferson* (the ship involved in the altercations at North Cape) had arrived at Kororaareka. There had been a disagreement with Tara, and a sailor from the ship had threatened to shoot the ariki. His people decided that if Tara was harmed, the *Jefferson* would be cut off and all her crew killed. The chiefs asked Marsden to go on shore and find out the cause of the quarrel. Marsden assured them that if Tara had been hurt, the guilty party would be arrested and taken to Port Jackson. He took the largest carpenter's axe on the ship and went to see Tara at Kororaareka.

At Kororaareka, Marsden found Tara at home. Giving the ariki the axe, he asked what had happened. Tara said that when he had boarded the *Jefferson*, one of the crew had pointed a pistol at his chest and threatened to shoot him. Marsden suggested that they should go to the ship to settle the matter. Tara, one of his brothers and another chief went with Marsden to the *Jefferson*, where he pointed out the man who had threatened him and gave an account of what had happened. The matter was peacefully settled and Marsden offered no further comment, except that 'it appeared to me that the Europeans were wholly to blame' for the dispute.[93]

Marsden and Tupi stayed on board the ship that night. The next morning there was another ugly incident. A young sailor had struck Tupi's wife several times with a sword, and when Tupi protested, jabbed at him several times with the weapon. Tupi was pointing to the masthead and telling his men to string up the sailor when Marsden intervened. He remonstrated with the young man, who swore at him and refused to apologise for his behaviour. Marsden ordered the officers to bring the sailor before Kendall, as resident magistrate. A hearing was held where the chiefs laid their complaints, so that these could be placed before Governor Macquarie at Port Jackson. Although the chiefs were contented with Marsden's handling of the matter, he was frustrated: 'Masters of vessels should be very particular and not to place swords in the hands of young thoughtless sailors when they are among savage people. The numbers of natives then on board and alongside the Jefferson could have taken her in one moment. The Natives should either be prohibited altogether, excepting the Chief of the District from coming on board, or care should be taken not to insult any of them, to whom this permission may be given.'[94]

As Marsden added, 'the New Zealand Chiefs are a warlike race, proud of their rank, and jealous of their dignity. They seemed to be men who never forget a favour or an injury. They retain a grateful remembrance of those Europeans who have been kind and faithful to them:– and a spirit of sovereign contempt and revenge to such as have abused their confidence or otherwise injured them.'[95] He was also annoyed to find the *Jefferson* swarming with local women. He had forbidden them to come on board the *Active*, and now they jeered at him, saying that the *Jefferson* was not tabooed and that on this ship 'there was no iriauta [haere atu – go away]'. When Marsden retorted that its crew were 'all very bad men', they smiled and replied that they were sure 'they would not be molested'.

On Sunday, 12 February, Kendall read the service at Rangihoua in Marsden's absence. Ruatara had attended, dressed in his European clothes, but the next day he began to run a high fever. When Nicholas visited him the following day, he thought Ruatara was suffering from a violent cold with 'inflammatory symptoms'. He went to the mission to fetch a dose of rhubarb, which he hoped might be helpful. Kendall and the other missionaries accompanied him back to the shed where Ruatara lay, surrounded by his head wife and other anxious relations. He was in a state of tapu, however, and visitors, food and drink were prohibited. After some anxious debate, and rituals of expiation, his family allowed the Europeans to enter the shed as a special favour. They may have hoped that if Ruatara's illness was European in origin, his European friends could help him. Despite their attentions, however, over the next few days the rangatira's condition rapidly worsened.

On 16 February, Nicholas tried to visit Ruatara again, but his relatives told him that the sick man was sleeping. Shortly afterwards a whaleboat pulled into the beach, carrying Mr Jones, the first mate of the *Jefferson*, to Rangihoua. He knew Ruatara from a previous visit to the Bay of Islands and was sorry to hear of his illness. Nicholas, Kendall and Jones went to pay their respects to the chief, finding him wrapped up in European blankets and sweating profusely. Ruatara remembered Jones well and promised to visit his ship as soon as he had recovered.

That afternoon Nicholas and Kendall accompanied Jones to the *Jefferson* and slept overnight on the vessel. As they sat down to breakfast the next morning, Tupi came to join them but was told that he would have to eat later. He went back to shore in a fury, and soon afterwards the sailors on land were refused permission to cut firewood. Nicholas and Jones went to Kororaareka to try to smooth things over, but Tupi and Tara made further loud complaints against the crew of the *Jefferson*. According to Tara, they had already taken three loads of wood without payment. When Nicholas asked Tara to come back to the ship, he refused, saying that after being threatened with a pistol on the *Jefferson* he had decided to have no further dealings with the vessel. Jones expressed sympathy for Tara, telling Nicholas that during a previous visit to the Bay with the *King George*, his captain and that of the *Jefferson* had got drunk every evening and entertained themselves by tormenting local people. Women were harassed, and if their husbands protested, they were threatened and sent off the vessel, and cannons were fired at their settlements. Tara and his wife had been singled out for particularly abusive treatment. Jones assured both Kendall and Nicholas that he had nothing to do with such abuses, and Nicholas believed him, saying, 'I am fully persuaded that such barbarous practices were abhorrent to his disposition.'[96]

When Kendall and Nicholas returned to Rangihoua on 17 February, they found Ruatara exhausted and visibly weakened. The next day his family forbade them to go near his shed. They had concluded that by allowing the missionaries to visit Ruatara with medicine and food, they had broken the tapu and put his life in danger. According to Nicholas:

> [They asserted] that the Etua would not yet have fixed himself in the stomach of the chief, had they not in their unhallowed temerity suffered us to see him while he was tabooed against such visitors. I remonstrated with them in urgent terms,

and thought to prevail on them to admit me; but it was of no use, they all cried out with one voice, 'nuee nuee taboo taboo', and forbidding me to approach the shed, they would, as I believe, have killed me on the spot, had I presumed to disobey.[97]

Ruatara's kinsmen told Kendall that on the night after the missionaries' visit, a shooting star had streaked across the sky over Rangihoua.[98] The next day Ruatara had become delirious and the tohunga told his family that an atua in the form of a lizard had entered his body, where it was eating his hau and his vital organs.[99] The missionaries considered this explanation a gross error of superstition. They were horrified that Ruatara was forbidden food and drink, which they thought would weaken his resistance to the illness. Kendall hurried to the *Active* to tell Marsden that Ruatara was seriously ill, and Marsden soon came back to Rangihoua.

On 19 February, Marsden attempted to visit Ruatara. The people forbade him to go into the shed, but after 'some serious expostulation' they finally relented and let him take the chief food and medicines. Marsden found Ruatara running a high fever, suffering from acute bowel pains and evidently dying. He was appalled:

> At the very time of these arrangements [for the mission] being made, Duaterra was laid on his dying bed. I could not but look on him with wonder and astonishment, as he lay languishing under his affliction, and scarcely bring myself to believe that the Divine goodness would remove from the earth a man whose life was of such infinite importance to his country, which was just emerging from barbarism, gross darkness, and Superstition. No doubt he had done his work, and finished his appointed course, though I had fondly imagined that he had only begun his race.[100]

When he asked Ruatara if he had had anything to eat and drink, the chief replied that he had only had potatoes and water. Marsden said that he could have whatever he wanted, and ordered a supply of tea, sugar, rice and wine to be brought to his enclosure. He gave him a few sips of wine and water, some rice and a little tea, which Ruatara drank gratefully. He told Marsden that as soon as he was better they would finish their work together.

As soon as Marsden returned to the *Active*, however, the tapu was reinstated. Nicholas was turned away from the enclosure on two successive days, for fear of the wrath of the atua. On 21 January, Mrs King gave birth to a fine baby boy. The local people were amazed by her grimaces and groans, which they mimicked mercilessly. Nicholas reproached one man who was imitating her writhings for being so heartless, but he was not in the least repentent:

> He descanted in a strain of arch ridicule on the extreme timidity of our countrywomen in this situation, compared to the hardy resolution of the New Zealand ladies. The latter, he said, never experienced any inconvenience from child-birth; but sitting down in the open air, surrounded by a concourse of both sexes, were delivered without uttering a single groan, while the spectators, who stood carefully watching the process, shouted out tarnee! tarnee! [boy, boy!], as soon as nature had executed her office; when the mother, after cutting the umbilical cord, rose up as if no such occurrence had taken place, and resumed her

ordinary occupations. But, said he, 'Europee woman be no like New Zealand woman; she cry out, Measser King! Measser King! for ittee ittee tarnee:' meaning, that his countrywomen would have more spirit than to use such an exclamation in so trifling an affair as the delivery of a little infant.[101]

On 22 February, Captain Barnes of the *Jefferson* brought two runaway convicts to Marsden (in his role as magistrate). Meanwhile, Nicholas had gone to Rangihoua, where he found Waari, Kanae's brother, cutting his wife's hair with flakes of obsidian. He had cut her hair very short in front but left the back untouched. When he finished, he carefully collected all the hair (which was sometimes called 'hau', since it embodied the life force) and took it outside the town for disposal. He explained to Nicholas that if the hair was left in the settlement, the atua would be angry and kill the person from whose head it had been taken. When Nicholas attempted to take one of the flakes he had used, he told him not to touch it, and that if he did, the atua of New Zealand would kill him. When Nicholas began to laugh and to ridicule the idea of the tapu, Waari replied by ridiculing Marsden's 'crackee crackee' (karakia). At the same time, though, he asked Nicholas to pray over his wife, perhaps hoping that this might serve as a new kind of spiritual protection.

By 22 February, the *Active*'s cargo was complete and Marsden brought the brig back to Rangihoua. When he tried to visit Ruatara the next morning, however, the people again refused to allow him into the enclosure. They were obdurate, despite his arguments and protests. Marsden knew he would shortly be leaving the Bay, and told the people that if they persisted in their refusal, he would order the *Active*'s cannons to be turned on the town and 'blow it about their ears'. They begged him to understand the power of their atua and the harm that they would suffer, but Marsden would not listen. Finally, Kanae, Ruatara's heir, who had spent a good deal of time with the Europeans during their visit, intervened:

> [He] spoke in a bold strain of sarcastic eloquence, not only against the impropriety of refusing free access to Duaterra, but against the *taboo* itself, which, as he expressed it, was 'no good in New Zealand, but only henerecka;' and he told them openly, that it ought not ever again to be feared or regarded. The other natives looked upon Gunnah as a blasphemous sceptic for making this declaration, yet his consequence as a rungateeda [rangatira] had some weight with them; but Mr Marsden's threat was more efficacious than all, and their fearful scruples being at length obliged to yield to it, they found themselves under the necessity of consenting to his ingress.[102]

Ruatara, although he was in considerable pain, seemed glad to see Marsden on this occasion. Some days earlier, when the tohunga had tried to have him carried to an island where his people were customarily buried, he had picked up the pair of pistols the Europeans had lent him and threatened to shoot anyone who laid hands on him.[103] He asked Marsden for some wine, and instructed his people to give the Europeans the iron he had been holding. They refused, on the grounds that it was tapu. When Kendall tried to take away the decanter in which the wine had been brought, Ruatara begged him to leave it, saying that if it were taken away, the atua would kill him. Kendall gave him some rice and he ate a little, but when the rice was offered to Miki, his head wife, and to the tohunga, they refused, saying that they were also tapu.

As Ruatara's illness worsened, he began to give away his belongings. When the Europeans visited him on 24 February, they found him racked with convulsions. Miki, hollow-eyed with sorrow and exhaustion, held him in her arms. Knowing that Marsden and Nicholas were about to leave on the *Active*, Ruatara instructed his wives to present Marsden with five fine mats, and Nicholas with three mats and a pig. The next day Marsden visited him again and found him still breathing but in great distress. He hurried out of the enclosure, thinking that Ruatara might die any moment. Various items that the Europeans had given to Ruatara were now handed back, including the pair of pistols he had had beside him in the enclosure. After leaving the enclosure, Nicholas went down to the beach and fired off one of these pistols as a signal to the *Active*'s captain to send off the boat. With a loud report, the powder in the pistol exploded. The weapon flew up out of his hand and struck his forehead, knocking him unconscious. Far from expressing any sympathy, the local people 'only upbraided me with my impiety for meddling with a pistol that was tabooed, and considered me as justly punished by the indignant wrath of the Etua'.[104] Although Nicholas had flouted tapu frequently, he could see its uses. He remarked:

> Though [the word *taboo*] subjects them . . . to many absurd and painful restrictions, it serves them in the absence of laws, as the only security for the protection of persons and property, giving them an awful sacredness which no one dares to violate . . . The New Zealanders make no idols, nor have they any external form of worship; their conceptions of a supreme power being shewn only in the veneration they have for the above-mentioned superstition, and in the single word *taboo* all their religion and morality may be said to consist.[105]

That afternoon Marsden concluded the exchanges for the transfer of the mission site with Te Uri o Kanae, presenting him with twelve axes and a parchment deed that had been drawn up at Port Jackson. Hongi took the parchment and carefully drew a representation of Kanae's moko on it, and Kanae added his mark to ratify the agreement. Kendall and Nicholas witnessed the deed for the settlers, and another local man witnessed it for the Rangihoua people, drawing the moko of one of his cheeks on the parchment. Kanae and Waari declared the area of the mission (about two hundred acres) now tapu to all but the white people. They announced that it could only be entered with the missionaries' permission. Marsden described this transaction as a purchase, but it was rather a ritual transfer of mana over the land to the Europeans. By the agreement of the rangatira, as represented by the marks on their faces, the place was placed under the mana of the Europeans' gods and ancestors. This made it tapu to others, unless they were given permission to enter. The 'deed of purchase', the first to be signed in New Zealand, read as follows:

Know all men to whom these presents shall come, That I, Ahoodee O Gunna, King of Rangee Hoo, in the Island of New Zealand, have, in consideration of Twelve Axes to me in hand now paid and delivered by the Rev. Samuel Marsden, of Parramatta, in the territory of New South Wales, given, granted, bargained and sold; and by this present instrument do give, grant, bargain, and sell unto the Committee of the Church Missionary Society for Africa and the East, instituted in London, in the kingdom of Great Britain, and to their heirs and successors, all that piece and parcel of land situate in the district of Hoshee, in the Island of New Zealand, bounded on the south side by the bay of Tippoona and the town of Ranghee Hoo, on the north side by a creek of fresh water, and on the west by a public road into the interior; together with all the rights, members, privileges, and appurtenances thereunto belonging; To have and to hold, to the aforesaid Committee of the Church Missionary Society for Africa and the East, instituted in London, in the kingdom of Great Britain, their heirs, successors, and assigns, for ever, clear and freed from all taxes, charges, impositions, and contributions whatsoever, as and for their own absolute and proper estate for ever:

In testimony whereof, I have, to these presents thus done and given, set my hand, at Hoshee, in the Island of New Zealand, this twenty-fourth day of February, in the year of Christ one thousand eight hundred and fifteen.

THOS. KENDALL.
J. L. NICHOLAS.[106]

This document was in English, which few of the local people understood. It is not known how the transaction had been explained and understood in Maori. The legal terms in the document, which denoted European notions about land as property and its transfer, had no close equivalents in Maori. Rangihoua was in a country run by Maori, not in England or in Port Jackson. The expectation that European law and ideas about property could be instated there by simply writing on a piece of paper was, in its own way, breathtaking.

Having concluded this transaction, Marsden baptised Mrs King's baby while local people watched with astonishment. Marsden and Nicholas, with a number of chiefs and their attendants who were making the voyage to Port Jackson, now boarded the *Active*. After poignant scenes of farewell, they sailed from the Bay for Port Jackson, leaving Ruatara on his deathbed.[107]

Thomas Kendall and the other missionaries who had been left behind at Rangihoua continued to visit Ruatara daily. On one of these occasions, Kendall brought him rice water in a decanter. When he went to take away the vessel to refill it, Ruatara said:

'You are very unkind Mr Kendall, if the Decanter is taken away Atua will kill me this very day.' I told him the Atua must be very cruel, and reminded him of the God whom we worshipped, who was infinitely kind; and as he had heard, had given his own Son who had suffered, bled and died for the Sin of Man, in order that man might live and die happy. He made no reply to my observation.[108]

Ruatara's friends probably interpreted these gifts of food and drink from the missionaries as oo matenga, or food for the death journey. Before dying, a person might ask for the flesh of kurii (dog), or kiore (rat) or tangata (human), or earthworms of a special sweet kind, or water from a particular stream, to sustain them on the pathway to Te Rerenga Wairua (the leaping place of spirits near the North Cape).[109] A man who had lived with Europeans for so many years might well ask for wine and rice water. Whether foreign or not, though, such foods were in the shade of the Poo, and so were intensely tapu.

On 2 March 1815, Ruatara was carried on a litter to a hill about eight miles away from Rangihoua, where he had planned to build his town. The dying man gave his cow and calf to the senior woman of his kin group, and his military uniform to his baby son, asking that he should be sent to Sydney when he was old enough, to be brought up at the Orphan School among Europeans. Early the next morning he died. His body was trussed in a sitting position and wrapped up in his garments. His head was decorated with a coronet of feathers and his face covered with a small piece of English scarlet cloth. His head wife sat beside him to the right, weeping bitterly and cutting herself, while his sister and other female relatives sat beside him to his left. Kaingaroa and Hongi, his senior relatives, arrived soon afterwards, and Hongi wept as he lamented over his kinsman, grasping a blade of green flax in one hand and occasionally taking hold of Ruatara's hair, a ritual that assisted his hau to leave his body.[110]

The next day, while the mourning ceremonies were still going on, Ruatara's head wife, an adept weaver, canoe-paddler and weapon-handler, left the enclosure and hanged herself. Her mother wept for her daughter, but her father and brothers seemed glad that she had gone to join her husband. Their bodies were lain together on a stage, with their tapu possessions around them. The chiefs who participated in the rituals were tapu'd for days, and had to be fed by others. Ruatara's body was now termed 'Atua'; as Kendall remarked, 'Whenever we come near a piece of Taboo'd ground and ask the reason why it is taboo'd; if a person has been buried in it, we always receive for an Answer, "Atua lies there".' He was told that one eye each of Ruatara and his wife had become living spirits on earth, and their other eyes had become stars in the heavens.[111]

Conclusion

TAPU AND RELIGION

> [A human being] is an existence carving itself out in space, shattering in chaos,
> exploding in pandemonium, netting itself, a scarcely breathing animal, in the webs
> of death.
>
> — Michel Foucault, in Introduction to *Le Rêve et L'Existence*

Death provokes thought about the meaning of life. Life is understood in its absence. As breath ceases, and a person no longer moves, something is seen to have departed. For Maori, Ruatara's hau had returned to its source; for the missionaries, his soul had left his body. The struggles over his death reflected a life that had been lived at the edges of cross-cultural encounter.

The arrival of Ruatara and Hongi with Marsden and his missionaries at the Bay of Islands was a cosmological event for local people. A number of Maori leaders had visited Port Jackson and Norfolk Island, and experienced European life in those harsh Antipodean 'thief colonies'. They knew that Europeans had atua of their own, with powers that could harm Maori. The burning of the ship *Boyd*, for instance, had been partly provoked by an epidemic that broke out after the captain of a European ship had dropped his watch, which local people thought was an atua, into the waters of their harbour.[1] Europeans and their things alike — ships, guns, iron, animals, plants and other paraphernalia, including watches — were imbued with supernatural power for Maori. The landing of the missionaries focused that power at Rangihoua, with their rituals and taonga (treasured items), for better or for worse.

When Ruatara complained of a 'lack of breath [hau]' and fell ill, the scene was set for a cosmological collision. Competing philosophies swirled around his sickbed. Ideas of tapu and Christianity, hau and the immortal soul, ora and life, mate and death battled it out over his sweating, increasingly emaciated body. The signs of approaching death provoked a debate over the meaning of life, which the missionaries had come in fact to initiate with Maori. There were arguments over how best to handle his affliction, which each side was determined to win. On one side of this ontological tug of war were the tohunga, or priests, who were concerned about Ruatara's hau. On the other were Marsden and his missionaries, who were trying to save his soul, so that he could go to heaven. They wanted to bring him into the light of God, to free him from the Prince of Darkness.

It is possible that a philosophy based on balanced exchange was a source of vulnerability for Ruatara, and other Maori. Relational logic worked well with people who shared in its assumptions. When other people assumed the superiority of their own forms of life, however, one could be faced with one-way relationships and constant failures of reciprocity. Failure to receive as well as to give was hau whitia in Maori – hau turned away; and this in its turn engendered hauhau aitu – harm to the hau – leading to illness and sometimes to dying.

In Maori accounts, as we have seen, the world was ordered by networks of kinship and alliance. The old cosmological chants recounted the emergence of the world in a language of whakapapa, or genealogical engagement. In everyday life, these links emerged as nets of relationship between people and places, animated by reciprocal exchanges. The dynamics of these exchanges were described in relational terms such as mana and tapu, and in everyday interactions. Maori diplomacy often converted former enemies (hoariri) into friends (hoa), by exchanges of gifts, strategic marriages and mutual assistance, weaving the strands of life together. Underlying all this was utu, the principle of balanced return. Within this philosophy, Ruatara's self was understood as a named set of links in the network of exchange relations. His death was a rupture in this net, to be repaired by ritual action.

In Europe, by way of contrast, reason was becoming a dominant value. Once mind was split from matter, thinking was understood as the mind's 'I' (or cogito) at work, reflecting on a detached reality. People were divided from each other and increasingly understood as autonomous beings. Thinkers and thought were separated from 'the world', understood as 'object' or 'subject matter'. Knowledge became the divided product of this fragmented labour. The disciplines carved up the world in an imperium of reflection.[2] As Foucault has pointed out, early modern thinkers used analytical grids to order people and places – in maps, blocks of land, countries, borders, bureaucracies based on filing systems, measurement and quantification, taxonomic hierarchies, censuses and cultures,[3] leading to forms of life based on surveillance and domination.[4] This was equally true of early modern science, 'rational administration', missionary enterprise and imperialism (which may be just one type of evangelism). In such systems, exchange was almost always unequal. Most Europeans, for instance, saw themselves as having everything to offer, and Maori as having nothing to teach them. Within this system of thought, the missionaries understood Ruatara as an individual with a soul to be 'saved', in a population of unimproved heathens. His death was seen as a moment of choice between heaven and hell, between grace and eternal torment.

TE PAE: THINKING FROM BETWEEN

> The rituals of meeting . . . the act of embrace, the greeting made in tears, the
> exchange of presents . . . In short, this represents an intermingling. Lives are
> mingled together, and this is how, among persons and things so intermingled,
> each emerges from their own sphere and mixes together.
>
> — Marcel Mauss, *The Gift*

On the face of it, Maori and European philosophies at the time of Ruatara's death
were so different that they might have been incommensurable. In practice, though,
from the very first, Maori and Europeans negotiated working understandings with
one another. From the earliest years of contact, Maori such as Ruatara, and some
Europeans crossed into each other's communities, learning local languages and
habits. Some of these contacts generated hybrid ways of living – on the whaling
ships, for example, where white, black and native Americans, Indians, Europeans,
Cape Verde Islanders and Pacific Islanders lived and worked in mixed shipboard
communities. Ruatara himself was planning a shore-based community at Rangihoua
with European-style houses and streets, and fields of European crops raised for
export, worked by Maori and artisan missionaries. The idea of the hau suggests
that 'rough intelligibility' and cultural hybridity occur because the members of
different societies have fundamental qualities in common.

According to the learned men of the waananga (schools of learning), hau
animated all kinds of being. People, animals, plants, mountains, rivers and rocks
had hau, or vitality, and ancestral power, or tapu. This power came to rest within
plants, animals or people in the mauri, its abiding place. The mauri protected the
hau, or breath of life, just as the wairua or immaterial being protected its physical
basis, the body (tinana). In fact, all things in the world of light had a tinana, a
wairua, a mauri and a hau, for in Maori cosmological theory the same fundamental forces gave form and energy to all matter.

People could communicate with the world by means of tinana, hau and wairua.
They received information through the senses: 'Ka kite te kanohi, ka rongo te
taringa, maatau ana ki te ngaakau' (The eyes see, the ears hear, the mind-heart
understands). At the same time, hau was communicated through exchanges of
breath (in the hongi, or pressing of noses in greeting), names, clothing or prized
weapons; while wairua could be reached through dreams, rituals or the visions of
matakite ('eyes that can see' – prophets or seers). Encounters with new kinds of
people, plants and animals happened on all of these dimensions. The senses were
the first point of engagement. New foods could be tasted, as well as seen, smelt
and touched. New people could be fingered, their skin stroked or sucked. New
kinds of clothing could be picked up and worn. New animals could be handled
and their habits observed. New tools could be tried and adapted. New sexual
games could be attempted and new diseases suffered. Red paint could be splashed
on the skin, and mirrors could reflect mirth or amazement. All of this could

happen without much language being used, in snatches of experience.

On both sides of such encounters, people tried to understand who they were meeting. Some individuals, more intrepid than others, pushed at the boundaries – sleeping on shore (in the case of some Europeans) or on ships (in the case of some Maori), and making their way into each other's communities. When this happened over any length of time, communication became less superficial. The 'mind-heart' (or ngaakau) came into play, allowing closer relationships to develop. People began to learn each other's languages, haltingly at first, and then with some fluency. With language came ideas, ways of crafting the world, and new possibilities for understanding. Hau was being intermingled. It was not so much people or even cultures that met in this way, but whole life worlds, with their ancestral powers, plants, animals and diseases.

In the Bay of Islands by 1815, the ancient world (Ao Tawhito) was spinning into a new configuration. Some rangatira were sporting muskets and pistols, as well as carved taiaha and greenstone patu. They wore uniforms for European rituals, and dogskin or feather cloaks for ceremonial kinship occasions. Children were given European beads for their ears, and dollar coins from the wreck of the *Boyd* as neck ornaments. A chief's wife wore a red petticoat and skirt at her husband's request, although her female friends mocked her unmercifully. In the gardens, potatoes were taking over as the staple crop (although kuumara, taro, yams and gourds were still being grown). Peas, corn, turnips, parsnips, carrots, onions and cereals were cultivated. Orange and peach trees were planted, and cabbages grew wild in the valleys. Some cattle, horses, goats and chickens had been introduced, while roaming pigs were becoming a menace. Fences had to be built around cultivations to keep these creatures out. Some iron tools – hoes, adzes, axes, chisels and scissors – were being used, and sharpened. Iron bars were shaped into swords or patu. Metal fish-hooks were acquired, and mirrors. Some travellers had learned to eat with knives and forks, to drink tea and to enjoy alcohol (which most local people still detested). A steel mill had been brought to the Bay, and wheat had been ground into flour. Bread had been cooked in a frypan.

In some hilltop paa, flagpoles were erected and flags flown as a sign of mana. Other paa, such as Okuratope, had been modified for musket fighting. Muskets and pistols were used in ceremonies of greeting, as well as in battle. On Te Pahi's island, a prefabricated house had been built (and later burnt down by the whalers). Ruatara had laid out a European-style town, with streets and houses. Many young men had travelled on European ships, around the New Zealand coastline, to Norfolk Island and Port Jackson, across the Pacific and to more remote destinations – India, South-East Asia, North and South America, and Europe. Some of these were mookai (war captives), eager to escape the constraints of their own society. Others were rangatira, or their sons, exploring European places. They learned a kind of pidgin (including curses and swear words) or, in a few cases, quite fluent English. They brought new practices back home; for instance, flogging and hanging for theft and adultery. They also brought back new carpentry, agricultural and seafaring techniques, as well as knowledge of shoe- and nail-making. Waiata (chants) had been composed about their adventures. Hongi Hika carved a self-portrait in wood with iron tools, made a cartridge box and re-stocked a musket. Like several of his companions, he learned how to write, or at least to copy out letters and documents. Tuki and Korokoro both drew maps for curious Europeans. People in the Bay had seen books, letters and proclamations, and religious tracts distributed by Kendall. They had handled compasses and watches, telescopes and spectacles. Tara had acquired a rowboat and a certificate of good character. At the same time, many rangatira, including Tara and his arch-enemy Te Pahi, had experienced bitter humiliations at the hands of Europeans.

As increasing numbers of Europeans, and several blacks, Pacific Islanders and Indians arrived at the Bay, local politics became increasingly volatile. Rangatira vied with each other to control useful Europeans, or other strangers, and access to their goods. In the process, they maligned and conspired against their rivals. As labour was diverted to felling and hauling timber for spars, or raising crops to trade with the whalers and sealers, the health of many local people suffered. They had infectious diseases to contend with for the first time, including venereal infections and consumption. Other, unidentified epidemic diseases had wreaked havoc in Whangaroa as well as the Bay of Islands, contributing to the *Boyd* killings. Tapu began to be mocked by young iconoclasts, and the status of chiefly women came into question. As tapu were broken, rangatira were flogged or cursed, and old habits like cannibalism and polygamy were derided, it seemed the new world was attacking the hau of the old. As one chief after another fell ill and died, this theory began to seem certain.

According to waananga teachings, the cosmic process was represented by the double spiral, in carving and moko, swirling into and out of a primal centre. Mana, the power of the gods, could work for good or for evil. People, and their gods, struggled for mana and survival. Each chevron etched into the spiral represented a key link in the unfolding of the cosmos. This image evoked the growth of fern fronds, the twining tendrils of gourd plants (painted in kowhaiwhai patterns on the rafters of meeting houses), and the spinning power of whirlpools (an image of death) and whirlwinds (which carried Taane to the highest layer of the universe to find knowledge for humankind), depicting life as a dynamic force, sometimes creative and sometimes destructive. As Patu Hohepa has put it: 'Time is a moving continuum if seen through Maori language, with ego being a particle whose own volition and direction is not bound to time. Time swirls like koru patterns, three-dimensional spirals.'[5] As it spins, the world continues to unfold, bringing new kinds of being together. New experience is grasped, but at the same time, people try to control it in the interests of their kinsfolk. This leads to entanglement and struggle, often across cultural boundaries.

In Western thinking, though, the notions of irreducible values, separate, maybe incommensurable cultures, and bounded, autonomous selves, make it hard to understand how such entanglements happen. It is difficult to think about cross-cultural exchanges, their paradoxes and ironies, within an Enlightenment model. The bounded, divided self projects human life as similarly bounded and divided. Separated 'cultures' and autonomous 'selves', spirit split from mind and the senses, and religion split from science and the arts are the products of this mirroring process. In this style of reflection, the processes and patterns of inter-connection are elusive (in the natural sciences as well as the humanities, if David Bohm is to be believed[6]). If 'cultures' are taken to be radically divided, questions of 'authenticity' arise and cross-cultural hybridity comes to seem an anomaly. If 'selves' and 'others' are radically set apart, mutual understanding may come to seem an illusion. If thinking is separated from the senses, wisdom will ever be wanting.

The great philosophical questions – What is it to be human? What do we have in common as human beings, and what divides us? – have lost none of their piquancy in a post-colonial order. What is needed, perhaps, are practical and ethical attitudes that give up the West's attempt to control the Rest; that seek answers to these questions (which are not just Western questions) in ways that allow other knowledges to speak.

On this basis, the practice of utu, or balanced exchange, and the idea of the hau may offer something to contemporary social theorists. Marcel Mauss certainly thought so, and I agree. The 'wind of life' still blows through the world, with its memories of cosmic connection. According to this philosophy, one form of life studying all others is hau whitia, fundamentally out of kilter. Human under-standing (as opposed to human control) requires reciprocal exchange, for all its hazards – your wisdom for mine (waananga atu, waananga mai), as we cross our thoughts together (whakawhitiwhiti whakaaro). In New Zealand, at least, a collaboration between Maori and Western knowledges seems possible. It may lead, eventually, to studies of cross-cultural encounters that do justice to the ancestors on both sides, and the potent, perilous pae – the edge between them.

As Eruera Stirling, eminent tribal scholar and my long-time mentor, once advised:

> E tamariki ma – study your whakapapa, and learn to trace your descent lines to all your ancestors, so you can join yourselves together. Do not use these treasures to raise yourselves above others – ko mea, ko mea, ko 'hau! But if you are chal-lenged, or if somebody throws words at you on the marae, then it is proper to stand up and reply. The old people said to us, be humble; work amongst the people and they will learn to praise you. That was the wisdom of our ancestors, brought from the ancient houses of learning in Hawaiki. The old men told us, study your descent lines, as numerous as the hairs upon your head. When you have gathered them together as a treasure for your mind, you may wear the three plumes, 'te iho makawerau', 'te pareraukura' and 'te raukura' on your head. The men of learning said, understand the learning of your ancestors, so you can talk in the gatherings of the people. Hold fast to the knowledge of your kinship, and unite in the knot of humankind.

Let me end these reflections with his favourite chant, a karakia of binding:

Whakarongo! Whakarongo! Whakarongo!	Listen! Listen! Listen!
Ki te tangi a te manu e karanga nei	To the cry of the bird calling
Tui, tui, tuituiaa!	Bind, join, be one!
Tuia i runga, tuia i raro,	Bind above, bind below
Tuia i roto, tuia i waho,	Bind within, bind without
Tuia i te here tangata	Tie the knot of humankind
Ka rongo te poo, ka rongo te poo	The night hears, the night hears
Tuia i te kaawai tangata i heke mai	Bind the lines of people coming down
I Hawaiki nui, I Hawaiki roa,	From great Hawaiki, from long Hawaiki
I Hawaiki paamamao	From Hawaiki far away
I hono ki te wairua, ki te whai ao	Bind to the spirit, to the daylight
Ki te Ao Maarama!	To the World of Light!

Postscript

By 1815, Maori in many parts of Aotearoa had met with Europeans. In Totara-nui (Queen Charlotte Sound), Tamatea (Dusky Sound), Hauraki (Thames) and the Bay of Islands, European ships had been arriving since 1769–70. After the killings at Grass Cove in 1773, though, Europeans shied away from Totara-nui. At Tamatea, after the contacts with Cook's men in the same year, local Maori avoided the Europeans. In both Hauraki and the Bay of Islands, on the other hand, the response to European arrivals was outgoing. Perhaps because the population of both districts was wealthy and large, their rangatira remained confident and assertive. They challenged the visitors, engaged in barter and other exchanges with them, and recruited their leaders as allies. In the early years, Europeans who transgressed local rules and restrictions were punished by mock attacks, ridicule and the confiscation of their goods by muru, and sometimes by killing and cannibalism.

In these districts, the European vessels were a travelling sideshow, a diversion from intertribal exchanges. In Hauraki, for instance, the ariki Te Haupa seemed preoccupied with local diplomatic and military adventures. At the Bay of Islands, the ariki Kaingaroa similarly spent little time with visiting Europeans. Just because so much of our understanding of early Maori life comes from European arrivals, it does not mean that all local people regarded these encounters as momentous. More likely they seemed curious and challenging, but on the edge of kin-group interests. Perhaps for this reason, Maori accounts of early encounters with Europeans are few and fragmentary. Usually they were collected by later Europeans (notably John White and William Colenso, from the 1830s) who were curious about Maori memories of Maori–European encounters.

If some of the most distinguished leaders of Maori communities invested little effort in their European visitors, though, others seized the opportunity to engage with them. Te Wahanga in Totara-nui, after visiting Cook on board the *Resolution* in 1773, collected greenstone tools to exchange with his men during Cook's next visit to the Sound. His young relatives Te Weherua and Koa later accompanied Cook and Mai on an epic voyage through Polynesia. At Hauraki, Te Haupa invited Thomas Taylor and his companions ashore, and encouraged his people to exact iron axes and other European items from visiting vessels in exchange for timber. These were no doubt used in the military campaigns that Te Haupa was leading against Tai Raawhiti (East Coast) and other kin groups. In the north, the most lasting relationships with Europeans were established. First,

515

Tuki and Huru were taken to Norfolk Island, where they forged a friendship with Philip Gidley King, the Lieutenant-Governor of that island. Both men were of chiefly descent, and they lived for six months in Government House on Norfolk with King, his wife and family. Subsequently, Te Pahi and his sons visited King at Port Jackson and stayed at Government House in Sydney. Thereafter, northern leaders regarded Europeans much as they did members of their own society, with aristocratic discrimination. Te Pahi, for example, dismissed William Stewart, the captain of the *Venus*, as a mookai, or man without mana, for his ill-mannered behaviour. He despised some of the Port Jackson colonists and was contemptuous of local Aboriginals. Like Tuki and Huru, he saw the convicts as taurekareka, or 'slaves' (that is, war captives). In this colonial context, chiefly Maori took it for granted that they were the equals of European leaders.

Governor King, in particular, fostered this expectation. In his months spent with Tuki and Huru, and later Te Pahi and his sons, he was impressed by their character and conduct. Close personal contact made it difficult for him to uphold habitual stereotypes about tattooed 'savages' and 'cannibals'. After King, successive governors upheld, at least rhetorically, the principle of just treatment for Maori and other Pacific Islanders. Their proclamations deserve further study, as foreshadowing the Treaty of Waitangi and later constitutional arrangements. It cannot be said, though, that all Europeans worried about honour, or mana. The Sydney traders, the sealers and whalers were hard-nosed men, and some were disreputable villains. Most convicts, as outcasts from their own society, were all the more eager to lord it over Maori. The fact that so many early European visitors to New Zealand came from, or through, penal colonies, deserves further historical reflection.

European visitors to Maori territories soon became embroiled in inter-tribal jousting. The records of Marsden's first visit to the Bay of Islands illustrate the complexity of such interactions. Many Europeans, however, were impatient and uninterested, as well as ignorant of, Maori geo-politics. Their interventions, from Marion du Fresne onwards, were often disastrous. As the fate of Te Pahi at Tara's hands shows, they could be easily manipulated by local leaders. Rangatira turned their guests against rivals, and deployed unwitting Europeans as mercenaries in inter-tribal battles.

Leaders like Honekai in the south or Te Pahi in the north were cross-cultural strategists, who employed many devices. On occasion, they married their daughters to stray Europeans (James Cadell and George Bruce, in those instances) who assisted them in fighting as well as in dealing with visiting compatriots. They sent their sons and other young relatives on board European ships, as scouts, spies and ethnographers. These young travellers came home with European goods, some English, a close knowledge of European seafaring habits, and European diseases. Sometimes the chiefs travelled to European places themselves, to conduct their own enquiries. They give the lie to those Western theorists who argue that 'primitives' are characterised by 'closed minds', incapable of systematic enquiry and investigation.

The impact of such scrutiny of Europe was uneven in different regions of New Zealand and different sectors of Maori society. In many inland districts, for instance, the news of European arrival must have seemed mythical. Some people (for instance, most ariki, or high chiefs, and tohunga, or priests) stayed aloof from the new arrivals. In Maori society, as in all human communities, there were those who mistrusted strangers and alien customs. It was the young men, in particular, who looked for adventure on European ships, and travelled to distant places. They suffered the frustrations of all travellers – disinterest from those who have stayed at home, and disbelief in the extraordinary things they had witnessed.

Slowly and unevenly, Te Ao Tawhito (the ancient world) was shifting on its foundations. New plants and animals came ashore, new people, and new and devastating illnesses. Perhaps, after all, the epidemic diseases, plants and animals were Europe's most eloquent emissaries. Even more than the first Europeans who came ashore at this time, they changed Maori life forever. At the same time, there was little sense that the ancient world was ending. Only Ruatara, and perhaps some of his companions on the *Active*, foresaw what might follow when the first European families arrived in the Bay of Islands. Even he dismissed these fears, at least on the surface. At this time everything still seemed possible. The risks seemed worth it. Nobody could tell what the future would bring.

Nor are our understandings any more final. The spiral is still spinning. James Cook and Kahura; Governor and Mrs King, Tuki and Huru; Te Pahi, George Bruce and Te Atahoe; James Cadell, Tokitoki and Honekai; Thomas Taylor and Te Haupa; Samuel Marsden, Ruatara, Miki, Thomas Kendall and Hongi Hika – their meetings still haunt us. The past never ends.

The following appendices are intended to indicate to readers the extent, complexity and frequency of visits by European shipping to New Zealand during the period covered by this work. They include voyages intended to harvest seals, whales, flax and timber on the mainland or seas and islands around New Zealand. The appendices also serve as a guide to a 'Ships Archive' now lodged in the University of Auckland Library, which includes a master index of documents, archival search books, and a collection of files for each vessel named in the Appendices. Each file contains documents relevant to that particular ship, and a summary sheet of shipping details. The archive has been donated to the Library so that researchers interested in any of these voyages can consult the copies of original documents collected for the *Between Worlds* project. I also commend to researchers the invaluable, if antique, index of Colonial Office correspondence between London and Port Jackson up to 1815, held in the Mitchell Library, Sydney.

Note that logs were kept in 'ship's time' (noon to noon, twelve hours ahead of civil time); whereas civilians' journals and most other records were kept in civil time (midnight to midnight). This may account for some variations of dates from original manuscripts; days are given uniformly in this account in civil time.

I: VISITS TO THE SOUTHERN SEALING GROUNDS

1773

26 March – 11 May: *Resolution* (Captain James Cook; 462 tons; Royal Navy) visits Dusky Sound (Tamatea) on exploring visit; sailors kill numbers of seals.

Seals reported at Tamatea (Dusky Sound).

1791

2–22 November: *Discovery* (Captain George Vancouver; 330 tons; Royal Navy) and *Chatham*; (Lieutenant William Broughton; brig; Royal Navy) visit Tamatea for supplies; seals killed; find the Snares; the *Chatham* finds the Chatham Islands.

Sealing at Dusky begins.

1792–93

23 October 1792: *Britannia ii* (Captain William Raven; 296 tons; St Barbe of London) leaves Port Jackson for the Cape of Good Hope via Dusky Sound for sealing; 6 November: drops off sealing party at Dusky; 1 December 1792: carries on to the Cape of Good Hope; returns to Port Jackson June 1793.

8 September 1793: *Britannia ii* and *Francis* (Captain House; 42 tons; colonial schooner) leave Port Jackson to collect sealing party in Dusky Sound; *Britannia* arrives 27 September; *Francis* caught in storm and arrives two weeks later; both leave for Norfolk Island 20 October

1793, where *Britannia* is commandeered by Lieutenant-Governor King to take Tuki and Huru back to Muriwhenua.

1795–97

18 September 1795: *Endeavour* (Captain William Wright Bampton; 800 tons; Bampton of Calcutta) and *Fancy* (Captain Thomas Dell; 150 tons; Bampton) leave Port Jackson for India via New Zealand and Norfolk Island; in Dusky 12 October; *Endeavour* abandoned there; some passengers and crew leave in *Providence* and *Fancy* 7 January 1796; others leave somewhat later on the *Assistance* (*Endeavour*'s longboat); rest picked up by *Mercury i* (Captain William Barnet) in May 1797.

1800

March: HMS *Reliance* (Captain Henry Waterhouse) leaves Port Jackson for England; finds the 'Pentantipodes', or Antipodes Islands.

1801

23 November: *Venus ii* (Captain George Bass; 142 tons; Creighton, Bass and Bishop of London) leaves Port Jackson for Tahiti to get pork; in Tamatea collecting sealskins and timber for pork chests, and iron from the *Endeavour*'s wreck 5–21 December; at Tahiti January 1802; returns to Port Jackson 14 November 1802 with 50 tons of pork.

Sealing begins in Bass Strait, Australia; sealing at Dusky continues.

1803

5 February: *Venus ii* leaves Port Jackson for Tahiti via Dusky, and disappears.

19 April: *Endeavour ii* (Captain Joseph Oliphant; 31 tons; Kable and Underwood of Port Jackson) leaves Port Jackson for Bass Strait; arrives at Dusky Bay 9 May 1803; explores southern coast and islands; returns to Port Jackson 7 October with 2,000 sealskins, leaves for Bass Strait 17 January 1804, arrives at Dusky in January.

December: HMS *Scorpion* (Captain William Dagg; 343 tons; James Mather; British 'South Whaler' sailing under Letter of Marque) at Dusky, Dagg Sound and southern fiords; returns to Port Jackson 31 March 1804.

1804

August: *Contest* (Captain Joseph Oliphant; 44 tons; Kable and Underwood) leaves Port Jackson for east coast of New Zealand with Jorgen Jorgensen as mate; in Dusky c. January 1805; returns to Port Jackson under Jorgensen's command 9 February with 7,000 skins, leaving two small boats at Dusky.

28 August: *Independence* (Captain Isaiah Townsend; 35 tons; Lord, Pendleton and Boston of Port Jackson) leaves Port Jackson; arrives at Stewart Island late 1804; meets *Contest* at Dusky January 1805; lands sealing gangs at Antipodes c. February; returns to Port Jackson 23 April.

c. December: *Honduras Packet* (Captain Owen Bunker, cousin of Eber Bunker; 143 tons; Hurrys of London, contracted by Simeon Lord) at east coast of Stewart Island; Owen Folger Smith on board; finds Foveaux Strait, and returns to Bass Strait.

Dusky rookeries in decline; Antipodes rush begins.

1805

26 April: *Governor King* (Captain Edward Edwards; 75 tons; Kable and Underwood) leaves Port Jackson for New Zealand; returns 31 July after being damaged in severe storms.

11 June: *Favorite* (Captain Jon Paddock, 245 tons; Gardner and Co. of Nantucket, chartered by Simeon Lord of Port Jackson) and *Independence* leave Port Jackson for the Antipodes; Owen Folger Smith in charge of *Independence* sealing gang.

29 July: *Venus iii* (Captain William Stewart; 45 tons; Robert Campbell of Port Jackson) leaves Port Jackson with sealing gang of fifteen men; calls at Norfolk Island; delivers animals to

Te Pahi at Bay of Islands c. late August 1805; takes Te Pahi and sons to Norfolk; arrives at Antipodes c. 20 November 1805; returns to Port Jackson with few skins 24 January 1806.

1 August: *Speedwell* (Captain John Grono; 18 tons; Andrew Thompson of Port Jackson) leaves Hawkesbury for south coast of New Zealand; returns 21 September 1806.

20 September: *Honduras Packet* (Captain William Edwards) leaves Port Jackson for Antipodes.

5 November : *Governor King* leaves for Antipodes, lands sealing gang there c. December; goes on to Dusky; returns to Port Jackson 1806 with 12 tons of iron from wreck of the *Endeavour*.

20 November: *Favorite* in Antipodes; returns to Port Jackson with 60,000 sealskins from 'East Coast of New Zealand' 10 March 1806; leaves for Canton 29 July 1806.

c. 20 November: With arrival of *Venus iii* at Antipodes, conflict between the men of *Venus iii* and those of *Favorite*, *Honduras Packet* and *Independence*; these vessels leave soon after. *Honduras Packet* returns c. late December.

1806

24 January: *Ceres* (Captain Edward Sharpe; 125 tons; Stevens of London, contracted by Simeon Lord of Port Jackson) leaves Port Jackson to collect 20,000 skins from Antipodes for London.

25 March: *Star* (Captain James Birnie; 119 tons; Birnie and Co. – but in fact Lord) leaves Port Jackson; arrives Antipodes in May (probably in Chathams meanwhile); assists William Stewart's sealing gang and takes Stewart himself back to Port Jackson; returns to Port Jackson 21 June; leaves again 30 July (Captain J. Wilkinson) for 'southward islands'; visits Whangaroa, where 'George', or Te Aara, joins the ship; travels to Antipodes; returns Te Aara to Whangaroa; returns 30 December with 14,000 skins; delivers 19,000 skins in London.

March: *Governor King* reports eighty sealers at Antipodes.

18 August: *Ocean* (Captain Abraham Bristow; 401 tons; whaler; Enderbys of London) finds the Auckland Islands.

October: *Contest* leaves Port Jackson for Dusky Sound; wrecked south of Port Stephens 28 February 1807.

The seal rush to the Bounty and Auckland Islands begins

1807

Sarah (Captain Abraham Bristow; whaler; Enderbys) visits Auckland Islands and takes formal possession of them.

9 April: *Dart* (Captain Richard Smith; 189 tons; Hulletts of London, in partnership with John Macarthur) sails to 'the fishing'; returns 'deeply loaded with salt skins' 4 February 1808.

11 June: *Brothers ii* (Captain Oliver Russell; 252 tons; Hulletts) leaves Port Jackson; returns 30 January 1808 with 38,000 skins; leaves for England 2 May.

10 July: *Santa Anna* (Captain William Moody; 220 tons; Lord, Kable and Underwood) leaves Port Jackson; in the Bay of Islands in July; leaves a gang of ten Europeans, two Tahitians, two Maori (including Ruatara) at the Bounty Islands in November; c. September 1808 the *King George* (Captain Samuel Chace; 185 tons; Kable and Underwood) arrives; by then two Europeans and one Tahitian had died of thirst and hunger; relieved by the *Santa Anna* c. October.

c. October: *Antipode* (Captain Scott; 58 tons; Blaxland and Lord of Port Jackson) leaves Port Jackson for sealing grounds.

24 October: *Sydney Cove* (Captain William Edwards; 282 tons; Plummers of London) leaves Port Jackson for Norfolk Island and New Zealand.

20–26 November: *Topaz* (Captain Mayhew Folger; Boston) off Chathams; meets the *Antipode* there 22 November; *Antipode* may have been in company with *Brothers* (256 tons; Mitchell of Nantucket); finds two sealing gangs at the Antipodes 17 December .

1808

6 February: *Commerce* (Captain James Ceroni; 225 tons; Lord) leaves Port Jackson with Jacky

Marmon on board; visits Bounty, Auckland and Chatham Islands; returns via Mercury Bay and Bay of Islands; Te Pahi, three sons and several attendants come on board as passengers; arrives Port Jackson 10 July with 3,000 skins, and logs and spars.

Sealing at Bass Strait and the Antipodes in decline; Foveaux Strait rush begins.

8 August: *Perseverance* (Captain Faulkner; then Kierumgaard; 136 tons; Campbell) leaves Port Jackson.

26 August: *Pegasus* (Captain Eber Bunker; Spanish prize; 325 tons; Lord and Moore of Port Jackson) leaves Port Jackson; arrives at Foveaux Strait mid-February; Bunker recharts the strait; speaks *Antipode* and *Governor Bligh*, which had sighted *Fox* and *Adventure* (Captain Keith, from England); returns to Port Jackson 15 March 1809 with 12,600 skins.

27 August: *King George* leaves Port Jackson; visits Bounty Islands where Ruatara and other sealers from the *Santa Anna* in dire straits; returns 13 March 1809 with 8,000 skins

c. August: *Antipode* (Captain John Birbeck; 58 tons; Blaxland and Lord) leaves Port Jackson for Foveaux Strait; reported at Bay of Islands 'very short of provisions' in December; returns to Port Jackson 22 March 1809 with 4,000 skins.

c. September: *Governor Bligh* (Captain John Grono; 100 tons; Thompson) leaves Port Jackson for Foveaux Strait; returns 11 March 1809 with 10,000 skins.

30 September: *Fox* (Captain William Cox; 45 tons; Campbell) leaves Port Jackson for the southern isles; speaks the *Governor Bligh* on 3 January; had lost a boat, and anchors and cables, and had twenty-six out of twenty-eight men down with scurvy; probably leaves a gang on Solander Island, which was not picked up until 2 May 1813; returns to Port Jackson 15 March 1809 with 14,000 skins; leaves again 7 May 1809; lands gang under Robert Murry in Foveaux Strait.

15 October: *Santa Anna* leaves Port Jackson for the fishery and England; picks up gang from Bounty Islands including Ruatara c. October 1808; arrives in London July 1809 with Ruatara on board.

1809

Late January: *Star* (Captain Wilkinson; 110 tons; Lord) leaves Port Jackson; returns 31 August with 2,000 skins.

Mid-February: *Adventure* (Captain Keith; British) arrives at Foveaux Strait direct from London.

15 March: *Unity i* (Captain Daniel Cooper; 160 tons; Plummers) arrives at Port Jackson on a sealing voyage from England with 2,000 skins, for repairs; damaged in a gale off Bay of Islands.

16 March: *Otter* (Captain Hopper, England) arrives at Port Jackson from sealing voyage at Cape Circumcision; has been to Bay of Islands, where met the *Antipode* in great want of provisions; and *Santa Anna*, which was going to England with 25,000 skins; leaves Port Jackson 2 April on sealing voyage.

13 April : *Governor Bligh* leaves for southern New Zealand; returns 19 January 1810 with 10,000 skins from around Thompson Sound.

3 May 1809 *Pegasus* (Captain Samuel Chace) leaves Port Jackson with convicts and supplies for Hobart, and a cargo of thousands of skins belonging to Lord for England; arrives Pegasus Island 16 July; finds Port Pegasus; at Stewart Island 7 August; charted by William Stewart first officer; circumnavigates Stewart Island; visits Pitt Island in Chathams; visits east coast of New Zealand north of Cook Strait; down to Banks Peninsula; returns to Port Pegasus 20 October for two months; collects gang from Pegasus Island January 1810; returns through Foveaux Strait and back to Chathams; leaves 4 February for England.

2 June: *Brothers iii* (Captain Robert Mason; 40 tons; hired by Campbell) leaves Port Jackson for the 'Isle of Wight' (White Island off St Kilda, Dunedin) off south-east New Zealand; lands gangs on the coast; returns to Port Jackson 15 January 1810 to collect more supplies.

18 June: *Endeavour* (Captain Phillip Goodenough; 31 tons; Kable and Underwood) reported at Bay of Islands; plunders Te Pahi's potato gardens; returns to Port Jackson 25 August 1809.

June: *King George* (Captain Samuel Chace; 185 tons; colonial vessel; Kable and Underwood) leaves Port Jackson for Auckland Islands; in Bay of Islands c. February 1810; prevented from entering by news of the *Boyd*; returns to Port Jackson 9 March.

18 July: *Sydney Cove* (Captain Charles McLaren; prize ship; 282 tons; Underwood and Plummer of London) leaves Port Jackson; lands gang in 'Molyneux Strait' (Foveaux Strait) in November; the sealers travel to Otago Peninsula then Foveaux Strait, where they are killed and eaten; lands gang on Stewart Island 10 January 1810; some of these men killed by Honekai; James Cadell survives.

22 August: *Unity i* leaves Port Jackson for Foveaux Strait and Thompson Sound; returns 15 August 1810 with 6,000 skins.

September: *Antipode* leaves Port Jackson for southern New Zealand; returns February 1810 'in distress'.

10 October: *Star* leaves Port Jackson; returns 26 March 1810 with 600 skins from the sealing islands and Mercury Bay, New Zealand.

22 October: *Perseverance* (Captain Hasselberg; 136 tons; Campbell) leaves for Auckland Islands; Ceroni on board as passenger; arrives late November; finds Campbell Island 4 January 1810; sails to Bay of Islands; hears of *Boyd* disaster and takes part in punitive raid on Te Pahi's island; takes evidence and letters, as well as spars, back to Port Jackson; arrives 28 April.

28 October: *Unity ii* (Captain John Grono; 36 tons; Benn and Webb of Port Jackson) arrives at Botany Bay from New Zealand with 3,600 skins.

11 December: *Active* (Captain John Bader; Phipps and Phillips of London) leaves Port Jackson, arrives at Open Bay on the west coast of New Zealand 2 January 1810; leaves a gang on an island there; the ship is never seen again; gang rescued 27 November 1813 by Captain Grono on *Governor Bligh*.

1810

2 March: *Brothers iii* leaves Port Jackson for Open Bay on west coast of South Island; collects two men from south-east coast 3 May, including William Tucker – called 'Wioree' by local Maori – may have taken a preserved head to Sydney; three members of the gang are collected by *General Boyd*, arrive back in Port Jackson 30 January 1811; four others are killed by Maori in Molyneux Harbour. Sails from there along the north coast to Cook Strait; to 'Banks Island' and Port Daniel (Otago Harbour); then back to Cook Strait and Cape Egmont; returns to Port Jackson 14 July with 2,100 skins.

27 March: *Governor Bligh* leaves Port Jackson with supplies for William Leith's flax-collecting party; spoken by the *Lady Nelson* in April; finds that the party has already left on the *New Zealander* (Captain Elder); returns via Foveaux Strait and Stewart Island; collects gang left by the *Fox*; arrives at Port Jackson 18 August with 1,600 skins.

25 June: *Perseverance* leaves Port Jackson; at Bay of Islands in March– April ; finds Macquarie Island 11 July; drops gang at Campbell Island and returns to Port Jackson for more sealers and supplies; leaves 7 September for Macquarie and Campbell Islands, accompanied by Robert Murry and a 'New Zealand boy'; sights *Aurora* (Captain Owen Smith) at Campbell Island; Murry passes on location of Macquarie to Smith; leaves Campbell 20 November; arrives Port Jackson 8 January 1811.

15 August: *Unity i* arrives from south coast of New Zealand; describes 'the natives as particularly friendly'; her foremast had been struck by lightning in Thompson Sound.

Foveaux Strait rookeries in decline; Macquarie Island rush begins.

18 September: *Aurora* (Captain Owen Smith; Samuel Chace on board as sailing master and

Lord's agent; 180 tons; Woolden of New York, chartered by Lord) leaves Port Jackson; drops gang on Macquarie Island early December; to Campbell Island; returns to Port Jackson 30 December with 100 skins and 140 gallons of elephant-seal oil.

2 October: *Star* leaves Port Jackson; at Macquarie Island February 1811; sails directlyto England.

20 October: *Unity i* leaves Port Jackson; arrives Macquarie Island in December; loads skins and leaves for London.

21 October: *Elizabeth and Mary* (Captain James Gordon; 80 tons; Thorley and Abbott, chartered by Hook) leaves Port Jackson for Macquarie Island via the Derwent; arrives 31 December and lands gang; reports *Sydney Cove* and *Unity* (arrived December 1810) both there; returns Port Jackson 2 March 1811 with 20.000 skins.

October– November: *Sydney Cove* sails from Norfolk Island to pick up her gangs in Foveaux Strait; on to Macquarie Island; *Governor Bligh* reports her at Foveaux and at Stewart Island; at Macquarie 11 March 1811; returns to Port Jackson 12 April with 1,000 skins and 5 tons of sperm oil.

14 December: *General Boyd ii* leaves Port Jackson to relieve *Fox*'s gang; at Port William finds a whaleboat with seven men from the *Brothers*.

1811

c. February: *Sydney Cove* reported at Port William proceeding to Macquarie Island by *Boyd ii*; returns to Port Jackson 10 April. *Mary and Sally* (Captain Charles Feen; 130 tons; Sarah Wills of Calcutta) leaves Port Jackson for Macquarie and Campbell Islands.

9 March: *Concord* (Captain Thomas Garbutt; 150 tons; Alexander Birnie of London) leaves Port Jackson, with Joseph Marmon (boy), on board; arrives Macquarie Island 1 April; leaves a gang of sealers and returns to Port Jackson 1 May.

26 March: *General Boyd ii* (Captain William Holford) returns to Port Jackson with gangs from Foveaux Strait; met with a whaleboat in the strait manned by seven sealers left by the *Brothers iii* in October 1809; several boats' crews had been 'barbarously murdered, and mostly devoured by the natives'.

12 April: *Unity i* reported at Macquarie Island; leaves for London.

4 May: *Governor Bligh* leaves Port Jackson; arrives Macquarie Island and services gangs left by *Aurora*; returns to Port Jackson 7 November.

18 May: *Mary and Sally* leaves Hobart for Macquarie Island; blown off course to Campbell Island; gang dropped off; five of six men died; one survivor rescued by *Cumberland* (Captain William Stewart; 80 tons; Blaxcell) in December.

1 June: *Concord* leaves Port Jackson; arrives Macquarie Island 12 July, where several gangs suffering extreme privation; returns to Port Jackson 1 October .

9 June: *Perseverance* (Captain Gordon; returns under Captain Holding) leaves Port Jackson with 'Jackie Mytye'(Maitai) in crew; arrives Macquarie Island 25–26 September; returns to Port Jackson 31 October .

21 September: *Sydney Cove* leaves Port Jackson; arrives Macquarie Island c. January 1812; driven off 11 March; sails to London.

28 November: *Cumberland* leaves Port Jackson; to Macquarie Island, then Campbell; returns to Port Jackson 3 July 1812 having rescued a survivor from *Mary and Sally*'s gang.

14 November: *Concord* leaves Port Jackson;a boat is wrecked in the surf at Macquarie Island and six men drowned; sails for London 10 March 1812 with 13,700 skins and 50 tons of oil.

28 November: *Governor Bligh* leaves Port Jackson; arrives Macquarie Island 20 December; returns 9 June 1812 with 4,000 skins.

1812

15 February *Mary and Sally* leaves Port Jackson; reaches Macquarie Island; bound for Campbell Island 20 March.

23 February: *Perseverance* (Captain Miles Holding) leaves Port Jackson with 'Jacky Maitai' in crew; leaves Macquarie Island 7 April; arrives Port Jackson 7 May with 9,000 skins and 65 tons of elephant-seal oil.

21 May: *Campbell Macquarie* (Captain Richard Siddons; 248 tons; Alexander) leaves Kangaroo Island; wrecked Macquarie Island 10 June; crew picked up by *Perseverance* 13 October; leaves behind one European, four 'Sea Cunnies', twenty-six Lascars; *Perseverance* arrives back in Port Jackson 1 November.

4 July: *Perseverance* leaves Port Jackson for Macquarie Island; picks up men from the wreck of the *Campbell Macquarie* 13 October; returns 1 November .

1 September: *Governor Bligh* leaves Port Jackson; picks up gang at Macquarie Island; returns 16 December 1813.

7 November: *Elizabeth and Mary ii* (Captain Richard Siddons) leaves Port Jackson for Macquarie Island to relieve the gang from the *Campbell Macquarie*; returns 28 January 1813 with Maori on board, 1,700 skins, and rigging and stores from the wreck of the *Campbell Macquarie*.

11 December: *Perseverance* leaves Port Jackson for Macquarie Island with 'Jacky Mytye' and 'Dick, a New Zealander' (or maybe a Tahitian) in crew.

1813

The sloop *William and Anne* sailed between Shoalhaven and Port Jackson with Maori sailors 'John Peter, Jackey Warree, Harry, John Brownie and R. George' on board.

22 February: *Elizabeth and Mary* leaves Port Jackson; crew includes two Lascars; returns empty 2 August; leaves again for Bass Strait 14 August.

19 April: *Perseverance* leaves Port Jackson for New Zealand with a Tahitian and 'Mahomet Cassim' in crew; returns in July.

4 August: *Matilda* (Captain Samuel Fowler; 75 tons; Lord) leaves Port Jackson; ship's officer and six Lascars desert at Port Daniel (Otago Harbour), later killed and eaten; altogether loses fourteen men and three boats.

16 November: *Mary and Sally* (Captain Kelly) leaves Hobart; arrives Macquarie Island 30 November; returns to Hobart 1814 with 80 tons of oil.

16 December: *Governor Bligh* returns to Port Jackson from west coast of New Zealand with 14,000 skins, 3 tons of oil and ten men from the gang left by the *Active i* (Captain Bader) on 16 February 1810 at a small island off the west coast.

1814

9 February: *Elizabeth and Mary ii* leaves Port Jackson for Bass Strait with 'Paddy' and 'Tommy', New Zealanders, on board.

4 September: *Elizabeth and Mary* leaves Port Jackson; drops gang at Macquarie Island; returns 17 December.

6 December: *Cumberland ii* (Captain Cubitt) leaves Port Jackson; to Macquarie Island; returns to Port Jackson for Campbell and Macquarie Islands 28 March 1815.

6 December: *Endeavour iii* (Captain Powell; 58 tons; Nichols of Port Jackson) leaves Port Jackson for Campbell and Macquarie Islands with several Tahitians in crew; returns 9 March 1815 with 3 tons of oil.

28 December: *Betsey iii* (Captain Phillip Goodenough; 222 tons; Underwood) leaves Port Jackson; lands gang on Macquarie Island 13 February 1815; to Auckland Islands; returns to Macquarie in August; ship abandoned off Bay of Islands 23 October; survivors rescued by *Active i* 23 Feb-ruary 1816.

1815

14 January: *Elizabeth and Mary ii* leaves Port Jackson for Macquarie Island; returns 2 March with 2,700 skins; leaves again for Macquarie in April; returns 23 June with 4,700 skins.

16 June: *Cumberland ii* leaves Port Jackson for Campbell and Macquarie Islands; no further record found.

8 August: *Elizabeth and Mary ii* (Captain Theodore Walker) leaves Port Jackson; returns from Macquarie Island 11 November with 40 tons of oil.

II: WHALING AND TIMBER VOYAGES TO NORTH-EASTERN NEW ZEALAND

1791

22 November: *William and Ann* (Captain Eber Bunker; 370 tons; St Barbe of London) leaves Port Jackson on a whaling voyage; leaves Norfolk Island 19 December to visit Doubtless Bay to try to secure 'natives' for Lieutenant-Governor King at Norfolk Island.

1794

29 September: *Fancy* (Captain Thomas Dell; 150 tons; William Bampton of Calcutta) leaves Port Jackson for Norfolk Island and New Zealand; in Tokerau (Doubtless Bay) 12–14 November; in Hauraki 20 November – 21 February 1795; returns to Port Jackson 15 March from 'River Thames' with flax and spars.

1798

20 August: *Cornwall* (Captain William Swain) leaves Port Jackson to go whaling at New Zealand.

20 August: *Hunter i* (Captain James Fearn; 300 tons; Campbell and Co. of Calcutta) leaves Port Jackson to collect spars from the 'River Thames'; c. October sails for China; returns to Port Jackson 14 February 1800 under the command of William Anderson.

1799

7 October: *Hunter ii* (Captain William Hingston; Simeon Lord and William Hingston of Port Jackson) leaves Port Jackson for Bengal via the 'River Thames' to collect timber; four men remained behind at Waihou; arrives at Calcutta in 1800 and is sold there.

1800

11 May: *Betsey i* (Captain Glasse; 316 tons; Daniel Bennett of London) leaves Port Jackson for Peru; spends three days at Hauraki collecting 'some very fine spars'.

1801

5 January: *El Plumier* (Captain William Reid; 250 tons; Reid and Co. of Port Jackson) leaves Port Jackson for the Cape of Good Hope; stops to collect timber at Hauraki 2 March – 20 August; leaves for the Pacific.

26 March: *Britannia i* (Captain Robert Turnbull; 301 tons; Enderbys of London) arrives at Port Jackson from London; leaves for the fishery in May; returns 19 October with 550 barrels of sperm oil; leaves Port Jackson 3 November for the fishery; returns 12 May with 1,300 barrels of oil; leaves Port Jackson 12 June 1802 for the fishery and England.

28 March: *Royal Admiral* (Captain William Wilson; 923 tons; Gabriel Gillet and William Wilson of London) leaves Port Jackson for China via the 'River Thames' and Tahiti to collect timber with party of LMS missionaries; in Hauraki 20 April – 15 June; leaves for Tahiti.

29 May: *Greenwich* (Captain Alexander Law; 338 tons; Enderbys) arrives at Port Jackson from London; leaves for the fishery 16 July; returns 25 June 1802 with 1,000 barrels of oil; leaves 10 August for the fishery.

June: *Albion* (Captain Eber Bunker; 362 tons; Champions of London) arrives at Port Jackson from London; leaves 26 August for the fishery and England with 155 tons of oil.

11 July: *Speedy* (Captain George Quested; 313 tons; Enderbys) arrives at Port Jackson from the

fishery; leaves for fishery 8 August; returns 30 April 1802 with 170 tons of oil; leaves for fishery 6 June.

20 August 1801 *Harriet* (Captain Samuel Chace; 227 tons; Mathers of London) leaves Port Jackson to go whaling; returns 11 August 1802 with 840 barrels of oil; leaves 20 August 1802 to go whaling; reported at the Bay of Islands in 1802.

16 September: *Venus i* (Captain Barnabas Gardner; 295 tons; Champions) arrives at Port Jackson; leaves for the fishery 13 October; returns 10 May 1802 with 550 barrels of oil; leaves again for the fishery 26 June 1802.

31 December: Governor King reports the *Eliza*, *Britannia i* and *Albion* have returned home laden with oil; and 'six [whalers] are now on the coast and off the north end of New Zealand'.

1802

21 May: Governor King puts a list of questions to the masters of the *Britannia i*, *Speedy* and *Venus i* about whaling off the New Zealand coast.

26 June: *General Boyd* (Captain Owen Bunker; 302 tons; Watson and Co.) arrives at Port Jackson with 5 tons of oil; leaves 10 August to go whaling off the New Zealand coast and to England.

1803

15 February: *Greenwich* (Captain Alexander Law; 338 tons; Enderbys) arrives at Port Jackson from New Zealand with 209 tons of oil; leaves for England 18 May. Law reports *Venus i*, *Alexander* (Captain Robert Rhodes; 301 tons; Hurrys of London) and *Albion* cruising off the New Zealand coast.

6 March: *Venus i* arrives at Port Jackson with 1,400 barrels of oil from New Zealand; Captain Gardner reports *Albion* and *Alexander* cruising off the New Zealand coast; leaves for England 18 May.

1 June: *Alexander* arrives at Port Jackson from New Zealand with 50 tons of oil; 'Tyeena' (Teina) on board; leaves with Teina 19 September for New Zealand.

7 July: *Albion* arrives at Port Jackson from New Zealand with 65 tons of oil); leaves again 6 October for New Zealand.

1804

13 May: *Britannia i* (Captain George Quested) arrives from New Zealand with 126 tons of oil; leaves 1 August for the fishery.

21 May: *Alexander* arrives at Port Jackson from New Zealand; leaves for the fishing 4 July; delivers Teina with a gift of pigs at the Bay of Islands; returns to Port Jackson 14 December with 210 tons oil and 70 tons of whalebone.

31 March: *Scorpion* (Captain William Dagg; 343 tons; Mathers of London) arrives at Port Jackson with 4,759 sealskins from Dusky Bay and 20 barrels of sperm oil; leaves 7 November for the fishery with 4,750 skins and 94 tons of oil.

3–12 June: *Lady Nelson* (Lieutenant James Symons; 60 tons; Government armed tender) visits North Cape, Bay of Islands and 'Cavalle's Bay', returns to Port Jackson 8 July.

5 July: *Albion* arrives at Port Jackson from New Zealand and Sandy Cape with 1,400 barrels of oil and 13,000 skins; leaves for the fishery and England 21 August.

25 August: *Adonis* (Captain Robert Turnbull; 290 tons; British) arrives at Port Jackson from New Zealand with 1,000 barrels of oil; leaves for the fishery 19 September.

October: *Greenwich* and *Venus i* leave Timor with 40 barrels of oil each, bound for New Zealand.

14 November: *Hannah and Eliza* (Captain Micajah Gardner; Benjamin Rotch of Milford Haven, Wales) arrives at North Cape from New Bedford via Cape of Good Hope and Tasmania; speaks *Britannia I* 29 November; speaks *Ann* (Captain James Gwynn; 288 tons; William Rock jnr of New Bedford) and *Harriet* (Captain Thaddeus Coffin) 3 December; speaks *Adonis* 6 December; speaks *Ferret* (Captain Philip Skelton; 208 tons; Bennet) 18 December –

Maa-Tara on board; sails in company with *Ferret* until 20 January 1805; takes local man on board for a cruise 23 January –15 February; speaks *John Sebastian* (Captain Smith) 31 January; takes another New Zealander on board 23 March; speaks *Harriet* 2 April; speaks *Ocean* (Captain Abraham Bristow; 401 tons; Enderbys) 20 December; speaks *Ann*, *Brothers i* (Captain Benjamin Worth; 256 tons; Mitchell of Nantucket) and *Aurora* (Captain Andrew Meyrick) 26 December; speaks *Brothers i* and *Carleton* (Captain Allerow) 12 January 1806; speaks *Vulture* (Captain Thomas Folger) 2 February; speaks *Argo* 7 February and *Atlantic* (Captain William Swain) 31 March – all off North Cape.

1805

5 January: *Richard and Mary* (Captain James Lucas; 215 tons; Spencer and Co. of London) arrives at Port Jackson from England; goes whaling off the coast of New Holland 26 January; returns to Port Jackson 9 February; sails for the coast 15 March; returns 24 April; sails for the Derwent 24 May with 170 barrels of oil; returns 12 October; leaves 3 November for New Zealand; returns 17 July 1806 with 100 tons of oil; sails for England 8 September.

27 February: *Alexander* leaves Port Jackson for Tahiti and London with 200 tons of sperm oil, 14,000 sealskins, some kangaroo skins and 22 tons of elephant-seal oil; in Bay of Islands en route to England. Teina comes on board; the ship goes whaling off the north end of the North Island; returns to the Bay of Islands; Teina and Maki come on board; the ship sails to Tahiti, Brazil and St Helena; arrives at Portsmouth 13 June 1806; at Gravesend 27 June. Teina and Maki left without pay in London; cared for by Sir Joseph Banks; Teina dies; Maki kidnapped by a crimp and taken back to sea.

26 March: *Scorpion* returns to Port Jackson from the coast of New Zealand with 700 barrels of oil, 4,750 sealskins; 94 tons elephant and whale oil; crew member 'Thomas Tewhee' on board; reports the *Harriet*, *Ann*, *Elizabeth and Mary* (Captain John Hingston; 235 tons; Spencer and Co. of London); *John Sebastian* (Captain Smith; London) and *Adonis*; *Adonis* collects eighteen sows and two boars at Norfolk to deliver to Te Pahi at Bay of Islands; visits Bay of Islands at end of year; *Britannia* and *Hannah and Eliza* at the fishery.

25 April: *Harriet* arrives at Port Jackson from New Zealand with 1,160 barrels of oil; sails for England 29 May.

16 May: *Ann* arrives at Port Jackson from New Zealand with 130 tons of oil; leaves again for the fishery 6 June.

9 June: *Ferret* arrives from fishery off New Zealand with Maa-Tara on board.

16 July: *Brothers i* arrives at Port Jackson with 200 barrels of oil; leaves again 1 November.

29 July 1805 *Venus iii* (Captain William Stewart; 45 tons; Campbell and Co. of Calcutta) leaves Port Jackson for 'Coast Peru' with Maa-Tara on board; collects two sows and two nanny goats at Norfolk Island for Te Pahi; goes to Bay of Islands where she lands Maa-Tara; collects Te Pahi and four sons and takes them to Norfolk Island. They are then carried by HMS *Buffalo* (Captain Houston) from Norfolk to Derwent, and then to Port Jackson, arriving 27 November.

15 September: *Ferret* leaves Port Jackson for Bay of Islands and London with John Savage on board; arrives Bay of Islands 20 September; Te Mahanga joins ship at Bay of Islands and travels to England; off St Helena 31 January 1806; arrives at Gravesend 27 April; leaves again from London for Port Jackson 13 June with Mahanga on board.

15 September: *Argo* (Captain John Bader; 221 tons; Hullets) leaves Port Jackson for New Zealand; collects six sows and two boars from Norfolk c. October 1805 to deliver to Te Pahi at the Bay of Islands; Te Pahi has left for Port Jackson; Ruatara and two of his countrymen join the crew; cruise off the coast about five months.

28 September: *Elizabeth and Mary* arrives from New Zealand with 800 barrels of oil; leaves for New Zealand and England 8 November.

20 October: *Elizabeth i* (238 tons; Campbell) arrives at Port Jackson from New Zealand with

oil; leaves again for the fishery 20 November; returns to Port Jackson August 1806 from Rio de Janeiro (Captain Eber Bunker).

22 October: *Ann* arrives at Broken Bay with 1,400 barrels of oil; leaves in company with *Ann and Eliza* (Captain Gardner; American) for the coast of New Zealand 20 November.

22 October: *Ann and Eliza* arrives at Broken Bay with 850 barrels of oil; leaves for New Zealand 20 November.

c. December: *Ocean* arrives at Norfolk en route to the whaling at New Zealand; finds Auckland Islands 18 August 1806.

1 December: *King George* (Captain Moody; 185 tons; Kable and Co.) leaves Port Jackson for the 'sperm fishery off the coast of New Zealand'; returns almost empty (1 ton of black whale oil) 5 April 1806.

1806

25 February: *Lady Nelson* returns Te Pahi and four sons to New Zealand; George Bruce deserts the ship at North Cape; vessel sails from Bay of Islands 7 May.

7 April: *Argo* arrives at Port Jackson from New Zealand with 27 tons of oil; reports *Aurora* (Captain Andrew Meyrick; 302 tons; Daniel Sterbeck of England) at Norfolk, proceeding to the coast of New Zealand; *Richard and Mary* spoken several times off the New Zealand coast; *Brothers i* and *Betsey ii* (Captain Richardson; 75 tons) also off New Zealand. Bader had visited Bay of Islands late 1805 to drop off stock from Norfolk for Te Pahi and returned on 18 March 1806, finding the place deserted. leaves Port Jackson 13 May; whaling off coast of New Holland; returns 20 September; Ruatara discharged without pay; transfers to *Albion*.

3 March: *Eliza i* (Captain William Richardson; 185 tons; Jerathmiel Peirce and Aaron Wait of Salem) leaves Port Jackson for Norfolk Island and China; fishing off New Zealand; takes 800 barrels of oil; at Bay of Islands, where Richardson collects Maori 'curiosities' now in the Peabody Museum, Salem.

22 April: *Aurora* arrives at Port Jackson from New Zealand with 40 tons of oil; leaves again 24 April; returns 26 May; leaves 30 June; returns 1 October with 44 tons of oil and 500 sealskins; leaves 24 October; returns 14 September 1807 with 130 tons of oil; leaves 19 October.

3 May: *Atlantic* (Captain William Swain) arrives at Port Jackson from New Zealand with 80 barrels of oil; visits Bay of Islands in April; leaves again for the fishery c. July.

17 June: *Venus iii* (Captain Samuel Chace; 45 tons; Campbell & Co. of Calcutta) piratically taken at Port Dalrymple; sailed to Bay of Islands; kidnaps various women at the Bay, takes them to Thames and East Cape, where they are killed; vessel disappears soon after.

16 July: *Richard and Mary* arrives at Port Jackson from New Zealand and Sandy Cape with 100 tons of oil.

21 July: *Brothers I* arrives at Port Jackson from New Zealand with 700 barrels of oil; leaves for the fishery 16 August.

22 July: *Vulture* (Captain Thomas Folger; 312 tons; Mathers of London) arrives at Port Jackson from New Zealand with 500 barrels of oil.

19 August: *Albion* (Captain Cuthbert Richardson; 362 tons; Campbell, Wilson and Page of England) arrives at Port Jackson from England; leaves for New Zealand fishery 12 October; Ruatara joins crew; cruising six months off New Zealand coast, treated well, paid and dropped off at Bay of Islands; vessel reported at Bay of Islands with the *Inspector* April 1807.

8 September: *Richard and Mary* leaves Port Jackson for London with Maa-Tara, son of Te Pahi, on board; arrives under Captain Leikins at Gravesend 17 April 1807.

14 October: *Elizabeth i* leaves Port Jackson for the fishery; goes to Norfolk Island and then to New Zealand.

7 November: *Atlantic* (Captain William Swain; 223 tons; Enderbys) arrives at Port Jackson with

New Zealanders in crew; one New Zealander killed 25 November by lightning that struck a boat belonging to the ship; vessel leaves December for fishery with 750 barrels of oil.

1807

6 February: *Commerce* (Captain Birnie; 225 tons; Lord) leaves Port Jackson; arrives Antipodes for sealing early March; collects gangs left by *Independence* in February 1805 and *Venus iii*; calls at Bay of Islands, where well received by Te Pahi; returns to Port Jackson 8 April; reports *Inspector* (Captain Poole) and *Albion* at the Bay of Islands, and on the arrival of the *Venus iii* pirates at the Bay.

13 February: *General Wellesley* (Captain David Dalrymple; 400 tons; Dalrymple) arrives at Port Jackson from Pulo Penang; leaves 24 April for Pulo Penang via New Zealand for spars; takes George Bruce and Te Atahoe from New Zealand to Fiji and Penang; reports *Santa Anna* and *Inspector* at Bay of Islands.

17 February: *Ferret* touches at Sydney Heads to land despatches and leaves again; returns Mahanga to Bay of Islands c. March.

27 February: *Argo* leaves Port Jackson for the fishery.

1 March: *Elizabeth ii* (Captain William Stewart; 160 tons; colonial brig; McArthur and Co.) leaves Port Jackson for Tahiti; Gregory Warner (medical missionary), William Shelley (missionary), Charles Savage (beachcomber), two Tahitians and two Tongans on board; calls at Bay of Islands 30 March – 11 April, where the actions of the whalers horrify Warner.

30 March: *Star* (Captain J. Wilkinson; 119 tons; James Birnie) leaves Port Jackson for sealing islands and London.

8 April: *Elizabeth i* arrives at Port Jackson from Bay of Islands; had spoke the *Indispensible* (Captain Robert Turnbull; 351 tons; Bennett) off the north end of New Zealand in December and learned more news of the *Venus iii*; leaves 20 April for the fishery via the Derwent; returns to Port Jackson 26 September; leaves 7 November under Alexander Bodie for the fishery and England.

14 May: *Albion* arrives in Port Jackson from New Zealand with 75 tons of oil; leaves for Port Dalrymple and the fishery 26 May; returns 21 September with 150 tons of oil; leaves for the fishery 20 October; returns 11 July; sails for the fishery 8 August; returns 23 September; sails for England 12 November.

10 July: *Santa Anna* (Captain William Moody; 220 tons; Lord, Kable and Underwood) leaves Port Jackson with James Kable, John Jones and two Tahitians on board; calls at Bay of Islands; picks up two Maori (including Ruatara) as sealers and drops them at Bounty Islands; returns to Port Jackson 8 June 1808.

16 September: *Indispensible* arrives at Port Jackson from the fishery with 138 tons of oil; leaves leaves Port Jackson under Captain Henry Best for the fishery and London 26 September.

26 September: *Grand Sachem* (Captain C. Whippey; Benjamin Roach; American) leaves Port Jackson for the fishery.

10 December: *Mercury ii* (Captain Thomas Reibey; 53 tons; colonial schooner) leaves Port Jackson en route to Tahiti with the *King George*; visits the Bay of Islands late December for refreshments; returns to Port Jackson 10 May 1808.

10 December: *King George* (Captain Richard Siddons; 185 tons; Lord, Kable and Underwood) leaves Port Jackson for Tongatapu and Fiji; returns 21 July 1808 with 110 tons sandalwood; 27 August 1808 leaves Port Jackson under Captain Samuel Rodman Chace for the fishery; returns 13 March 1809 with 8,000 sealskins and 1,800 gallons of oil.

1808

7 February: *Elizabeth ii* leaves Port Jackson for Fiji on a sandalwood voyage; visits Bay of Islands en route for 'vegetable comforts'; to Tongatapu and Fiji; returns to Port Jackson 16 October with 120 tons of sandalwood.

14 April: *Parramatta* (Captain John Glenn; 102 tons; Hullets) leaves Port Jackson for Bay of Islands; wrecked there and all the crew killed.

22 April: *Eliza ii* (Captain Corey; 135 tons; Brown and Ives of Providence) leaves Port Jackson for Fiji on a sandalwood voyage; calls at Bay of Islands en route.

10 May: *Venus iv* (Captain John Birbeck; 70 tons; John Macarthur) arrives at Port Jackson from Bay of Islands and Tahiti; had been in Bay October 1807 with *Inspector* (Captain Poole) and *General Wellesley* (Captain Dalrymple).

15 May: *Harrington* (Captain William Campbell; 180 tons; Chace and Co.) piratically seized at Sydney by Robert Stewart and forty other convicts; thought to be taken to the Bay of Islands.

18 May: *Pegasus* (Lieutenant Symonds; Captain Eber Bunker and detachment of NSW Corps; prize ship) sets off in unsuccessful pursuit of *Harrington* to Bay of Islands; reports *Commerce* (Captain James Ceroni), *Inspector*, *Seringapatam* (Captain Edward Clarke) and *Grand Sachem* at the Bay; returns to Sydney 22 July. Former missionary James Elder had boarded *Seringapatam* in Tahiti en route to Port Jackson; cruised off New Zealand for two months with eight other ships, before calling at the Bay; horrified at behaviour of whalers.

16 June: *Favorite* (Captain William Campbell; 158 tons; American brig) returns to Port Jackson; leaves for Fiji 9 September; returns 21 November under Fisk, first officer, having left Campbell at Fiji; leaves 14 December for Fiji to collect sandalwood, and China; in Bay of Islands c. December; returns 14 February 1809 under Campbell's command with 'upwards of' 100 tons of sandalwood.

10 July: *Commerce* arrives at Port Jackson from sealing islands via Bay of Islands and Whangaroa, where Ceroni dropped his watch into the harbour; Te Pahi and three sons on board; carries a cargo of 3,000 sealskins and some 'desirable fine logs, fit for flooring boards, and spars for masts, just imported from New Zealand'; reported that she had sailed from the Bay of Islands with *Inspector*, *Grand Sachem* and *Seringapatam*; sails again for New Zealand 26 September with Te Pahi and his sons.

11 July: *Bom Cidadao* (Captain Demaria, who had died at sea; Portugese vessel) arrives at Port Jackson on a sandalwood voyage to China; had been dismasted off New Zealand; towed in by colonial schooner *Estramina*.

17 September: *Ann* arrives at Port Jackson; in Bay of Islands c. July; leaves again for the fishery in November.

17 September: *Seringapatam* arrives at Port Jackson from New Zealand with 170 tons of oil; leaves again 30 October for the fishery.

15 October: *Mercury ii* (Captain Richard Siddons; 53 tons) sails from Port Jackson to Fiji, calls at Bay of Islands for provisions c. November. *Santa Anna* leaves Port Jackson for sealing islands and England; Ruatara picked up from Bounty Islands and taken to England; landed ill, without pay; transferred to the *Ann ii* (Captain Charles Clarke), which arrives in London July 1809.

15 November: *Speke* (Captain John Hingston) arrives at Port Jackson from England with Maa-Tara on board and ninety-seven female convicts. leaves for the fishery 11 January 1809; visits Bay of Islands, where Hingston has Te Pahi flogged when he could not produce an axe stolen from a woodcutting party; returns to Port Jackson 29 September with 150 tons of black oil and 30 tons of sperm oil.

1809

27 January: *City of Edinburgh* (Captain Simeon Pattison; 526 tons) leaves Port Jackson with Maa-Tara on board and Captain Ceroni as passenger; arrives Bay of Islands 1 March and stays until end of May while refitting ship; Ceroni again drops his watch overboard; six or eight New Zealanders join the journey to Fiji for sandalwood.

16 March: *Otter* (Captain Hopper) arrives at Port Jackson from England on sealing cruise via

Bay of Islands, where she arrived 6 March; found the *Antipode* (Captain Birbeck; 58 tons; Blaxland and Lord) there in great want of supplies; *Antipode* arrives at Port Jackson 22 March.

6 April: *Diana* (Captain Parker; 286 tons; Bennett) and *Inspector* (Captain Walker) reported at the Derwent, both 'five months from England and about to proceed immediately for the fishery off the coast of New Zealand'.

24 July: *Ann* arrives at Port Jackson from Bay of Islands with 1,500 barrels of oil; leaves again 26 September for the fishery.

19 August: *Indispensible* (Captain Henry Best; 350 tons; Bennett) arrives from England; leaves for the fishery 21 October; returns 18 April 1810 with 60 barrels of oil; leaves again 26 April for the fishery.

21 September: *Inspector* arrives at Port Jackson from New Zealand with 160 barrels of oil.

October: *Perseverance* (Captain Hasselberg) leaves Port Jackson for the fishery; returns 28 April 1810 with a load of spars from Bay of Islands.

16 October: *Mary* (Captain Simmons) leaves Port Jackson for the fishery; lost off East Cape, New Zealand; crew saved by the *Inspector*.

Late October: *City of Edinburgh* (Captain Simeon Pattison) returns to Bay of Islands from Fiji; Alexander Berry goes to Whangaroa late December; reports the loss of the *Boyd*; carries the three surviving passengers and one surviving crew member to Peru.

November: *Mercury ii* (Captain Theodore Walker) at Bay of Islands with Peter Dillon on board; on voyage from Sydney to Tahiti for pork.

8 November: *Boyd* (Captain John Thompson) leaves Port Jackson with Te Aara ('George') on board; calls at Whangaroa for spars in December; cut off, burnt and all the crew bar one killed.

1810

18 January: *Union* (Captain William Collins, although Bruce reported Captain Luttrill; 300 tons; Loane and Co.) arrives from Calcutta with Atahoe and George Bruce on board.

Late January: *Cumberland* (Captain William Swain; 268 tons; Enderbys), which had left Port Jackson in September 1809 for the fishery, came into Bay of Islands. Tara showed Swain letters about the loss of the *Boyd* left in his keeping by Berry; was given several gallons of oil as reward.

Mid February: *Ann i*, which had left Port Jackson on 26 September 1809, and *Albion* (Captain Cuthbert Richardson) came into the Bay; Tara told them the news and also showed them the letters left by Berry.

28 February: *Ann ii* (Captain Charles Clarke; 627 tons, convict transport; Jacobs of London) arrives at Port Jackson from London with Marsden, Hall, King and their families, and Ruatara on board.

18 February: *Ann i* and *Albion* leave the Bay of Islands; meet the colonial sealing vessel *King George* (Captain Samuel Chace; 185 tons; Lord, Kable and Underwood) 19 February; Chace comes on board the *Ann* and is told the news of the burning of the *Boyd*; Chace sends a Maori sailor on shore in a whaleboat with a local man, with a letter warning any passing ships' captains about the loss of the *Boyd*; Chace reaches Sydney 9 March and is the first to report the news there.

17 March: *Experiment* (Captain Joseph Dodds; 146 tons; Mestaers of London) hired by Simeon Lord, Francis Williams and Andrew Thompson to take a party headed by William Leith to set up a flax-collecting settlement in the North Island; leaves for Bay of Islands; Lieutenant-Governor Foveaux and his secretary Lieutenant Finacune on board as passengers; arrives at Bay 5 April.

Late March: *Inspector* (Captain John Walker), which had left Port Jackson 16 October 1809);

Atalanta (Captain Joshua Morris; 137 tons; Wilson and Co. of London), which had also left 16 October; *Speke*, which had left November 1809; *Diana* (Captain William Parker); and the sealer *Perseverance* (Captain Frederick Hasselberg), which left Port Jackson October 1809 – each sent an armed boat to attack Te Pahi's island. Soon after, *Spring Grove* (Captain William Mattinson; 256 tons; Wilson and Campbell), which left Port Jackson 28 November 1809, and *New Zealander* (Captain William Elder; 256 tons) arrive at the Bay.

27 March: *Governor Bligh* (Captain Samuel Chace) leaves Port Jackson with supplies for *Experiment*; arrives at Bay of Islands and is told of attack on Te Pahi's island; Mahanga delivers letters from Captain Charles Clarke of *Ann* and from Leith, telling him the probable course of *Experiment*.

27 March: *Star* (Captain John Wilkinson; 119 tons; Plummers of London) arrives in Port Jackson with 600 skins from sealing islands via Mercury Bay, where locals hostile; calls at Bay of Islands; surrounded by armed warriors at watering place.

30 July: *Spring Grove* (Captain William Mattinson) arrives in Port Jackson with 53 tons of oil; leaves again for the fishery 22 October.

17 August: *Diana* (Captain William Parker; 286 tons; Daniel Bennett of London) arrives in Port Jackson with 140 tons of oil; leaves again for the fishery 15 September.

Mid-August: *Unity* arrives at Port Jackson from coast of New Zealand.

1 October: *New Zealander* (Captain William Elder; 258 tons; Daniel Bennett of London) arrives at Port Jackson with 110 tons of oil; leaves again for the fishery 13 October.

28–30 October: *Atalanta* leaves Port Jackson for the fishery and London; in Queen Charlotte Sound in November.

1811

7 February: *Santa Anna* arrives at Port Jackson from New Zealand with 45 tons of oil; reports *Industry* (Captain Walker), *Indispensible* and *Spring Grove* off the New Zealand coast; leaves again for the fishery and England 10 April; wrecked in Straits of Timor.

13 February: *Active ii* (Captain William Richardson; 206 tons; James Cook and Co. of Salem) leaves Port Jackson for Fiji; arrives at New Zealand, where Richardson collects Maori curiosities now in Peabody Museum of Salem.

c. 10 April: *Hawich* (Captain Simmons; 500 tons) battered in storm; puts in to Bay of Islands.

16 July: *Indispensible* arrives at Port Jackson from New Zealand with 175 tons of oil; leaves again for the fishery and London 18 September.

25 July: *New Zealander* arrives at Port Jackson with 1,300 barrels of oil; had spoken *Indispensible*; caught in gales off New Zealand coast that lasted ten weeks.

7 October: *Frederick* (Captain Alexander Bodie; 240 tons; Wilson and Co.) leaves Port Jackson for the fishery and London with Ruatara and Te Pahi's son on board as crew; Ruatara left at Norfolk Island without pay; Te Pahi's son taken forcibly on voyage to England; ship captured in English Channel; Ruatara taken by Captain Gwynn of *Ann i* from Norfolk Island to Port Jackson, arriving 1 August 1812.

15 December: *King George* (Captain Lasco Jones) leaves Port Jackson for the fishery with Jacky Marmon, and 'Bevan and Jack, New Zealanders' in crew.

1812

12 March: *Governor Macquarie* (Captain Eber Bunker), with William Leith on board, returns to Port Jackson with a cargo of spars from New Zealand.

25 March: *Cato* (Captain J. Lindsay; 186 tons; Birnie and Co.) arrives at Port Jackson from the New Zealand fishery with 55 tons of oil; reports *Frederick* with 1,050 barrels; *Ann i* with 600 barrels; *Cumberland* with 750 barrels; *Thames* (Captain Bristol) with 350 barrels at the fishery; *Cato* leaves again for the fishery 21 May.

March 1812: *King George* in the Bay of Islands; complaints later laid at Port Jackson by John

Besent, who ran from the ship and lived in the Bay for twelve months, that Captain Jones had ill-treated the New Zealanders.

2 May: *Mary* (Captain David Lachlan; 360 tons; Boyd of London) arrives at Port Jackson from London and Rio (where on 10 January 'came on Board a Native of New Zealand to work his passage to Port Jackson').

13 June: *Active iii* (Captain Robert Leslie; 120 tons; Hook and Co. of Calcutta) leaves Port Jackson for the Derwent and New Zealand.

18 July: *Atalanta* leaves Port Jackson for the fishery; returns 20 July 1813 with 84 tons of oil.

Later in 1812: *King George*, *Phoenix* and *Ann* reported whaling in company off Macauley Island in the Kermadecs; Jones warns whaling captains of 'Otaheite Jack', left in New Zealand by *Seringapatam* four years earlier, offering his services to obtain spars and decoying seamen away; *King George* returns to Port Jackson 15 February 1813.

1 August: *Ann i* arrives at Port Jackson with 140 tons of oil; brings Ruatara back from Norfolk Island; leaves 19 September and returns Ruatara home after five months at sea.

September: *Daphne* (Captain Michael Fodger [Folger]) leaves Port Jackson for New Zealand, en route to the Pacific for pork.

24 December: *Brothers* (Captain James Kelly) leaves Port Jackson for New Zealand.

1813

19 April: *Perseverance* (Captain Robert Murry) leaves for New Zealand to find a site for harvesting and manufacturing flax; returns 20 July.

19 May: *King George* leaves Port Jackson for Derwent with 'Peter, Cooper, Harry, Jack Wurree, Jemmy Bond, New Zealanders' in crew.

9 June: *Jefferson* (Captain Robert Barnes; 247 tons; Roche of Milford Haven) leaves Port Jackson for the fishery.

22 June: *Phoenix* (Captain William Parker; 320 tons; Bennett) returns to Port Jackson with 205 tons of oil; had visited the Bay of Islands and was treated kindly by Ruatara.

5 December: *King George* leaves Port Jackson for the fishery with Jacky Marmon, Hooroo, Harry, Jemmy Bond, George and Joseph, all 'New Zealanders', in crew.

15 December: *Governor Bligh* (Captain John Grono) arrives at Port Jackson from New Zealand.

1814

15 January: *Cumberland* (Captain Philip Goodenough; 80 tons; Blaxcell) leaves Port Jackson for Tahiti on a sandalwood voyage; in Bay of Islands c. January; returns to Port Jackson in October with 60 tons of 'Yellow wood'.

5 March: *Spring* (Captain Richard Brooks; 150 tons) arrives at Port Jackson from London via Bay of Islands.

2 June: *James Hay* (Captain Thomas Folger; 186 tons; Blaxcell and Co.) leaves Port Jackson for London; in Bay of Islands in June.

10 June – 25 July 1814 *Active iii* (Captain Peter Dillon; 120 tons; Church Missionary Society) in Bay of Islands with Thomas Kendall and William Hall; returns to Sydney 23 August with Ruatara, Hongi Hika and Korokoro.

13 July: *Catherine* (Captain Simmons; 304 tons;Bennett) leaves Port Jackson for the fishery; in Bay of Islands c. August.

16 October: *Jefferson* leaves for the fishery with 95 tons of oil; in Bay of Islands in December.

28 November: (after unsuccessful attempt to leave on 19 November) *Active iii* leaves Port Jackson with Samuel Marsden, Thomas Kendall, William Hall, J. L. Nicholas, Hongi Hika, Ruatara and Korokoro as passengers; arrives Bay of Islands 22 December; leaves 26 February 1815.

c. December: *King George* in Bay of Islands.

Notes and
References

Key to archives abbreviations

ANL National Library of Australia, Canberra, Australia.

APL Auckland Public Library, Auckland, New Zealand.

ATL Alexander Turnbull Library, National Library of New Zealand, Wellington, New Zealand.

AUL University of Auckland Library, Auckland, New Zealand

DL Dixson Library, State Library of New South Wales, Sydney, Australia.

HO Hocken Library, University of Otago, Dunedin, New Zealand.

ML Mitchell Library, State Library of New South Wales, Sydney, Australia.

NLS National Library of Scotland, Edinburgh, United Kingdom.

PRO Public Record Office, London, United Kingdom.

SOAS School of Oriental and African Studies Library, London, United Kingdom.

Prologue

(pages 17–27)

1. Toiroa's prophecy is cited in Binney 1995: 11–12.
2. 'No mua noa atu tera kitenga i te waka i te taenga mai o te kaipuke o Kapene Kuki ka titiro atu nga koroua me nga kuia ka karanga, he motuu he motu tere mai no tawhiti ina e tere mai nei. Ka titiro atu ki nga heera ka karanga, ahahaa me he kapua i te rangi nga ra o te motu e tere mai nei. No te tukunga o nga heera, no te riwhi-tanga, ka titiro atu ki nga rewa; ara ki nga maihi, me nga kurupae, me nga rikini; ka karanga ano, e i me he uru rakau tonu no tahaki hikitia ai ki te moana te motutere e tu mai nei. He maanu mai te poti ka karanga ano, ka maanu mai nga waka o te motu e tu mai nei.' (*Te Pipiwharau- roa* 153, January 1911: 5.)
3. Salmond 1991: 123–24; 'Tipihaere' in *Te Pipi- wharauroa* 104, 1906: 6.
4. Salmond 1991: 150–51.
5. Ibid: 87–88. A number of scholars, notably Gananath Obeyesekere (1993), have questioned my use of this and other tribal historical accounts, on the grounds that such material is inherently unreliable and should not be taken seriously as

evidence of the past. In response I would argue that oral memory was highly developed among Maori, especially those (like Te Taniwha) who were repositories of kin-group accounts of the past; furthermore of Te Taniwha's account, that it survives in a number of versions that are mutually consistent but give different levels of detail on particular incidents, and one of which was recorded as an official affidavit in 1852; and that other accounts of Cook's first voyage were being collected at about the same time, for instance from an old lady called Hine Kapu, who spoke with Donald McLean in 1851: 'I met an old deformed woman shrunk up from age who had seen Captain Cook . . . she describes herself to have been 16 years old, she is quite clear in intellect and retentive in memory describing minutely every small circumstance connected with Capt. Cook's visit.' (McLean 1851). My own experiences in collecting Eruera and Amiria Stirling's autobiographical memories, which could be checked against documentary evidence in many instances, convinced me that Western scholars' dismissals of oral histories are often simply prejudice, based on a privileging of written materials (their own most characteristic medium) and ideas about memory based on a literate way of life. While there may be inconsisten- cies and inaccuracies in oral accounts, this is also true of documents. The best approach is to check each source against the widest possible array of other evidence.

6. White ATL Ms 75, nd, Folder 19: 87.
7. White 1888 V: Maori texts 105–6; English texts 122–26. 'Ka noho ra matou i Whitianga ka puta taua kaipuke nei ki reira, ka kite atu a matou kaumatua i taua kaipuke ka mea ratou he atua, a he tupua nga tangata o taua kaipuke, a ka tu te kaipuke a ka hoe mai nga poti ki uta, ka mea aua kaumatua, "Koia ano he tupua, he kanohi kei nga muri-kokai, ina e hoe tuara mai ana ki uta," ka u mai aua tupua ki uta ka mataku atu matou nga wahine me nga tamariki a ka oma matou ki te tahora, ko nga toa anake i noho i aro atu ki aua tupua, ano ka roa, a kahore kau he he o aua tupua ki o matou toa, ka taki hokihoki mai matou, a ka matakitaki ki aua tupua, a ka mirimiri o matou ringa ki o ratou kakahu, a ka mihi matou ki te ma o a ratou kiri me te kahurangi o nga kanohi o etahi.

'Ka mahi ka kohi tio aua tupua, a ka hoatu he

kumara, he ika, he roi e matou ki aua tupua, pai
tonu mai ratou, a ka noho matou nga wahine me
nga tamariki ka tunu pipi ma aua tupua, a ka kite
atu matou e kai ana taua hunga i te kumara, me
te ika me te pipi ka oho mauri matou ka mea, "E
hara pea i te tupua penei me nga atua maori nei,
ina hoki e kai ana i nga kai o te ao maori nei." Ka
haere aua tupua ki te ngahere, piki haere ai ki to
matou Pa i Whitianga, me te kohi otaota i nga
pari, me te patoto haere i nga kohatu o te akau,
ka mea matou, "Hei aha ra aua mea ma aua
tupua?"

'A ka kohia atu hoki e matou e nga wahine me nga
tamariki, nga kohatu noa, nga tarutaru noa ka hoatu ki
aua tupua, he kohatu i paingia a ka kohia ki a ratou
putea, he mea i makaa, ko nga tarutaru me nga peka
rakau i hoatu, ka tu ka korero, he ui pea, ko te reo koa
kihai i mohiotia, kata atu ai matou, a ka kata hoki aua
tupua, a pai noa iho matou.'

8. Salmond 1991: 427.
9. Ibid: 388.
10. Ibid: 387.
11. Ibid: 401. 'Ka kainga . . . a Mariao e Te Kauri raua ko
   Tohitapu, he tohunga hoki raua, a ma raua e kai taua
   maitai, kia kore ai he aitua ki a raua iwi mo te tapu o a
   raua tupapaku i takahia e te iwi o Mariao. A, ko nga
   wheua o te hunga maitai i patua nei he mea mahi hei
   tirou kai, a, a, ko nga wheua o nga huha he mea mahi hei
   torino, ara, hei rehu.'
12. *Te Pipiwharauroa* November 1910: 7; December 1910:
   2–3; January 1911: 4–5. See also Atkinson 1892,
   Williams 1893, Nahe 1894. In 1963, Wilson
   suggested that the term 'Pakeha' comes from the
   sailors' frequent use of 'Bugger you'. Baker, however,
   had already dismissed this derivation in his 1945 work
   on New Zealand slang as appealing 'to popular
   imagination at the expense of common sense'. I agree
   with Baker. The scholarly opinions given by Nahe and
   Williams accord with that given by Mohi Tuurei and
   cited above. I suspect one must look to twists in the
   settler psyche, rather than etymology, to understand
   why so many 'Pakeha' prefer to think that the word is a
   transliteration of a dismissive curse.
13. Van Nierop 1674: 58–59.
14. Prévost 1746 in Ollivier 1987: 209.
15. See Ollivier 1987: 210-11.
16. Salmond 1991: 112–13.
17. *Gazette de France,* 5 October 1770: 324; 26 July
   1771: 247; 79: 323; 80: 327.
18. *Critical Review* XXXII 1771: 256–61; *London Chronicle,*
   27–30 July 1771: 102; 30 July – 1 August: 109; 8–10
   October: 349.
19. Benjamin Franklin 19 August 1771, ATL qMS 0809.
20. Plan for Benefiting Distant Unprovided Countries,
   Dodsley's Annual Register for 1771, in ATL qMS
   0809.
21. Boswell 1891 II: 124–25.
22. Cook 1771 in McNab 1914 II: 79–80.

Introduction I
(pages 31–33)

1. Quoted in Salmond 1991: 95.
2. Quoted in ibid: 264.
3. Francis Bacon, cited in Slawinski 1991: 81, 109.
4. Heidegger 1978: 267.

One: The *Resolution* and *Adventure*
(pages 36–44)

1. Banks in Beaglehole (ed.) 1962 II: 38–41.
2. Franklin and Dalrymple 1771.
3. Beaglehole (ed.) 1962 I: 69.
4. Quoted in Beaglehole 1969 II: xxx.
5. Elliott in Holmes (ed.) 1984: 7.
6. Beaglehole 1969 II: clxviii.
7. Cook in ibid: 13.
8. Admiralty Secretary in ibid: 923–34.
9. Elliott in Holmes (ed.) 1984: xxx.
10. J. Forster quoted in Beaglehole 1969 I: xlv.
11. Ibid: xlvi.
12. Shapin and Schaffer 1985.
13. Larson 1971: 97,143–44; Barber 1980: 51–52.
14. Elliott in Holmes (ed.) 1984: 11.
15. J. Forster in Hoare (ed.) 1982 I: 156.
16. Ibid: 153–54.
17. G. Forster in Kahn (ed.) 1968: 53.
18. Elliott in Holmes (ed.) 1984:14.
19. J. Forster in Hoare (ed.) 1982 II: 233–34.
20. Pickersgill in Holmes (ed.) 1984: 67.
21. Cook in Beaglehole 1969 II: 110.

Two: Tamatea (Dusky Sound)
(pages 45–64)

1. Beattie 1949: 7–12.
2. Beaglehole 1969 I: 27; Beattie 1915: 110–11;
   Beattie 1917: 76–78.
3. Beattie 1915: 99–100.
4. Ibid: 100–1. According to White (1887: 195–97),
   Ngaati Mamoe were descended from Awatopa, the
   elder brother of Rauru son of Toi (see also Beattie
   1917: 79–80), whereas Mackay (1873: 40) traces
   them to Turi of the *Aotea* canoe.
5. Mackay 1873: 44–45; see also White III 1887: 311–
   13; Pybus 1954: 38–40.
6. Off Anchor Island.
7. G. Forster 1777 I: 123–24.
8. Ibid: 126, Coutts 1969: 186.
9. Pickersgill in Holmes (ed.) 1984: 68. This was
   Whetuu, or Pickersgill Harbour.
10. Wales (in Beaglehole [ed.] 1969 II: 777) says one
   canoe; Cook says two or three; Pickersgill says two.
11. Wales in ibid: 777.
12. J. Forster in Hoare (ed.) 1982 II: 242.
13. For instance, Cowan 1926: 161; Fildes 1936;
   Beattie 1945; 103–5. Cowan says that 'some old
   natives of Murihiku' gave him 'the names of Maru,
   Te Ao-paraki and a woman named Ki-mai-waho as

those of the three principal inhabitants of Dusky at this period', but this identification is very late. According to some accounts, Maru was a Ngaai Tahu/Ngaati Mamoe contemporary of Tarawhai, whose story was recounted at the beginning of this chapter.

14. Wales in Beaglehole (ed.) 1969 II: 777.
15. Ibid.
16. Begg and Begg 1966: 133.
17. Wales in Beaglehole (ed.) 1969 II: 778–79.
18. G. Forster 1777 I: 125.
19. J. Forster in Hoare (ed.) 1982 II: 241.
20. Blunt 1971.
21. J. Forster in Hoare (ed.) 1982 II: 251.
22. G. Forster 1777 I: 128.
23. J. Forster in Hoare (ed.) 1982 II: 257.
24. Ibid: 245.
25. Ibid: 248.
26. See Salmond 1991: 82.
27. Elliott in Holmes (ed.) 1984: 17–18.
28. Tikao 1939: 154–55. Tikao also reported that on one occasion Te Ihukakaru, father of Karetai, saw Cook smoking a pipe and decided to test whether he was atua or human. He doused Cook's head with water, the pipe went out and he decided that Cook was human. There is no mention of any such incident, however, in any of the journals from Cook's three expeditions; and if it had happened it would have been a great insult to Cook. Pouring water on a person's head attacked their tapu.
29. Marra says these spears were eighteen feet long – they were bird spears (Marra 1967: 25).
30. Elliott in Holmes (ed.) 1984 II: 17.
31. J. Forster in Hoare (ed.) 1982 II: 248–49.
32. Marra 1967: 26.
33. Pickersgill in Holmes (ed.) 1984: 69.
34. Coutts 1969: 200–1.
35. South Island Maori was a different dialect from those spoken in the North.
36. Pickersgill 1984: 69; Wales in Beaglehole (ed.) 1969 II: 780; J. Forster in Hoare (ed.) 1982 II: 254.
37. Wales in Beaglehole (ed.) 1969 II: 780.
38. Marra 1967: 31–32.
39. J. Forster in Hoare (ed.) 1982 II: 258.
40. G. Forster 1777 I: 160.
41. Cook in Beaglehole (ed.) 1969 II: 122.
42. J. Forster in Hoare (ed.) 1982 II: 259.
43. Ibid I: 102.
44. Clerke in Beaglehole (ed.) 1969 II: 123.
45. J. Forster in Hoare (ed.) 1982 II: 262.
46. Cook in Beaglehole (ed.) 1969 II: 124–25.
47. Strands and lines were often used in ceremonies to allow spiritual transfers to take place – to let a spirit leave a dying body, to call upon ancestral gods and so on. Michael King has pointed out that this kind of ceremony was retained by Maori in the far south and by Moriori in the Chatham Islands. It may have been a survival from ancient peaceful protocols of greeting (King, pers. comm. 1997).
48. G. Forster 1777 I: 171–72.
49. Wales in Beaglehole (ed.) 1969 II: 783.

50. G. Forster 1777 I: 165–66.
51. Elliott in Holmes (ed.) 1984: 17.
52. Clerke in PRO Adm 55/103: 71.
53. Coutts 1969: 188–89.
54. G. Forster 1777 I: 177–79.
55. See also George Forster's comments on Tahitians, 1777: vii.
56. Sparrman 1944: 46.
57. Pickersgill in Holmes (ed.) 1984: 70.
58. See, for instance, Begg and Begg 1966: 113–27.
59. G. Forster 1777 I: 179.

For manuscript records of Cook's second expedition visits to New Zealand, see British Museum Cook's Second Voyage Fragments, Add Ms 27889; South Sea Voyages Drawings and Prints, Add Ms 23920; Charts of Cook's Voyages, Add Ms 31360; Logbook of *Resolution*, Add Ms 27 887 ff 43–46B; 47; 70B–71B; 125A–126B; Logbook of *Resolution*, Add Ms 27956 ff 5B–7; 79–81; 31 James Cook's holograph *Resolution* Logbook, Add Ms 27886 ff 76–90; 95–112; 96B–105; 163B–168B; 315–319B; Cook's draft *Resolution* Journal, Add Ms 27888; Charles Clerke's *Resolution* Logbook, Vol. I, Add Ms 8951, ff 66A–72B; 76A–78A; Vol. II, Add Ms 8952, ff 46B–48B; Vol. III, Add Ms 8953, ff 28 A–29A; Charts Add Ms 31360; William Hodges's Views, Add Ms 15743; John Elliott's *Resolution* Memoirs, Add Ms 42714, f 1B, ff 16–17; 22–23B; 34B–35; Charts, Add Ms 15500, 3, 4; Cook's *Resolution* Journal, Eg Ms 2178, ff 164–199B; James Cook's *Resolution* Journal, Eg 2177A, ff 69–93; 2177B, ff 5–17; Public Record Office James Cook's Resolution journal (copy) Adm 55/108, ff 267–70; James Cook's *Resolution* Letters, Adm 1/1610, ff 86–154; Robert Cooper's *Resolution* Journal, Adm 55/104, ff 64–65B; 68; 94B–98; Robert Cooper's *Resolution* Log, Adm 55/109, ff 35–35B; Charles Clerke's *Resolution* Log, Adm 55/103, ff 67B–71, 73–74; 105–109; 193–194; Richard Pickersgill's *Resolution* Log, Adm 51/4553/5, ff 250B–254; 256–256B; /6, ff 288–292B; Joshua Gilbert's *Resolution* Log, Adm 55/107, ff 69–76; ff 108–108B; Isaac Smith's *Resolution* Log, Adm 55/105, ff 72B–75; 77B–78B; 108–113; 187–188; John Burr's *Resolution* Log, Adm 55/106, ff 72B–75; 77–78; 106–110B; 180B–182; Thomas Willis's *Resolution* Journal, Adm 51/4554/199; ff 134B–140; 148B–151; / 200, ff 379B–382; /201, ff 186–188; 190–190B; 218B–222B; /202, ff 293–293B; William Harvey's *Resolution* Journal, Adm 51/4553/185 ff 52B–61; /186, ff 89B–92; /187, ff 157B–160; Joseph Price's *Resolution* Log, Adm 51/4556/189, ff 54B–57B; Joseph Price's *Resolution* Journal, Adm 51/4556/190, ff 112–116B; Anon. *Resolution* log, Adm 51/4555/218, ff 201–204; 206–207; 238B–240; John Elliott's *Resolution* Log, Adm 51/4556/208, ff 255B–260B; 288–291B; Alexander Hood's *Resolution* Log, Adm 51/4554/182, ff 41B–48; 58B–63; /183, ff 97B–100; Charles Loggie's *Resolution* Journal, Adm 51/4554/207, ff 350B–355; James Maxwell's *Resolution* Log, Adm 51/4555/206, ff 33–36; 38B–39; 66B–70B; 136–137B; Bowles Mitchel's *Resolution* Log, Adm 51/4555/194, ff 280–287; 289–292; 323–328; /195, ff 402–403; Tobias Furneaux's *Adventure* Log, Adm 55/1, ff 43B–49; 62B–75; Tobias Furneaux's Captain's Letters,

Adm 1/1789; Arthur Kempe's *Adventure* Log, Adm 51/4520/1 (2), ff 63–67B; 96B–108A; Adm 51/4520/2, ff 191B–197; 4520/3, ff 212B–219A; James Burney's *Adventure* Journal Adm 51/4523/2, ff 38–41; 70B–83; /5, ff 115B–121; /6, ff 143B–152; Constable Love, Adm 51/4520/8, ff 212B–219A, 238B–245; Adm 51/4520/7, ff 289B–294; Henry Lightfoot's *Adventure* Log, Adm 51/4523/5, ff 203–205; 235–241; 244B–246; Anon *Adventure* Journal, Adm 51/4524, /17, ff 145B–150B; 170–176; 178–182; Robert Browne's *Adventure* Journal, Adm 51/4521/9, ff 22B–27A; /10, ff 41B–48; Thomas Dyke's *Adventure* Log, Adm 51/4521/12, ff 258–260B; 289–294; 294–299B; John Falconer's *Adventure* Log, Adm 51/4524/1, ff 35–36B; /2, ff 66B–72; 76–77; William Hawkey's *Adventure* Log, Adm 51/4521/11, ff 128–131B; 161B–165; 166–167; 167B–170B; Richard Hergest's *Adventure* Journal, Adm 51/4522/13, ff 54B–62; 91B–107; 168B–173; 186B–197; John Wilby's *Adventure* Journal, Adm 51/4222/14, ff 166B, 168B–173; 189B–197; National Maritime Museum, James Cook's Journal copy; Richard Pickersgill's *Resolution* Journal, JOD/56, ff 49–83; Royal Greenwich Observatory; William Wales' *Resolution* Logbook; National Library of Australia, letter to Cook from Sir Phillip Stephens, 20 July 1776, Mss 688; Mitchell Library, Sydney, James Cook Log Leaves, Safe PH 17/2; Cook holograph fragments, Safe PH 17/2, 4, 12; William Wales Safe PH 18/4; Alexander Turnbull Library, Sandwich family papers, WTU Ms Papers 841

Three: Totara-nui I

(pages 65–88)

1. See Salmond 1991: 241. See also the excellent reconstruction of eighteenth-century Maori occupation of Totara-nui by Mitchell and Mitchell nd: 2–73–92.
2. Banks quoted in Salmond 1991: 252–53.
3. White 1888 V: 120–21.
4. O'Regan in Barratt (ed.) 1987: 147–53.
5. Furneaux in Beaglehole (ed.) 1969 II: 737.
6. Burney in Hooper 1975: 48–49.
7. Salmond 1991: 254.
8. G. Forster 1777 I: 202.
9. Bayly in McNab 1914 II: 203–4.
10. Ibid: 204.
11. Burney in Hooper (ed.) 1975: 50.
12. Furneaux in Beaglehole (ed.) 1969 II: 738.
13. Ibid: 741.
14. J. Forster in Hoare (ed.) 1982 II: 284.
15. G. Forster 1777 I: 203.
16. J. Forster in Hoare (ed.) 1982 II: 284–85.
17. Wales in Beaglehole (ed.) 1969 II: 788–89.
18. Mitchell Ms 4-90, for the Koraki identification; Simmons in Barratt (ed.) 1987: 42, and Mitchell Ms 4-89 identify him as Korako.
19. Mitchell prefers 'Taiaroa', derived from 'Tiarooa', Cook's transcription of this young man's name (see Mitchell Ms 4-92). I note, however, that the best Maori linguist on board, Samwell, called him 'Taywe-herooa', as did Edgar – a name for which Te Weherua seems a better Maori equivalent.
20. G. Forster 1777 I: 209.
21. J. Forster in Hoare (ed) 1982 II: 288.
22. This family seem to have had kin links further south, for in later life a man named Korako (who Simmons claims was 'Kollakh' [Simmons in Barratt 1987: 42]) spent much of his time at Murdering Beach, where one of the second voyage medals was found. In 1848 he traded a tomahawk received from Cook with a European settler there. Mitchell argues that this Korako (whose whakapapa he cites) could not have met with Cook, since in 1773 he was the father of a thirteen-year-old boy named Taiweherroa (or Taiwahirooa), and must have been around thirty years old at least (Mitchell Ms 4-90); and suggests one Koraki of Ngaati Mamoe instead. A close reading of the manuscripts suggests, though, that Te Weherua's father was 'Kutughhaa' (Toka), not 'Kollakh' (J. Forster in Hoare [ed.] 1982 II: 287), and that 'Kollakh' may have been quite young in 1773, so Simmons' identification remains possible. The distribution of second voyage medals and Cook artefacts do, however, suggest a chain of kinship links to the south.
23. Marra 1967: 45.
24. Cook in Beaglehole (ed.) 1969 II: 174–75.
25. G. Forster 1777 I: 212.
26. A red-headed, bearded man was described to Edwin Palmer in the 1820s as having been fathered by one of Cook's men (Anderson 1991: 2).
27. Sparrman 1944: 56.
28. Cook in Beaglehole (ed.) 1969 II: 168–69.
29. Mitchell Ms 4-94. Mitchell supplies a whakapapa for this man, gleaned from Rangitaane whakapapa books.
30. G. Forster 1777 I: 218.
31. Ibid: 219.
32. J. Forster in Hoare (ed.) 1982 II: 290.
33. Burney in Hooper (ed.) 1975: 56–57.
34. Cook in Beaglehole (ed.) 1969 II: 170. George Forster elaborates on this story in his retrospective account, transposing it to 10 November 1773, when the *Resolution* visited the Sound for the second time.
35. J. Forster in Hoare (ed.) 1982 II: 291.
36. Burney in Hooper (ed.) 1987: 57.
37. G. Forster 1777 I: 224.
38. Bayly in McNab (ed.) 1908 II: 209.
39. G. Forster 1777 I: 225.
40. Ibid: 227.
41. Ibid: 225.
42. Ibid: 229–30.
43. Marra 1967: 38.
44. Bowles in Adm 51/4555: 292.
45. Wales in Beaglehole (ed.) 1969 II: 790.
46. Elliott in Holmes (ed.) 1984: 18.
47. J. Forster in Hoare (ed.) 1982 II: 303–4.
48. G. Forster 1777 I: 243.
49. Elliott in Holmes (ed.) 1984: 19.
50. G. Forster 1777 I: 483.
51. Colenso 1877: 146.
52. Marra 1967: 73.
53. Cook in Beaglehole (ed.) 1969 II: 279.

54. G. Forster 1777 I: 485.
55. Colenso 1877: 146.
56. J. Forster in Hoare (ed.) 1982 III: 410.
57. Wales in Beaglehole (ed.) 1969 II: 815.

Four: Totara-nui II

(pages 89–108)

1. G. Forster 1777 I: 494.
2. J. Forster in Hoare (ed.) 1982 III: 419.
3. G. Forster 1777 I: 496–97.
4. Cook in Beaglehole (ed.) 1969 II: 288.
5. Ibid: 289.
6. G. Forster, 1777 II: 503.
7. J. Forster in Hoare (ed.) 1982 III: 422.
8. Salmond 1991: 243–45.
9. Cook in Beaglehole (ed.) 1969 II: 291.
10. G. Forster 1777 I: 508.
11. Cook in Beaglehole (ed.) 1969 II: 292.
12. J. Forster in Hoare (ed.) 1982 III: 426.
13. See, for instance, Marsden 1932: 128, 193, 283; Taylor 1855: 165; Colenso 1875: 30.
14. Clerke in Beaglehole (ed.) 1969 II: 293.
15. Ibid: 293.
16. Cook in Beaglehole (ed.) 1969 II: 294.
17. G. Forster 1777 I: 517.
18. Sparrman 1944: 115–16.
19. Wales in Beaglehole (ed.) 1969 II: 819.
20. For instance, during the French Revolution it was reported in an English newspaper that, after the fall of the Tuileries, a man was seen drinking the blood of a Swiss Guard and that the hearts of Guards were eaten by some of the people (*St James's Chronicle*, 21 August 1792).
21. Duffy 1987: 262.
22. Baynham 1969: 79–80, for instance, quotes this sailor's description of a fight at sea: 'The din of battle continued. Grape and canister shot were pouring through our port-holes like iron hail, shaking her to the very keel, or passing through her timbers and scattering terrific splinters, which did a more appalling work than even their own death-giving blows . . . I now went below to see how matters appeared there. The first object I met was a man bearing a limb which had just been detached from some suffering wretch. Pursuing my way to the wardroom I necessarily passed through the steerage which was strewn with the wounded; it was a sad spectacle, made more appalling by the groans and cries which rent the air. Some were groaning, others were swearing most bitterly, a few were praying, while these last arrived were begging most piteously to have their wounds dressed next. The surgeon and his mate were smeared with blood from head to foot: they looked more like butchers than doctors.' One could multiply ad nauseum such accounts of the results of battle in eighteenth-century Europe.
23. Cf. Obeyesekere 1992: 630–54.
24. J. Forster in Hoare (ed.) 1982 III: 429.
25. G. Forster 1777 I: 523.
26. Bayly in McNab 1914 II: 211.
27. Quoted in G. Forster 1777 I: 477–78.
28. Burney in Hooper (ed.) 1975: 87.
29. Ibid: 89.
30. Bayly in McNab 1914 II: 216.
31. See Salmond 1991: 249–50.
32. Furneaux in Beaglehole (ed.) 1969 II: 744.
33. Burney in Adm 51/4523/2: 82.
34. See *Monthly Miscellany*, December 1774: 298–99, quoting from Marra 1967: 96. It does not seem likely that Marra was in fact an eyewitness, however, so there was some creative editing involved.
35. Burney in Adm 51/4523/2.
36. G. Forster 1777 I: 458.
37. Browne in Adm 51/4521/10: 48.
38. Marra 1967: 97. It was a sailors' custom to auction the clothes of dead shipmates so that the proceeds could be given to their families.
39. Cited in McCormick 1977: 95.
40. Cited in ibid: 94.
41. Ibid: 96.
42. J. Forster in Hoare (ed.) 1982 III: 438.
43. Cook in Beaglehole 1969 II: lxxxvi.
44. Sparrman 1944: 119.

Five: Totara-nui III

(pages 109–140)

1. G. Forster 1777 II: 452–53.
2. Cook in Beaglehole (ed.) 1969 II: 571.
3. J. Forster in Hoare (ed.) 1982 IV: 676.
4. Bowles in Adm 51/4555: 402b.
5. Clerke in Adm 55/103: 193b.
6. O'Regan 1987: 148–55.
7. G. Forster 1777 II: 471.
8. Ibid: 472.
9. Ibid: 474.
10. Ibid: 476.
11. Cook in Beaglehole (ed.) 1969 II: 576–77.
12. Cook in ibid: 576 fn.
13. J. Forster in Hoare (ed.) 1982 IV: 684.
14. Cook in Beaglehole (ed.) 1969 II: 653. See also Cook to John Walker, 14 September 1775: 'That the New Zealanders are Cannibals will no longer be disputed, not only from the Melancholy fate of the Adventure's people and Captain Marion and his fellow sufferers, but from what I and my whole crew have seen with our own eyes. Nevertheless I think them a good sort of people at least I have always found good treatment among them.' ATL qMS 1775 P C00: 5.
15. See McCormick 1977: 151.
16. Cook in Beaglehole 1969 II: 657.
17. Solander quoted in O'Brien 1987: 189. In his *Observations*, George Forster (1777 I: 512) noted: 'This head is now deposited in the collection of Mr. John Hunter F.R.S.' Hunter was a noted anatomist of the time.
18. Cook in Beaglehole (ed.) 1969 II: cxiii.
19. Munford 1963: xxiii.
20. Ryskamp and Pottle 1963: 308–10.

21. Cook in Beaglehole (ed.) 1967 III (i): 23.
22. *London Magazine*, quoted in McCormick 1977: 150.
23. Samwell in Beaglehole (ed.)1967 III (ii): 994–95.
24. Samwell in ibid: 995.
25. Samwell in ibid: 995.
26. Cook in Beaglehole (ed.) 1967 III (i): 60–61.
27. Samwell in Beaglehole (ed.) 1967 III (ii): 996.
28. Gore in Adm 55/120: 79b.
29. Williamson 12.2.1777.
30. Rickman 1785: 50–51.
31. Samwell in Beaglehole (ed.) 1967 III (ii): 998.
32. Rickman 1785: 41.
33. Anderson in Adm 51/4560: 88.
34. Clarke 1903: 27.
35. White 1888 V: 120–21.
36. Rickman 1785: 53–54.
37. Ibid: 55–56.
38. Burney in McNab 1914 II: 198–99.
39. Home quoted in Beaglehole 1967 III (i): xcviii–iv.
40. See Darnton in *The Great Cat Massacre* 1985: 75–106.
41. Gilbert in Holmes (ed.)1984: 24.
42. Burney in McNab 1914 II: 198–99.
43. Gore in Adm 55/120: 80.
44. Rickman 1785: 63.
45. King in Adm 55/116: 52.
46. Cook in Beaglehole (ed.) 1967 III (i): 70; and Bayly in McNab 1914 II: 220.
47. Ledyard in Munford (ed.) 1963: 19–20.
48. I am not sure about the status of this part of the 'Gowhanahee' story. Ledyard was something of a romantic, and in any case copied much of his account from Rickman, who does not mention her lover's attempted desertion. This episode thus lacks independent corroboration and, while it is appealing, is either exaggerated in some of its details, or could be pure fiction on Ledyard's part.
49. Cook in Beaglehole (ed.) 1967 III (ii): 68.
50. McEwen in Beaglehole (ed.) 1967 III (ii): 1299–1300.
51. Edgar in Adm 55/21: 59.
52. Samwell in Beaglehole (ed.) 1967 III (ii): 1298–99.
53. Ibid: 1009.
54. King, quoted in McCormick 1977: 213.
55. Samwell in Beaglehole (ed.) 1967 III (ii): 1031.
56. Clerke in Adm 55/22: 57b.
57. See Beaglehole 1967 III (i): cii–civ.
58. Rickman 1785: 131–33.
59. Samwell in Beaglehole (ed.) 1967 III (ii): 1063.
60. Williamson quoted in Beaglehole (ed.) 1967 III (i): 231.
61. Samwell in Beaglehole (ed.) 1967 III (ii): 1072.
62. Ibid: 1072–73.
63. Ibid: 1073.

Six: Cook's Visits to Totaranui

(pages 141–160)

1. Pickersgill quoted in Salmond 1991: 259.
2. See Anderson 1991: 2.
3. J. Forster in Hoare (ed.) 1982 III: 412.
4. Wales in Beaglehole (ed.) 1969 II: 800–1.
5. Quoted in Gascoigne 1994: 137.
6. See ibid: 134, 188.
7. Anderson in Beaglehole (ed.) 1967 III (ii): 802.
8. Ibid: 809.
9. Cook in Beaglehole (ed.) 1967 III (i): 72.
10. Anderson in Beaglehole (ed.) 1967 III (ii): 803.
11. Walker, quoted in Gascoigne 1994: 188.
12. Anderson in Beaglehole (ed.) 1967 III (ii): 802–3.
13. Ibid: 805.
14. Ibid: 804–5.
15. J. Forster in Hoare (ed.) 1982 II: 297–8.
16. Bayly in McNab 1914 II:206.
17. Anderson in Beaglehole (ed.) 1967 III (ii): 806.
18. Ibid: 808.
19. Ibid.
20. Ibid.
21. Ledyard 1963: 13.
22. Furneaux in Beaglehole (ed.) 1969 II: 739–40.
23. J. Forster in Hoare (ed.) 1982 II: 299–300.
24. Bayly in McNab 1914 II: 205.
25. J. Forster in Hoare (ed.) 1982 II: 301.
26. Anderson in Beaglehole (ed.) 1969 II: 812–13.
27. J. Forster in Hoare (ed.) 1982 II: 301.
28. Anderson in Beaglehole (ed.) 1967 III (ii): 812.
29. Ibid: 810–11.
30. Furneaux in Beaglehole 1969 II: 739.
31. J. Forster 1996: 152.
32. For example, the *Royal Admiral* missionaries in Hauraki in 1801 thought that there must be 'many hundred thousand of natives at New Zealand'; and William Ellis, who visited the Bay of Islands in 1816, wrote: 'The population of New Zealand has been estimated at half a million; which estimate must, from the unorganized state of society, be mere conjecture, so that it may exceed this number' (Ellis 1969: 341).
33. J. Forster 1996: 184–90.
34. Anderson in Beaglehole 1967 III (ii): 816.
35. Ibid.
36. Ibid.
37. J. Forster in Hoare (ed.) 1982 II: 298.
38. Anderson in Beaglehole 1967 II (ii): 813–14.
39. Ibid: 817.
40. Cook in Beaglehole (ed.) 1969 III (i): 71.
41. Anderson in Beaglehole (ed.) 1967 III (ii): 814–15.

For manuscript records of Cook's third Pacific expedition visits to New Zealand, see British Museum, James Cook *Resolution* Journal, Eg. Ms 2177A, B; 2178–9; James Burney's *Resolution* Journal, Add Ms 8955; John Webber Drawings, Add Ms 15, 513, 6, 10; John Webber Drawings, Add Ms 17277, Nos 7, 8, 36; George Gilbert's *Discovery* Journal, Add Ms 38,530 ff 10B–16B; David Samwell's *Discovery* Journal, Eg. 2591, ff 10–19; Thomas Edgar's *Discovery* Journal, Add Ms 37, 528, ff 17–23; Public Record Office, James Cook's *Resolution* Journal (copy), Adm 55/111, ff 56–63B; John Gore's *Resolution* Log, Adm 55/120, ff 79–81; James King's *Resolution* Log, Adm 55/116, f 129, ff 1–3B; 51–53; George Gilbert's *Resolution* Log, Adm 51/4559/213, ff 152B–154; John Williamson's

Resolution Log, Adm 55/117, ff 44B–45; William Lanyon's *Resolution* Log, Adm 51/4558/196, ff 96–97B; William Lanyon's *Resolution* Log, Adm 51/4558/196, ff 96–97B; John Watts's *Resolution* Log, Adm 51/4559/212, ff 27B–29; William Charlton's *Resolution* Log, Adm 51/4557/191, ff 21B–23B(?); William Charlton *Resolution* Log, Adm 51/4557/4, ff 160–169; /5, ff 241–242B; William Harvey's *Resolution* Log, Adm 55/110, ff 98B–100B; William Anderson's *Resolution* Log, Adm 51/4560/203, ff 85–111; Mathew Paul's *Resolution* Log, Adm 51/4560/4, ff 328B–329; Anon *Resolution* Log, Adm 55/114, ff 51B–52; William Shuttleworth's *Resolution* Log, Adm 51/4561/220, ff 181–181B; Charles Clerke's *Discovery* Log, Adm 55/22, ff 56–57B; James Burney's *Discovery* Journal, Adm 51/4528/45, ff 184–187; John Rickman's *Discovery* Log, Adm 51/4529/46, ff 163–164; Thomas Edgar's *Discovery* Log, Adm 51/4529/41, ff 370–371; William Bayly's *Discovery* Observations, Adm 55/115, ff 55B–58; William Bayly's *Discovery* Journal, Adm 55/20, ff 47B–48B; William Lanyon's *Resolution* Log, Adm 51/4558/196, ff 96–97B; William Harvey's *Discovery* Log, Adm 55/110, ff 98B–100B; Anon *Discovery* Log, Adm 51/4528, ff 111–119B; Anon *Discovery* Log, Adm 51/4530, ff 89–92; John Martin *Discovery* Log, Adm 51/4531/47, ff 17B–20; Anonymous *Discovery* Log, Adm 55/22, ff. 56–57B.

Seven: Later Scientific Voyages

(pages 161–169)

1. Malaspina, quoted in Kendrick and Inglis 1991: 10.
2. Quoted in Hall-Jones nd: 11–12. See also McNab 1908 I: 161–65.
3. Quoted in Hall-Jones nd: 17.
4. *A Voyage Round the World, under the Command of J. F. G. de La Pérouse*, translated from the French, 1799 I: 27.
5. De Suffren 1785 quoted in Frost 1980: 96.
6. Quoted in Doyle 1978: 327.
7. Quoted in Dunmore 1965 I: 283.
8. The library is listed in Ollivier (ed.) 1986: 17–21.
9. D'Entrecasteaux in ibid: 27–29.
10. Avignon in ibid: 54.
11. D'Auribeau in ibid: 39.
12. See Salmond 1991: 83–84, 365.
13. D'Auribeau in Ollivier (ed.) 1986: 31.
14. Ibid: 33.
15. De Labillardière in Ollivier (ed.) 1986: 57–58.
16. Ibid.
17. D'Auribeau in ibid: 33.
18. Raoul in ibid: 49–51.
19. De Labillardière in ibid: 59–60.
20. Wigglesworth 1981: 4

Conclusion I

(pages 170–172)

1. Birch *History* 1677, quoted in Shapin and Schaffer 1985: 36.

2. Taylor 1855: 14–16.
3. According to Fox (1993), such categories are widespread across the Pacific in Austronesian-speaking communities, even in those that do not focus on genealogy and descent. He talks of these as 'relative relational' terms, dual rather than binary, and capable of being applied recursively to form ordered series of relationships. One of his most interesting comments is that across Austronesian-language communities, relationships between categories may stay the same, even when cognate terms change. This raises the possibility that the genealogical language in which such categories in Maori are typically expressed may be epiphenom-enal, just one way of talking relationships whose basic patterns may also be expressed in other idioms. 'Relational thinking' clearly has deep origins in Pacific societies, and Fox's comparative work is crucial in delineating some of its more fundamental features.
4. Foucault 1980: 157.
5. Some European thinkers, furthermore, although taking the concept of 'civilisation' for granted, could imagine future worlds not ruled by Europe. The English translator of D'Entrecasteaux's *Voyage*, for instance, inspired by Edward Gibbon's conceit in *The History of the Decline and Fall of the Roman Empire* that 'New Zealand may produce, in some future age, the Hume of the Southern Hemisphere' (1781 II: 1001), wrote in 1800: 'Without obtruding our own sentiments on the reader, we may be permitted to ask, whether appearances do not justify a conjecture, that the Great Arbiter of the destinies of nations may render that zeal [for exploration] subservient to the moral and intellectual, not to say the religious, improvement, and the consequent happiness, of our whole species? Or whether, as has hitherto generally happened, the advantages of civilization may not, in the progress of events, be transferred from the Europeans, who have but too little prized them, to those remote countries which they have been so diligently exploring? If so, the period may arrive, when New Zealand may produce her Lockes, her Newtons, and her Montesquieus; and when great nations in the immediate region of New Holland, may send their navigators, philosophers, and antiquaries, to contemplate the ruins of *ancient* London and Paris, and to trace the languid remains of the arts and sciences in this quarter of the globe. Who can tell, whether the rudiments of some great future empire may not already exist at Botany Bay?' (Quoted in Colenso, William, 1883. *On 'Macaulay's New Zealander'*. Napier, Daily Telegraph Office). My thanks to Robin Skinner for these references.

Introduction II

(pages 175–179)

1. Cf. Macpherson 1962.
2. Hobbes 1968.
3. Locke quoted in Macpherson 1962: 211–12. For a

—

—

—

—

—

—

—

—

—

—

—

—

—

—

—

—

—

—

—

—

—

—

—

—

—

—

—

—

—

—

—

—

—

—

Notes and References

contrary argument, see Jean-Jacques Rousseau in his *Discourse on the Origin of Inequality* (1755): 'The first man who, having enclosed a piece of land, thought of saying, *This is mine*, and found people simple enough to believe him, was the true founder of civil society. How many crimes, wars, murders, miseries and horrors, might mankind have been spared, if someone had pulled up the stakes or filled in the ditch, and shouted to his fellow-men: "Beware of listening to this imposter; you are ruined if you forget that the fruits of the earth are everyone's and that the soil itself is no-one's."' (quoted in Hankins 1985: 174).

4. Ranaipiri quoted by Best in Mauss 1993: 11.
5. Cook in Beaglehole (ed.) 1969 II: 653.
6. Pièces originales, 372–74, quoted in Foucault 1977: 3.
7. Baynham 1969: 62–66.
8. Glover 1963: 162–96.
9. Ford 1989: 234.

Eight: Introducing Law and Commerce

(pages 180–204)

1. Phillip in HRNSW I (ii): 53.
2. Linebaugh in Hay et al. 1975: 65–117.
3. McLynn 1989: 545–46.
4. Hay in Hay et al. 1975: 17–63.
5. Howard 1929: 203.
6. Frost 1980: 15, 23, 25; 1994: 102. See also 'An Anonymous Proposal for the Settlement of New South Wales' in McNab 1908 I: 58–66. Note that in June 1780, William Fullerton had proposed an expedition to South America via the Phillipines and New Zealand to harass the Spaniards. They should rest the men 'at some healthy spot in New Zealand', and then proceed directly to South America (King 1987: 203). New South Wales was also thought to be suitable for such a purpose.
7. For an authoritative account of the factors leading up to this decision, see Mackay 1985.
8. Bentham 1812: 7
9. See Frost 1994: 87–97.
10. Matra in HRNSW I (ii): 1.
11. Ibid: 2–4; see also 'An Anonymous Proposal for the Settlement of New South Wales' in McNab 1908 I: 58–66, which makes very similar arguments.
12. Heads of a Plan, HRNSW I (ii) 18–19.
13. Note his letter to Under-Secretary Nepean on 1 March 1787: 'That [I am instructed to] send one of the ships to Charlotte Sound, in the Island of New Zeland, for the flax-plant, and to the Friendly Islands for the breadfruit, and . . . women will be there procured' (HRNSW I (ii): 55).
14. Hill in HRNSW I (ii): 367.
15. Frost 1994: 116. Sir Joseph Banks, 4 June 1806, quoted in McNab 1908 I: 271–72.
16. Sir Joseph Banks, 4 June 1806, in McNab 1908 I: 2171–72. See also PRO BT 6/88:212–20.
17. *London Chronicle*, cutting in NLA Ms 4658.
18. Vancouver, quoted in Lamb (ed.) 1984 I: 272–73.
19. Convention between His Britannic Majesty and the King of Spain, 28 October 1790, quoted in Frost 1994: 182.
20. Admiralty in Lamb (ed.) 1984 I: 287.
21. Lamb (ed.) 1984 I: 40.
22. For accounts of Vancouver's expedition in Tamatea and the Chatham Islands, see BM Add Ms 17543 ff 14b–17, 'Logbook of the Chatham Tender', Lt. W. R. Broughton; BM Add Ms 17545 ff 28b–35, 'Logbook of the Discovery', Anon: BM Add Ms. 32641 ff 40–51, 'A. Menzies Journal of Vancouver's Voyage 1790–1794', Archibald Menzies; PRO Adm 51/4532/62 ff 87b–89, 'A Log of the Proceedings of His Majesty's Ship Discovery . . . kept by Spelman Swaine'; Adm 51/4533/53 ff 47b–48b, 'Browne'; Adm 51/4533/52 ff 46–7, 'Anon'; Adm 51/4534/58 ff 32b–33b, 'A Log of His Majestys Sloop Discovery, by Edward Roberts'; Adm 51/4534/73 ff 57–58, 'Anon'; Adm 53/403 ff 225–26, 'The Log of His Majesties Sloop Discovery, Thomas Manby Third Lieutenant'; Adm 55/13 ff 34b, 47b–48, 'Log of H.M.S. Chatham, Anon'; Adm 55/14 ff 18b–19, 21, 'Lt. Scott's Log, H.M.S Chatham'; Adm 55/15 ff 49–52b, 'Thos. Heddington'; Adm 55/32, ff 71–74b, 'A Log of His Majesty's Ship Discovery, kept by Josh. Baker, 3rd Lieutenant'; Adm 55/25 ff 49b–50b, 'A Log of the Proceedings of His Majesty's Sloop Discovery, kept by John Sykes'; Adm 55/26 ff 54b–58b, 'A Journal of a Voyage to the North West Coast of America and Round the World, performed in His Majesties Sloop Discovery & Brig Chatham, kept by Harry Humphrys, Midshipman, Master's Mate and Master'; Adm 55/28, ff 39–40b, 'Log of H.M.S. Discovery, Lieut. Stewart'; Adm 55/29, ff 47b–48, 'A Log of the Proceedings of His Majesty's Ship Discovery, by . . . Ballard;' Adm 55/30 ff 47, 'A Log of the Proceedings of H.M. Sloop Discovery, kept by Robt. Pigot'; Adm 55/27, ff 51–52, 'A Log of the Proceedings of His Majesty's Sloop Discovery, kept by Lieutenant Peter Puget'; Adm 53/334, ff 19–21, 'Chatham's Log Book, John Sherriff'.
23. Frost 1980: 138–41.
24. Menzies in McNab 1914 II: 483.
25. Anonymous, Adm 55/13: 39.
26. Anonymous in ibid: 40a.
27. Menzies in McNab 1914 II: 485.
28. Ibid: 486.
29. Ibid: 487.
30. Anonymous in Adm 55/13: 43.
31. Menzies in McNab 1914 II: 494.
32. Ibid: 492.
33. Ibid: 490.
34. Anonymous in Adm 55/13: 41.
35. Manby in ATL Micro Ms 8537.
36. Quoted in King 1989: 18–19.
37. Ibid: 17–38.
38. Ewing 1873: 545.
39. Bell in McNab 1914 II: 503.
40. Broughton in Lamb (ed.) 1984 I: 382–83.
41. Shand 1904: 151.
42. Broughton in Lamb 1984 I: 387.

43. Ibid: 383–84.
44. Ibid: 384.
45. Ibid: 386–87.
46. Ibid: 385–86.
47. Ibid: 386.
48. Shand 1904: 151.
49. Cited in King 1989: 45.
50. Ewing 1873: 549. My thanks to Michael King for corrections to the Koche story.
51. Ibid.
52. Ibid: 545, 547–48.
53. My thanks to Michael King and David Simmons for their help in finding sources for this section.
54. McNab 1908 I: 159–60.

Nine: The Hunt for Flax

(pages 205–233)

1. Call and Young to the East India Company, 21 June 1785, quoted in Frost 1994: 55.
2. See Frost 1994: 58–86.
3. Letterbook of Philip Gidley King ML C187, 1788–99: 59.
4. McNab 1908 I: 126.
5. King Letterbook: 225. See also King to Sir Joseph Banks, 25 October 1791 in ML A78-6: 25–26, followed by the gift of a stone adze sent in 1792 to Banks, presumably one of those found on Norfolk Island (ML A 78-6: 69).
6. Lamb (ed.) 1984 II: 450–55.
7. Norman 1994: pers. comm.
8. James Hanson to Philip Stevens, 30 May 1790, in Adm 1/2917.
9. King Journal ML A1687: 179–80.
10. Bell in McNab 1914 II: 540–41. See also Vancouver's much less detailed account in ibid III: 1081.
11. Ibid II: 541.
12. Salmond 1991: 340. Maori text as follows: 'Ka puta te awha, ka noho te hunga turoro o au maitai ki uta, a na te iwi o Te Patu aua turoro ra i whangai, he aroha atu hoki ki aua pakeha . . . a herea ana taua rangatira o Te Patu a Rangi nui e te upoko o aua maitai, a rere atu ana taua kai-puke me te Rangi-nui, a ngaro atu ana ki te rere noa atu i te moana, kahore kau he take a aua mai tai i herehere kau ai i a te Rangi-nui a i maua noatia ai aia ki waho ki te moana, na aua mahi nei te Maori i mahi raruke ai i te mai tai, u noa mai ki enei motu, kia taea ai te utu mo ana mate ano a te Maori i te mai tai.'
13. White ATL MS 75, Folder B19: 90. Maori text as follows: 'E rua o matou i riro i te Pakeha ki te kai-puke, he mea kia akona te pakeha ki te haro muka. Ka hoe te tokorua nei a Tuki raua ko Huru-kokoti, ara a Toha-mahue, ko te Tohunga me tana hoa, ki te aruaru kahawai i waho i te moana, a ka hi raua, a ka puta te kai-puke, a ka eke atu raua ki taua puke, a ka utaina hoki ta raua waka ki taua puke, a ka rere te puke ra i te moana, po maha ka u te puke ra ki te tahi moutere, he tini te pakeha o taua motu ra . . .'
14. King, 26 May 1793, CO201/9: 207.
15. Collins 1891 I: 270, 273.
16. Grose in McNab 1908 I: 165.
17. Specht gives tentative dates of AD 1000–1400, possibly with a second Polynesian settlement in AD 1400–1750: Hoare in Nobbs (ed.) 1988: 18–22; King in HRNSW I (2): 187, 296; ANL Ms 9/94a, King to Banks 24 May 1793: 3; Merval Hoare 1991: pers. comm.
18. King Letterbook ML C187, 15 1792: 90.
19. King to Sir Joseph Banks, 8 May 1792, ML A78-6: 67; King to Eber Bunker, 17 January 1792, CO201/9: 79.
20. King to Bunker 17 January 1792, CO201/9: 79.
21. King Journal ANL Ms 70: 13.
22. Ibid, April 1793: 146.
23. Nobbs (ed.) 1988: 5; King Journal ANL Ms 70: 63–64.
24. HRNSW 1891 I: 228.
25. Phillip in ibid: 596.
26. The record of punishments administered during 1790–91 by the Acting Commandant, Major Ross, and his quartermaster, Lieutenant Ralph Clark, gives a chilling calendar of floggings of male and female convicts (including both the young and the very old), and convicts being put in the stocks, chained to the grindstone, or confined in the island's jail:

    'Jany. 1 1791 Majr. Ross ordered Mary Nash a female convict out at Charlotte Field both Legs in Irons on my Representing to him that all the people Say that She is the person they Believe that Steal all ther things and goes to town to Sell them to the Seamen – She is big with child otherwise Should have flogged her Yesterday for she is a D. . . B . . .

    'Tues 15th Feb, Elizh. Breeze a notarious thief was Punished today with 75 Lashes for killing and Stealing a hen . . . Vinry male Convict Punished with 100 lashes for Stealing Cobbs of Indian Corn – Jno. Hudson a Convict Boy Punished with 50 lashes for been out of his hutt after nine oclock . . .

    'Monday 7th Mar, John Gualt and Strong were Punished with one hundred lashes each for attempting to break open the Public Store – when there backs are well the[y] are each to Receive two hundred lashes more.'
    (Clark ed. Fidlon and Ryan: 178, 183, 187, 197, 207.)
27. Nobbs (ed) 1988: 118.
28. Ibid: 119.
29. Victualling Book Norfolk Island ML A1958: 8a; King Journal ANL MS 70, 10 March 1793: 62.
30. King Journal 1793 ML A1687: 129–30.
31. 'Their method of preparing the flax is this, the leaf is plucked green, the longer the better, the middle part of the leaf is stripped off with the finger & thumb & thrown away being too hard – the leaf is then split into narrow Stripes, and each Stripe cut across, in the middle, but great nicety is required here, so as not to separate the filaments, the Stripe is then held between the finger & Thumb of the left hand, whilst the right holds the Knife or a Sharp shell, on the under part just below the cut across; It

32. King to Banks, 24 May 1793, AN Ms 9/94a.
33. King Journal 1793 ML A1687:136.
34. Jamison in McNab 1908 I: 183.
35. King to Banks, 10 November 1793, ANL Ms 9/95.
36. Collins 1798 I: 519–20. See also King to Banks, 10 November 1793, ANL Ms 9/95.
37. Roe 1963: 24.
38. King Letterbook ML C187: 225.
39. Chapman letters ML A1974, 3 November 1793.
40. King to Banks, 10 November 1793.
41. Chapman letters ML A1974, 19 November 1793.
42. King Journal 1793: 82, 86, 87.
43. McNab 1908 I: 262–68.
44. King Letterbook ML A1687: 187.
45. Ibid: 61.
46. King to Banks, 10 November 1793.
47. Ibid.
48. Ibid.
49. King Journal ML CY Safe 1/10: 173–88.
50. McNab 1914 II: 543.
51. Ibid: 543–44.
52. King in Fidlon and Ryan (ed.) 1980: 364.
53. King in McNab 1914 II: 544–45.
54. Ibid: 545.
55. White ATL Ms 75, Folder B19: 81, 90.
56. Salmond 1991: 221.
57. King to Banks, 10 November 1793: 2, 3.
58. McNab 1914 II: 542.
59. Collins 1798: 521–22.
60. See in particular Milligan 1964.
61. Including one that tribal accounts say was drawn for Cook on the deck of the *Endeavour* at Whitianga (Salmond 1991: 207), another for Nicholas by Koro-koro in 1814 and others for Shortland in the 1840s.
62. The most serious error in Milligan's interpretation of Tuki's map occurs here, when he assumes that the promontory marked at the west boundary of Muriwhenua is Cape Maria Van Diemen. I am certain that this is Tauroa Point at the end of Te Oneroa-a-Tohe (Ninety Mile Beach). Many of Milligan's subsequent disagreements with tribal authorities follow from this mistaken identification.
63. King Journal ML A1687: 185.
64. Ibid: 183.
65. Milligan 1964.
66. King Journal ML A1687: 171.
67. King in McNab 1908 I: 168.
68. King to Dundas, 7 November 1793, CO201/9.
69. King, Necessary arrangements for Settling a Colony of Six Hundred people in New Zealand, CO201/9: 304–6.
70. King in CO201/9: 307a.
71. King Journal ML A1687: 193–94.
72. Robert Murry's *Britannia* journal, 12 November 1793, Essex Institute, Salem Massachussetts.
73. King Journal ML A1687: 195–96.
74. William Chapman letter ML A1974 19.11.1793
75. King to Dundas, 19 November 1793, CO201/9: 309.

76. King Journal ML A1687: 199.
77. Ibid: 200.
78. Ibid: 201.
79. King in Fidlon and Ryan (ed.) 1980: 367.
80. William Chapman letter ML A1974: 37.
81. King to Nepean in McNab 1908 I: 181.
82. P. P. King letter, ML AK1.
83. King Journal ML A1687: 318–22.
84. White ATL Ms 75 Folder B 19: 81, 90.
85. King 1806, ML C186: 135.
86. Milligan 1964: 138.

Ten: The Timber Voyages 1794–1797

(pages 234–251)

1. J. Thomson to H. Dundas, 22 November 1792, CO201/7: 360–64.
2. Furber 1970:160–90.
3. Ferguson 1767, ed. Schneider 1991: 206–7.
4. J. M. Matra, 23 August 1783, in McNab 1908 I: 39.
5. See Albion 1965 for a trenchant commentary on 'The Timber Problem of the Royal Navy' in this period.
6. Grose to Dundas, 19 April 1793, in HRA I: 419–20. Contract 10 April 1793 in CO201/8: 16–22; and HRA I: 423–27.
7. Grose to Dundas, 31 August 1795, in HRA I: 482–83; W. W. Bampton to Lieutenant-Governor Paterson, 1 June 1795, CO201/12:53-4.
8. See Judge Advocate's Records, Ships' Protests and Protests of Bills, in NSW Archives, 5/1162 COD 193: 29–31.
9. Collins 1798 I: 391–92.
10. Dell 1795 in CO201/18: 7.
11. Ibid: 8.
12. Ibid: 10.
13. I am indebted to Caroline Phillips, Louise Furey and Paul Monin for reading the Hauraki reconstructions, and for their many helpful comments and suggestions.
14. Best 1980.
15. Banks in Beaglehole (ed.) 1962 I: 435–36.
16. Ibid II: 4.
17. Phillips 1994: 182.
18. White 1888 V: 131–32.
19. See Phillips 1994, various sections.
20. Yate, quoted in Park 1995: 33–34.
21. Dell 1795: 10a.
22. From the *Royal Admiral* chart of the area in 1801, this sandbank was by Te Totara Pa, near the mouth of the Kauaeranga River.
23. Dell 1795: 12.
24. This outbreak was dated to about 1790 by Thomson(1859: 219).
25. Tapp 1958: 51. One such voyage that has been reported is that of the *Mermaid*, Captain Jonathan Trevarthen, a whaler owned by Master Joseph Thoms and Sons, of Billiter Street, London, which was supposed to have left England on 20 September 1795 and to have visited Aotea (Great Barrier Island) on 3 November 1796. This voyage was

discussed by 'Lee Fore Brace' (the nom de plume of an amateur maritime historian called Forbes Eadie) in an article in the *Weekly News* of Sydney on 14 April 1937, who claimed to have purchased the original logbook of the *Mermaid* in a second-hand bookstore in Sydney. The article quotes extensively from the log, mentioning that after taking a French Guineaman prize, the *Mermaid* proceeded to the Sargossa Sea, where she took a number of whales; then south to Rio de Janeiro, where she met a Bristol barque, *England's Glory*, which was homeward bound from the New Holland fisheries. At Rio Captain Trevarthen exchanged a scurvied sailor for 'an Indian of New Zeeland, and signed him as boatsteerer and pilot on a lay of thirty of one thousand. The Indian speaks good English and was a pilot on the Endeavour with Captain Cook.' From Rio the *Mermaid* sailed around Cape Horn to Juan Fernandez Island, and then to Easter Island, and across the Pacific. On 26 October 1796, off the coast of New Zealand north and east of Cook Strait, a brown bird, which the Indian pilot called a 'peepee forarroah' [pipiwharauroa – shining cuckoo] flew on board. The whaler made her way up the East Coast, making sporadic contact with local people in canoes, past White Island in the Bay of Plenty, to 'Oa tea Heerikeematter' [Aotea – Great Barrier Island], where they had extensive contacts with relatives of their Maori pilot. When the ship sailed from the island on 8 January 1797, four local men were on board as crew. The ship cruised off the east coast for two months, and by the beginning of March was fullly laden. Trevarthen paid off his pilot and signed on six Maori for the passage to Australia. Unfortunately, the log of the *Mermaid* has not been sighted, and all enquiries have failed to turn it up. Nor have the two ships mentioned been located in other shipping records, despite enquiries at the National Maritime Museum and with Ian Nicholson in Australia. Forbes Eadie had something of a reputation as a yarn-spinner, although he is said to have been very knowledgeable about maritime matters. On current evidence, I agree with Harry Morton's verdict that the *Mermaid*'s voyage is a hoax. ['The Voyage of the *Mermaid* . . . was published in the *Weekly News* of Sydney on 14 April 1937 . . . There are good reasons to think that the *Mermaid* log, so fortuitously discovered and so conveniently lost, is a very well-done fake. But the author obviously knew South Pacific whaling. It is just possible he might have heard of Maoris serving on British whaleships in the early 1790s' Morton 1982: 166.] See also an authoritative footnote on the *Mermaid* by Rhys Richards in Richards 1996: 90–91, which comes to essentially the same conclusion.

26. Dell 1795: 13.
27. Ibid: 16a.
28. Ibid: 18.
29. I am indebted to Roger Morris, author of *Pacific Sail*, maritime historian and artist, and formerly master of the *Bounty* replica, for his meticulous reconstruction

of the movements of the *Fancy* during this visit, both in the gulf and upriver. He used his mastery of the navigational information given in the *Fancy*'s log to produce annotated charts as well as an authoritative text, and I am deeply grateful. I also thank Caroline Phillips, with her expert knowledge of Hauraki's historic landscapes, for working through the same material. In the end, those who wish to assess it should examine their reconstructions, now lodged in the *Fancy* file in the Ships Archive, University of Auckland Library.

30. Dell 1795: 19.
31. Ibid: 19a.
32. My thanks to Patu Hohepa for this suggestion.
33. See also Hauraki Minute Book 26: 328: 'A kauri tree was of great value to Maories – no one would dare to make a canoe from a kauri tree growing on another person's land – there was another valuable tree on this land (Moutere / Coromandel) the totara but it was small.' My thanks to Paul Monin for this quote.
34. King in CO201 / 12: 25a, to Lieutenant-Governor Grose. Note 'The Master of the *Fancy* . . . having favoured me with his Journal whilst that Vessel staid here, I made such extracts from it, as appeared to contain the most information the substance of which I have in a private Letter communicated to Mr. Secretary Nepean, but as that information is not so perfect, as the whole Journal would be if transcribed which I had not time to get done, during her stay here, I beg to suggest with much defference to you whether a full Copy of that Journal being transmitted to His Majesty's Ministers might not tend to some Publick advantage.' Grose had formerly reprimanded King for going to New Zealand without permission, and may not have been inclined to attend to this request. If a full copy of the *Fancy*'s journal was taken, it does not appear in any of the dispatches from Port Jackson to the Colonial Office. (See also King Letterbook ML C187: 284.)
35. Collins 1798: 410–11.
36. Thomson 1859 I: 219.
37. Paterson in CO201 / 12: 11–11a

Eleven: The Timber Voyages 1798–1801
(pages 252–281)

1. Settlers to Secretary of State, 1 February 1800, in HRA II: 442–43, Return of Spirits in ibid: 550; Collins 1802 II: 126–27; Colllins 1802 II: 116; Cumpston 1977: 33.
2. HRA III: 453.
3. Collins 1802 II: 127.
4. See Hunter in CO201 / 15: 55; J. Thomson in CO201 / 15: 187a; Collins 1802 II: 205, 318.
5. For instance, McNab 1914: 89–90.
6. Collins 1802 II: 267–68.
7. Hainsworth 1981: 66.
8. See Cumpston 1977: 34; Hainsworth 1981: 40, 65–66.

9. HRNSW IV: 271–73.

10. HRA II: 570.

11. Richards 1990: 1–14.

12. Vason 1840: 43.

13. Myers 1817: 202–4.

14. White 1888 V: 126.

15. Hunter, 3 January 1800, in CO201/16: 37; and in HRA II: 425–27; and in HRNSW IV: 163.

16. Hunter to Portland 25 September 1800 in HRA II: 570; Return of Spirits in HRA II: 550; Collins 1802 II: 274–75. See also HRA III: 129.

17. Banks papers, 26 January 1801, in ML A78/3: 13–14; see also Meikle 1912: 112–36; *Monthly Magazine*, February 1804; and Thomas Fyshe Palmer letters NLA Ms 761.

18. Meikle 1912: 135.

19. Under-Secretary King to Lieutenant-Governor Grose, 14 February 1794, in HRA I: 463. For Muir, Palmer and Skirving's request that their sentence be understood as one of banishment from Great Britain, rather than restriction to Port Jackson only, see Muir, Palmer and Skirving to Governor Hunter, 14 October 1795, HRA I: 543–45, 568–69, 599.

20. *Australian Dictionary of Biography*: 126–27, 312–13; Fowler 1980: 37.

21. *Australian Dictionary of Biography*: 312–13; 126–27.

22. Missionaries' Journal, 24–25 January 1801, School of Oriental and African Studies CWM Archives, Journals South Seas 1796–1803 Box 1 Folder 11. This mutiny was perhaps inspired by lack of confidence in the captain as well as the vessel. As Fergus Clunie has pointed out, Reid had already grounded Boston and Co.'s *Martha* off the Australian coast in 1800 (Clunie, pers. comm. 1997).

23. See the Missionaries' Journal from Rio de Janeiro to Port Jackson, 10 December 1800: 'Mr. Puckey, late Missionary to Otaheiti, and afterwards employed in this Colony as a Store Keeper under Government; having lost that Office he determined to leave the Colony and go to the Cape of Good Hope with that intention he entered on board the Pluma as a second Officer.'

24. Cumpston 1977: 35.

25. HRA III: 129.

26. *Sydney Gazette*, 12 May 1804; see also Wharton (ed.) 1922: 178–79.

27. For a full list of the crew, see William Wilson Journal India Office L/MAR/B/338 I.

28. HRA III: 127.

29. See HRA II: 470, 493; HRA III: 16–18, 129, 159–61; HRNSW IV: 76–77, 256–63.

30. King to Portland, 30 November 1800, in HRA II: 697; King to Hobart, 30 October 1802, in HRA III: 583.

31. This vocabulary had been compiled before the *Royal Admiral* left England from the vocabularies of Cook and Bougainville; and the missionaries had been enjoined to study it throughout their voyage (Davies ed. Newbury 1961: xlvi).

32. Lovett 1899: 20.

33. Thomas Haweis, Letters to Sir Joseph Banks about

34. missionary work in the Pacific, in ATL qMS 932; Banks note on Haweis to Banks, 23 September 1799.

34. Lovett 1899: 158.

35. See ibid, and Davies ed. Newbury 1961.

36. After his escape from Tahiti, Smith tried to get a passage from Port Jackson to India on Campbell and Clarke's ship the *Hunter*, but was twice refused by her captain, James Fearn. Robert Campbell, a partner in the Calcutta company who had come to the penal colony on the *Hunter* to investigate business prospects there, had decided to move to Port Jackson, but first he had to return to India. When he met Smith, a former linen draper, he left him in temporary charge of his affairs, but Smith had made some disastrous decisions. To make matters worse, Campbell's house was burgled while Smith was living there, and he tried to charge Campbell an exorbitant commission. Campbell took the matter to court, charging Smith with dishonesty, and had Smith thrown into gaol for debt. Smith had tried to escape on *El Plumier*, but after a spell of freedom with his servant Patrick Riley, he was captured and returned to prison. He was still there when the *Royal Admiral* arrived in Port Jackson (see Smith 1813: 129–200).

37. Elder to Rev. Alex Waugh, 6 May 1801.

38. Rev. Samuel Marsden to Capt. William Wilson of the Royal Admiral, November 1800, in ANL Rex Nan Kivell collection Ms 4197. This letter also contained advice on how to set up and maintain a successful mission; viz. by sending sufficient numbers of missionaries with adequate means of self-defence; a wise and judicious man to lead them, the power to expel back-sliders; a proper system of self-government; wives to keep the missionaries away from local women; and with the means of introducing the 'arts of civilized life' among the local people.

39. Missionaries' Journal, *Royal Admiral*, New Zealand, 16 June 1801.

40. Wilson in India Office L/MAR/B/338 I: 19 April 1801. See also Wilson's chart, which shows the ship's track and the anchor that was lost in the storm.

41. Smith 1813: 228; see also Missionaries' Journal, SOAS, 19 April 1801.

42. It is conceivable that this man was Tutaua, a Ngaati Maru chief descended from Rautao through Kuriuaua and Pautangi (Caroline Phillips, pers. comm. 1996).

43. Smith 1813: 57, 193.

44. Missionaries' Journal, 19 June 1801.

45. Monin typescript 1996: 5.

46. See, for instance, the division of roles between the ariki Kaingaroa and his younger brother, Hongi Hika, in the inland Bay of Islands during the early years of the nineteenth century (Sissons, Wi Hongi and Hohepa 1987: 19–21).

47. Monin typescript 1996: 6–7, ref. to Hauraki Minute Book 8: 133.

48. Missionaries' Journal, 2 May 1801.

49. James Elder to Rev. Alex Waugh, 24 June 1801, in SOAS, CWM Archive, South Seas Inwards Correspondence, Box 1, Folder 3.
50. Savage 1807: 21–22.
51. Nicholas 1818 I: 51–53.
52. Forster 1996: 152.
53. After a visit to the Bay of Islands in 1816, William Ellis wrote: 'The population of New Zealand has been estimated at half a million; which estimate must, from the unorganized state of society, be mere conjecture, so that it may exceed this number. The inhabitants are certainly far more numerous than those of the Society Islands, and appear exempt from many of the diseases which afflict their northern neighbours' (Ellis 1969: 341). Although after his visit to the Bay of Islands in 1814–15, J. L. Nicholas guessed at a national population of 150,000 (Nicholas 1817 II: 299), informed estimates of the Bay of Islands population circa 1830 by Shawcross (1966) suggest a figure of about 15–20,000. If the prior introduction of epidemic diseases, VD and muskets to this region are taken into account, and other regions of dense population are brought into the equation (Taranaki, Waikato, Hauraki, Bay of Plenty, the inland volcanic areas and the East Coast bays, for example), an estimate of 100,000 for the entire country seems far too conservative.
54. Smith 1813: 230.
55. Quoted in Sherrin 1890: 119.
56. Missionaries' Journal, 12 March 1801.
57. See the ancestor of this name in Hauraki Minute Book 7, 25.11.1872: 372.
58. Missionaries' Journal, 19 June 1801.
59. Elder to Rev. Alex Waugh, 24 June 1801. See also Deposition of Mr. James Elder, Court House Parramatta, 12 November 1813, submitted by Samuel Marsden, in HO Ms 54A/18: 81–84.
60. Elder deposition, 12 November 1813, Samuel Marsden correspondence, HO Ms 54a.
61. Missionaries' Journal, 13 May 1801.
62. For example, Shortland 1856: 92. My thanks to Patu Hohepa for the identification of 'Wannugu' as Uenuku.
63. Missionaries' Journal, 18 May 1801.
64. Elder to Rev. Alex Waugh, 24 June 1801. For a vivid account of the custom of muru, see Maning 1964: 97–108.
65. Smith 1813: 234–35.
66. The missionaries accurately translated 'warreekee' (ariki) as 'chief' at the very beginning of their visit, and applied the term at different times to both Tautaua and Tauarange (Taurangi?). As well as I can judge, Tautaua was the ariki controlling the coastal district around Te Puru Paa, while Taurangi was ariki for the inland river district.
67. Davies 1961: 31.
68. Lockerby 1925: xxxviii-ix, 177–79.
69. Sydney Gazette, 12 May 1804.
70. For an informative recent account of El Plumier's voyage, see Richards 1990: 6–9.
71. Charles Wilson, Royal Admiral, New Zealand, 16 June 1801, in ATL fMs Papers 4386.
72. Wilson to his cousin, 16 June 1801.
73. Smith 1813: 239.
74. My thanks to Caroline Phillips for this suggestion.
75. Tribal accounts given in the Native Land Court tell of at least two epidemics in the region before 1820; one of 'rewharewha' (Phillips 1994: 219, 325).
76. Missionaries' Journal, 19 June 1801.
77. William Wilson, 15 March 1802.
78. Charles Wilson to his cousin, 16 June 1801.
79. Smith 1813: 240.
80. For mention of the vocabulary, see Elder to Waugh, 23 July 1801; Davies to Rev. Haweis, 25 July 1801.
81. My thanks to Caroline Phillips for this suggestion.
82. Smith 1813: 242–43.
83. Youl to Rev. Alex. Waugh, 26 July 1801.
84. Elder to Rev. Alex Waugh, 28 July 1801.
85. Missionaries' Journal, 19 June 1801.
86. Ibid. My thanks to Patu Hohepa for the translation of pungapunga – raupo-pollen bread.
87. Horeta Te Taniwha seems to have been referring to the Royal Admiral when he claimed in this same statement that after the Endeavour and another ship (probably one of the Hunters) had visited the gulf, a much larger ship had arrived. Either this ship picked up two local people, as he claimed, from a storm-bound canoe as she left the gulf, or Horeta muddled in elements of the Tuki and Huru story, which was apparently in circulation in Hauraki by 1801: 'As this ship was leaving Hauraki she fell in with a canoe which had been driven some distance away by bad weather. The people of this canoe were taken on board of this ship. There were only two in the canoe, but, as the gale continued, these two could not be landed anywhere on the coast, and they were taken away to the other side in this ship, and were away two years, and were brought back in another ship. It was from this ship that we, the Hauraki people, obtained pigs' (White 1888 V: 126–27).
88. Elder to Rev. Alex Waugh, 6 May 1801.

Twelve: Sealing in the South
(pages 282–313)

1. J. Forster ed. Hoare 1982 II: 275.
2. Sir Joseph Banks, 4 June 1806, in BT 6/88: 215b; and McNab 1908 I: 273.
3. Heaphy, quoted in Richards 1982: 3–4.
4. De Blosseville in McNab 1907: 220–21.
5. Grose to Dundas, 3 September 1793, CO201/8: 77. See also Samuel Enderby, 13 October 1790: 'Since I had the pleasure of seeing you a Mr. St. Barbe, who is concern'd in the South Whale Fishery has apply'd to me about carrying the Convicts to Botany Bay, he thinks it may answer to take them all in a joint Account with us, and afterwards to prosecute our Fishery in those Seas' CO201/3: 302.
6. See Judge Advocate's Records, Ships' Protests and Protests of Bills, NSW Archives 5/1162 COD 193:

6.

7. Grose to Phillip, 4 October 1792; CO201/7: 63–64; and in HRNSW I (2): 652.

8. Phillip to Dundas, 4 October, 1792; CO201/7: 61–62, 71–72; and in HRNSW I (2): 651–53.

9. Contract in CO201/12: 49a.

10. Murry, Log of the *Britannia* 1792, Peabody Museum of Salem; and in McNab 1914 II: 511. Checked against the original by A.S. and corrected in Salem.

11. Ibid: 509–17

12. Raven to King, 2 November 1793, CO201/9: 273–75b.

13. Collins 1798–1802 I: 293; and Paterson in CO201/12: 9a–11.

14. Charter in HRA I: 448–51.

15. Grose to Dundas, 3 September 1793, CO201/8: 77–79; and in McNab 1908: 167.

16. Collins 1798–1802: 321.

17. Raven to King, 2 November 1793, CO201/9: 273–75b; and in McNab 1908 I: 179.

18. Ibid: 177–79.

19. Murry, Log of the *Britannia* 1793, Peabody Museum of Salem; and in McNab 1914 II: 516.

20. Collins 1798–1802 I: 322.

21. Bampton to Paterson, 1 June 1795, CO201/12: 53–54; and in HRA I: 507; Paterson to Dundas 15 June 1795 in HRA I: 498.

22. Collins 1798: 417–18.

23. Cobley 1963: 39; '24 May 1789. The Reverend Mr. Johnson christened James Hatherly . . . James was the son of James Hatherly, a ship's carpenter, and a convict named Elizabeth Bason.'

24. Bampton said twenty-five to thirty in his report to King at Norfolk, but he was probably trying to minimise the scale of the mass escape. (Bampton to King CO201/18: 52.)

25. Murry, Journal of the *Endeavour* 1795, Peabody Museum of Salem; and in McNab 1914 II: 518–34.

26. Although on the *Shaw Hormuzear*, Bampton had travelled with his wife, and merchantmen often had women on board as passengers.

27. Murry, Journal of the *Endeavour*.

28. King in CO201/18: 49a–55.

29. Forty-three people from the *Endeavour* are listed in the 1796 entries of the Norfolk Island Victualling Book (ML A 1958: 39–41). See also Bampton's report and letters, and King's list in CO201/18: 52–58, which names thirty people whose terms of transportation had expired, including Elizabeth Heatherly and her young son James; and eighteen escaped convicts who had been brought to Norfolk on board the *Endeavour*; and twenty more freed convicts, and seventeen escaped convicts, including Ann Carey, who were expected to arrive on the *Resource*. For mention of the Lascars and Portugese seamen, see McNab 1914 II: 553. See also King Letterbook ML C187: 310–11.

30. Murry, Journal of the *Endeavour*.

31. Busch speculates that the *Mercury* may have been a sealer; certainly her itinerary makes this likely (Busch 1985: 29).

32. Hunter to the Duke of Portland, 10 January 1798, CO201/14: 116–18; Collins 1802 II: 48–49; although as Rhys Richards (1996: 87–88) has noted, one of Captain Gardin's crew was later reported as saying, 'We had, for the sake of a cargo from her, gone and brought them off, consisting of *fifteen* [italics mine] persons, part of whom he had since left at Norfolk Island' – in which case twenty people had either died, or been left at Tamatea.

33. See King to Hobart, 1 March 1804, BT 6/88: 190–90b; 14 August 1804, BT 6/88: 183–85b.

34. Campbell to Commissioner Bigge, 1820, quoted in Abbott & Nairn (ed.) 1969: 288–89.

35. Bass to King, 31 January 1802, ML B1374.

36. Bass to Waterhouse, 30 January 1802, 5 January 1803; Bass to King, 30 January 1803; Bass to Waterhouse, 2 February 1803, in McNab 1908 I: 240–45.

37. Bass to King, 30 January 1803, in McNab 1908 I: 243–44; see also King to Lord Hobart 9 May 1803, in HRA Series I, Vol. 4: 147.

38. Bass to Waterhouse, 2 February 1803, in McNab 1908 I: 245.

39. McNab 1907: 70–77.

40. *Sydney Gazette*, 29 May 1803.

41. Stewart, quoted in Murray-Smith 1973: 172.

42. See, for instance, *William and Ann* 1813, bound for Bass Strait, listed 'John Peter, Jackey Warree, Harry, John Brownie, R. George, all New Zealanders' among her crew; *Elizabeth and Mary* 1814 headed for Bass Strait with 'Paddy and Tommy, New Zealanders' among her crew; *Glory* 1819 sailed for the seal fishery with 'Jacky Mity, New Zealander' on board (Cumpston 1970: 36, 37, 53); *Governor Brisbane* 1825 sailed to Bass Strait with 'William Hook, a New Zealander'; sealers at Hunter Island in 1830 included 'a native of New Zealand named John Witieye [from the Bay of Islands] . . . He had two women and was the head man among the sealers and considered the most honourable.' (Plomley & Henley 1990: 43, 48).

43. Ross 1987: 12; Fowler 1980: 37.

44. *Sydney Gazette,* 9 October 1803.

45. Ibid, 16 October 1803.

46. Balmain to D. A. Wentworth, 1 June 1803, ML A 754-2, Supplementary Papers: 122.

47. Shipping Returns, in McNab 1908 I: 253; *Sydney Gazette,* 1 April 1804.

48. Published in the *Sydney Gazette,* 29 September 1805.

49. Proclamation by Philip Gidley King, 26 May 1804, BT 6/88: 187; General Order 11 August 1804, see Ross 1987: 29; King to Hobart, 14 August 1804, BT/6/88: 183–85b; see Fowler 1980: 73–76.

50. Ross 1987: 33–34.

51. Translated copy of Jorgensen's pamphlet *Observations on English and North American Voyages and Trade in the South Seas*, edited by Rhys Richards and translated by L. Knight; and copy of Jorgensen's *A Shred of Autobiography*; in ATL Ms Papers 78217, ed. Rhys Richards. I am very grateful to Mr Richards for access to this invaluable collection of edited and translated accounts.

52. *Sydney Gazette* of 11 February 1805 reported that the *Contest* returned with only 5,000 sealskins.

53. Jorgensen, *A Shred of Autobiography*: 125.

54. Jorgensen, *Observations*: 27–32.

55. This account of the complex movements of the *Contest, Union, Endeavour, Honduras Packet* and *Independence* is taken from the excellent reconstruction by John Ross (1987: 25–37).

56. See Appendix I, Sealing Voyages, which gives fuller details of these visits.

57. King in HRA Series I/V: 55.

58. Ross 1987: 42, 49; Richards 1977: 15–16.

59. Ewing 1873: 549.

60. Captain Mayhew Folger's log of the *Topaz*, Nantucket Historical Association.

61. John Cumpston has calculated that at least 250,000 skins were taken from the Antipodes in the five seasons 1804–09 (cited in Richards 1995: 28); and over fifteen months to July 1808, the cargoes of the *Commerce* fell in three voyages from 39,000 to 3,000.

62. I. S. Kerr, Sealers in Southern New Zealand 1803–12, ATL Ms Papers 1685-2: 16a.

63. See Samuel Enderby to Sir Joseph Banks, 21 July 1809, reporting the discovery of the islands, MLA 83.

64. For a scholarly critique of the various 'memoirs' based on Marmon's life, see Wigglesworth 1974. His guesses about the provenance of the shorter and more accurate *New Zealand Herald* memoir, published in 1880, and the later, more elaborated and fanciful 'Memoirs' published in the *Auckland Star* and the *Otago Witness* in 1881–82 are interesting, but highly hypothetical. If two original versions of the memoirs existed, as Wigglesworth suggests, they may have been an earlier and a later, more detailed version of Marmon's life crafted by the same person (probably Mrs Alice Bennett, for Chief Justice Gillies), and that differences among the versions can be explained as editorial and journalistic licence, attributable to the staff of the relevant newspapers.

65. *The Life and Adventures of John Marmon*, Fern Album APL, Grey MS 920 MAR.

66. Ibid.

67. Bathgate 1969: 354.

68. Ibid.

69. *New Zealand Times,* 15 November 1913, cited in Richards 1995: 24.

70. De Blosseville in McNab 1907: 220–21.

71. *Sydney Gazette,* 25 August 1810, and Richards 1995: 23.

72. Ibid.

73. Richards 1995: 21.

74. *Sydney Gazette,* 30 March 1811.

75. 'Geographical Account of New Zealand &c' in *Nouvelles Annales des Voyages*, Paris, quoted in McNab 1907: 217–18; and Carrick 1905: 85–88.

76. *Dictionary of New Zealand Biography* 1990 I: 553.

77. Anderson 1991: 4–5.

78. Quoted in Carrick 1905: 86–88.

79. See also a description of Foveaux Strait life collected from Caddell by Thomas Shepherd in 1826, quoted in Richards 1995: 37–38.

80. e.g. Houghton 1980: 97–98.

81. For example, the individuals said to have been young at the time of Cook's visits, who reported their memories in the 1840s and 1850s (cf Sherrin 1890: 19, who cites Colenso's meeting with an old chief called Hakahaka near Uawa in 1841, who recollected Cook's visit there in 1769 'although he was but a little boy at the time'; and Salmond 1991: 87, 128).

82. Richards 1995: 22.

83. *Hobart Town Gazette,* 28 March 1818.

84. *Sydney Gazette,* 2 December 1815.

85. Richards 1995: 20.

86. Visits recorded in greater detail in Appendix I.

87. This process of hybridisation is discussed in interesting detail by Atholl Anderson (1991).

Thirteen: Whaling Voyages and Maori Explorers

(pages 314–330)

1. See Royal Instructions to Governor Arthur Phillip: 'It is our royal will and pleasure that you do not on any account allow craft of any sort to be built for the use of private individuals which might enable them to effect . . . intercourse [with the Pacific Islands, the East India Company settlements, or the coast of China]'; Governor Hunter's instructions, 9 October 1797, strictly forbidding the building of boats whatsoever for the use of private persons (Cumpston 1977: 3,7); Governor King's instructions, 26 May 1804, prohibiting the building of vessels with keels over fourteen feet long without explicit permission, in CO201/33: 169; and King to Hobart, 20 December 1804, limiting permissions to three ships of not more than 200 tons each, in CO201/33: 182.

2. Clark 1992 I: 197.

3. *Britannia* (i) Transport/Whaler (Captain Thomas Melvill, 320 tons, Enderby of London); 10 November 1791 arrives at Port Jackson, 22 November goes cruising for whales; 16 December returns; 7 January 1792 leaves Port Jackson for coast of Peru; 17 November 1792 arrives there; 7 September 1793 returns to Dover. Not to be confused with *Britannia* (ii) Storeship (William Raven, 296 tons, St Barbe of London), which in 26 July 1792 arrives at Port Jackson from Falmouth with stores; 23 October 1792 leaves for Dusky Sound and the Cape of Good Hope; 20 June 1793 returns to Port Jackson; 8 September 1793 leaves for Dusky Sound, Norfolk Island and India; 27 September 1793 arrives at Dusky; 20 October leaves for Norfolk Island, where the ship is commandeered by Lieutenant-Governor King to take himself, Tuki and Huru and a party of others to northern New Zealand.

4. 11 November 1791, Arthur Phillip to Viscount Sydney in Dixson Ms Q162, CY Reel 223: 32. For the *Britannia* transport, see also Dixson Ms Q36, *Whaling Voyages Round the World in the Britannia and Speedy Transports, Capt. Thomas Melvill, 1791. 1792.*

1793. 1794. 1795. 1796. in Which is Introduc'd a few Remarks on the Spanish South America and an Essay on the Whale Fisherys; PRO CO201/5: 83; /6: 133–159, 232–38, 391–92; HRA I: 303, 307, 312, 347, 354, 380, 397, 400; HRNSW I (2): 558; Hunter 1793: 556–59, 566; Collins 1798 I: 182, 187–91.

5. Jackson 1978: 103–6.

6. For the *William and Ann,* see PRO CO201/8: 174, 196; /9: 51, 54, 68, 77–80, 90, 98, 148, 154, 157.

7. Jackson 1978.

8. Samuel Enderby, Evidence in Report to the Select Committee of the House of Lords, cited in Richards 1996: 45. It is possible, though, that Enderby had muddled his dates and that he was referring to the 1792 visit by the *William and Ann*.

9. Cumpston 1977: 33.

10. 'The ship Albion which left London in February 1799 cost the owner about ten thousand pounds Sterling. The ship itself had cost five thousand pounds, and provisions, food and the rest of the appliances, five thousand Pound as well. It was a beautiful fast sailing ship of 320 English tons, had a new copper bottom and was under the command of Hiber Bunker, an American, but was owned by Mr. Champion, a London merchant.' (Jorgensen 1996: 17.) See also Collins II: 215, 223, 299; HRA III: 109, 268. 1786 Statute 26 Geo. III, c.50 allowed southern whaleships to go as far east as 51°E; 1798 Statute 38 Geo III, c.57 opened Australian and New Zealand waters to whaleships, provided they didn't go northward of 15°S; 1802 the area was extended; 1814 Act 59 Geo. III, c.155 ended almost all the East India Company's privileges except trade with China and trade in tea.

11. King in McNab 1908 I: 224.

12. King to Messrs. Turnbull, Quested & Gardiner, 21 May 1802, in CO201/21: 218–19; King to Sir Joseph Banks, 5 June 1802, in CO210/23: 290–92; King to Sir Joseph Banks, 5 June 1802, in McNab 1908 I: 234–40.

13. In 1802, Daniel Ward donated three items from New Zealand; and in 1803 a patu onewa was donated by 'Captain J. F. Jeffrie, an Englishman, on behalf of Captain John Holman of Salem' (Richards 1996: 70).

14. A report on the southern whale fishery in 1804, which included an inventory of the seventy-five British ships on the fishery and their muster lists (giving the names and nationalities of each crew member), gives the composition of shipboard populations. PRO BT1/25: 276–349, Muster Lists of Ships on the Southern Whale Fishery. For documents relating to the fishery, see collection of items from BT1/15, 20, 21, 25,33; BT/6/88 in Ships' Archive, University of Auckland Library.

15. Jackson 1978: 91–92.

16. This doggerel poem recites the names of the Nantucket families involved in whaling in the mid-eighteenth century:

    Out of Nantucket their's Whalemen seventy-five,
    But two poor Worths among them doth survive:

    Their is two Ramsdills & their's Woodbury's two,
    Two Ways there is, chuse which one pleaseth you,
    Folgers thirteen, & Barnards there are four
    Bunkers their is three & Jenkinses no more,
    Gardners their is seven, Husseys their are two,
    Pinkhams their is five and a poor Delano,
    Myricks there is three and Coffins there are six,
    Swains their are four and one blue gally Fitch.
    One Chadwick, Cogshall, Coleman their's but one,
    Brown, Baxter, two & Paddacks their is three,
    Wyer, Stanton, Starbuck, Moorse is four you see.
    But if for a Voyage I was to choose a Stanton,
    I would leave Sammy our & choose Ben Stratton.
    And do not forget that Bocott is alive,
    And that long crotch makes up the seventy-five.
    This is answering to the list, you see,
    Made up in seventeen hundred & sixty three.

17. Comstock 1838: 5.

18. Starbuck 1989: 19–20, 90.

19. Byers nd: 167.

20. Doane 1987: 76–78.

21. Ibid: 71.

22. For another good account of the techniques used to 'cut in' a whale, see Jorgensen 1996: 15–16.

23. For example, in the stories of Paikea, who came to the East Coast either in the shape of, or on the back of a whale (Salmond 1991: 157). I have often wondered whether, since whales navigate using geo-magnetic sensing and some of their Pacific pathways take them to the coasts of New Zealand, voyaging canoes might not have followed migrating pods of whales to Aotearoa.

24. Salmond 1991: 220.

25. John White collected an account of the killing of Marion du Fresne from a Ngaa Puhi source in about the 1830s, which said: 'The canoes from the other side of that sea did that which was evil, they dragged their net to take fish in the beach of Manawa-ora where some corpses had laid, which had been drowned in the sea, belonging to the Hii-kutu tribe, and these Europeans were attacked and killed by the resident natives called the Nga-ti-uru and Nga-ti-pou, this they did to save themselves from an attack by the relatives of the drowned people of the Hii-kutu, and the chief of these salts called Marion was cooked and eaten by these two tribes, that is by the chiefs Te-Kauri and Tohi-tapu as they were Priests, and it was for them to eat these salts, so the evil might not come on their tribes for the evil of the salts, for ignoring the sacredness of the beach where corpses had lain' (John White ATL Ms 75 Folder B19: 88).

26. HRA I Vol. 4: 18, 365, 526; HRNSW 5: 165, 270, 532–34, 587; *Sydney Gazette,* 12 March, 5 June, 11 September, 25 September, 16 October 1803; 20 May, 27 May, 17 June, 26 August, 16 December 1804; 6 January, 3 March 1805; 7 December 1806.

27. The *Alexander* (Captain Robert Rhodes, 301 tons, six guns, twenty-nine men) was built in 1801 for Hurrys of London; leaves England at the beginning of April 1802, arrives at Port Jackson from New

Zealand 1 June 1803 with Teina on board; leaves for New Zealand 19 September 1803, returns to Port Jackson 21 May 1804; leaves again 4 July 1804 for the fishery, at Adventure Bay in Tasmania 30 July 1804, at Derwent 10 August – 7 September 1804, where she catches the first whale in the river, at Adventure Bay 23 October – 14 November 1804 (according to Nicholson's *Shipping Arrivals and Departures – Tasmania*, however, this whale was taken during the *Alexander*'s visit to the Derwent from 10 August to 7 September 1804, after her visit to New Zealand, so Jorgensen has confused the sequence of events); returns to Port Jackson 14 December 1804; sails from Port Jackson on the return voyage to England 27 February 1805, arrives in England at Portsmouth 13 June 1806; at Gravesend 27 June 1806 (Jones 1986: 37). See also 'Account of Sundry Disbursements & Expenditure made by Robert Rhodes Master of the Ship Alexander', ML ZA 1442.

28. *Sydney Gazette*, 1 June 1803, see also 12 March, 11 September, 25 September, 16 October, 1803; 20 May, 27 May, 17 June, 26 August, 16 December, 1804; 6 January, 3 March, 1805; 13 July, 24 August, 31 August, 21 September, 5 October, 12 October, 26 October, 2 November, 16 November, 7 December 1806.

29. Ibid: 16 October 1803.

30. Ibid: 5 June 1803. See Marsden in Elder (ed.) 1932: 155.

31. Philip Gidley King, 11 September 1803, ML MS A4042.

32. John White, ATL Ms 75 Folder B20: 84–85. Patu Hohepa (pers. comm. 1997) notes that when Ngaati Pakau killed some of the progeny of these pigs, there was fighting in which Muriwai was killed.

33. ATL Ms McNab notebook Vol. I: 24.

34. See Richards 1996: 57–74.

35. *Sydney Gazette*, 31 March 1805.

36. Jorgensen, *Observations*: 11–12.

37. Jorgensen's letter to the *Courier*, London, 10 October 1817, quoted in Richards 1996: 75–79.

38. See notes from Jorgensen [John Johnson] and Banks, and Johnson's bill for clothing the two Otaheitean boys in ANL Ms 9/91.

39. Banks to Rev. Joseph Hardcastle, 24 July 1806; 'Is grateful to him for taking under the protection of his Society the deserted islanders; they will soon be embarked on a ship for New South Wales and recommended to the Governor and Chaplain Marsden; advises that they should be inoculated by the Jennerian Society before sailing'; Kew: B.C. 2. 327.

40. Banks notes the name of the ship and captain, but both are illegible (ANL Ms 9/91). See Richards 1996: 78.

41. Jorgensen, *A Shred of Autobiography*: 125–28. See also Richards 1996: 57–68 for the voyage of the *Alexander*.

42. Sir Joseph Banks actively supported and promoted this strategic use of whaling and sealing, c.f. 'Whale and Seal Fisheries &c: Sir Jo. Banks' Remarks' and statistical sheets, ML A78-3: 226–39; 281.

43. *Sydney Gazette*, 15 June 1804; Lee 1815: 233–39.

44. Log of the *Hannah and Eliza*, Nantucket Whaling Museum. See Appendix II on Whaling Voyages.

45. See Log 93, *Hannah and Eliza*, Nantucket Whaling Museum.

46. These Maori sailors were by no means exceptional. Of the ships to visit New Zealand during these early years, at least thirty (and probably many others where the presence of Maori on board went unremarked) were to carry Maori as crew or passengers, some on wide-ranging voyages – to the Pacific, the East Indies and India, South America, North America and Britain, viz: *Active, Albion, Alexander, Ann, Anne, Argo, Atlantic, Boyd, Britannia, Buffalo, City of Edinburgh, Commerce, Cumberland, Daedalus, Elizabeth, Fancy, Ferret, Frederick, General Wellesley, Hannah and Eliza, Jefferson, Kangaroo, King George, Lady Nelson, Perseverance, Resolution, Richard and Mary, Santa Anna, Scorpion, Speke, Star, Venus.*

47. King to Earl Camden, 30 April 1805; quoted in McNab 1908 I: 253–57.

48. King to Commandant Captain John Piper, Sydney, 30 April 1805, in ML Safe 1/51.

49. Government and General Order, *Sydney Gazette*, 26 May 1805, and in McNab 1908 I: 257–58.

50. Sir Joseph Banks, ANL Ms 9/139.

51. See Sissons, Wi Hongi and Hohepa 1987: 14–15, 34–35, 111–13, 120–22; for whakapapa, see ibid: 35, 56. According to S. Percy Smith, Ngaati Uru had migrated to Whangaroa after being driven from Whangamumu and the southern shores of the Bay of Islands, because their chief Te Kuri [Te Kauri] had killed Marion du Fresne' [Smith 1897: 13]. This seems to be a confusion, because early accounts collected by John White make it plain that while Ngaati Uru did indeed join Ngaati Pou in killing Marion, it was because members of both groups had accompanied Marion on a fishing expedition when he insisted on hauling his seine on a beach where the corpses of some drowned men belonging to Te Kauri's people, Te Hikutuu, had lain. They were forced to kill him as utu for this offence, and to save themselves from being killed and eaten by Te Hikutuu in revenge [John White ATL Ms 75, Folder B20: 79–88]. It is clear from early Wesleyan missionary records from Whangaroa that Ngaati Uru were related to the Ngaa Puhi descendants of Auha and Whakaaria.

52. This son of Te Pahi's was variously called 'Ma-Tara' or 'Materie' (by Christopher Spencer in London), 'Maitai' (by Governor King), 'Jacky Myetye' (by the *Sydney Gazette*) and 'Ma-Tamai' (by Sir Joseph Banks in London). When he went to London in early 1807, he was placed under the protection of Banks, who noted that 'The Young Man Ma-Tamai had been sent by his Father on the Ferrett Capt. Skelton a year and a half before [i.e. before Te Pahi's visit to Port Jackson in November 1805] in order that he might see the English at their settlement' (ANL Ms

9/139).

53. Log 93, Nantucket Whaling Museum, 18 December 1804.

54. On 31 January 1804, the *Ferret*, South Whaler, owned by Mr D. Bennett of London, sailed from Port Jackson for Norfolk Island, arriving there on 11 February 1804 and returning to Port Jackson from Norfolk Island and the Coast on 9 June 1805 with 108 tons of sperm oil. Her visit to Norfolk was recorded in a letter from Colonel Foveaux to Governor King, 22 February 1804: 'Lieutenant Houston and Captain Piper arrived on the Ferret on the 13th inst' (ML A1444) and in the *Sydney Gazette*, 11 March 1804. Her return to Port Jackson from the fishery and Norfolk was reported in the *Sydney Gazette*, 16 June 1805.

55. King, 'The Legality of Government and General Orders', in McNab 1908 I: 261–68.

56. McNab 1914: 102.

57. King to Captain Piper, 24 July 1805, in ML A2015: 490.

58. The itinerary of the *Venus* (iii) on this voyage was as follows: arrives from Calcutta May 1805 at Port Jackson, leaves 29 July 1805 'for the coast of Peru', but actually on a sealing voyage to the Antipodes, via Norfolk Island, New Zealand and Norfolk. See also Ross 1987: 38–40.

59. *Sydney Gazette*, 1 December 1805.

60. King to Captain Piper, February 1806, in ML A2015: 517.

61. *Sydney Gazette*, 13 April 1806.

Fourteen: John Savage and Te Mahanga
(pages 331–348)

1. *Sydney Gazette*, 28 July 1805: 'On Friday morning sailed for England, to touch at St. Helena, the *Ferret* south whaler, Capt. Skelton; with whom went passengers: Mr. and Mrs. Savage, and Mr. and Mrs. Hartley.' See *Australian Dictionary of Biography*: 419; New South Wales Archives, Colonial Secretary's papers, fiche 3268, 9/2731: 150. The *Ferret*, Captain Philip Skelton, left Port Jackson on 26 July 1805; returned leaking, for repairs, on 21 August, and again on 8 September 1805, finally sailing for England on 15 September 1805. The ship arrived off North Cape on 18 September 1805. See also Colonial Secretary's Papers, NSW Archives Fiche 3268, 9/2731: 150, 1 May 1805, Extract from Letter to Sir Charles Morgan re. Surgeons Savage and Mileham being tried for offences by General Court Martial. For arrival at St Helena and Gravesend, see Jones 1986: 36–37.

2. ML A78-6, Banks correspondence, Philip Gidley King to Banks, Sydney, 20 July 1805.

3. Title page, Savage 1807.

4. The British whalers *Scorpion*, *Elizabeth and Mary*, *John Sebastian*, *Adonis*, *Britannia*, *Alexander*, *Argo*, *Betsey, Harriet, Ocean*, *Richard and Mary* and *Ferrett*; and the American whalers *Ann and Eliza*, *Hannah and Eliza* and *Ann* of New Bedford, and the *Brothers* of Nantucket (see Appendix I).

5. Savage 1807: 3–4.

6. Ibid: 11.

7. Ibid: 14.

8. Ibid: 18.

9. Ibid: 22.

10. Ibid: 25.

11. Ibid: 27.

12. Ibid: 30–31.

13. See Sissons, Wi Hongi and Hohepa 1987: 15.

14. Savage 1807: 31–32.

15. Ibid: 32.

16. Ibid: 34–35.

17. Ibid: 43.

18. Ibid: 44-48.

19. Ibid: 48–53.

20. Ibid: 54–57.

21. Ibid: 58–59.

22. Ibid: 61.

23. Ibid: 63.

24. In an early account collected by John White, the adventures of 'Mohanga of Nga-puhi' were described, in ATL White Ms 75, Folder 19. According to Sherrin & Wallace (1890: 131), 'Moehanga was a representative or connection of several hapu – of Te Para Whau of Whangarei, of Ngatiwai of Whangaruru, and of Te Tawera of Te Rawhiti; but his father was of Te Para Whau.' Unfortunately, they do not acknowledge their source for these identifications.

25. My thanks to Hori Parata of Ngaati Wai for his account of contemporary knowledge held by the descendants of Te Mahanga.

26. Savage 1807: 68.

27. Ibid: 78–79.

28. Ibid: 85.

29. Ibid: 89–90.

30. Sherrin & Wallace (1890: 121–22) identify this child as one Tauke, whose mother belonged to Ngawhitu, a settlement between Pakaraka and Ohaeawai in the Bay of Islands, and was of the Urikapana hapuu of Ngaa Puhi. They added that she married a European and left issue one daughter named Te Tauhara, who lived in Whangarei. It is, however, uncertain on what basis they identified the child seen by Savage as Tauke.

31. Savage 1807: 93.

32. Ibid: 97.

33. Ibid: 103.

34. Ibid: 105.

35. Ibid: 39–40.

36. During this encounter with Dillon, Mahanga had also talked of a voyage to India, which Dillon later discovered was an invention, 'no doubt to serve some purpose or gratify some purpose of his own'. Mahanga begged Dillon to take him to Bengal to see his friend Mr. Savage, and Dillon agreed, giving him a red jacket to match an old soldier's cap that he had kept in his possession. Mahanga had accompanied him on a cruise to Tongatapu and other Pacific Islands, but when they returned to New Zealand before proceeding to Calcutta, he decided to leave the ship and return home. (Dillon 1829: 192, 199–203, 214, 248, 324, 355).

37. *Sydney Gazette*, 7 December 1806: 'The *Alexander*, Captain Rhodes, we are happy to learn, arrived in England the 12th of June, the day before the *Ferret* sailed.' But for the *Alexander*'s arrival at Portsmouth, see Jones 1986: 37.

38. White ATL Ms 75, Folder B20: 91.

39. Nicholas 1817 I: 431.

Fifteen: Te Pahi, Governor King, George Bruce and Atahoe

(pages 349–367)

1. King private papers, quoted in McNab 1908 I: 262–63.

2. See Adm 51/1694, 'Journal of the Proceedings of His Majesty's Storeship Buffalo' part 2 – but on the relevant dates there is no mention of Te Pahi and his sons coming aboard.

3. King in McNab 1908 I: 263–64.

4. *Sydney Gazette*, 1 December 1805. HMS *Buffalo*, Acting Captain Lieutenant Houston, had arrived in Port Jackson on 27 November 1805 from Norfolk Island.

5. King private papers, quoted in McNab 1908 I: 264.

6. King to Sir Joseph Banks, 8 January 1806, ANL Ms 9/98.

7. McNab 1908 I: 267.

8. *Sydney Gazette*, 22 December 1805.

9. Nicholas 1817 I: 9–10.

10. King in McNab 1908 I: 267–68.

11. Ibid: 264–65.

12. Nicholas 1817 I: 10–11.

13. King's reports on Te Pahi's visit are to be found in his private papers, quoted in McNab 1908 I: 262–68; and in King to Sir Joseph Banks, Sydney, 8 January 1806, ANL 9/98; King, visit to Sydney of Chief of the Bay of Islands, ML Ab 67/16; King, despatch to Lord Camden, 15 March 1806, ML C186, and CO201/39: 31–33.

14. *Sydney Gazette*, 23 February 1806.

15. King to Sir Joseph Banks, 8 January 1806, ANL Ms 9/98.

16. King to Edward Cooke, 31 December 1805, CO201/37: 337–39.

17. For the 1804 and 1806 voyages of the *Lady Nelson*, see J. Symons's Logbook, PRO Adm 51/1666; and Lee 1915.

18. For a more detailed account of George Bruce's early life, see DL Ms 165, 'The Life of a Greenwich Pensioner, an Abridgement of his Autobiography'; ML A1618-1, 'The Life of a Greenwich Pensioner 1778 to –'; ANL Ms 3608, 'The Life of A Greenwich Pensioner, by Himself'; and Orchiston 1972.

19. Bruce, 'The Life of A Greenwich Pensioner, by Himself', 1806, ANL Ms 3608: 62–63.

20. *Sydney Gazette*, 22 June 1806.

21. Ibid, 15 June 1806.

22. Ibid; Lee 1915: 278–95.

23. Bruce, 'The Life of A Greenwich Pensioner, by Himself', 1806, ANL Ms 3608: 63.

24. Ibid: 64.

25. *Sydney Gazette*, 13 July, 20 July 1806.

26. The *Richard and Mary* sailed from Port Jackson for England on 8 September 1806. Correspondence relating to Maa-Tara's stay in London includes Spencer and Co. to Sir Joseph Banks, 11 May 1807; Christopher Spencer to Sir Joseph Banks; note by Sir Joseph Banks, in ANL Ms 9/139. See also a comment in the *Sydney Gazette*, 17 September 1809: 'This plan appears to have been agitated by King Tippahee and Prince Matarra, his son, who went to England . . .'

27. *Sydney Gazette*, 12 April 1807; *London Chronicle*, clipping in ANL Ms 4658: 9.

28. *NZDB* I:11; Belich 1996: 133.

29. King to Sir Joseph Banks, 26 November 1807, ML A83.

30. *NZDB* I: 11.

31. Marsden, ed. Elder 1932: 142, 155, 172–73; White ATL Ms 75, Folder B20: 95–99.

32. *Sydney Gazette*, 29 May 1808.

33. *Evangelical Magazine*, May 1807: 468.

34. *Sydney Gazette*, 12 April 1807.

35. See McNab 1914: 114–15; and the *Sydney Gazette*, 30 October 1808, listed 'George and Teara, New Zealander' as about to leave Port Jackson in the *Star*.

36. Esther Spalding, otherwise Knowland; Mary Riley, otherwise Toaling; Martha Simmonds, otherwise Petrie; Sarah Hughes, otherwise Atkins; Sarah Brooks; Elizabeth Bennet; the wife of Edward Robarts (*Sydney Gazette*, 29 March 1807, 5 April 1807, 19 April 1807).

37. Dening 1974: 1–12.

38. HO 54/1: 84–86; Robarts ed. Dening 1974: 178–80. Edward Robarts claimed that these people had tried to cut off some of the *General Wellesley*'s crew who were out on the reef collecting oysters and looking for pearls.

39. Ibid: 185; Robarts, NLS Adv. Ms 17.1.18: 95.

40. *Sydney Gazette*, 15 May 1808.

41. Robarts, NLS Adv. Ms 17.1.18: 97.

42. Ibid: 98.

43. Ibid: 100; Dening 1974: 194.

44. Miller 1854: 44.

45. *Calcutta Gazette*, 11 May 1809.

46. Memorial from George Bruce to the Earl Bathurst, 4 June 1813, CO201/69: 51–53. In this memorial, Bruce also attributed the burning of the *Boyd* to anger over the kidnapping of his wife, and asked to be returned to New Zealand, where he had already partially persuaded the local people of the superiority of his own religion. He added, 'If furnished with proper books, he would be of great service in this respect, and might at least pave the way for the success of future Missionaries of the Gospel.'

47. *Sydney Gazette*, 3 March 1810.

48. J. Arnold, Letters 1810, ML A1849-2; quoted in Dening 1974: 199.

49. Memorials from George Bruce CO201/59: 308;

CO201/69: 51–53; 82–85; CO201/70: 78–79; and letter from Macquarie, 12 May 1814, in CO201/73: 6–7. For George Bruce's adventures, see Bruce, ML Ms 3608; *Calcutta Gazette*, 11 May 1809; Bruce, NLS Ms 11064: 99–110; Macquarie to Lord Minto, Governor-General, Calcutta, 7 April 1810, NLS Ms 11331: 59–60. Although Macquarie argued forcibly that Bruce was much despised and disliked by the New Zealanders for his ill-treatment and neglect of his wife, his drunkenness and lack of principle, the tombstone inscription suggests that Bruce did care for his wife. Interestingly, in 1805 one of Marsden's correspondents reported: 'There is a New Zealander at this time in England as Mr. Pratt informs me, who speaks English fluently, and is a man of rank in his own country, which he quitted a few years ago from motives of curiosity, and Lord Minto allowed him an equipage and a handsome establishment. In the vicissitudes of his life he has in this country fallen into the work-house at Shoreditch' – evidently a reference to George Bruce (ML A1992: 196).

Sixteen: The Burning of the Boyd

(pages 368–394)

1. Ex-Governor King to the Commissioners of the Board of Revision, December 1807, in McNab 1908 I: 286–87.
2. John Besent deposition in HO CMS 54a: 78–79; and McNab 1908 I: 423–24. See Muster List of *Parramatta* in PRO BT1/25: 282.
3. James Gordon deposition in HO CMS 54a: 69–70.
4. McNab 1914: 116–17.
5. Deposition of James Elder, Court House Parramatta, 12 November 1813, in HO Ms 5: 81–89.
6. *Sydney Gazette*, 17 July 1808.
7. John Marmon, APL Grey 920.
8. Berry in *Adventures of British Seamen in the Southern Ocean* 1827: 330–31.
9. Ibid: 331–32.
10. *Sydney Gazette*, 17 July 1808.
11. Berry 1912:14–26.
12. Kendall ML Bonwick Transcipts.
13. Captain James Gordon to Rev. Samuel Marsden, 8 November 1813, in HO Ms 5: 69.
14. Cumpston 1977: 62.
15. King to E. Cooke, 8 February 1808, in CO201/48: 36, 42.
16. Berry 1827: 332–33. It was later claimed in the *Sydney Gazette* that 'Prince Matarra . . '. went to England in the Buffalo, and returned hither on the Porpoise, and . . . had been favored with a passage back to New Zealand in the Edinburgh'. We know from Banks's correspondence, however, that Maa-Tara arrived in England on the *Richard and Mary,* and was there by May 1807; and from the shipping returns that the *Porpoise* was working along the New South Wales coast during this time until she sailed for England with Governor Bligh on 17 March 1808, so

this report is incorrect on almost all scores. Maa-Tara did, however, return to the Bay of Islands on the *City of Edinburgh*.

17. Bligh to Castlereagh, 10 June 1809, in McNab 1908 I: 289.
18. For more background on Alexander Berry and his speculations, see Kociumbas 1992: 109–11.
19. Berry 1827: 33.
20. See Sissons, Wi Hongi and Hohepa 1987: 22, 39, 40, 41 (whakapapa), 42, 44, 46–48.
21. Berry 1827: 33–34. Fergus Clunie points out the importance of the Red Ensign as a signal of ranga-tira status to Maori (Clunie pers. comm. 1997).
22. Berry 1827: 336–37.
23. Berry 1912: 33–34.
24. Ibid: 39–44; see also *Sydney Gazette*, 17 September 1809, for Ceroni's account of this episode.
25. See Sissons, Wi Hongi and Hohepa 1987: 37–38.
26. Berry 1912: 47.
27. Ibid: 54.
28. Ibid: 83.
29. For an extended discussion of such exchanges, see David Chappell's thesis, 'Beyond the Beach: Periplean Frontiers of Pacific Islanders Aboard Euro-American Vessels 1768–1887', University of Hawaii 1991.
30. Captain James Gordon to Rev. Samuel Marsden, 8 November 1813, in HO Ms 5: 69.
31. The Depositions of Jacob Williams of the *Mercury*, William Burnett of the *Mary*, and Peter Dillon of the *Mercury*, 20 November 1813, in a complaint preferred by Rev. Samuel Marsden against Mr. Theodore Walker, late Master of the *Mercury* schooner in McNab notebooks ATL Ms 81943, Vol I: 1–7. See also Deposition of Jacob Williams, 19 November 1813, at the Courthouse, Parramatta, in HO CMS 54a: 96–98.
32. 'The Boyd Massacre' by Alexander Berry, DL Ms Q330: 15–16.
33. Berry 1912: 102–3.
34. Berry 1827: 344–45.
35. Owens 1974: 34.
36. See *Sydney Gazette*, 12 November 1809.
37. Kelly *JPS* 49: 400; Owens 1974: 39.
38. Berry 1827: 348.
39. By the Wesleyan missionary Nathaniel Turner; see Owens 1974: 53.
40. Alexander Berry, 'The Boyd Massacre', DL Ms Q330: 6.
41. Berry 1827: 350–51.
42. Alexander Berry Account, ATL qMs 0163: 7.
43. 'The Boyd Massacre' by Alexander Berry, DL Ms Q330: 10.
44. Ibid: 12.
45. 'Notice! All Masters of Ships frequenting New Zealand are directed to be careful in not admitting many natives on board, as they may be cut off (in a moment) by surprise', in CO201/53: 87–88; see also *Sydney Gazette*, 21 April 1810.
46. HRA I /7: 294.
47. See *Sydney Gazette*, 10 March 1810.

48. Deposition of Samuel R. Chace and Philip Goodenough before Robert Campbell, 12 March 1810, in CO201/53: 85–86.

49. *Sydney Gazette*, 10 March 1810.

50. Governor Macquarie to Viscount Castlereagh, 12 March 1810, in CO201/53: 33–40. Also Macquarie to Lord Minto, 7 April 1810, in NLS Ms 1131: 59–60.

51. 'Atrocious and Horrible Massacree', St Bride's Printing Library, London.

52. New Zealand flax had been tested and shown to have a high breaking strength, and it was lightweight compared with other kinds of cordage (*Sydney Gazette*, 30 June 1805). Lord and Williams hoped to set up a settlement for three years to begin with (*Sydney Gazette*, 28 January 1810), and had originally recruited Bruce and Atahoe to lead it (*Sydney Gazette*, 3 March 1810). See the correspondence between Lord and Williams, and Secretary Campbell and Governor Macquarie: Lord and Williams, Alexander Riley and Thomas Kent to Governor, 27 January 1810; Thomas Campbell to Messrs Lord and Williams, Alexander Riley and Thomas Kent, 2 February 1810 and 20 February 1810; Lord and Williams to Governor, 12 March 1810; in CO210/53: 93–101; and in HRA I/7: 294–300.

53. For the correspondence relating to this venture, see a Despatch from Governor Macquarie to the Earl of Liverpool, notifying him that Lord and his partners had asked for an exclusive privilege to the New Zealand flax trade for fourteen years, submitting their proposals to the Earl and asking for ministerial approval (30 April 1810); from Lord and Williams, Riley and Kent, putting these proposals (27 January 1810); a further letter from the merchants, suggesting that storeships sent out with supplies from England should be directed to take on cargoes of hemp and timber from this venture (20 February 1810); and a letter from Lord and Williams notifying the Governor that Riley and Kent had withdrawn from the venture after hearing of the destruction of the *Boyd*, but that they were determined to proceed with it and had taken on Andrew Thompson (owner of the ship *Governor Bligh*) as a new partner (12 March 1810); see PRO BT1/64: 56–67. See also CO201/54: 43; /56: 175.

54. *Sydney Gazette*, 28 April 1810.

55. In CO201/53:89.

56. Kendall to Secretary, 25 March 1814, in HO CMS 54a: 175n.

57. *Sydney Gazette*, 8 October 1809; see also McNab 1908 I: 301–6.

58. The *Spring Grove* and *New Zealander* arrived soon after this incident, and Philip Tapsell, a Danish sailor on board the *New Zealander*, later gave a hearsay account of the raid. The local people had attacked the sailors with spears and muskets, but were outgunned and driven off the island. One sailor from the *Inspector* was killed in the raid, a death that they blamed on the defenders. Te Pahi himself was shot in the chest or neck by Captain Parker, but managed to escape to the mainland, swimming with the assistance of two women. The woman who had incited the whalers to attack Te Pahi for the *Boyd* killings was no longer safe among her own people, and she later arrived in Sydney (with the *Boyd*'s longboat) on the *Perseverance*, recommended by Colonel Foveaux to the care of the Governor (McNab 1908 I: 301–4; Tapsell ed. Cowan 1935: 43–44; and ATL Tapsell papers: 22–29).

59. Ibid.

60. PRO PC1/396; CO201/59: 391–96.

61. Bligh to Richard Ryder, 11 August 1810, in CO201/56: 175.

62. McNab 1908 I: 301–4.

63. *Sydney Gazette*, 25 August 1810.

64. Dillon reported that this was because the boy had been kind to George, while William Swain of the *Cumberland* reported that it was because he had a club foot and they took him to be 'a son of the devil' (McNab 1908 I: 312).

65. McNab 1908 I: 306–9; *Sydney Gazette*, 4 September 1810.

66. Thomas Kendall to Secretary, 6 September 1814, in HO CMS 54b: 325

67. Letter from George, Wangaroa, 6 November 1823, ATL Ms Papers 983-01.

68. See also an account collected in 1827, when Mahanga gave Peter Dillon a version of events at the Bay of Islands that added a few final details. He told Dillon that the head chief of Whangaroa, a man called 'Pipi', had asked Captain Wilkinson of the *Star* in about 1806 to take his son to Europe, to get toki (adzes) and fish-hooks for their people. This young man, whom they nicknamed 'George', boarded the *Star* and went to the seal fishery at the Antipodes Islands. In 1808, the *Elizabeth*, Captain 'Stuard' (William Stewart), called at Whangaroa, and 'Prince George' had joined that vessel. He went to Fiji and then to Port Jackson, where he joined Captain Wilkinson of the *Star* for another voyage to the sealing islands. This time they took no seals, so George received no payment. When they returned to Port Jackson, he shipped on the *Boyd*, commanded by Captain John Thomson. One of the passengers on board the ship was a wealthy East India captain called Burnsides, who was returning home to England, and it was rumoured that he brought £30,000 with him. During the voyage the cook accidentally threw overboard a dozen pewter spoons belonging to the captain. Apprehensive of getting a flogging, he blamed George instead, and the captain ordered George to be punished by the boatswain. George protested that he was a chief, who should not be flogged, but Thompson retorted that he was a 'cokey' (kuki, or slave).

When they anchored at Whangaroa, George showed his friends and family his lacerated back, and told them what had happened. The next day George and his people went with Captain

Thompson in three armed boats up the river, where George threw off his cloak and pointed to the marks on his back. At that moment his brother Te Puhi (the 'Tippoohee' mentioned in earlier reports) knocked out Thompson's brains, and all of the other sailors were killed. George and his men then dressed themselves in the Europeans' clothes and got on board the ship, where they killed all but some sailors who escaped into the rigging; Mrs Marley, the wife of a publican; Miss Broughton, daughter of the Deputy Commissary at Port Jackson; and the cabin boy George, whose club foot seemed a sign of supernatural power and who had been kind to the chief during the voyage. When Te Pahi arrived at Whangaroa the next day on a fishing party, the sailors who were still perched in the rigging begged him to save them. He told them to jump overboard and swim to his canoe, but they were caught in the water. The next day all of the gunpowder was brought up on the deck to be shared out amongst the local warriors. A chief (usually identified as Te Aara's father, Pipikoi-takere) snapped his musket over some loose gunpowder, which exploded, killing a number of people and setting fire to the ship, which burned down to the water (Dillon 1829: 214–25).

An account collected in Maori by John White some years later tells a similar story: 'Tara [Te Aara] told the following to us, soon after the time he and his people killed and eat the crew of the vessell they took in Whanga-roa. He said he went from Whanga-roa in a vessell to kill whales, and after he had worked for a long time in the ship, he was not paid for his work, and he stayed in Port Jackson, where he was called George by the Europeans, from where he came in a vessell to Whanga-roa, and when out at sea, he was charged with having taken some of the things [according to other accounts, pewter spoons] the Cook of the vessell had in charge for which he was flogged on his back with a rope, the vessell came into Whanga-roa where Tara showed his back that had been beaten to his people, and the people planned to take revenge, and they invited the people of the ship to go and look at a kauri forest at the head of the Whanga-roa harbour where the Maori killed all those who went to look at the forest, the clothes of those killed the Nga-ti-uru men put on themselves and pulled back to the ship and killed all those who were there save one woman, a little girl and two small boys, these the women of the Nga-ti-uru saved in spite of the men of the tribe, and the vessell caught fire and was burnt' (John White ATL Ms75, Folder B19: 94).

69. Hainsworth 1981: 74, 126n, 152n, 194, 238.
70. For letters illustrating the commercial difficulties of the period, see Macarthur papers, ATL Ms Papers 0725, from ML A2808, A2900.
71. McNab 1908 I: 293; CO201/50: 284–87.

Introduction: The Evangelical Voyages

(pages 401–404)

1. Smith 1913: 12.
2. Taylor 1855: 14–16.
3. Lovejoy 1950.

Seventeen: Ruatara and Samuel Marsden

(pages 405–447)

1. For mention of this trip on the *Fancy* (Captain Dell) shortly after Dell's return to Port Jackson from New Zealand, see W. Paterson to Governor Hunter, 15 June 1795, in CO 201/12.
2. Marsden to Rev. Josiah Pratt, 24 March 1808, in Havard-Williams 1961: 11–12.
3. Marsden, 'Observations on the Introduction of the Gospel into the South Sea Islands', HO Ms 176A: 21–24.
4. Ibid: 8–9.
5. Marsden to Pratt, 24 March 1808, in Havard-Williams 1961: 13–14.
6. Marsden did not graduate from Cambridge. He was recruited for the New South Wales position before he had time to sit the examinations (My thanks to M. G. S. Parsonson for this information). For background on Marsden's chaplaincy, see ML A1992, CO201/14: 184–87; /17: 45–47; 280; ML A78-3: 98–99; ML A1677-2; and Yarwood 1996.
7. Marsden, quoted in Yarwood 1996: 98.
8. Yarwood 1996.
9. Ibid: 104.
10. Salmond, in press.
11. Marsden to Joseph Hardcastle, 25 October 1810, in ML A1993: 677.
12. Marsden to Pratt, 7 April 1808, in Havard-Williams 1961: 15.
13. Nicholas 1817 I: 17.
14. Marsden to Pratt, 7 April 1808, in Havard-Williams 1961: 15.
15. Marsden, in HO Ms 176A: 11.
16. For an early Ngaa Puhi account of 'Ruatara and his travels', see John White AU MIC 78-249, Folder B20: 92.
17. For the itinerary of the *Argo*, see Appendix II; and *Sydney Gazette*, 9 June, 28 July, 11 August, 18 August, 25 August, 8 September, 15 September, 1 December, 1805; 13 April, 11 May, 27 July, 21 September, 28 September, 7 December, 14 December, 28 December 1806; 4 January, 11 January, 25 January, 8 February, 22 February, 1 March 1807.
18. For the itinerary of the *Albion*, see Appendix II; and *Sydney Gazette* 10 August, 24 August, 31 August, 21 September, 5 October, 12 October, 1806; 25 January, 12 April, 7 June, 1807; 15 May, 22 May, 10 July, 14 August, 18 September, 25 September, 2 October, 9 October, 23 October, 30 October, 1808. Also Elizabeth Bligh to Sir Joseph Banks 30 March 1809; ML Ms A78-5: 148–149a.
19. For a vivid account of a whaling voyage to New

Zealand on the *Santa Anna* (Captain Dagg), leaving Port Jackson in late November 1810 and returning 20 February 1811, see George Miller 1854, *A Trip to Sea from 1810 to 1815*. This includes a detailed description of contemporary techniques of harpooning and cutting-in whales.

20. For an itinerary of the *Santa Anna*'s voyage, see Appendix II, and *Sydney Gazette* 22 February, 15 March, 22 March, 29 March, 5 April, 7 June, 14 June, 28 June, 5 July, 1807; 15 May, 5 June, 12 June, 17 June, 14 August, 21 August, 28 August, 25 September, 2 October, 9 October, 23 October, 1808.

21. Miller 1854: 16–17.

22. Ibid: 12–13.

23. *Proceedings of the Church Missionary Society* 3, 1810: 112.

24. Elder (ed.) 1932: 63–68.

25. John Mason Good to Marsden, 29 April 1810 ML A1992: 485.

26. Mauss 1990: 20.

27. Marsden to Pratt, 15 November 1809, in Havard-Smith 1961: 24.

28. For material from the *Ann*'s voyage, see University of Birmingham Library, CMS Archives N/E 1–5; CN/061/28.

29. Sissons, Wi Hongi and Hohepa 1987: 37–38. Miki seems to have been Ruatara's favorite wife at this time. He was also married to Rahu, the daughter of Raakau, the tohunga at Rangihoua (ibid: 15, 34–35).

30. Marsden to Good, Rio de Janeiro, 15 November 1809, in *Proceedings of the CMS* 3, 1810: 111–26.

31. See Grey 1923: 6–23.

32. For Elsdon Best's commentaries on Rona, see Best 1972: 25. None of the various versions he cites echoes Nicholas' acoount very closely.

33. See William Colenso's version of the fable of the shark and the large lizard, in *TNZI* 11: 101. According to Colenso, the lizard wanted to live on land. When his brother the shark asked him to stay in the sea he cursed him, saying, 'Go out to sea, and become a relish for the basket of cooked roots!' The shark retorted, 'Go on land, to be smothered with the fire of green fern (i.e. be smoked out of your burrow)!' The lizard answered, 'I will go on shore, where I will terrify everyone, with my spines and ridgy crest, the personification of the war god Tuu.'

34. There was a constellation known as 'Te Waka' – Canoe. Nicholas gave a virtually identical description of Maori beliefs in his book, evidently borrowed from this account by Marsden (see Nicholas 1817 I: 55–62).

35. See Best 1982: 32–33.

36. My thanks to Fergus Clunie for this insight.

37. Marsden in *Proceedings of the CMS* 3, 1810: 119–20.

38. Colenso 1868: 35–36.

39. See whakapapa in Sissons, Wi Hongi and Hohepa 1987: 14, 16, 33, 37, 134.

40. Marsden in *Proceedings of the CMS* 3, 1810: 120–21.

41. For instance, the Tauranga chief Tuuhopetiki, who upon destroying Whitianga Paa and killing its chief Koropiritoetoe, took his wife and renamed himself Pirimaupakanga (Piri who won the battle) after her former husband (Salmond 1991: 202).

42. See whakapapa in Sissons, Wi Hongi and Hohepa 1987: 37, 38.

43. Marsden in *Proceedings of the CMS* 3, 1810: 121–22.

44. The systematic listing of warrior numbers for each main kin group in the far north given to Governor King by Tuki in 1793 is probably the result of such musters, which were also described by the missionary William Williams.

45. See Williams in AUL Ms 366, Journal, 317–, 1833.

46. See, for instance, Maning's comments on the role of rangatira in the north (Maning 1964: 36).

47. For examples, see Colenso 1879: 115–22.

48. Marsden in *Proceedings of the CMS* 3, 1810: 123.

49. Good to Marsden, 29 April 1810, in ML A1992/89: 82–100.

50. A theory subsequently pursued by a number of scholars in New Zealand (see Sorenson 1979).

51. Ibid: 98.

52. See also letter from M. Atkinson to Marsden, 24 March 1803, in ibid: 27; and Anna Barbauld's poem *1811* (Barbauld 1812: my thanks to Joanne Wilkes for this reference). *Horace Walpole's Correspondence* gives earlier intimations of these attitudes: e.g. Vol II, ed. W. S. Lewis, 1937: 225: Walpole to Rev. Mr. Cole, 15 June 1780: 'How I abominate Mr Banks and Dr Solander who routed the poor Otaheitens out of the centre of the ocean, and carried our abominable passions amongst them. Not even that poor little speck could escape European restlessness – well! I have seen many temptestuous scenes and outlived them! The present prospect is too thick to see through – it is well Hope never foresakes us! Adieu!'; Volume 7, Walpole to Sir Horace Mann, 13 July 1773: 'Yet if the merit of some historian does not interest posterity by the beauty of his narration, this age will be as little known as the annals of the Byzantine Empire, marked only by vices and follies. What is England now? – A sink of Indian wealth, filled by nabobs and emptied by Maccaronis! A senate sold and despised! A country overrun by horse-races! A gaming, robbing, wrangling, railing nation, without principles, genius, character or allies; the over-grown shadow of what it was!'; Volume 25, Walpole to Sir Horace Mann, 2 December 1784: 'If air-balloons could reach the moon, I believe the first inquiry of philosophers would be after the specie in the planet. Otaheite and all the Owyhees and New Holland and New Zeland will be left to return to their primitive obscurity, because they have nothing more intrinsic than hogs and red feathers. Yet science pretended to make the expedition! Science is perfectly content with the very little it has learnt!'; and Volume 33, Walpole to Lady Ossory, 4 January 1781: 'Our ruin seems to me inevitable. Nay, I know those who smile in the Drawing-Room, that groan by their fireside – They own we have no more men to send to America, and think our credit almost nearly as exhausted . . . Oh no! Nor can I be sorry to be on

the verge – does one wish to live to weep over the
ruins of Carthage?'

53. See Pick 1989 for a fascinating discussion of
European ideas of progress and degeneration.

54. Play with the idea of 'savage' witnesses to the
degeneration and follies of Europe goes back at least
to Montaigne, (discussed in Salmond 1991: 307–8),
although it was 'savages' other than Maori who
peopled the trope. The notion that 'New Zealanders' might one day survey the ruins of London
seems to have sprung from an editor of d'Entrecasteaux's *Voyage* (see Colenso 1883), which led to
Edward Gibbon's 1812 conceit that in his own time,
tribes once savage (i.e. the English) were sending
pilgrims to muse over the ruins of Rome (*The
History of the Decline and Fall of the Roman Empire*, e.g.
Vol. XII: 431). Thomas Macaulay, another English
historian, picked up this notion and played with it in
his 1840 review of Ranke's *History of the Popes of
Rome* (Macaulay 1840: 228), while discussing the
Catholic Church, 'She was great and respected
before the Saxon had set foot on Britain – before
the Frank had passed the Rhine – when Grecian
eloquence still flourished at Antioch – when idols
were still worshipped in the temple of Mecca. And
she may still exist in undiminished vigour when
some traveller from New Zealand shall, in the midst
of a vast solitude, take his stand on a broken arch of
London Bridge to sketch the ruins of St. Pauls.' In
1855, Anthony Trollope began his book *The New
Zealanders* with a reference to Macaulay's phrase,
asking 'Is the time quickly coming when the New
Zealanders shall supplant the Englishman in the
history of the civilization of the world? Have the
glories of Great Britain reached their climax, and
begun to pale? Is England in her decadence?'
(Trollope ed. N. J. Hall 1972: 3. My thanks to the
Reverend Dr Allan Davidson and Robin Skinner for
tracking down these references).

55. John King to Deputy Secretary, 25 April 1810,
University of Birmingham Library CMS C N/O
61/28.

56. William Hall and John King to Deputy Secretary,
ibid: O 61/27.

57. Hall and King to Deputy Secretary, 2 November 1811,
N/E2.

58. Marsden to Secretary, 18 June 1813, in HO
CMS54a: 40.

59. Report of the Committee delivered to the Annual
Meeting, 4 June 1811, at the New London Tavern,
Cheapside, ML BT49: 299–302.

60. My thanks to Fergus Clunie for this point.

61. See Kociumbas 1992: 117–18; Yarwood 1996: 134.

62. Alexander Huey, Journal aboard H.M. Store Ship
Dromedary, ML B1514.

63. Marsden to Pratt, 29 July 1810, in Havard-Williams
1961: 30.

64. Marsden to Secretary, March 15th 1814, in HO
CMS54a: 146.

65. Marsden to Secretary, 16 August 1813; Marsden to
Hall, 20 November 1813, HO CMS 54a :62–

63,104; Marsden to Pratt, 19 November 1811, in
Havard-Williams 1961: 38.

66. Marsden to Pratt, 20 November 1811, in Havard-
Williams 1961: 40–41.

67. Ibid.

68. Ibid.

69. See William Colenso (1880: 33) for informed
comment on this point.

70. Again, Colenso (1868: 68–73) makes strong
statements about the rapid decline in the Maori
population after contact .

71. Marsden to J. Pratt, 15 November 1815, in Havard-
Williams 1961: 36.

72. Hall and King to Deputy Secretary, 2 November
1811.

73. Marsden, Ho Ms 176A: 21–22. The master of the
Frederick who suffered capture at sea was Alexander
Bodie, who had been ill and unable to take the ship
to the fisheries in 1810, and was replaced tempo-
rarily by Eber Bunker. Bunker took the *Frederick* to
the fisheries on 30 November 1810, and returned
to Port Jackson on 21 August 1811. By then Captain
Bodie had recovered from his illness, and commanded the ship on her return voyage to the
fisheries and England in October 1811. In 1813, the
ship was taken by a French privateer in the English
channel, when Te Pahi's son was either killed or
captured (see Hodgkinson 1975: 27–28). It was
reported that Ruatara had been returned to New
Zealand by the ship; which report was duly passed
on to the Church Missionary Society, who sent this
news to Marsden at Port Jackson (Pratt to Marsden,
22 March 1813; HO Ms 54a: 22). Marsden later
responded with a précis of Ruatara's account, given
to him at Port Jackson, and asked the CMS to try to
find news of Te Pahi's son, who had been carried off
on the *Frederick* to England, and if possible to send
him home (Marsden to Secretary, ibid: 42–43).

74. Marsden to Secretary, 15 March 1815, in HO CMS
54a: 137.

75. HO CMS 54a: 66,74; and Marsden to Secretary, 15
March 1814, in ibid: 127.

76. Ibid: 74–77. Te Aara also noted that when he had
completed his second voyage on the *Star,* he was
paid his lay by Captain Wilkinson, who also gave
him a musket. Some muskets evidently came on
shore as payment to Maori sailors, as well as
through barter with visiting vessels.

77. Marsden report to CMS, in ML BT49: 301–2.

78. Marsden to Secretary, 18 June 1813, in HO CMS
54a: 37.

79. Marsden in HO Ms 176A: 26.

80. Pratt to Thomas Kendall, 18 August 1814, in HO
CMS 54a: 237.

81. James Gordon deposition, 8 November 1813, in
HO CMS 54a: 71–72. For the Maori sailors on
board, see the *Sydney Gazette,* 28 November, 5
December 1812.

82. For information on Williams, and correspondence
about this expedition see McNab 1908 I: 315–16;
457–74. See also Wigglesworth 1981: 31–34.

83. Marsden to Secretary, 18 June 1813, in HO CMS 54a: 37–44.

84. *Sydney Gazette*, 4 September 1813.

85. Report on New Zealand Flax, by R. Williams (Ropemaker), McNab 1908 I: 457–66.

86. Ibid: 463.

87. Good to Marsden, 10 March 1813, in ML A1992: 151–56.

88. For example, in Marsden to Secretary, 16 August 1813, in HO CMS 54a: 57.

89. Marsden to Secretary, 23 June 1813, HO CMS 54a: 45–47.

90. John White Ms 75, Folder 19B: 84.

91. See Marsden's note on Maaui in HO CMS 54a: 108; and HO Ms 176A: 33–34.

92. Marsden to Secretary, 16 August 1813, in HO CMS 54a: 60.

93. Lesson in Ollivier 1986: 139. My thanks to Fergus Clunie for reminding me of this scandalous tid-bit.

94. Binney 1968: 13.

95. Secretary to Hall and King, 22 March, 1813; Secretary to Kendall, 18 March 1814; Secretary to Hall and King, 18 March 1814, and Rev. D. Wilson to King, 18 March 1814, in HO Ms 54a: 24, 147–60. For an insightful account of the background and life of Thomas Kendall, see Binney 1968.

96. Marsden to Hall, 28 November 1813, in HO CMS 54a: 100–7.

97. Marsden in HO CMS 54a: 65–99; and 202–6.

98. Marsden to the Secretary, 15 March 1814, in HO CMS 54a: 127.

99. Macquarie to Bathurst, CO201/72: 3–7. See also McNab 1908 1: 316.

100. Minutes in HO CMS 54b: 287.

101. Marsden to Secretary, 15 March 1814, in HO CMS 54a: 127.

102. The cost of this purchase was met when Marsden sold £900 worth of sheep, and gave a promissory note for the remaining £500. Kendall contributed with a draft on his salary for £120, and a draft on the CMS for £100. It cost a further £500 to outfit the vessel. Marsden anticipated that he might have to draw on the CMS for £700 of this expenditure (Marsden to Pratt, 15 March 1814, in HO 54A: 30; Yarwood 1996: 164; Elder 1934: 40). For Marsden's account of the purchase, see Marsden to Secretary, 15 March 1814, in HO CMS 54a: 139–46. Kendall also explained that Marsden had tried to hire a small schooner, the *Elizabeth*, but the owners wanted him to pay for the ship 'in the event of the Natives attacking her, and destroying her.' After thinking about it for a few days, Marsden had agreed, but by then someone else had hired her. After this Marsden tried to hire the *Perseverance*, but this arrangement also failed (Kendall Journal ML A1443: 2–3).

103. Macquarie to Bathurst, 24 May 1814, in CO201/73: 12–15; 'I consider Mr. Marsden's Objections as very frivolous and ill-founded; arising from Illiberal Sentiments and bigotted Principles which on all Occasions pervade, and strongly mark his Conduct, both on Political and Religious Subjects.'

104. For instance, a despatch of 8 October 1814, which complained that while 'considerable sums had been spent by the missionary societies on the cannibalistic and treacherous natives of New Zealand and Tahiti, the Aborigines of New South Wales . . . had been left to waste their lives in wandering through their native woods, ignorant of the duties they owed their kindred and society in general' (6 October 1814 Macquarie to Bathurst CO201/73); and Macquarie to Bathurst, 8 October 1814, in CO201/73: 190).

105. Kendall to Secretary, 25 March 1814, in HO CMS 54a: 172.

106. Marsden to Secretary, 15 March 1814 in HO CMS 54a: 130. Kendall listed their names as 'Peter Dillon, Ireland; David Siepky, Germany; John Wilson, England; John Hunter, New Holland; Thos. Hamilton, Ireland; Wm. Mansel, N. America; Abrham Wilson, Norway; Bobbahee, Owhyhee; Dickhahee, Otaheite; Frederic Wormberg, Sweden; Henry May, England; Bobaro, Otaheite; Wm. Jones, England, Toi, New Zealand' (Kendall Journal, ML A1443: 4; see also Kendall to Rev. B. Woodd, 23 April 1814, in HO CMS 54a: 195).

107. Samuel Marsden in ibid: 143.

108. Marsden to Duaterra King, in HO CMS 54b: 312–13. For this letter in another version, and for Marsden's instructions, see also Kendall Journal ML A1443: 5–7, 21–22.

109. The *Active* sailed from Port Jackson on 14 March 1814, and anchored near Hobart Town on 12 April. On 23 May she left the River Derwent for the Bay of Islands, anchoring at Te Puna on 10 June. The *Active* sailed from the Bay on 25 July, anchoring at Port Jackson on 22 August 1814.

110. Kendall to Rev. B. Woodd, 11 March 1814, in HO CMS 54a: 124–26.

111. Marsden to Secretary, 15 March 1814, in HO CMS 54a: 137.

112. Kendall to Woodd, 23 April 1814, in HO CMS 54a: 194–95. See also Kendall Journal ML A1443: 15.

113. Kendall Journal, ML A1443: 18–19.

114. Kendall to Secretary, 25 March 1814, in HO CMS 54a: 176.

115. Kendall to Governor Davy, 18 May 1814; to James Gordon Esquire, 20 May 1814; in ML A1443: 11–12.

116. Kendall to Secretary, 6 September 1814, in HO CMS 54b: 308–9.

117. See Shawcross 1966: 204–8.

118. Described by Kendall as a 'Hipwah a Towa' (he paa a taua – a fighting paa), in Kendall Journal ML A1443: 23.

119. During the voyage to Port Jackson on the *Earl Spencer*, for instance, he wrote: 'Children are generally fond of receiving Religious Instruction, and they will listen with interest when it is given in a plain, easy and an affectionate manner. To those who can condescend to sit down amongst

little Children, and, encircled by their numbers
can point out to them the way to be truly happy
both here and hereafter the task must be truly
delightful' (in HO Ms 54A: 162).

120. Hall to Secretary, 15 June 1814, in HO CMS 54a:
231–32.

121. Marsden to Secretary, 30 September 1814, in ibid:
271.

122. Kendall Journal, ML A1443: 20–21.

123. Although Kendall's journal reverses the sequence,
putting the meeting with Hongi before that with
Tara; ibid: 29–30.

124. Listed as 'Homah Peddie (Omaapere), Tawai matta
(Te Waimate), Tatoo Hoonah (Te Tuhuna?), Phah
roa (Paaroa), Mongehayro (Maungaroa), Kiddie
Hokay (Kirioke), Pookay Kohee (Pukekohe),
Quoiwatta (Kauwhata), Shokee Hangha (Hokianga),
Poonahkee Terra (Punaakitere), Heeco Pooha
(Hikupua), Pah Keongha, Ahou Kenna (Ahukena),
Pookay moede (Puke maire?) Pyhangha Noa
(Paihanga noa), Mangho Caheeah (Mangakaahia),
and Hoota Hoodah (Utakura)'.

125. Kendall Journal, in HO CMS 54b: 315–16; see
also Kendall Journal ML A1443: 28–29.

126. According to Te Aara of Whangaroa, in about 1806
Captain Wilkinson of the *Star* gave him a musket,
in part payment for his services as a sailor.

127. My thanks to Fergus Clunie for these insights.

128. Thomas Kendall Journal, ML A1443: 31.

129. Ibid: 33.

130. Ibid: 68.

131. Ibid: 50.

132. Marsden to Secretary, 30 September 1814, in HO
CMS 54b: 278.

133. Nicholas 1817 I: 21.

134. Marsden to Secretary, 12 October 1814, in HO
CMS 54a: 289.

135. Marsden to Secretary, 30 September 1814, in ibid:
274–75.

136. Ibid: 271.

137. Marsden to Secretary, 12 October 1814, in ibid:
289–92.

138. Marsden to Secretary, 28 September 1814, in ibid:
244–45.

139. Kendall to Secretary, 26 September 1814, in ibid:
236–37; Kendall to Secretary, 3 October 1814, in
ibid: 336–37.

140. Marsden to Secretary, 30 September 1814, in HO
CMS 54b: 278–90.

141. S. Lord, G. Blaxcell, R. Brooks, W. Hovell, E. Hall
to Governor Macquarie, 3 October 1814, in
HRNZ I: 323–24.

142. Government and General Order, 12 November
1814, in McNab 1908 I: 329–30.

143. Government and General Order, 9 November 1814,
in ibid: 328–29; *Sydney Gazette,* 12 November 1814;
Nicholas 1817: 30–33.

144. Ibid.

145. My thanks to Judith Binney for an important
correction at this point; Nicholas had got the
names of Kendall's sons wrong, and I quoted him.

146. For the complement of the *Active*, see Marsden to
Secretary, 28 November 1814, in McNab 1908 I:
69–70; and Nicholas 1817 I: 36–38.

147. Ibid: 23.

Eighteen: The Mission at Rangihoua
(pages 449–507)

There are three primary accounts of Marsden's first visit
to New Zealand: (i) a manuscript (not in Marsden's
handwriting, with some of its pages missing, which is
annotated in a hand that looks like Marsden's) in the
Mitchell Library, Sydney (ML A1997); (ii) a manuscript
written in another hand, which includes some of the
annotations and appears to be a later, neat copy) in the
Hocken Library (HO Ms 176A); and (iii) J. L. Nicholas's
two-volume work *Narrative of a Voyage to New Zealand*
(1817). In this work, I have quoted Marsden from the
earlier, Mitchell Library manuscript. Dates given below
are usually taken from Nicholas, who seems to have
based his work on a daily journal. His *Narrative* is much
more detailed and circumstantial than Marsden's account
in most places, and follows a stricter chronological
sequence. Of the two edited versions of Marsden's
account, that by McNab (1908 I: 331–99) is more
accurate than Elder's (1932) version. Elder has an
uncomfortable habit of including elements of free
composition in his editions of both Marsden's and
Kendall's accounts.

1. Nicholas 1817 I: 2–7.

2. Ibid: 41.

3. Ibid: 39–44.

4. Ibid: 50.

5. Ibid: 53.

6. For Nicholas's transcription of the words of these
waiata, see ibid: 69–71.

7. Ibid: 23–24.

8. Ibid: 51.

9. According to Elsdon Best, all of the stars together
were referred to as Te Apa Whatu of Te Ahuru, 'The
Eye-like Company of Te Ahuru', Hine-te-Ahuru
being the Star Mother; he identified Te Waka-o-
Tamarereti (The Canoe of Tama-rereti) as the tail of
the Scorpion. For his comment on Nicholas's
report, see Best 1972: 50.

10. Nicholas 1817 I: 65.

11. Ibid: 86–87.

12. Ibid II: 252.

13. Ibid I: 28–29. See a similar comment from Colenso
(1868: 39).

14. Ibid: 27.

15. 'Tenpenny nails' were three-inch nails, a hundred of
which cost tenpence (Clunie 1997: pers. comm.).

16. Nicholas 1817 I: 96–97.

17. For descriptions of tutu juice, see Colenso 1868:
26; and Shortland 1974: 191–92.

18. Nicholas 1817 I: 113–14.

19. Marsden in ML A1997: 11.

20. Ibid: 67–68.

21. Nicholas 1817 I: 117.

22. Ibid: 136–37.

23. Ibid: 140–41.
24. Marsden in ML A1997: 19.
25. Ibid: 82.
26. For an explanantion of the protocols of gift exchange, see Colenso 1868: 17.
27. Nicholas 1817 I: 171–72.
28. Ibid: 177.
29. Ibid: 181.
30. Ibid: 194.
31. Ibid: 200.
32. Marsden in ML A1997: 28.
33. Ibid: 29–30.
34. See Shawcross 1966: 238–42.
35. Nicholas 1817 I: 208–9.
36. See Shawcross 1966: 233–37.
37. Sissons, Wi Hongi and Hohepa (1987: 42) state that the name of Te Kokee does not appear on any of the whakapapa from the region; it seems likely that this chief went under another, Maori name. He was, however, extensively mentioned by early Europeans to visit the Bay – see Shawcross (1966: 235) for some references.
38. Nicholas 1817 I: 222–23.
39. Ibid: 226–27.
40. See Shawcross 1966: 216–20.
41. This remained a contentious issue; on 13 February 1815 Kendall wrote to the Secretary of the Church Missionary Society expressing their discontent that Marsden had ordered them to settle at Rangihoua: 'We think we ought now to be left to the free exercise of our own judgment with respect to the choice of a Situation where the Land is good and where we think we should be best able to preserve our neutrality and to gain the good will of the neighbouring chiefs as well as Duaterra' (in ML A1443: 56). For an excellent discussion of the dilemma in which Marsden had left his missionaries, see Binney 1968: 32.
42. Nicholas 1817 I: 248.
43. Colenso 1868: 7. See also J. Montgomerie, *Journal of the Polynesian Society* 97 (2): 115–52.
44. Nicholas 1817 I: 258–59.
45. Sissons, Wi Hongi and Hohepa 1987: 42.
46. Shawcross 1966: 242–47.
47. See also Colenso 1868: 26.
48. Nicholas 1817 I: 274.
49. Ibid: 276.
50. Ibid: 255. For information about talking tuuii, see Colenso 1868: 27; 1891: 456–57.
51. For a perceptive commentary on Maori leadership and property, see Colenso 1868: 21–23. He explains that a person's portable property, including his or her house and canoe, and gardens they had made, were their own.
52. Ibid: 293.
53. A remark echoed by Colenso (1868: 33).
54. See for instance Ambrose Serle to Marsden, 15 April 1805, in ML A1992.
55. Nicholas 1817 II: 398.
56. Ibid: 318.
57. Marsden to Joseph Hardcastle, 25 October 1810, in ML A1993.
58. Ibid: 322–23.
59. See Shawcross 1966: 210–16. My thanks here to M. G. S. Parsonson for pointing out that the falls visited at the head of the inlet were the Wharepoke Falls, not the Waianiwa.
60. Sissons, Wi Hongi and Hohepa 1987: 16.
61. See Shawcross 1966: 220–30.
62. Nicholas 1817 I: 334.
63. Ibid: 344.
64. Ibid: 346–47.
65. Ibid: 365.
66. Ibid: 365–66.
67. My thanks to Fergus Clunie for this identification.
68. Nicholas 1817 I: 392–93.
69. Ibid: 395.
70. Marsden in ML A1997: 56–57.
71. At Peach Cove on Bream Head (Elder 1934: 108 fn).
72. Nicholas 1817 I: 428–29.
73. Marsden in ML A1997: 67–68.
74. Ibid: 70.
75. Nicholas 1817 II: 45.
76. Ibid: 58–59.
77. Ibid: 68.
78. The nature of such transactions has been extensively debated in recent scholarship (cf. the Muriwhenua Land Report of the Waitangi Tribunal, 1997, including my own submissions). As Colenso (a reliable authority on such matters) asserted last century (1868: 17, 23–24), the idea of buying and selling was unknown at first, as was the concept of a commodity. Such early transfers were understood in the local context of gift exchange, rather than the foreign context of industrial capitalism.
79. Nicholas 1817 II: 87.
80. Ibid: 98–99.
81. In fact, Colenso (1868: 7) comments that hunchbacks were not uncommon in Maori communities. He thought that children were perhaps often injured when passing through low doorways on their parents' backs, although Maori people denied this.
82. Nicholas 1817 II: 106–7.
83. See Colenso 1868: 42; 1878: 83–100.
84. Such constant requests for utu are also commented on with irritation by Colenso (1868: 31): 'Their disagreeable ever-asking for some utu – return, payment, recompense, or equivalent – for the least assistance or thing, (quid pro quo), is more a matter of growth during the last twenty-five years, at all events if latent it has wonderfully developed.' It is scarcely a matter of surprise, though, that people brought up in a world based on reciprocity, having once realised that Europeans did not necessarily respect the rules of utu, began to insist upon it.
85. Marsden in ML A1997: 75–76.
86. Nicholas 1817 II: 301–2.
87. Marsden in HO Ms 176A: 137.
88. Ibid: 181–82.
89. Marsden in ML A1997: 82–83.
90. Marsden in HO Ms 176A: 175.

91. See Colenso 1868: 20.
92. Nicholas 1817 II: 307–8.
93. Marsden in HO Ms 176A: 152.
94. Ibid: 153–54.
95. Ibid: 174–75.
96. Nicholas 1817 II: 165.
97. Ibid: 166–67.
98. Comets (and presumably shooting stars) were a tohu, or omen, of death in many tribal areas (Best 1905: 158).
99. Nicholas 1817 II: 166–67; Kendall in Binney transcript: iv. See also Colenso 1868: 42.
100. Marsden in HO Ms 176A: 32.
101. Nicholas 1817 II: 171–72. See also Colenso 1868: 6–7.
102. Nicholas 1817 II: 178–80.
103. Ibid: 167.
104. Ibid: 191.
105. Ibid: 309–11.
106. Ibid: 194–95.
107. See *Sydney Gazette*, 6 May 1815, for a report of this voyage.
108. Kendall in Binney transcript: iv.
109. Best 1905: 162–64.
110. Ibid: 165.
111. Kendall in Binney transcript: iv.

Conclusion III

(pages 508–514)

1. Salmond, in press.
2. Salmond in Fardon (ed.) 1995: 23.
3. Foucault 1966: 50–162.
4. Foucault 1977.
5. Hohepa nd, A note on Mua and Muri (pers. comm.).
6. I have found Bohm's demonstration of the limits of the mind-matter split, and of the fragmentation arising from analytical thinking in contemporary science, fascinating (Bohm 1980).

Bibliography

Abbott J., and Nairn, B., 1969. *Economic Growth of Australia 1788–1821.* Carlton, Melbourne University Press.

Albion, R. G., 1965. *Forests and Sea Power: The Timber Problem of the Royal Navy 1652–1862.* Connecticut, Archon Books.

Allen, D. E., 1976. *The Naturalist in Britain: A Social History.* London, Allen Lane.

Alpin, Graeme (ed.), 1988. *A Difficult Infant: Sydney Before Macquarie.* Kensington, New South Wales University Press.

Almond, Philip C., 1994. *Heaven and Hell in Enlightenment England.* Cambridge, Cambridge University Press.

Anderson, Atholl, 1991. *Race Against Time: The Early Maori-Pakeha Families and the Development of the Mixed-race Population in Southern New Zealand.* Dunedin, Hocken Library.

Anderson, Benedict, 1983. *Imagined Communities.* London, Verso.

Andrews, J. R. H., 1987. *The Southern Ark: Zoological Discovery in New Zealand 1769–1900.* London, Century.

Atkinson, A. S., 1892. What is a Tangata Maori? *Journal of the Polynesian Society* 1: 183–86.

Aymler, Captain Fenton, 1860. *A Cruise in the Pacific, from the Log of a Naval Officer, Volumes I and II.* London, Hurst and Blackett.

Baker, Sidney, 1945. Origins of the Words Pakeha and Maori. *Journal of the Polynesian Society* 54: 223–31.

Barbauld, Anna, ed. W. McCarthy and Elizabeth Kraft, 1994. *The Poems of Anna Letitia Barbauld,* Athens, University of Georgia Press.

Barber, Lynn, 1980. *The Heyday of Natural History 1820–1870.* New York, Doubleday.

Barratt, Glynn (ed.), 1987. *Queen Charlotte Sound, New Zealand: The Traditional and European Records, 1820.* Ottawa, Carleton University Press.

Bathgate, Murray, 1969. Maori River and Ocean-Going Craft in Southern New Zealand 1773–1852. *Journal of the Polynesian Society* 78: 344–77.

Baynham, Henry, 1969. *From the Lower Deck: The Old Navy 1780–1840.* London, Hutchinson.

Beaglehole, J. C. (ed.), 1962. *The Endeavour Journal of Joseph Banks 1768–1771, Volumes I and II.* Sydney, Angus and Robertson.

Beaglehole, J. C. (ed.), 1967. *The Journals of Captain James Cook on His Voyages of Discovery; Vol. III: The Voyage of The Resolution and Discovery 1776–1780, Parts (i) and (ii).* Cambridge, Hakluyt Society.

Beaglehole, J. C. (ed.), 1969. *The Journals of Captain Cook On His Voyages of Discovery, Vol. II: The Voyage of The Resolution and Adventure 1772–1775.* Cambridge, Hakluyt Society.

Beattie, Herries, 1915–1922. Traditions and legends collected from the Natives of Murihiku (Southland, New Zealand). *Journal of the Polynesian Society,* XXIV: 99–112; 130–39; XXV: 9–17, 53–65; XXVI: 75–85; 110; XXVII: 137–61, 212–25; XXVIII: 51; 152–59; XXIX: 128–38, 189–98; XXXI: 134–44; 193–97.

Beattie, Herries, 1945. *The Maori Lore of Lake, Alp and Fiord.* Dunedin, Otago Daily Times and Witness Newspapers.

Beattie, Herries, 1949 *The Maoris and Fiordland.* Dunedin, Otago Daily Times and Witness Newspapers.

Beattie, Herries, 1950. *Far Famed Fiordland: Historic and Descriptive.* Dunedin, Otago Daily Times and Witness Newspapers.

Beattie, Herries, 1954. *Our Southernmost Maoris.* Dunedin, Otago Daily Times and Witness Newspapers.

Beattie, James Herries, 1994. *Traditional Lifeways of the Southern Maori: The Otago Museum Ethnological Project, 1920.* Otago, University of Otago Press.

Bebbington, D. W., 1989. *Evangelicism in Modern Britain. A History from the 1730s to the 1980s.* London, Unwin Hyman.

Begg, A. C. and Begg, N. C., 1966. *Dusky Bay.* Christchurch, Whitcombe and Tombs.

Begg, A. C. and Begg, N. C., 1973. *Port Preservation*. Christchurch, Whitcombe and Tombs.

Belich, James, 1996. *Making Peoples. A History of New Zealanders*. Auckland, Penguin.

Bentham, Jeremy, 1812. *Panopticon versus New South Wales: Two Letters to Lord Pelham*. London.

Berry, Alexander, 1827. Adventures of British Seamen, in *Constable's Miscellany*. London, Willison.

Berry, Alexander, 1912. *Reminiscences of Alexander Berry*. Sydney, Angus and Robertson.

Best, Elsdon, 1900. Spiritual Concepts of the Maori. *Journal of the Polynesian Society* IX:173–99; X: 1–20.

Best, Elsdon, 1906. Maori Eschatology: The Whare Potae (House of Mourning) and its Lore. *Transactions of the New Zealand Institute* XXXVIII: 148–239.

Best, Elsdon, 1976. *Maori Religion and Mythology I*. Wellington, Government Printer.

Best, Elsdon, 1982. *Maori Religion and Mythology II*. Wellington, Government Printer.

Bickers, Robert and Seton, Rosemary, 1996. *Missionary Encounters: Sources and Issues*. Richmond, Surrey, Curzon Press.

Binney, Judith, 1968. *The Legacy of Guilt: A Life of Thomas Kendall*. Auckland, Oxford University Press.

Binney, Judith, 1995. *Redemption Songs: A Life of Te Kooti Arikirangi Te Turuki*. Auckland, Auckland University Press and Bridget Williams Books.

Bladen, F. M., 1894. *History of New South Wales from the Records, Volumes I and II*. Sydney, Government Printer.

Blunt, Wilfred, 1971. Linnaeus and Botany. *History Today*, XXI: 107–15.

Blunt, Wilfred, 1978. *The Complete Naturalist: A Life of Linnaeus*. London, Collins.

Blunt, Wilfred, 1978. *In For a Penny: A Prospect of Kew Gardens: Their Flora, Fauna and Falballas*. London, Hamish Hamilton.

Bohm, David, 1980. *Wholeness and the Implicate Order*. London, Routledge.

Boswell, James, 1891. *The Life of Samuel Johnson, L.L.D.*, H. Morley (ed.). London, George Routledge and Sons.

Bowden, Keith, 1952. *George Bass 1771–1803*. Melbourne, Oxford University Press.

Brailsford, Barry, 1981. *The Tattooed Land: The Southern Frontiers of the Pa Maori*. Wellington, A. H. and A. W. Reed.

Brailsford, Barry, 1984. *Greenstone Trails: The Maori Search for Pounamu*. Wellington, A. H. and A. W. Reed.

British Museum Yearbook, 1979. *Captain Cook and the South Pacific*. London, British Museum Publications.

Brockway, Lucille M., *Science and Colonial Expansion: The Role of the British Royal Botanic Gardens*. New York, Academic Press.

Brooke, John Hedley, 1991. *Science and Religion: Some Historical Perspectives*. Cambridge, Cambridge University Press.

Buffon, M. le Compte, 1777. *Histoire naturelle, générale et particulière servant de suite a l'Historie Naturelle de l'Homme*. Paris, de l'Imprimerie Royal.

Busch, Briton Cooper, 1985. *The War Against the Seals: A History of the North American Seal Fishery*. Kingston, McGill-Queen's University Press.

Byers, Edward, 1987. *The 'Nation of Nantucket' Society and Politics in an Early American Commercial Centre 1660–1820*. Boston, Northeastern University Press.

Carrick, Robert (ed.), 1903. *Historical Records of New Zealand South Prior to 1840*. Dunedin, Otago Daily Times.

Carter, Harold B., 1987. *Sir Joseph Banks (1743–1820): A Guide to Biographical and Bibliographical Sources*. London, St Paul's Bibliographies.

Carter, Paul, 1987. *The Road to Botany Bay: An Essay in Spatial History*. London, Faber and Faber.

Churchward, L. G., 1949. Notes on American Whaling Activities in Australian Waters 1800–1850. *Historical Studies Australia and New Zealand* 4: 59–63.

Clark, Manning, 1992. *A History of Australia I: From the Earliest Times to the Age of Macquarie*. Carlton, Melbourne University Press.

Clarke, George, 1903. *Notes on Early Life in New Zealand*. Wellington, J. Walch and Sons.

Clarke, Marcus, 1991. *For the Term of His Natural Life*. Pymble, Angus & Robertson.

Clune, F. and Stephensen, P. R., 1954. *The Viking of Van Diemen's Land: The Stormy Life of Jorgen Jorgensen*. Sydney, Angus and Robertson.

Cobley, John, 1963. *Sydney Cove 1789–1790*. Sydney, Angus and Robertson.

Cohen, Anthony P., 1994. *Self Consciousness: An Alternative Anthropology of Identity*. London, Routlege.

Colenso, William, 1868. On the Maori Races of New Zealand. *Transactions of the New Zealand Institute* 1: 339–424.

Colenso, William, 1878. Contributions towards a Better Knowledge of the Maori Race. *Transactions of the New Zealand Institute* 11: 77–118.

Colenso, William, 1880. Historical Incidents and Traditions of the Olden Times. *Transactions of the New Zealand Institute* : 38–84.

Colenso, William, 1881. Historical Incidents and Traditions of the Olden Times. *Transactions of the New Zealand Institute* 3–33.

Colenso, William, 1877. Notes on the ancient Dog of the New Zealanders. *Transactions of the New Zealand Institute* X: 146.

Collins, David, 1798. *An Account of the English Colony in New South Wales, With Remarks on the Dispositions, Customs, Manners &c. Of the Native Inhabitants of that Country*, Volumes I and II. London, T. Cadell Jun. and W. Davies.

Comaroff, Jean and John, 1991. *Of Revelation and Revolution: Christianity, Colonialism and Consciousness in South Africa.* Chicago, University of Chicago Press.

Comstock, William, 1838. *A Voyage to the Pacific, Descriptive of the Customs, Usages, and Sufferings on Board of Nantucket Whale-Ships.* Boston, Oliver L. Perkins.

Cottingham, John (ed.), 1992. *The Cambridge Companion to Descartes.* Cambridge, Cambridge University Press.

Coutts, P. J. F., 1969. The Maori of Dusky Sound: A Review of the Historical Sources. *Journal of the Polynesian Society* 78: 179–211.

Coutts, P. J. F., 1969. Merger or Takeover. A Survey of the Effects of Contact Between European and Maori in the Foveaux Strait Region. *Journal of the Polynesian Society* 78: 495–516.

Cowan, James, 1926. *Travel in New Zealand: The Island Dominion.* Auckland, Whitcombe and Tombs.

Cowan, James, 1935. *A Trader in Cannibal Land. The Life and Adventures of Captain Tapsell.* Dunedin, A. H. and A. W. Reed.

Craik, George L., 1830. *The New Zealanders.* London, Charles Knight.

Crosby, Alfred W., 1986. *Ecological Imperialism: The Biological Expansion of Europe 900–1900.* Cambridge, Cambridge University Press.

Cumpston, J. S., 1968. *Macquarie Island.* Melbourne, Antarctic Division, Department of External Affairs.

Cumpston, J. S., 1970. *Kangaroo Island 1800–1836.* Canberra, Roebuck.

Cumpston, J. S., 1977. *Shipping Arrivals & Departures, Sydney 1788–1825.* Canberra, Roebuck.

Dakin, William, 1963. *Whalemen Adventurers: The Story of Whaling in Australian Waters and other Southern Seas related thereto from the Days of Sail to Modern Times.* Sydney, Angus and Robertson.

Dallas, K. M., 1968. Commercial Influences on the First Settlements in Australia. *Tasmanian Historical Research Association* 16: 36–49.

Dalrymple, Alexander, 1778. *New Discoveries Concerning the World and its Inhabitants.* Parts I and II. London, J. Johnson.

Darnton, Robert, 1985. *The Great Cat Massacre, And Other Episodes in French History.* New York, Vintage Books.

Davies, J., ed. C. W. Newbury, 1961. *The History of the Tahitian Mission 1799–1830.* Cambridge, Cambridge University Press.

Davies, Rhys, 1940. *Sea Urchin: Adventures of Jorgen Jorgenson.* London, Duckworth.

David, Andrew, 1992. *The Charts & Coastal Views of Captain Cook's Voyages: Volume II: The Voyage of the Resolution and Adventure 1772–1775.* London, Hakluyt Society.

Davidson, J. W., 1975. *Peter Dillon of Vanikoro.* Melbourne, Oxford University Press.

Dawson, Warren, 1958. *The Banks Letters. A Calendar of the Manuscript correspondence of Sir Joseph Banks.* London, British Museum.

Delano, Amasa, 1970. *A Narrative of Voyages and Travels in the Northern and Southern Hemispheres, Comprising Three Voyages Round the World.* New York, Praeger Publishers.

Dening, Greg (ed.), 1974. *The Marquesan Journal of Edward Robarts 1797–1824.* Canberra, Australian National University Press.

Dening, Greg, 1992. *Mr Bligh's Bad Language: Passion, Power and Theatre on the Bounty.* Cambridge, Cambridge University Press.

Dillon, Peter, 1829. *Narrative and Successful Result of a Voyage in the South Seas, Performed by Order of the Government of British India, To Ascertain the Actual Fate of La Perouse's Expedition, Volumes I and II.* London, Hurst, Chance, and Co.

Doak, Wade, 1984. *The Burning of the Boyd. A Saga of Culture Clash.* Auckland, Hodder and Stoughton.

Doane, Benjamin, 1987. *Following the Sea.* Halifax, Nova Scotia.

Dodge, Ernest, 1965. *New England and the South Seas.* Cambridge, Mass., Harvard University Press.

Dow, George Francis, 1925. *Whale Ships and Whaling: A Pictorial History of Whaling during Three Centuries.* Salem, Marine Research Society.

Doyle, William, 1978. *The Old European Order 1660–1800.* Oxford, Oxford University Press.

Druett, Joan, 1983. *Exotic Intruders: The Introduction of Plants and Animals into New Zealand.* Auckland, Heinemann.

Duffy, Christopher, 1987. *The Military Experience in the Age of Reason*. London, Routledge and Kegan Paul.

Dunbabin, Thomas, 1954. The First Salem Vessel in Sydney and Fiji. *The American Neptune* XIII: 275–81.

Dunmore, John, 1969. *French Explorers in the Pacific, Volumes I and II.* Oxford, Clarendon Press.

Elder, John (ed.), 1932. *The Letters and Journals of Samuel Marsden 1765–1836.* Dunedin, Coulls Somerville Wilkie.

Elder, John (ed.), 1934. *Marsden's Lieutenants.* Dunedin, Coulls, Somerville Wilkie.

Ellis, William, 1782. *An Authentic Narrative of a Voyage Performed by Captain Cook and Captain Clerke, in His Majesty's Ships Resolution and Discovery during the Years 1776, 1777, 1778, 1779 and 1780.* London, G. Robinson.

Ellis, William, 1829. *Polynesian Researches: Society Islands, Tubuai Islands, and New Zealand.* Rutland, Charles E. Tuttle.

Evison, Harry. C., 1993. *Te Wai Pounamu The Greenstone Island: A History of the Southern Maori during the European Colonization of New Zealand.* Christchurch, Aoraki Press.

Ewing, C., 1873. Koche, King of Pitt. *Catholic World*, July: 545–57.

Fardon, Richard (ed.), 1995. *Counterworks: Managing the Diversity of Knowledge.* London, Routledge.

Fildes, Horace, 1936. *The Last of the Ngati Mamoe.* Dunedin.

Fisher, R. and Johnston, H. (eds.), 1979. *Captain James Cook and His Times.* Canberra, Australia National University Press.

Fisher, R. and Johnston, H. (eds.), 1993. *From Maps to Metaphors: The Pacific World of George Vancouver.* Vancouver, UBC Press.

Ford, Franklin L., 1989. *Europe 1780–1830.* London, Longman.

Forster, George, 1777. *A Voyage Round the World in His Britannic Majesty's Sloop, Resolution.* Volumes I and II. London, B. White.

Forster, Honore, 1985. *The South Sea Whaler: An Annotated Bibliography.* Sharon, Massachusetts, Kendall Whaling Museum.

Forster, Honore, 1991. *More South Sea Whaling. A Supplement to the South Sea Whaler: An Annotated Bibliography.* Canberra, Research School of Pacific Studies.

Forster, John Reinhold, 1778. *Observations Made During a Voyage Round the World, on Human Geography, Natural History and Ethic Philosophy.* London, G. Robinson.

Forster, John Reinhold, ed. Nicholas Thomas et al., 1996. *Observations Made During a Voyage Round the World.* Honolulu, University of Hawaii Press.

Foucault, Michel, 1954 in Binswanger, Ludwig, 1954. *Le Réve et L'Existence.* Paris, Desclee de Brouwer.

Foucault, Michel, 1977. *Discipline and Punish: The Birth of the Prison.* London, Penguin Books.

Foucault, Michel, 1980. *The Order of Things: An Archaeology of the Human Sciences.* London, Tavistock Publications.

Fowler, R. M., 1980. *The Furneaux Group, Bass Strait. A History.* Canberra, Roebuck Books.

Fox, Aileen, 1985. Okuratope Pa, Waimate, Bay of Islands. *Rec. Auckland Institute and Museum* 22: 1–15.

Fox, James, 1993. *Inside Austronesian Houses.* Canberra, Australian National University.

Frangsmyr, T. et al., 1990. *The Quantifying Spirit in the 18th Century.* Berkeley, University of California Press.

Frost, Alan, 1980. *Convicts and Empire: A Naval Question 1776–1811.* Melbourne, Oxford University Press.

Frost, Alan, 1994. *Botany Bay Mirages: Illusions of Australia's Convict Beginnings.* Melbourne, Melbourne University Press.

Furber, H., 1970. *John Company at Work: A Study of European Expansion in India in the late Eighteenth Century.* New York, Octagon Books.

Gascoigne, John, 1994. *Joseph Banks and the English Enlightenment : Useful Knowledge and Polite Culture.* Cambridge, Cambridge University Press.

Gay, Peter, 1969. *The Enlightenment: An Interpretation : The Science of Freedom.* New York, W. W. Norton.

Gibbon, Edward, 1812. *The History of the Decline and Fall of the Roman Empire, in Twelve Volumes.* London, John Stockdale.

Glover, Richard, 1963. *Pensinular Preparation: The Reform of the British Army 1795–1809.* Cambridge, Cambridge University Press.

Goodman, D. and Russell, C. A., 1991. *The Rise of Scientific Europe 1500–1800.* London, Hodder and Stoughton.

Grady, Don, 1986. *Sealers and Whalers in New Zealand Waters.* Auckland, Reed Methuen.

Grayland, Eugene, 1963. *Coasts of Treachery.* Wellington, A. H. and A. W. Reed.

Gunson, Niel, 1978. *Messengers of Grace: Evangelical Missionaries in the South Seas 1797–1860.* Melbourne, Oxford University Press.

Hagberg, Knut, 1952. *Carl Linnaeus.* London, Jonathon Cape.

Hainsworth, D. R., 1968. *Builders and Adventurers: The Traders and the Emergence of the Colony*. Melbourne, Cassells.

Hainsworth, D. R., 1981. *The Sydney Traders: Simeon Lord and His Contemporaries 1788-1821*. Melbourne, Melbourne University Press.

Hall-Jones, F. G., 1945. *Historical Southland*. Dunedin, Otago Daily Times.

Hall-Jones, John, nd. *Doubtfull Harbour*. Invercargill, Craig Printing.

Hall-Jones, John, 1994. *Stewart Island Explored.* Invercargill, Craig Printing Co.

Hankins, Thomas L., 1985. *Science and the Enlightenment*. Cambridge, Cambridge University Press.

Hawkins, Clifford W., 1969. His Majesty's Armed Tender Lady Nelson 1799–1825. *The Mariner's Mirror: The Journal of the Society for Nautical Research* 55: 417–35.

Hay, Douglas et al, 1975. *Albion's Fatal Tree: Crime and Society in Eighteenth-Century England*. Harmondsworth, Penguin.

Hedges, James and Black, Jeanette, 1963. Disaster in the South Seas: The Wreck of the Brigantine *Eliza* and the subsequent Adventures of Captain Corey. *The American Neptune* XXIII (I): 233–54.

Heidegger, Martin, 1978. *Basic Writings*. London, Routledge and Kegan Paul.

Hoare, Michael, nd. *Enlightenment and New Zealand 1773–1774 : Essays Commemorating the Visit of Johann Reinhold Forster and George Forster with James Cook to Queen Charlotte and Dusky Sound*. Wellington, National Art Gallery.

Hoare, Michael, 1975. *Three Men in a Boat: The Forsters and New Zealand Science*. Melbourne, Hawthorn Press.

Hoare, Michael E., 1976. *The Tactless Philosopher: Johann Reinhold Forster (1729–98)*. Melbourne, Hawthorn Press.

Hoare, Michael E. (ed.), 1982. *The Resolution Journal of Johann Reinhold Forster 1772–1775, Volumes I, II, III and IV*. London, Hakluyt Society.

Hobbes, Thomas, 1985. *Leviathan*. London, Penguin.

Hogan, J. F., 1891. *The Convict King, Being the Life and Adventures of Jorgen Jorgenson.* London, Ward and Downey.

Hodgkinson, R., 1975. *Eber Bunker of Liverpool*. Canberra, Roebuck.

Hogan, James F., 1891. *The Convict King, Being the Life and Adventures of Jorgen Jorgenson*. London, Ward and Downey.

Holmes, Christine (ed.), 1984. *Captain Cook's Second Voyage*. London, Caliban Books.

Hooper, Beverly (ed.), 1975. *With Captain James Cook in the Antarctic and Pacific. The Private Journal of James Burney*. Canberra, National Library of Australia.

Houghton, Phillip, 1980. *The First New Zealanders*. Auckland, Hodder and Stoughton.

Howard, Basil, 1974. *Rakiura: A History of Stewart Island, New Zealand*. Dunedin, A. H. and A. W. Reed.

Howard, John, 1929. *The State of the Prisons*. London, J. M. Dent and Sons.

Howay, F. W. 1929. *Zimmermann's Captain Cook*. Toronto, The Ryerson Press.

Howe, K. R., 1984. *Where the Waves Fall: A New South Sea Islands History from First Settlement to Colonial Rule*. Sydney, George Allen and Unwin.

Houghton, Philip, 1980. *The First New Zealanders*. Auckland, Hodder and Stoughton.

Hughes, Robert, 1987. *The Fatal Shore: A History of the Transportation of Convicts to Australia, 1787–1868*. London, Collins Harvill.

Hunter, John, 1793. *An Historical Journal of the Transactions at Port Jackson and Norfolk Island*. London, Stockdale.

Jackson, Gordon, 1978. *The British Whaling Trade*. London, A. and C. Black.

Jardine, N., Secord, J. A., and Spary, E. C., 1996. *Cultures of Natural History*. Cambridge, Cambridge University Press.

Johnson, Donald D., 1992. *The United States in the Pacific: Private Interests and Public Policies 1784–1899*. Westport, Praeger.

Johnson, Paul, 1991. *The Birth of the Modern: World Society 1815–1830*. London, Weidenfeld and Nicolson.

Jones, A. G. E., 1986. *Ships Employed in the South Seas Trade 1775–1861*. Canberra, Roebuck.

Joppien, R. and Smith, Bernard, 1985. *The Art of Captain Cook's Voyages: Volume II: The Voyage of the Resolution and Adventure 1772–1775*. Melbourne, Oxford University Press.

Joppien, R. and Smith, Bernard, 1987. *The Art of Captain Cook's Voyages: Volume III: The Voyage of the Resolution and Discovery 1776–80, parts (I) and (II)*. Melbourne, Oxford University Press.

Kant, Immanuel, 1974. *Anthropology from a Pragmatic Point of View*. The Hague, Martinus Nijhoft.

Keane, John, 1995. *Tom Paine: A Political Life*. London, Bloomsbury Publishing.

Kelly, Leslie G., 1939. Some New Information Concerning the Ship Boyd. *Journal of the Polynesian Society* 49: 600.

Kendrick, John and Inglis, Robin, 1991. *Enlightened Voyages: Malaspina and Galiano on the Northwest Coast 1791–1792*. Vancouver, Vancouver Maritime Museum.

Kerr, Ian S., 1976. *Campbell Island: A History*. Wellington, A. H. and A. W. Reed.

King, Michael, 1989. *Moriori: A People Rediscovered*. Auckland, Viking.

King, Robert J., 1987. 'Ports of Shelter, and Refreshment . . . Botany Bay and Norfolk Island in British Naval Strategy, 1786-1808. *Australian Historical Studies* 22: 199–213.

Kociumbas, Jan, 1992. *The Oxford History of Australia, Volume 2: 1770–1860: Possessions*. Melbourne, Oxford University Press.

Lakoff, George and Johnson, Mark, 1980. *Metaphors We Live By*. Chicago, University of Chicago Press.

Lamb, W. Kaye (ed.), 1984. *A Voyage of Discovery to the North Pacific Ocean and Round the World 1791–1795, by George Vancouver*, Volumes I–IV. London, The Hakluyt Society.

Larson, James, 1971. *Reason and Experience: The Representation of the Natural Order in the Work of Carl von Linne*. Berkeley, University of California Press.

Lee, Jack, 1983. *'I Have Named it the Bay of Islands . . .'* Auckland, Hodder and Stoughton.

Locke, John, 1993. *Two Treatises of Government*. Cambridge, Cambridge University Press.

Lockerby, William, 1925. *The Journal of William Lockerby: Sandalwood Trader in the Fijian Islands during the Years 1808–9*. London, Hakluyt Society.

Lovejoy, Arthur O., 1950. *The Great Chain of Being: A Study of the History of an Idea*. Cambridge, Mass., Harvard University Press.

Lovett, Richard, 1899. *The History of the London Missionary Society 1795–1895, Volumes I and II*. London, Henry Frowde.

McConville, Sean, 1981. *A History of English Prison Administration*. London, Routledge and Kegan Paul.

Mackay, Alexander, 1873. *A Compendium of Official Documents Relative to Native Affairs in the South Island, Volume I*. Wellington, Government Printer.

Mackay, David, 1985. *In the Wake of Cook: Exploration, Science and Empire, 1780–1801*. Wellington, Victoria University Press.

Mackay, David, 1985. *A Place of Exile: The European Settlement of New South Wales*. Melbourne, Oxford University Press.

McCormick, E. H., 1977. *Omai: Pacific Envoy*. Auckland, Auckland University Press.

McDowell, R. B. (ed.), 1991. *The Writings and Speeches of Edmund Burke: Volume IX 1794–1797*. Oxford, Clarendon Press.

McEwen, J. M., 1987. *Rangitane: A Tribal History*. Auckland, Heinemann Reed.

MacLeod and Rehbock, P., 1988. *Nature in its Greatest Extent: Western Science in the Pacific*. Honolulu, University of Hawaii Press.

McLynn, F. J., 1989. *Crime and Punishment in Eighteenth Century England*. London, Routlege.

McNab. Robert, 1905. *Murihiku: Some Old Time Events*. Gore, Southern Standard.

McNab, Robert, 1914. *From Tasman to Marsden: A History of Northern New Zealand from 1642 to 1818*. Dunedin, J. Wilkie.

McNab, Robert, 1907. *Murihiku and the Southern Islands. A History of the West Coast Sounds, Foveaux Strait, Antipodes, Auckland, Campbell and Macquarie Islands, from 1770 to 1829*. Invercargill, William Smith.

Macpherson, C. B., 1962. *The Political Theory of Possessive Individualism: Hobbes to Locke*. London, Oxford University Press.

Marchant, Leslie, 1982. *France Australe: A Study of French Explorations and Attempts to Found a Penal Colony and Strategic Base in South Western Australia 1503–1826*. Perth, Artlook Books.

Marra, John, 1967. *Journal of the Resolution's Voyage in 1771–1775*. Amsterdam, N. Israel.

Maude, Harry, 1968. *Of Islands and Men*. London, Oxford University Press.

Mauss, Marcel, 1990. *The Gift. The Form and Reason For Exchange in Archaic Societies*. London, Routledge.

Meikle, Henry W., 1912. *Scotland and the French Revolution*. New York, Augustus M. Kelley.

Merrill, Elmer, D., 1954. *The Botany of Cook's Voyages and its Unexpected Significance in Relation to Anthropology, Biogeography and History*. Waltham, Mass., Chronica Botanica.

Millar, David P., 1971. Whalers, Flax Traders and Maoris of the Cook Strait Area. An Historical Study in Cultural Confrontation. *Dominion Museum Records in Ethnology* 2 (6): 57–74.

Miller, David and Reill, Peter, 1996. *Visions of Empire: Voyages, Botany and Representations of Nature*. Cambridge, Cambridge University Press.

Miller, George, 1854. *A Trip to Sea From 1810 to 1815*. Long Sutton, John Swain.

Milligan, R. R. D., ed. John Dunmore, 1964. *The Map Drawn by the Chief Tuki-tahua in 1793*. Mangonui.

Mitchell, L. G. (ed.), 1989. *The Writings and Speeches of Edmund Burke: Volume VIII: The French Revolution*. Oxford, Clarendon.

Monin, Paul, 1995. The Maori Economy of Hauraki. *New Zealand Journal of History* 29 (2): 197–210.

Morton, Harry, 1982. *The Whale's Wake*. Dunedin, University of Otago Press.

Moyal, Ann, 1986. *'A Bright and Savage Land': Scientists in Colonial Australia*. Sydney, Collins.

Munford, James Kenneth (ed.), 1963. *John Ledyard's Journal of Captain Cook's Last Voyage*. Oregon, Oregon State University Press.

Murray-Smith, Stephen, 1973. Beyond the Pale: The Islander Community of Bass Strait in the 19th Century. *Tasmanian Historical Research Association Papers and Proceedings* 20 (4): 167–200.

Myers, John, 1817. *The Life, Voyages and travels of Capt. John Myers, detailing his adventures during four Voyages round the World*. London, Longman, Hurst, Rees.

Nahe, Hoani, 1894. Maori, Tangata Maori. *Journal of the Polynesian Society* 3: 27–35.

Neal, David, 1991. *The Rule of Law in a Penal Colony : Law and Power in Early New South Wales*. Cambridge, Cambridge University Press.

Nicholas, John Liddiard, 1817. *Narrative of a Voyage to New Zealand, Performed in the Years 1814 and 1815, in Company with the Rev. Samuel Marsden, Volumes I and II*. London, James Black and Son.

Nicholson, Ian, 1983. *Shipping Arrivals and Departures, Tasmania*. Canberra, Roebuck.

Nicholson, Ian, 1993. *Log of Logs. A Catalogue of Logs, Journals, Shipboard Diaries, Letters, and all forms of Voyage Narratives 1788 to 1988, for Australia and New Zealand, and Surrounding Oceans, Volumes I and II*. Nambour, Queensland, Roebuck.

Nierop, Dirk van, 1674. *Eenige Oefeningen in God-lijcke ... Pt. 2: 56–64: 'Een kort Verhael uyt het Journael van den Komm. Abel Jane Tasman'*. Translated by Barbara Andaya, 1989.

O'Brien, Patrick, 1988. *Joseph Banks: A Life*. London, Collins Harvill.

Obeyesekere, Gananath, 1992. 'British Cannibals': Contemplation of an Event in the Death and Resurrection of James Cook, Explorer. *Critical Inquiry* 18: 630–54.

Obeyesekere, Gananath, 1992. *The Apotheosis of Captain Cook: European Mythmaking in the Pacific*. Princeton, New Jersey, Princeton University Press.

Oliver, W. H., 1990. *The Dictionary of New Zealand Biography, Volume I*. Wellington, Allen and Unwin and Department of Internal Affairs.

Ollivier, Isabel (ed.), 1986. *Extracts from New Zealand Journals Written on Ships Under the Command of d'Entre-casteaux and Duperry, 1783 and 1824*. Wellington, Alexander Turnbull Library Endowment Trust with Indosuez New Zealand.

Ollivier, Isabel (ed.), 1987. *Extracts from Journals Relating to the Visit to New Zealand of the French Ship St. Jean Baptiste in December 1769 Under the Command of J. F. M. de Surville*. Wellington, Alexander Turnbull Library Endowment Trust with Indosuez New Zealand.

Oman, Charles, 1914. *A History of the Peninsular War, Volumes I–V*. Oxford, Clarendon Press.

O'Regan, Tipene, in Barratt, G.(ed.) 1987. *Queen Charlotte Sound, New Zealand; The Traditional and European Records, 1820*. Ottawa, Carleton University Press.

Orchiston, D. Wayne, 1974. Cook Voyage 'Trading Stations' in Early Protohistoric New Zealand, *Dominion Museum Records in Ethnology* 2 (12): 134–56.

Orchiston, D. Wayne, 1975. Maori Material Culture Change in Early Protohistoric New Zealand: The Greenstone Trade at Queen Charlotte Sound, *The Artefact*: 39: 40–77.

Orchiston, D. Wayne, 1975. Contact and Conflict: the Rowe Massacre in Early Proto-historic New Zealand, *Historical Studies* 16(65): 518–38

Orchiston, D. Wayne, 1978. Preserved Maori Heads and Captain Cook's Three Voyages to the South Seas: A Study in Ethnohistory, *Anthropos* 73: 798–816.

Orchiston, D. Wayne, 1972. George Bruce and the Maoris (1806–8), *Journal of the Polynesian Society* 81 (2): 248–54.

Overing, Joanna (ed.), 1985. *Reason and Morality*. London, Tavistock Publications.

Owens, J. M. R., 1974. *Prophets in the Wilderness: The Wesleyan Mission to New Zealand 1819–27*. Auckland, Auckland University Press.

Partington, J. Edge., 1899. Extracts from the Diary of Dr. Samwell (Surgeon of the Discovery During Cook's Third Voyage, 1776–9. *Journal of the Polynesian Society* 8: 250–63.

Park, Geoff, 1995. *Ngaa Ururoa: The Groves of Life*. Wellington, Victoria University Press.

Plomley, Brian and Henley, Kristen, 1990. *The Sealers of Bass Strait and the Cape Barren Island Community. Tasmanian Historical Research Association Papers and Proceedings* 37 (2–3): 37–68.

Porter, Roy and Rousseau, G. S., 1980. *The Ferment of Knowledge: Studies in the Historiography of Eighteenth Century*

Science. Cambridge, Cambridge University Press.

Pratt, Mary Louise, 1992. *Imperial Eyes: Travel Writing and Transculturation*. London, Routledge.

Pybus, T. A., 1954. *The Maoris of the South Island*. Wellington, A. H. and A. W. Reed

Rediker, Marcus, 1987. *Between the Devil and the Deep Blue Sea: Merchant Seamen, Pirates, and the Anglo-American Maritime World, 100–1750*. Cambridge, Cambridge University Press.

Richards, Rhys, 1977. *Whaling and Sealing at the Chatham Islands*. Canberra, Roebuck.

Richards, Rhys, 1990. Indigenous Beachcombers: The Case of Tapeooe, a Tahitian Traveller from 1798 to 1812. *The Great Circle* 12 (1): 114.

Richards, Rhys and Chisholm, J., 1992. *Bay of Islands Shipping Arrivals and Departures 1803–1840*. Wellington, Paremata Press.

Richards, Rhys, 1993. *Into the South Seas: The Southern Whale Fishery Comes of Age on the Brazil Banks 1765–1812*. Wellington, Paremata Press.

Richards, Rhys, 1995. *Murihiku Re-Viewed*. Wellington, Hand-in-Hand Press.

Richards, Rhys (ed.), 1996. *Jorgen Jorgenson's Observations On Pacific Trade; and Sealing and Whaling in Australian and New Zealand Waters Before 1805*. Wellington, Paremata Press.

Rickard, L.S., 1965. *The Whaling Trade in Old New Zealand*. Auckland, Minerva.

Rickman, John (attributed), 1785. *Journal of Captain Cook's Last Voyage, to the Pacific Ocean on Discovery: Performed in the Years 1776, 1777, 1778, 1779, and 1780*. London, E. Newbery.

Robotti, Frances Diane, 1983. *Whaling and Old Salem. (A Chronicle of the Sea)*. New York, Fountainhead Publishers.

Robinson, Portia, 1993. *The Women of Botany Bay*. Ringwood, Penguin.

Robson, L.L., 1994. *The Convict Settlers of Australia*. Carlton, Melbourne University Press.

Rockmore, T. and Margolis, J., 1992. *The Heidegger Case: On Philosophy and Politics*. Philadephia, Temple University Press.

Rodger, N. A. M., 1986. *The Wooden World : An Anatomy of the late Georgian Navy*. Annapolis, Naval Institute Press.

Ross, John O. C., 1987. *William Stewart. Sealing Captain, Trader and Speculator*. Canberra, Roebuck.

Ryskamp, Charles and Pottle, Frederick, 1963. *Boswell: The Ominous Years 1774–1776*. London, Heinemann.

Sahlins, M., 1983. Other Times, Other Customs: The Anthropology of History. *American Anthropologist* 8: 517–44.

Sahlins, M., 1985. *Islands of History*. Chicago, University of Chicago Press.

Sahlins, M., 1989. Captain Cook at Hawaii. *Journal of the Polynesian Society* 98: 371–425.

Sahlins, M., 1995. *How Natives Think, About Captain Cook, For Example*. Chicago, University of Chicago Press.

Saine, Thomas P., *George Forster*. New York, Twayne Publishers.

Salmond, A., 1978. Te Ao Tawhito: A Semantic Approach to the Traditional Maori Cosmos. *Journal of the Polynesian Society* 87 (1): 5–28.

Salmond, Anne, 1980. *Eruera: The Teachings of a Maori Elder*. Auckland, Oxford University Press.

Salmond, Anne, 1982. Theoretical Landscapes: On Cross-cultural Conceptions of Knowledge, in David Parkin (ed.), *Semantic Anthropology*. London, Academic Press.

Salmond, Anne, 1985. Maori Epistemologies, in Joanna Overing (ed.), *Reason and Morality*. London, Tavistock Publications.

Salmond, Anne, 1989. Tribal Words, Tribal Worlds: The Translatability of Tapu and Mana, in *Culture, Kin and Cognition in Oceania: Essays in Honour of Ward Goodenough*. Special Publication of the *American Anthropologist* 25, Washington.

Salmond, Anne, 1990. *Two Worlds: First Meetings Between Maori and Europeans 1642–1772*. London, Penguin.

Salmond, Anne, 1991. Tupuna: Ancestors. Aspects of Maori Cognatic Descent, in Andrew Pawley (ed.), *Man and a Half: Essays in Pacific Anthropology and Ethnobiology in Honour of Ralph Bulmer*. Auckland, Polynesian Society.

Salmond, Anne, 1995. Self and Other in Contemporary Anthropology, in Richard Fardon (ed.), *Counterworks: Managing the Diversity of Knowledge*. London, Routledge.

Savage, John, 1807. *Some Account of New Zealand, Particularly the Bay of Islands and Surrounding Country* ... London, J. Murray.

Shapin, Steven and Schaffer, Simon, 1985. *Leviathan and the Air Pump: Hobbes, Boyle, and the Experimental Life*. Princeton, Princeton University Press.

Shapiro, Irwin and Stackpole, Edouard, nd. *The Story of Yankee Whaling*. New York, American Heritage Publishing.

Sharp, Andrew (ed.), 1971. *Duperrey's Visit to New Zealand in 1824.* Wellington, Alexander Turnbull Library.

Sherrin, R. A. A., (ed.) Thomson. W. Leys, 1890. *Early History Of New Zealand, From Earliest Times to 1840.* Auckland, Brett Printer.

Sherman, Stuart C., 1965. *The Voice of the Whaleman.* Providence, Providence Public Library.

Sherman, Stuart C., 1986. *Whaling Logbooks and Journals 1613–1927: An Inventory of Manuscript Records in Public Collections.* New York, Garland Publishing.

Shineberg, Dorothy, 1967. *They Came for Sandalwood: A Study of the Sandalwood Trade in the South-West Pacific 1830–1865.* London, Melbourne University Press.

Sissons, J., Wi Hongi, W., and Hohepa, P., 1987. *The Puriri Leaves Are Laughing: A Political History of Ngaa Puhi in the Inland Bay of Islands.* Auckland, Polynesian Society.

Slawinski, Maurice, 1991. *Science., Culture and Popular Belief in Renaissance Europe.* Manchester, Manchester University Press.

Smith, Adam, 1986. *The Wealth of Nations, Books I–III.* London, Penguin.

Smith, Bernard, 1985. *European Vision and the South Pacific.* Sydney, Harper and Row.

Smith, Bernard, 1992. *Imagining the Pacific: In the Wake of the Cook Voyages.* Melbourne University Press.

Smith, S. Percy, 1897. *Maori Wars of the Nineteenth Century: The Struggle of the Northern against the Southern Maori Tribes prior to the Colonisation of New Zealand in 1840.* Christchurch, Whitcombe and Tombs.

Smith, William, 1813. *Journal of a Voyage in the Missionary Ship Duff, to the Pacific Ocean in the Years 1796, 7, 8, 9, 1800, 1, 2, &c.* New York, William Smith.

Sorrenson, M. P. K., 1979. *Maori Origins and Migrations: The Genesis of Some Pakeha Myths and Legends.* Auckland, Auckland University Press.

Spate, O. H. K., 1988. *Paradise Found and Lost.* Rushcutter's Bay, Australian National University Press.

Spears, John, 1908. *The Story of the New England Whalers.* New York, Macmillan.

Stack, Canon James, 1898. *South Island Maoris: A Sketch of their History and Legendary Lore.* Christchurch, Whitcombe and Tombs.

Stackpole, Edouard, 1972. *Whales and Destiny. The Rivalry Between America, France, and Britain for the Control of the Southern Whale Fishery, 1785–1825.* Boston, University of Massachusetts Press.

Stackpole, Edouard, 1953. *The Sea Hunters: The New England Whalemen during Two Centuries 1635–1835.* Philadelphia, J. B. Lippincott Co.

Stafleu, Frans, 1971. *Linnaeus and the Linnaeans: The Spreading of their Ideas in Systematic Botany, 1735–1789.* Utrecht, A. Oosthoek's Uitgeversmaatschappij N.V.

Starbuck, Alexander, 1989. *History of the American Whale Fishery.* Secausus, N.J., Castle Books.

Steven, Margaret, 1965. *Merchant Campbell 1769–1846: A Study of Colonial Trade.* Melbourne, Oxford University Press.

Stewart, Larry, 1992. *The Rise of Public Science: Rhetoric, Technology, and Natural Philosophy in Newtonian Britain, 1660–1750.* Cambridge, Cambridge University Press.

Strathern, Marilyn, 1988. *The Gender of the Gift. Problems with Women and Problems with Society in Melanesia.* Berkeley, University of California Press.

Tamati, Tuta, 1893. A Reply to Mr. A. S. Atkinson's Paper, 'What is a Tangata Maori?' *Journal of the Polynesian Society* 2: 60–62.

Tapp, E. J., 1958. *Early New Zealand: A Dependency of New South Wales 1788–1841.* Melbourne, Melbourne University Press.

Taussig, Michael, 1987. *Shamanism, Colonialism and the Wild Man. A Study in Terror and Healing.* Chicago, University of Chicago Press.

Taylor, Richard, 1855. *Te Ika a Maui, or New Zealand and its Inhabitants.* London, Wertheim and Macintosh.

Tewsley, V. (trans.), 1926. *Zimmermann's Account of the Third Voyage of Captain Cook 1776–1780.* Wellington, Government Printer.

Thomas, Nicholas, 1991. *Entangled Objects : Exchange, Material Culture and Colonialism in the Pacific.* Cambridge, Mass., Harvard University Press.

Thomas, Nicholas, nd. 'On the Varieties of the Human Species': Forster's Comparative Ethnology.

Thomson, Arthur S., 1859. *The Story of New Zealand: Past and Present — Savage and Civilized, Volumes I and II.* London, John Murray.

Tikao, Teone Taare. *Tikao Talks: Ka Taoka Tapu o Te Ao Kohatu.* Auckland, Penguin.

Townsend, Charles Haskins, 1935. The Distribution of Certain Whales as shown by the Logbook Records of American Whaleships. *Zoologica* XIX (1): 3–50.

Trollope, Anthony, ed. N. John Hall, 1972. *The New Zealander*. Oxford, Clarendon Press.

Turnbull, John, 1813. *A Voyage Round the World, in the Years 1800, 1801, 1802, 1803 and 1804*. London, A. Maxwell.

Vason George, 1840. *The Life of the Late George Vason of Nottingham, One of the Troop of Missionaries first sent to the South Sea Islands by the London Missionary Society in the Ship DUFF, Captain Wilson* 1796. London, John Snow.

Veit, Walter (ed.), 1972. *Captain James Cook: Image and Impact, Vol. I*. Melbourne, Hawthorn Press.

Veit, Walter (ed.), 1979. *Captain James Cook: Image and Impact, Vol II*. Melbourne, Hawthorn Press.

Walpole, Horace, ed. W. S. Lewis, 1937. *The Yale Edition of Horace Walpole's Correspondence*. London, Oxford University Press.

Ward, John, 1948. *British Policy in the South Pacific 1786–1893*. Sydney, Australasian Publishing Co.

Weibust, Knut. *Deep Sea Sailors: A Study in Maritime Ethnology*. Nordiska museets, Handlingar 71.

White, John, 1888. *Ancient History of the Maori, Tainui*. Vol. V. Wellington, Government Printer.

Withey, Lynn, 1987. *Voyages of Discovery: Captain Cook and the Exploration of the Pacific*. London, Hutchinson.

Williams, William, 1989. *Christianity Among the New Zealanders*. Southhampton, The Banner of Truth Trust.

Wilson, Ormond, 1963. Maori and Pakeha. *Journal of the Polynesian Society* 72: 11–20.

Wilson, Ormond, 1985. *From Hongi Hika to Hone Heke: A Quarter Century of Upheaval*. Dunedin, John McIndoe.

Wilson, Ormond, 1990. *Kororareka and Other Essays*. Dunedin, John McIndoe.

Wohlers, Rev. J. F. H, 1881. On the Conversion and Civilization of the Maoris in the South of New Zealand. *Transactions and Proceedings of the New Zealand Institute* XIV: 12353.

Woloch, Isser, 1982. *Eighteenth-Century Europe, Tradition and Progress 1715–1789*. New York, W. W. Norton.

Yarwood, A. T., 1977. *Samuel Marsden: The Great Survivor*. Wellington, A. H. and A. W. Reed.

Yates, Frances, 1966. *The Art of Memory*. London, Routledge and Kegan Paul.

Young, John M. R. (ed.), 1967. *Australia's Pacific Frontier: Economic and Cultural Expansion into the Pacific: 1795–1885*. Melbourne, Cassell.

Theses and research essays

Blair, Simon, The Attack on the Boyd: A Study of an Early Incident of Violence. Research essay in History, Massey University.

Chappell, David, 1991. Beyond the Beach: Periplean Frontiers of Pacific Islanders aboard Euro-American Ships, 1768–1887. PhD thesis in History, University of Hawaii.

Davidson, J. W., 1942. European Penetration of the South Pacific, 1779–1842. University of Cambridge.

Fallas, Victoria, 1990. Kai Tangata: A Study of Maori Cannibalism. Research essay in History, University of Newcastle.

Hutchinson, Marian, 1995. Bound for New Zealand. Seamen Under Sail and Steam in the Nineteenth Century. MA thesis in History, University of Auckland.

Orchiston, D. Wayne, 1978. Studies in South Island New Zealand Prehistory and Protohistory. PhD thesis in Anthropology, University of Sydney.

Phillips, Caroline, 1994. The Archaeology of Maori Occupation along the Waihou River, Hauraki. Ph D thesis, University of Auckland.

Schaniel, William Carl, 1985. The Maori and the Economic Frontier: An Economic History of the Maori of New Zealand, 1769–1840. PhD dissertation, University of Tennessee.

Strauss, Wallace Patrick, 1958. Early American Interest and Activity in Polynesia 1783–1842. PhD thesis in Political Science, Columbia University.

Turner, Stephen, 1995. Cultural Encounter, Aesthetics, and the Limits of Anthropology: Captain Cook and the Maori. PhD dissertation, Cornell University.

Wigglesworth, Roger, 1974. The Myth and the Reality. A Study of the Adaptation of John Marmon with comments on his three newspaper autobiographies. Research essay in History, Massey University.

Wigglesworth, Roger, 1981. The New Zealand Timber and Flax Trade 1769–1840. PhD thesis in History, Massey University.

Published collections of manuscripts

Britton, Alexander (ed.), 1892. *Historical Records of New South Wales, Volume I, Part 2 – Phillip 1783–1792*. Sydney, Government Printer.

Bladen, F. M. (ed.), 1893. *Historical Records of New South Wales, Volume II: Grose and Paterson, 1793–1795*. Sydney, Government Printer.

Bladen, F. M. (ed.), 1895. *Historical Records of New South Wales, Volume III: Hunter, 1796–1799*. Sydney, Government Printer.

Bladen, F. M. (ed.), 1896. *Historical Records of New South Wales, Volume IV: Hunter and King, 1800, 1801 and 1802*. Sydney, Government Printer.

Library Committee of the Commonwealth Parliament, 1914–25. *Historical Records of Australia, Series I, Governors' Despatches to and from England. Volumes I–III*. Sydney, Library Committee of the Commonwealth Parliament.

McNab, R. (ed.), 1908. *Historical Records of New Zealand, Volume I*. Wellington, Government Printer.

McNab, R. (ed.), 1914. *Historical Records of New Zealand, Volume II*. Wellington, Government Printer.

Manuscripts (not referenced in endnotes)

Kerr, I. S., Sealers in Southern New Zealand 1803–1812. ATL Ms papers 1685-2.

Kugler, Richard C., nd. The Penetration of the Pacific by American Whalemen in the 19th century. Whaling Museum, New Bedford, Massachusetts.

McNab, Robert. Evidence given before the Judge Advocate in the Sydney Courts in 1811–12. ATL qMs-0457.

Mitchell, Maui John and Hilary, 1996. Te Tau Ihu o Te Waka. A History of Maori of Nelson and Malborough.

Morris, Roger, 1996. Suggestions concerning the Anchorage of the Snow 'Fancy', Dec. 6 1795.

Phillipson, Grant, 1994. Maori Occupation of Te Tau Ihu o Te Waka a Maui.

Renelle, Mme Lucie, 1789. *Nouvelle Géographie a L'Usage des Instituts et des Gouvenantes Françoises*. Trans. Isabel Ollivier 1994.

Richards, Rhys (ed.) and L. Knight (trans.), nd. Jorgen Jorgensen's Observations on English and North American Voyages and Trade in the South Seas. ATL Ms Papers 78217.

White, John. Northern Manuscripts. ATL Ms 75 B19.

Wigglesworth, Roger, 1974. The Myth and the Reality: A Study of the Adaptation of John Marmon (1800?–1880), with comments on his three newspaper autobiographies. Research essay, Massey University.

Newspapers

Calcutta Gazette, 1809.

Evangelical Magazine.

Gazette de France, 1770, 80: 324; 1771, 60: 243; 61: 247; 79: 323; 80:327; 1772, 27: 125; 1774, 60: 267; 61: 275; 62: 280: 1784, 92.

Hobart Town Gazette, 1818.

London Chronicle, 1771, 13–16 July: 51a; 20–23 July: 75a; 27–30 July: 102a–b; 28 September – 1 October: 315–17b; 8–10 October: 349a–c; 14–17 December: 580a; 1772, 9–11 June: 559a.

Monthly Miscellany, 1774.

Proceedings of the Church Missionary Society.

Sydney Gazette, 1803–15.

Index